Experimental Psychology and Information Processing

Experimental Psychology and Information Processing

DOMINIC W. MASSARO

University of Wisconsin

Rand McNally College Publishing Company · Chicago

Credits for chapter numerals, and figures and tables taken from other sources appear on pp. 633–634.

Cover: Detail from *Sunday Afternoon on the Island of La Grande Jatte* by Georges Seurat. Courtesy Art Institute of Chicago. Helen Birch Bartlett Collection.

MARKHAM PSYCHOLOGY SERIES
Howard Leventhal, advisory editor

ai miei genitori

til min kone

Preface

When I began teaching courses in Experimental Psychology and Information Processing at the University of Wisconsin, Madison, four years ago, the tradition in the experimental course here, as in most universities, was to teach methodology relatively independent of content and theory. This seemed to me to be an impossible task, so I set out to integrate methodology, content, and theory in teaching the course. An information-processing approach was utilized because it provided a framework for work in all of the areas of experimental psychology. With this framework, one did not need entirely different conceptualizations to study such varied topics as perception, memory, and decision-making. The potential contribution of the information-processing approach promised an exciting adventure. My goal was to define and develop an information-processing framework for experimental psychology and to communicate it to my students and colleagues. This volume is the outcome of that venture.

The goal here is to articulate a paradigm for experimental psychology. The paradigm, consisting of metaphysical, conceptual, theoretical, and methodological commitments, defines a set of standards for scientific exploration into the human mind. Calling the paradigm "information processing" is not as important as the articulation of the paradigm itself. The success of the present articulation will not only be evaluated by the reader, but will be tested against the development of experimental psychology.

The development of the first half of the book proceeds from the experimental course, which deals with more traditional areas of research such as reaction times, psychophysics, and visual sensation and perception. Most of the second half of the book is based on an undergraduate course called human information processing. The topics here concern attention, visual information processing, auditory information processing, short-term memory, long-term memory, and learning. The organization is not necessarily front-to-back or middle-to-back sequence. Rather, sections and even chapters can be read independently. If the reader finds that some earlier development is necessary, the table of contents and indices should be sufficient to direct him to the necessary material. Also, cross-references across chapters are included throughout the text. Further study of each topic should be facilitated by the suggested readings given at the end of the book.

This volume is meant to be basic and yet advanced. It is basic because the level of material covered is exactly that taught to sophomores and juniors. Undergraduates have no more trouble dealing with contemporary concepts than they have with traditional concepts. For example, there is nothing inherently more difficult in the method of signal detection theory than in the method of constant stimuli. At the same time, it is advanced because it represents the current state of the art in Experimental Psychology and Information Processing. My belief is that this book is appropriate for courses in Experimental Psychology, Perception, Memory and Attention, Information Processing, and Cognitive Psychology.

It is difficult to say whose assistance was most crucial in a project of this sort. The abstract goal of writing such a book developed into a concrete commitment because of Howard Leventhal. I appreciate the comments and helpful reactions of Peter W. Frey, Andrew Goldman, and Harold L. Hawkins. Their ability to react to the material as would students, teachers, and scientists improved the book considerably. Finally, Michael Olson provided good feedback from the undergraduate point of view.

Susan Case enthusiastically and energetically transcribed my sixty or seventy lectures and helped organize the book. Marion Masse has been a most dependable secretary, and Lynne Heinneman and Kathy Schmit also contributed to the typing. Peter Lang kindly provided the brain waves shown in Figure 1.2, Michael Cohen contributed many of the spectrograms in the auditory information-processing section, and Wendy Idson proofread many of the typed chapters. Karen T. Massaro photographed the Roman mosaics shown on the opening pages of Sections I, III, and V, and the Borromini colonnade. Finally, Bob Erhart, Charlotte Iglarsh, and Jenny Gilbertson at Rand McNally aided in the materialization of the book.

Some of my research reported in the book was supported financially by the Wisconsin Alumni Research Foundation and the National Institute of Mental Health. The final version was written while I was a John Simon Guggenheim Memorial Foundation Fellow. Their support and that of the Wisconsin Alumni Research Foundation allowed me to spend the year in a way that such work could materialize. In this regard, I would like to thank the people at the Institute of Psychology of the Central Research Council in Rome for their hospitality.

I am obliged to the many scientists who gave their permission to reproduce findings from their work. Thanks also are due to the artists, museums, and collectors who permitted reproduction of their works of art.

D. W. M.

Contents

Experimental Psychology and Information Processing

Overview

Mind is a mass of tangled processes. Our problem is to dissect this complex, and to discover if we can, its plan of arrangement.
—Edward B. Titchener (1899)

The goal of this book is to present the current state of the art in *Experimental Psychology*. By experimental is meant scientific; by psychology is meant the study of psychological phenomena. We focus, therefore, on the scientific study of psychological phenomena. As has been traditional in Experimental Psychology since Woodworth's (1938) book of the same title, the study of abnormal, developmental, and social psychology is not included. We further limit ourselves to the study of human psychology. Our focus is on the scientific study of sensation, perception, memory, decision-making, psychophysics, attention, imagination, and learning. These topics concern the ways in which the individual derives knowledge, that is, information, from his environment. We assume that psychological functions or processes intervene between the stimulus environment and the knowledge the subject finally realizes. Therefore, we consider the study of experimental psychology equivalent to the study of information processing—the processes that allow the individual to take the potential information from the environment to its utilization by that individual.

The central assumption of this book is that psychological functions, operations, or processes intervene between stimulus and response. As psychologists, we study what these processes do, rather than what they are. The question of what psychological processes are is a metaphysical one, which cannot be answered experimentally. The problem of the nature of psychological events is known in philosophy as the mind-body problem. The solutions to this problem are analyzed in Chapter 1 and one solution is developed as the metaphysical basis for the information-processing approach.

Chapter 2 discusses the role of theory and method in experimental research. One observation that is made throughout this book concerns how experimental method follows theoretical development. The information-processing approach also prescribes a particular methodology since its goal is to provide information about the sequence of processes that intervene between stimulus and response. This methodology follows directly from the development of the experimental method in psychology during the last one hundred years. After covering the foundation of experimental method in Chapter 2, we develop its utilization in psychological research throughout the book.

The information-processing approach is illustrated nicely in the methods that have been developed to measure the time it takes for psychological operations (see Chapter 3). The goal of this procedure, established by Donders in the 1860's, is to measure the exact time it takes to perform certain psychological events, such as selecting the appropriate response from a set of alternatives. Although there are certain problems with Donders' exact method, a modification, the additive-factor method, can be used to study the nature of psychological processing. As an example, in one task discussed in Chapter 4, a subject is given a short list of target items and then presented with a given test item. His task is to indicate whether the test item was contained in the target set. For example, if the target set was 4, 9, 7, 2 and the test item 8, the answer would be "no." The dependent variable is the time it takes the observer to make his decision. By manipulating a number of independent variables and analyzing the data appropriately, this paradigm illuminates the nature of certain psychological operations.

Psychophysics, or the relationship between the physical and the psychological worlds, is one of the earliest areas of psychological study (see Chapter 5). Fechner established the experimental study of the relationship between sensation and perception in the middle of the 19th century. Fechner's goal was to describe the subject's response as a direct function of the stimulus. Fechner discovered, however, that there is no one-to-one relationship between stimulus and response. Psychological operations intervene between stimulus and response and these must be accounted for in the psychophysical situation. Chapters 5, 6, and 7 show how two operations occur in a simple psychophysical task in which a subject is asked to interpret a stimulus event; for example, was a stimulus presented? These operations involve a perceptual and a decision process, respectively. The experimenter cannot understand the relationship between stimulus and response unless he accounts for both of these processes. We shall see that the decision process is a critical stage of information processing and must be accounted for in all experimental tasks.

Visual information processing is discussed in Chapter 8–12. The process of visual detection is introduced in Chapter 8 when we seek the answer to the question: What is the minimal amount of light an observer can detect under optimal conditions? Answering this question requires a knowledge of stimulus, physiological, anatomical, psychological, and mathematical variables in the experimental situation. The study of visual perception in Chapter 9 utilizes works of art in addition to the experimental method to learn how we perceive the visual world. Many art works function as controlled experiments and can be used to demonstrate the rules of visual perception. In Chapter 10 the interaction of theory and research is clearly seen in the study of visual illusions. Illusions in themselves continue to intrigue the scientist and can be utilized to illustrate some of the operations in visual perception.

We perceive a constant three-dimensional world although the stimulus input continually changes over time. A given object is perceived reliably under a wide variety of instances and orientations which drastically change the retinal input. This perceptual constancy has generated much theory and research, some of which is discussed in Chapter 11. We are interested in the operations responsible for veridical perception and the time it takes for these operations to occur.

Chapter 12 concerns the interaction between visual recognition and short-term memory. The research and techniques discussed there make apparent that the simplest recognition experiment requires two stages of information processing: perception and memory. Each of these stages of processing must be accounted for in the task before the experimenter can isolate the rules of processing of any one stage.

The experimental and theoretical study of attention receives our attention in Chapters 13–16. The information-processing approach to the study of attention attempts to answer two questions. First, at what stages of information processing does attention operate? That is to say, at what stages of information processing can a limited processing capacity be utilized for one task at the expense of another? For example, excluding changes in eye movements, can we selectively attend to a given location of a visual display? Second, can processing at one stage influence the processing capacity available for another stage of information processing? Does an increased memory requirement decrease the efficiency of the recognition process?

The rules of the visual recognition process in reading are

studied in Chapters 17–19. We assume that the visual stimulus is transformed by the visual receptor system and a preperceptual representation of the stimulus is stored in preperceptual visual storage. The visual recognition process transforms the preperceptual representation into a synthesized visual percept which corresponds to the phenomenological experience of seeing. The time needed for the visual recognition process as well as methods for its study are discussed in detail in Chapters 17 and 18. We also use these methods to define the properties of preperceptual visual storage.

The information necessary for visual recognition is in the nature of the figure-ground contrast of the visual image. This stimulus does not change continuously in time, but is held in a relatively steady-state form during every eye fixation between saccadic eye movements. During this time, we assume that the light wave pattern is held in preperceptual visual storage. The visual recognition stage involves a readout of the information in the preperceptual visual image. An analysis of the visual information available in the image takes time and it is assumed that the preperceptual visual image holds the information for recognition to take place. Recognition of a visual pattern produces a synthesized percept in synthesized visual memory, which holds this information long enough to allow us to see more than just the visual input from one eye fixation.

The characteristics of the auditory stimulus are discussed in Chapter 20 as preparation for our study of auditory information processing. The production and characteristics of speech stimuli is included, since we also study the perception of speech. The auditory recognition process is studied in Chapters 21–23. Auditory information processing is assumed to be exactly analogous to visual information processing. The auditory stimulus is transformed by the auditory receptor system into a representation held in preperceptual auditory storage. The auditory recognition process involves a transformation of the preperceptual representation into a synthesized auditory percept.

The information necessary for auditory recognition is in the nature of the temporal changes of sound pressure over time. The process of recognition requires an analysis of the acoustic information available in the sound pattern. This analysis cannot take place while the stimulus is occurring, since a complete sound pattern is necessary for recognition. The preperceptual storage holds the information in the sound pattern so that recognition can occur. Until the sound pattern is complete, recognition cannot begin, since all of the stimulus information is necessary for the recognition process. Recognition of an auditory pattern produces a synthesized percept held in synthesized auditory memory.

Chapters 24–27 examine the properties of immediate or short-term memory. We divide short-term memory into three structural components: synthesized auditory and visual memory, which are modality-specific, corresponding to the experience of the immediate present, and generated abstract memory, which is not modality-specific, but is in an abstract form. We study the properties of synthesized auditory memory in Chapters 24 and 25 and the properties of synthesized visual memory in Chapter 26.

Synthesized memory is made available by the recognition of information in preperceptual storage. This memory is the structure responsible for experience of what we are currently seeing, hearing, or dreaming. Synthesized memory differs from preperceptual information in that preperceptual information is tied to the stimulus, whereas synthesized information is not. Information can be synthesized and experienced without a recent stimulus, such as is the case in dreaming. With little effort, we can silently imagine the sound quality of a friend's voice or what he looks like. The studies discussed in Chapters 24, 25, and 26 demonstrate that synthesized information usually lasts some seconds following stimulus presentation.

Meaning is derived from synthesized auditory and visual memory and is placed in generated abstract memory. This stage of processing corresponds to the processing stage studied by most immediate memory studies. In the model developed in this book, the same structure is used to store meaning derived from auditory, visual, and other sensory stimuli. One structure seems to be sufficient since the information is not modality-specific, but appears to be in a relatively abstract form. The storage and forgetting of information in generated abstract memory are discussed in Chapter 27.

In Chapter 28, we study the structure of long-term memory, our storehouse of knowledge, and discuss methods used to determine how information is stored there and what processes are responsible for its utilization. Chapter 29 presents methods of the study of learning. Learning appears to be made up of all of the component processes discussed in this book. Hence, all of these component processes must be accounted for in the learning task. Finally, we summarize the information-processing model developed in our study.

INTRODUCTION

Psychology: the science of mental life

Psychology is the Science of Mental Life, both of its phenomena and their conditions.
—*William James (1890)*

Our study of psychology follows in the tradition of William James, who in 1890 defined psychology as the science of mental life. What James meant by a science of mental life was nothing more or less than understanding the psychological processes of perception, imagination, memory, thinking, and decision-making. These processes seem to be fundamental to man's existence qua man. For example, one important problem in perception is how the reader derives meaning from a page of text. How is he or she able to imagine the theme of Beethoven's ninth symphony? How does a person remember what he was doing one year ago today? Think of a four-letter word that ends in *eny*. Should you continue reading or consider some of the thoughts generated by these questions?

James' definition of the content of psychology appears reasonable and provides a fascinating challenge to the experimental psychologist. Before accepting this challenge, however, we need to explore the assumptions that are implicit in James's definition about the nature of man as the subject of science. The assumptions are first, that mental phenomena exist, and, second, that these phenomena can be subjected to the scrutiny of scientific endeavor. These assumptions have rival assumptions, and although the issue among them cannot be decided with the certainty of science, they can be subjected to rational, critical examination.

MIND-BODY PROBLEM

Early in the history of philosophy the mind was isolated and identified as distinct from the body. Immediately the relationship between mind and body became a central problem of human thought. The ingenuity of generations of philosophers provided various models of man, all starting from the dualism of mind and body. One of the first great thinkers to reflect on this problem was Plato. He observed that whereas the body follows laws embedded in physical events and circumstances, the mind appears to be free from these events. Building on the mind as the agent of man's incorporeal acts—perceiving, thinking, decision-making, and so on—and on the vague cultural concept of spirit Plato conceived the soul. Immortal and incorporeal, the soul in this life is imprisoned by the body. Its escape is death, when it breaks free of the body's limitations and exists as pure thought. Plato's notion of the soul was adopted by religion, and the concept that the soul or mind is free from the demands and laws to which the body is subject permeated Western culture. This dualism still determines the framework in which most of us think about man: we study him either as biology or as psychology.

Plato's formulation—called Platonic dualism—immediately raised a problem that has exercised philosophers ever since: How can these two distinct entities, with their two distinct sets of functions, be related within one entity? The mind-body problem is a metaphysical one. No experimental paradigm can be set up to solve it, and no final answer is possible with presently available techniques. We can only analyze it carefully and review the answers that philosophers arrived at by using the methods of metaphysical speculation.

Interactionism   About 20 centuries after Plato, Descartes, a Catholic scientist, came up with a famous solution to the problem. As a good scientist, Descartes maintained that the human body, like all physical entities, could be described by mechanical laws. Accordingly, through mechanical laws, we would understand the functioning of the human body as human physical behavior. In this respect, the physical body was no different from other physical objects. As a good Catholic, however, Descartes also maintained that the human soul was not subject to the laws that governed the body. Being spiritual, immortal, and eternal, the soul was free of physical necessity and could not be understood by the laws of science.

Descartes' solution to Plato's problem was to accept that the mind and body must somehow meet, since their operations are in some ways interlinked. For this meeting place Descartes chose the pineal gland; he was drawn to it as the seat of the interaction between mind and body because this gland is not duplicated as are most of the brain structures (one hemisphere of the brain being a mirror image of the other). In the pineal gland, according to Descartes, spiritual fluids interacted with bodily fluids, with the result that some control of the body by mind was possible.

Cartesian interactionism is represented graphically in Figure 1 (upper left), in which we have the human body interacting with the human mind. Cartesian interactionism maintains that a person is made up of two different things: mind and body. Two things ought to be capable of being thought about independently of each other. For example, this book and a table are separate entities, and one should be able to think about them separately. One can, indeed, think about the book without thinking of the table, and about the table independently of the book. But to attempt to do the same with the two entities of interactionism causes some difficulty. When thinking of the body, thoughts of the mind arise. Thoughts of the mind also give rise to those of the body. The manner of our thinking, therefore, poses a problem for Descartes' theory.

Philosophers have been unhappy with the Cartesian proposition that a person is two separate things that somehow interact and have evolved alternative theories. One of the most influential of these is materialism, shown in graphic form at the lower left in Figure 1.

Materialism

FIGURE 1. Graphic representations of four solutions to the mind-body problem.

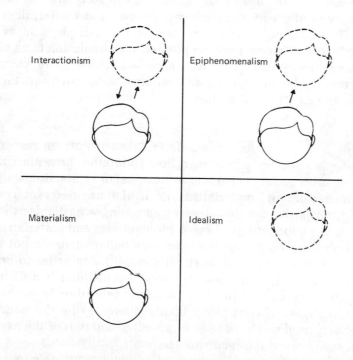

Interactionism

Epiphenomenalism

Materialism

Idealism

Materialism simply denies the existence of the mind. If the mind does not exist, then to understand man we need understand only his behavior. A materialist rejects James' definition of psychology as the study of mental life. For the materialist, there is no mental life and no need to study it. The proper subject of psychology is, rather, observable behavior; materialism is the metaphysical foundation of behaviorism.

Epiphenomenalism Another solution to the mind-body problem is epiphenomenalism, which holds that consciousness—or mental life—is nothing more than the by-product of material life, an epiphenomenon with no consequence of its own. The mind can be compared to the glow around a lightbulb that in no way influences the behavior of the bulb itself. Epiphenomenalism, then, rejects Descartes' conviction that the mind interacts with the body. Rather, the body controls the functions of the mind without being at all influenced by it. To understand man, therefore, it is not necessary to study his mental life.

Idealism Do you deny mind? I'll deny matter. Thus said Bishop Berkeley, some time after the age of Descartes, and in so doing formulated the theory of idealism. For Berkeley, the body, as matter, does not exist. Therefore, only the mind need be studied; physical events may be ignored. Samuel Johnson put Berkeley's solution to a unique test; maintaining that there was a material reality, he kicked a stone, thereby hurting his toe and proving, to his own satisfaction at least, the existence of matter.

Best Choice We now have discussed four different theories of the respective roles of mind and body in human life. Today the three most influential theories among scientists are Cartesian interactionism, epiphenomenalism, and materialism. Each of these deserves careful thought, given the consequences of accepting a particular theory. Consider the implications of epiphenomenalism and materialism. If mental phenomena do not influence our behavior or do not even exist, then we need not understand mental life in order to understand behavior. On introspecting, however, we find it difficult to believe that our mental life has no influence on bodily processes. In fact, methods of controlling bodily processes by the mind are now widely used and have become an important part of the psychological study called bio-feedback training.

Employing electronic devices, psychologists are able to record a number of physiological responses, such as heart rate, brain waves, and galvanic skin potentials of human observers. Electrodes can be attached to an observer's head so that the electrical changes in his brain activity can be monitored. The electrodes pick up these brain waves, take their electrical potential, and put it through an amplifier (analogous to the amplifier of your record player). The amplified signal is then fed into an oscilloscope which, in essence, renders a graphical analysis of the electrical changes in the observer's brain. With an oscilloscope, time is represented along the horizontal axis, and a relative change in electrical current along the vertical axis. Figure 2 presents an oscilloscopic display of two prominent brain waves: the alpha wave and alpha blocking.

FIGURE 2. The alpha wave shown at the top oscillates regularly at about 9 cycles per sec. The wave produced by alpha blocking shown at the bottom oscillates at a much higher frequency in a highly irregular fashion.

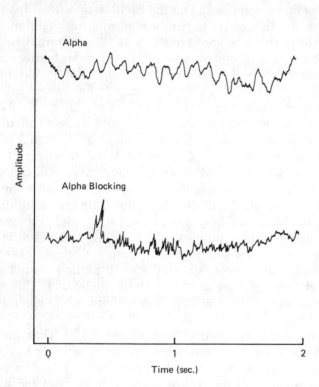

An observer with attached electrodes can be seated at the oscilloscope so that he can observe his own brain waves. This touches on the question of whether a mind can look upon itself. Experimental studies indicate that observers *can* control the nature of their brain waves. Indeed, as you may already know, yoga has provided a system of mental exercises allowing the yogi to control his body with his mind. By thinking the right thoughts, the yogi can change his heart rate and the wave shape of his brain activity. This has great implications for our metaphysical problem, implications that are fortified by data gathered from observers controlling their brain waves in the laboratory.

Different types of brain waves can be distinguished by the amplitude (the height of the wave) and the number of repetitions of the wave per second. The alpha wave is very regular, has a high amplitude, and usually cycles between eight and fourteen times per second. A second wave, alpha blocking, is more irregular, has a smaller amplitude, and repeats at a much higher frequency than the alpha wave. With a little training, an observer finds that he can produce these two brain waves at will. Alpha blocking is produced by attending to an interesting scene, or by forming a visual image if the eyes are closed, or merely by attending to the changes in the brain waves that are appearing on the oscilloscope. The alpha wave state is a meditation state; to produce it, one but maintains a relaxed alertness, thinking about nothing at all, or alternatively, one concentrates on something mundane, like a regular bodily process. An observer concentrating on the steady beating of his heart rate to the exclusion of everything else produces alpha waves.

What does this phenomenon imply for our theories of the relationship between mind and body? The brain pattern constitutes a physical behavior of man; the epiphenomenalist, or behaviorist, should be able to predict it. On the contrary, however, it is the observer alone who can predict which wave shape will come next. He controls the phenomenon, and he may choose, from the point of view of the behaviorist, quite arbitrarily. This creates difficulties for both materialism and epiphenomenalism. Mental processes, say epiphenomenalists, play no part in controlling the body. But here we have an experimental situation in which a mental event does control a behavioral event. Materialists tell us that mental events do not exist. But here they are, controlling the body. In this experiment we can, and must, grasp the real existence of something we call mental processing.

So the mind exists and influences the body. That the body affects the mind is also known. Recalling one's last trip to the dentist should remove any doubt of that; pain hurts. Hurt is a perception, a phenomenon of mind. We seem to have been led back to interactionism, to the theory, originally espoused by Descartes, that mind affects body and body affects mind. Unfortunately the problems in this theory still remain. *How* do body and mind interact? If a spiritual entity can affect a physical one and vice versa, this seems to imply that anything can cause anything. Here are two things, mind and body, which can neither be related to one another satisfactorily, nor thought of separately.

At this point it is necessary to retrospect and ask why mind and body have been postulated as separate and distinct in the first place. The philosophers from whom we inherit this distinction were unable to conceive that a physical entity could be conscious, that is, lead a mental life. They experienced consciousness as altogether other than a corporeal function. Consciousness, they believed, was free of all but its own dictates, whereas the body was subject to the accidents of time and place, the random influence of exterior events, the laws of nature, and death. It was not logical that thought, an incorporeal function, could be caused by, produced by, and be dependent upon a mortal body. Plato had the only possible solution. There must be a second entity, a spiritual being, to do the thinking.

Attributing mental processing to an incorporeal entity does not, however, resolve the problem. The operations of consciousness are not in any sense easier to understand if they are assumed to be independent of the body. Conversely, in the age of computers and other nonhuman information-processing systems, it is much easier to accept the fact that physical things think. Computers, to whose absolute corporeality man can attest since he made them, do perform incorporeal operations with incorporeal results. We ourselves have designed their operations, and can usually understand the rules by which they occur. Many of the internal operations of computers seem to be analogous to the mental operations of man. So it is simply not unreasonable or illogical that some physical things are conscious and can lead a mental life. Nor is it inconceivable any longer that certain physical organisms can perceive, imagine, and remember. Our task is to describe how these physical entities—ourselves—perform these internal operations.

Monism

These observations lead us to a distinctly different alternative solution to the mind-body problem, which is called monism. The term monism is used to describe this solution because the mind and body are not considered to be separate entities whose interaction must be explained. Rather, it is assumed that human beings are highly complex organisms with a number of complex visible attributes such as a complex brain and nervous system. One of the properties of this complex being is that it leads a mental life. To understand man, we must understand these mental processes.

One critical attribute or dimension of the physical entity, man, is consciousness. Throughout history, consciousness has been attributed to a nonphysical entity, the mind or soul. However, it is more logical to conceptualize consciousness as a dimension of human beings in the same way that the thumb and forefinger arrangement represents one of their characteristics. Mental life is the distinguishing feature that qualifies man as the unique subject of psychological study. When we say that the contribution of the mind is critical to understanding man, we are not positing another entity; rather we are referring to a dimension or attribute of man himself. In studying the processes that William James laid down in 1890, we shall be studying neither mind nor body, but the internal mental operations of the whole person.

Psychology was defined here as the science of mental life. To build our metaphysical foundation, it was necessary to determine how our mental life related to our behavioral life: how the mind related to the body. Popular solutions to the mind-body problem were discussed. Materialism and epiphenomenalism were rejected because mental events or processes exist, and these affect our behavioral life. Descartes' interactionism was rejected because it is not logical that the nonphysical should affect the physical. We were left with the monistic solution, which posits that the physical nature of a person possesses the attributes that allow him to lead a mental life.

Mental processes are tied to physical systems but cannot be reduced to physical processes. Man is organized with a conscious awareness that is integrated with the different sense modalities. Visual perception is an example. Input for vision comes by way of our eyes; but they are not sufficient for perceiving. We actively construct and synthesize our view of the world. Later, with no visual input, we can reconstruct what we saw earlier and form a mental image of the scene. This is what is referred to as a mental process. Mental events exist and must be studied to understand human behavior. Accordingly, the subject of psychology as seen here is the study of man's mental processes.

MENTAL OPERATIONS

Earlier researchers assumed that mental processes could be ignored because the stimulus situation alone would be sufficient to predict response. This expectation has not turned out to be the case. For instance, it would have been nice to predict the simple detection response (in which the subject reports whether or not a stimulus was presented), based on the intensity of the stimulus. Indeed, it was long assumed that there existed a threshold of intensity above which the observer would detect a stimulus and below which he would not. On investigation what actually happens is that, although subjects grow increasingly more likely to detect (experience) a stimulus as its intensity is increased, their response on any given trial is also a function of a decision or a response rule. The response rule governs how often the subject will say "yes" or "no" to a given experience and is influenced by the attitudes and motivations of the subject. Subjects, therefore, may claim to hear a sound that is well below any possible threshold; later they may ignore one that is surely above it. In these experiments it is clear that in some way the subject has acted upon the information derived from the stimulus before he produced the response. He does not constitute a passive reactor, but is himself an agent that influences the final outcome—the response. The response cannot be understood without understanding how the subject acts upon the information in the stimulus.

Some might object that no reliable method exists for studying the mental processes of the subject. This is no longer true. The information-processing approach provides us with a model which has proved extremely fruitful in generating experimental designs for studying the sequence of operations between stimulus and response. Each mental process is looked upon as an operation on the information made available to it by an earlier operation or by the stimulus itself. What this means can be illustrated by an analysis of the creative process in human invention and discovery and also by the sequence of operations performed by a general purpose computer.

Creativity and Computers

The creative process is a large, ill-defined process at present and as such is not studied by experimental methods, but the data received from introspection can be analyzed in the framework of information processing. Most creative people report that they go through a series of operations or stages of processing from the inception of a project until its publication. The first of these is a preparation stage in which the problem takes shape as such, and relevant information in the person's storehouse of knowledge is called up and sensitized and made available for the solution. This information is now available for the next stage of the creative process, in which the individual stops consciously processing the information. We know nothing about this incubation stage, which is widely reported by creative people, except that the processing taking place here is accomplished at a subconscious level, and that when the problem emerges again into the creative person's consciousness, it has been transformed into a new conceptualization.

Under the new formulation a solution may now be possible. If so, the person experiences an insightful stage of processing. He or she may now see the theoretical revision that will permit a solution, or the link between this and other problems in his area, or the key piece of knowledge that will furnish a solution. Finally, the creative person must go through the final editing, or mopping-up, stage in which he must validate his insight. The implications of the solution must be worked out to verify its consistency. He may refine it by mapping it into mathematical or logical terms, which are a further check on its validity. Whatever his tests, if his solution passes them it is now ready to be made public.

In each of the stages of creativity a certain amount of information is made available. The operation of a particular stage transforms the information and passes it into the next stage of processing. A computer's operations on a computer program follow the same pattern. Figure 3 illustrates the series of operations between the input of the program and the output of its solution. The series is initiated by an input; the first stage transforms the input into a

FIGURE 3. Computer Behavior: A graphic representation of the sequence of component operations between the input of a program and the output of its solution.

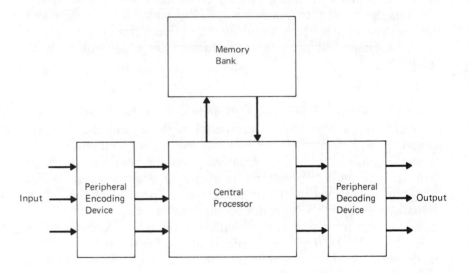

language comprehensible to the computer. After this peripheral encoding, the central processor of the computer routes the information into the memory bank, where it remains available as needed for execution of the program. The central processor executes the program and produces an output which must pass through the peripheral decoding device before it can be communicated to the outside world.

A computer is usually equipped with devices to read cards, paper tape, or magnetic tape; information meant for ears and eyes is meaningless to it. The input designed to be encoded by a card-reading device arrives in the form of a card punched with holes. The area of the card is arranged in rows and columns so that the location of each hole can be precisely identified. The card reader has a set of photoelectric cells that send light through each hole in the card. The device can therefore move from one position to the next, asking in each location whether or not a light shows through. The presence or absence of light can be transformed into a more useful form, for instance whether or not a particular magnetic core is magnetized. At the end the computer has a set of "yeses" and "nos" or 1s and 0s in the form which it was specifically designed to handle directly.

The central processor now places the information in memory, which is made up of a set of locations. Each location in memory has an address, and the information stored there is its content. Now the central processor can refer to the contents by their addresses only. The central processor can then begin to execute the program. The execution of the program involves performing the sequence of operations listed in the instructions of the program. The outcome of the program is the solution or information wanted by the computer user. In order to communicate the solution, the central processor must translate it into a form that is intelligible to the computer user.

The goal of this book is to present methods of experimental psychology that will enable the experimenter to understand the sequence of operations that occur between stimulus and response. We have noted that to understand the creative process it is necessary to understand the sequence of events that occurred between the inception of the problem (stimulus) and its solution (response). Analogously, to understand a computer's behavior it is necessary to understand the internal set of operations and transformations of information between input and output. The study of man is fundamentally no different. To understand man we must determine and understand the sequence of mental processes that occur between the observed stimulus and response.

Information-Processing Model

The guide we use in our study of psychology is an information-processing model. The central assumption of the model is that a number of mental operations, called processing stages, occur between stimulus and response. A stimulus has potential information and its presentation initiates a sequence of processing stages in which each stage operates on the information available to it.

The operations of a particular stage take time and transform the information in some way, making the transformed information available to the following stage of processing. Two theoretical components or constructs are important in the model. First, the *structural* construct describes or defines the nature of the information at a particular stage of processing. Second, the *functional* component describes the operations of a stage of information processing. Figure 4 illustrates the graphic representation we shall use for the structural and functional components between stimulus and response.

FIGURE 4. Information-Processing Model: A graphic representation of the structural and functional components between stimulus and response.

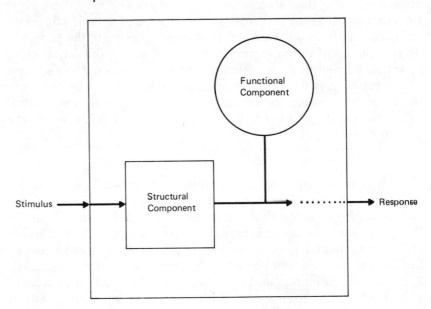

The information-processing model will be utilized to study sensation, perception, memory, attention, learning, and decision-making. Its main purpose is to formally represent the psychological processes that are important in a given experiment. By delineating the psychological processes, an understanding is obtained that not only clarifies the stimulus-response relationship but also illuminates the processes themselves. Our goal is to understand what the psychological processes do and how they do it. The model functions as a formal representation of our knowledge of these processes and forces us to be consistent in our psychological research. It enables us to study methodological, logical, and theoretical issues in a consistent and coherent manner. The model also provides a tool we can use to summarize our findings and predict the results of new experimental and real-life situations. Remember that a model is used to represent the phenomena under study as simply as possible; it is not meant to correspond to the phenomena exactly. If it did, it would no longer be a model but would be identical to the phenomena.

Our psychological model is built by a method of successive approximations in order to demonstrate how knowledge is accumulated in science. Chapter 2 begins our study with a short discussion of the development of theory and scientific method in psychology. One of our goals there and throughout the book is to show how the method of experimentation follows from psychological theory, whether or not it is explicitly articulated by the experimenter.

Methods of psychology

No psychologist is likely to make pertinent contributions
to the field if he still hesitates to remember that the
armchair is the most indispensable piece of hardware
we own.
—*Rudolf Arnheim (1971)*

Given that psychological phenomena exist, how do we go about understanding them? No single set of methods is correct for psychological study in the same way that no single set of rules is followed for proposing marriage. The method used in both cases is critically dependent upon one's perception of the situation and what one wants to know. In most cases, a "yes" or "no" answer is not sufficient; there is concern for other aspects, such as the rationale for the answer. In psychology, the methods we use to study psychological processes can only follow, not precede, the questions we wish to ask. Scientists with different questions or conceptions of the topic to be studied develop different experimental methods. They then use the results of the experiments to argue for the importance of asking just these questions in their particular experimental manner.

Consider the change from the Aristotelean to the Galilean view of motion. Aristotle saw a falling stone as a change of state rather than a process. For him, the relevant dependent measures of motion were the total distance covered and the amount of time elapsed. From these two observations the Aristotelean could compute the average speed or the average distance covered per unit of time. In contrast, Galileo, like some of the men before him, saw the falling of a stone as a process; therefore, it was reasonable to speculate on the operations of this process. One hypothesis put forward was that stones fall with a uniformly accelerated motion. This idea led to new methods of experimentation and data analysis which were unlikely in the conceptual framework of Aristotle's view of motion.

THE ROLE OF THEORY IN RESEARCH: A BRIEF HISTORY

Research in psychology has also been dictated by the theories and conceptual ideas of the investigator. A brief review of some different psychological theories will indicate how the methods of research followed directly from these theories. The British Empiricists (John Locke, George Berkeley, and David Hume) of the 17th and 18th centuries provided a model of human psychology that stimulated the beginning of its systematic study in the 19th century. The empiricists rejected the venerable philosophical notion of innate ideas as the working material for thought to take place. Instead, they postulated that all knowledge is acquired through experience. According to Locke, experience consists of sensation and reflection. Sensation is what we see, hear, feel, or touch. Reflection is a process of the mind and involves building directly on our sense experiences. Accordingly, phenomena such as knowing are a direct consequence of the reflective process operating on our sense experiences. Thus sensation—a phenomenon with observable, tangible properties—becomes the basic unit of human psychology.

Thomas Reid, an 18th-century empiricist, was the first to further refine empirical psychology by distinguishing sensation from perception. Sensation, according to Reid, is the impression that an object makes on the mind; it constitutes the bare content, the raw materials, of the mind. Perception, on the other hand, includes a further step or operation by which that content is supplied with meaning. Perception is the apprehension or recognition of an object; it contains not only the sensation of the object, but a concept of it.

Reid answered the question of how the mind took this step—of applying meaning to the bare sensation and transforming it into a perception—by appealing to the Supreme Being. We need not look so far. The source of the meaning by which the observer transforms the sensed or detected object into the recognized one is his storehouse of knowledge, his memory. William James made this point by stating: "We perceive only that which we preperceive." For example, we hear, or detect, a foreign language as well as we do our native tongue, but very little if any meaning can be attached to the message. Certain syllables may be recognized as corresponding to some that we know in English, but even these do not have the same meaning. The words of the foreign language are not making contact with our semantic memory that continuously provides meaning to the words of our own language.

Introspection

The empiricist theory of knowledge emphasized a process, sensation, that could be observed and measured; and in the 19th century people who had been influenced by the empiricists began to think of doing so systematically. Wilhelm Wundt set up the first laboratory dedicated to experimental psychology in 1879. Wundt was, at least functionally, a dualist; he believed that the study and description of mental phenomena should differ from that of physical phenomena. Fixed laws could be developed to describe physical phenomena, he believed, but mental phenomena could be characterized only by normative rules. For example, Wundt utilized different methods of study for sensory motor events and cognitive mental events. To study the former, he employed the empiricistic concepts of association and contiguity of events. In studying the latter he relied on developments of Kant and his followers. As an example, he formalized and tested the concept of apperception to describe the focus of attention in which the observer selects and structures his conscious experience.

Given his belief in conscious experience, Wundt proposed to analyze this experience into its elements. In order to do this, he developed the method of introspection. In this method observers were trained to report the elements of their conscious experience. Carefully collecting and systematically analyzing their own and others' reports of mental processes, the introspectionists defined some of the most important areas of psychological investigation, such as attention and the analysis of consciousness. In his best known finding, Wundt claimed that conscious feeling could be described on values on three basic dimensions: pleasant-unpleasant, excitement-calm, and strain-relaxation. Titchener and his students also utilized Wundt's experimental methods but found slightly different results. They argued that there were only two basic dimensions to feeling since Wundt's excitement-calm and strain-relaxation dimensions measure the same psychological experience. Unfortunately, this disagreement grew into a controversy which could not be resolved by the introspective method itself. Accordingly, no advancement in knowledge could occur until psychologists agreed on a new method of analysis within Wundt's general paradigm or until a new paradigm was developed.

Although the introspective method sometimes proves valuable as an adjunct to the experimental method, it does not, by itself, lead to precise and quantitative knowledge. We have all been dissatisfied with someone else's subjective report of some psychological experience. Consider St. Theresa's description of a mystical experience known as the Ecstasy of St. Theresa.

Introspective method

> Beside me on the left hand appeared an angel in bodily form, such as I am not in the habit of seeing except very rarely. Though I often have visions of angels, I do not see them . . .

He was not tall but short, and very beautiful. . . . In his hands I saw a great golden spear, and at the iron tip there appeared to be a point of fire. This he plunged into my heart several times so that it penetrated to my entrails. When he pulled it out, I felt that he took them with it, and left me utterly consumed by the great love of God. The pain was so severe that it made me utter several moans. The sweetness caused by this intense pain is so extreme that one cannot possibly wish it to cease (from Hibbard's *Bernini*, 1965).

Bernini, in his famous baroque sculpture inspired by this description (see Figure 1), represented the hallucinatory event in as real and concrete a depiction as possible.

To see the uses and limitations of introspection itself, consider the question: "In the house that you lived in two houses ago, was the front doorknob on the right side or the left side of the door?" How do you retrieve this memory? Most likely you will first fix on the house in which you live at present, go back one step to the house before that, and then to the house before that one. In other words, you trace back your history until you have arrived at the correct house, when you gradually recall details that build a picture of the front door. At some point it becomes clear on which side the door opened. In the final step, one person might be picturing himself coming home in the evening after a hard day's work; another might see himself leaving. One might remember the position of his own body as he went through the door; another might remember the door itself as it opened.

The introspective method can tell us a great deal about the psychological processes involved in answering this question. The task is a difficult one and involves a sequence of processing operations or stages between question and answer. Employing the experimental method to study this task would not be informative, due to the complexity of the task. The performance of this task, however, involves the performance of myriad smaller tasks, such as those involved in the perception of a message or in the retrieval of a single item in memory. Some of these processes do not lend themselves to introspection at all, but each of these processes can be studied and evaluated by the experimental methods articulated in this book.

Act psychology   Rather than accepting Wundt's definition of psychology, Franz Brentano argued against focusing the study of psychology on the *contents* of consciousness; instead, psychologists should be concerned with the *acts* of consciousness. In this sense, Brentano saw the importance of mental processes, or psychological functioning

FIGURE 1. Ecstasy of St. Theresa as represented by Bernini.

over time. Freud, a student in Brentano's psychology courses, developed the first systematic psychological theory that emphasized dynamic processes. The critical weakness in Brentano's contribution was that his theoretical development did not include a new method or paradigm for research. Thus, although Wundt emphasized the contents or structure of consciousness while Brentano attended to the acts or function of consciousness, both thought in terms of the introspective method.

Behaviorism   John B. Watson (1913), primed with the findings and methods of Pavlov and Thorndike in the study of animal behavior, rejected the methods of Wundt and Brentano. Watson proposed, instead, an entirely objective psychology in which public observable behavior was the focus of study. In his favor, Watson cited the current controversies that grew out of defining psychology as the study of consciousness and the use of the introspective method. He concluded that introspection was an invalid scientific method; hence, because he believed that mental processes were not discoverable in any other way, they were not a proper study for psychology at all. Only behavior, observable, measurable, and controllable, could be studied scientifically.

Watson correctly realized that advancement in any scientific discipline requires methods of study the results of which can be agreed upon by the scientific community. Since introspections were not directly observable, they were open to alternative interpretations, whereas all scientists would agree on some observable behavior, such as whether a rat turned left or right. In this respect, Watson was entirely correct and was following in the methodological development in the physical sciences. However, Watson went beyond arguing for observable behavior as the basic dependent variable, and denied that any theoretical references to consciousness or other mental processes could increase our understanding of behavior. Watson's argument reached its logical consequence with B. F. Skinner's (1950) proposal that psychologists should develop a stimulus-response psychology with no reference to any psychological processes between stimulus and response. Given this framework, proponents of the paradigm set about attempting to define functional stimulus-response relationships without reference to intervening psychological processes.

Watson's and Skinner's elimination of any reference to mental processes in psychological study is not a logical consequence of demanding observable dependent measures. Although two psychologists might agree on *when* a rat turned right or left, they might not agree on *why* the rat turned in a particular direction. In order to explain and to predict the direction of turning, it might be necessary to propose intervening processes which cannot be directly observed. To return to our physical example of motion, Aristotle and Galileo would agree on Aristotle's observation of the relationship between the distance that an object moves and the time taken for the movement. However, Galileo proposed an unobservable intervening process—uniformly accelerated motion—that predicted the relationship and allowed him to predict results in other experimental situations. Although it may be argued that, with present techniques, a uniformly accelerated motion can be observed directly, it could not at the time of Galileo's proposal. In the physical sciences today, the idea of an unobservable process is not bothersome and is considered essential to theory and accurate prediction.

Another paradigm of psychology was Gestalt, developed by Max Wertheimer and his students (Koffka, 1935; Kohler, 1929). Wertheimer and his followers objected to the introspective methods of Wundt and Titchener and to Watson's behavioristic approach. Against Watson they maintained that immediate conscious experience was an essential subject for psychology. Against Wundt and Titchener they asserted that experience could not be reduced to the elements of sensation, that indeed the experience cannot be understood through analysis of any of its parts. To illustrate, let us consider the experience of hearing a symphony. The important thing about this act is clearly the mental processes involved. The behavior of the listener is insignificant in comparison and consists for the most part in abstaining from activity in order that something might happen inside his head. At the same time, an introspective analysis, which would have us attend to the quality, intensity, and duration of the experience, says really little more than behaviorism does about the experience of listening to a symphony although it might be an accurate list of its parts. The experience is somehow greater than the sum of its parts.

Gestalt Psychology

Gestalt psychologists assumed that the physical universe contains organized information and that we preserve this organization in our perception. Accordingly, the study of psychology should focus on the description of this organization. A series of dots arranged to form a circle appear as a circle, not as an unrelated series of dots. Psychology should develop methods and theories that delineate the rules of our perceptual organization. Although the Gestalt psychologists argued against both the introspective and behavioristic approaches, they shared with them some critical assumptions about the content and method of psychological study. In agreement with the introspectionists, they viewed consciousness as a structure rather than a process, even though they differed in their conceptualization of this structure. Accordingly, they mainly were concerned with rules that describe the structure rather than with processes. In many of their studies, they relied on phenomenological reports similar to the introspective reports utilized by Wundt and his followers. In a manner similar to the behaviorists, they refused to postulate intervening psychological processes to account for observed behavior. Rather, their primary assumption was that our nervous system was wired in a certain way to resonate to particular configural stimulus situations in the real world. Similarly, Gibson (1950, 1966) ignores intervening psychological processes given his assumption that perceptual systems respond directly to invariant aspects of the stimulus environment.

The theories of Donders, Fechner, Helmholtz, and Broadbent have also influenced the development of certain methods of psychological study. These theories and methods will be scrutinized in detail in subsequent chapters. We shall also contrast each of these theories to our present information-processing approach. The aim of this brief discussion has been to show how the method of study followed from, not preceded, the psychological theory. In this respect, the methods of experimental psychology can be articulated only in the framework of a psychological theory.

The central assumption of the development of theory and method in this book is that psychological phenomena are conceptualized as processes, not as stimulus-response relationships. In this case we are primarily interested in what psychological events do, even though we may be somewhat foggy about what they are. We address ourselves to the psychological processes that intervene between some stimulus and some response for two central reasons. First, explanation and prediction of stimulus-response relationships fail without prior understanding of the intervening sequence of mental processes. Second, we are interested in developing a psychological explanation of exactly those processes that lead to the response. Our inquiry into psychology is primarily directed at understanding the form of psychological behavior, not at merely predicting simple cause-effect relationships between stimulus and response.

The goal of this book is to illuminate the proper methods of psychological study. However, the illustration of these methods is completely interwoven with the study of the psychological processes themselves. As illustrated above and throughout this book, the methods of psychology cannot be discussed independently of the theory and content of psychology. Also, the knowledge of the proper methods of psychology is acquired by doing science rather than by learning a set of abstract rules for doing it. Accordingly, all of the appropriate experimental techniques are illustrated in the context of specific experiments and theories rather than in isolation.

Throughout this book, the experimental method will be used to study the psychological processes that intervene between stimulus and response. Before beginning these experimental approaches, it is necessary to briefly discuss the experimental method itself. In this method the experimenter manipulates nature, in the form of his independent variable, and looks for the effect of the changes that he makes in the independent variable upon changes in a dependent variable. The dependent variable is the indicator of the psychological event of interest.

EXPERIMENTAL METHOD

For example, an experimenter might be interested in finding out how many letters a subject can perceive in a single eye fixation as a function of the number of items in the visual display. Visual

Dependent Variables

How does the experimenter find a good dependent variable? Most experimental psychologists agree that a dependent measure should be reliable, valid, and sensitive. Validity refers to how accurately the dependent variable measures the psychological process of interest. If a psychologist is interested in how well an observer detected (experienced) a stimulus, the proportion of times he said he detected it may not be a valid measure. In this case, the psychologist is interested in a psychological process (detection) and the subject's observed behavior may not be a true (valid) index of that process. The validity of dependent measures in psychological experimentation is one of the central themes of this book.

The second criterion, reliability, refers to the desire to have as little random variability in our measure as possible. For example, distance might be measured by counting the number of steps one takes between the two points or by utilizing a yardstick. The first measure would have more variability than the second and although both measures would increase our knowledge about the distance between the points, we use the least variable measure possible in the experiment.

The third criterion, sensitivity, is bound up with validity. Most experimental design books tell us to find a dependent measure which is sensitive to changes in our independent variable. Those that vary most with variations in the independent variable are preferred. However, here our interest is in a dependent variable that reflects the operation of a psychological process. So we look for variables that are sensitive to changes in the psychological process itself. Accordingly, in our approach we look for dependent variables that are (1) valid, reflecting accurately the operations of a psychological process, (2) reliable, fluctuating or changing very little for other reasons, and (3) sensitive, changing with changes in the psychological process they measure.

displays can be presented for a very short time, so that their duration does not exceed a single eye fixation. The experimenter presents the subject with a variety of trials containing anywhere from 1 to 9 letters per trial. On each type of trial, he records the number of letters correctly reported. From this data a functional relationship can be plotted between the number of letters reported and the number of letters in the display. The independent variable, that which is under the experimenter's control and manipulated by him, is the number of letters presented on each trial. The dependent variable is the number of letters reported correctly on each trial. Results of this experiment are plotted as a functional relationship in Figure 2. The number of correct letters is plotted on the Y ordinate as a function of the number of letters in the display plotted on the X abscissa.

FIGURE 2. The number of letters correctly reported as a function of the number of letters in the display (after Sperling, 1960).

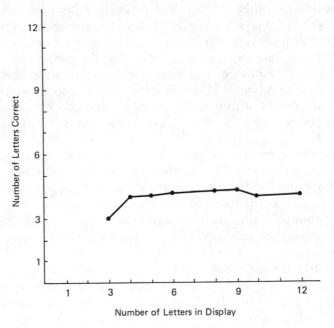

Experimental Design and Control

In an experimental design, the experimenter seeks to establish a functional relationship between an independent variable and a dependent variable. In order to assure that this relationship is reliable, all other variables must be accounted for in the experimental task. If they are, the experimenter is safe in assuming that changes in the dependent variable were caused by changes in the independent variable. This is only the first step—but a critical one—in defining the experimental task. The experimenter must also account for the sequence of mental processes or processing stages that the task requires before he can understand the functional relationship between stimulus and response. The central theme of this book is the presentation of experimental methods for understanding the processing stages between stimulus and response. Before discussing these methods, however, it is necessary to describe how to establish a proper experiment design for investigation.

Methods of control over experimental design are available to the experimenter. These controls are used to prevent other variables besides the independent variable from influencing or confounding the observed relationship between stimulus and response. A second variable is confounded with the independent variable if it is possible that changes in the second variable are partially responsible for the observed relationship between stimulus and response. Some methods of control are (1) eliminate the variables, (2) hold them constant, (3) counterbalance or randomize their effects in the experimental task.

The experimental question in the sample experiment presented above concerned how many items an observer could recognize in a single glance. This question was answered by varying the number of items in a display and recording the number that the observer recalled correctly. The answer to the question is seen in a functional relationship between the independent variable and the dependent variable. A number of other variables, however, could affect this relationship. These variables must be controlled so that the relationship will reflect the direct influence of the independent variable on the dependent variable.

Some of the variables that can influence the experimental results are (1) how long the observer looks at the display, (2) the nature of the test items, (3) the size of the test field, (4) the acuity of the subject, (5) the figure-ground contrast of the items in the display, (6) the amount of practice, and (7) the opportunity that the subject has for chance guessing. Controlling for these variables should provide the desired functional relationship between the independent and dependent variables, supplying an answer for the experimental question.

Our experimental question requires that subjects get only a single glance at the visual display for recognition. Therefore, the effective duration of display must be controlled to eliminate additional glances. Evidence that will be presented later shows that we cannot take discrete looks at the world faster than about five times per second. To give the subject only one look, then, it is necessary that the display be presented for a duration less than 200 msec. Presenting the display for 50 msec. at each experimental condition will hold display duration constant and will also eliminate additional looks at the visual display.

The test items chosen must be items that can be recognized; in other words, they must be meaningful to the observer. The letters of the alphabet provide a good population of items for our experiment; since we operationally define test items as letters, it is necessary to prevent the subject from employing other test items in his recognition strategy. For example, if the letters in the display spell words, the subject could possibly treat the whole word as a single item. Accordingly, the experimenter would overestimate the number of items an observer could recognize, since the experimenter counts each letter as a test item. The experimenter can eliminate this possible confounding by making sure that the letters in the visual display do not spell words or wordlike items.

When the experimenter increases the number of items in the visual display it would be only natural to increase the overall size of the visual display. In this case, he has completely confounded the size of the visual display with the number of items in the visual display. This confounding creates a particular problem since the acuity of the observer decreases as letters are removed from the center of the visual display. It is necessary, therefore, to control for the visual display size as the number of items in the display presentation increases. One way to do this is to define a given display size, for example, a 4 x 4 matrix of cells. The subject is instructed to fixate at the center of the matrix. Now on each trial, the experimenter can choose the cells randomly for his item presentation. In this case, even single item displays would contain letter presentations that lie off the center of the display. This procedure randomizes the location of the items in the visual field to eliminate a confounding of display location with the independent variable (the number of items in the display).

Acuity of the subject is an important variable. We can hold this variable constant by testing the same subject under all the experimental conditions. If we tested different subjects under different experimental conditions, the results might differ simply because the subjects differed in acuity (or some other ability), not because of differences in our independent variable. Another solution to this problem would be to test a very large number of subjects at each of the levels of our independent variable in order to average out any differences in the different subjects. Although there are times when such a design is appropriate, we shall see that the best control for individual subject differences is to test each subject at all of the experimental conditions.

Figure-ground contrast (legibility) of the display is also an important variable that can affect performance. Performance would be positively correlated with the figure-ground contrast of the display. To control for this variable, the experimenter should print the display letters so as to optimize legibility and to maintain the same legibility at all levels of the independent variable.

The amount of practice an observer gets in this task will affect his performance. Observers show some rapid improvement over the first few trials in almost any experimental task. To eliminate this large practice effect, some general practice should be given before the experiment proper is carried out. Also, the experimenter must not confound the order of presentation during the experiment with the levels of the independent variable. The order of presentation in the experiment can be randomized. Assume that there are five levels of the independent variable in the experiment: test displays of 1, 3, 5, 7, and 9 items. The experimenter can, therefore, perform one replication of the experiment every five trials. Each of the five levels must be presented once within the five trials. To do this, the experimenter can have five cards, each of which represents one of the five experimental conditions. He mixes the cards randomly, in a hat, for example, and draws one card for the condition to be presented on each trial. Since he wants to present all five trial types once before he repeats a given trial type, he does not replace the cards into the hat until the hat is empty. This is called sampling without replacement. Sampling with replacement involves replacing the cards into the hat after each draw.

The opportunity that the subject has for chance guessing must also be controlled with changes in display sizes. If subjects were simply required to recall the letters that had been presented on a given trial, they would be more likely to guess correctly an item with large display sizes, since they would feel free to name more items at test. One control for this is to have the subject also indicate the location of the letter in the display. In this case, the subject would write the letters in the appropriate cells in a 4 x 4 response sheet on each trial. A reported letter would be scored as correct only if it were written in the appropriate cell.

As one learns more about this visual information-processing task, other variables in the situation become important. The present design provides a good first approximation to an experiment that answers the question asked. The findings of this particular experiment are discussed in the section on the span of apprehension (Chapter 12). The results are presented there because the number of items that can be recalled in this task defines the span of apprehension, which represents the number of items that subjects can process and hold together simultaneously in short-term memory.

Confounding Processes The experimental psychologist has traditionally been interested in the effects of one variable, called his independent variable, on the dependent variable. His goal, in this case, is to eliminate the influence of other irrelevant variables on his dependent measure. When the experiment has failed to adequately control for the effects of an irrelevant variable on his dependent variable, we say he has confounded their effects and his results are invalid. Confounding variables are easily spotted by the experimenter himself or his colleagues so that this is not a major problem in psychology.

The problem of experimental psychology examined in this book is the confounding of psychological processes in an experiment. This confounding invalidates the experiment in the same way as a confounding of variables. Consider the previous question of the effects of the size of the display on perception as measured by the number of items correctly reported from a visual display. We shall see in Chapter 12 that the memory process is a critical one in this task and its effects must be accounted for before any conclusions about perception can be reached. That is to say, increasing the number of items in the display not only affects the perceptual process, but also influences memory so that the results reflect some combination of both of these processes. The experimenter must design his study so that he can isolate the effects of each of these processes before conclusions about either process can be reached. If he fails to pull apart their effects, his dependent measure gives no information about the functioning of psychological processes in this task. Our goal is to discuss designs and analytic methods that can be used to study one psychological process without the confoundings of other processes. We shall find that the traditional experiment which manipulates only one independent variable is usually insufficient to accomplish this.

What characterizes a good scientific investigation of a psychological problem? It is impossible to respond to this question with exactitude because there is no fixed set of rules or properties an experiment must meet. The easiest way to answer the question is in terms of what a psychological experiment does, rather than what it is. The central goal of a psychological experiment is to increase our knowledge about some psychological process. A given experiment may conform to all of the requirements of proper experimental design and control and yet fail to be a good experiment. If it does not increase our knowledge beyond the specific outcome of the experiment itself, it fails. Psychological investigation is an art and requires much more artistry than merely following an experimental psychology cookbook.

Consider an experiment in which an experimenter investigates whether schizophrenics differ from normals; or children from adults; or males from females; or students on the left side of the room from the students on the right. In all these cases, the experimenter will probably find a difference between the groups. But what have we actually learned from the study? Nothing, since it was already highly likely the two groups would differ before the experiment. What the scientist should learn is not simply how well a subject performs in a given experimental test; rather, the results should shed light on the psychological processes required by the test, the rules by which these processes operate, and, finally, the way in which one subject differs from another with respect to one or more of these processes. As can be seen in this example, scientific investigation cannot begin testing between different groups of subjects until something is known about the psychological processes involved. Research in social, clinical, or developmental psychology needs to be concerned with the psychological processes between stimulus and response in the same way that we are in this book.

The duration of mental processes

*Would it not be possible to determine the time required
for shaping a concept or expressing one's will? For years
this question intrigued me.*
—Franciscus C. Donders (1869)

An experimental psychologist studying human information
processing is concerned with the psychological processes that intervene between stimulus and response. This chapter discusses a
technique for studying these processes. The logic of the experimental approach tells us that in order to interpret response data
properly, we must ask how many processes occur between a
stimulus and a response in an experimental task. How do these
processes work? What rules describe the operations of each
process? How long does each operation last? What variables influence each of the mental processes?

For example, suppose a student is sitting in a classroom and
a fire alarm goes off. The appropriate response would be to leave
the room. The siren functions as the stimulus, and walking out of
the room would usually be an appropriate response. The amount
of time that elapses between the onset of the siren and the onset
of walking out of the room is referred to as reaction time (RT)
or latency.

Our interest lies in the processes that occur internally between the
onset of the stimulus and the onset of the response. We can identify the probable stages of mental processing hypothetically by
a logical analysis of the fire alarm scenario. First the observer
must certainly become aware that some new stimulus has occurred.
This reminds us of the British Empiricists' concept of sensation—
the imprinting, as they thought of it, of the stimulus upon the sensory system. Sensation, or detection, is the process that initiates
the flow of information through the human processing system. This
takes an amount of time which we can call T_d.

Second, before he can act appropriately the observer must
recognize the siren and identify it as a symbol indicating that a

**STAGES OF
MENTAL
PROCESSING**

Stages of Information Processing

The processes we have identified between stimulus and response in the fire alarm scenario can be clarified in terms of our information-processing analysis. Each process has some information available to it and transforms this information, making the transformed information available to the next processing stage. The information available to the detection process is the stimulus. The detection process transduces the physical signal into a neurological code. At this point in the processing chain, the observer has enough information to report that something has occurred. He cannot, however, say what it is.

The detection process makes available the neurological code to the recognition process. The recognition process must transform this preperceptual information into a perceptual form. There are actually two stages to the recognition of a fire alarm. First, the recognition process must resolve the sound quality so that it can be distinguished from other possible sounds, such as the bell that signals the end of the class period. Second, the observer must know that this particular sound means "fire alarm." For example, if he had never heard a fire alarm before, he may recognize the sound as one of a certain quality but it would have no meaning. In order to recognize its meaning, he must first perceive the sound of the alarm and, second, know that this sound signifies a fire alarm.

The recognition process, therefore, must translate the neurological code given by the detection process into a code that its meaningful to the response selection process. The knowledge that the fire alarm is ringing is the outcome of a successful recognition. This information or symbolic encoding of the sound of the fire alarm is meaningful to the response-selection process. The response-selection process, therefore, receives the information from the recognition stage that the fire alarm is ringing. The response-selection process could have received this information in other ways; a deaf person, for example, could see someone ringing the alarm. The response-selection process must answer the question: Given that there is a fire alarm, what response should be executed?

The response-selection process is similar to the decision process discussed in detail in Chapters 5, 6, and 7. It is influenced by the subject's knowledge of the likelihood that, given a fire alarm, a fire did indeed occur. For example, there may have been a number of false alarms recently, which could lead the response-selection process to wait rather than to execute a "leave the room" command to the response-execution process. Payoffs for different responses also are important for response selection. The situation might be one in which a person could be arrested and fined if he does not leave the building during a fire alarm. In this case, the response-selection process might be biased to leave the room even though a fire is unlikely.

fire, hence danger, may be in the building. The stimulus has now been given a meaning by making contact with some knowledge in memory. If this process does not take place, if the observer experiences the alarm simply as an extraneous event without meaning, then it provides no reason to leave the building. Recognition is similar to the concept of perception used by the British empiricists —the point at which mere sensation has acquired meaning. It also takes a certain amount of time which we will call T_r.

After the observer has recognized the stimulus, he must select a response. He might stand on his head, or jump out the window, or do one of any number of things; we may assume he will pick the response most appropriate to the situation. The choice may be more or less difficult. For instance, if the observer has experienced a number of false fire alarms in the same building and, moreover, is engaged in important work with a deadline to meet, he may hesitate to leave. In any case, selection of the appropriate response also takes some time, which we will abbreviate as $T_{r.s.}$

Finally, the response must be executed after it is selected. In our fire alarm scenario, however, we are not interested in response-execution time per se, but rather in the processing that led up to the execution of the response. Therefore, we measure reaction time from the onset of the stimulus to the onset of the response, so that response-execution time contributes very little to the overall reaction time.

Detection, Recognition, Response Selection

Detection, recognition, and response selection, then, can be identified as three mental processes that would be expected to occur between stimulus and response. We expect also that each of these processes consumes a certain amount of time and the duration of each of these three processes contributes to the total reaction time (RT) from the onset of the stimulus to the onset of the response. The average RT of leaving, given a fire alarm in a classroom, might lie between 2 and 10 seconds, with most of the time taken up by response selection. Detection and recognition of the meaning of the alarm would probably occur in less than 1/2 sec. These mental processes are referred to here as sequential stages in the overall process. Think of a stage as one step in the progression toward the final outcome. Figure 1 presents a flow diagram representation of these stages in the task. Thus, in this example, there are at least three stages between stimulus and response. Of course the observed RT will be longer than the sum of these three times since other events, such as nerve conduction time, will contribute to the overall RT.

FIGURE 1. Three psychological operations or stages of information processing that occur between stimulus and response.

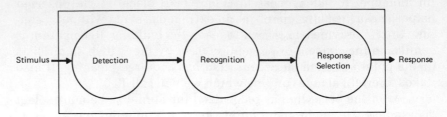

REACTION TIME

The first experimenter to study mental life in terms of stages of processing between stimulus and response was F. C. Donders, a Dutch scientist best known for his work in ophthalmology. Donders described his work in psychology in a paper (1869) entitled "On the Speed of Mental Processes." In this article Donders recalled the pronouncement of physiologist Johannes Müller, twenty-five years before, that the time required for a stimulated nerve to carry its message to the brain and for the brain to activate the muscles was "infinitely short," and that therefore the velocity of nerve conduction could never be measured. Donders pointed out, however, that by 1850, Helmholtz, the famous German scientist, was doing exactly that. Helmholtz worked out a technique for measuring nerve condition velocity in frogs, and subsequently applied the same principles to a series of experiments with humans. The experiment measured the time between the presentation of a stimulus on the skin and an involuntary reflex to the stimulus. Helmholtz compared two conditions of RT. In one, the muscles of the ball of the thumb were stimulated at a point on the wrist (the subject's hand and arm were immobilized). Reaction time was measured between onset of this stimulus and the onset of muscle contraction reflex of the thumb. In the other condition, the same muscles were stimulated at a point just above the fold of the elbow. The RT required for muscle contraction to the stimulus at this point was also measured and was found to be more than in the first condition.

Subtractive Method

The logic of this experiment was founded on the belief that the two RTs should differ only with respect to how far the nerve impulses had to travel between the point of stimulation and the nerve-muscle junction. The basic task did not differ under the two conditions, and therefore the time for all other elements of processing between the stimulation and muscle reflex could be assumed to be constant. Thus, all Helmholtz had to do in order to arrive at the nerve conduction velocity was to determine the extra time required for the longer distance and divide this time by the difference between the two distances. In this way, Helmholtz was able to estimate human nerve conduction velocity at 100 ft./sec. This result was surprisingly accurate, given the speed of nerve conduction time and the short distance between the two points.

Helmholtz also was able to employ this paradigm with voluntary responses. He stimulated the skin at either of two different distances from the brain. The subject was instructed to respond to the stimulus as rapidly as possible with a movement of the hand. The two conditions, therefore, only differed with respect to how far the nerve impulses had to travel to the brain. All other components of the task were assumed to be constant in the two conditions. Thus the difference in the reaction times provided an estimate of the difference in nerve conduction times for the two distances.

Donders was stimulated by another set of experiments also, those of the French astronomer Hirsch. Hirsch measured the RTs of simple detection responses (moving a hand) to stimuli presented to the eye, ear, and skin, respectively. Hirsch found that stimuli to the eye produced slower RTs than stimuli to the ear, which produced slower RTs than stimuli to the skin. Donders replicated these conditions and found that a reaction to a visual stimulus took 1/5 sec.; to an audio stimulus 1/6 sec.; and to a touch stimulus 1/7 sec. It should be noted that the RTs in these experiments would have been affected by the intensity of the stimuli used, although the investigator did not appear to be aware of this.

Today a number of studies have shown that RTs to a stimulus decrease as the intensity of the stimulus increases. Thus, an observer instructed to press a lever as soon as he hears a tone will respond sooner, as the loudness of the tone is increased. Logically, this effect should probably influence the sensation stage, the process of becoming aware of the stimulus. This logical analysis is supported by physiological studies, which have actually shown that nerve conduction time across the synapses on the way to the brain is inversely related to stimulus intensity. Consequently, it appears that stimulus intensity affects the detection or sensation stage in a simple signal detection task. According to a sequential process model, stimulus intensity is unlikely to also affect response selection because response selection occurs after the stimulus is detected and should be relatively independent of stimulus variables (see Chapter 7).

Intensity of Stimulus

Given Helmholtz's measure of nerve conduction velocity and Hirsch's and Donders' absolute RTs, Donders correctly reasoned that nerve conduction time could only account for a small portion of the total RT. What Donders wanted to know, however, was what process or processes took up the rest of the RT. Although Donders' indicated that there was at least 1/10 sec. consumed by mental processes, his analysis did not allow one to measure the time it took for each mental process.

Helmholtz's experiment had taken the activity of the nerves out of the realm of the unfathomable. Donders was inspired to hope that the same might be done for mental processes. "Would thought also not have the infinite speed usually associated with it?" he asked. Helmholtz's method gave Donders a clue, and in time he devised a method for studying the speed of mental activities, employing the Helmholtz principle of subtraction in his research.

Simple vs. Choice RT Tasks

Donders devised several experimental situations based on this principle. In one paradigm, an electrode was placed on each of the subject's feet and hooked up so that Donders could stimulate either foot as he wished. There were two conditions. In the first, Donders told the subject that he was going to stimulate the left (or the right) foot, and asked the subject to make a response as rapidly as possible with the hand on the same side. Thus, in this condition, the subject knew which foot would be stimulated and was prepared to respond with the correct hand. His task, therefore, was simply to detect that a stimulus occurred and give the predetermined response as fast as possible.

In the second condition, the subject was told that the stimulus might be given to either foot and was instructed to respond with his left hand if his left foot was stimulated, and with his right hand if his right foot was stimulated. Donders would stimulate one or the other foot randomly from trial to trial. In this situation the subject did not know in advance which foot would be stimulated and, therefore, which hand would be the correct one for his response. Thus, two additional operations in the mental processing that occurred between stimulus and response were required in the second task. The subject had to first identify which of his two feet were stimulated and then select the appropriate hand for the response. The first condition is referred to as a simple RT task; the second is called a choice RT task.

Consider at this point what your intuition would predict as the result of the experiment. This can be a helpful tool in analyzing both one's own experiments and those of others. In this case, one would certainly predict that choice RT would be larger than simple RT. This was indeed true of the data Donders obtained. On the average, choice RT took longer than simple RT by 1/15 sec. (67 msec.).

Donders reasoned that since all other aspects of the experimental situation had been held constant in the two conditions, the additional time necessary for completion of the task in choice RT could only be explained by the presence of the two additional mental processes. He concluded, therefore, that 1/15 sec. or 67 msec. was "the time required for deciding which side had been stimulated and for establishing the action of the will on the right or left side." That is, by comparing two tasks, the second identical to the first except for the addition of a recognition and a response-selection stage, Donders could isolate out and identify the duration of these two stages as 67 msec. He found from this experiment that it requires 67 msec. for an observer to recognize one of two possible stimuli and to choose between two responses when only one response was possible. It also seems reasonable that a larger number of possible stimuli and responses to choose among would take even longer.

Donders' experimental design was such that the subject in the simple RT task, knowing which foot would be stimulated and all prepared to respond, could possibly respond before he actually detected the stimulus. We all jump the gun now and then. The measured RT would be affected, of course. It would no longer accurately reflect the duration of the mental events. Psychologists are careful to remain aware of the possibility that the subject might start to respond before information is sensed or perceived; such responses are called anticipation errors. How could a psychologist check for anticipation errors in the simple RT experiment?

Donders repeated the same experimental design for the visual modality, using a red and a white light in place of the right-left feet. Again, the first condition required a predetermined response to one of the lights; the second required a choice between the right or left hand, depending on which of the two randomly varied stimuli was perceived. His results averaged over five subjects indicated that the extra time required for choice RT over simple RT was 154 msec. The difference between the simple and choice RT was over twice as long (154 vs. 67) when the stimulation was visual rather than tactile. Why would recognition and/or response selection be more difficult in the visual than in the tactile experiment?

In a third set of experiments, the nature of the response was changed. The stimuli now were two letters of the alphabet, and

Visual presentation

the response required was to pronounce aloud the name of the letter presented on each trial, again (as always) as fast as possible. Thus if the subject saw an E, for example, his task was to say "E" as quickly as he could. Again RTs were observed under two conditions: in one, the subject knew which of the two alternative letters of the experiment would be presented on each trial and thus was ready with his response; in the other, one of the two letters was presented randomly from trial to trial and the subject was not told which letter, so that he could only choose between the two responses after the stimulus was presented and correctly recognized. The extra processing in the choice task required an average of 166 msec. longer than the simple RT task.

Auditory presentation   Donders' stage-process model implied that insertion of additional stages would increase reaction time for all the sensory modalities, and he therefore took care to demonstrate that the results of an experiment using one modality could also be replicated for another. Thus the above visual experiment was also done with auditory stimuli. Subjects were presented with vowel sounds and asked to respond as soon as possible by repeating the sound presented. For example, the two-alternative experiment was done using the vowel sounds /e/ and /i/. In the choice reaction condition either of two vowel sounds, /e/ and /i/, could be presented on a given trial, and the subject had to distinguish the sound and repeat back the vowel. This condition was compared with the simple reaction condition in which the subject knew in advance which vowel sound would be presented and repeated the sound as quickly as possible.

Insertion of the recognition and response-selection stages also added to reaction time with auditory presentations, but the amount of additional time was greater in the visual task (166 msec.) than in the auditory task (56 msec.). Either recognition, or response selection, or both, was easier in the auditory task with spoken vowel stimuli, than in the visual task with printed symbols. Donders believed that the differences in the two tasks must be due to the recognition stage rather than the response-selection stage since response selection is the same in the two tasks. To account for the results, Donders actually presented a detailed description of how the auditory identification of a vowel sound was not as complex as the visual identification of a vowel symbol.

Donders was aware that choice RT tasks differed from the simple detection task with respect to two processes: stimulus recognition and response selection. So he devised another series of experiments to isolate the contributions of each of these stages. To determine the time for the recognition stage, Donders set up two experimental conditions. In the first condition, a subject would be required to push a button as rapidly as possible when he saw a light go on. In another condition, the light could be one of two colors, and the subject was instructed to respond only when one of the lights came on. In this case, the subject had to identify the color of the light after he had detected it in order to insure that he would only respond to the indicated light. Thus the second condition required a second stage, recognition, in addition to the detection stage required by both conditions. Donders considered that he had held the detection stage constant and that response selection did not occur in the two conditions. He believed that when only one response was required, the subject could select this response before the stimulus was presented. Therefore, any difference in RTs would represent the time required for the recognition stage inserted in the second condition.

To determine the time for response selection between two alternatives, Donders devised another experimental comparison. The subject would be required to recognize the stimulus in both conditions, but should have to select a response in only one. In the first condition, the subject could be presented with either of two signals but was required to respond to only one. In this case, the subject could conceivably select the response before the stimulus is presented. In the second condition, the subject is required to respond differentially to both stimuli; therefore, he could not select his response in advance. Hence, the second condition requires all the processing of the first, plus the time for response selection. It follows that the difference in RTs between the two conditions represents the time for response selection.

In order to estimate the time for mental processes, Donders' classic comparisons involve three different experimental conditions, A, B, and C: the detection task, the detection-identification-response selection task, and the detection-identification task, respectively. In Condition A, the subject is told that a certain stimulus, let us say the letter X, will appear on every trial and he is instructed to pronounce the letter X as soon as he sees it. Once he has detected the presence of a stimulus, he can execute the appropriate response immediately. The stimulus does not have to be identified and a response does not have to be selected, since it has been chosen in advance.

In Condition B, the subject knows that the stimulus will be one of two letters, say X and O, and he must respond appropriately to both stimuli. Therefore, he must detect the presence of the stimulus, identify it as either one or the other, and select his response. Although the subject knows the stimulus must be one of two alter-

A, B, and C Tasks

natives, it must be identified on every trial. Similarly, although he can narrow his response down in advance to the two alternatives, he cannot select a response until identification is complete. Therefore, in Condition B, the subject is required to identify the stimulus and select the appropriate response after the stimulus is recognized. In this case, detection, recognition, and response selection contribute to the RT.

In Condition C, either X or O can be presented on any trial, but the subject has been told to respond only when one of them, say X, is present. Therefore, he must detect the presence of the stimulus, identify it as either X or O, and if it is X, respond by pronouncing "X." Donders believed that the response-selection stage in this task was equivalent to the same stage in the simple detection task; that is, there is only one correct response, which the subject can prepare in advance and have ready whenever the stimulus is presented. Accordingly, response-selection time should not contribute to the overall RT in Condition C.

If Donders' analysis is correct, the time for the identification process should equal the difference in RT between conditions C and A. Similarly, the RT difference between conditions B and C estimates the time for response selection. Donders' original results employing these three conditions were very promising. The RTs were ordered as predicted by the stage analysis. In one study reported, with vowel sounds Donders found reaction times of 201, 284, and 237 msec. for Conditions A, B, and C, respectively. Using the subtractive method, he was able to estimate the time for recognition or identification as 237 minus 201, or 36 msec., and the time for response selection as 284 minus 237, or 47 msec. Of course, the time for detection cannot be estimated, since other events contribute to the reaction time in the task. That is to say, the RT in the simple RT task does not simply represent the time for detection.

Criticism of Donders' methods

Donders believed that he could insert a stage of processing in an experimental task and estimate its time using the subtractive method. For example, the difference in reaction time between Conditions B and C was assumed to represent the time for response selection. It is assumed that Condition B contains response selection, whereas Condition C does not. But we can look at Condition C in a slightly different manner; there are two stimuli, X and O, and there are two responses, "X" and silence. That is, after identifying the stimulus as either X or O, the subject must decide whether the appropriate response is now to say "X" or not to say anything. Indeed, there is a sense in which the subject can be said always to have to select a response; that is, he must always decide whether to respond or not, even in a simple detection task. Accordingly, we cannot say that the response selection stage was present in Condition B and not present in Condition C. Condition C required the subject to select between responding and not responding, depending on the stimulus presented. In Condition B he was required to respond to both stimuli, but to select a response depending upon the stimulus presented.

It appears then, that rather than inserting or deleting a stage of processing in the task, the different conditions changed the nature of the response selection process. Donders' assumption that the experimenter could devise two experimental tasks which differed only with respect to an additional stage of processing is, therefore, untenable, and without this assumption his results cannot be used to estimate the duration of a processing stage. Indeed, it is difficult to see what meaning his results would have even if the method of insertion were a valid one. Even if we knew the duration of each stage, we would still be in the dark about how these mental processes operate. Donders' work, having proved at least that perception and cognition were not instantaneous, failed to open further doors and lent itself to criticisms that undermined what little it had seemed to achieve.

At the turn of the century, Külpe and his coworkers criticized the central assumption of Donders' subtractive method: the additivity of the times for mental events. They asserted that stages cannot be added in a task without affecting the time to complete other stages. Their central argument was that typical tasks compared in the subtractive method differ by more than one or two stages: rather, the overall quality or gestalt of the tasks differ. Accordingly, the subtractive method cannot indicate the duration of a particular stage of mental processing. Being introspectionists, they did not present any RT evidence supporting this criticism of the Donderian subtractive method. Rather, they relied on the introspective reports of the observers. After this criticism, investigators lost interest in Donders' insertion method as a tool for studying mental processes.

Donders' stage model of mental life remained dormant along with his techniques until the 1960s, when it was revived by Saul Sternberg (1969a,b). Sternberg accepted as valid the conclusions of Donders' critics that one cannot insert one stage without affecting the operations of other stages, and that the new reaction time will confound the duration of the new stage with changes in the duration of the original stages. The method he devised avoided this problem while capitalizing on the possibilities in the stage notion. Sternberg's idea was to introduce changes in the experimental situation that affected the amount of processing or the number of

Sternberg's modification

operations required within a single stage, rather than the number of stages present in the task.

For instance, using Sternberg's principle we might set up an identification experiment in which the subject was asked to push a button to a red light. In one condition, we would randomly mix red light presentations with blue light presentations. In the other condition we would randomize red light trials with pink light trials. Therefore, the task remains exactly the same in both conditions—respond only to red—but the colors are more similar to each other in the second condition than in the first. We can test whether this variable might affect the time needed to complete the recognition stage; it seems logical that the observer would find it harder to discriminate between very similar stimuli than between very dissimilar stimuli. The detection stage, however, in which the subject in either case notices that something is out there, should not be affected; nor would we expect the variable to affect the response-selection stage, which in both cases, given one of two identifications, requires deciding on one of two possible responses.

To test these expectations, the experimenter must choose other independent variables that would be expected to affect other processing stages of the task. He assumes that the color of the stimuli does not affect response-selection time, but he could vary an independent variable that is expected to influence this stage of processing. The experimenter might vary response compatibility in the task, since this is expected to influence response-selection time, but not recognition time. In our task, for example, we can also have the subject respond verbally with the word "red" when it is presented under the red-pink and red-blue conditions. Hence, we have four experimental conditions and measure the RT in each condition.

We expect significant differences in RT as a function of both of our independent variables. Reaction time should be larger in the red-pink condition than the red-blue conditions and button pushing might take longer than verbal reaction. More importantly, if the two variables affect two independent processes (stages) in the RT task, their effects on RT should be additive. That is to say, the effect of the red-pink variable would be the same under each response compatibility condition and, analogously, the effect of response compatibility should be the same under both color conditions.

Thus, if our results show that it takes 50 msec. longer to respond when the alternative stimuli are red and pink than when they are red and blue under both response compatibility conditions, we have evidence that indicates it is more difficult to distinguish red from pink than red from blue. We still do not know the absolute identification times in either case. Rather, the 50 msec. is a measure of the increased difficulty of the recognition stage in the red-pink relative to the red-blue condition. By choosing other stimulus pairs according to increasing or decreasing color similarity, we should be able to determine the psychophysical similarity of the colors, using reaction times as our dependent measure.

Donders assumed that it was possible to introduce an entire stage without affecting the difficulty of the other stages. Sternberg assumes that one can introduce a variable that will selectively increase or decrease the difficulty and, thus, the time to complete a single stage without affecting the others. He has formalized a method to validate the assumption that a given variable selectively affects the processing of only one stage. This procedure, known as the additive-factor method, will be discussed in detail (see below).

With Sternberg's method we have indeed abandoned Donders' hope of obtaining the absolute time to complete mental stages of processing. Donders was searching for some sort of platonic ideal of each stage, even if it were only quantitative: he wanted to be able to state that recognition takes 100 msec., detection 50 msec., and so on. As the example just described demonstrates, however, recognition time fluctuates from one condition to another, making the platonic ideal of recognition time a meaningless concept. Rather, it is the fluctuation itself that will interest us, not only because it alone can be studied, but also because it is far more useful information than the absolute time required for identification in any particular task. Sternberg's paradigm, by allowing us to understand how variables affect the duration of mental processes, informs us about the nature of those processes themselves, an accomplishment which lay beyond the hope of Donders.

ADDITIVE-FACTOR METHOD

In Sternberg's formalized method of study, called the additive-factor method, each experimental task can be analyzed logically to determine the number of stages involved in the task. The experimonter then chooses an independent variable that is expected to affect the processing or operation of a particular stage. For example, the experimenter could choose two levels of stimulus discriminability (red-blue, red-pink) as a variable that affects recognition time. By pairing each level of this variable with levels of another variable that is expected to affect another stage, the experimenter can provide a test of his experimental assumption that the two variables affect different stages of processing. In our example, we

Factorial Designs

The design of the tone detection experiment is typical of experiments using the additive factor method. It is called a factorial design because each level of one independent variable is crossed with every level of the other independent variable. The two independent variables are stimulus intensity and response compatibility, with two levels of each variable, which gives $2 \times 2 = 4$ experimental conditions. It will become apparent that the additive-factor method could not be used if the experiment was not a factorial one.

In this experiment, as in most of the experiments in this book, the subject goes through all of the experimental conditions. Accordingly, the experimenter must present the different conditions in such a way that the condition is not confounded with the temporal order of presentation. One way to do this is to first practice the subject sufficiently under all experimental conditions, say, for example, one hour. Then the subject is required to participate for four additional days. The conditions could be presented in the following order. On each day, we present all four conditions so that each experimental condition is pre-

	Order			
	1st	2nd	3rd	4th
Day 2	a	b	c	d
Day 3	b	c	d	a
Day 4	c	d	a	b
Day 5	d	a	b	c

sented once at each of the 4 possible temporal orders. This counterbalances for any possible learning or fatigue effects that may be present on each day. For a second subject, the experimental conditions can be presented in an entirely different sequence, but with the same counterbalancing constraints, and so on for the different subjects. This counterbalancing technique, although completely straightforward, is an important one in this kind of psychological experimentation.

Each condition is preceded with a number of practice trials under that condition. For example, we might have 25 practice trials before each condition, followed by 100 experimental trials. Also, the experimenter should not tell the subject which are practice trials, since the subject might be likely to treat these trials differently. The subject should be precisely instructed in the task and reminded to keep a constant motivation throughout the study.

chose a second variable—response compatibility—that is believed to affect response selection time. If the two variables affect two independent stages in the RT task, their effects on RT should be additive. If not, their effects would most likely combine in a non-additive fashion, that is, they would interact.

The method of studying mental processes, in which the effects of two or more independent variables are evaluated, is an important one. We shall, therefore, analyze yet another task, in which the subject has to respond to a stimulus as soon as he detects it, using the additive-factor method. In this task there are two stages; first, the subject must detect the stimulus, which will take up a certain amount of time. Then he must select his response; he must remember which of the innumerable actions possible to him at the moment is the correct one, given the information put out by the detection stage. This selection also takes some finite time; the two times should contribute to the total RT of the task.

Now we choose two independent variables to study in this task, asking whether each one affects only one or both stages. Stimulus loudness, it would seem, is a variable that should affect only the detection stage. The more intense the stimulus, the easier it is to detect; we shall be surprised, on the other hand, if the more intense stimulus results in a shorter response selection time. We might choose response compatibility as the second variable, requiring subjects to use their dominant hand in one condition and their nondominant hand in the other, pushing a button with the index finger in each case. People are able to respond much more rapidly with their dominant hand than with their nondominant hand, and thus we can expect RT to be longer in the nondominant than in the dominant case. Response compatibility should affect the response selection stage, but again, we will be surprised if it affects the detection stage. Logically, it should not be easier to detect a signal simply because the appropriate response is easier to make.

The experiment will thus have four separate conditions:

1. A tone of the intensity of a whisper; subject required to respond with his dominant hand.
2. A louder tone, of normal speaking intensity; subject required to respond with his dominant hand.
3. The soft tone of condition 1; subject required to respond with his nondominant hand.
4. The loud tone of condition 2; subject required to respond with his nondominant hand.

This experiment can be represented by a 2 x 2 matrix, shown in Figure 2.

FIGURE 2. An experiment that covaries two levels of two independent variables: stimulus intensity and response compatibility. The numbers refer to the experimental conditions described in the text; t_i, where $i = 1,2,3$, or 4, represents the RT for each condition.

Response Compatibility

		dominant hand	nondominant hand
	soft	(1) $\quad t_1$	(3) $\quad t_3$
Stimulus Intensity			
	loud	(2) $\quad t_2$	(4) $\quad t_4$

The experimenter runs many trials under each experimental condition and records the reaction time. The dependent variable in the experiment would be the mean RT under each experimental condition. This RT is assumed to be the sum of the duration of the two stages plus the time taken up by other internal events. It should be stressed that the time taken for the other internal events, called t_o, is assumed to be the same at each condition. If one variable only affects one stage, and the second affects the other stage, then the effects of two independent variables, each of which affects the duration of only one stage, should be additive. That is, there is a time required for detection of a soft tone and another time required for detection of a loud tone; there is a time for selecting a response with the dominant hand and a different time for selecting a response with the nondominant hand. In Condition (1) the total reaction time should include the time it takes to detect a soft tone, plus the time to respond with the dominant hand. In Condition (2) reaction time includes the time for detection of a loud tone, plus the time for selecting a response with the dominant hand. Reaction time in Conditions (3) and (4) will contain the time required for detection of the soft and the loud tones, respectively, plus the time needed to respond with the nondominant hand.

If the additive factor holds, that is, if the independent variables affect different stages, the sum of the RTs of Conditions (2) and (3) will be equal to the sum of the RTs of Conditions (1) and (4). The contribution of t_o can be ignored, since it is assumed to be constant under all experimental conditions.

$$t_2 + t_3 = t_1 + t_4 \tag{1}$$

If the assumptions are correct, the RTs will take on a definite form. If we plot RT as a function of stimulus intensity and response compatibility, the two curves will be parallel as seen in Figure 3.

FIGURE 3. Predicted RTs if stimulus intensity and response compatibility only affect the detection and response-selection stages, respectively.

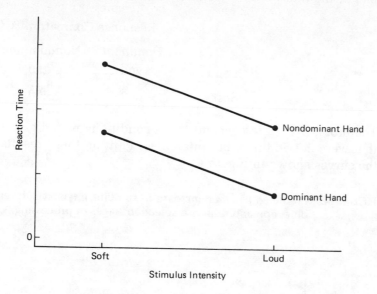

Assume, however, that stimulus intensity affects not only the time it takes to detect the stimulus, but also the time it takes to select a response. In this case, the two curves probably would not be parallel because a decrease in stimulus intensity will change both detection time and response-selection time. Since response compatibility affects response-selection time, both of our variables affect response-selection time, and it is unlikely that their effects would be additive since they are in some sense compounded.

As an example of this case, assume that response-selection time takes 100 and 150 msec., respectively, for the dominant and nondominant responses with a loud tone. If the loudness of the tone also affects response-selection time, we can expect that it might have a larger effect with the nondominant than with the dominant hand. Therefore, the soft tone may slow down the dominant response by only 50 msec. and the nondominant response by 100 msec. Accordingly, the results would not be additive but would interact, since response selection time would have the following times under the four experimental conditions.

		Response Compatibility	
		Dominant	Nondominant
Intensity	Loud	100	150
	Soft	150	250

Now if loudness affected detection so that detection time was 100 and 150 msec., respectively, for the loud and soft tones, the sum of the times of the two processes would be

		Response Compatibility	
		Dominant	*Nondominant*
	Loud	200	250
Intensity	Soft	300	400

Therefore, if t_o were constant these conditions would give results that were not additive, but interacted. Plotting these results gives the curves shown in Figure 4.

FIGURE 4. Predicted RTs if an increase in stimulus intensity shortens both detection and response-selection stages of processing.

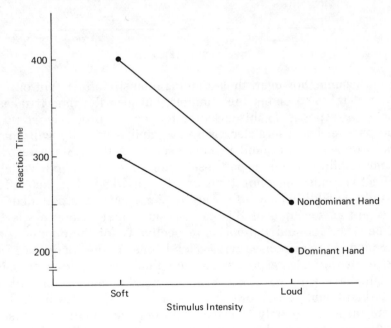

The concept of two variables affecting the same stage of processing and leading to an interaction is a difficult one and deserves another example. Although the additive-factor method was developed for RTs, the concept of interaction is easily seen in an example using 'percentage correct' as a dependent measure.

Consider two variables that affect legibility of printed text: lighting and letter size. First, make the task 20 percent more difficult by decreasing the lighting from an optimal level until the reader is performing 20 percent poorer. Now return to the optimal lighting and decrease the letter size until the reader again performs 20 percent poorer. Then combine the lower levels of lighting and letter size found in the previous two conditions and measure performance. Since both lighting and letter size affect legibility, the task should be much more difficult than the 40 percent below optimal performance predicted by additivity of the two effects of our variables. The foregoing example supports the notion that if decreases in stimulus intensity slow down both detection time and response-selection time, the curves will appear as in Figure 4. Therefore, if the results show diverging curves, one possibility is that the two independent variables interact. That is to say, at least one variable in the task affects two stages of processing.

To see how the additive-factor method improves on Donders' method of subtraction, let us consider an experiment by Donders and discuss its limitations. Then we can continue his study in the framework of the logic of the additive-factor method. Recall Donders' comparison of simple and choice RT tasks in naming visually presented letters. Donders found that the choice RT experiment took an average of 166 msec. longer than the simple RT task.

To this experiment, Donders added one more condition, testing the effect of enlarging the number of alternative responses in the choice reaction time task. The subject was instructed as before to pronounce the name of the letter as rapidly as possible on each trial. This time, however, there were five possible test letters instead of only two. Donders expected that this task would be harder than the two-choice RT tasks and, therefore, would require more time for identification and response selection.

Donders saw that the difference between the two- and five-choice RT experiments measured the processing time difference for at least two stages, identification and response selection. If Donders found that the five-choice reaction time experiment gave longer RTs than the two-choice experiment, he would not know whether the increased time was required because the subject must prepare himself for five possible responses instead of two, or because identification among five alternatives requires finer discrimination and therefore more time than between two. Where the response was to be one of a number of known alternatives, a subject could prepare these responses in advance and select among them when the time came. Obviously, it would be easier to select between two than among five. The subject could use an analogous strategy for identification as well. In the two-alternative case, he might say to himself on any trial that the stimulus out there has to be either X or O, and identify it by means of a single distinguishing characteristic or feature. In this case, a curved or straight line would be sufficient to discriminate between the two letters. To use the same strategy among five alternatives, the subject would have to consider a larger number of distinguishing features, for example, if the alternatives Y, Q, and M were added.

Naming and Button-pushing Task

What Donders didn't realize, however, was that manipulation of this independent variable—number of alternatives—could be co-varied with a second independent variable to isolate the contributions of stimulus recognition and response selection. As was mentioned above, increasing the number of alternatives could conceivably affect stimulus recognition and/or response selection. However, logically, we should be able to find independent variables that affect only one of these stages. For example, Donders required his subject to respond by naming the letter symbol on each trial. Response selection in this case would involve determining the appropriate response and executing the necessary articulatory commands to name the stimulus. As a second condition, Donders could also have required his subjects to push a button for their response. In this case, the number of different button responses would increase with increases in the number of alternatives.

This manipulation of the nature of the response should affect response-selection time. Button pushing would probably take longer than naming, since naming a letter symbol is an over-learned response, whereas button pushing is not. The subject in the choice RT task would find it much more difficult to keep track of the appropriate stimulus-button pairings than the stimulus-name pairings. Moreover, the difficulty of the response-selection task would increase much more rapidly with increases in the number of alternatives in the button-pushing task relative to the naming task.

Whether the subject names or pushes the appropriate button to give a letter alternative, however, should not affect stimulus recognition time. The stage model of the task is a sequential one. Stimulus recognition occurs before response selection and its duration cannot be affected by the duration of mental events that follow it. Therefore, it is logical to assume that the type of response should not affect stimulus identification time. In the fire alarm example, the time to identify the warning siren was independent of the difficulty of selecting the appropriate response.

Our experiment would accordingly manipulate the number of alternatives and the nature of the response in a reaction time task. For example, we could choose 2-, 4-, or 8-letter alternatives and have the subject name or push the appropriate button to each stimulus. Reaction time would be measured from the onset of the stimulus to the onset of the response. This design gives six experimental conditions. Each subject would go through all conditions. The order of the conditions across different subjects could be counterbalanced to control for order effects in the task. In each of the six sessions, the subject would be told the stimulus alternatives and the appropriate response to each alternative. Some practice should be given at each experimental condition before the experimenter records the results.

The results of the experiment could be presented graphically, plotting mean RT on the Y ordinate as a function of the number of alternatives on the X abscissa. Two curves would be plotted; one for each response condition. Some hypothetical results of the experiment are presented in Figures 5 and 6.

Recall that the experimental question was whether the increase in RT with increases in the number of alternatives was due to stimulus identification time, response selection time, or both. If this increase was due only to stimulus identification time, the increase should be independent of the nature of the response. If the increase was due only to response selection time, the increase should be directly related to the difficulty of the response. The

FIGURE 5. Hypothetical results of an experiment in which increasing the number of alternatives affects only the stimulus recognition stage.

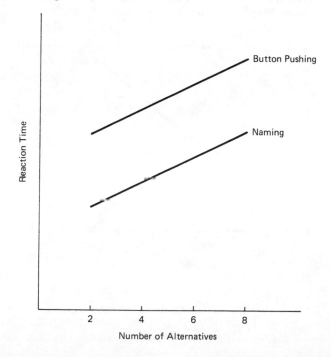

hypothetical results in Figure 5 show that the increase in RT with increases in the number of alternatives was the same for the naming and button-pushing tasks. These results would indicate that increasing the number of alternatives increases stimulus-identification time and does not appear to influence response-selection time. Button pushing is more difficult than naming, but this difficulty does not interact (change) with changes in the number of alternatives.

Figure 6 plots another set of hypothetical results where the increase in RT with increases in the number of alternatives is flat between 2 and 8 alternatives in the naming case, but increases sharply in the button-pushing task. What mental process accounts for the increase in RT with increases in the number of alternatives? The results in Figure 6 indicate that response-selection time can account for all of the increase in RT from 2 to 8 alternatives. This follows from the fact that the naming function between 2 and 8 alternatives is flat. If the response is an overlearned one, increasing the number of alternatives does not increase overall RT. Requiring a button-pushing task instead of naming should not change stimulus-identification time since the button-pushing condition simply changes the response selection process, not the identification process. Accordingly, the increase in RT with increases in the

FIGURE 6. Hypothetical results in which response-selection time accounts for the increase in RT with increases in the number of alternatives in the button-pushing condition.

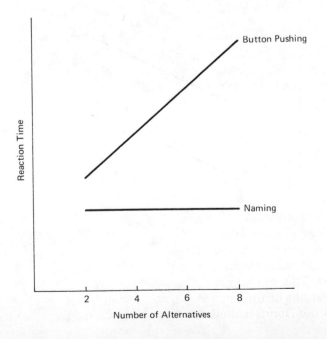

number of alternatives in the button-pushing task cannot be accounted for by stimulus-identification time, but is due to response selection time. When this experiment is carried out, the results actually correspond to those shown in Figure 6 (Theios, 1973).

The simple RT condition was not included in this experiment since this condition changes the overall nature of the task by eliminating the identification stage. Accordingly, we would expect RT to increase in both the naming and button-pushing tasks from a simple to a two-choice situation. If the subject is faced with two or more alternatives, stimulus identification is necessary for the response to be given. In the simple RT task, stimulus detection is sufficient for response selection to begin. We can see that the overall nature or quality of the task changed in going from the choice to the simple task. Therefore, RT will be shorter in the simple than in the two-choice task for both the naming and the button-pushing conditions. This result indicates that stimulus-identification time must be different in the two cases. However, response-selection time also differs since the subject can prepare his response exactly in one task but not in the other. Therefore, the comparison between the one- and two-alternative conditions does not illuminate the operations of stimulus identification and response selection processes.

The experimental conditions from 2 to 8 alternatives are illuminating in our modification of Donders' experiment. If the alternatives are overlearned stimuli such as letters, it appears that stimulus-identification time is independent of the number of alternatives larger than two. Response-selection time is also independent of the number of alternatives larger than two if the responses are highly compatible and overlearned, as in the naming condition. If, however, the responses are not compatible and overlearned, response-selection time is a direct function of the number of alternatives in the experimental task.

In summary, covarying two independent variables using the additive-factor method can illuminate the nature of psychological processing. In this paradigm, the experimenter does not attempt to insert a stage of processing but simply to influence the amount of processing at a given stage. In the choice RT task with two or more alternatives, a stage of processing was not inserted when the number of alternatives was increased. Rather, the experiment tested whether the operations of each stage, as reflected in the time to complete each stage, differed with changes in the independent variables. This experiment, therefore, makes transparent some of the operations of the recognition and response-selection processes, whereas the Donders method of insertion does not.

Operations of mental processes

We may be able in the future to use "brain waves" as indicators of the beginning and end of a mental process; but in general it has seemed necessary to let the timed process start with a sensory stimulus and terminate in a muscular response.
—Robert S. Woodworth (1938)

This chapter discusses the techniques of decomposing RTs to study the operations of mental processes. One psychological process that can be studied very easily using RTs is memory search. To answer the question, where would you like to eat dinner? involves some form of memory search. We search in memory for restaurants we know about and test their qualities against our current appetite, budget, and whatever other considerations we deem important. The main concern of this chapter will be to see how the time it takes to search memory illuminates the nature of the memory search process.

MEMORY SEARCH

Sternberg (1966, 1967) used the additive-factor method to design a series of experiments for studying memory search processes. The experimental task is slightly more involved than the tasks Donders employed. The subject is told that the experimenter is going to present a target list of digits of a certain size, say 4 digits. He will then present some sort of warning signal—a buzz perhaps—and finally one more digit, the test digit. The task of the observer is to respond "yes" by pushing one lever if the test digit was one of the digits in the preceding list, and to respond "no" by pushing another lever if it was not. Thus the subject might hear 0, 2, 6, 7, buzz, 6. The correct response would be "yes," since the test digit was equal to one of the memory list digits. Had the test digit been "3," the correct response would be "no."

Given this paradigm, Sternberg could vary the difficulty of the search task by varying the number of digits in the memory list. Thus the independent variable in this task is the number of digits in the list; the dependent variable is the reaction time measured from the onset of the test digit to the onset of the subject's response, pushing the appropriate lever. All other factors can be held constant, such as the rate at which the digits are presented (usually at 1 test digit/sec.).

Stages of Processing
What stages of psychological processing does this task involve? First, it is clear that a good deal of processing goes on both before and after the test digit presentation. To respond correctly, the subject must first learn and remember the target list of digits. This requires accurate recognition and memory of the target set. Recognition and storage of each target item may take from 250 to 500 msec. In the typical memory task in which the items are presented at 1/sec., we can assume that the processing is complete before the test item is presented. Therefore, the time it takes to perform this processing does not affect the RT to the test item.

Processing and responding appropriately to the test item determines RT in this task. First, the subject must detect and recognize the test item. To determine whether the test item was a member of the target set, the subject must perform some sort of search and comparison of the test item with the target items in memory. The outcome of the search and comparison provides the necessary information for the response-selection process. We can discern, then, detection, recognition, memory search and comparison, and response selection as the processing stages in this task. Figure 1 presents a flow diagram of these stages of information processing in the memory search task.

FIGURE 1. A flow diagram of the intervening stages of information processing between presentation of the test digit and execution of the appropriate response.

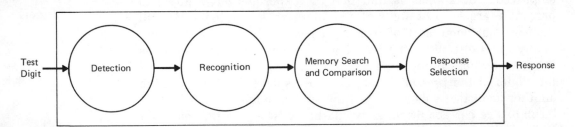

Which of these stages will be affected by the independent variable—changes in the number of items in the target list? The detection stage clearly would not be, nor should recognition of the test digit be affected by the number of preceding target items. Undoubtedly, however, a change in the number of items in the target set is going to affect the difficulty of the memory search and comparison. Once the search is performed, on the other hand, and the observer knows whether or not the test item was present in the target set, the nature of the response selection task should still be the same: given that the item was or was not present in the list, is the appropriate response pushing the left or right lever?

Analysis of the task, then, allows us to test the assumption that changes in the independent variable (number of items in the target list) affects only the memory search and comparison stage. If this assumption is correct, if RTs change as set size is increased or decreased, it can tell us a good deal about the nature of the memory search process. For instance, we can hypothesize a search algorithm, a sequence of operations that might be used to perform the memory task and determine the expected changes in RT as a function of increase in memory set size. Two very different algorithms, or strategies, will be analyzed for their prediction of how RT will change as a function of change in the independent variable. The experiment, then, can provide a test of these two hypotheses. If the actual results match the function predicted by one of them, the results will support the assumptions about the processing stages in the task, and provide evidence that a particular algorithm was used. If, however, the results match neither prediction, the results imply that either the assumptions about the processing stages were incorrect or that a different search algorithm was used.

One source of hypotheses concerning the strategies of human subjects is provided by the general purpose digital computer. Computers are characterized by three distinct structures: The most critical is the central processing unit, which is the workhorse of the machine. The second is the computer's memory, which holds both

---

Models

In studying memory search and comparison operations, we use the computer program as a model of the psychological processing of humans. Models are useful in scientific study because they provide a description of a process that helps make it understandable. When we ask how a human does something, any answer is essentially in the form of an analogy; he acts as if he were doing the following. Models not only make psychological processes understandable, but they also are useful as a guide or heuristic to further research and theorizing. The model that the scientist uses is his reality; he sees the psychological process in this form. Other models are not as understandable or as meaningful to him in his search.

the computer programs and any necessary data information. The third structure contains the communication links to the computer user. The central processor can communicate with both the memory and the communication links referred to as input/output devices. The memory bank contains a set of locations each of which has a specified address and contents. The central processor can read the commands or data coming over an input device and can also execute instructions to present information over output devices. A teletype similar to an electric typewriter usually functions as both an input and output device for computers.

Computers can be programmed to perform Sternberg's task and, of course, these programs are known in full detail. There are two basic search algorithms that can be employed using a digital computer. The search algorithm is in the form of a computer program which lists a sequence of operations. Each operation takes a certain amount of time so that the RT of the computer can also be used as an index of a particular search strategy. If we perform the task analogous to a particular computer program, the number of operations the program executes is taken as a relative index of the time it takes us to perform the task. Therefore, we can analyze each program and compare the predicted results with the results obtained from humans.

Serial Search: Self-terminating

The programs specify how the central processor of the computer stores the target list in memory and how this list is searched, given the test item. The first strategy considered is a serial search. Initially, the central processor assigns a location in memory, the address TARGET LIST. The first item in the target list is recognized and is stored in the contents of TARGET LIST. When the second item is recognized, it is stored in the next adjacent location, called TARGET LIST + 1. The third digit goes into TARGET LIST + 2 and so on, until each item in the list is entered into memory in serial order. The computer has to be informed that it has come to the end of the list, so the programmer instructs it to enter some code such as "end" in the next location when the buzz is presented. Table 1 presents an outline of the computer program which stores the target items in serial order.

Now the central processor is ready for the test item, which comes in, is recognized, and is stored in location TEST. The central processor takes TEST and compares its contents to the contents of TARGET LIST, then TARGET LIST + 1, and so on in serial order. At each comparison the program asks first whether the contents of the target location are equal to "end"; if so, the search is terminated and the program moves on to the next stage of processing. If the contents do not contain "end," the central processor compares it to the contents of TEST. If the TEST and TARGET LIST + x are equal, the central processor places a "yes" in the contents of ANSWER. At this point the program instructs the central processor to terminate the search. The program then determines the contents of ANSWER and selects the appropriate response. Table 1 presents the program for this algorithm, which is referred to as a serial self-terminating search. The search is self-terminating because no further comparisons are made once a match has been found.

TABLE 1

Outline of a computer program specifying the processing of the target list and the test item for a serial self-terminating search of the target items in memory. (Each instruction or step in the program is executed before going to the next instruction.)

Processing the target list

1. make the variable x equal to zero
2. wait for input; when input detected, go to step 3
3. recognize input; if not target digit or buzz, go back to step 2
4. if input is buzz, go to step 8
5. if input is digit, store it at location TARGET LIST + x
6. increment the variable x by 1
7. go to step 2
8. store the symbol "end" at location TARGET LIST + x
9. make the variable x equal to zero

Processing the test digit——serial self-terminating search

10. wait for input; when input detected, go to step 11
11. recognize input; if not test digit, go back to step 10
12. store test digit at location TEST
13. determine contents of TARGET LIST + x
14. if it is the symbol "end," go to step 20
15. if it is equal to the test digit, go to step 18
16. increment the variable x by 1
17. go to step 13
18. store the symbol "yes" at location ANSWER
19. go to step 21
20. store the symbol "no" at location ANSWER
21. determine the contents of ANSWER
22. typo this symbol
23. stop

By contrast, in a serial-exhaustive search (shown in Table 2), the central processor proceeds to the next comparison and does not output the contents of ANSWER until the list has been exhausted and it has reached "end."

Serial Search: Exhaustive

TABLE 2

Outline of a computer program performing a serial-exhaustive search
of the target items in memory. (Program for processing the target list
before the test item presentation is the same as that given for the
serial self-terminating search in Table 1.)

Processing the test digit——serial-exhaustive search

10. store the symbol "no" at location ANSWER
11. wait for input; when input detected, go to step 12
12. recognize input; if not test digit, go back to step 11
13. store test digit at location TEST
14. determine contents of TARGET LIST + x
15. if it is the symbol "end," go to step 21
16. if it is equal to the test digit, go to step 19
17. increment the variable x by 1
18. go to step 14
19. store the symbol "yes" at location ANSWER
20. go to step 17
21. determine the contents of ANSWER
22. type this symbol
23. stop

In a self-terminating search, the number of items actually searched varies, ranging from all items on "no" trials and on trials in which the last digit in the list is equal to the test digit, through one item only on trials in which the first item is equal to the test digit. On the average, the central processor would have to search $\frac{N + 1}{2}$ items on "yes" trials, where N is the number of items in the target list. In a serial-exhaustive search, it exhausts the list on "yes" and "no" trials alike.

To demonstrate whether either of these algorithms describes the performance of human subjects in Sternberg's task, we must analyze each one for its predictions regarding changes in reaction times as a function of changes in memory set size. Begin with the processing of the test digit since the RT is measured from its onset. First, the computer program has instructions corresponding to the detection and recognition of the test digit and the response-selection stage. We can see that these instructions and the number of times they are executed do not vary with changes in the size of the target list. The memory search and comparison stage, however, is affected by target list size: the more items to be searched, the larger the number of instructions to be executed and the longer the search should take. Looking only at "no" trials, which would be the same whether the search was exhaustive or self-terminating, the number of instructions to search each target location is the same; therefore, the time required to search each item is equal. Each additional item in the target set will add a constant increment to the reaction time. Thus, if detection plus recognition time equals x, memory search and comparison per item equals y, and response-selection time equals z, then the total RT to say "no" will be equal to

$$RT = x + yN + z + o \qquad (1)$$

where N is the number of items in the target set, and o is equal to the time for other events necessary in the memory search tasks.

Figure 2 plots "no" RT as a function of target set size according to Equation 1. With one item in the target set, $RT = x + y + z + o$. With two items in the target set, $N = 2$, $RT = x + 2y + z + o$. The results, when plotted, give a linear function, intercepting the Y ordinate at $x + z + o$, with a y msec. increase in reaction time for every increase in target set size.

FIGURE 2. Predicted reaction time function for "no" responses for both the serial self-terminating and serial-exhaustive searches of the target list.

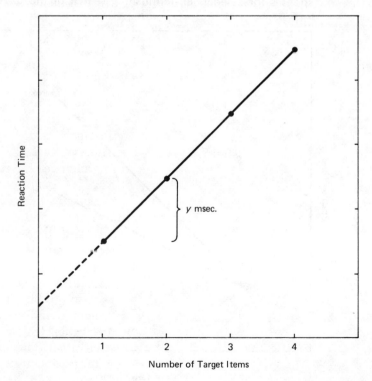

In the serial-exhaustive search, the slope of the function will be the same for "yes" and "no" responses. The slope of the function will not be the same, however, for trials in which ANSWER equals "yes," when the program instructs the central processor to terminate the search whenever it finds a match. In the case of the self-terminating search, on each "yes" trial the central processor searches some proportion of the list. If the test digit is equally likely to occur at any serial position on "yes" trials, it will search $\dfrac{N+1}{2}$ items on the average, whereas on "no" trials it will search the entire list. If the strategy is a serial self-terminating search, therefore, we can expect the rate of increase in reaction time as a function of target set size to be 1/2 that of "no" trials. Figure 3 presents the curves for "yes" and "no" responses under the assumption of a serial self-terminating memory search. If, on the other hand, the entire list is searched on both kinds of trials, it follows that the function will be the same for both "yes" and "no" trials. Therefore, the "yes" and "no" curves will be parallel when the search algorithm is a serial-exhaustive one.

FIGURE 3. Predicted reaction time functions for "yes" and "no" responses for a serial self-terminating search of the target list.

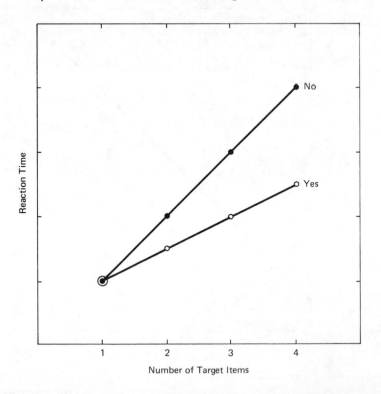

The computer can also be programmed to use a different search algorithm, called a content-addressable search, to perform this task. In this strategy, somewhat more processing of the target list makes possible a shorter search time, so that a different reaction time function is obtained. The program tells the computer that in this task any of the digits 0 through 9 may be fed into its memory, and instructs it to set aside 10 locations, assigned the names TARGET LIST, through TARGET LIST + 9. All 10 locations are assigned the contents "no." As each digit in the target list comes in, the central processor goes to the location with the address of the target digit and changes its contents from "no" to "yes." For example, if the digits in the list are 3, 7, and 2, the central processor changes the contents of TARGET LIST + 3, TARGET LIST + 7, and TARGET LIST + 2, respectively. Thus, in this example, at the end of this operation there are three locations containing "yes" and seven containing "no." At test, the test digit is recognized and the program instructs a search of TARGET LIST plus the value of the test digit. If the test digit was contained in the target list, that location should contain a "yes"; otherwise, it would contain a "no." This program is shown in Table 3.

Content-Addressable Search

TABLE 3
Outline of a computer program specifying the processing of target list and test item for a content-addressable search of target items in memory.

Processing the target list

1. make the variable x equal to zero
2. store the symbol "no" in TARGET LIST + x
3. increment the variable x by 1
4. if the variable x is equal to 10, go to step 6
5. go to step 2
6. wait for input; when input is detected, go to step 7
7. recognize input; if not target digit or buzz, go back to step 6
8. if input is buzz, go to step 12
9. if input is digit, make variable x equal to this value
10. store the symbol "yes" at location TARGET LIST + x
11. go to step 6

Processing the test digit — content-addressable search

12. wait for input; when input is detected, go to step 13
13. recognize input; if not test digit, go back to step 12
14. make variable x equal to test digit
15. determine the contents of TARGET LIST + x
16. store it at ANSWER
17. determine the contents of ANSWER
18. type this symbol
19. stop

In this strategy, changes in the number of items in memory will affect the amount of processing before the onset of the search operation. A larger number of items will require a longer time for the storing of the digits in their proper memory locations. No matter how many digits are in memory, however, once they are stored and the test digit is presented, the operations are always exactly the same; the central processor reads the test digit, addresses the location TARGET LIST plus test digit, and reads its contents. Since RT in this task is measured from onset of the test digit to the onset of the response, the slope of the RT function with increases in target set size given this strategy would be zero; it would be plotted as a horizontal line (see Figure 4). The horizontal function would be obtained for both "yes" and "no" responses.

The major difference between the serial search and content-addressable search is the way target items are retrieved from memory. In the first case, the subject has the names of the target items in a particular part of memory and he searches those locations for a target item equal to the test item. In the second case, the target items are not restricted to one area of memory, rather, all digits are

FIGURE 4. Predicted reaction time function for "yes" and "no" responses for a content-addressable search of the target list.

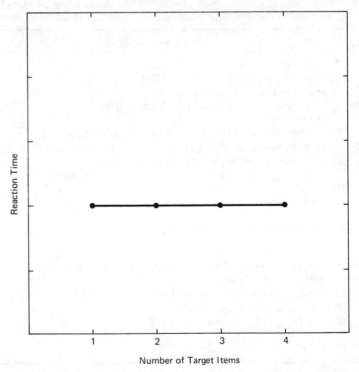

Number of Target Items

represented in memory and the subject simply inquires about the status of the test digit. In the serial search, the target items must be systematically retrieved from memory, whereas in the content-addressable search the only retrieval is that of the contents or status of the test item itself. Therefore, RT is dependent upon the number of target items in the serial search but is unaffected by this variable in the content-addressable search.

These two search strategies are probably utilized at different times in normal cognitive functioning. If you are asked whether there is a given number—for example, "one"—in your telephone number, you will probably use a serial search. A content-addressable search seems unlikely since it is improbable that contents of the memory location of "one" would have information about whether or not it is contained in your telephone number. Rather, you must go to the location or address of your telephone number and inquire there whether a "one" is represented. In contrast, when asked if you keep your butter in the refrigerator, you do not search through all the foods you have stored in memory under refrigerator. Rather, the concept of butter is enough to tell you whether you store it in the refrigerator. Therefore, the time to answer this question should be independent of the number of foods kept in the house.

Here, then, are two hypothetical strategies that generate two different reaction time functions across changes in memory set size. These predicted functions can be compared to the function obtained in the actual experiment with humans. If the latter is a horizontal line, we have evidence that humans use something analogous to a content-addressable strategy in this task. If the results show a linearly increasing function, the serial search algorithm is supported. One other possibility is some combination of the two, perhaps a flat line up to 3 or 4 items in memory, followed by a linear increase; this would imply that at a memory list size of 3 or 4, subjects changed from a content-addressable to a serial search strategy.

Memory Set Size

In fact, Sternberg's results plotted in Figure 5 showed a linear increase in reaction time as a function of memory set size, supporting the hypothesis that humans perform this task by employing a serial search strategy. Moreover, the function was the same for both "yes" and "no" responses, indicating that the subject exhausted the memory list on "yes" trials. The results, then, support the serial-exhaustive search algorithm.

It might be hypothesized that this search and comparison operation is performed during subvocal rehearsal that subjects em-

FIGURE 5. Observed "yes' and "no" reaction times in the memory search task as a function of the number of items in the target list (after Sternberg, 1969).

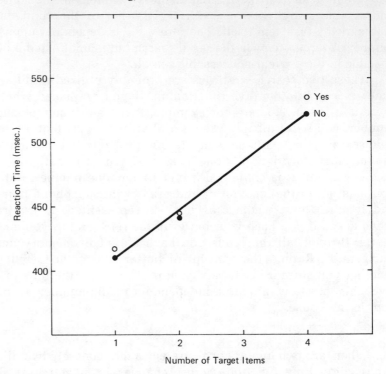

ploy in the task. Subjects report reciting the numbers to themselves in order to keep them fixed in memory. This hypothesis would predict that each additional item in the target set would require at least an additional 160 msec. for search and comparison, since the rate of implicit speech is about 6 items per second. Sternberg's results, however, show the increment of additional time for each additional item to be about 40 msec., demonstrating that the serial search and comparison cannot take place at the level of subvocal speech.

The additive-factor method can be used to clarify further the operations of the search process in the search task. Simultaneously, this method can be used to substantiate the independence of the processing stages. Consider the three stages—recognition, memory search and comparison, and response selection—and independent variables that might affect each stage. The recognition process is dependent on the clarity of the test digit; if we present the test digit in degraded form, it should take the subject longer to recognize the test digit but should not necessarily affect the time to complete the following processing stages. We have seen how the number of items in the target set appears to affect only the memory search and comparison stage. Finally, the response selection stage might be affected by the contents of ANSWER. The subject may find it more or less difficult to select a "yes" than a "no" response.

Quality of Test Stimulus

This armchair analysis leads to further experiments which simultaneously vary these three independent variables. In one experiment, Sternberg (1967) manipulated the visual quality of the test digit, presenting it in degraded form on half the trials, and intact on the remaining trials. The stimulus was degraded by placing a masking screen of dots over the test digit. In this study, subjects were given a fixed target set for a whole block of trials. For example, the subjects might be given the target list containing the digits 4 and 7. Then each trial would be initiated with the onset of the test digit. After a series of trials, the subjects would be given a new target list followed by a block of trials. The quality of the test digit was also varied between trial blocks. (Work out a counterbalancing scheme for this factorial experiment of four levels of target size and two levels of visual quality.)

In this study, Sternberg covaried two independent variables. The test digit appeared either intact, or was embedded in the visual noise and the number of items in the target set was varied. The reaction time function under the intact condition was compared to the reaction time function in the degraded condition. Logically, one would predict that the case in which the test stimulus was embedded in noise would take longer than the intact stimulus case. In particular, one would expect that recognition of the test digit would be more difficult. Thus, the overall reaction time function would be higher than the typical function found with intact stimuli. One might expect, however, that the slope of the function would not change, that is, that the stimulus quality manipulation would not affect the difficulty of the memory search process. It seems reasonable to suppose that once the recognition stage has given the test digit a label, however easy or difficult it may have been to do so, the rate of memory search would be the same. If this is the case, the slopes of the two functions will be parallel. If not, if changes in stimulus quality *do* affect the memory comparison stage, the results of the experiment will show diverging lines.

Thus, we can expect one of two alternative functions, both of which would be informative. In Figure 6, the two independent variables have additive effects, the degraded function is parallel to the intact function, and we can conclude that the two variables affect different stages. If the two variables interact, their effects will be compounded, resulting in the interaction presented in Figure 7. This result might imply that the subjects employ some

Analysis of Variance

The analysis of variance is the best statistical tool to analyze experiments with two or more independent variables that are combined in a factorial fashion, as is required by the additive-factor method. The analysis essentially evaluates the treatment effect against the chance variability found in the experiment. Consider an experiment with two levels of an independent variable in which we test the subject 3 different times under each level so that we have 3 scores at each level. Assume that in two different experiments the scores are those given in the table below, where I_1 and I_2 are the two levels of the independent variable.

Experiment 1		Experiment 2	
I_1	I_2	I_1	I_2
80	100	73	87
60	90	70	90
70	80	67	93

In both experiments, the subject averaged 70 at I_1 and 90 at I_2. However, we have more confidence in the difference between I_1 and I_2 in the second experiment than in the first. In the first experiment, the difference (20) between I_1 and I_2 is not any larger than the difference between the 3 scores at the same level of I_1 or I_2. The differences between the scores at the same level of our independent variable must be attributed to chance variability since there is nothing the experimenter can point to as a causal factor. Since chance variability was so much larger in the first experiment than the second, we have more faith in the significance of the results in the second experiment than the first. However, statistical significance itself is not the major issue and our analysis is focused on the psychological significance of a given result.

The analysis of variance provides the experimenter with an index of the size of the treatment effect measured against the chance variability in his experiment. In a two-factor design—an experiment with two independent variables—the analysis of variance provides this index for the effect of each of the independent variables and their interaction. The experimenter should design his experiment as carefully as possible to keep chance variability to a minimum. After the experiment, he computes the statistical significance using the analysis of variance. His task then is to evaluate the size of these effects and what these effects say about psychological processes and current models or theories of the processes. Our knowledge comes from evaluating the meaningfulness of the effects of independent variables rather than simply from their statistical significance.

FIGURE 6. Predicted reaction time functions if the quality of the stimulus affects only the recognition stage of processing in the search task.

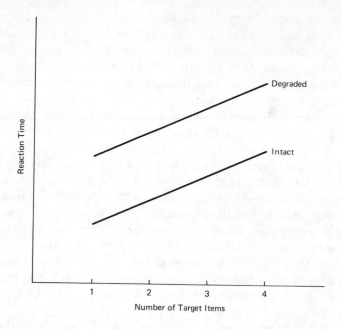

FIGURE 7. Predicted reaction time functions if the quality of the test stimulus affects both the recognition stage and the memory search and comparison stage of processing in the search task.

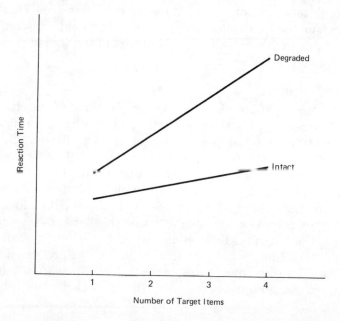

direct representation of the test digit in the memory search and comparison so that the degraded digit not only increases recognition time but slows down the rate of memory search.

On the second day of the experiment, Sternberg found that the RT function in the degraded condition described a straight line above and parallel to the function of the intact condition, supporting the hypothesis that stimulus quality affected only the recognition stage. This result tells us something about the connections between the stage of recognition and the stage of memory search and comparison. If degrading the stimulus had affected the reaction time of the memory search stage, then that would imply that the information in the recognition is handed over raw to the memory search and comparison stage. Sternberg's results, however, tell us that the recognition stage transforms the degraded information to produce an unequivocal digit value for the memory search stage. This lends credence to the information-processing model, in which stages of processing are seen as producing successive transformations upon the information as it moves through them.

Note that Sternberg designed his experiment so that either result would have been informative. A good experimenter first asks: What are the possible outcomes of the experiment? What theories can be rejected or supported by the study? If the results do not distinguish between theories, they are not informative in the sense of reducing uncertainty about the psychological processes responsible for the results. The psychologist is primarily interested in what the experiment can indicate about psychological processing; behavioral data are not sufficient in and of themselves. He, therefore, designs the experiments so that every possible outcome will be informative with respect to psychological functioning.

VISUAL SCANNING About the time that Sternberg was doing his memory search experiments, Neisser and his colleagues devised another paradigm that approached the study of memory search from a different direction (Neisser, 1963, 1964; Neisser, Novick, & Lazar, 1963). In Neisser's task, the subject was given a target item, perhaps a letter of the alphabet, and told to find this item in a list of letters that he was then given. The list contained a column of letters with usually 4 or 6 letters per row. Upon presentation of the list the subject read (scanned) the list from the top and pushed a lever as soon as he found the target letter. On each trial, then, he was presented with a list of, say, 50 rows of 6 letters each, which he searched for the target item. As soon as he found it, the subject pushed a button.

Reaction time was measured from the presentation of the list to the onset of the response.

Sternberg's additive-factor method allows us to determine the time for memory search by accounting for the times of other processes in the task. The slope of the function relating reaction time to the number of items in the target set provides an index of memory search and comparison time. Neisser estimated memory search and comparison time in a similar fashion. The independent variable in Neisser's task is the location of the target letter in the test list. Reaction time should be a direct function of what row in the list contains the target letter. Since the subjects begin scanning at the top of the list, we would expect RT to increase as the target letter is placed lower down in the test list. Logically, each letter in the test list requires the same amount of processing until the subject finds the target letter. For example, if the subject is looking for the letter *K*, we would expect that his search rate through the list would be constant. That is to say, the time to process the test letters should be independent of their serial position in the test list. Since the response selection time should also be independent of where the subject finds the letter in the list, we would expect that reaction time should be a linear function of the serial position of the target letter.

The results of Neisser's experiment, shown in Figure 8, support the logical analysis. Reaction time is well described by a linearly increasing function of position of the target letter in the test list. The fact that the intercept of the function is close to 0 sec. shows that other processes such as response-execution time account for very little of the reaction time. The slope of the function provides an index of the time it takes the subject to recognize, to compare, and to select a response for each letter. That is to say, for the subject to perform the task correctly, he must process each letter to the degree that he knows enough about whether it is or is not the test letter and must select the appropriate response given this information. If it is not the target letter, he goes on to the next letter; if it is, he pushes the lever.

Neisser's paradigm is very similar to the experimental task used by Sternberg. The target item in Neisser's task is analogous to the target set in Sternberg's task; Neisser's test list is analogous to Sternberg's test item. Given Sternberg's results, we might expect subjects to perform Neisser's task by comparing each item on the presentation list to the target item in memory. Since they are instructed to start at the top of the list, they could proceed in serial order until a match is found.

In Sternberg's task, the subject has several items in memory and one test item to be recognized and compared serially to the items in memory. In Neisser's task, the subject has one item in memory, and up to 50 rows of letters to be compared to it. Reaction time in Neisser's task should vary, therefore, not as a function of the number of target items, which is constant, but rather as a function of the position of the target item in the list; that is to say, RT should vary as a function of the number of test items that must be searched before the subject reaches the one that corresponds to the item in memory. This function should be linear, as in Sternberg's task, i.e., each item to be searched should add a constant increment to the reaction time. In fact, Neisser's results confirm this prediction, indicating a linear increase in RT as the target item is moved further and further down the list. Up to this point, Neisser's and Sternberg's experiments confirm each other nicely.

Having established the reaction time function in the case of one target, Neisser presented subjects with a larger number of target items. For example, the subject would be given two targets, perhaps K and O, and told to respond as soon as he found either one in the list. We would expect, according to what both Sternberg and Neisser have shown so far about how subjects perform this sort of task, that each item in the list would be matched against one target letter first and then against the other, proceeding serially down the list, and generating a linear function that would have a steeper slope than the function with the same list and only one of the targets. That is, twice as many comparisons will have to be made for the same number of test items, since now the subject has to check each test item against two targets instead of just one.

This is not what Neisser found with practiced subjects. Although RT was a linear function of the position of the target item in the test list, it did not vary at all as a function of the number of targets in memory. A target that was 1 out of 10 was found as quickly as the same target when it was the only one the subject was looking for. Subjects could search the test list for 8 letters and 2 numbers as quickly as they could search for the letter K alone. This means that the rate of memory search and comparison was independent of the number of target items in memory.

Neisser's results can be described by a slight variation on the content-addressable search algorithm discussed earlier. Subjects would ticket only the target items in advance; negative items would remain unmarked. Therefore, each test item would take the search process to a specific location in memory corresponding to that test item. If it was ticketed, it would be a positive (target) item and the subject should push the lever. If it was unticketed the subject could reliably conclude that it was a negative (nontarget) item and proceed to the next test item. In this way, reaction time would not be dependent upon the number of target items in memory. All that is required is a check of the status of each test item without referring to the target items at all.

FIGURE 8. Reaction time as a function of the serial position of the target item in the test list (after Neisser, 1967).

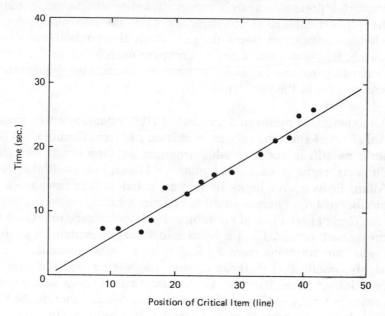

The difference in the way the subjects performed these two tasks must reflect differences in the two experimental paradigms. Unlike Sternberg's subjects, Neisser's were practiced and highly motivated. They returned day after day, and were able to decrease their overall reaction time remarkably. Moreover, the targets which they had to keep in memory while searching the lists did not vary. A subject would be given 10 target letters; on one day he might look for 5 of these, and on another day he might look for all 10. Over time he learned the targets quite thoroughly. Sternberg's subjects, on the other hand, came in once for a few hours. They had little practice with the search operation, and very little opportunity to rehearse the target items. In addition, Sternberg emphasized perfect performance with his subjects, keeping the rate of errors down to about 2 or 3 percent. Neisser, on the contrary, allowed his subjects to make many errors, about 25 percent; the emphasis in his experiment was on speed of reaction.

Neisser compared the performance of his subjects to that of employees in news-clipping services, who contract with clients

Differences Between Sternberg and Neisser Tasks

to search the newspapers for any mention of clients' names. The people who perform this work learn to scan newspapers at astonishing rates. They report they do not need to read the material in any sense. Somehow the clients' names just pop out at them. In the same way, Neisser's subjects reported that after practice, the target letters just leaped out at them from the list. According to our content-addressable search model, ticketing the target items has the phenomenological consequence of these items popping out, whereas unticketed items do not. With the content-addressable search, it was not necessary to compare each letter in the test list to the target items in memory. Rather, the necessary information was present in the test item itself.

Specific practice An experiment performed by Graboi (1971) demonstrated the critical effect of specific practice on memory search. Graboi used Neisser's paradigm and English surnames as target and list items. Subjects were given such names as Hicks, James, Blake, Klein, Allan, Brown, and Joyce to find in a list of similar names; the number of target names could vary from 1 to 7.

Graboi first allowed his subjects to become very practiced with the same 7 names. Each subject had 7 targets which he searched for in combinations from 1 to all 7 in list after list, until he was highly practiced with these targets. Measuring reaction time as a function of target list size, Graboi found that there was some increase in time, but this increase was not a linear function. Subjects took longer to search with 3 targets than with 1, but beyond 3 targets reaction time did not increase. Seven targets took no longer than 3; finding James in a list took no longer if the possible targets were Hicks, James, Brown, Jones, Klein, Blake, and Joyce, than if they were Hicks, James, and Brown.

Subjects all reported that this was a skill they had learned. After so much practice, they felt they no longer gave the list the active attention they had at the beginning of the experiment; rather, they seemed to need only glance through the list, thinking of nothing in particular, to have the relevant names pop out at them.

Now Graboi gave subjects a new set of target names and 15 minutes in which to study them. When the same subjects performed the same task with a different set of names, the reaction time was found to increase sharply with increases in the number of items in memory. Subjects who had had much practice in the task and who had learned to search for one set of targets according to a content-addressable search fell back on a serial search when presented with a new set of targets. This study demonstrates that practice affects the type of search algorithm used. Humans probably choose one of a number of search algorithms depending upon the conditions and requirements of the task at hand. If subjects are highly practiced with the target set and errors are not critical, something analogous to a content-addressable search can be used. If accuracy is critical and the subjects are unpracticed, a serial search seems more appropriate.

SENSATION

Los Angeles County Museum of Art, <u>Serape Style, 1850–1865</u>, Natural History Museum of Los Angeles County (detail).

Psychophysics

Psychophysics should be understood here as an exact theory of the functionally dependent relations of body and soul or, more generally, of the material and the mental, of the physical and the psychological worlds.
—Gustav T. Fechner (1860)

The methods developed by Donders and Sternberg have allowed us to partition the time between stimulus and response into a series of psychological processing stages. We now begin to study how these processes operate in more detail. The initial stage of processing is what we call detection and is very similar to the British Empiricists' concept of sensation. The outcome of the detection process provides information about whether or not a stimulus was presented. Traditionally, the study of the relationship between stimulus and sensation has been called psychophysics. The goal of this research has been to describe and understand the relationship between the physical stimulus signal and the psychological experience it creates.

Given the current advanced state of technology, the experimental psychologist is now able to control and measure the stimulus signal exactly. In contrast, the psychological sensation of the observer remains unobservable and the experimentalist must resort to asking the observer about his experience. From his answer, the experimenter must be able to derive a measure of the observer's sensation. The development of experimental and analytical techniques for deriving a measurement of sensation based on the response of the subject has gone hand in hand with theoretical advances, so that today the experimenter is able to measure the unobservable psychological experience of the observer.

In the mid-19th century, Gustav T. Fechner, a physicist recovering from a nervous breakdown, took up the study of philosophy. At that time the fashion in metaphysics was materialism, but Fechner was not convinced by it. He rejected the notion that the mind was forever closed to the scientific explorations that had been devel-

CLASSICAL PSYCHO-PHYSICS

oped for the study of the physical universe. On the contrary, it seemed to him certain that mind and matter were two aspects of one world. The mind was only a different sort of manifestation of the same universe (completely separated and different in kind, but in constant correspondence with the body). Thus, internal psychological experience should correspond directly to changes in the physical environment. These beliefs correspond to the epiphenomenalists' solution to the mind-body problem (see Chapter 1). It followed that internal experience could be studied through manipulation of the environment. Changes made in a stimulus under carefully controlled experimental conditions should be reflected directly in changes in sensation. Sensation, a mental event, could thus be an object for scientific study on the same level and under the same scientific constraints as physical phenomena.

Fechner inaugurated the study of psychophysics, whose goal was to determine the laws of correspondence between the outer world and inner experience. For example, the sensory threshold seemed a clear case of the link between mental and physical phenomena. Since the time of the ancient Greeks it had been taken as self-evident that for each individual there is some value on a given stimulus dimension—sound intensity, for instance—such that stimuli above this value produce a sensation, whereas stimuli below it do not. A sound that is one unit more intense than the individual's threshold would be heard, and a sound that is one unit less intense goes unnoticed. No one had ever subjected the assumption of a sensory threshold to experimental study; the threshold for sound intensity, or indeed for any other stimulus dimension, had never been determined for any individual. Yet here was a clear instance of the direct relationship between mental and physical events, one that could be observed and measured under controlled conditions.

Accordingly, Fechner set about studying individual threshold values. His first problem in this new science was to devise experimental methods for measuring the correspondence between the physical and mental worlds. The three experimental methods that he employed, (1) the method of limits, (2) the method of constant stimuli, and (3) the method of adjustment, were carefully described along with his results in the treatise *Element der Psychophysik,* published in 1860. These three methods continued to be used in all psychophysical research as recently as fifteen or twenty years ago, when their inadequacies began to emerge and better methods were introduced. Indeed, Fechner's methods are still favored by some researchers and are assumed to be valid in some practical applications. These experimental methods will be discussed in some detail, showing in just what way they fail to provide the experimenter with a reliable measure of the observer's sensation. Following this discussion of classical psychophysics, a more recent and sophisticated psychophysical experiment will be presented. In the two chapters following, we shall discuss and evaluate alternative models of the psychological processes involved in the psychophysical task.

To determine the threshold value along a given stimulus dimension, Fechner and his successors in classical psychophysics presented the subject with a stimulus and asked him to report whether or not he detected it. The independent variable in this simple experimental design is the intensity of the stimulus; the dependent variable is the subject's response. Fechner's three methods represent three different ways of presenting the stimuli and measuring the response.

FECHNER'S PSYCHO-PHYSICAL METHODS

In the method of limits, subjects are tested by presenting stimuli in an ascending or descending series of intensities. For example, an experimenter can choose a tone of a certain frequency and vary its intensity from trial to trial within a range that is both well above and well below what is known to be audible. On each trial, subjects are asked to say whether or not they heard the tone during a certain interval, and their answers are recorded. Somewhere on the continuum of intensities the subject's response should change. In an ascending series, the tone is presented at a weak enough intensity to assure that the subject will respond "no." Then, the tone is incremented by a small amount on each successive trial until the subject says "yes." In a descending series, the first tone is intense enough so that it is consistently detected and then made slightly less intense on each successive trial until the subject reports "no." Each series is always started at a different intensity so that the subject will not become accustomed to always changing his response at a given serial position in the series.

Method of Limits

If the classical threshold model of sensation is correct, there will be a stimulus value along the continuum of values where the subject's response changes from "yes" to "no" or from "no" to "yes." This value should, therefore, correspond to the sensory threshold of the subject, the point at which he ceases to hear nothing and begins to hear something. Fechner's original threshold model predicted that this value would be definite and unconditional.

Table 1 presents the results of a hypothetical experiment employing the method of limits to measure the detectability of a tone as a function of its intensity. As Fechner and all other experiment-

TABLE 1
Determination of the Detectability of a Tone
as a Function of its Intensity by the Method of Limits

Stimulus intensity (arbitrary units)	Alternating descending and ascending series						
−5				N			
−4			N	N			N
−3	N	N	N			N	N
−2	N	N	N			N	Y
−1	Y	N	Y			N	
0		N	Y		Y	N	
1	Y			N		Y	N
2	Y	N		Y		Y	Y
3	Y	Y		Y		Y	Y
4	Y	Y					Y
5	Y						Y

ers using this method have found, no point exists in these data at which the response consistently changes from one category to the other. Instead, the transition point differs for the ascending and descending series and also varies from series to series within a particular type of series. Faced with this variance, Fechner and later experimenters have usually averaged the transition values and defined the threshold as the mean of all of the transition values. Clearly, these results indicate that the classical concept of a threshold will require modification.

Method of Adjustment
In the method of adjustment, the intensity of the stimulus is under the subject's control and he is required to maintain it at a barely detectable level. In the popular Békésy audiometer application of this method, the observer sits listening to a tone whose intensity is slowly decreasing. He controls a button which increases the intensity of the tone as he presses it. The subject's task is to maintain the tone at a barely audible level. Thus, he presses the button as soon as the tone becomes inaudible and holds it down until it is audible again, at which point he releases the button and the tone is allowed to decrease again. The subject is actually engaged in tracking a certain intensity, corresponding to the limits of his hearing. The experimenter can calculate the intensity that the subject attempts to maintain and thus arrive at an estimate of the subject's threshold.

In the method of constant stimuli, the experimenter chooses a population of stimuli that differ in intensity around the limits of audibility. The subject is then given a series of trials in which the stimulus for each trial is chosen randomly from this set. (Although this stimulus set corresponds to the set of stimuli used in the method of limits, the constant stimuli method usually requires more trials than does the method of limits, since the experimenter can terminate the series after a response transition in the method of limits.) The experimenter records the responses to each stimulus and the dependent variable is the proportion of "yes" responses. As shown in Figure 1, the proportion of "yes" responses in a typical experiment rises continuously with increases in intensity. There is no precise threshold level; the subject is more and more likely to say "yes" as the intensity increases, but there is no clearly defined transition between "yes" and "no" responses.

Method of Constant Stimuli

In these psychophysical methods, the experimenter must attend carefully to the levels of intensities of his independent variable. The

Choice of Stimulus Levels

FIGURE 1.   The percentage of "yes" responses as a function of the stimulus intensity of a tonal signal utilizing the method of constant stimuli procedure.

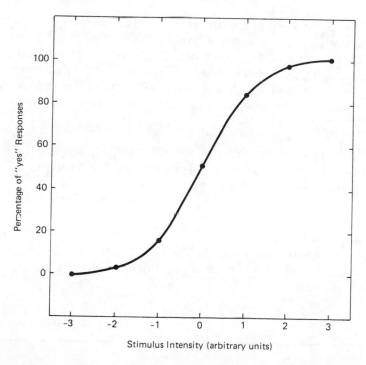

series of intensities must be neither too close to one another nor too distant. Consider an experiment using the method of limits, for example. If the intensities are chosen so that they are very close to one another, no change will occur in the subject's response with changes in intensity. By contrast, if the intensities are chosen so that they are too distant, the change in the subject's response with a change in intensity will not be informative. In this case, the experimenter cannot interpolate—speculate on the responses for the intervening intensities—between the observed responses. Therefore, in this task, as in most psychological experiments, the experimenter must choose the levels of his independent variable cautiously.

Choosing the appropriate stimulus levels usually requires a series of miniature experiments. For example, in the method of constant stimuli, the experimenter might choose seven levels of intensity, the extremes of which are known to be well above and well below threshold. The experimenter presents these levels in random order and records the responses to each stimulus. The experimenter could easily find that the subject consistently responded "yes" to some of the stimulus levels and "no" to the other levels. Since the response of the subject changed in an all-or-none manner, does this result support Fechner's idea of a threshold? Not necessarily; the

---

Logarithms

Consider the case in which each of the successive levels of an independent variable is 10 times the value of the preceding level. If the first level was 1 unit, the following six levels would be 10, 100, 1000, 10,000, 100,000, and 1,000,000 units, respectively. Rather than dealing with these large numbers, they are more easily expressed as logarithms to the base 10. The seven levels (X) of our independent variable are easily expressed in terms of 10 raised to the appropriate power Y.

$$X = 10^Y.$$

The seven levels would be 10^0, 10^1, 10^2, 10^3, 10^4, 10^5, 10^6, respectively. The logarithms of our values X are the respective powers Y of the value 10. In this way we define Y as the logarithm of X to the base 10 as

$$Y = \log_{10} X.$$

Then the logarithm Y of X to the base 10 is the power to which we must raise 10 to get X. In other areas of psychological study, it is useful to use logarithms to the other bases besides 10. The same general principles hold, so that Y is the logarithm of X to the base b.

$$Y = \log_b X.$$

---

intensity levels may have been too far apart, with the result that some of the stimuli were too far above and the other stimuli too far below the limits of audibility. The experimenter should now choose seven new levels between the two levels at which the subject changed from "yes" to "no" responses in the first experiment. If he repeats the experiment and continues in this manner, he will eventually find the appropriate levels that allow him to provide a valid test of Fechner's all-or-none threshold concept.

Fechner had centered his study of the relationship between stimulus and sensation on the sensory threshold concept. Below the threshold, changes in stimulation do not effect changes in sensation; sensation does not occur at all. Above the threshold value, Fechner assumed that the magnitude of the sensation increases with increases in the absolute intensity of the stimulus. This central assumption was represented by Fechner's equation:

THE THRESHOLD AND FECHNER'S PSYCHO-PHYSICAL LAW

$$S = K \log_{10} I, \tag{1}$$

where S measures the magnitude of the sensation, I the intensity of the stimulus, and K is a constant of proportionality. The stimulus intensity I is measured with the threshold value as the unit of measurement. Accordingly, the value I, substituted in Equation 1, is a ratio of the absolute intensity of the stimulus to the threshold value. For example, if the threshold of sound intensity for a subject corresponds to a sound pressure of .0002 dynes/cm^2, each value of I is obtained by dividing the sound pressure value of the stimulus by .0002 dynes/cm^2. Therefore, when the stimulus presented is at threshold value:

$$S = K \log \frac{.0002 \text{ dynes/cm}^2}{.0002 \text{ dynes/cm}^2}, \tag{2}$$

$$S = K \log 1 = 0.$$

Dynes

A dyne is a measure of force or pressure, and dynes/cm^2 measures the amount of pressure per square centimeter. One dyne of force applied to a mass of 1 gram for 1 sec. will move it at a velocity of 1 cm. per sec.

The value .0002 dynes/cm^2 is equal to the atmospheric sound pressure of a 1000 Hz. tone that is barely detectable. Sixty dB with a reference source pressure of .0002 dynes/cm^2 would be equal to 1000 $\times$ .0002 dynes/cm, or .2 dynes/cm, which is roughly equivalent to conversational speech at a distance of 3 ft.

That is, when the stimulus is at threshold, no sensation occurs, since $S = 0$. As stimulus intensity increases over this threshold value by the smallest amount, S is immediately greater than zero, and a noticeable sensation occurs.

According to this model, data from an experiment in detection should correspond to the curve shown in Figure 2. First, note that we have transformed our measure of sound pressure from dynes/cm² to decibels. A decibel is a unit that describes the sound pressure of a sound wave relative to some other sound pressure value. The decibel, therefore, refers to a sound pressure ratio and is equal to 20 times the logarithm to the base 10 of that ratio. Accordingly, 100 times the sound pressure is equivalent to 40 dB since 20 times $\log_{10}100$ equals 40. A doubling of sound pressure gives an increase of 6 dB since 20 times $\log_{10}2 = 6$. The reference sound pressure level is usually taken to be .0002 dynes/cm², since this value approximates the limits of audibility.

As noted above, Fechner's actual results looked rather different from those predicted in Figure 2. The results presented in Table 1 and Figure 1 show that subjects are not completely consistent in the psychophysical task; they do not give the same response to the same stimulus trial after trial. However, the results in Figure 1 indicate that the observers have a higher probability of saying

FIGURE 2. Predicted results of a detection experiment according to a simple threshold model.

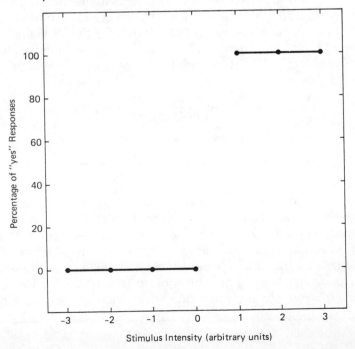

Normal Distributions and Ogive Curves

The normal distribution is a frequently encountered distribution in psychology and other scientific disciplines. If we set a radio dial between stations, we hear static, referred to as white noise. If we took isolated samples of this static —for example, recording 100 msec. segments on a tape recorder—and measured the sound pressure level (SPL), we would find that the different samples differed. A frequency distribution of the SPL for each sample could then be plotted. If we took a very large number of samples and converted our frequency histogram to a probability distribution, this distribution would approximate a normal curve. The curve would be symmetrical and would have the shape shown in Figure 3. If the probabilities of the normal curve from left to right were cumulated, we would produce the ogive curve shown in Figure 1.

"yes" to the more intense than to the less intense stimuli. The graph of this data actually approximates an ogive curve; the increase in percentage "yes" responses is less at the high and low values of sound pressure than in the middle.

If Fechner was disappointed to find that the sensation of an observer cannot be exactly predicted by knowledge of the intensity of the stimulus, the results he obtained were nevertheless reassuringly orderly and systematic. The probability that a stimulus exceeded threshold was directly related to the intensity of the stimulus. Thus, although his data did not support the assumption of his original model, that for each sensory system there is an absolute threshold of detection, the threshold concept could be applied if modified from the all-or-none to a probabilistic model.

After looking at the results, Fechner defined the threshold as that point at which the observer detects the stimulus 50 percent of the time. This definition maintains the concept of a threshold but assumes that the threshold value varies from trial to trial. With this assumption, the results indicated that the threshold value varies in a very specific fashion. The function in Figure 1 shows that the variation is symmetrical; the momentary value of the threshold is just as likely to be above as below the defined 50 percent threshold value. The ogive curve actually implies that the threshold value follows a normal distribution, with a mean at the 50 percent value. Figure 3 represents graphically the distribution of threshold values that will predict the results shown in Figure 1.

Noise in the sensory system might account for the variability in the threshold values that Fechner observed. Noise is a concept that will be used continuously throughout our psychological study.

Variability of the Threshold

Stars

Although Fechner's original model did not predict the results of his detection experiments accurately, his Equation 1 did capture an important relationship between stimulus intensity and the magnitude of sensation. Equation 1 specifies a logarithmic relationship between the magnitude of the sensation and the intensity of the stimulus. This means that it takes a much larger increase in the intensity of a bright light than of a dim light to give the same increase in the magnitude of the sensation. The subjective classification of the brightness of the stars by the ancient astronomer, Hipparchus, illustrates this fact. Wishing to describe the brightness of stars, Hipparchus placed the stars in six or seven categories based on their apparent brightness. The first category contained the stars that were barely visible and each succeeding category contained stars that were perceived to be one order of magnitude brighter than the stars in the previous category. When precise measurement became possible, it was found that the physical intensity of the stars in each category was about 2 1/2 times more intense than the intensity of the stars in the preceding category. If the physical intensity of the stars in the first category is arbitrarily defined as 1 unit, then the stars in the second category would be 2 1/2 units in brightness. The stars in the third category would be 2 1/2 x 2 1/2 or 6 1/4 units and so on. This means that, as described by Equation 1, equal increments in sensation required equal ratios between the stimulus intensities.

FIGURE 3. The probability distribution of momentary threshold values that will predict the results shown in Figure 1.

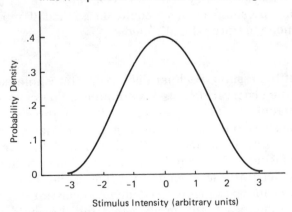

Stimulus Intensity (arbitrary units)

It is not unlikely that the momentary state of the sensory system would fluctuate rather than remain exactly constant. That is to say, although the subject is in a quiet room in the experiment, we can expect there to be a certain amount of background noise, for example, from the heating and ventilating system or the lights, etc. This noise would most likely fluctuate according to a normal distribution. That there is internal noise in the sensory system is also likely. Our receptors are continuously firing at a low level even though no stimulus is present. The number of receptors firing could also vary randomly from moment to moment. Therefore, it seems probable that existing external and internal noise in the experimental situation will make itself visible in the results of the experimental situation. We shall see in Chapter 7 that the concept of noise is an important one in the most recent approach to the study of sensation and detection.

A far more serious problem was posed for Fechner's model by his discovery that the probabilistic threshold could be affected by the attitude of the observer. The results he obtained from his wife seemed to be entirely different from those of his next-door neighbor; furthermore, he found that he could raise or lower the threshold of the same observer by instructions affecting his attitude. If he instructed one group of observers that they were to respond positively only when they were absolutely certain that they had detected the tone, he would find a much higher threshold than that from a group not so instructed.

Attitude of Observer

Although noise in the sensory system could account for the variability in the threshold that led to Fechner's probabilistic modification, nothing in Fechner's model could account for the effect of attitude on the subject's response. According to this model, the threshold of detectability is wired into the sensory system. Whether or not a stimulus is detected can be determined only by the limits of that system and by variables that affect the sensory system. How could changes in attitude affect the measured sensitivity of the sensory system?

But since attitude could affect the observed threshold value, Fechner faced the problem that this measure could not be a valid index of the sensitivity of the sensory system. Logically, the sensory system probably does operate independently of the observer's attitudes and motivations. But the decision or response of the subject in a psychophysical task does not. What Fechner needed was an index of the attitude of the observer so that he could correct his data to account for this attitude and get an independent measure of the sensitivity or detectability of the sensory system under study. The experimental methods that Fechner employed, however, could not provide such an index.

Consider for instance the fact that Fechner presented a stimulus on every trial. Some of his stimuli were assumed to be audible and some were not, but even on those trials in which no subject ever detected a stimulus, a stimulus was in fact presented. Very likely most subjects were aware of this or, if not, would sooner or later become aware of this circumstance as the experiment progressed. Perhaps they just might realize that there was a higher probability that a stimulus was present than that it was not. Intuitively we would all expect a subtle change in the subject's response pattern given this knowledge. Even without reference to such an influence, however, there is the undeniable possibility that subjects could lie in this task. Knowing that a stimulus was always present, they could say that they detected it, when in fact they had not.

Modifications to keep observer honest

A partial solution to the problem of the effect of attitude on the observer's performance, therefore, is to include no-signal trials in the experiment on which no stimulus is presented. The subject's task remains the same; he simply reports whether he detected a stimulus. If 50 percent of the trials are "blank" and if signal and no-signal trials are randomly presented, the subject has no cue to the presence or absence of the signal other than the sensitivity of his sensory system. A 2 x 2 confusion matrix, shown in Figure 4, is used to analyze performance in this task. The criterion of performance changes from "trials on which the stimulus is detected" in the classical methods to "trials on which subject's response correctly reflects the real state of the world" in the new psychophysical method with blank trials.

FIGURE 4. A two-by-two confusion matrix used to analyze performance in the yes-no signal detection task.

	Response	
	yes	no
Stimulus signal	hit $P(\text{yes}\,|\,\text{signal})$	miss $P(\text{no}\,|\,\text{signal})$
no signal	false alarm $P(\text{yes}\,|\,\text{no signal})$	correct rejection $P(\text{no}\,|\,\text{no signal})$

$$P(\text{yes}\,|\,\text{signal}) + P(\text{no}\,|\,\text{signal}) = 1$$
$$P(\text{yes}\,|\,\text{no signal}) + P(\text{no}\,|\,\text{no signal}) = 1$$

There are, therefore, two kinds of correct trials: those in which a signal is present and the subject says "yes," called "hit trials," and those in which a signal is not present and the subject says "no." Incorrect trials are those in which a signal is present but the subject says "no"—equivalent to Fechner's missed trials—and those on which no stimulus is present but the subject says "yes," called "false alarm trials." The experimenter tabulates the frequency of each of these four possibilities and computes the probability for each cell. As the figure shows, only two of the probabilities are independent of each other: the two probabilities that come from different stimulus trials. The standard data analysis of this task employs the proportion of times the observer said "yes" given that a signal was present, $P(\text{yes}|\text{signal})$, and the proportion of times he said "yes" given that no signal was present, $P(\text{yes}|\text{no-signal})$. These are the two probabilities we will be concerned with; the results in the confusion matrix can be represented completely by these two alone, since each of the remaining two can be generated from these.

Consider an experimental situation in which the subject says "yes" on most trials, not because he actually hears the stimulus, but for other reasons; for example, he decides that the experimenter will present a stimulus on most trials. His hit rate—the probability of "yes" given signal—will be very high. But so will his false alarm rate—the probability that he says "yes" given no signal. By contrast, if another subject actually heard the stimulus trials and responded "yes" to these trials and "no" to the blank trials, his hit rate would be high but his false alarm rate would be low. We can see that the correct measure of performance in this task must include some analysis of the relationship between these two probabilities. A high hit rate means one thing when the false alarm rate is low, and another when the false alarm rate is high.

Consider, for example, an experiment of 100 trials in which subjects are awarded 5¢ for every correct "yes" response and 1¢ for every correct "no" response. The signal is presented on one-half the trials, and the subjects know this. If these subjects simply disregard the sensory information entirely and say "yes" on every trial, they will get every signal trial correct and receive $2.50. At the same time, every no-signal trial will be a false alarm, and they will not collect for any of these trials. The no-signal trials are worth only 1¢, however; if they got all of them correct, they would receive only 50¢. Obviously, it is better to bias one's response in this situation in favor of "yes," since a correct "yes" is worth more than a correct "no." Indeed, if they attempt to respond simply on the basis of sensory information, then their unbiased performance must be 84 percent correct in order to earn slightly more than the amount they can earn by simply saying "yes" on every trial.

Since the experimenter controls the difficulty of the detection experiment, and since it is he who will have to pay, it seems the wisest choice might very well be to say "yes" on every trial. The hit rate of a subject who so chooses—the probability that he says "yes" given the presence of a signal—will be 100 percent. Fechner would wish to conclude that the subject therefore detected the signal on every trial in which it was present. But we know that this is not the case because the false alarm rate is also 100 percent. Neither of these figures alone—the 100 percent hit rate nor the

Motivation of observer

100 percent false alarm rate—accurately reflects the sensitivity of the subject's sensory system.

Fechner, you will remember, experimented with inducing changes in the subjects' attitude by instructing them on how confident they should be before reporting that a signal was presented. In this way he could raise or lower the subject's probability of saying "yes" quite independently of the difficulty of the detection task. When a high confidence was required, the "probabilistic threshold"—the intensity at which the subject said "yes" half the time—was far greater than when he encouraged the subject to say "yes" with just a low confidence. Clearly Fechner's subjects had some decision rule, held more or less consistently throughout the experiment, by which they selected their response given the sensation on a particular trial. In the earlier example, where hits were rewarded over correct "no" responses, the best rule might be to disregard the percept entirely or to respond "yes" to the smallest possible sensation. By changing the payoff, then, the experimenter could induce a subject to change his decision rule affecting the proportion of times he says "yes" in a given experiment.

Fechner intended to study the relationship between the intensity of the stimulus and sensation, that is, how the subject's experience was dependent upon the stimulus environment. He assumed that the subject's response was a direct indication of the sensation, but by logical analysis we see that another stage of processing intervenes, the decision process. How an observer responds in a given psychophysical situation is influenced by factors other than the information in the sensation. An adequate method for the study of sensation or the detection process, therefore, requires that the operation of the decision system be understood so that we can account for its effect on the response. Some alternative solutions to the problem are presented in Chapters 6 and 7.

The concept of threshold can be traced back to the ancient Greeks and psychologists have traditionally called it *limen,* derived from the Greek word. Subliminal perception, then, translates as a perceptual experience that is below the threshold for the stimulus involved. To take an example from science fiction, Ballard's (1964) story, *The Subliminal Man,* depicts a society that is entirely dependent on a consumer economy, making it necessary to convince the public of the value of buying. To accomplish this, huge signs are placed along the expressways, displaying advertisements at durations too short to be seen, but somehow long enough to influence the commuter to BUY NOW. This concept of subliminal perception is critically dependent on the threshold concept that a barrier exists which must be exceeded before we become aware of the stimulus presented to the senses. Somehow, stimuli below this level have an effect, but we are unaware of the impact of the message.

One could, therefore, equate subliminal perception with perception without awareness. It cannot really be denied that we seem to continually process information without a conscious awareness. Walking with a friend while simultaneously carrying on an intellectual discussion requires the participants to avoid bumping into trees and walls, and tripping over curbs, holes, and other people. The participants have no trouble doing this although they may not be consciously aware of their decisions. Or to take another example, we continually learn about people through certain interactions without making conscious conclusions about the basis for our information. We find ourselves giving an opinion when, in fact, none had been developed consciously. These examples are meant to illuminate the difficulty of relating perceptual processing to conscious awareness. There are probably many states of awareness; hence, the dichotomous assumption necessary for the subliminal perception concept is not justified.

The concept of a threshold is itself the weakest link in the subliminal perception idea. In the chapters that follow we consider alternatives to Fechner's threshold concept. Chapter 7 presents evidence that persons have any one or more of a range of sensations to a given stimulus. The observer, therefore, always has some information about the stimulus situation, and there is no such thing as a stimulus going unnoticed because it is below threshold. Without a threshold barrier to overcome, subliminal perception is not a meaningful issue. Subliminal advertising need not worry us, either, although, as Freud pointed out, we must realize that some of our values and actions may be based on processing not immediately available to conscious introspection.

Two-stage models of detection

A way is suggested to graft onto this sensory threshold model a decision process which predicts in some detail the biasing effects of information feedback, payoffs, and presentation probabilities.
—R. Duncan Luce (1963)

The last chapter showed how our description of the observer's task in the psychophysical situation must include and account for two stages of information processing between stimulus and response. We must understand both the sensation or detection stage and the decision stage before we can isolate the relationship between the stimulus and sensation. Fechner's original experiments cannot make this possible; his measure of sensitivity (sensation) can be influenced by both the sensory system and the decision system. His data cannot discriminate between a change in the sensory system and a change in the decision system. We do not know whether a change in the measured threshold following some experimental manipulation is due to a change in what the subject experiences, i.e., in the sensation, or results from a change in his decision rule.

Figure 1 shows graphically the sequence of operations that is assumed to occur in the psychophysical task. Notice that contact with external events is limited for both stages. The sensory stage's input is the stimulus, which can be objectively observed and mea-

STAGES BETWEEN STIMULUS AND RESPONSE

FIGURE 1. A flow diagram of the two operations that occur between stimulus and response in a detection task.

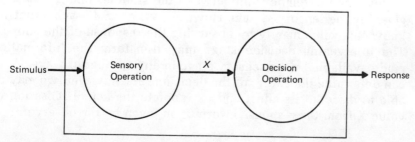

sured, but its output is an unobserved sensation, which can be represented by the value X. The value X is made available to the decision stage and is operated on before the subject tells the experimenter his answer. The output of the decision operation determines the response, but its input is the information value X given by the outcome of the sensory operation rather than the stimulus itself.

To understand the implications of this stage model, let us look more closely at the contribution of each stage to performance, and the variables by which each is affected. Each stage operates upon its input and transforms it. The stimulus information first enters the detection stage. This stage can be thought of as the operation of the sensory system. Its output is some value X that reflects two things: the properties (e.g., intensity) of the stimulus and the state (e.g., sensitivity) of the sensory system. This value X is the input to the decision or response-selection stage. This stage asks the question: Given X, which of my alternative responses is most appropriate? A decision is then made according to some decision rule and the response is then executed. The sensory stage performs the operation of transforming the stimulus into a sensory experience. For example, in auditory detection, the sensory system includes the hearing apparatus and other physiological structures that carry the stimulus message to the homunculus. Therefore, the output of the sensory system—the sensation value—should be a direct function of the characteristics of the stimulus and the state of the sensory system.

By contrast, the operations of the decision stage are affected by variables that determine the appropriateness of a response, for example, knowledge of the experimental situation, payoffs, attitudes, and motivations. If we could measure the two processes independently, the outcome of each process should be affected only by the variables that influence that process alone. Accordingly, we expect the rule of the decision system to be independent of the intensity of the stimulus signal. Similarly, the sensitivity of the sensory system should be independent of the decision rule employed by the decision system.

In terms of our information-processing model, Fechner wanted to describe the relationship between the stimulus and the value X given by the sensory system. However, we cannot assume that we know this value merely by observing the response of the subject. The intervening decision stage may transform the information made available by the sensory stage in any number of ways. If we can determine the nature of the decision rule, however, we may be able to discount its effect and extrapolate the actual sensation or value X from the response information given by the observer.

Given this stage model of performance in the psychophysical task, we can formalize various models of the detection process. Any threshold model implies that the output X from the sensory system can take on only one of two possible values. If the stimulus intensity is greater than the sensory threshold, the sensory system outputs a sensation value s. If the stimulus intensity is below the threshold, the sensory system outputs the value n, since no sensation was experienced. In the all-or-none threshold model, a given stimulus intensity and the output of the sensory system are consistently related. If a stimulus intensity I is greater than the threshold T, the conditional probability of s, given the stimulus, is one. This can be written $P(s|I>T) = 1$. Analogously, according to the all-or-none model, $P(s|I\leq T) = 0$. That is to say, the probability of s given a stimulus whose intensity is at or below threshold is zero.

Fechner's original conception of psychophysics, then, was that the probability of a "yes" response, given a fixed stimulus, was either zero or one. But as we have seen, this expectation was not confirmed by the results. In order to save the concept of a threshold, it is necessary to propose a probabilistic threshold, which is assumed to be unstable. That is, the probability that a stimulus exceeds the threshold will not always be zero or one. It is assumed that, owing to noise in the sensory system, the threshold itself varies somewhat.

A given stimulus, then, due to noise on the system may fall above threshold on one occasion, below it on another. Fechner's test tone, presented around the threshold value, will sometimes exceed the threshold and sometimes fall below it. The probability of the stimulus exceeding the threshold, if it is heard by the subject 80 percent of the time, is .8. As the intensity of the stimulus increases, the probability of its being detected increases also. If we take two stimuli, S_1 and S_2, such that S_1 is more intense than S_2, we can ask: What is the probability that S_1 and S_2 give rise to s, a sensation output from the sensory system? This probability is no longer 1, but varies between 0 and 1. If the sensory system gives value s to S_1 eight out of every 10 times it is presented, then the probability that S_1 gives rise to s is .8. We have said that S_2 is less intense than S_1; the probability that S_2 gives rise to s would therefore be less than .8.

The probabilistic theory assumes that the threshold varies from moment to moment, and that therefore a stimulus of given intensity will exceed it only with some probability. The probabilistic threshold concept appears to be consistent with Fechner's results; it explains the effect of noise in the system, and, as will be shown below, can be incorporated into a theory with a decision process. Therefore, it can also account for changes in attitude on the part of

MODELS OF THE SENSORY SYSTEM

the observer. This concept is formally represented as the high threshold theory.

It is necessary to evaluate the high threshold theory and any alternatives in a signal detection task in which both signal and no-signal (blank) trials are presented. As noted previously, Fechner's classical methods cannot derive independent measures of the sensitivity of the sensory system and the decision rule of the decision system. In contrast, the signal detection task with blank trials allows the experimenter to derive indices of the two stages of processing that operate in the task. To do this, he must first formalize the operations of these two stages of processing and, then, derive the indices of each process, based on this formal model. He must also provide evidence that the model adequately describes performance in the experimental task before the indices can be taken as valid measures of the two stages of information processing.

High Threshold Theory In the high threshold theory, it is assumed that blank trials never exceed the threshold. Signal trials exceed the threshold with some probability (p), where $0 \leq p \leq 1$ and the value of p is directly related to the intensity of the signal. The decision system is assumed to operate according to the following algorithm: An observer will respond "yes" in the experimental situation with probability 1 when the stimulus exceeds the threshold and probability g when the stimulus does not exceed the threshold. As the observer is induced to say "yes" more often, he will increase the probability (g) of saying "yes" on those trials on which the threshold is not exceeded.

Assuming no-signal or noise (N) trials and signal-plus-noise (SN) trials, the two possible sensory states, s and n, correspond to whether the stimulus presented on that trial exceeded or did not exceed the threshold, respectively. Let p represent the probability that SN exceeds the threshold, that is, produces output s from the sensory system. Therefore, the probability that SN does not exceed the threshold, that is, produces output n from the sensory system, must be $1 - p$. Given that N cannot exceed the threshold, the probability that N produces output s is zero. Therefore, N produces output n with probability 1. These assumptions of the high threshold theory can be formalized in a two-state transition matrix.

Sensory State

$$
\text{Stimulus} \quad
\begin{array}{c}
\\
\text{SN} \\
\text{N}
\end{array}
\begin{array}{cc}
s & n \\
\left[\begin{array}{cc}
p & (1-p) \\
0 & 1
\end{array}\right]
\end{array}
$$

Transition matrices are used in this section because they are convenient forms for presenting theories with two intervening stages between stimulus and response. Each matrix represents one stage and has an input and an output. The entries in the matrices represent the probability of the output given (conditional upon) the input. Consider the two matrices:

$$A = \text{input} \quad \begin{array}{c} a \\ b \end{array} \overset{\overset{\text{output}}{\overset{c \qquad d}{}}}{\begin{bmatrix} P & 1-p \\ q & 1-q \end{bmatrix}} \qquad B = \text{input} \quad \begin{array}{c} c \\ d \end{array} \overset{\overset{\text{output}}{\overset{e \qquad f}{}}}{\begin{bmatrix} g & 1-g \\ h & 1-h \end{bmatrix}}$$

The matrix A has as input the events a and b and as output the events c and d. The entries represent the probabilities of the output given the input. Since there are only two possible outputs, the entries across the rows must add to 1.

If we were interested in the relationship between the inputs a and b and the outputs e and f, we would want to know the probability of output e given input a and so on. This relationship could also be represented in a 2 x 2 transition matrix with inputs a and b and outputs e and f. The entries in the matrix would be determined by multiplying matrices A and B.

$$AB = \begin{array}{c} a \\ b \end{array} \overset{c \qquad d}{\begin{bmatrix} p & 1-p \\ q & 1-q \end{bmatrix}} \times \begin{array}{c} c \\ d \end{array} \overset{e \qquad f}{\begin{bmatrix} g & 1-g \\ h & 1-h \end{bmatrix}}$$

$$= \begin{array}{c} a \\ b \end{array} \overset{e \qquad\qquad\qquad\qquad f}{\begin{bmatrix} pg + (1-p)h & p(1-g) + (1-p)(1-h) \\ qg + (1-q)h & q(1-g) + (1-q)(1-h) \end{bmatrix}}$$

Put into words, Event e can occur—given the Event a—in two different ways. First, if Event a produces Event c and c produces Event e. This occurs with probability pg. Second, if Event a gives rise to event d and d gives rise to Event e. This occurs with probability $(1-p)h$. Therefore, Event e can occur given Event a with probability $pg + (1-p)h$, and so on for the other entries

---

The inputs in the transition matrix are the two stimulus events and the outputs are the two sensory states that can be produced by the sensory system. The entries in the transition matrix represent the probability of a particular sensory state given a particular stimulus trial. For example, the sensory state s will occur with probability p given stimulus SN. This matrix describes the relationship between the stimulus and the output of the sensory system, the first stage of the two-stage model shown in Figure 1. The experimenter does not have an observable measure of this output in the experimental task. The decision system intervenes between output of the sensory system and the observable response of the subject. Therefore, it is also necessary to describe the relationship between the output of the sensory system and the response of the subject. The high threshold theory assumes that the subject employs a specific decision rule that can be represented by a two-state transition matrix which describes the relationship between the output of the sensory system and the response of the subject.

$$\begin{array}{c} \text{Response} \\ \begin{array}{cc} \text{yes} & \text{no} \end{array} \\ \begin{array}{cc} \text{Sensory} & s \\ \text{State} & n \end{array} \begin{bmatrix} 1 & 0 \\ g & 1-g \end{bmatrix} \end{array}$$

In this case, the transition matrix represents the relationship between the input to the decision system and its output. Since the input to the decision system is the output of the sensory system, the possible inputs are s and n. Given that the subject must make one of two responses on each trial, the outputs are limited to "yes" or "no." The entries in the transition matrix define the decision rule used by the decision system. In the high threshold theory, it is assumed that the observer always says "yes," given that the stimulus exceeded the threshold, producing sensory state s. Accordingly, the transition probability from s to "yes" is 1. The probability that the observer responds "yes" on trials on which the threshold was not exceeded is dependent on the motivations and attitudes of the observer and his knowledge of the likelihood of a signal trial. Therefore, the transition probability from n to "yes" is represented by the value g, which can take on values between 0 and 1.

Measure of sensitivity   Given this model of the sensory and decision system, how does the experimenter account for the contribution of the decision system, and derive a true measure of the sensitivity of the observer in the experimental task? The measure of sensitivity, according to the high threshold theory, is the parameter p, the proportion of times the stimulus exceeded the threshold. The parameter p represents a true measure of sensitivity since it indexes exactly the relationship between the stimulus and the output of the sensory system. According to this two-stage theory, the operation of the sensory system is not influenced by the decision system. Therefore, the value p is uncontaminated by changes in the response bias of the subject; that is, p remains constant with changes in g. The value p can, therefore, be used as a dependent variable that describes the sensitivity of the sensory system, assuming this formal probabilistic threshold theory. Keep in mind, however, that the high threshold theory must be shown to accurately describe performance on this task before this dependent variable can be used.

Thus, the high threshold theory will be tested against the empirical data in our psychophysical task. A series of trials is presented, randomly choosing between signal (SN) and no-signal (N) trials. The observer might be tested for a series of 600 trials. The experimenter records the trial type and the response in a 2 x 2 confusion matrix (see Figure 4 in Chapter 5). Performance can be completely described in this task by the two independent probabilities: $P(\text{yes}|\text{SN})$, the probability that the subject says "yes" given that SN is presented; and $P(\text{yes}|\text{N})$, the probability that the subject says "yes" given that N is presented. These are our observed hit and false alarm probabilities, respectively.

The predicted values of these two probabilities can be derived from the assumptions of the high threshold theory. According to this theory, a hit—saying "yes" on an SN trial—can occur in one of two independent ways. First, if the signal exceeds the threshold and the subject says "yes"; second, if the signal does not exceed the threshold but the subject says "yes," anyway. This verbal description must be presented in terms of probabilities. The probability that the subject says "yes" on a signal trial is equal to the probability that the signal exceeds threshold and the subject said "yes," plus the probability that the signal did not exceed threshold but the subject said "yes," anyway. Stated mathematically:

$$P(\text{yes}|\text{SN}) = P(s|\text{SN}) \cdot P(\text{yes}|s) + P(n|\text{SN}) \cdot P(\text{yes}|n). \qquad (1)$$

Substituting the entries of the transition matrices for the respective probabilities, we get

$$P(\text{yes}|\text{SN}) = p \cdot 1 + (1 - p)g. \qquad (1a)$$

Analogously, we see that

$$P(\text{yes}|\text{N}) = P(s|\text{N}) \cdot P(\text{yes}|s) + P(n|\text{N}) \cdot P(\text{yes}|n) \qquad (2)$$
$$P(\text{yes}|\text{N}) = 0 \cdot 1 + 1 \cdot g = g. \qquad (2a)$$

These equations predict the hit and false alarm probabilities in terms of the high threshold theory. Given these equations, it is now possible to determine p, the measure of sensitivity according to high threshold theory. Since $P(\text{yes}|\text{N}) = g$, we can substitute value $P(\text{yes}|\text{N})$ in place of g in Equation 1a, which gives

$$P(\text{yes}|\text{SN}) = p + [1 - p] \cdot P(\text{yes}|\text{N}). \qquad (3)$$

Multiplying and rearranging terms gives

$$P(yes|SN) = p + P(yes|N) - p \cdot P(yes|N) \qquad (3a)$$

$$P(yes|SN) = P(yes|N) + p[1 - P(yes|N)] \qquad (3b)$$

It follows that the value p is given by

$$p = \frac{P(yes|SN) - P(yes|N)}{1 - P(yes|N)} \qquad (4)$$

Accordingly, given the hit and the false alarm probabilities, it is possible to determine a measure (p) of the magnitude of the sensation of the observer that is uncontaminated by the operation of the decision system. Before we can employ the measure p as an index of the sensitivity of the sensory system, however, it is necessary to demonstrate that the high threshold theory accurately describes our two stages of processing in the psychophysical task. A critical test of the theory is to hold the signal characteristics constant and to vary the decision bias of the observer. In this case, the experimenter performs a number of small experiments that differ only with respect to the instructions given the subject. In one case, the subject is instructed to be relatively certain that a signal was presented before he says "yes"; in another, he is told to say "yes" if he has the slightest indication that a signal was presented. These instructions, according to high threshold theory, are assumed to affect the value of g, the decision bias of the subject.

ROC curves It is possible to graphically represent the results from this set of experiments in which the sensitivity of the observer remains constant and the decision rule changes. This representation, called a receiver operating characteristic (ROC) curve, plots the hit rate, $P(Yes|SN)$, on the Y ordinate as a function of the false alarm rate, $P(Yes|N)$, on the X abscissa. According to the high threshold theory, an unbiased observer would respond "yes" given SN trials with probability p and would never respond "yes" on N trials. Therefore, his performance would be represented by the point (p,0). Hence, the ROC curve must intersect the Y ordinate at the value p when the X abscissa is equal to zero. Now, as the observer became biased to respond "yes," both $P(yes|SN)$ and $P(yes|N)$ will increase accordingly. Equation 5 describing the relationship between $P(yes|SN)$ and $P(yes|N)$ is in the form of a linear equation: $y = a + bx$

$$P(yes|SN) = p + [1 - p] \cdot P(yes|N) \qquad (5)$$

This shows that $P(yes|SN)$ is a linear function of $P(yes|N)$. Therefore, the ROC curve will be described by a straight line beginning from the point (p,0). The most biased observer will be one that sets the value $g = 1$. In this case, $P(\text{Yes}|N) = 1$ by Equation 2a and $P(\text{Yes}|SN) = 1$ by Equation 5. Therefore, the straight line must go through the upper right-hand corner of the *ROC* curve intersecting at the point (1,1). This analysis indicates a critical test of the high threshold theory: that an *ROC* curve drawn through the results of the experiment manipulating the observer's decision rule should be a straight line function similar to those shown in Figure 2. In Figure 2, the intersection point on the Y ordinate would be our estimate of the value p, our index of sensitivity.

FIGURE 2. *ROC* curves predicted by high threshold theory.

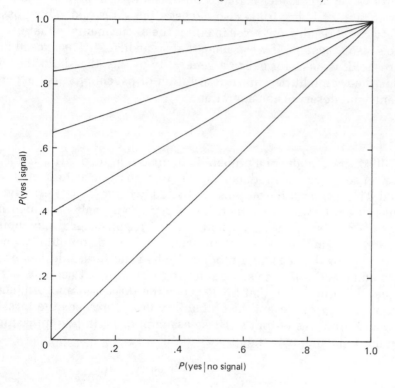

The mathematical formulation of high threshold theory is analogous to the classical correction for chance guessing, so often employed in psychological testing. The assumption here is that the observer either knows the answer or guesses randomly from the possible set of response alternatives. The chance factor is taken as $1/n$ where n is the number of possible response alternatives. Therefore, the classical correction for chance guessing is given by the equation

Classical correction for guessing

$$p = \frac{P(C) - 1/n}{1 - 1/n} \qquad (6)$$

where p is the true proportion correct and $P(C)$ is the observed proportion correct in the experimental task. We shall see throughout this volume that the assumptions underlying the correction are false.

Empirical tests The predictions of the high threshold theory that the *ROC* curve should resemble a straight line fails empirical tests. The results indicate that the observer cannot maintain a substantial hit rate with a negligible false alarm rate. Experiments show that if $P(\text{yes}|N)$ is close to zero, so is $P(\text{yes}|SN)$. An alternative possibility we shall consider is that if there is a threshold, a substantial proportion of blank trials also exceeds the threshold. This possibility could result from noise in either the experimental situation or the sensory system. If we assume that some blank trials exceed the threshold, we can formalize a general two-state threshold theory. This theory might provide a description of psychophysical experiments and deserves consideration.

GENERAL TWO-STATE THRESHOLD THEORY In this formal model of a probabilistic threshold theory (Luce, 1963) the sensory system produces one of two possible values on each trial. These alternative outputs are tied to two stimulus alternatives, but in a probabilistic manner. Let N represent trials on which no signal or noise alone is present; SN represents signal-plus-noise trials. Let s and n represent the sensory system outputs, with s standing for the sensation produced when the threshold has been exceeded, and n for the sensation produced when it has not. Let p equal the probability that SN exceeds the threshold and produces output s; let q represent the probability that N exceeds the threshold and produces output s. These assumptions can be represented by the following two-state transition matrix:

Sensory State

$$
\text{Stimulus}\quad
\begin{array}{c}
\\
\text{SN} \\
\text{N}
\end{array}
\begin{bmatrix}
s & n \\
p & (1-p) \\
q & (1-q)
\end{bmatrix}
$$

The input to the decision process is the output of the sensory system—the sensation s (stimulus exceeds threshold) or n (no signal is detected). The decision process is controlled by a decision rule. The operation of the decision rule is affected by the subject's knowledge of the likelihood of a signal (SN) trial, the reward contingencies in the experimental situation, and the attitudes and motivation of the observer. The output of the decision process prescribes the observable response of the subject in the experimental situation. The following transition matrix represents these assumptions:

Response

$$
\begin{array}{cc}
& \text{yes} \quad\quad \text{no} \\
\begin{array}{c} \text{Sensory} \\ \text{State} \end{array}
\begin{array}{c} s \\ n \end{array}
& \begin{bmatrix} f & (1-f) \\ g & (1-g) \end{bmatrix}
\end{array}
$$

The value f represents the probability that subject responds "yes" given sensory input s; the probability that he responds "no" given sensory input s is therefore $1 - f$. Similarly, g represents the probability of a "yes" response given sensory input n, and the probability of the "no" response given this input is $1 - g$. These probabilities, f and g, are determined by the class of variables mentioned above—those that influence the decision bias of the subject. For example, if an observer won a nickel every time he correctly identified a signal present and lost 3¢ every time he missed a signal, he should be more likely to indicate "signal" on both SN and N trials. Or, if he were told that 9 out of 10 trials would be signal trials, he should say "yes" most of the time, independent of which sensory state was elicited, if he wants to maximize the number of correct answers. In this example, simply responding "yes" all the time would allow the observer to be 90 percent correct.

It should be noted that the high threshold theory merely represents a special case of the general two-state threshold theory. If q is made equal to zero and f is set equal to 1, the general two-state theory reduces to the high threshold theory. We can see that the general two-state theory *is* more general and, therefore, should be able to provide a better description of the results than does the high threshold theory. However, two additional parameters, q and f, must be estimated by the experimenter from his results. As we shall see, this limits the practical or heuristic value of the general two-state theory, since its parameter estimates cannot be derived from one set of hit and false alarm probabilities.

Thus, performance is determined by two processes, the sensory system and the decision system. The probability of a particular response, given a particular stimulus, cannot be calculated from either transition matrix alone. The first matrix gives the probability of each sensory state given the stimulus; the second gives the probability of each response given those sensory states. To find our two predicted response probabilities in the experiment—the hit rate (probability of "yes," given signal-plus-noise) and the false alarm rate (probability of "yes," given noise alone)—we must multiply these two matrices.

The predicted hit rate can be obtained as follows: The hit rate refers to the probability of a "yes" response conditional on an SN trial. An SN trial can give rise to one of two sensory states. Therefore, the probability of the "yes" response given stimulus SN is the sum of two probabilities: (1) the probability that stimulus SN elicited sensory state s and the subject said "yes," and (2) the probability that stimulus SN elicited state n and the subject said "yes." Hence the equation for the hit rate is:

$$P(\text{yes}|\text{SN}) = P(s|\text{SN}) \cdot P(\text{yes}|s) + P(n|\text{SN}) \cdot P(\text{yes}|n). \quad (7)$$

Substituting our parameter values for these probabilities, this equation can be expressed as:

$$P(\text{yes}|\text{SN}) = pf + (1 - p)g. \quad (7a)$$

The equation for the false alarm rate can be derived in the same manner, giving:

$$P(\text{yes}|\text{N}) = P(s|\text{N}) \cdot P(\text{yes}|s) + P(n|\text{N}) \cdot P(\text{yes}|n), \quad (8)$$

which we simplify as

$$P(\text{yes}|\text{N}) = qf + (1 - q)g. \quad (8a)$$

In the two-state model, performance in a psychophysical task can be described by the values of the parameter estimates, since these determine our observed response probabilities. The probability p represents the probability that a signal trial exceeds the threshold. It is influenced, therefore, by variables affecting whether or not a stimulus exceeds threshold—namely, the energy of the signal and the state of the sensory system. The probability q is likewise dependent upon the properties of stimulus and sensory variables—the background noise on no-signal trials, for example. The probabilities f and g, on the other hand, represent the probabilities of a particular response decision, given one or the other sensory state. These probabilities are affected by variables influencing the subject's decision rule. We expect f and g to increase as the observer becomes more biased toward the "yes" response. If we assume that the observer modifies his bias to optimize his decision, then some simplifying constraints can be applied to the values f and g. With a bias toward correctly identifying SN trials, it would be optimal to give this response every time the sensory output is s, and to deviate from it only on occasions when the sensory output is *n*. The parameter *f* in that case is equal to 1. The value *g*, which is the probability of "yes" given *n*, would lie between zero and 1, and would increase with increases in the bias toward "yes." Likewise, with a bias toward "no" or correctly identifying no-signal (blank) trials, the value *g* is optimally set at zero and *f* lies between zero and 1. An observer with no bias toward either response is assumed to map the output of the sensory system directly into a response. With this decision rule, a given sensory state would determine a given response with probability 1. Since in this case $f = 1$ and $g = 0$, Equations 7 and 8 give

$$P(\text{yes}|\text{SN}) = p,$$
$$\text{and}$$
$$P(\text{yes}|\text{N}) = q.$$

These two probabilities, equal to *p* and *q*, respectively, represent performance of an unbiased observer in the signal detection task. According to the general two-state model, the index of performance of the sensory system is described by the values of *p* and *q*. Analogously, the values of *f* and *g* describe the decision rule of the subject in the experimental task.

By varying the decision bias of the observer while holding sensory variables constant, we can also generate a hypothetical *ROC* curve that is predicted by the general two-state threshold theory. As mentioned above, the point (*p,q*) will represent performance of an unbiased observer in the psychophysical task. If the observer was biased to respond "no," the parameter *g* would be zero and *f* would vary from zero to 1. When both *g* and *f* are zero, $P(\text{yes}|\text{SN})$ and $P(\text{yes}|\text{N})$ are also zero, as can be seen in Equations 7a and 8a. It can also be shown that increases in *f* produce increases in $P(\text{yes}|\text{N})$ that are linearly related, so that a straight line between the points—(0,0) and (*p,q*)—is obtained. Analogously, when *f* is equal to 1 and *g* increases from zero to 1, $P(\text{yes}|\text{SN})$ increases linearly with increases in $P(\text{yes}|\text{N})$ from the point (*p,q*) to the point (1,1). Figure 3 presents an *ROC* curve generated by the general two-state threshold model.

According to the general two-state theory, it is necessary to estimate four parameter values *p, q, f,* and *g* to predict the observed values of $P(\text{yes}|\text{S})$ and $P(\text{yes}|\text{N})$. But it is not possible to derive a single set of these parameter values from a simple experiment with only these two observed response probabilities. That is to say, there is a whole family of values for each of the parameters that will predict the results accurately. Having only one point on the *ROC* curve does not uniquely determine the placement of the two lines predicted by the general two-state theory. At least two points are needed on the *ROC* curve to uniquely determine the placement of the two lines. (Two points are sufficient since the two lines must intersect at the points 0,0 and 1,1, respectively.) Any experiment, therefore, that is based on the model of the general two-state threshold theory must include measures of performance along at least two points on the potential *ROC* curve. Our evaluation of the general two-state threshold theory will be deferred until another conception of the signal-detection problem is presented in the next chapter.

The goal of this chapter has been to account for two stages of processing in a psychophysical task. A theory of psychological performance must describe the operations of each stage, and the experiment must be designed in a way that will allow a measure of performance for each of the processing stages. Although we are currently concerned with psychophysical problems, the approach should be taken as prototypical for all psychological problems. Every experiment in all areas of psychology requires a task with a number of processing stages, and each of these stages must be accounted for before the experimenter learns something about the exact process of interest. For example, learning tasks also require decision operations which must be understood and incorporated into the theoretical and empirical study of learning phenomena. Hence, our interest in the development of theory and experiment in psychophysics is not only for the purpose of studying psychophysical phenomena but also has the aim of making transparent all operations of the human mind.

FIGURE 3. An *ROC* curve predicted from the general two-state threshold theory.

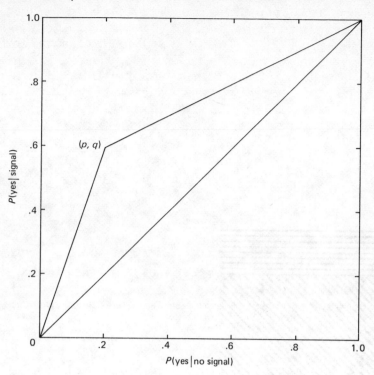

Theory of Signal Detectability

The methods that permit separating the criterion and sensitivity measures, and a psychophysical theory that incorporates the results obtained with these methods, stem directly from the modern approach taken by engineers to the general problem of signal detection.
—*John A. Swets (1961)*

There are only two possible states of the world in the psychophysical task: SN (signal present) and N (no signal). Accordingly, it is only natural to assume that there are only two possible outputs of the sensory system: s (sensation) and n (no sensation). However, according to a multistate theory—the theory of signal detectability (Green and Swets, 1966)—many sensory states are possible. The central assumption of this theory is that no threshold or barrier exists that must be overcome for a sensation. Rather, there is always some background noise in the sensory system, which always produces some positive sensation value. Therefore, even though there are only two stimulus trials, many possible outputs of the sensory system can occur when it processes either of these two stimulus inputs. Although the subject could be presented with a constant stimulus from trial to trial, he actually knows a different amount on each trial, a difference that can extend over a wide range. For a given stimulus event, the sensory system can output any of a number of sensation values corresponding to the magnitude of the sensation.

The transition matrix corresponding to the sensory system of multistate theory, therefore, consists of two stimulus states and m sensory states.

MULTISTATE THEORY: SENSORY SYSTEM

$$
\begin{array}{c}
\text{Sensory State} \\
\begin{array}{cccccccc}
 & s_1 & s_2 & s_3 & \cdots & s_i & \cdots & s_m \\
\text{SN} & \begin{bmatrix} p_1 & p_2 & p_3 & \cdots & p_i & \cdots & p_m \\ \\ q_1 & q_2 & q_3 & \cdots & q_i & \cdots & q_m \end{bmatrix}
\end{array}
\end{array}
$$

Stimulus

$$\sum_{i=1}^{m} p_i = 1 , \ \sum_{i=1}^{m} q_i = 1$$

As can be seen in the transition matrix, a signal gives rise to sensory state s_i with probability p_i and a no-signal trial gives rise to this state with probability q_i. It is assumed that the sensory states are ordered in magnitude along some dimension, for example, the magnitude of sensation. In this case, the magnitude of sensation given by sensory state s_i is less than that given by sensory state s_{i+1} ($s_i < s_{i+1}$).

If s_1 is the smallest magnitude for a sensory state, then we would expect q_1 to be larger than p_1. In other words, it should be more likely for a no-signal trial to elicit sensory state s_1 than for a signal trial to do so. In contrast, if sensory state s_m is the largest magnitude of sensation, we would expect that $p_m > q_m$. Somewhere along the continuum of sensory states, then, the relative values of p_i and q_i reverse. Furthermore, we might expect that the differences between p_i and q_i are larger at the extreme values of s_i than in the middle range of values.

MULTISTATE THEORY: DECISION SYSTEM

According to multistate theory the decision system is faced with any of a whole range of sensation values X, given by the sensory system. The task facing the decision system in the multistate theory, therefore, differs significantly from its task in the threshold models. In a two-alternative task, however, the decision system can divide the range of sensory output into two classes: those that are smaller than some sensation value s_i and those that are larger than this sensation value. In multistate theory, these two sets of values are treated differently by the decision system. It is assumed that the decision system responds "no" for sensation values that are below the cutoff sensation value and "yes" for sensation values that are larger than this cutoff value.

In this model, then, it is assumed that the decision system chooses a cutoff or criterion value C such that if the sensory value s_i from the sensory system is equal to or exceeds this value, a "yes" response is executed; otherwise, the observer says "no." This decision rule can be represented by the following transition matrix:

Response

		yes	no
Sensory	$s_i \geq C$	1	0
state	$s_i < C$	0	1

As can be seen in the transition matrix representing the decision system, the decision rule is assumed to be deterministic rather than probabilistic. Given a total value from the sensory system, the response is determined with probability 1. This decision rule con-

In the mathematical formulation of the theory of signal detectability, the decision rule of the subject is assumed to be analogous to one in statistical decision theory. It is assumed that the decision system assigns conditional probabilities to the output of the sensory system. The decision system computes the conditional probability that the output X from the sensory system arose from an SN trial, $P(X|SN)$, and the probability that it arose from an N trial, $P(X|N)$. The likelihood ratio L is a ratio of these two probabilities:

$$L = \frac{P(X|SN)}{P(X|N)}$$

The decision system has a criterion value, so that if the likelihood ratio exceeds this value it responds "yes"; otherwise it responds "no." The unbiased observer would have a criterion value set at 1, the point at which it is equally likely that X came from an SN or an N trial.

---

trasts with the probabilistic decision rule of the general two-state model.

The exact predictions of multistate theory are not easily derived from the transition matrices of the sensory and decision systems because of the large number of sensory states. The theory, however, can be formalized and actually simulated or modeled in a straightforward manner. First, we shall describe how the multistate theory can be simulated, using a dice game analogy. For this analogy we imagine an experimenter with 3 dice, including one stimulus or signal die. The signal die is imprinted on three of its sides with the value 3, and on the remaining three sides with the value zero. The other two dice in the game are normal dice with the values 1 through 6 on their six respective sides. The experimenter rolls the three dice and announces the sum of the values on their faces. A subject must decide, on the basis of the total of all the values, whether the value showing on the signal die was a 3 or a zero.

The dice in this game are analogous to the stimulus trial in a simple detection experiment; the total dice value presented to the subject by the experimenter represents the sensation—the information from the sensory system. The subject in the dice game performs the task of the decision system, judging whether the signal die is 3 or zero on the basis of the total value. We use a dice game analogy because, in a real psychological task, we cannot observe the value

DICE GAME ANALOGY

X that is produced by the sensory system. We do not know what sensation a stimulus produces in a subject; we only know the response he chooses to make. If we do not know the nature of the sensation, we do not know the exact decision problem he faces in choosing that response.

In a dice game model of a particular sensory system, on the other hand, we have direct control over the possible outcomes of the roll of dice, and, therefore, over the values that can be transmitted from the sensory system to the decision system. Thus we can change our dice game to represent different experiments in which variables are manipulated to affect the operations of the sensory and decision systems. Such a representation of a particular model of the sensory system clarifies the operation of the sensory system and the task that the decision system faces, given the output of the sensory system.

The multistate theory challenges the assumption that there is a threshold. Although the experimenter presents either a signal or no-signal trial, the sensory system always gives a certain positive sensation value. This theory can best be understood by simulating it with our dice game. The multistate theory assumes that the output of the sensory system is analogous to the total number of points obtained from the three dice. One die is our special signal die with three 3s and three 0s; a 3 corresponds to those trials on which a signal is presented and zero corresponds to no-signal or blank trials in the psychophysical task. The other two dice are normal dice whose six sides each have a number from 1 to 6; these dice are analogous to the noise that multistate assumes to exist in the sensory system. We roll all three dice; the decision system, given only the combined total, must say "yes" or "no" whether the stimulus die is showing a 3 (signal) or a zero (non-signal), respectively.

In this case we have a range of possible combined totals from 2 (0 + 1 + 1) to 15 (3 + 6 + 6). Given the total value of 2, the decision system can say "no" with absolute confidence. Similarly, it can say "yes" to the value of 15 with 100 percent accuracy. In fact, the combined values up to 4 could not occur if the signal die is 3; and the combined values of 13 and over could not occur if the special die is zero. So up to 4, and over 13, the decision system can be 100 percent correct. For all values in between, the decision system cannot be absolutely certain of its decision. The possible outcomes in this dice game given that a 3 or zero is showing on the signal die are presented in Table 1. The total value 6 can occur in seven ways; five ways with a zero on the signal die and two ways given a 3 on the signal die. Therefore, given the total value of 6, the probability of a signal being present is 2 out of 7 or 2/7.

TABLE 1
Frequency of possible totals given the signal die showing 3 or 0
for a block of 72 trials.

Dice total	Frequency given signal die is	
	3	0
2	0	1
3	0	2
4	0	3
5	1	4
6	2	5
7	3	6
8	4	5
9	5	4
10	6	3
11	5	2
12	4	1
13	3	0
14	2	0
15	1	0
total combinations	36	36

This particular dice game can be analyzed in terms of a transition matrix of the sensory process. Since the dice totals are in the range of 2 to 15, and these correspond to the possible number of sensory states, we have 14 possible sensory states. Of course, there are only two possible stimulus trials, signal (3) or no signal (0). Therefore, the sensory process can be represented by the following transition matrix

$$\text{Sensory State}$$

$$\text{Stimulus} \quad \begin{matrix} & 2 & 3 & 4 & 5 & 6 & 7 & 8 & 9 & 10 & 11 & 12 & 13 & 14 & 15 \\ 3 \\ 0 \end{matrix} \begin{bmatrix} 0 & 0 & 0 & 1 & 2 & 3 & 4 & 5 & 6 & 5 & 4 & 3 & 2 & 1 \\ 1 & 2 & 3 & 4 & 5 & 6 & 5 & 4 & 3 & 2 & 1 & 0 & 0 & 0 \end{bmatrix}$$

Each entry in the matrix is divided by 36.

For example, if the odd die is showing a 3, the probability that the sensory system will output a total value of 10 points is 6/36. In this case, $p_{10} = 6/36 = 1/6 \approx .17$.

The multistate theory assumes that the detection system transmits a wide range of values as in the totals in the dice game. The decision maker receives one of these values, computes—in some sense—the likelihood of a signal being present given this value, and makes his response according to some decision rule. This theory does not require the concept of a threshold—a barrier that must be over-

Value of Signal

come before a sensation is possible. On the contrary, it assumes that the detection stage always has a sensation value, and that the sensation can vary across a wide range. In our dice game simulation, the output of the detection system is very informative when the value is 2 or 15, but essentially uninformative when the value is 8 or 9. The optimal decision procedure in this situation is to establish a cutoff point, say the total 8½, at which the decision maker would cease to respond "no" and begin to respond "yes."

In the dice game model of this theory, the decision maker is faced with one of many possible values from 2 through 15. His task is to translate the value he received into one of only two possible responses. For a few of the combined totals he might receive, this could be done with confidence. Combined totals of 2, 3, or 4 mean that the signal die could only be showing zero, and, therefore, the correct response could only be "no." For combined totals above 12, on the other hand, the signal die would have to be showing 3. Given a combined total of 13, 14, or 15, therefore, the decision process could choose a "yes" response with absolute confidence. Values between 5 and 12, however, represent varying probabilities of either condition.

Another way of seeing the relationship between the sensory and decision systems, is to plot the distribution of total scores given in Table 1. The expected distribution of totals given that the signal die contains a zero or a 3 are shown in Figure 1. The total number of points represents the output of the sensory system, the values given to the decision system. These values, then, make up a decision continuum, with some total values giving 100 percent probability of a correct "yes" at the extreme right, and those giving 100 percent certainty of "no" at the extreme left. As the values given to the decision process increase from left to right, uncertainty grows; at 8 and 9, it is very unsure of the answer. Thereafter the probability of "yes" over "no" increases, until at 13 and beyond the decision maker again knows 100 percent of the information needed to choose a response correctly. The subject in our dice game arrives at his decision choosing some criterion value C, such that if the total is equal to or exceeds that value, he says "yes"; otherwise he says "no." The criterion value that the subject chooses is influenced by experimental variables assumed to affect the decision system.

As in the two-state models of detection, two processes in the multistate model contribute independently to the final result. The output of the sensory system is affected by the nature of the stimulus and the state of the sensory system. The decision rule is affected by the subject's knowledge of the probability of a signal trial, the payoffs in the experimental situation, and the attitude of the observer.

FIGURE 1. The expected distribution of totals as a function of whether the signal die showed 3 or 0.

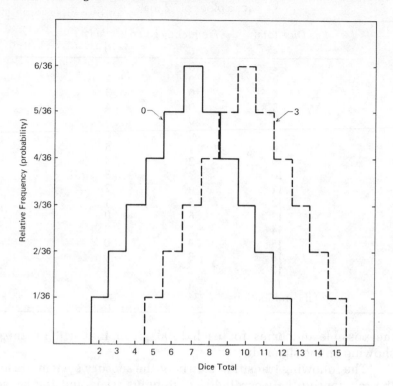

Returning to the dice game model of multistate theory, let us change the nature of the stimulus by changing the number representing an SN trial on the signal die from 3 to 6. We now have, as before, three dice: two of them are normally marked with the values 1 through 6, each imprinted on one of the six sides. The signal die is now marked 6 on three of its sides and zero on the remaining three. Again, the decision maker is told only the combined value showing on all three dice, and his task is to say "yes" or "no," given this combined value, whether the number showing on the signal die is 6 or zero.

The range of possible totals will now be from 8 to 18 when 6 is on the signal die, and from 2 to 12 when zero is on the signal die. Therefore, changing the signal level from 3 to 6 changed the possible outputs of the sensory system, as represented by the total number of points showing on the three dice. The decision maker in this case can be certain that 6 is not present given 2, 3, 4, 5, 6, and 7, and that it is present given 13 through 18. The number of trials on which he can be absolutely certain has increased significantly and his performance should be correspondingly better. Table 2 presents

TABLE 2
Frequency of possible totals given the signal die showing 6 or 0
for a block of 72 trials.

Dice total	Frequency given signal is	
	6	0
2	0	1
3	0	2
4	0	3
5	0	4
6	0	5
7	0	6
8	1	5
9	2	4
10	3	3
11	4	2
12	5	1
13	6	0
14	5	0
15	4	0
16	3	0
17	2	0
18	1	0
total combinations	36	36

the possible outcomes for each total given that a 6 or zero is showing on the signal die.

The following transition matrix of the sensory system presents the relationship between the two stimulus trials and the sensory state outputted by the sensory system.

$$\text{Sensory State}$$

$$\text{Stimulus} \begin{array}{c} 6 \\ 0 \end{array} \begin{array}{ccccccccccccccccc} 2 & 3 & 4 & 5 & 6 & 7 & 8 & 9 & 10 & 11 & 12 & 13 & 14 & 15 & 16 & 17 & 18 \\ \left[\begin{array}{ccccccccccccccccc} 0 & 0 & 0 & 0 & 0 & 0 & 1 & 2 & 3 & 4 & 5 & 6 & 5 & 4 & 3 & 2 & 1 \\ 1 & 2 & 3 & 4 & 5 & 6 & 5 & 4 & 3 & 2 & 1 & 0 & 0 & 0 & 0 & 0 & 0 \end{array} \right] \end{array}$$

Each entry in the transition matrix is divided by 36.

As can be seen in the transition matrix, there is a much larger number of sensory states in which the decision system can be confident about its decision. Figure 2 presents the distribution of total values from the sensory system given the values 6 and 0 showing on the signal die. It should be noted that the distance between the two distributions corresponding to the 6 and 0 on the signal die is twice the distance between the 3 and 0 distributions shown in Figure 1.

Correspondingly, we can change the signal die in the opposite direction and choose two very similar numbers, zero and 1, representing no-signal and signal trials, respectively. Now the decision system is faced with a much more difficult task; of the 72 possible

FIGURE 2. The expected distribution of totals as a function of whether the signal die showed 6 or 0.

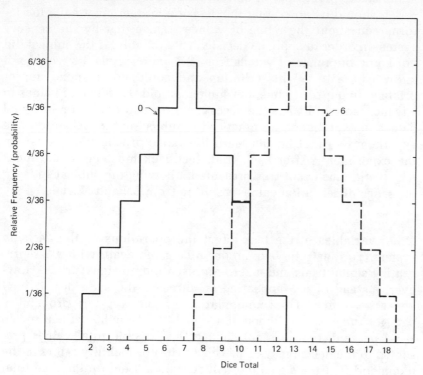

combinations of the three dice, on only two of them will the probability of a correct response be 1. As an exercise, work out the possible outcomes for each total given that a 1 or zero is showing on the signal die, and represent the distribution of these outcomes along a decision continuum as in Figures 1 and 2.

These variations of the signal die can be thought of as reflecting ways in which the efficiency of the sensory system can be made to vary. Analogously, we could change the nature of the noise (the numbers on our normal dice), which would also affect the efficiency of the sensory system. If stimuli are very different from each other, they will be easier to distinguish than if they are very similar. We are very much more sensitive to the difference between a red light and a green one, than to that between a red and a red-orange light. The absolute values on the signal die—the stimulus variables in the experimental situation—determine the values that the sensory system transmits to the decision system; the signal die values do *not* influence the operations of the decision system since the same decision rule or algorithm can be maintained. In both cases, the decision system will want to choose a criterion value that lies halfway between the means of the two distributions. This value will optimize the percentage of correct responses in both cases.

It should be noted that the decision system must have the information about the range of values transmitted by the sensory system in order to apply its decision rule reliably. If the subject did not know the range of values from SN and N trials, he would not know where to set his criterion and could not respond appropriately. In our dice game, the subject is told the range of values in advance, so that he has the necessary information. In a real signal detection experiment, we practice the subject in the task before the experiment so that he can learn the range of sensation values in the experiment. After each trial, feedback must be given about which stimulus event was presented, allowing the subject to learn the range of sensation values resulting from SN and N trials.

A Priori Probability of Signal

Other variables in the task affect the operations of the decision system. To illustrate, take up our dice game again with a 3 representing signal trials and a zero representing no-signal trials. However, instead of a 3 appearing on three of the six sides, it now appears on five. This manipulation of the a priori probability changes the prior likelihood of a signal trial from 50 percent to 5/6 $\approx$ 83 percent, but does not change the possible total values presented to the decision system. The a priori probability refers to the likelihood that the signal die will contain a 3 before the dice total is known. On a given role of the dice, the sensory system possesses no more or no less knowledge about the stimulus than it did when the 3 occurred on only three sides. The values transmitted by the sensory system, or the range of totals given by the three dice, does not change with changes in the a priori probability. All that has changed is the likelihood or the probability that any of the ambiguous values given by the sensory system represents the presence of a 3 on the odd die. The expected frequency of occurrence of 3 and 0 given the possible totals when the a priori probability of 3 is 5/6 is shown in Table 3. This difference in a priori probability should accordingly change the rule of the decision system. The decision system should be biased to say "yes, a 3 was presented," much more often than in the previous example where zero and 3 trials were equally likely.

To determine the relative frequency of possible totals with an a priori probability of a signal trial (3) being 5/6, we can simply weight the frequencies given in Table 1. Before the total is determined, we know that on the average, a 3 will be presented five out of six times. Accordingly, for each of the possible totals from the two normal dice, on 5/6ths of the trials, a signal (3) will be added to

TABLE 3

Frequency of possible totals given the signal die showing 3 or 0
when the a priori probability of 3 is 5/6 for a block of 216 trials.

Dice total	Frequency given signal is	
	3	0
2	0	1
3	0	2
4	0	3
5	5	4
6	10	5
7	15	6
8	20	5
9	25	4
10	30	3
11	25	2
12	20	1
13	15	0
14	10	0
15	5	0
total combinations	180	36

this total and on 1/6th of the trials, no signal (0) will be added to the total. For example, given the total value five from the three dice, the relative frequency of a signal (3) will be five times the relative frequency of no signal. With equally likely signal and no-signal trials, the total 5 arises from 3 one out of five times, and from 0, four out of five times. If the a priori probability is 5/6ths, the total five will result from a signal trial five times as often, relative to a no-signal trial. Therefore, multiplying the relative frequencies 1 and 4 for the total 5 by five and one, respectively, gives the relative frequencies of 5 and 4 when the a priori probability is 5/6.

The frequencies in Table 3 are converted into relative frequencies or probabilities in the following transition matrix of the sensory system:

$$\text{Sensory State}$$

$$\text{Stimulus} \quad \begin{matrix} & 2 & 3 & 4 & 5 & 6 & 7 & 8 & 9 & 10 & 11 & 12 & 13 & 14 & 15 \\ 3 \\ 0 \end{matrix} \begin{bmatrix} 0 & 0 & 0 & 5 & 10 & 15 & 20 & 25 & 30 & 25 & 20 & 15 & 10 & 5 \\ 1 & 2 & 3 & 4 & 5 & 6 & 5 & 4 & 3 & 2 & 1 & 0 & 0 & 0 \end{bmatrix}$$

The entries in the first and second rows are divided by 180 and 36, respectively.

The transition matrix is identical to the matrix generated when the a priori probability of a 3 was 3/6. The number and the values of the sensory states are the same and the transition probabilities are identical in the two cases. The sensory system only makes contact with the stimulus events on a trial. Therefore, manipulations in the a priori probability cannot affect the operations and hence the outputs of the sensory system. Accordingly, our measure of the sensitivity of the sensory system should not change with changes in a priori probability. Since the transition matrix for the sensory system does not change with changes in a priori probability, neither does the distribution of sensory states as plotted in Figure 1. Changes in a priori probability do not affect the relative frequency of occurrence of each total given the value "3" showing on the signal die. Although it increases the number of signal (3) trials relative to no-signal (0) trials in the experiment, it does not affect the relative frequency of occurrence of each total given the value showing on the signal die. Therefore, a change in a priori probability does not affect the shape of the distributions or the distance between the means of the two distributions. This contrasts with the manipulation of signal intensity (6 or 3) which directly affects the distance between the two means of the distributions.

"Percent Correct" Invalid Index

According to this analysis, our measure of the sensitivity of the sensory system should not change with changes in a priori probability, and with the placement of the criterion, since these changes do not affect the operations of the sensory system. We can see that the percentage of correct responses in the task cannot be used as a measure of the sensitivity of the sensory system. Assume that the observer knows that the a priori probability of a 3 is 3/6 in one case and 5/6 in another. If he simply responded on the basis of this information, he could achieve a performance of only 50 percent correct in the former case but could maintain a performance of 83 percent correct in the latter. He would simply respond "yes" on every trial regardless of the total value. Then if "percent correct" were used as a measure of the sensory system, we would conclude that the system was more sensitive with increases in a priori probability—an incorrect conclusion since the actual operations of the sensory system did not change.

Note that the decision system must have access to the a priori probabilities in the experimental situation to use an optimal decision rule. The experimenter might either tell the observer the a priori probabilities or give the observer feedback from trial to trial so that the latter could discover this fact for himself. As noted, the decision rule can also be affected by the payoff in the situation. If the observer is rewarded for saying "yes" correctly by a greater increment than he is punished for saying "yes" incorrectly, it will pay off for him to say "yes" more often even when the probability is relatively low that "yes" is the correct response.

According to multistate theory, the a priori probability of a signal trial (3) affects the decision system's choice of a criterion value. We can actually determine the receiver-operating characteristic predicted by multistate theory with changes in the criterion value. Assume first, for example, that the observer has a strong bias to say "no"—the a priori probability of a signal trial is very low. The observer may respond "no" all the time. Therefore, $P(\text{yes}|3) = 0$ and $P(\text{yes}|0) = 0$. As the observer becomes more willing to respond 3, the $P(\text{yes}|3)$ increases but so does $P(\text{yes}|0)$ as demonstrated in Figure 3. Figure 3 presents the $P(\text{yes}|0)$ and $P(\text{yes}|3)$ at each possible criterion value on the dice game task when the signal die contains a 3 as the signal trial and a 0 for a no-signal or blank trial.

FIGURE 3. An *ROC* curve which represents $P(\text{yes}|3)$ and $P(\text{yes}|0)$ for each possible criterion value in the dice game task. The subject responds "yes"—a 3 was presented—if the total is larger than or equal to the criterion value. Otherwise, he responds "no."

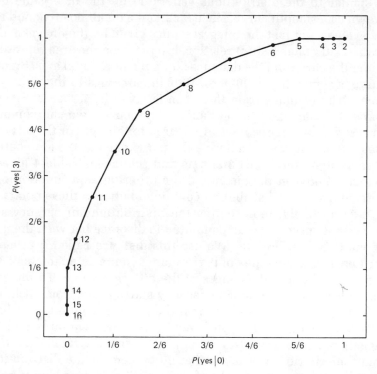

Now it is necessary to provide a measure of the sensitivity of the sensory system that is invariant with changes in the criterion value. This is given by the distance between the means of the two distributions. How can this distance be calculated in a signal detection

Measure of Sensitivity

task? In this task, we are given the results represented by a confusion matrix. From our hit and false alarm probabilities, we can determine the criterion value of the subject with respect to the means of each of the two distributions and, therefore, compute the distance between the means of the distribution. Assume that in our experiment, an observer responded $P(\text{yes}|\text{signal}) = .9$ and $P(\text{yes}|\text{no-signal}) = .3$. Therefore, the distribution for the signal trial would be drawn so that 90 percent of it lies to the right of the criterion value. Similarly, the distribution for the no-signal trial would be drawn so that 30 percent of it lies to the right of the criterion value.

Normal distribution and z scores

Since the experimenter does not know the number or values of the sensory states in an actual experiment, multistate theory assumes that the sensory states are distributed normally in a bell-shaped curve with variance equal to 1. This distribution is called the normal distribution and is shown in Figure 4. The normal distribution is similar to the distributions generated by the dice game but is drawn as a smooth curve, since it can take on all positive and negative values, not just the integral values given by the dice game. The normal curve has a strict relationship between the area represented under the curve and the distance along the horizontal axis. Since the curve is symmetrical, 50 percent of the area lies to the right of the mean. The distance from the mean is given by z scores. Since we know the shape and the variance of the curve, we can compute a z score for each percentage of the area to the right or the left of the mean. Similarly, we can derive the percentage of the area between a point along the horizontal axis and the mean. Table 4 gives the distance between the mean and the criterion as a function of the percentage of the distribution contained between these points.

Accordingly, representing the distributions of sensory states by normal curves, we can compute the distance between the means of the two distributions. We use this distance called d prime and written as d' as an index of performance in the detection task, since it remains fixed with changes in the criterion value. To the extent that the two distributions of sensory states differ from each other, d' will be large. To the extent that the two distributions are similar, d' will be small. In our hypothetical experiment we said that $P(\text{yes}|\text{signal}) = .9$ and $P(\text{yes}|\text{no signal}) = .3$. The hit rate of .9 means that the criterion was set so that 90 percent of the distribution of signal trials was to the right of the criterion. This is shown graphically in Figure 5.

Figure 6 is a graphic representation of the normal curve of the no-signal distribution, with 30 percent of the curve to the right of the criterion. The relationship between the two curves is given in

FIGURE 4. The normal distribution with a mean of 0 and a variance of 1. The values along the X abscissa are called z scores.

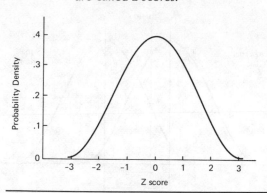

FIGURE 5. The criterion value is drawn so that 90 percent of the possible values of a signal trial lie above the criterion.

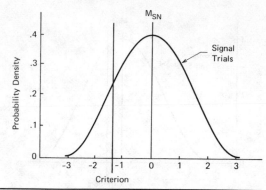

TABLE 4
The z score distance corresponding to the percentage of the distribution between the mean and the criterion value. (If the criterion lies to the left of the mean, the z scores are negative.)

Percentage	z score	Percentage	z score
0	0	26	.707
1	.025	27	.739
2	.050	28	.772
3	.075	29	.806
4	.100	30	.842
5	.125	31	.878
6	.150	32	.915
7	.176	33	.954
8	.202	34	.995
9	.223	35	1.037
10	.253	36	1.080
11	.280	37	1.126
12	.306	38	1.175
13	.332	39	1.226
14	.358	40	1.282
15	.385	41	1.340
16	.403	42	1.405
17	.440	43	1.476
18	.468	44	1.555
19	.496	45	1.645
20	.524	46	1.751
21	.553	47	1.882
22	.584	48	2.054
23	.610	49	2.327
24	.643	49.5	2.575
25	.675	49.9	3.085

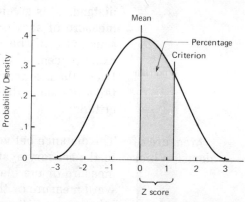

FIGURE 6. The distribution representing no-signal trials is placed so that 30 percent of the no-signal trials lie above the criterion.

FIGURE 7. The relationship between the signal (SN) and no-signal (N) curves shown in Figures 5 and 6.

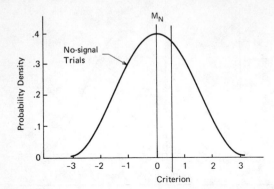

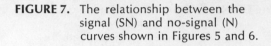

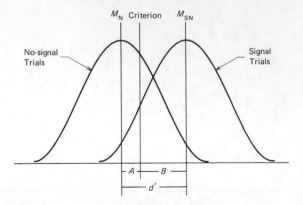

Figure 7. Accordingly, the distance between the means is given by the sum of the absolute distance of A and B. To determine the distance B between the criterion point and the mean of the signal distribution, we want the value of the z score of a point that lies 90 percent to the left of the distribution or 40 percent to the left of the mean of the distribution, since the curve is symmetrical around the mean. Table 4, (p. 133) shows that the z score which represents this distance along the X abscissa is −1.28. (The value is minus since the criterion lies to the left of the mean.) Analogously, to find the distance of the same criterion point from the mean of the no-signal distribution, we want the distance between the mean of this distribution and a point that lies 20 percent to the right of the mean. This distance as shown in Table 4 corresponds to a z score of .52. Given that the criterion lies between the means of the two distributions, the distance between the means of the two distributions is given by the sum of the positive values of A and B. Therefore, the distance d′ is given by the sum of 1.28 and .52, which is 1.80. Our measure of sensitivity in this task (1.8) provides an index of the sensitivity of the sensory system that is uncontaminated by the exact placement of the criterion value. Given a fixed distance between the means, the calculation of this distance using z scores obtains the same distance value regardless of the placement of the criterion.

Measure of decision bias The distance between the means provides a measure of sensitivity of the sensory system. Sometimes it is also informative to have a measure of the bias in the decision system. The most straightforward measure of this bias is simply the overall or marginal probability of a "yes" response. This probability lies between zero and 1 and reflects the willingness of the observer to say "yes." To calculate the marginal probability of a "yes" response, we take the average of the conditional probabilities of a "yes" response given signal and no-signal trials, weighted by the probability of occurrence of the signal and no-signal trials.

$$P(yes) = P(SN) \cdot P(yes|SN) + P(N) \cdot P(yes|N)$$

This measure of P(yes), then, indexes the willingness of the observer to say "yes," independent of sensitivity of the sensory system.

The multistate theory provides a method of data analysis in order to provide a measure of the sensitivity of the sensory system that is independent of changes in the decision system. This method of analysis allows the experimenter to compare sensitivity values between experimental conditions even though the variables affecting the decision rule differ in the different situations. This method achieves Fechner's original goal: to relate the sensation of the observer to the stimulus situation although the response of the subject does not appear to be directly related to the stimulus situation.

    Let us go over the basic design of the signal-detection experiment in detail. First, an observation period is defined for the observer. For example, in an auditory detection task we can define the observation interval by turning on a light; during the light presentation the subject attends and then reports to the experimenter that a stimulus tone either was or was not presented. The stimulus tone may or may not be presented; to preserve the subject's honesty, we want to keep him uncertain. So we present the tone on 50 percent of the trials, deciding randomly, perhaps by flipping a coin. Therefore, if the subject says "yes" on every trial throughout the experiment, he will only be 50 percent correct. If he can detect the signal on every trial on which it is presented, and does not falsely detect it on any of the trials on which it is not presented, performance will be 100 percent.

This experimental method and data analysis can be used in any two-stimulus–two-choice experimental task. For example, instead of the auditory alternatives of tone and no-tone, the subject could be asked to distinguish between two visual alternatives, the letters D and O presented briefly in a tachistoscope. On each trial, one of these two letters is chosen randomly and presented; the subject's

ANALYSIS OF SIGNAL-DETECTION EXPERIMENT

Experimental Method and Data Analysis

task is to report which one he sees. Here, instead of the magnitude of the sensation, the sensory system has a measure of the amount of O-ness and D-ness that was present on a given trial. We can think of the information available to the sensory system as falling on a single D–O dimension. A large amount of O-ness implies a small amount of D-ness and indicates that an O was more likely presented. Similarly, a large amount of D-ness implies a small amount of O-ness and indicates that a D was more likely presented. Given the complementary relationship between O-ness and D-ness, it is sufficient for us to specify the information available to the sensory system in terms of O-ness. Therefore, the amount of O-ness produced by either letter must fluctuate from trial to trial and, on occasion, the letter D will actually produce more O-ness than will the letter O on another occasion. Thus, just as in the dice game analogy the two stimulus states of signal-plus-noise and noise alone could result in a range of possible combined total values, in this experiment the two stimulus alternatives of O and D can result in a number of different values of O-ness.

We think of O-ness, then, as a continuum on which the letter O will, on the average, produce more O-ness than the letter D. If we assume that the noise effect is randomly distributed in a bell-shaped curve, then the amount of O-ness perceived by the subject varies from trial to trial. Drawing the distribution of O-ness perceived by the subject for O trials and for D trials, Figure 8 shows that the two curves can overlap. This overlap represents the range of uncer-

FIGURE 8.   The distributions for O and D when the observer responds O given O 85 percent of the time and O given D 65 percent of the time.

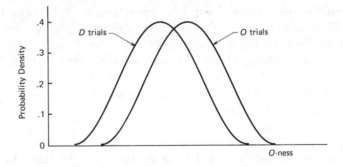

tainty in the information passed on to the decision system by the sensory system. Within this range the observer cannot be 100 percent correct, but must establish a decision rule, or criterion, that translates "maybe" into "yes" or "no" with an optimal degree of accuracy. It is assumed that the observer establishes some criterion along the O-ness scale. Whenever the output of the sensory system exceeds this criterion value, the observer says O; otherwise he says D.

After running repeated trials, the experimenter sets up a confusion matrix with two stimuli and two responses. The stimulus

Stimulus

$$\text{Response} \quad \begin{array}{c} O \\ D \end{array} \begin{bmatrix} \overset{O}{F_1} & \overset{D}{F_2} \\ F_3 & F_4 \end{bmatrix}$$

can be O or D, and the observer can say O or D. The two independent probabilities are the probability that the observer said O, given that the stimulus presented was O (the hit rate), and the probability that he said O, given that the stimulus presented was D (the false alarm rate). We can count up these two outcomes over the course of the experiment and compute their probabilities. To compute $P(O|O)$, we first count up all the trials in which an O was presented (i.e., the sum of F_1 and F_3). Then the proportion of trials that subject said O, given O, is the number of these trials (F_1) divided by F_1 plus F_3. Similarly the proportion of D responses to the D stimulus is equal to F_4 divided by F_2 plus F_4. Our second independent probability of interest, $P(O|D)$, is equal to F_2 divided by F_2 plus F_4, or 1 minus $P(D|D)$.

Therefore, if in a particular experiment the observer responded O 85 percent of the time when presented with an O, the probability of O given O is .85. If he responded D 35 percent of the time when presented with a D, the probability of D given D is .35 and the probability of saying O given D is .65. These independent response probabilities allow us to draw in the distributions for O and D on the O-ness axis (see Figure 8). The line drawn perpendicular to the axis represents the criterion (C). This is the point in the O-ness continuum where the subject ceased to respond D and began to respond O. Therefore, the normal distribution for the stimulus alternative D would be drawn so that 35 percent of it lies to the left of this line, representing the .35 probability of D given D. The distribution of O-ness for the stimulus letter O is drawn so that 85 percent of it lies to the right of the criterion line, representing the probability of responding with O given O.

Our goal is to find some sensitivity parameter for a dependent variable that is changed by variables affecting the sensory process, but is not changed by variables affecting the decision process. These conditions are fulfilled by employing the distance between the means of the two distributions. This distance is measured using the z scores of the normal distribution as shown in Figure 4. Imagine a subject in the same experiment who for some reason is especially partial to responding O. His criterion will move to the left, so that more of the O and D distributions will lie on the right of the line. That is, both the hit rate and the false alarm rate will increase. The distributions of O-ness on D trials and of O-ness on O trials will remain at the same distance from each other. The sensory system of this subject is able to discriminate O from D as well as he could with a lower criterion, and the difference between the means of the two distributions expresses this discriminability alone.

On the other hand, imagine a different subject whose results show the same hit rate but a higher false alarm rate. The distribution of O-ness and O trials will be the same with respect to the criterion value, but a larger proportion of the distribution of O-ness on D trials must now lie to the right of the criterion, and the two distributions will therefore be closer together. This subject is less able to discriminate between the two letters than our first subject. If a third subject's false alarm rate is lower than that of the first subject, his D distribution is farther to the left of the criterion, and therefore the distance between the two means is greater. He is better able to discriminate the two letters than either of the other two subjects.

The distance between the two means therefore provides us with an index of the sensitivity of the subject; it takes into account both the hit rate and the false alarm rate, and is completely independent of the decision rule the subject may use. This distance is called d' and can be computed by the following equation:

$$d' = z[P(\text{yes}|N)] - z[P(\text{yes}|SN)] \tag{1}$$

where $z[P(\text{yes}|N)]$ is the z score for the false alarm rate, $P(\text{yes}|N)$, and $z[P(\text{yes}|SN)]$ is the z score for the hit rate, $P(\text{yes}|SN)$.

In this equation, the sensitivity measure d' is obtained by subtracting the z score transformation of the hit rate from the z score transformation of the false alarm rate. In our sample experiment of discriminating D and O, the hit rate $P(O|O)$ was .85 and the false alarm rate $P(O|D)$ was .65. The 85 percent hit rate means that the criterion value was set so that there was 35 percent of the area of the O distribution between its mean and the criterion. Since the criterion is to the left of the mean, we take the negative z score for 35 percent in Table 4 (−1.037). The 65 percent false alarm rate places the criterion value to the left of the mean of the D distribution, with 15 percent of the distribution between its mean and the criterion value, giving a z score of −.385. Substituting these values in Equation 1 gives

$$d' = -.385 - (-1.037) = .652$$

for the d' value in our sample experiment.

Multistate theory and two-state threshold theory differ significantly in their descriptions of performance in the psychophysical task. The major difference concerns the assumption of a threshold. Two-state threshold theory assumes that the signal on a given trial either does or does not exceed the threshold. Accordingly, the output of the sensory system can take on only one of two values. In contrast, the theory of signal detectability disposes of the concept of a threshold and assumes that the output of the sensory system can take on a whole range of values even though there are only two trial types. How do we decide between these two theories?

The first source of evidence supportive of multistate theory comes from the phenomenological experience of the observer in the signal detection task. He reports that he seems to have more information on some trials than on others. If he were a gambling man, he would be willing to bet more on the correctness of some answers than others. To test this experimentally, studies have been done in which subjects have been provided with the means to record their degree of confidence about their response to each trial. These experiments follow from the fact that, if observers have more information on some trials than others, they should be able to estimate the degree of information reliably.

In the signal-detection experiments, subjects are asked to rate their confidence in each "yes" or "no" judgment on a scale, for example, from 1 to 5. Thus one response "yes" might be accompanied by the rating 5, meaning the subject is very sure that a signal is out there; the same response on another trial might be rated 3 by the subject; and on a third trial rated 1, meaning that he is very uncertain, perhaps just guessing. His confidence could then be compared to his actual performance. The experimenter can look up the trials for each rating and compute the probability that the response was correct. According to multistate theory, if the subject says he is positive that a stimulus signal is out there, his response should almost always be correct. If he says he is not very certain, a correct response should be less likely. Actual confidence ratings done during experiments have yielded results that support the multistate model (Green & Swets, 1966; Swets, 1961). Threshold theory, on the other hand, cannot easily predict this result since the theory was not developed to predict confidence judgments. In its present formulation there is no immediate mechanism available to incorporate the results. In this regard, then, multistate theory is preferred since it is relevant to a larger class of psychophysical experiments and results.

MULTISTATE vs. TWO-STATE THEORY

Confidence Ratings

A Priori Probability and Payoffs	Another way to distinguish between the two theories is to compare their quantitative predictions of performance in a signal-detection task as a function of changes in the a priori probability of a signal trial, or of changes in the monetary payoffs in the experimental situation. As seen in the last chapter, the two-state threshold theory predicts an *ROC* curve with two straight-line segments. In contrast, the multistate theory predicts a curvilinear *ROC* curve similar to that generated by the dice game presented in Figure 3. The results of experiments in audition, vision, and taste have agreed with the predictions of multistate theory (Linker, Moore, & Galanter, 1964; Swets, 1961; Swets, Tanner, & Birdsall, 1961).
Other Evidence	A straightforward test between multistate and two-state theories is an experiment in which the observer is asked to attend to four observation intervals on each trial. The signal is presented in one of the four intervals chosen randomly on each trial. Two-state theory says that each interval either will or will not exceed the threshold. In contrast, multistate theory predicts that the observer will have a measure of the likelihood that the signal was presented in each of the intervals. The two-state sensory system can only categorize each interval in terms of a "yes" or "no," whereas in the multistate sensory system each interval's sensation state can take on many values. If we ask the observers to rank order the four observation intervals in terms of the likelihood that the signal occurred in each of the intervals, the multistate theory predicts their ability to do so more reliably than does the two-state theory (Swets, Tanner, & Birdsall, 1961).

An observation by Nachmias and Steinman (1963) provides further evidence against the two-state threshold model. They found that the estimate of q—the probability that the threshold was exceeded on noise trials—was not independent of the strength of the stimulus on signal trials. The estimated value of q decreased with increases in the intensity of the stimulus on signal trials. There is no way that two-state theory can handle this result since it assumes a fixed threshold; hence the probability that noise trials exceed the threshold must remain independent of the intensity of the signal on stimulus trials. In contrast, this result can be predicted by the multistate theory. If the subject establishes his criterion at the intersection of the signal and no-signal distributions, increasing the intensity of the signal will pull the distributions apart, increasing the hit rate and decreasing the false alarm rate simultaneously. (This result is exactly analogous to our previous description of the dice game in which the value of the signal was changed from 3 to 6.)

A final reason why most investigators have accepted the multistate theory over the two-state threshold theory is a practical or heuristic one. The two-state theory does not allow the investigator to derive an index of the operation of the sensory system from just one set of hit and false alarm probabilities, whereas the multistate theory does. Therefore, if the experimenter wants to use the two-state model he must simultaneously vary the a priori probability, or the payoffs, in the task to generate an ROC curve. Then he must fit the curve and estimate the values of p and q in the task. This increases the complexity of the experiment because usually the experimenter is interested in signal-detection performance as a function of some other independent variable. Accordingly, using the two-state theory increases the number of subject hours by a factor of 3 or 4 over using the multistate model. Finally, the index d' describes sensory performance with only one value, whereas the two-state theory needs two values, p and q, to describe performance. Accordingly, the two-state theory really only leaves us with something very similar to hit and false alarm probabilities, still making it necessary to analyze the relationship between the values p and q. We know performance is better to the extent p is larger than q, or the hit rate is larger than the false alarm rate. The theory of signal detectability allows us to reduce these independent observations into one value that represents a direct index of performance. Given the relative simplicity of multistate theory and the supporting evidence, it is now generally accepted by most investigators of sensory processes.

In summary, we have seen how the multistate theory can be used to derive an index of sensory performance that is unaffected by biases in the decision system. The decision system plays a role in all experiments, whether sensory, perceptual, mnemonic, or whatever. In each case, the experimenter wants an index of performance that is free from any decision bias. The multistate model allows this by using the d' index to describe what a sensory, perceptual, or mnemonic system knows under a given set of experimental conditions. In this case, the experimenter can observe directly the effects of his independent variable on the psychological process of interest. The advantages of the multistate theory will be apparent when we utilize the d' index in the analysis of experiments and the development of theory throughout this book.

Detection of light

*Obviously the amount of energy required to stimulate
any eye must be large enough to supply at least one
quantum to the photosensitive material. No eye need be
so sensitive as this. But it is a tribute to the excellence
of natural selection that our own eye comes so
remarkably close to the lowest limit.*
—Selig Hecht, Simon Shlaer & Maurice Pirenne (1942)

Light is radiant energy which makes up only a minute part of the electromagnetic spectrum. Along the spectrum energy is described by its wavelength and its intensity. The visible part of the spectrum contains wavelengths longer than X-rays and ultraviolet waves and shorter than radio waves and infrared waves.

Within the visible portion of the electromagnetic spectrum, the intensity of light is primarily responsible for its perceived brightness. The wavelength mainly determines which hue, usually called color by the layman, is perceived. White light is a combination of all visible wavelengths. When it enters a prism, it slows down and is bent, since the medium of the prism is denser than air. The amount of bending differs for the different wavelengths making up the white light, producing a rainbow on the other side of the prism. White light leaves a prism as different hues, ranging from violet, blue, green, yellow, orange, to red. The wavelengths of these hues range between 400 and 700 nms. (One nanometer is equal to one billionth of a meter.)

A description of the electromagnetic spectrum in terms of waves does not describe or explain all of its known properties. Accordingly, physical scientists find it useful to describe light in terms of a quantum theory. This theory assumes that radiant energy is emitted in discrete units, one at a time, not in a continuous train of waves. Each unit or particle of energy is called a quantum. Although the quantum theory solves many of the physicists' problems, they still find it necessary to treat light as a wave phenomenon in some situations. We shall see in our discussion of the research in light detection that both theories are also utilized by psychologists studying visual information processing.

FIGURE 1. Structure of the human eye.

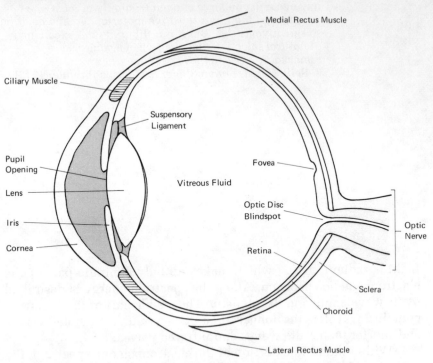

The appropriate stimulus for seeing is light entering the eye. Figure 1 illustrates that when light enters the eye, it first passes through the cornea, the protective window of the eye. The curvature of the cornea and the shape of the lens focus the light entering the eye so that a reasonably accurate inverted picture of the visual field is formed on the retina, the back of the eye. Before light reaches the retina, however, it has to pass through the nerve fibers connected to the light receptors, since the nerve fibers lie directly in the path of the incoming light. The retina contains the rods and cones, the light-sensitive receptors. The cones are packed at the center of the eye, called the fovea, whereas the rods are more prevalent in the periphery. The rods and cones transform the light into nerve impulses as a result of their photochemical reaction to the light. These impulses are passed on to the brain via the optic nerve fibers.

VARIABLES INFLUENCING LIGHT DETECTION

What is the minimal amount of light that is visible to the human observer under optimal conditions of seeing? This experimental question was asked by Hecht, Shlaer, and Pirenne in 1942. We shall discuss the research generated by this question in detail, since it provides an excellent example of how knowledge is compiled in science. More importantly, it also demonstrates that the answer to a psychological question requires a knowledge of stimulus, physiological, anatomical, psychological, and mathematical variables in the experimental situation. Hecht et al. found that the answer to their question was dependent on the answer to a number of related questions. First, it was necessary to analyze the results from a number of previous experiments that were relevant to these related questions.

To find optimal conditions for the visual system was the significant aspect of the experimental question. To optimize visual detection it is necessary to consider a number of variables that affect how well an observer can detect a light. For example, the adaptation state of the observer could be very important. Visual detectability will be poorer if the observer has been exposed to a bright light recently, than if the observer has been in the dark for a while.

A second variable that must be dealt with is the location of the test stimulus in the visual field. Whether the observer is looking directly at the stimulus or whether it is off to one side could make a difference.

The size of a visual stimulus of constant intensity is also an important stimulus variable. As the area of a fixed amount of light becomes larger, there would be less light in any given area. Logically, then, we would not see the flash as well.

Another important variable is the duration of the light flash. Visual detectability should be dependent upon whether the light is presented for a brief moment, or whether this same light intensity is spread out over time.

And finally, the hue of the test flash should make a difference for optimal detection. As mentioned earlier, visible light is only a small portion of the electromagnetic spectrum. It seems reasonable that we would be less sensitive to colors presented at the extremes than in the middle range of the visible spectrum.

Hecht et al. had to find the optimal visual condition for each of these variables. The optimal conditions could then be employed to determine the minimal intensity of light at which the observer could reliably report, "I see some light out there." The experimental apparatus was designed so that the stimulus variables could be precisely controlled. Figure 2 illustrates the optical system and the experimental situation used in the study. The duration, location, size, wavelength, and intensity of the light could be controlled by Hecht et al. They measured the sensitivity of the subject by asking at what point his responses were reliable in predicting whether a light had been presented.

FIGURE 2. An illustration of the Hecht et al. experimental situation.

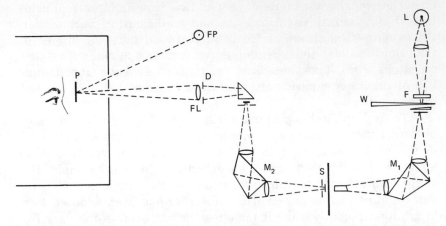

The subject sits in a dark room; his head is held in a fixed position by keeping his teeth in a "bite" rest—a hard impression of the upper jaw. His left eye is next to the artificial pupil *P* and by fixating on the red fixation point *FP,* he sees the field lens *FL.* The light source is a ribbon filament lamp *L* focused on the slit of a double monochromator $M_1 M_2$ which controls the wavelength of the light sent on to the field lens *FL.* The light intensity is controlled by the filters *F* and neutral wedge and balancer *W.* The size of the test field is controlled by the diaphragm *D.* The shutter *S* controls the exposure (after Hecht et al., 1942).

Dark-Adaptation of Observer

The first variable to consider, then, is the state of the subject. What becomes important here is the phenomenon of dark-adaptation. Going for a walk on a dark night demonstrates this phenomenon. At first, nothing is visible and it is very difficult to find one's way around. After strolling for 5 or 10 minutes, however, the shapes of trees and flowers become visible. What is happening in this case is that the walker is becoming dark-adapted and his sensitivity to the amount of light there is increases. This phenomenon is only partly due to chemical changes in the visual receptors in the retina and is not completely understood. In any case, psychologically, the ability to see light increases with increases in the duration of dark-adaptation. To find the optimal level of adaptation to the dark, it is necessary to measure experimentally the sensitivity of the observer after different amounts of dark-adaptation.

Such an experiment had already been done a number of times. The sensitivity to a flash of light was measured after different periods of dark-adaptation. The results indicated that subjects need less and less light as they become dark-adapted for detecting that light. There are two ways to plot this data with respect to the independent variable.

First, we plot the minimal intensity of the light that is required for the subject to report "I see it," as a function of the duration of dark-adaptation. The results of a typical experiment are presented in Figure 3. When the subject is not dark-adapted after exposure to a high-intensity field of light, he needs a relatively bright test flash for him to report it. As he dark-adapts, the amount of light necessary for detection decreases. The results indicate that the intensity necessary for detection before dark-adaptation is 4 log units more intense than that needed after 30 minutes in the dark. (Four log units indicates that one light was 10,000 times as intense as the other.)

FIGURE 3. The minimal intensity of light necessary for visual detection as a function of the duration of dark-adaptation, after a preliminary light-adaptation to a high intensity field of light (after Hecht, 1934).

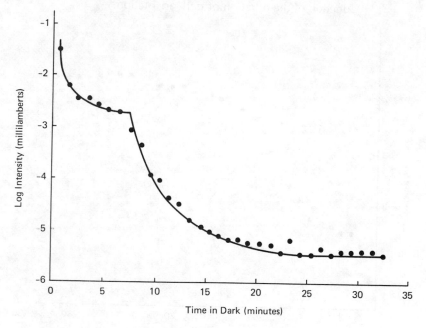

Another important thing to notice in Figure 3 is that the dark-adaptation curve is actually the combination of two curves. The detection of light in the first 7 or 8 minutes of dark-adaptation is due to the detection of the light that hits the central or foveal region of the retina. In the last 20 minutes, detection of the light is dependent upon the light falling on the periphery of the retina. Accordingly, dark-adaptation in the foveal region becomes asymptotic much earlier than adaptation in the peripheral region of the retina. Given this interpretation, the two curves show that a visual stimulus, to be seen by a dark-adapted subject, must be more intense if it is presented to the foveal region than to the periphery. Hence, this experiment indicates that Hecht et al. should dark-adapt their subjects for at least 30 minutes and that the light should also be presented somewhere in peripheral vision.

We can also plot these dark-adaptation results on a relative sensitivity curve. If an observer needs 100 units for detection at time t_1 and 10 units at time t_2, he is 10 times more sensitive at t_2 than at t_1. An increase in sensitivity, then, simply means a decrease in the intensity of the light necessary for the subject to report, "I detect it." The dark-adaptation curve in terms of sensitivity is shown in Figure 4. At the first point in time, much more light is needed for the subject to see it than at a later point in time. Per-

FIGURE 4. Results in Figure 3 plotted in terms of relative sensitivity as a function of the duration of dark-adaptation.

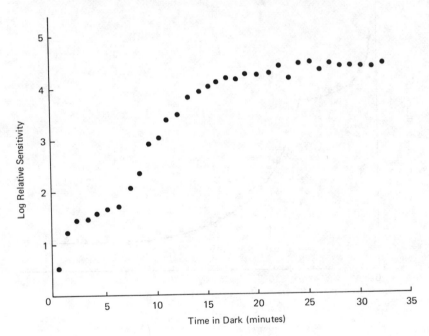

formance reaches a steady state after about 30 minutes of dark-adaptation. This would then be the level of dark-adaptation at which to test the observer for optimal performance. To determine the minimal amount of light necessary for detection, we must dark-adapt the observer for 30 minutes.

Location of Test Flash   The second variable to consider is the exact location in the test field for presenting the test stimulus. Hecht et al. had the subject viewing with one eye and looking at a dim red light as a fixation point. The experimenters were able to present the text flash anywhere in the visual field. To clarify the discussion, some method is needed to describe the location where the test flash is presented. The easiest way of describing the location is according to the angle of viewing with respect to a fixation point. If the subject is looking directly at a point in space, then this fixation point is arriving at the center of the subject's eye. Figure 5 presents a top view of one eye of a subject looking at a fixation point.

FIGURE 5. Locating a test stimulus with respect to the fixation point.

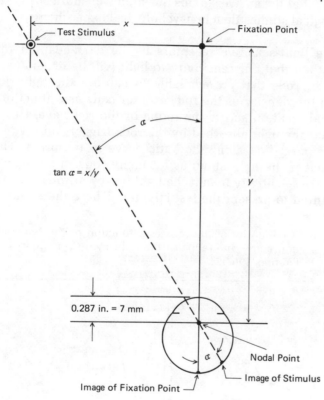

We can now describe how far away our test stimulus is from the center of the eye in the horizontal plane. A single value can describe the location of the test flash in Figure 5, that is, the visual angle between a line drawn through the test stimulus and a line drawn through the fixation point. The lines intersect at the nodal point of the eye, which remains constant with changes in the location of the test flash. Using trigonometry, we can compute the angle α for any test stimulus if we know the distance between the eye and the fixation point and the separation between the fixation point and the test stimulus. The value of α for the test stimulus in Figure 5 can be determined by determining the angle whose tangent is x/y. This value is sufficient to tell another experimenter exactly where the test light was presented. It does not matter where along the dashed line the test stimulus is presented. It will hit the eye in the same position as long as it is on this line.

Hecht et al. were interested in determining the location of the visual field that is optimal for stimulus detection. To determine this location, they could have tested the observer under all locations to find the retinal area of greatest sensitivity. This would have been very time-consuming, however, as well as a waste of energy. Hecht et al. saw that the answer to this question was more easily found in physiological studies than in psychological experiments.

Physiological structure of retina Rods are light-sensitive receptors in the dark-adapted retina. It follows then that our sensitivity to light will be dependent on the number of rods that are available to capture the light. Figure 6 presents the density of the rod receptor cells as a function of the horizontal location across the retina of the right eye. Hecht et al. knew that the light absorbed by the rods triggers a nerve impulse, which is passed on along the optic nerve to the brain. They reasoned that if the light stimulus hit many rods, the subject would show more sensitivity than if the light hit fewer rods. Accordingly, they wanted to present the test stimulus where there was a maxi-

FIGURE 6. The density of the rods as a function of the horizontal location across the retina of the right eye (Cornsweet, 1970; after Pirenne, 1967).

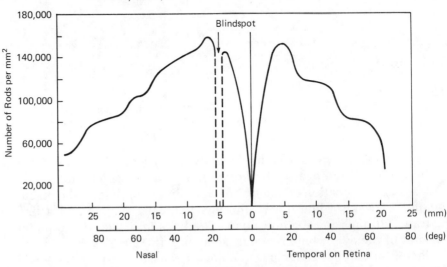

FIGURE 7. Relative sensitivity as a function of the horizontal position of the test flash with respect to the fixation point when viewing with the right eye (Cornsweet, 1970; after Pirenne, 1967).

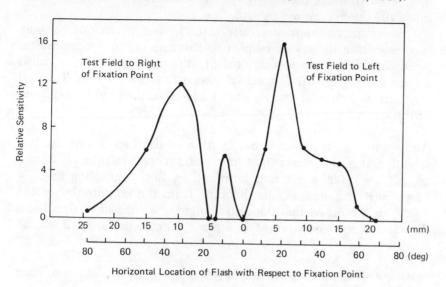

Horizontal Location of Flash with Respect to Fixation Point

mum density of rods. In looking at the physiological data, then, they found that if they presented the test stimulus about 20° off the fixation point, they would hit a maximum number of rods. Figure 7 shows that the sensitivity to light is highly correlated with the density of the rods. When Hecht et al. chose to present their test flash 20° to the left of the fixation point, they were stimulating the most sensitive area of the dark-adapted retina.

About 5° on the nasal side of the retina is the blindspot—an area that does not contain any visual receptors. This is the area where the nerve fibers and blood vessels enter the eyeball. How would you demonstrate that light striking this area is not visible?

Size of Test Flash

The next thing to be considered was the size (area) of the test stimulus. At this point it is necessary to understand something about light itself. Recall that light can be described as a stream of discrete energy particles, referred to as quanta. Since a quantum cannot be broken into smaller pieces, varying the intensity of light varies the number of quanta emitted from the test stimulus. When the size of the test stimulus is varied to find which size is optimal for detection, its intensity will be given by the number of quanta in the test stimulus. If we want to compare the detection of two stimuli of different sizes, we must, of course, hold constant the number of quanta. By increasing the size, then, for a given number of quanta of light, the quanta must necessarily spread over larger and larger areas. For example, if we have 100 quanta in our light, we can focus the light within a small area or we can spread those 100 quanta out over a wide range.

The experimenters were interested in finding the optimal way to present the light with respect to the size of the test stimulus. Accordingly, it was necessary to vary the size of the test stimulus and to measure relative sensitivity as a function of size. The test stimulus was circular and its size can be described by the diameter of the circle.

Visual angle   Analogous to our angular specification of the location of the test stimulus, it is also convenient to express its size in terms of visual angle. The visual angle is determined by first computing the size of the test stimulus and its distance from the nodal point of the eye. Figure 8 shows that the visual angle of an object of size S at a distance D corresponds to the angle β. The visual angle β can be

FIGURE 8.   Determining the visual angle of the test field given its size and its distance from the observer.

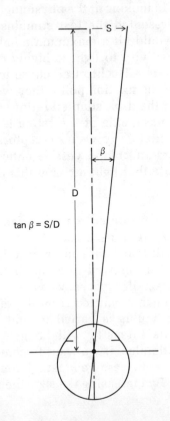

$$\tan \beta = S/D$$

determined by trigonometry, computing the angle whose tangent is equal to S/D.

The results of the previous experiments indicated that the test flash must be contained in a very small region for maximal sensitivity. If the test flash is smaller than 10 minutes (10') of visual angle, sensitivity is maximal. (One degree contains 60 minutes.) Ten minutes of arc represents the approximate size of a thumbtack at a distance of 10 ft. Increasing the size of the test flash beyond 10' decreases the sensitivity; the light must be made more intense for the observer to detect it.

This result also tells us something about the physiological structure of the visual system. Looking in the eye at the rod receptors, we find that the rods are distributed in a certain way, according to spatial summation areas. One spatial summation area corresponds to about 10' of visual angle. All the rods within a given summation area go to the same optic nerve fiber, where their effects are summated. If a rod receptor is stimulated outside the summation area, it sends its message—the nerve impulse—along a different optic fiber. For optimal sensitivity, the light should be contained in one spatial summation area.

Hecht and his coworkers could choose any test flash that was smaller than 10' of visual angle for optimal sensitivity. They decided to choose a test flash of 10' because smaller test flashes can present a problem. With very small test flashes, it is possible that a piece of dust could actually reflect the light and by so doing interfere with the light's path coming to the observer.

Duration of Test Flash

Another variable that Hecht et al. had to account for was the duration of the test flash. When a light is presented, its duration must be specified. It is possible to have the quanta of light coming out at a very fast rate—a lot of light presented in a very short time—or the quanta can come out of the electrical filament at a very slow rate. Hecht et al. were interested in the relative sensitivity of the observer as a function of the duration of the light flash with all other variables held constant.

Previous studies had measured the relative sensitivity of observers while varying the duration of the test flash. In a number of studies, the sensitivity did not vary if the duration was varied between 1 and 100 msec. After 100 msec., sensitivity decreased with further increases in duration. If the same intensity of light, as defined by the number of quanta in the light, were presented within 100 msec., the sensitivity to that light would be greater than if it were spread out and presented over the time course of a second. The most interesting thing about these results is not that sensitivity decreases with increases in duration but that sensitivity does not drop off until a duration of about 100 msec. It is possible to spread out the light over a good period of time without affecting sensitivity. This finding reflects a process called integration, in which the light is integrated or summated over a short period of time. For example, with 100 quanta, we can present all 100 quanta within a msec., or we can present 1 quantum/msec. over the time course of 100 msec., and there will be no difference with respect to sensitivity. Similarly, 50 quanta could be presented in the first msec. and 50 quanta in the 100th msec., with nothing in between, and performance in that condition would not be any different from the condition in which 100 quanta were presented within 1 msec.

Wavelength of Test Flash

The final variable Hecht et al. had to consider was the wavelength of the test flash. As discussed above, light can be described in terms of energy by defining the number of quanta it contains. Another way to describe light is in terms of a sine wave phenomenon. One of the properties of light, the wavelength of the sine wave, is the physical characteristic of light that gives us the psychological experience of hue. Wavelength and intensity of light can be independently varied. Intensity can be varied by varying the number of quanta in the light, thus determining the perceived brightness of the light. The hue of the light is primarily determined by the wavelength of the quanta of the light. Hecht et al.'s experimental question was "What is the sensitivity of the observer to light at different wavelengths?"

When Hecht et al. studied earlier experiments of light detection, they saw that sensitivity was critically dependent on the wavelength of the test flash. Figure 9 indicates optimal sensitivity to the middle of the visible spectrum—the blue-greens—and least sensitivity to the two extremes. The minimum point on the curve corresponds to about 510 nm. Therefore, the light in the test stimulus should be at 510 nm. in the main experiment.

Subjects in the experiments varying the wavelength of the light did not see different hues of the test stimulus at the different wavelengths. Since the observers were dark-adapted and the stimulus was presented in peripheral vision, the color receptors (the cones) in the fovea were not operational. The rods were responsible for seeing the test stimulus and these receptors do not transmit information about hue, but only about brightness. The flash of light that the observers saw looked colorless or grey, just as at night one can see the shape of flowers in a garden, but cannot see their color. The objects out there have not changed; they are still reflecting the

FIGURE 9. Log relative sensitivity as a function of the wavelength of the test flash (after Wald, 1945).

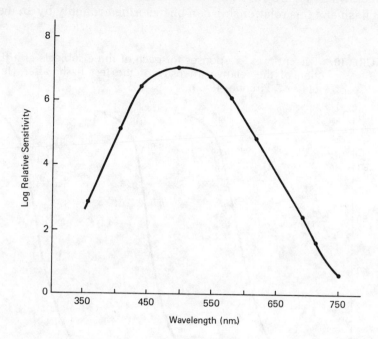

wavelengths of yellows and reds and blues, but they are simply not seen in that way.

With these five variables defined, Hecht et al. were ready for the main experiment. The subject could now be tested under optimal conditions for detecting light in the real world. The subject was dark-adapted; a flash of 10′ of visual angle was used, it was presented 20° off the point of fixation, the duration of the flash was 1 msec., and the energy in the flash was concentrated at a wavelength of 510 nm.

Hecht et al. determined the observer's sensitivity by employing the method of constant stimuli (see Chapter 5). The experimenters chose randomly one of 6 intensities for presentation on a given trial. The subject sat at the apparatus, had a fixation point, and on each trial pressed a button which initiated presentation of the visual target. He then reported whether or not he saw a test flash. Hecht et al. were interested in the relationship between number of quanta in the test flash and the probability of the observer saying, "Yes, I detect it."

OPTIMAL DETECTION

The results for three subjects from the Hecht et al. experiment are shown in Figure 10. Detection is related to the intensity of the test flash and this relationship can be described roughly by an ogive

FIGURE 10. Percent "yes" responses for each of three subjects as a function of the relative intensity of the test flash (after Hecht, Shlaer & Pirenne, 1942).

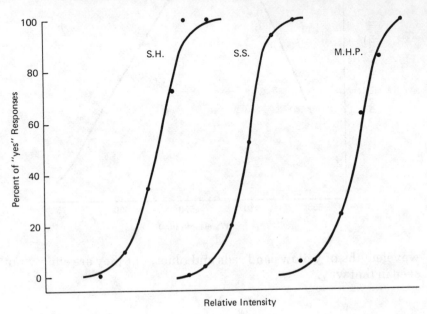

curve. The shape of the function agrees with most functions obtained using the method of constant stimuli (see Chapter 5). To test whether the decision system distorted Hecht et al.'s results, the experiment should be replicated using a signal detection task. The Hecht et al. task was carried out in 1942, and signal detection theory was not yet available to experimental psychologists. Since Hecht's subjects were very practiced and very well-trained, we can hope that their attitudes played a very small role.

When Hecht and his associates did this experiment, they found the subject detected the light about 50 percent of the time when the light stimulus contained only about 90 quanta. Upon examining the physiology of the ocular system, Hecht et al. found that the system is even more sensitive than their result first indicated. First of all, as the test flash comes into the eye, about 3 percent of the 90 quanta are reflected back out into the real world. In other words, these quanta never get to the receptor system. Then, 50 percent of the remaining light is absorbed in the eye itself before it reaches the light-sensitive area. As mentioned before, our eyes are built backwards. The light-sensitive area lies behind the optic nerve fibers and other neural tissue. Light has to get through this other pigment before it reaches the retina. Therefore, about 50 percent of the 97 percent of light that enters the eye is absorbed, leaving about 48 percent that hits the light-sensitive part of the retina. Accordingly, about 44 quanta enter the spatial summation area. Within a spatial summation area, there is pigment between the rods that does not function as a receptor; this pigment, therefore, cannot signal light or no light. When the light absorbed by this pigment is accounted for, only about 9 or 10 quanta are found to be captured by the rods. Hecht et al. knew that there were about 300 rods in the spatial summation area covered by the test flash. Therefore, it was very unlikely that 2 of the 9 or 10 quanta would hit the same rod. Hence, we need about 9 or 10 rods catching a quanta each in order to detect, under optimal conditions, that a light stimulus is out there in the real world.

When the experimenters analyzed the physics of their light stimulus, their interpretation of the results could be made even more precise. The stimulus was an electrical filament that emitted quanta of light. But they found that the number of quanta coming from the filament varied from trial to trial, even though the intensity of the light was experimentally held constant. When they thought they were putting out 90 quanta, on some trials they were putting out even less quanta and on other trials they were putting out more quanta. Light behaves according to a Poisson process, such that at any point in time the probability that a quantum will be emitted is described by some probability value. Since the number of quanta emitted per unit of time varies, Hecht et al. had variability in their stimulus. This variability in the stimulus could, therefore, account for some of the variability in the response to a given stimulus.

Stimulus and Receptor Variability

In any task, we also have variability due to the subject. By variability due to the subject we mean that sometimes one of the rods fires without a light quantum hitting it. So we have background activity in our receptor system. The background activity of the rods is one example of noise in the sensory system postulated by the theory of signal detectability. The number of rods firing per unit of time varies and this variation could conceivably follow a normal distribution. Accordingly, the subject's task is actually one of determining when the activity outputted by the sensory system is from background activity alone or background activity plus activity due to the test flash. Taking into account this variability of the physiological receptor, we see that the eye is indeed a very sensitive apparatus, in the sense that you have to add only about 9 or 10 quanta to its background activity for the light to be seen.

What is the minimal amount of light that is visible to the human observer under optimal conditions? This was the experimental question asked by Hecht, Shlaer, and Pirenne in 1942 and posed early in this chapter. The question led to a series of experiments that required precise stimulus and experimental control and measurement in a psychophysical situation. The answer indicated that under optimal conditions for seeing, an observer was essentially as sensitive as he or she could possibly be.

VISUAL PERCEPTION

The art of monocular perception

*For the psychologist green is not a property of the leaf,
nor of light rays, nor of the excitation of the inner eye,
but rather a subjective phenomenon, a conscious content
of a definite quality.*
—Ewald Hering (1878)

The perception of the visual world appears to be direct and straight-forward. We easily recognize objects of different sizes, shapes, and colors at varying distances and orientations in the real world. The act of visual perception is so familiar that, upon introduction to the topic, many students do not see the necessity of psychological investigation. Our phenomenological experience might easily lead to the position that we see the world in a certain way because that's the way the world is. Perception, therefore, simply involves walking up to an object and resonating to the information that is contained within it.

Nevertheless, eye contact with the visual world is not sufficient to see it in an orderly, organized, and predictable way. Gregory (1966) reports the experiences of a man who, blind from the age of ten months, had his sight restored at the age of fifty-two. When he was shown a simple lathe, he could not recognize it or see it clearly although he knew what a lathe was and how it functioned. When he was allowed to touch it, he closed his eyes and ran his hands over the parts of the lathe. Afterwards, when he stood back and observed it, he said, "Now that I've felt it I can see it." Apparently this man had learned a set of operations which allowed him to see the world by touch but not by sight. But after learning about the shape and function of a particular object by touch, he could use this information to see the object as it should have been seen. Without knowing what to look for, or how to look for it, the object could not be perceived. This example, given its complexity, is meant only to show that visual perception is a complicated and time-consuming process that deserves careful psychological study.

Visual perception involves the interaction of two sources of information available to the perceiver. The first is the visual stimulus available to the visual sensory system and the second is the knowl-

**PERCEPTION
AND
KNOWLEDGE**

edge of the perceiver. This chapter utilizes two-dimensional works of art as experimental demonstrations of how both of these factors contribute to our experience of the visual world. Two dimensions are sufficient because the visual phenomena they illustrate are not dependent upon a two-eyed observer viewing a three-dimensional scene. The richness of our monocular perception, however, should not lead one to question the advantages of having two eyes. The chapter on binocular perception will show that two eyes are better than one.

An example of how the visual information available to the observer and his knowledge interact in perception is illustrated by a passage taken from *Robinson Crusoe*.

> When, one morning the day broke, and all unexpectedly before their eyes a ship stood, what it was was evident at a glance to Crusoe. But how was it with Friday? As younger and uncivilized, his eyes were presumably better than those of his master. That is, Friday saw the ship really the best of the two; and yet he could hardly be said to see it at all.

What Crusoe possessed that Friday did not was knowledge of how to operate on the visual information transduced by the eye in order to recognize a ship on the horizon. Without these operations, the visual input was not sufficient for perception of a ship.

PERCEPTION AND ART

There are a number of basic perceptual phenomena that demonstrate how the eye and psychological processes operate together in visual perception. Many of these phenomena can be seen in the perceptual consequences of viewing art. Abstract art, for example, provides a very good tool for analyzing how visual perception works because the abstract artist presents a well-controlled demonstration; usually all stimulus variables but one are precisely controlled. He manipulates one variable in the painting and observes its perceptual consequence. The reader should be warned, however, that experiencing art, like interpreting experimental results, can lead to alternative conclusions.

EYE MOVEMENTS

The first demonstrations seem to be dependent upon normal eye functions, of which we are usually not aware. Figure 1, *Cinematic Painting* by Wolfgang Ludwig, is appropriately titled; no matter how much we try to stabilize the scene, the two patterns do not remain stable. One hypothesis is that this effect occurs because the eye has a fine high-frequency tremor or nystagmus. This movement is an involuntary rapid oscillation of the eyeballs of between 30 and 100 cycles per sec. The eye moves only a very small distance in nystagmus—about 17 sec. of arc. Accordingly, the retinal image of a scene is continually jerking (moving) slightly on the retina, even though one usually sees a stable world.

Has the artist, therefore, succeeded in devising a scene that takes advantage of the eye's nystagmus? Normally, the visual scene has a more defined figure-ground relationship, so small eye movements go unnoticed. In the painting in Figure 1, however; the lines become very fine towards the middle of the patterns so that acuity breaks down. The thin portion of the line becomes fuzzier at the

Nystagmus

1964. Oil on composition board, 24⅛ x 48⅛". Owned by the artist.

FIGURE 1. *Cinematic Painting* by Wolfgang Ludwig

center and one tends to see a grey patch that vibrates. One test of the eye movement explanation of visual effects in Figure 1 is to produce in a dark-adapted subject an afterimage of the painting, by illuminating it with a very short and bright light. The electronic flash used in photography is excellent, since it presents the light in less than 1 msec. In this case, eye movements cannot change the position of the image on the retina as they do in normal viewing. If a positive afterimage is obtained, the viewer can observe whether he experiences any movement within the picture. If he does not, this provides good evidence that eye movements are, at least, partially responsible for the effects observed in Ludwig's disturbing painting. Some corroboration for this comes from Evans and Marsden (1966), who showed that movement in patterns similar to Ludwig's painting disappeared when viewed as positive afterimages.

Accommodation   Another possible cause of the movement in Ludwig's painting could be fluctuations in the accommodation of the lens of the eye. In order to bring a retinal image into sharp focus, the curvature of the lens must be changed, that is, it must accommodate. When the object is brought closer to the viewer, the lens must accommodate at a larger thickness in order to focus the image properly on the retina. The method of stabilizing the retinal image by a bright flash producing an afterimage would not only eliminate the small nystagmus movements, but would also eliminate movements of the retinal image due to fluctuations in accommodation. Therefore, either or both of these movements could be responsible.

Another method of stabilizing the image on the retina projects the image on a contact lens. The contact lens moves with movements of the eye so that the image on the retina does not change its position with eye movements. Although this method eliminates changes in the retinal position due to eye movements, it does not eliminate changes in the image produced by changes in accommodation. Therefore, using this stabilization method when observing the painting could isolate the critical variable. If nystagmus were responsible, no movement should be visible. MacKay's (1957) observations implicate accommodation as the responsible mechanism, since he still observed movement of similar figures using the contact lens stabilization technique.

Millodot's (1968) observation also tends to support the accommodation hypothesis. His experiment was based on the observation that the momentary fluctuations in accommodation were smaller when objects were viewed at greater distances. Accordingly, the perceived movement should be larger when the figure is viewed at a shorter than a longer distance if accommodation is responsible for the effect. His observations supported this hypothesis when subjects viewed concentric circles similar to those embedded in our chapter numbers. Furthermore, one of his subjects who had no accommodation in one eye, only saw the illusion with the other eye. These observations point to accommodation changes rather than nystagmus eye movements as responsible for the movement seen in Ludwig's painting and in Millodot's concentric circles.

Eliminating nystagmus as a causal agent for perception of movement is consonant with other observations that nystagmus appears to have no important function in visual processing. It is best thought of as meaningless background noise in the visual system. In no way does nystagmus help one to encode information, nor does it add to the information in the visual stimulus. The assertion of some investigators that these small, high-frequency oscillations allow the light pattern to hit more receptors and, therefore, improve the figure-ground contrast is unfounded. When an image is stabilized on the retina, so that nystagmus is eliminated, visual acuity is just as sharp as with normal nystagmus movements (Keesey, 1960).

Figure 2, *Current* by Bridget Riley, gives similar effects of movement. Riley's canvas usually covers a whole wall, and should

FIGURE 2. *Current* by Bridget Riley

1964. Polymer paint on composition board, 58⅞ x 58⅞". Collection, The Museum of Modern Art, New York. Philip Johnson Fund.

be viewed at a distance. The viewer can then observe that the whole wall is vibrating. The fine lines in Riley's painting are responsible for this effect, similar to the effect of the thin lines in Figure 1. Did the artist knowingly design her painting this way, or was the perceptual effect discovered?

Saccades   A second kind of eye movement, called saccades, are much larger movements than high-frequency nystagmus and do not occur more frequently than 4 or 5 times per sec. Viewing a painting, for example, the eyes jerk across the painting and obtain a succession of discrete looks during the fixation time between eye movements. The saccadic eye movement is programmed by the viewer before it is initiated. Once it begins, the direction and distance of the movement cannot be modified. The movement is called ballistic and is very rapid, covering about 360° per sec. for large eye movements.

Again, in normal perception, we are not usually aware of this very fast eye movement. Perception is suppressed during the saccadic eye movement, and the views from successive fixations are integrated into a continuous picture. Since saccadic eye movements are extremely fast, the image of the visual scene moves rapidly across the retina. We do not notice this for at least two reasons. One is that the stimulation from any point on the visual scene occurs only on a given point on the retina for a brief period of time so that the intensity of the stimulation is very low. The second reason is that very little time elapses to process the stimulation once initiated, since it is replaced immediately by another part of the visual scene. The role of the visual integration of light over time and the temporal course of seeing is discussed in detail in Chapters 8, 11, 17, and 18.

Bridget Riley's *White Discs I* (Figure 3) takes advantage of our saccadic eye movements, and also of the momentary state of excitation of the light receptors, the rods and cones. Normally we are not aware of these discrete series of eye movements. We seem to perceive the world continuously rather than in discrete chunks. The perceptual system has mechanisms, which are not well understood, that correct for the discrete eye movements and allow us to perceive a continuous world. Riley bypasses this correction procedure by simplifying the visual scene so that the view from one fixation is not completely integrated with the next. Observing *White Discs I,* we see not only black discs but white discs jumping out at different places on the figure. The white discs appear out of nowhere, during a given fixation, because of the differences in adaptation of the light receptors from the previous fixation. Walking into

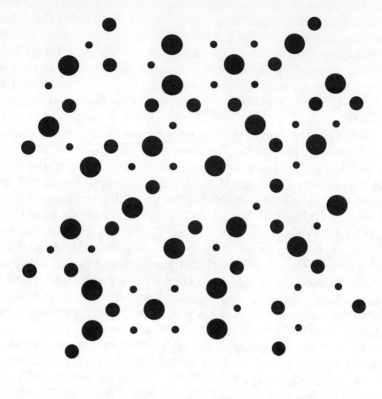

FIGURE 3. *White Discs I* by Bridget Riley

a movie theater, we all have experienced momentary blindness followed by increased visual sensitivity as we become dark-adapted. In this case, the eyes were light-adapted when we walked in and became dark-adapted when the light reaching the eye was reduced. We saw in the preceding chapter that the temporal course of this process is much longer than the one Riley is working with, but the principles are the same. During one fixation, the amount of light reaching the receptors from the white background is much greater than the light being reflected from the black discs. Accordingly, the receptors receiving the light from the white of the canvas are being washed out (light-adapted) relative to the receptors receiving light from the black discs.

Now when the eyes make their next saccadic movement, the receptor's view of the scene changes. A saccadic eye movement essentially shifts the scene on the retina. After an eye movement, most of the receptors that previously received light from the black discs are now fixated on the white canvas. Those receptors that had contact with the black discs during the previous fixation are much more sensitive to the light from the white of the canvas than their surrounding receptors, which were fixated on white. Therefore, the receptors previously fixated on the black discs give a larger light response to the white than do the surrounding receptors, so that we see very white discs on a white background. The discs come from nowhere, since the black discs themselves are integrated between eye fixations.

Why does the previous view not always mix with the current view in normal situations? The answer to this question may be a long time in coming. Does the complexity of the typical visual scene make it very easy to integrate the successive views exactly? Riley reduced the complexity of the visual scene by imposing a large background with small figures and, more importantly, she chose two extreme values of brightness for figure and ground. Accordingly, when the eye moves, the receptors previously exposed to black are much more sensitive than those exposed to white. In typical visual scenes, we do not have such extreme values of intensity for figure and ground or such simple figure-ground relationships. Riley's demonstration should come to mind when we discuss the temporal course of seeing (Chapters 17 and 18).

Saccadic eye movements are critical for visual perception. It is important to refresh our view of the world every ¼ sec. or so; otherwise, it might disappear entirely. This is demonstrated in the painting *Minimum* by Alexander Liberman (Figure 4). Fixating on a point in the center of the painting will cause the thin circle to blend with the background and disappear. The small saccadic movements when we try to hold our fixation steady do not change the visual scene significantly, indicating that simple scenes can be made to disappear with steady fixation. This demonstration shows that nystagmus movements, which cannot be controlled voluntarily, are not sufficient to maintain the appearance of the scene, again pointing up their lack of function.

Viewing Liberman's painting we mix the background with the figure, losing sight of the figure-ground. The visual system continually mixes light at the eye when acuity—the ability to resolve the figure-ground contrast—breaks down. In *Vega* by Victor Vasarely (top panel of Figure 5), the small areas of black and white are easily seen. Each small area is capable of being resolved as figure. This would not be the case if the distance were increased between the viewer and the display. As the distance increased, as each square would hit a smaller portion of his retina, his acuity would eventually break down so that the outlines of the areas

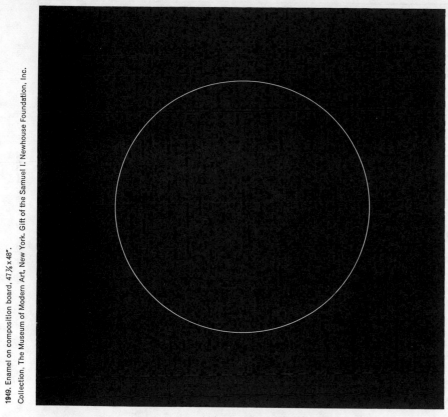

1949. Enamel on composition board, 47⅛ x 48". Collection, The Museum of Modern Art, New York. Gift of the Samuel I. Newhouse Foundation, Inc.

FIGURE 4. *Minimum* by Alexander Liberman

would disappear. The resulting perception is a complete mixture of the colors in small areas, giving continuous grays that can be seen in the out-of-focus photograph of *Vega* shown in the bottom panel of Figure 5.

A number of painters have relied on this mixing phenomenon for obtaining figure-ground relations in their work. A specialist in this technique, known as pointillism, was the impressionist Georges Seurat. Seurat painted with points or dots of different colors, knowing that these dots would mix into the appropriate color when the painting was viewed from the correct distance. Notice that if the Seurat painting in Figure 6 is viewed from too close a distance, the dots themselves are seen and we miss the intended color and texture of the work. A good example is the cover of this book, which utilizes a detail from another Seurat painting.

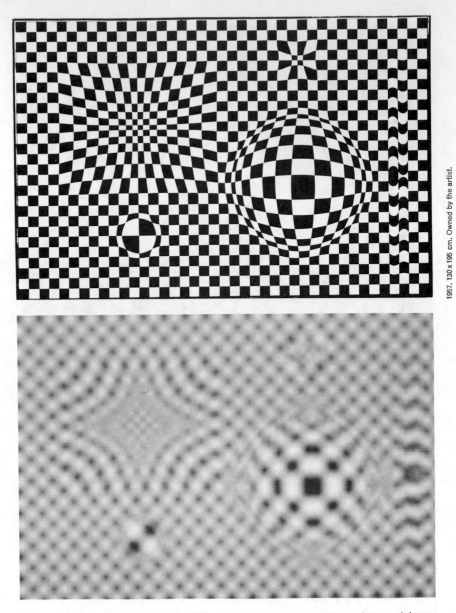

1957. 130 x 195 cm. Owned by the artist.

FIGURE 5. *Vega* by Victor Vasarely. In focus (top panel) and out of focus (bottom panel).

PERCEPTION AND MEMORY Recall that Gregory's patient could not see the shape of an object accurately if he first did not learn about it by touching it. Similarly Crusoe's man Friday was not able to discern a ship on the horizon, being young and inexperienced on the seas. These observations agree with the statement of William James, who said we can per-

FIGURE 6. *Poseuse Debout (Vue de Face)* by Georges Seurat

ceive only what we have preperceived. Gregory's patient was able to build up a memory representation of the object by touching it, which later facilitated his visual perception of it. Crusoe's experience allowed him to spot the ship with very little visual information. Our knowledge continually facilitates perception by allow-

FIGURE 7. *Cathedral* #3 by Roy Lichtenstein

FIGURE 8. *Rouen Cathedral* by Claude Monet

ing us to build a figure-ground relationship with the processing of a minimal amount of visual information.

To perceive a figure-ground relationship it is necessary to have information in memory to help identify what is seen. Figure 7 shows a lithograph by Roy Lichtenstein. By viewing the work from a distance, the dots can also be mixed in the way intended by Seurat. But Lichtenstein's print is much more ambiguous than Seurat's painting and usually is not perceived at first glance. Even its title, *Cathedral #3,* does not help most observers. The most help comes from viewing Claude Monet's *Rouen Cathedral* (Figure 8), which Lichtenstein used as a model for his lithograph. With an idea or conception of what we should see, we have no problem seeing the intended figure-ground relationship.

As noted earlier, in visual perception both the visual stimulus and the knowledge of the observer are essential ingredients. One problem that has intrigued philosophers and psychologists for centuries is how to see a three-dimensional world given only a two-dimensional visual image. This problem is easily resolved if we recognize the contribution of what the observer knows. Gregory's patient, we noted, could not perceive the visual input accurately in three dimensions. Here we discuss how the knowledge of the observer takes advantage of visual features, or cues in the visual scene, to perceive a three-dimensional world.

CUES TO PERSPECTIVE

There are many two-dimensional cues that aid us in perceiving a three-dimensional world. These cues are referred to as two-dimensional, since they are not dependent on actual depth relationships, nor do they have to be viewed binocularly. The role of each cue can be localized in abstract art because the artist usually makes only one cue available. Its perceptual consequences can thus be viewed directly.

Size

The first perspective cue we consider is size. Relative size is a cue that can be used for determining relative depth. Discs perceived in Figure 3 (p. 167) seem to be at different distances from the viewer. The larger discs appear closer; the small ones appear far away. This painting has no other cue to depth but size, indicating that relative size is a powerful depth cue. Usually, larger things appear nearer than smaller things. This phenomenon can also be observed in the moon illusion; the moon at the horizon looks both large and close, whereas the zenithal moon appears small and far away.

Lighting and Shadow

We have no problem perceiving a weeping willow in the pastel by Wayne Thiebaud (Figure 9). The differential lighting and the shadow convey a message of figure, ground, and depth. Of course, contemporary artists were not the first to use shadow as a perspective cue. In fact, lighting and shadow were used as cues to depth long before linear perspective cues. Thiebaud, however, by eliminating other depth cues in this work, demonstrates that the nature of the lighting is a sufficient cue for depth.

Interposition

Figure 10 (*Black Cross* by Georgia O'Keeffe) demonstrates the role of interposition in perceiving depth. One cue to depth in the real world is that an object appearing in front of, or interposed, between you and another object is perceived as nearer. It is very easy to

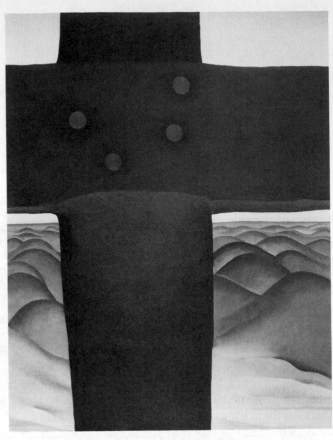

FIGURE 9. *Weeping Willow* by Wayne Thiebaud

FIGURE 10. *Black Cross* by Georgia O'Keeffe

Courtesy Allan Stone Gallery, New York.

Courtesy of the Art Institute of Chicago.

perceive the black cross and the mountains extending in depth, because the cross is interposed in front of the mountains and each mountain covers another mountain behind it.

Josef Albers' *Homage to the Square* (Figure 11), gives a purer demonstration of interposition. The squares can be viewed as a series of colored sheets. The smaller sheets must therefore lie in front of the larger sheets. The black sheet must be in front of the gray sheet since it is interposed between the viewer and the gray square. The only possible alternative is that the gray sheet is nearer and the black is seen through a square cut out of the gray sheet. However, it is more likely that the squares are complete; accordingly, it is very easy to perceive the black sheet as being nearer to you. Since no other cues to depth are apparent, the painting demonstrates that interposition can function as a sufficient cue for depth.

1961. Oil on composition board, 40 x 40".
Collection, The Museum of Modern Art, New York. Dr. and Mrs. Frank Stanton Fund.

FIGURE 11. *Homage to the Square: Silent Hall* by Josef Albers

Linear perspective is a very important cue to depth. Two converging lines are usually perceived as extending in depth if they are assumed to be parallel in the actual three-dimensional scene. Victor Vasarely uses perspective very nicely in the painting shown in Figure 12, which gives a receding hallway effect. Since it is usually assumed that hallways do not change their shape, the converging lines, conveyed by the rectangles becoming smaller, allow the viewer to look down the hallway receding into the distance. In this painting, it is very difficult to compete against the linear perspective cues by consciously trying to see the narrow part of the hallway as actually closer. **Linear Perspective**

Another cue for depth is surface texture. If the texture of an object remains constant, then as it recedes into the distance the gradient **Surface Texture** of the texture appears smaller. In *Equivocation* by Benjamin Cunningham (Figure 13), the relative sizes of the squares give a cue to their distance, since it is usually assumed that the texture of the object is made of constant size squares. The object must be receding in depth if the squares become smaller. The change in the projected size of the squares is called a texture gradient. Texture gradients provide information about relative depth and simultaneously give a cue to the slant of the surface. Cunningham's work

FIGURE 12. *Vonal-KSZ* by Victor Vasarely

1964. Polymer paint on gesso panel, 26 x 26". Collection, The Museum of Modern Art, New York. Larry Aldrich Foundation Fund.

FIGURE 13. *Equivocation* by Benjamin Cunningham

shows that texture gradients can convey not only relative depth but the actual shape of the surface seen in depth. Texture allows Cunningham to display a fascinating three-dimensional scene in only two dimensions.

In *Betelgeuse I* by Victor Vasarely (Figure 14) the depth we see is dependent on the figure we see. We tend to perceive as figure the simplest possible object in the real three-dimensional world. In other words, it is easiest to form perceptions as figures, those objects that are familiar or simple—circles, squares, rectangles, etc.

    The simple or good figure—such as the circle—is most easily seen, and the perceived depth is made congruent with this perception. An ellipse is more likely to be seen as a circle rotated in depth.

**Simplicity
of Figure**

By contrast, circles are seen as flat, in a plane parallel to the viewer's forehead. Figure 14 shows that different depth relationships can be seen in the same two-dimensional representation, depending upon the simplicity of the possible figures in the three-dimensional world.

1957. 195 x 130 cm. Owned by the artist.

FIGURE 14. *Betelgeuse I* by Victor Vasarely

Illusory Contours The visual system does not always need complete information to form a figure-ground relationship. Figure 15 (*Capella II* by Vasarely) shows how very easy it is to see shapes as complete even though they are not. The borders of the squares and circles are not continu-

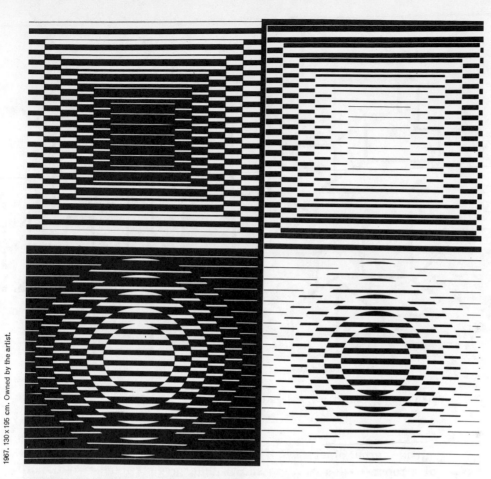

FIGURE 15. *Capella II* by Victor Vasarely

ous even though we see them that way. We can fill in the missing parts to form a figure-ground relationship that is meaningful. Vasarely demonstrates this perceptual process in a very simple situation; we might expect from this demonstration that the process also plays a role in seeing the three-dimensional world.

In Figure 16 (Al Held's *Blk/Wt#16*) we see that a given two-dimensional display can be interpreted in different ways. The boxes do not remain fixed; the top of one box may become the bottom of another, and so forth. Looking at a particular box, if an intersection of two sides appears nearer to you, try to reverse it so that it now appears farther away. In other words, instead of looking at the

Reversibility

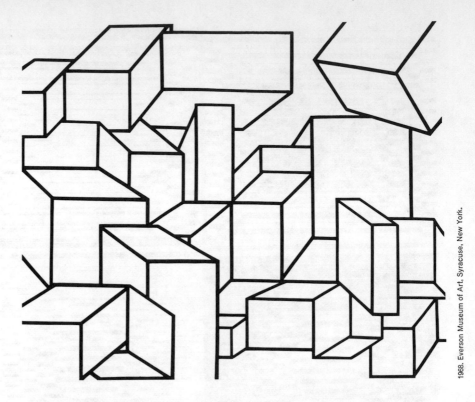

1968. Everson Museum of Art, Syracuse, New York.

FIGURE 16. *Blk/Wt #16* by Al Held

outside corner of a box, look at the intersection as the inside corner of a room. Held's painting shows that, given a fixed two-dimensional scene, we can interpret it in a variety of ways. Our perceptions, then, are not always determined by the visual information present in the scene. The alternative interpretations of the Roman mosaic shown on the opening page of this section also provide an example of reversibility. In a number of situations, we perceive what we expect, desire, or try to see.

Impossible Scenarios

Two-dimensional perspective cues can also be used to create impossible three-dimensional scenes. Figure 17, *Satire on False Perspective,* an engraving by William Hogarth (1754) presents an impossible town scenario. Although the depth relationships in any small portion of the engraving are reasonable, combining the various scenes boggles the mind. Artists usually incorporate two-dimensional depth cues to convey realistic three-dimensional scenes. In this engraving, Hogarth has done the opposite; he has used the depth cues to make the scene impossible.

FIGURE 17. *Satire on False Perspective* by William Hogarth

Logic of illusion

So, Socrates, you have made a discovery—that false judgment resides, not in our perceptions among themselves, nor yet in our thoughts, but in the fitting together of perception and thought.
—Plato's Theaetetus

The last chapter discussed the many visual features of the two-dimensional scene that are sufficient for the phenomenological experience of size, shape, and so on. These features were interpreted correctly in the sense that we experienced the visual message intended by the artist. Similarly, in normal perception the visual features are interpreted correctly and experience is veridical; that is to say, it accurately represents the scene as it is. Sometimes, however, the visual features give misleading information so that phenomenological experience does not accord with the way things are. In this case, we say we have experienced an optical illusion.

OPTICAL ILLUSIONS

Optical illusions are not only fun but important in the study of perception. Understanding the mechanisms or processes that underlie illusory perception should give some insights into such basic perceptual processes as form and space perception. For example, how is it that three-dimensional shapes in space can be seen when only a two-dimensional representation is given? The most popular illusions are geometric, such as the Müller-Lyer, Ponzo, and Poggendorf figures shown in Figure 1. However, new illusions continue to be discovered and the impossible figures are gaining in popularity. Figure 2, known as a "blivet," appeared on the cover of the March, 1965, issue of *Mad Magazine*. The cover showed Alfred E. Neuman, with two extra eyes, trying to balance a blivet on his index finger. More recently, the *National Lampoon* did a take-off on apparent illusions that were not actually illusory. For example, although the blivet shown in Figure 3 is not impossible, it could easily seem so, since it is so difficult to resolve in just one or two glances.

FIGURE 1. Popular illusions.

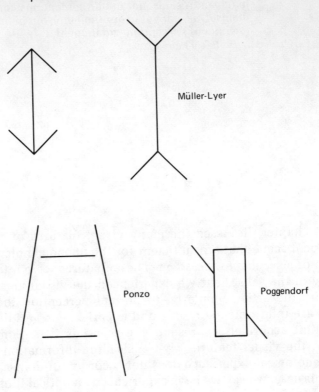

Müller-Lyer

Ponzo

Poggendorf

FIGURE 2. A blivet. This figure could not exist in a three-dimensional world.

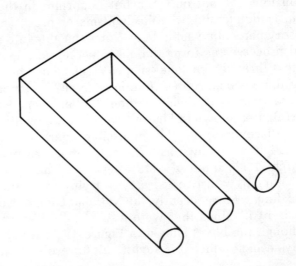

FIGURE 3. An illusory blivet. This figure could exist in a three-dimensional world.

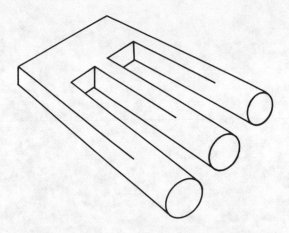

Illusions are not restricted to perceptions of two-dimensional scenes but can also be found in three-dimensional representations. Furniture designers and architects often distort their creations from their geometrical or pure forms to take into account certain perceptual distortions. For example, the arm of a chair usually looks most pleasing when it appears parallel to the floor. In some chair designs, the front of the arm is made higher than the back in order to counterbalance the sloping seat and back of the chair.

The artist employs a number of visual devices in his painting to represent a three-dimensional scene in two dimensions. Perception of depth relationships in painting can be considered illusory since they do not actually exist in the real world. The term illusory, however, is usually given to perception that does not agree with another measure of the visual scene. For example, Figure 4 is a photograph of the Palazzo Spada restoration by the well-known Renaissance architect Borromini. The photograph indicates that a viewer standing at one end of the palazzo sees a long colonnade, beyond which is a large open space with a life-size statue at the far end. However, in actual fact, Borromini had only a limited area and expanded the available space by magnifying the perspective features. Rather than erecting all the columns the same size as we would expect, he made them shorter and closer together as they were placed farther from the observer. Moreover, the statue at the far end of the palazzo is not life size, but was reduced by a factor of 1/2. Hence, the colonnade is perceived as much longer than it is, making the statue seem much farther away than it actually is. Figure 5 is a photograph of the same scene with a person in it. Here we

FIGURE 4. Palazzo Spada colonnade and statue.

see that something is wrong. It can be said, therefore, that Borromini achieved an illusory situation, since our perception of it conflicts with its actual physical representation.

Illusions continue to persist even though we know what we are seeing is illusory. Figure 6 gives an example of a man holding an umbrella over himself and a woman (Kanizsa, 1969). The shaft of

FIGURE 5. Same scene as Figure 4 with a person alongside statue.

the umbrella appears to be extended through the woman's hair even though we know this cannot be the case. Here we have a stimulus property of the display playing a larger role in what is seen than the knowledge of the observer. The umbrella shaft and the hair are the same color and the viewer must fill in the outlines of the object that is closer to—that is, in front of—the other object.

Apparently, it is easier to close off the outlines of the woman's hair over the shaft of the umbrella than to see the outlines of the shaft in front of her hair. In the first case, only a very small area has to be closed off, whereas completing the outlines of the shaft requires closing off a very large area. Figure 7 presents another impossible scene of this type. These examples stand in marked contrast to those in the last chapter in which knowledge critically influenced what was perceived. The stimulus properties in Figures 6 and 7 determine what is seen and our knowledge is unable to influence this impossible interpretation. Both the stimulus characteristics and the knowledge of the observer are important contributions to our experience of the visual world.

The Moon Illusion

On evenings when the sky is clear and the moon makes an appearance, one might say, "Look at that huge moon." This observer probably would be looking towards the horizon; the key word here is "huge." If the moon is overhead at the zenith, one might say, "The moon is out," or "full," or "lovely," but the adjective would probably not be in terms of size because the perceived size of the moon at the zenith is not impressive and appears significantly smaller than the horizontal moon. The moon illusion has been represented in a number of paintings; apparently the artists were unaware of

FIGURE 7. What properties of this visual scene are responsible for its impossible interpretation (after Kanizsa, 1969)?

their illusion. For example, Van Gogh's *The Sower*, a scene showing a farmer sowing his fields near a tree, has an enormous moon at the horizon. Comparing the painting to a hypothetical photograph of the scene, it can be shown that in relation to other details of the painting, Van Gogh has enlarged the moon by a factor of ten. The perception of a larger horizontal than zenithal moon is illusory, since the moon reflects the same size image at the horizon and zenith. One way to see this is to photograph the moon in different celestial positions. Cameras are not sensitive to the moon illusion and record the same size image at the horizon as at the zenith. However, the photographer must be sure to measure the size of the images physically since some people report a moon illusion even in photographs.

The moon illusion has been known and discussed at least since the time of the astronomer Ptolemy in the second century A.D. Ptolemy proposed that the apparent distance of the moon is responsible for its perceived size. The horizontal moon viewed across a terrain appears farther away than the zenithal moon, which is viewed through empty space. This explanation rests on the perceptual phenomenon of size constancy: an object retains a relatively constant apparent size at different distances from the

Constancy scaling

The apparent size of the moon is a critical factor in achieving the sense of space in Henri Rousseau's *The Sleeping Gypsy* and *Carnival Evening*.

observer. As one moves towards an object, the size of the retinal image increases so that if the distance is halved, the retinal image increases by a factor of two. Psychologists have, therefore, proposed a psychological mechanism which operates to evaluate the relative size of the retinal image of an object with respect to the perceived distance of the object. This mechanism is referred to as constancy scaling since it scales the relative size of the image based on perceived distance.

How does constancy scaling account for the moon illusion? If the view of the moon gives more depth cues at the horizon than overhead, it should appear larger at the horizon. Although the moon

gives the same retinal image at both locations, constancy scaling would expand the image of the horizontal moon more than the zenithal moon since the horizontal moon appears farther away due to the depth cues. However, one also hears how near the moon appears at the horizon: "It looks as if it's just behind that building."

Boring (1943) and his colleagues at Harvard University tested our phenomenological experience by asking people to judge the relative distances of the horizontal and zenithal moon. The observers tended to see the zenithal moon as farther away than the horizontal moon. This result led Boring to reject the constancy scaling explanation of the moon illusion.

Boring believed instead that the moon illusion was due to the different angles of viewing by the observer. To demonstrate this, Boring required observers to judge the size of the horizontal and zenithal moon by matching its apparent size with one of a series of comparison stimuli. The comparison stimuli were discs of light projected on a nearby screen. He found that when observers looked at the horizontal moon with their eyes level and the zenithal moon with their eyes raised, they chose a disc 1½ or 2 times larger to match a horizontal moon than the disc chosen to match the zenithal moon. However, if they observed the zenithal moon with tilted heads or in a supine position, so that it was not necessary to raise their eyes, the zenithal moon was not perceived smaller than the horizontal moon. When two of these observers bent their necks forward so that they had to raise their eyes to observe the horizontal moon, it appeared smaller than the zenithal moon. Although Boring could not discover a psychological process to explain his results, he argued very convincingly that the apparent size of the moon was inversely related to the raising of one's eyes.

Rock and Kaufman (1962) were unconvinced by Boring's results since they noticed no apparent size changes in the moon if their eyes were level or elevated. They were also unhappy with Boring's experimental set-up since they felt it might be difficult for subjects to match the size of the moon with the size of a disc nearby. To convince yourself of this difficulty, attempt to formulate the instructions you would give to the subjects in this task.

To overcome the experimental difficulties in studying the moon illusion, Rock and Kaufman developed an artificial moon apparatus in which artificial moons could be seen against the sky. Observers could then be asked to compare directly a moon seen at the zenith with a moon seen at the horizon. The subjects observed a standard size moon in one sky position and determined when another variable comparison moon in another position was equal to it in size. The method of limits was used to change the size of the variable moon. The dependent variable was the actual size of the zenithal moon divided by the actual size of the horizontal moon when the two moons were perceived to be equal.

Rock and Kaufman found that the two moons were seen as equal in size when the zenithal moon was about 1½ times larger than the horizontal moon. Furthermore, they found no significant effect of eye elevation using their experimental set-up. They also showed that the view of the terrain was a necessary condition for the moon illusion. If the view of the terrain was eliminated by requiring the subject to view the moon through a small aperture in a large piece of cardboard, the moon illusion was eliminated. In this case, the horizontal moon was perceived as the same size as the zenithal moon. Rock and Kaufman believed that they had established unambiguous support for Ptolemy's hypothesis. Their results, they believed, supported the idea that the moon appears farther away at the horizon than at the zenith and that the constancy scaling mechanism operates to enlarge the retinal image of the horizontal moon relative to the zenithal moon. However, Rock and Kaufman did not provide any direct evidence that the moon at the horizon is actually seen as farther away than the moon at the zenith. To support Ptolemy's theory directly, we must show that the moon or other objects are seen as being farther away at the horizon than at the zenith.

The size constancy explanation of the moon illusion rests on the assumption that perceived distance influences perceived size. A view of the horizontal moon, which contains terrain, trees, and buildings, includes cues for depth, which expand its apparent distance. These cues are not seen in views of the zenithal moon, which consequently appears to be nearer. When the horizontal moon is observed without the view of the terrain, the horizontal moon appears to be about the same size as the zenithal moon.

Testing the size constancy explanation

Galanter and Galanter (1973) provide some direct evidence that objects at the horizon appear farther away than objects at the zenith. Their subjects estimated the distance of an aircraft flown at the horizon or directly overhead. A radar system was used to accurately measure the distance of the airplane as it flew at varying distances from the observer. In order to determine the relationship between perceived or apparent distance and actual distance, the psychophysical method of magnitude estimation was employed. In this experiment, the observer estimated the apparent distance of the airplane at different distances. The observer was first shown the airplane at a given distance and was told that the airplane is 100 units away. All subsequent judgments involved estimating the distance of the airplane relative to this standard distance, called 100 units. The airplane was shown to the observer at a number of different distances which were presented in random order. In most tasks employing the method of magnitude estimation, the magnitude of the perception can be described by a simple mathematical function of the physical magnitude of the stimulus. The function is a power function which can be represented by the equation

$$P = KS^n \qquad (1)$$

where P is the magnitude of the perception, S is the stimulus magnitude, K is a constant that corrects for the arbitrary unit of measurement used by the observer, and n is the power or exponent of the function. Power functions are more easily expressed in terms of logarithms. Using logarithms, Equation 1 can be represented as

$$\log P = \log K + n \log S \qquad (2)$$

Equation 2 is a linear equation of the form

$$y = b + ax \qquad (3)$$

where y is a linear function of x. Therefore, $\log P$ should be a linear function of $\log S$. The value $\log K$ is the intercept value and the value n is the slope of the linear function. Equation 2 can be represented graphically by plotting the observed values of the perceived magnitude P as a function of the values of the stimulus magnitude S on logarithmic graph paper.

If the power function holds in the present study, the perceived distance of the airplane should be a linear function of the actual distance when the results are plotted on a logarithmic scale. In fact, if perception is completely veridical, the slope n of the linear function should be 1, since $\log P = \log S$. In this case, the value of K would also be 1. Log K would, therefore, be zero. The function describing veridical perception is given by the continuous line in Figure 8. If actual distance is overestimated, the slope n of the function would be greater than 1; if actual distance is underestimated, n would be less than 1.

The results of the actual experiment gave slopes that differed significantly for the horizontal and zenithal judgments. The functions describing the results are shown in Figure 8. The function obtained with airplanes flying at the horizon indicated that the observers, when seeing an airplane that was 1000 units away, estimated that it was about 1250 units away. That is, at the horizon, the observers significantly overestimated the distance of the object. In contrast, the function obtained with an airplane flying overhead at the zenith indicated that the observers underestimated its distance: for example, the airplane appeared to be only 800 units away when it was actually 1000 units away. The Galanter study thus provides direct evidence that objects at the horizon appear farther away than objects at the zenith. The size constancy theory, dating back to Ptolemy, seems to be correct after all.

Earlier we said that the moon at the horizon also impresses us because of how near it appears. How can the moon appear near, and at the same time provide depth cues such as the terrain for con-

FIGURE 8. Perceived distance as a function of actual distance for airplanes seen at the horizon and the zenith. Veridical perception is given by the solid line (after Galanter & Galanter, 1973).

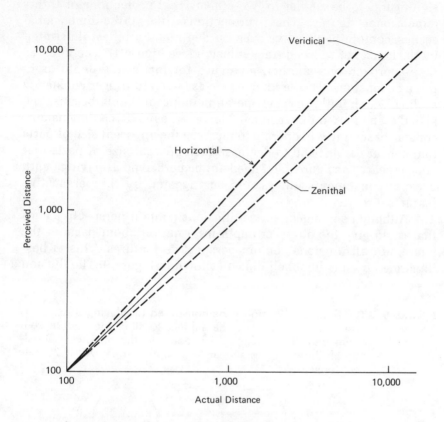

stancy scaling? Rock and Kaufman handle this paradox by assuming that the subject may not be consciously aware of the registered distance used by the constancy scaling mechanism. Therefore, when asked to evaluate the distance of the moon, he does not report the registered distance used for constancy scaling but rather bases his judgment on the conscious perceived size of the moon. The evidence for this assumption is that subjects presented with two moons, one much larger than the other, always report the smaller moon as farther away, regardless of its location in the sky. For Rock and Kaufman, this shows that the larger moon will be seen as nearer, without reference to other factors that produce differences in perceived distance. The constancy scaling explanation of the moon illusion attained credence in the scientific community and also has been proposed for a number of other illusions.

GEOMETRICAL ILLUSIONS

The size constancy explanation known as perspective theory has been applied to the standard geometrical illusions by R. L. Gregory (1963, 1966, 1968). Perspective theory considers the geometric illusion figures to be similar to two-dimensional projections of three-dimensional figures. These projections, like three-dimensional scenes, contain perspective cues for depth and are best illustrated by the Ponzo, or railroad track, illusion (see Figure 1). The lines, as they approach one another, give cues for increasing depth as in three dimensions. The depth cues are assumed to trigger constancy scaling, which in this case is operating inappropriately because the actual scene is two-dimensional. However, as in three dimensions, constancy scaling will operate to increase the apparent size of parts that appear distant and to decrease the apparent size of parts that appear near. The figure itself need not be perceived as having depth because constancy scaling could be triggered by the perspective features directly.

Although some geometrical illusions contain perspective cues that could give the observer depth information about parts of the figure, not all illusions contain perspective features. This is best illustrated by the dumbbell illusion shown in Figure 9. The illusion

FIGURE 9. The dumbbell illusion is demonstrated by placing three coins in a row and requiring the subject to slide the middle coin down until the distance *AB* is equal to the distance *CD*. Although the distances appear to be about equal, AB is 20 percent longer than *CD*.

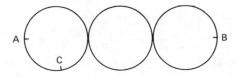

is easily demonstrated with three coins or discs: place the three coins in a row and have the observer slide the middle coin down until the distance *AB* seems equal to the distance *CD,* as in Figure 9. This illusion demonstrates that perspective theory cannot account for all geometrical illusions, because some illusions do not contain perspective cues. However, it is still necessary to test the perspective theory to account for other two-dimensional illusions. The standard Müller-Lyer figure is a good place to start because the processes operating with this illusion might also be operating in the dumbbell illusion.

Perspective theory assumes that Müller-Lyer figures are similar to projections of typical three-dimensional objects. For example, Figure 10a—with the wings directed outward—is similar to a projection of the corner of a room, where the central axis corresponds to the corner and the outside wings correspond to the intersections

Applications and Tests of Perspective Theory

FIGURE 10. The standard Müller-Lyer figures and the same figures with an enlarged width of the central axis.

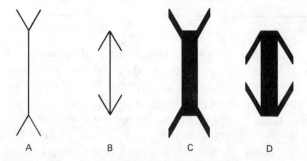

A   B   C   D

of the walls with the ceiling and with the floor. Due to the effect of the wings as perspective cues, the central axis is judged as if it were farther away than the wings. According to the theory, constancy scaling operates, and increases the apparent length of the central axis. Figure 10b—with the wings directed inward—has the perspective cues of a projection of an outside corner of a building. The central axis is thus judged as if it were closer than the wings and, therefore, appears smaller due to constancy scaling. Gregory (1968) presents evidence which he interprets as directly supportive of the perspective theory explanation of the Müller-Lyer illusion. He asked observers to make depth judgments of Müller-Lyer figures illuminated without a visible background so that they appeared suspended in space. To eliminate binocular cues to depth such as convergence (see Chapter 11), the figures were viewed with one eye.

Subjects judged the distance of the central axis of figures with ingoing and outgoing wings. The results, as predicted by perspective theory, showed that the axis with ingoing wings was judged as nearer than the axis with outgoing wings. However, although these results are in agreement with perspective theory, they cannot be taken as evidence that the perceived depth of the central axis caused or influenced its perceived length. Gregory's observation is a correlational one so that no conclusion about causation can be reached.

The perspective theory account of the Müller-Lyer illusion has been put to a number of experimental tests. Waite and Massaro (1970) observed that perspective theory makes an interesting prediction about the size of the central axis of the Müller-Lyer figures. Since the figure with outward-directed wings contains perspective features that make the central axis appear more distant, constancy scaling should affect both the apparent length and the apparent width similarly. That is, if constancy scaling is responsible for the illusion, then both the apparent length and the apparent width of the central axis should be increased.

Correlation

In a correlational design the scientist attempts to find a relationship between two variables. For example, he may collect data on the relationship between affection and juvenile delinquency. To do this he must first define a measure of each variable, such as number of hugs received and number of hubcaps stolen. He then goes from house to house recording the number of hugs each mother gives her children and the number of hubcaps these kids are stealing. Finally, he correlates these two variables and finds that kids who are not hugged steal a large number of hubcaps. Kids who receive a large number of hugs do not steal hubcaps, whereas kids who are hugged somewhat steal hubcaps now and then. Since the number of hubcaps stolen is inversely related to the number of hugs received, the investigator concludes that delinquency is directly related to lack of affection and so advises the mayor's commission.

The central weakness of this method is that the causal relationship between the two variables is not defined. Lack of affection may cause delinquency. On the other hand, delinquents stealing hubcaps may have less time available to be home receiving hugs. Or, both delinquency and lack of affection may be caused by a third variable; there may simply be more cars around in neighborhoods in which parents show less affection. In other words, all the correlational design can tell us is that A is somehow related to B. A may cause B; B may cause A; A and B may both be caused by C.

However, observing the standard Müller-Lyer figure, there are no noticeable differences in the apparent widths of the central axes. These lines are relatively fine and any change—-a 20 percent increase or decrease in the apparent width, for instance—would not be noticed. One way of overcoming this difficulty is to increase the width of the central axis. Any distortion of the width should now be discernible. If we assume that a change in the width does not make a significant change in the perspective cues—the wings and their directions—available in the Müller-Lyer figures, constancy scaling should also operate in the modified figures. According to perspective theory, both the length and the width of the central axis should change with changes in the directions of the wings. Waite and Massaro, therefore, required length and width judgments of modified Müller-Lyer figures, two of which are shown in Figures 10c and 10d.

In the Waite and Massaro (1970) study, a number of modified figures with inward and outward wings were used. Four different sizes of the central axis were used so that subjects would not learn that all the figures had the same-size central axis and respond accordingly. Figures were projected one at a time onto a screen and the subjects were told to judge the apparent length and width of the central axis of each figure. The response sheet contained a horizontal and vertical line which met at a point near the upper left corner of the sheet. The subject made his judgment by making a mark on each line to indicate the length and width of the central axis. Each subject judged each of the figures a number of times in randomized blocks of trials.

The results agreed exactly with what one observes phenomenologically in Figures 10c and 10d. The distortion of the width of the central axis is in the opposite direction of its length. That is, the figure with outward-directed wings appears longer than the figure with inward-directed wings, as is predicted by perspective theory. However, the apparent width of the figure with outward directed wings is slightly smaller than the apparent width of the figure with inward-directed wings. The fact that there was a significant distortion of the length of the central axis of the figures as a function of the direction of the wings supports the assumption that the modification of the figures did not significantly change the visual features of the Müller-Lyer figures. That is to say, since the illusion of the length of the central axis is the same in the modified figures as in the normal figures, the same mechanism is probably responsible. The Waite and Massaro (1970) study, then, appears to provide a critical rejection of perspective theory; the explanation of the Müller-Lyer illusion must be found elsewhere.

Total Impression Theory

One very old explanation of geometrical illusions is the total impression theory (Woodworth, 1938), which simply states that a part of a figure cannot be judged independently of its background or context. The total impression theory is a slight modification of the saying that a whole is greater than its parts; the perception of each part is dependent upon the whole. For example, one would expect the observer to show some distortion in judging the central axis of the Müller-Lyer illusion since he is affected by the figure as a whole. In the figure with outward-directed wings, the imaginary or undrawn lines parallel to the central axis and enclosed by the wings are longer than the central axis itself. If the observer cannot ignore the impression that the undrawn parallels are longer than the central axis, he might assimilate or average the length of these lines with the length of the central axis. In this case, he would judge the central axis to be longer than its actual size. In the Müller-Lyer figure with inward-directed wings the undrawn parallel lines are shorter than the central axis. Again, if the impression cannot be ignored, the observer would average these shorter lengths into his observation and would judge the central axis to be shorter than it actually is. One appealing aspect of the total impression explanation of the Müller-Lyer illusion is that it also explains the other versions, such as the dumbbell illusion.

Assimilation and contrast

The total impression of the figure can influence the judgment of a part of the figure in two ways: assimilation and contrast. Assimilation is operative in the Müller-Lyer figures; the length of the central axis is assimilated toward the lengths of the imaginary or undrawn parallel lines. The contrast effect is operative in other illusions, such as the Ebbinghaus illusion (see Figure 11), in which the size of the center circle may be thought to appear larger or smaller than it actually is due to the size of the surrounding circles. If the surrounding circles are smaller than the center circle, the center circle may appear larger than it actually is because it is larger relative to the small surrounding circles. The small circles function as compar-

FIGURE 11. Illustration of Ebbinghaus illusion. (Center circle has the same size in both panels.)

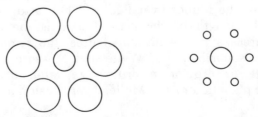

ison stimuli and influence the judgment of the center circle. If the surrounding circles are large, the comparative influence will reduce the apparent size of the center circle.

The conditions under which assimilation and contrast operate cannot always be specified. In fact, both assimilation and contrast can operate in the same illusion. If the outward-directed wings of the Müller-Lyer figure are extended beyond some point, a contrast effect will begin to appear. Figure 12a shows that although the central axis of the extended Müller-Lyer figure appears larger than it is due to assimilation, it appears slightly smaller than Figure 12b due to contrast.

FIGURE 12. The central axis of Figure A appears larger than it is due to assimilation, but smaller than Figure B due to contrast.

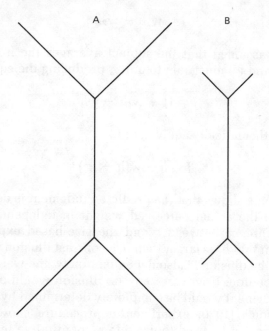

A mathematical formulation of the total impression theory has been applied to the size–weight illusion by Anderson (1970). The size of an object can influence its perceived weight, making the judgment of weight illusory. A pound of feathers is subjectively lighter than a pound of lead. We expect objects to weigh more as they increase in size and this expectation influences their perceived weight. If we have high expectations about an event, we are more likely to be disappointed than if our expectations are minimal. This is a contrast effect.

Mathematical formulation

In Anderson's formulation of the total impression theory, two values contribute to the perceived weight of an object: a heaviness value (h) directly related to the actual weight and independent of size and a heaviness value (h^*) which is a perceived weight dependent upon perceived size. The actual perceived or judged weight (J) is then a weighted average of these two values, giving the equation

$$J = w_1h + w_2h^* \tag{1}$$

where w_1 and w_2 are the weights given the two heaviness values, respectively. A contrast effect is operative in the size-weight illusion; to the extent h^* is large, J must be small. This means that w_2 must be negative, in which case larger values of h^* would lead to smaller values of J.

$$J = w_1h - w_2h^* \tag{2}$$

If it is also assumed that the subject averages the h and h^*, the weights w_1 and w_2 must sum to unity, producing the equation

$$J = (1 + w)h - wh^* \tag{3}$$

which is mathematically equivalent to

$$J = h + w(h - h^*) \tag{4}$$

Equation 4 shows that the predicted judgment is dependent on two factors: the actual perceived weight h, independent of size, and the difference between h and the size-based expectancy h^*. To the extent that h^* is larger than h, a contrast illusion is operative. The size of the illusion is also dependent on w, the weight attached to the expectation. If w were zero, no illusion would be operative, since the judgment would be completely determined by h.

Anderson's (1970) experimental procedure shows how factorial designs can be used to provide a quantitative test of mathematical formulations of the total impression theory. Subjects were required to judge the heaviness of blocks. The two independent variables covaried in the experiment were the weight and size of the blocks. Three different weights and five different sizes were chosen, giving 15 blocks in all. Subjects lifted each block and estimated its weight by marking a slash on a horizontal line from left (lightest) to right (heaviest). Two end anchors, one much lighter and one much heavier than the test blocks, were first presented for lifting and the subjects were told to respond near the left and right ends, respectively, for these stimuli. The perceived weights of the test blocks, therefore, would lie between these two values. The subjects judged each of the objects presented in randomized trials. The mean ratings of the blocks in terms of the distance from the left of the line to the slash are presented in Figure 13. The results show that the size of the block had a significant contrast effect on its perceived weight. A block of a given weight was perceived as

FIGURE 13. Mean line-mark judgments for the three values of block weight (in grams) as a function of block size.

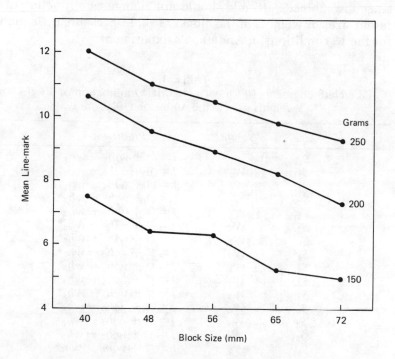

heavier when it was smaller in size. The second significant effect is that the actual weight of the block influenced its perceived weight.

How does the preceding mathematical formulation relate to the results of the present experiment? Equation 3 states that the judged weight is a weighted composite of two factors. To know the predicted value of J for any experimental condition, it is necessary to have values of w, h, and h^*. With only one experimental condition these values cannot be determined, since an infinite number of values could be combined to give J a given value. Therefore, the experiment must be designed so that values for the parameters w, h, and h^* can be estimated, and it can be determined whether a set of parameter values exists which provide a good description of the observed results.

In his factorial design Anderson employed 3 levels of actual weight. Since it is assumed that the actual weight will affect h, we must have a different value for h at each of the 3 levels of weight. Second, it is assumed that the size of the block affects h^* and we must estimate five different h^* values for the five block sizes. Finally, we must estimate a value of w which is assumed to remain constant under all experimental conditions. The value of w could be affected by the instructions or attitude of the observer, but it should not be affected by the different experimental conditions, since the subject's attitude should not change as a function of different sizes or weights of the blocks. Table 1 presents the equations for the 15 conditions in Anderson's experiment.

TABLE 1

Predicted judgments (J) for each factorial combination of 5 sizes and 3 weights used in the Anderson (1970) study.

Size	Weight	Prediction
S_1	W_1	$J = (1 + w)h_1 - wh_1{}^*$
S_1	W_2	$J = (1 + w)h_2 - wh_1{}^*$
S_1	W_3	$J = (1 + w)h_3 - wh_1{}^*$
S_2	W_1	$J = (1 + w)h_1 - wh_2{}^*$
S_2	W_2	$J = (1 + w)h_2 - wh_2{}^*$
S_2	W_3	$J = (1 + w)h_3 - wh_2{}^*$
S_3	W_1	$J = (1 + w)h_1 - wh_3{}^*$
S_3	W_2	$J = (1 + w)h_2 - wh_3{}^*$
S_3	W_3	$J = (1 + w)h_3 - wh_3{}^*$
S_4	W_1	$J = (1 + w)h_1 - wh_4{}^*$
S_4	W_2	$J = (1 + w)h_2 - wh_4{}^*$
S_4	W_3	$J = (1 + w)h_3 - wh_4{}^*$
S_5	W_1	$J = (1 + w)h_1 - wh_5{}^*$
S_5	W_2	$J = (1 + w)h_2 - wh_5{}^*$
S_5	W_3	$J = (1 + w)h_3 - wh_5{}^*$

Now we must find values for h_1, h_2, h_3, h^*_1, h^*_2, h^*_3, h^*_4, h^*_5, and w that give the closest correspondence between our observed values of J and the predicted values given by these equations. This can be done by utilizing a high-speed digital computer that performs a search for the best values. The program is given a range of values for each parameter and tries out different values in the range in order to give the closest correspondence between the observed and predicted scores. One index of correspondence is the average squared difference between the predicted and observed values. When the parameter values are found that best describe the observed data, some index of how well the predicted results match the observed can be computed. For example, the experimenter can

When one formulates a quantitative model of psychological functioning, it is usually necessary to include parameters that cannot be given a definite value. In Anderson's formulation of total impression theory, he cannot predict the magnitude of the illusion without first estimating values of the parameters from the observed data. We face the problem of how much of the data the theorist can use in making his predictions.

Consider the following model and experiment. In the model, perceived weight P is predicted to be a linear function of actual weight:

$$P = ax + b$$

where x is the actual weight. In this model, there are two free parameters (a and b) and the theorist is free to choose any values for a and b to predict results. Suppose an experiment that is carried out to test the theory measures perceived weight at two values of actual weight. This gives two observed data points to predict. However, in order to predict these points, the experimenter must also estimate the two parameter values a and b. He cannot disprove the theory, since a straight line can always be made to fit between only two points. Since it is impossible to reject the theory when performance is measured at only two levels of actual weight, this experiment is not a sufficient test of the theory. As the experimenter increases the number of levels, it becomes easier to disprove the theory. Three points do not necessarily describe a straight line, and so on. In general, we provide a more powerful test of the theory as we increase the number of observations relative to the number of parameters that must be estimated from the data.

determine the average percentage deviation between predicted and observed results.

In Anderson's experiment, 9 parameters must be estimated from the data in order to predict 15 data points. It is possible, therefore, to disprove the theory. More specifically, the equations in Table 1 show that the effects of block weight and block size should be additive. That is to say, the judgment is an additive combination of a heaviness value based on h and one based on h*. Accordingly, if we plot the judged weight as a function of actual weight and block size, the theory predicts a series of parallel curves. Hence, it is possible to test the theory by observing whether there is a significant interaction between the independent variables of actual weight and block size (see Chapters 3 and 4). We saw in Figure 13 that the observed curves are parallel, supporting this quantitative formulation of the total impression theory.

Experimental study of Ebbinghaus illusion

The total impression theory attempts to account for the contribution of the background or context on the observer's perception. In the Ebbinghaus illusion (Figure 11), if the surrounding circles influence judgment, this influence should be directly related to the number of surrounding circles, the relative size of the circles, and their proximity to the center circle. Experiments studying these stimulus variables have, in general, supported the total impression theory (Massaro & Anderson, 1971).

The experimental procedure of these studies illustrates one method of studying perception of illusions. The subject was instructed to judge the size of the center circle in the test figure. For his judgment, he chose a comparison circle that was presented alone without context. The subject rotated a wheel that presented single comparison circles one at a time through a window in the wheel. Accordingly, the subject could search through the comparison circles, one at a time, until he found the comparison circle that appeared to be equal to the center circle of the test figure. The subject judged each of the possible test figures repeatedly and in a random order. His average judgment could then be determined for each test figure condition.

Figure 14 presents the results of an experiment that varied the number of surrounding circles and their size relative to the center circle. In agreement with total impression theory, the illusion increased with increases in the number of surrounding circles. The figure also shows that the larger the size difference between the center and surrounding circles, the larger the illusion. The lines are the predictions of a quantification of total impression theory similar to that derived for the size–weight illusion (Massaro & Anderson, 1971). In a second experiment, the distance of the surrounding circles from the center circle was varied. The results showed that increasing the distance decreased the illusion, as was predicted by total impression theory.

Moon Illusion Revisited

Restle (1970) has utilized the general total impression theory to provide an explanation of the moon illusion. Restle assumes that the size of an object is always judged *relative* to other extents in the visual field. This assumption is similar to the contrast mechanism used to explain the size–weight and the Ebbinghaus illusion. According to Restle's application of the relative size hypothesis to the perception of the moon, the significant context effect is the empty space between the moon and the horizon. The moon appears small at the zenith because it is surrounded by large empty space, whereas the moon near the horizon appears large due to the small space between the moon and the terrain. Restle (1970) was able to

FIGURE 14. Observed (points) and predicted (lines) results of an experiment in which the number and relative size of the context circles in the Ebbinghaus illusion were varied. The value along each curve represents the size of the context circle minus the size of the center circle (after Massaro & Anderson, 1971).

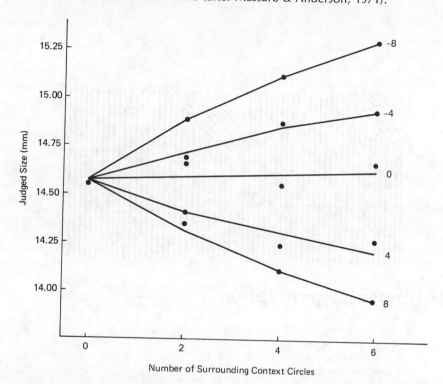

Number of Surrounding Context Circles

predict many of Rock and Kaufman's results quantitatively with his mathematical formulation of this assumption.

We have discussed in detail two widely different theories for visual illusions. Perspective theory is appealing because it attempts to relate mechanisms found in normal visual perception to illusory perception. In contrast, the total impression theory has not been utilized much in the study of normal perception. Although total impression theory seems to provide a more consistent description of illusions, it is unlikely to be accepted by the scientific community until it has been made relevant to much more of normal visual functioning. In the future, we can expect that innovative research and theory in the study of visual illusions will go hand in hand with the study of normal perception. We might predict, also, that neither perspective theory nor total impression theory will be the final answer since research, like perception, requires a constant revision and reconstruction of our hypotheses about the nature of reality.

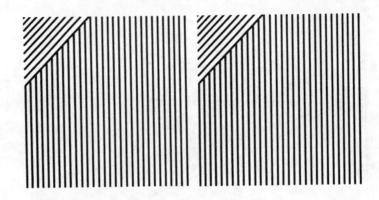

The art of binocular perception

Within-subject designs

The whole visual world and its content is a creation of our inner eye, as we may call the neural visual system . . . , in contrast to the dioptric mechanism, which may be designated the outer eye.
—Ewald Hering (1878)

Since the time of the British empiricists, philosophers and psychologists have distinguished between sensation and perception. Helmholtz, the famous 19th-century scientist, made the clearest distinction between these two processes and he also defined their relationship. Helmholtz thought of visual sensation as a two-dimensional impression but without meaning. Loosely speaking, sensation might accurately describe the response to Lichtenstein's *Cathedral #3* (see Chapter 9) before the figure-ground relationship was determined. Sensations, themselves, can be said to be always in flux. The retinal image changes with changes in eye and head movements and in the distance and orientation of the objects. Perception, on the other hand, gives us the phenomenological appearance of a stable and veridical world. Helmholtz proposed a straightforward process, taking us from sensation to perception. The central focus here is that process, which dominated much of the study of visual perception. The goal of this research is to account for the fact of veridical perception notwithstanding that our sensory inputs are always in flux.

Consider the problem of the perceived size of objects. If Galanter and Galanter (1973) would have asked their observers to judge the size of a series of airplanes at varying distances, the observers might have responded, "How can we accurately judge the size of planes when we don't know how far away they are?" Such an observation expresses the fact that, in order to judge size accurately, distance must be taken into account. Holway and Boring's (1941) experiment was designed to show that accurate perception of distance is necessary for accurate perception of size.

The subject in the experiment sat at the intersection of two

SIZE CONSTANCY

long hallways that met at a right angle. A disk of light that was adjustable in size, called the variable disk, was placed 10 feet away from the observer. In the other hallway, a standard disk was placed from 10 to 120 feet from the observer. The size of the standard disk was increased with increasing distance so that it always subtended a visual angle of 1 degree. The subject's task was to adjust the size of the variable disk of light so that the two disks appeared to be the same size. The independent variable was the distance of the standard disk from the observer and the dependent variable was his setting of the variable disk.

There are two orderly ways the subject can operate in this task. The subject can adjust the variable disk so that its real size is the same as the standard disk or he can adjust the variable disk so that it subtends the same visual angle as that subtended by the standard disk. When the standard and variable disks are the same distance from the observer, both strategies will give the same response. However, the responses of the two strategies diverge as the distance of the standard disk is increased. Figure 1 shows the predicted adjustments of the variable disk using these strategies as a function of the distance of the standard disk. We call the strategy of matching the true size of the standard disk *size constancy* and the strategy of matching the retinal size *retinal size match*. If the subject shows size constancy, the apparent size of the standard disk follows its true size, whereas a retinal size match follows its retinal projection.

FIGURE 1. The perception of size as a function of the distance of the object. The different conditions are described in the text (after Holway & Boring, 1941).

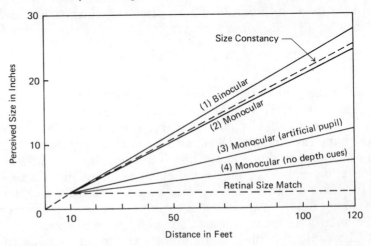

When Holway and Boring did this experiment under conditions of normal binocular (1) or monocular (2) viewing, the subject's adjustments of the variable disk matched the actual size of the standard disk. In Condition (3) however, when the subject had to view the standard disk monocularly through an artificial pupil—a small hole that eliminated some depth cues, such as the sides of the hallways—the judgments fell somewhere between the two strategies. When additional depth cues were eliminated by removing reflections in the hallway (4), the judgments were almost equivalent to the retinal size match. These results reveal that the apparent size of an object is critically dependent upon its perceived distance. If distance cues are available, subjects tend to perceive size veridically; when these cues are eliminated, performance deteriorates and tends towards a retinal size match.

Holway and Boring's experiment demonstrates that we are capable of perceiving the true size of an object at different distances. Their experiment was somewhat unnatural in the sense that the size of the standard had to be changed at different distances in order to maintain a fixed visual angle of 1 degree. Holway and Boring had to increase the size of the standard by a factor of 2 for every doubling of distance. The experimenters could have carried out their study in another manner by having subjects judge objects of the same size at different distances. They would have found that the same object can be perceived as the same size at different distances, which changes the retinal size significantly. Both results show that some process operates to incorporate distance information in the perception of size.

SHAPE CONSTANCY

Analogous to perceived size, perceived shape usually corresponds to objective shape, even though the retinal input changes with changes in spatial orientation of the object. Consider the retinal projections of a coffee cup as the cup is rotated in depth. When the viewer is looking directly inside the cup, so that the plane formed by the rim of the cup is parallel to the viewer's forehead, the projected image of the rim of the cup is a circle and, of course, a circle is seen. However, as the cup is rotated into an upright position, the projected image of the rim of the cup becomes elliptical until only a line is projected when the plane of the rim of the cup is perpendicular to the observer's forehead.

The most striking observation is that the rim of the cup continues to appear circular as the cup is rotated despite the projective transformations of the retinal image. We might assume that the observer has independent access to the object's real shape and that this accounts both for constancy and veridicality. For example, with a coffee cup, context cues such as the handle and other identifiable characteristics indicate that the object is a coffee cup. With these cues, the observer could infer directly that the rim of the cup is circular. In this case, the projected image transformations could be ignored and a circular rim perceived because this perception agrees with what is known about coffee cups. However, the appeal to nonvisual knowledge cannot account completely for shape constancy and veridicality since redundant cues are not in fact necessary for the perception of true shape. If, instead of the rim of a cup, a plain circular ring is viewed under different rotations, shape constancy and veridicality will still be found.

Without additional context cues, the spatial orientation of an object must be incorporated in the perception of shape. Analogous to size perception, we would expect that elimination of orientation cues would interfere with true shape perception and the observation would tend towards a retinal image match. In fact, a number of studies of shape perception have shown that shape constancy breaks down when cues to orientation are reduced or eliminated entirely (Epstein & Park, 1963; Winnick & Rosen, 1966). This analysis indicates that, analogous to the judgment of size, one cannot tell the true shape of an object without accounting for its spatial orientation.

INDUCTIVE INFERENCE

How can we account for veridical perception despite the changes in retinal information? Helmholtz, in the middle of the 19th century, proposed a solution which is still influential in much of today's research and theory in visual perception. Helmholtz first made a distinction between sense impressions and perceptual judgments. This distinction made by Helmholtz corresponds to the distinction made earlier by Reid between sensation and perception. Sensation was the raw impression made by an object, whereas perceptual judgments involved a further step in which the sense impressions were supplied with meaning. Helmholtz's significant contribution was the process he proposed for going from sensation to perception. He stated that our perceptions were determined by inductive inference—an unconscious mental process in which we derive inferences from our sense impressions. Inductive inference in perception was assumed to be analogous to the process of inference in more abstract mental functioning, such as inferences that can be made from a set of assumptions using laws of logic.

In making a distinction between sensations and perceptual judgments based on inductive inference, Helmholtz may have implied that there were two successive stages involved in the per-

Albrecht Dürer's *Draftsman Drawing a Lute* makes apparent Helmholtz's statement: "But objects of unknown and irregular shape baffle the skill of the most consummate artist. . . . Yet when we have these objects in reality before our eyes, a single glance is enough for us to recognize their form" (Helmholtz, 1867).

ceptual process. Helmholtz (1867) said, "We shall succeed much better in forming a correct notion of what we see if we have no opposing sensations to overcome, than if a correct judgment must be formed in spite of them." In our interpretation of Helmholtz, then, the first stage would involve the operations necessary for the sensations to become apparent. The second stage would involve the formation of a perceptual judgment based on inductive inference. In this formulation, the process of inductive inference must occur after the process of sensation, since inference operates on the output of the sensation stage. This model is illustrated in Figure 2.

FIGURE 2. Stage model representing Helmholtz's two-stage theory of perception. The operations of the first stage produce a sensation that becomes available to the second stage, the operation of inductive inference. The outcome of inductive inference is the conscious perception that can be reported by the observer.

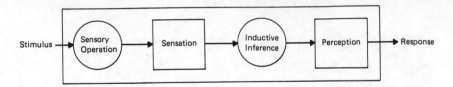

INVARIANCE HYPOTHESIS

A more specific application of Helmholtz's theory of inductive inference is the invariance hypothesis (Beck & Gibson, 1955; Hochberg, 1971; Koffka, 1935). The invariance hypothesis is a descriptive process that accounts for veridical perception, the fact that the perceived object usually corresponds to the real object even though the retinal input changes with changes in the object's distance and orientation. The invariance hypothesis of object perception uses laws of projective geometry to describe the stimulus circumstances that can provide veridical perception of an object.

Size Invariance

The invariance hypothesis of size perception provides the object's true size by incorporating retinal (projected) image size and perceived distance in an algorithm taken from the laws of projective geometry. In this case, size perception also follows a two-stage process similar to the process of inductive inference (see Figure 3).

FIGURE 3. A two-stage process representing the invariance hypothesis of size perception.

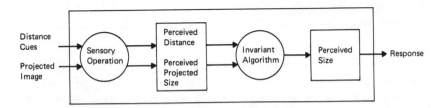

Distance cues and the projected image of the object enter the sensory system, are processed there, and transformed into actual values of apparent distance and apparent retinal image size. These values are then inserted in an equation called an invariance algorithm, which computes the size of the object. Mathematically, the invariance algorithm says that for some fixed retinal image, the ratio of perceived size S to perceived distance D is a constant K:

$$S/D = K \qquad (1)$$

Equation 1 can also be written in the form

$$S = D \cdot K \qquad (2)$$

which says that perceived size S is directly proportional to perceived distance D. For a fixed retinal image size, each doubling of distance should double the perceived size. This equation accurately predicts the results of the Holway and Boring experiment under the different conditions of viewing. When distance cues are available so that distance should be perceived veridically, the observers' judgments should be on the straight line generated by Equation 2. As cues to distance are removed, the sensory system cannot resolve a value for the distance D. In this case, the true size cannot be computed and the observers simply match the retinal images of the two disks.

Shape Invariance

The invariance hypothesis of shape perception provides the object's true shape by incorporating retinal image shape and spatial orientation (slant) in an algorithm based on the laws of projective geometry. This hypothesis can also be interpreted as a two-stage process, illustrated in Figure 4. Depth cues of the object and its

FIGURE 4. A two-stage process representing the invariance hypothesis of shape perception.

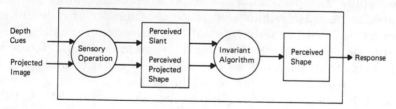

projected retinal image provide the sensory operation with information on slant and projected shape, respectively. The sensory system processes these two inputs and gives values of perceived slant and projected shape. These values are then inserted into the invariance algorithm, which then gives a unique value of perceived shape. Mathematically, for a fixed projected image, perceived shape S is some function of perceived orientation O.

$$S = F(O) \tag{3}$$

The invariance algorithm resembles Helmholtz's process of inductive inference, since its operation occurs after the process of sensation and operates on the values given by that stage. Furthermore, the rules of the invariance algorithm and of inductive inference are not dependent on the structural properties of the perceptual system.

The invariance hypothesis of shape perception can account for veridical perception of shape. The model illustrated in Figure 4 and expressed in Equation 3 shows that perceived shape is uniquely determined by projective shape and apparent slant (Koffka, 1935; Beck & Gibson, 1955). The projected shape is available in the retinal image and apparent slant is determined by depth cues. Support for the invariance algorithm has been found in two paradigms. First, investigators have shown a direct functional relationship between perceived shape and apparent slant as predicted by Equation 3. Second, a number of studies have shown that shape constancy breaks down when cues to orientation are reduced or eliminated entirely (Epstein & Park, 1963; Winnick & Rosen, 1966).

TESTING THE INVARIANCE HYPOTHESIS

Formulation of the inductive inference and the invariance hypothesis in terms of stages leads to a number of experimental questions which were not previously apparent. The rule of thumb of previous work in this field appears to have centered on the specification of stimulus-response relationships. Hence, investigators focused on testing the functional relationships given by Equations 1, 2, and 3 under different stimulus conditions. Our formulation, however, conceptualizing perception as a series of processes rather than as a stimulus-response relationship leads to a number of different experiments. These experiments not only provide information about perception as a process, they also allow us to test the applicability of the invariance hypothesis to a new set of experimental findings.

We seek the rules that describe each stage of processing involved in object perception. One method of discovering these rules is to measure the time it takes for each process as a function of certain independent variables. Using this logic, the present author carried out a series of experiments aimed at illuminating the shape perception process (Massaro, 1973). These experiments also allowed a test of the present formulation of the invariance hypothesis of shape perception. Following Donders, it was assumed that shape judgments involve a sequence of psychological processes (stages) between presentation of the stimulus and the observer's response.

In fact, the Donders type B reaction time (RT) paradigm was used. There were two possible stimuli and two possible responses. On each trial, one of the stimuli was randomly selected and shown to the observer who had to recognize it as quickly as possible by making the appropriate response. The stimulus figures were two-dimensional shapes cut out of plastic, chosen to be fairly similar. A circle and an ellipse (shown in Figure 5) were employed as the two figures. The observer was required to hit one button if the circle was presented and the other button if the ellipse was presented. The independent variable was the orientation (rotation) of the figure in

FIGURE 5. The circle and ellipse stimuli used in Massaro's (1973) study.

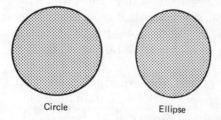

Circle   Ellipse

depth. The dependent variables were the RT and the percentage of correct responses in the task.

Figure 6 shows a simple stage model of this task. The observer can be conceptualized as first determining the shape of the figure in the perception stage. The perception stage corresponds to the stage of processing which is of central concern in this chapter. After perceiving the shape, some comparison must be made with the possible alternatives in the task. That is to say, the subject could perceive a figure of a certain shape before he knows which alternative it is. The comparison process allows the subject to compare the perceived shape with the alternatives in memory. The observer then selects the response that agrees with the outcome of the comparison process. The simplest assumption is that each of these stages is independent and sequential as indicated in Figure 6. Each stage takes

FIGURE 6. An information-processing model of the shape judgment task. The time to complete each state of processing is independent of the time taken by preceding or following stages.

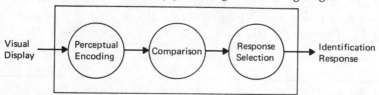

Within-Subject Designs

In the experiments carried out by Massaro (1973), practiced subjects were tested under all experimental conditions repeatedly throughout the study. The first day was completely devoted to practice and the data disregarded. On the next four days the subjects received repeated presentations of all of the experimental conditions in a randomized fashion. This kind of experiment allows us to derive a function for each subject that relates reaction time or percentage errors to the levels of the independent variable. A between-subject design in which different subjects are tested under different experimental conditions would be inefficient and inappropriate. The experiment can be considered a two-factor design with type of figure (circle or ellipse) and slant of figure (0, 13, 26, 39, 52, 65, or 78) as the two independent variables. To do a between-groups design would require seven groups of subjects, one for each slant condition. The type of figure must be a within-subject variable so that the subject would have two responses available. Otherwise, he could just hit the same button on each trial without looking at the figure.

In a between-groups design, the experimenter would probably need at least five or ten subjects for each group to eliminate major differences due to different subjects in each group. However, he probably will never eliminate individual differences completely in this task. Subjects tested under just one experimental condition might employ different strategies than if they were tested under all conditions. Since the subject in the between-group design knows the slant before the figure is presented, he might be able to short-circuit the normal shape perception process by simply operating on the size of the projected shape. Therefore, the between-groups design does not control for differences in strategies under the different experimental conditions. This is the same reason that the experimental conditions are randomized from trial to trial in the within-groups experiment. If the subject knew which condition was to be presented, he could switch strategies. Randomizing the trials is the best insurance for the subject to operate within the same strategy under all experimental conditions.

The subjects should be practiced on the task before the RTs are recorded, because other processes such as response selection and execution improve significantly and rapidly during the first 50 to 200 trials. Therefore, the average RT decreases markedly during this time. Since the early RTs are larger, they will contribute more to the overall average. Furthermore, early in the experiment, the subject makes more foolish mistakes, like hitting the wrong button even though he knows the right answer. Practicing the subject is also important for reducing his anxiety in the task. Early in the game he does not know what is involved and may feel threatened. The first series of trials is necessary to convince him that he can handle the task easily and to simply adopt a constant level of motivation.

some finite time and gives information to the following stage. The time to complete a stage is independent of the time it takes to complete preceding or following stages.

Shape Judgment Task

The task in the first experiment required observers to identify the physical shape of the single flat figures (circle or ellipse) presented either on a frontal parallel plane or at one of six rotations (13, 26, 39, 52, 65, or 78 degrees) about the vertical axis. The observers were explicitly instructed to respond to objective shape. The instructions encouraged the subject to respond as rapidly as possible but to avoid making errors. Each trial was initiated by the opening of a rotating shutter that exposed the test figure. The subjects pressed one button if the figure was a circle and another button with their opposite hand if the figure was an ellipse.

The five subjects were sufficiently practiced in the task on the day before the actual experiment began. The subjects were then tested an hour a day for four successive days. Accordingly, the results represent the judgments of highly sophisticated observers. Furthermore, all levels of the independent variables were presented randomly from trial to trial rather than between days or blocks of trials. The 14 possible combinations of 2 test figures x 7 rotation conditions were randomized within blocks of 14 trials. There were five blocks of trials per day, giving a total of 70 trials per day. The randomization of all events within a session is the best control for the effects of changes in motivation and strategies over the course of the experiment.

Figure 7 presents the RTs of the correct judgments as a function of angle of rotation. For all observers, increasing the angle of rotation beyond 26 degrees increased RTs in a positively accelerated manner. As shown in the figure, percentage errors also increased in the same way with increases in angle of rotation. This result is a common one in RT studies in which accuracy is stressed. Although the error rate is relatively low, there is usually a positive correlation between RT and percentage errors. What the correlation means here is that the RT function would have increased even more with increases in rotation if the experimenter had been successful in holding percentage errors constant at all levels of the independent variable.

The principal finding of this experiment is that the time necessary for performing the shape judgment task increases with degree of rotation. It is now necessary to identify the stage of processing that is responsible for this increase. It is possible that perception time

Responsibility for RT increases

FIGURE 7. Mean RTs of correct judgments and mean percentage errors as a function of angle of rotation of the circle and ellipse test figures (after Massaro, 1973).

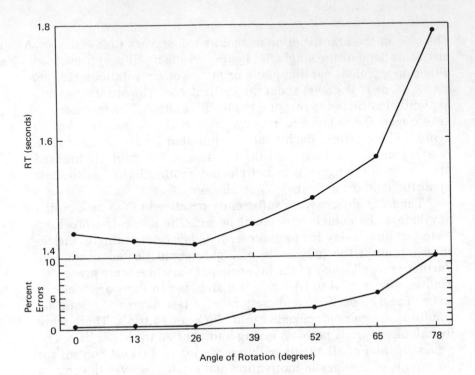

and comparison time could increase with increases in degree of rotation. However, it is unlikely that the increase in RT across rotation reflects increases in the response selection stage. Logically, there is no reason why rotation should affect response selection, since it is assumed that the shape judgment is completed before response selection begins. A number of previous studies have reported results that indicate response selection time is not dependent on the time needed to complete earlier stages of the RT task (see Chapters 3 and 4). Accordingly, we can safely reject the possibility that increases in rotation significantly affected the time for response selection.

The comparison stage might account for the RT increase with increases in degree of rotation. The observer, faced with an absolute judgment task, could have adopted the following strategy in the task. First, he would learn and remember the exact shape of the circle and ellipse used in the experiment. Then after he perceives the test figure on each trial, he could compare its shape with the memory representations of the circle and ellipse. This strategy involves a memory comparison that might account for the increase in RTs with increasing orientation. For example, it is possible that the observer would hold a visual image of the test figure as it was seen in the frontal-parallel plane. Accordingly, if the figure is presented in the frontal-parallel plane, matching time would be minimal. Increasing the rotation of the figure would slow down the matching process. The observer would have to operate on the shape of the figure presented or the representation of the standard in memory to align their orientations. A mental operation of this sort, a rotation in imagination, has been alluded to by Helmholtz (1867), and more recently by Shepard and Metzler (1971).

Shepard and Metzler (1971) have also studied shape judgments in an RT task. In their task, perspective line drawings of three-dimensional objects were used as stimulus figures. Figure 8 shows two pairs of objects, each of which was built with ten solid cubes attached face-to-face forming an arm-like structure with three right-angle elbows. Subjects were presented with two perspective views and had to report whether the two objects were the same or differ-

Shepard and Metzler task

FIGURE 8. Examples of the pairs of perspective line drawings used by Shepard and Metzler (1971). A is a "same" pair which differs by an 80° rotation in depth. B is a "different" pair which cannot be brought into congruence by rotation.

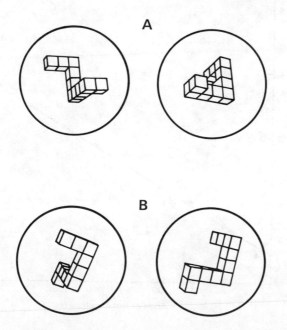

ent in actual shape. The two objects are the same if one of the perspective views can be rotated into the other. Subjects pressed one button if the figures were perspective drawings of the same object and another button if they were not. The investigators took different perspective projections corresponding to a complete rotation along the vertical axis, choosing different views of each figure for pairwise presentations. For the independent variable, the difference in orientation between the two perspective views of the same shape was systematically varied. The "different" trials contained one of the original figures of a "same" trial, but it was paired with the other figure reflected about some plane in three-dimensional space. The dependent variable was the RT in the same-different task recorded as a function of differences in orientation for the same pairs. The subjects were well-practiced and knew the direction of the required rotation that, in the case of "same" pairs, would bring the object on the left into congruence with the object on the right through the minimal angle.

The results shown in Figure 9 indicate that RT was a linear function of the angular difference between two projections of the

FIGURE 9. RTs for "same" responses as a function of the angular differences between two projections in depth of the same three-dimensional object (after Shepard & Metzler, 1971).

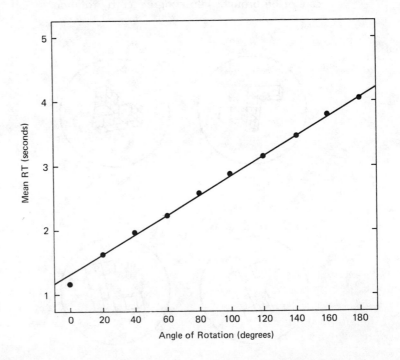

same three-dimensional object. Reaction times to different pairs cannot be plotted with respect to angular differences in rotation, since one figure does not rotate into the other. However, the overall mean RT for different pairs was nearly one second longer than the overall mean RT for same pairs.

Shepard and Metzler interpreted their results as reflecting a process of "mental rotation in three-dimensional space" (p. 703). The fact that RT was a linear function of rotation differences between the two projections is compatible with the idea that subjects rotated one figure into another at a fixed rate. Employing this interpretation, the slope of the "same" RTs indicated that the observers were able to rotate the objects at about 60 degrees per second.

The rotation hypothesis itself might even account for our task in which single figures—a circle or an ellipse—were presented and the observer had to identify the figure. In this experiment, we could assume that the observer maintains a mental representation of how the circle and ellipse look in the frontal-parallel plane. Presented with a figure oriented in depth, the observer first perceives the figure and then rotates that figure to the frontal-parallel plane, comparing it to his mental representations of how these figures look in the frontal-parallel plane. Given that the amount of rotation would increase with increases in angle of rotation, we could obtain the results that were observed in Figure 7.

Test of rotation hypothesis

It is, therefore, necessary to provide a test of the rotation hypothesis of the comparison stage in the experimental paradigm with circles and ellipses. Consider the following qualitative test of whether the rotation hypothesis can provide a sufficient account of the increase in RT with increases in orientation in depth experiments. The rotation hypothesis says that the important variable in the same-different experiment with two figures is the difference in rotation between the two figures. An experiment was conducted by Massaro (1973) which held the difference in rotation constant by presenting both figures at the same orientation while the absolute orientation was varied. Instead of making an absolute judgment, observers were now required to say whether the objects were the same or different in shape. The rotation theory of the comparison process predicts that RT should not differ across the conditions of absolute rotation, because no rotation is required to determine whether the figures are the same or different when the figures are presented in the same orientation. Therefore, RT should be constant across levels of absolute rotation if the rotation operation is critical in the shape judgment task with circles and ellipses rotated in real depth. The four possible figure pairs (circle/circle, circle/ellipse,

ellipse/ellipse, ellipse/circle) were presented at each level of rotation (0, 13, 26, 39, 52, 65, and 78 degrees) about the vertical axis. The observers performing the same-different task were informed that the two forms on each trial would always be presented in the same orientation. Both figures were rotated in the counter-clockwise direction so that the figures were presented in parallel planes.

The results presented in Figure 10 show that mean percentage RT increased with increases in absolute angle of rotation in a positively accelerated manner. When the figures were presented in parallel planes, comparison should not require any mental rotation since one figure does not have to be rotated into the other but can be compared directly. Even so, RTs increased with increases in degree of absolute rotation. The results disconfirm the rotation hypothesis as a sufficient condition for the RT functions in the

FIGURE 10. Mean RTs of correct "same" and "different" judgments as a function of the angle of rotation of both figures (after Massaro, 1973).

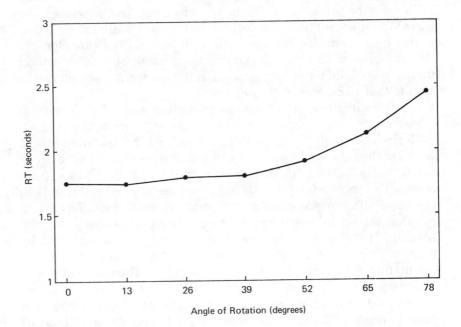

circle-ellipse experiment. Since the two figures were always equal in angle of rotation, no difference in RT should be expected if rotation was a sufficient condition for increases in RT. Therefore, the mechanism responsible for increasing RT with increases in absolute rotation is not due to processing at the comparison stage.

The experiments and analyses appear to show that the comparison and the response selection processes cannot account for the increase in RT with increases in degree of rotation. Accordingly, this increase must be located at the perception stage. The experiments, therefore, speak to the invariance hypothesis of the perception stage. Massaro now carried out a series of experiments that provided a test of the invariance hypothesis. According to the interpretation of the invariance hypothesis given here, the increase in RT with increases in degree of rotation could be caused by three possible functions. In the first stage, the subject determines the projected shape and the orientation of the figures. Either of these functions could take more time with increases in degree of rotation. After determining the projected shape and orientation, the invariance algorithm is performed at the second stage to determine actual shape. The time for this process might also increase with degree of rotation. The following experiments were carried out to see if the increase in RT could be located at one of these stages. If it cannot, the process responsible for the increase cannot be explained by the invariance hypothesis.

Testing the Invariance Hypothesis of the Perception Stage

FIGURE 11. Mean RTs of correct shape judgments as a function of the angle of rotation of the standard and comparison figures. (In this task, subjects were required to respond "same" or "different" with respect to objective shape.) (After Massaro, 1973.)

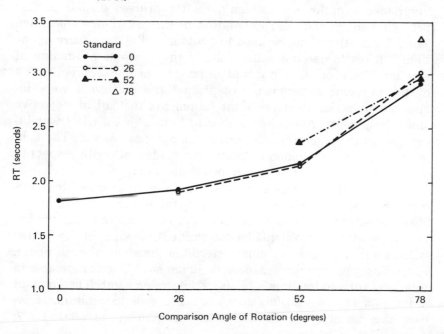

The first experiment is intended to replicate the earlier studies and to provide a paradigm for the tests of the invariance hypothesis. The same circle and ellipse figures were used and two figures were presented on a trial. The least rotated figure of the pair, designated the standard, was presented at rotations of 0, 26, 52, or 78 degrees. The other figure, designated the comparison, was presented at the same rotation as the standard, or rotated further in depth, giving 10 possible rotation combinations: 0–0, 0–26, 0–52, 0–78, 26–26, 26–52, 26–78, 52–52, 52–78, and 78–78. Of course, each of the 4 possible figure pairs was presented at each rotation combination. Again, the observers were told to respond "same" or "different" as rapidly as possible, with respect to objective shape, while maintaining a high level of accuracy.

Figure 11 presents the RTs as a function of the orientation of the two figures. The RTs are directly related to the absolute rotation of the two figures and cannot be described adequately as a function of the relative rotation differences. For example, both figures presented in the frontal-parallel plane give a mean RT of 1.823 sec., whereas both figures oriented at 78° give a mean latency of 3.336 sec.

Time needed to determine slant

The next experiment asks if the increase in RT with increases in rotation can be accounted for by the time it takes to determine the slant of the figures. To test this, instead of asking for true shape judgments, we ask for slant judgments directly. According to the invariance hypothesis, this eliminates the process of determining projected shape and the computation of the invariance algorithm. The RT can, therefore, be used to provide a direct measure of the time it takes to determine the slant of the figure as a function of rotation. The procedure of this experiment was an exact replication of the previous experiment except that the observers were instructed to make objective slant judgments instead of objective shape judgments. Also, the number of "same" slant trials was increased so that the probability of a "same" trial was .5. The subjects were told to respond to "same" or "different" with respect to slant and to ignore the actual shapes of the figures.

The results in Figure 12 indicate that the time needed to determine the slant of a figure is not directly related to increases in the absolute rotation of the figures. Consider the trials in which the figures were at the same slant. To determine if the slant of the figures is the same, the observer must determine the slant of each figure. Accordingly, if the increase in shape judgment RT with increases in rotation is due to the time it takes to determine slant, RTs for slant judgments should also increase with increases in rotation. However, they do not. The RTs for "same" responses are 1.637, 1.937,

FIGURE 12. Mean RTs of correct judgments as a function of the angle of rotation of the standard and comparison figures. (In this task, subjects were required to respond "same" or "different" with respect to objective slant.) (After Massaro, 1973.)

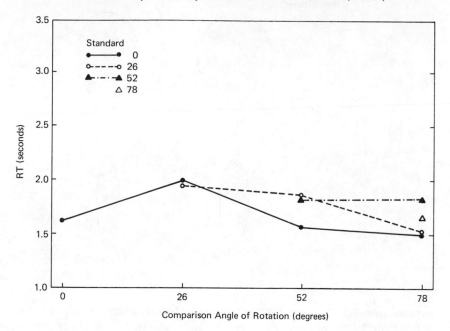

1.778, and 1.634 sec. for absolute slants of 0, 26, 52, and 78 degrees of rotation, respectively. Therefore, in judging true shape the increase in RT with increases in rotation cannot be attributed to the time it takes to perceive slant.

In the framework of the invariance hypothesis, the second and remaining possibility for the RT increase in the first sensory stage of processing is the time it takes to determine the projected shape. In this task as in most shape judgments, the projected images of the two figures (circle and ellipse) become more similar as the figures are rotated in depth. Figure 13, presenting the frontal-parallel projections of the circle and ellipse as the figures are rotated in depth, shows that the projections of the circle and ellipse become much more similar to each other. It seems highly possible, therefore, that determination of projected shape would become much more difficult as the figures are rotated in depth. For example, determination of the projected shape at the 26° rotation can be carried out fairly rapidly, since there is a large difference between the projections of the circle and ellipse. The observer can then respond more rapidly. On the other hand, at the 65° rotation, the projection of the circle

Time needed to determine projected shape

FIGURE 13. The projections of the circle and ellipse as the figures are rotated in depth to 26 and 65 degrees (after Massaro, 1973).

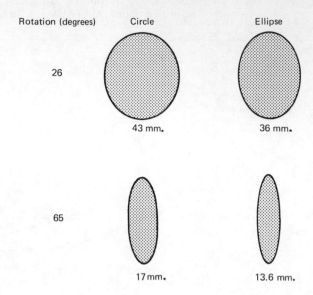

and ellipse are very similar to each other and might require much more time to process. Therefore, the increase in RT of shape judgments with increases in rotation might be due to the increase in similarity of the projections of the circle and ellipse as the figures are rotated in depth. This would influence the time it takes to determine projected shape in terms of the invariance hypothesis.

To test this, we must record the time it takes subjects to distinguish between the different projections and compare this time to the time found in our standard shape judgment task. To this end, the same-different shape judgment experiment was replicated. But trials were included that contained figures in the frontal-parallel plane which gave the same projected images as the figures rotated in depth. If there are no differences between these two types of trials (rotated and frontal-parallel), then we can conclude that RT increases with increases in rotation because of the corresponding increases in similarity of the two-dimensional projections. Accordingly, the RT increase could be accounted for by the invariance hypothesis with additional processing for determining projected shape when the figure is rotated in depth.

Since the two retinal projections of the figures differ, the projection of the figures was taken at a point halfway between the two eyes. The extreme slant of 78° had to be eliminated in the present experiment since the projections were very similar for the circle and ellipse, respectively. This fact is interesting in terms of the invariance hypothesis, which states that the projected image and slant are sufficient for reliable shape judgments. Accordingly, the observers should not have been able to perform the shape judgment task at 78° rotation if the invariance hypothesis were true. In the present study, figures were presented at 65° instead of 78°, so that all the figures representing projected shape in the frontal-parallel plane could have different and, therefore, discriminable projections for the circle and ellipse.

The same-different experiment was then replicated with the exception that 65° rotation was substituted for the 78° rotation. Projected shape trial types were added to provide a test of the hypothesis that the increase in RT with increases in angle of rotation is due to increased difficulty in determining projected shape. The pairs of projections were presented in the frontal-parallel plane. The projection trials correspond to the trials in which the figures are presented at the same slant. The figures were either the same or different in objective shape depending on whether the projections were from the same figure or from two different figures. Therefore, half of the projected shape trials were the same in objective shape. The projected shape trials will be compared directly to their analogous trials that involve a rotation in depth. For example, when the figures are rotated to 65°, the large RT could be due to the fact that the two-dimensional projections of the circle and ellipse are very similar. If this is the case, the RT to their corresponding projections in the frontal-parallel plane should also be very long and RT should not differ under the two conditions.

The results indicate that the similarity in projected shapes with increases in rotation cannot account for the increase in perception time in the shape judgment task. Figure 14 shows that RT increased from 1.948 to 3.280 sec. with increases in rotation of the figures presented at the same slant in depth. However, RTs to the projected shapes presented in the frontal-parallel plane increased only slightly (1.976 to 2.133 sec.) as the projected shapes became more similar. The results then support the idea that distinguishing between shapes may become slightly more difficult as their projected shapes become more similar. However, this process is not sufficient to account for the large increases in RT with increases in degree of rotation.

The results indicate that the increase in RT in shape judgments cannot be completely accounted for by extra processing time in the first stage of the two-stage model given by the invariance hypothesis. The final possibility is that the increase in RT is due to the

Time needed to compute invariance algorithm

FIGURE 14. The continuous curve gives mean RTs of correct "same" and "different" judgments of the circle and ellipse figures as a function of the angle of rotation. The dashed line function gives mean RTs to the corresponding projections of the rotated figures. The projections were presented in the frontal-parallel plane (after Massaro, 1973).

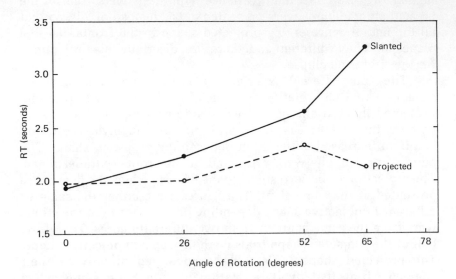

second stage of processing: the time to compute the invariance algorithm. This alternative, however, can be rejected on logical grounds. The time for the computational algorithm follows the determination of the values that are inserted in the equation. The time to compute the true shape should not depend on the actual values for projected shape and slant because the same equation is used in all cases. For example, if the invariance algorithm were implemented on a digital computer, the number of computational steps would not differ with changes in the values of projected shape and slant. Accordingly, the two stages of processing postulated by the invariance hypothesis cannot account for the time it takes to determine the shape of a figure rotated in depth.

The results contradict the assumption that shape perception can be understood by analyzing the processes involved in perceiving projected shape and slant of the figure. The experiments have shown that the time to perceptually encode shape is dependent on the degree of rotation of the figure. In contrast, the time to encode slant information and projected image information does not increase significantly with increases in degree of rotation. In the terminology of the invariance hypothesis, the time to obtain information about projected shape and slant does not depend on degree of rotation, whereas the time to perceive objective shape is critically dependent on degree of rotation.

Our empirical tests and logical analysis support our earlier statements concerning inductive inference and the invariance hypothesis. These theories seemed to be aimed at describing perception as a stimulus-response relationship rather than a dynamic process that occurs over time. Although the invariance hypothesis offers a method to compute the actual shape of an object given its projected shape and slant, it does not describe accurately how, in fact, shape perception occurs. Consider, for example, a model taken from the laws of mathematics to describe how two numbers are added. One problem of adding 3 to 5 can be described by a mathematical process of adding 1 to 5 three times. This mathematical solution is psychologically unrealistic if our solution involves a simple direct access to the answer in memory. Analogously, although the invariance hypothesis can describe the outcome of most shape judgments, it does not describe how humans do, in fact, make shape judgments. Even so, we cannot expect that the invariance hypothesis will be discarded until another theory takes its place. Conant (1947, p. 36) states that "a theory is only overthrown by a better theory, never merely by contradictory facts."

Rejection of Invariance Hypothesis

With these thoughts in mind, it is necessary to consider a perceptual processing model of shape judgments that can describe the effects of rotation on RT. This theory must be consistent with four results. First, the above experiments have located the effect of absolute rotation on the perception stage. Second, the time to perceive the true shape of a figure is critically dependent on the degree of rotation of the stimulus figure. Third, the increase in RT with increases in degree of rotation is not due to the fact that the two-dimensional projections of the figures become more similar as the figures are rotated in depth. Fourth, the time needed to determine the rotation (slant) of a figure does not depend on degree of rotation.

A MODEL OF THE PERCEPTUAL PROCESS

Figure 15 presents a flow diagram of our model of the shape perception process. Viewing a visual display produces two retinal inputs; the sensation process makes this information available to preperceptual visual storage. The recognition or perception process involves a readout of this information, which produces a percept in synthesized visual memory. The properties of preperceptual visual storage and synthesized visual memory are analyzed in detail in

FIGURE 15. A flow diagram model of the shape perception process.

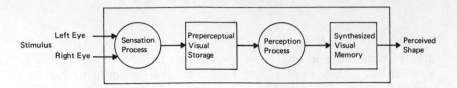

Chapters 12, 17, 18, and 26. For now, it is enough to know that preperceptual visual storage can hold the information from only one eye fixation. The recognition process transforms the preperceptual information into a synthesized percept in synthesized visual memory, which can integrate the percepts from the last three or four eye fixations. Before defining the model further, we must discuss properties of the visual system that are important in binocular visual perception.

The Horopter   When the eyes are looking at a point in infinity, the line of sight of the right eye is parallel to the line of sight of the left eye. In this case, the same image falls on each retina and stimulates corresponding retinal points. Corresponding retinal points are linked by the fibers of the optic tract to a common locus in the visual projection area of the cortex. For example, when one observes the sky at night and fixates on a star, the images of all the stars would fall on corresponding retinal points. But when one fixates on an object closer in space like the page of a book, only some of the objects in space will produce images that fall on corresponding retinal points. The loci of all points in space which stimulate corresponding retinal points is defined as the horopter. When the eyes are fixated on a point in space, the horopter approximates a circle passing through the points of fixation and the center of curvatures of the two eyeballs (shown in Figure 16). The perception of the points in space is critically dependent on their distance from the horopter. Points on or near the horopter are seen most clearly; points farther from the horopter appear blurred and sometimes double images can be seen. Figure 17 depicts Peter Paul Rubens' view of an early study of the horopter.

To demonstrate the horopter, put a coin in each hand, and hold out both hands side by side. Maintain your fixation on one coin while moving the other slowly closer or farther away. Do not change your fixation—concentrating on the writing of the coin may help. You should notice blurring of the one coin as it is moved off the horopter of the other.

FIGURE 16. In some cases the horopter approximates a circle passing through the point of fixation and centers of curvature of the two eyeballs.

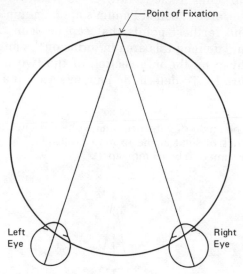

Point of Fixation

Left Eye

Right Eye

FIGURE 17. Rubens' drawing of the original horopter apparatus of Franciscus Aguilonius (1613). As can be seen in the drawing, the student assistants were extremely enthusiastic and took an active interest in their mentor's work.

Panum's Area The recognition process can only read out or resolve the figure-ground relationship of the points in space that are sufficiently close to the horopter. Exactly how close was first determined by Panum, and this area is called Panum's area. Panum's area includes the nearest and farthest points that can be seen clearly without blurring. Panum defined this area in terms of the angle of vergence —the angle given by the intersection of the two lines of sight as shown in Figure 18. To determine Panum's area at a given fixation,

FIGURE 18. The angle of vergence γ given by the intersection of the two lines of sight at the fixation point FP. The eyes L and R are assumed to be 65 mm. apart.

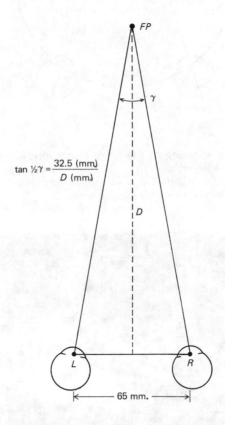

we subtract the angle of vergence given by the farthest points that can be seen clearly from the angle of vergence given by the nearest points. Panum defined this area to be about 6 to 10 min. of visual angle. It is possible that in our shape judgment task the recognition process during one fixation could only resolve the figure-ground relationship within Panum's area.

In our shape judgment task, an object rotated in depth outside of Panum's area could not be perceived completely in one eye fixation. In this case, additional eye fixations are necessary to perceive the complete figure. Two types of eye movements are important in the shape judgment task: saccadic and vergence eye movements. A saccadic eye movement is initiated to direct a given part of the visual display to the foveal region where best resolution can be achieved. Saccadic eye movements involve a sharp rotation of the optical axes and give nearly identical movements for both eyes. The duration of saccades is very brief, ranging between 10 and 70 msec., depending on the magnitude of the change in visual direction. The vergence eye movement is necessary to change the point of fixation in space, defining a new horopter for recognition. Vergence movements (convergence or divergence of the optical axes) are about ten to twenty times slower than saccades and occur independently of saccadic eye movements. In all cases the vergence movement achieves a change in the depth of the point of fixation. When an observer is presented with a two-dimensional object rotated in depth, both of these eye movements are necessary to determine the shape of the figure. A saccadic eye movement rotates the eyes to bring part or all of the figure into the foveal region. The vergence movement occurs to fixate the eyes at the appropriate point in space. It is necessary to fixate at the depth of the figure, so that the figure can be clearly seen, making recognition possible. Consider the case in which the figure is rotated in depth. This manipulation affects saccadic and vergence movements differently. As the figure is rotated in depth, it presents a smaller visual angle and, therefore, it will be easier for a saccade to bring the projection into foveal vision. The opposite is the case for vergence movements. If the observer verges at the axis of rotation of the figure, more of the figure will be off the horopter as it is rotated in depth and, hence, less of the figure can be recognized in one eye fixation. Accordingly, a greater number of vergence movements are necessary as the figure is rotated in depth.

Saccadic and vergence eye movements

Our analysis has shown that the perception process during a given eye fixation can occur only within a limited field of view. Recognition of a visual scene is limited by its horizontal extension, its vertical extension, and how far it extends in depth. The critical variable in the RT experiments was the extension in depth of the test figures. Rotation variations in the circle and ellipse experiments affected the extension in depth of the test figure. Table 1 presents the differences in the angles of vergence between the nearest and farthest points of the test figures as a function of degree of rotation. The

Extension in depth

TABLE 1

Differences in Angles of Vergence in Minutes between the Nearest and
Farthest Points of Different Test Figures as a Function of Degree of Rotation

Angle of Rotation (degrees)	Horizontal Diameter of Test Figures (cm.)			
	Circle and Ellipse		Two Ellipses	
	5.1	4.3	2.2	1.7
0	0	0	0	0
13	4	4	2	2
26	10	8	4	4
39	14	12	6	4
52	16	14	8	6
65	18	16	8	6
78	20	16	8	6

vertical axes of the figures were at a distance of 73 cm. from the observer. The circle had a diameter of 5.1 cm., and the ellipse had a vertical axis of 5.1 cm. and a horizontal axis of 4.3 cm. As can be seen in the table, the extension in depth of the figure increases significantly with increases in degree of rotation. Since recognition of the test figure can only occur within roughly 6 to 10 min. of the horopter, degree of rotation would determine how much of the figure was perceived in a given eye fixation. It follows that the number of eye fixations and, hence, the time needed to determine the shape of the figure would increase with increases in degree of rotation. The results in Figure 11 (p. 225) support this prediction since RTs increase with increases in degree of rotation of the figures.

Our recognition model can also account for the finding that the time to make slant judgments does not depend on degree of rotation. In the slant judgment task, the observer does not have to resolve the true shape of the figure but only has to process its slant. Since the figure is flat, its slant can be determined at any small portion of the figure. Therefore, even though the figure is rotated in depth, enough of it lies within Panum's area for slant recognition. In this case, additional eye fixations are not needed as the figure is rotated in depth, and perception time should not increase with increases in degree of rotation of the figure. Accordingly, our model is also consistent with the finding that the time for slant judgments remains constant across degree of rotation.

Test of Perceptual Process Model The present model assumes that the time needed to resolve the shape of a figure increases with increases in the extension in depth of the figure. The present model, therefore, can be distinguished from the invariance hypothesis, which assumes that degree of rotation is a critical independent variable. The critical test between the two theories is straightforward. If we choose two test figures that are much narrower than those used in our shape judgment task, the theories make different predictions. If angle of rotation is the critical variable, the results should resemble those shown in Figure 11 (p. 225). On the other hand, if extension in depth is critical, the increase in RTs with increases in degree of rotation should be diminished. We chose two ellipses with horizontal diameters of 2.2 cm. and 1.7 cm., respectively. The vertical diameter was kept at 5.1 cm. The extensions in depth of these figures as a function of rotation are given in Table 1. In this study we replicated the experiment whose results are shown in Figure 11. All procedural conditions were kept the same except that, in this experiment, a 65° rotation was used instead of the 78° rotation. This was necessary since very little of the surface area of the small figures was visible at 78°, making identification impossible.

The results disconfirm the invariance hypothesis and support the perceptual process model. Figure 19 shows that RTs to the narrow test figures do not increase sharply with increases in angle

FIGURE 19. Mean RTs of correct shape judgments as a function of the angle of rotation of the narrow standard and comparison figures. The three panels are for three different observers (unpublished data of Massaro, 1973).

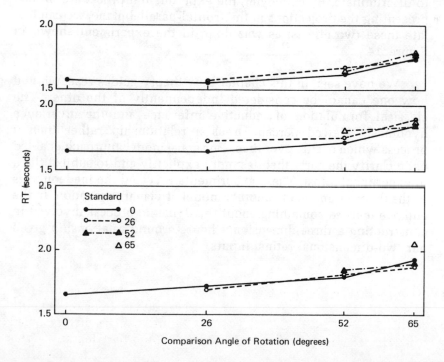

of rotation. These results, contrasted with those in Figure 11, show that extension in depth is the critical variable that affects perception time, not absolute degree of rotation. Reaction times to the figures in the frontal parallel plane did not differ significantly for the narrow and wide figures. In this case, both sets of figures lie on the horopter and perceptual processing time would be minimal. As the figures are rotated in depth, RTs increase sharply for the large figures relative to the small increase for the small figures.

Reaction time does show some increase when the small figures are rotated to 65°. This result cannot be accounted for by the additional processing time needed as the figure is extended farther in depth, since the 65° rotation does not extend the figure significantly farther in depth than the 52° rotation. The increase in RTs at 65°, then, is not due to the perceptual processing time necessary for additional vergence eye movements. The increase probably reflects the fact that the perceived figures become significantly more similar when the figures are rotated to 65°. Very little of the surface area of the small figures is visible at 65°. At 78° identification of the small figures is impossible since almost all of the surface area is rotated out of view. Therefore, the results indicate that rotation of figures in depth can increase RTs in two independent ways. First, rotation increases the extension of the figures in depth, which increases perceptual processing time. Second, rotation increases the similarity of the figures seen in depth, making them more difficult to discriminate. By employing the experimental procedure of also presenting the projections in the frontal-parallel plane, we can isolate these two effects, as was done in the experiment shown in Figure 14.

We have seen in this chapter how theory guides research and how one cannot be considered independently of the other. The classical formulation of inductive inference and the invariance hypothesis viewed perception as a relationship rather than a process which occurs over time. Our stage model approach enabled us to clarify the early theories more explicitly and to subject them to experimental test. These experiments revealed the inadequacies of the theories and led to another model of visual perception. In the end, we learned something about the dynamic process involved in constructing a three-dimensional figure-ground relationship given our two-dimensional retinal inputs.

ATTENTION

Los Angeles County Museum of Art, Serape Style, 1850–1860, Mr. William H. Claflin, Boston (detail).

The span of apprehension

This law is that the greater the number of objects to which our consciousness is simultaneously extended, the smaller is the intensity with which it is able to consider each.
—Sir William Hamilton (1859)

Since the invention of the tachistoscope, experimental psychologists and reading instructors have flashed visual displays for short time periods and required the observer to report what he saw. The paradigm gave results that agreed with Sir William Hamilton's law of the span of apprehension, which represents the number of items that can be processed and held in parallel. We can only report back four or five items in the visual display. Sperling (1960) carried out a series of studies for his doctoral dissertation which illuminated the processing stage responsible for the phenomenon. It is safe to say that Sperling's experiments have been one focal point in the last five to ten years of theory and research in visual information processing.

SPERLING STUDY

Sperling was interested in finding the amount of information a subject could take in during one fixation between saccadic movements. With a tachistoscope he presented a visual display to observers for 50-msec, a period shorter than the duration of a single eye fixation between eye movements. For his stimuli he chose letters of the alphabet, and as the independent variable he varied the number of letters in a single display from 3 to 12. Aware that subjects could remember more items if they recoded them, he prevented the recoding of letters into words by using only consonant letters. The observer was given a score sheet marked off like the actual display, and he was instructed to write down the letters in the same location on the sheet as they appeared to him on the display. A letter was recorded as correct if it was written in on the score sheet in the correct location.

Sperling's results can be plotted as the number of items reported correctly as a function of the number of items in the display.

If subjects were perfectly correct through 12 items, the graph would show a straight line at 45 degrees. This possible result and the actual results are shown in Figure 1. What Sperling found, however, was that the function leveled off or asymptoted at about 4½ items correct. Presented with a 3- or 4-item display, subjects could report all the items in their correct locations. With more than four items

FIGURE 1. Number of letters correctly reported as a function of the number of letters in the display. The 45° diagonal represents perfect performance (after Sperling, 1960).

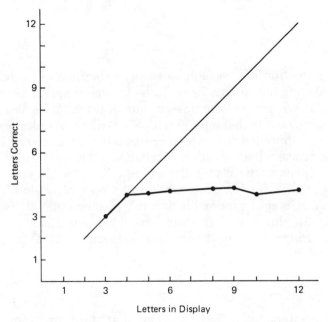

in the display, however, the correct number recalled averaged only about 4½ letters. Thus, the experiment demonstrated that subjects cannot report back more than 4 or 5 items, regardless of the display size.

Recognition and Memory

Sperling saw that this limitation could be due to two stages of information processing. To report the items correctly, the subject must first recognize and then remember the test letters. It was possible that subjects could not recognize more than four or five items, that this represented the limit of the amount of visual information that subjects had available. Given that the duration of the test flash was so short, subjects may have only had sufficient time to read (recognize) 4 or 5 items. In this case, Sperling would have obtained the answer to his question of how much information can be recognized during a single saccadic eye fixation. A second possibility had to be considered, however. The subjects might have recognized more than 4 or 5 letters, but were unable to remember more than 4 or 5 in order to report them when the display was terminated. This would be a limitation not of the visual system but of immediate memory.

Sperling reasoned that if the limitation lay only with the recognition stage, then increasing the duration of the display should overcome it. He therefore repeated the experiment, using 6 or 8 test letters and adding as an independent variable the duration of the display. If the amount of information recognized in one eye fixation was 4 items, the subject could then recognize 8 items in two eye fixations. Accordingly, a longer display lasting 500 msec. should permit him to recall all 8 items. In this experiment, however, as in the first one, subjects were unable to recall more than 4 or 5 items regardless of the duration of the display. Figure 2 shows that increasing the duration had a very slight effect, providing strong evidence that the memory system is limited in this situation. In order to evaluate the properties of visual recognition, then, he must bypass this memory limitation.

Sperling now knew his problem: how to study the visual recognition stage of processing a large display of items, when a limitation

FIGURE 2. Number of letters correctly reported as a function of exposure duration (after Sperling, 1960).

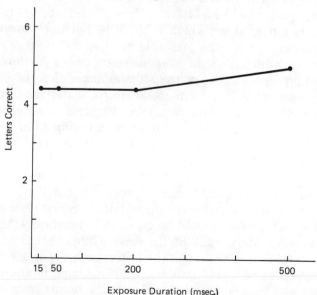

on memory prevented subjects from recalling more than 4 or 5 items. To get around this limitation, Sperling devised the following experiment. A 50-msec. visual display of 12 consonants was presented, arranged in three horizontal rows of 4 items each. Having shown in his earlier experiments that subjects could not recall this many items, he did not ask that they try to do so in this experiment. Instead he followed each display with one of three easily distinguished cues that instructed the subject to report either the top, the middle, or the bottom row. These cues were short tones differing in pitch: a high tone of 2500 Hz, signalling the subject to report the top row, a middle tone of 650 Hz, corresponding to the middle row, and a low tone of 250 Hz for the bottom row. Subjects were trained to interpret these cues quickly and had no problem learning since there was a high degree of response compatibility between each tone and the row it cued the subject to report.

Partial Cueing Thus the subject was asked to recall only 4 of the 12 items on each trial, which was within his memory limit. However, he did not know which row would be required for report until after the display was terminated. If he could see only 4 or 5 letters, then when the display went off and the tone came on, he would have available information about only 4 or 5 of the 12 letters. Knowing only half the total number of letters in the display, he would on the average be able to report only half the letters in the particular row indicated by the tone cue. If he knew 6 of the letters in the complete display, he would on the average recall 2 of the 4 required letters. The average partial report multiplied by a factor of three, therefore, would equal the number of letters about which subjects had visual information. This is no different from the principle used in the average course examination, in which the student is tested on only a portion of the information presented in the course. It is assumed that the student knows the same proportion of the total course material as the proportion correctly answered on the exam. A course containing, say, 300 facts, can be tested by an examination covering 50 of them; if the student knows 45 of those 50 facts, he is assumed to know 90 percent, or 270 of the 300 facts.

Sperling found that practiced subjects in this experiment recalled an average of three letters correctly when the tone cue followed the offset of the display immediately. Since the subjects did not know which row would be cued, they must have had this much information about each of the rows. Given that there were three rows, information about 9 of the letters in the 12-letter display was available at some level to the subject. This experiment demonstrated that although subjects could usually report only 4 or 5 items in a 12-item display, information about 9 of them actually existed somewhere after the display was turned off.

Sperling now had a complete demonstration that although subjects could recall only 4 or 5 items in a display, information about more of them actually existed at the time the display was terminated. How long did this information remain available? Sperling reasoned that extending the time between the end of the display and the onset of the tone cue would reveal how long the subject could outperform his limited span of apprehension. In the original partial report experiment, the cue had followed the display presentation immediately. Using a display of 9 or 12 consonants and holding its duration constant at 50 msec., Sperling now either presented the recall cue 50 msec. before the display or waited for varying lengths of time after the display was turned off before he turned on the recall cue. Thus for some varying length of time after the visual information was obtained, the subject did not know which portion of it he would be required to recall. Of course, delaying the tone cue increases the difficulty of the task. The subject must remember the names and locations of all of the items until the tone cue is presented, signifying which row to report.

Figure 3 shows both the percentage correct and the number of items the observers had available as a function of the interstimulus interval—the time between the offset of the 12-item display and the onset of the tone. If the tone appeared 50 msec. before the visual display, the subjects had 9.8 letters available. When the cue was delayed 300 msec. after the display was turned off, performance dropped to about 6.4 items available in the displays. Further delays of the cue lowered performance so that by a 1-sec. delay performance was close to that predicted by the limit of the span of apprehension. That is, the subject's partial report at this time could be predicted by the number of items he normally could recall in a whole report.

Sperling interpreted the results of these experiments to mean that, although a display presentation lasts for only 50 msec., the information about the items in the display must have remained available for a longer time. When the cue tone comes on, therefore, although the display is no longer out there in the real world, the subject can report the items signalled by the tone. The results discussed in Chapters 17 and 18 will indicate that the items could be held in a preperceptual visual image which persists for a slightly longer time than the display. The subject is able to continue to read out information from this image which remains after the stimulus is terminated. Indeed, Sperling checked with his subjects and found

Delaying the Report Cue

FIGURE 3. The number of letters available and the percentage correct as a function of the interstimulus interval—the time between the offset of the display and the onset of the tone cue. (The dashed line represents the number of letters recalled in a whole report.) (After Sperling, 1960.)

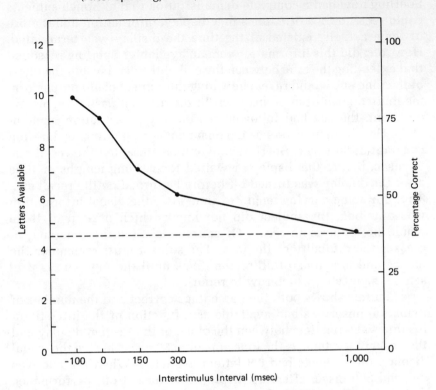

that they believed the display to last about 250 or 300 msec., when it actually lasted only 50 msec. What lasted, and what they interpreted as seeing, was the information in preperceptual visual store.

The duration of the preperceptual image is mainly determined by the physical properties of the stimulus and the visual system. The visual image is found to last much longer when it is followed by a dark field rather than a bright light. Other experiments have shown that the image is vulnerable to masking by other visual stimuli presented immediately afterwards (see Chapters 17 and 18). Unlike immediate memory, the visual image cannot be regenerated; since it is preperceptual, it cannot be rehearsed and the subject has no control over it. Sperling's results indicated that the subject may select portions of it to process, but by the time he returns to process the rest, it has disappeared.

If the items are being held in preperceptual visual store in Sperling's experiments, they may not be completely recognized at the time of the cue presentation. Consider the finding that the subjects had information about 9 of the 12 items when the tone cue followed the display immediately. The information about the 9 items could have been in two forms. In the first, the items would have already been recognized so that their names were immediately available for report. In the second form, the items have not been recognized, but information about the items exists in the form of a preperceptual image. The subject must still process, that is, recognize the letters after the tone occurs. Given these two alternative interpretations, Sperling devised the following experiment to test between them.

Subjects in the experiment were presented with displays of 8 items arranged in 2 horizontal rows of 4 items each. Each row contained 2 digits and 2 consonant letters randomly mixed. A high or low tone cued the subject to report, not the upper or lower row, but the category of digits or of letters. This was a very different task. The cue of spatial position used in the other partial report experiments required selection based on a physical characteristic of the display. Subjects did not have to recognize any of the letters in order to determine which was the top, middle, or bottom row. To report back the items of a given category, however, meant that letters and digits first had to be distinguished, i.e., had to be recognized.

Cueing by Name

When subjects are cued by spatial location, they can correctly report back the cued row if the cue comes on before the visual information is lost. If this visual information already has been named (categorized), then cueing by category class should also be an efficient method of selection. However, the partial report analysis indicated that subjects in this experiment only could recall about 2 items in a given category. Since there were two possible categories, this means that subjects only had information about 4 items. They knew no more than they would have if they had been required to recall all 8 items. Sperling's results show that a partial report can facilitate performance if the report cue specifies a physical location dimension, but not if the cue specifies a categorical name dimension.

Sperling's experiments thus revealed a sequence of events in the visual recognition task involving two kinds of memory. As shown in Figure 4, a visual stimulus presented to the observer is transformed by visual receptors, and stored in the form of a preperceptual visual image. In the process of recognition the observer reads out the information in the image and places the names in immediate memory. The names can be rehearsed until they are recalled. The subject can select which items to read out if the report

FIGURE 4. The storage structure and psychological process at each stage of processing in the visual recognition task.

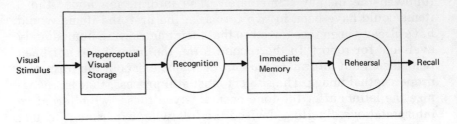

cue directs him to a spatial dimension of the display, since the pre-perceptual image holds its spatial representation intact. Therefore, the location report cue is effective if it occurs before the image is gone. The category report cue, on the other hand, is not helpful, since the subject does not have the names of the items in preperceptual store. So the subject has to recognize each item before he determines whether it belongs to the proper category. Sperling's results show that not only is immediate memory limited, but visual recognition is as well. We can read out only 4 or 5 items in one fixation but can selectively choose which items to read out if the cue directs us along a physical dimension. Logically, there is no reason to read out more than 4 or 5 separate items if we can only remember this number.

REHEARSAL Everyone seems to be aware of the rehearsal phenomenon. If the tone cue in Sperling's experiment had not occurred by the time the subject recognized some of the items in the display, he would have to rehearse them in order to remember them accurately. One form of rehearsal—repeating the items to oneself—is called subvocal rehearsal. In fact, Sperling found two kinds of errors in his experiments that might be attributed to the recognition and rehearsal processes, respectively. The first kind were visual confusions: subjects might report an E where they should have reported an F, or a B for an R, etc. Although the subject could not recognize all of the items accurately, this result shows that he did get enough visual information from some of them to make a good guess on this basis. The second kind of errors were not visual confusions, but articulatory or auditory ones. In this case, the subject might recall a T for a B or an F for an S. These pairs of letters are similar in the way they are pronounced and, therefore, in the way they sound. If subjects repeated the letters to themselves, and forgot some part of them, they might choose a similar sounding letter at the time of report.

For a more complete discussion of the role of visual and auditory similarity in letter recognition and memory, see Chapters 19 and 25, respectively.

Sperling knew when he began his experiments that his subjects would have done much better in the task had he used stimuli they could combine into words or pseudo-words. If each row of letters spelled a word, an item would no longer have been equivalent to a letter, but rather to one word. The span of apprehension would then have applied to 4 words, rather than 4 letters. If the subjects recognized 3 four-letter words, they could have recalled these correctly. Immediate memory is constrained by the number of labels it can hold and the amount of information covered by one label can vary considerably. Recoding can greatly increase the amount of information in immediate memory. What constitutes an item is determined by knowledge stored in long-term memory. For example, if someone is presented with sequences of letters that form words of an unknown language, he will not have the appropriate knowledge in long-term memory and, therefore, will not be able to recognize and remember words instead of single letters.

RECODING

One of the important variables in perception and immediate memory, then, is this recoding operation in which the number of items that must be rehearsed is reduced according to information stored in long-term memory. The letters can be recognized and recoded into words and rehearsed as such; then at recall the words can be decoded into the original sequence of letters. A telegraph operator performs an analogous task when he recodes the series of long and short beeps coming in, first into letters and then into words, so that his immediate memory is constrained not by 4 or 5 dots and dashes, which represent only a letter or two, but rather by 4 or 5 words. His task involves a continual recoding of the information coming in. In repeating the information, he may be required to decode the words back into letters and dots and dashes, for example, to telegraph the information elsewhere.

In a famous paper called "The Magical Number Seven Plus or Minus Two," published in 1056, George Miller discussed how recoding could operate in immediate memory. Miller presented an experiment originally carried out by Sidney Smith, who presented subjects with long sequences of 1's and 0's in random order and asked them to remember the sequences. Since it exceeded their immediate memory, they could not remember the entire sequence. Smith then taught them how to recode the sequences as octal numbers. (Table 1 gives the octal representation of all possible se-

TABLE 1
Octal Representation of All Possible Sequences
of Three Binary Numbers

Binary Sequence	Octal Representation
000	0
001	1
010	2
011	3
100	4
101	5
110	6
111	7

quences of three binary numbers.) That is, he introduced a new set of rules into long-term memory which now allowed subjects to group the bits of information into larger chunks. A 12-item sequence of binary numbers could be recoded into 4 octal numbers and remembered. At the time of test, the octal numbers could be decoded back to binary form to present the experimenter with all twelve 1's and 0's in their proper order.

Miller showed that immediate memory could hold any amount of information as long as it was grouped into a limited number of items. The limit Miller talked about was around 7, whereas Sperling found the limit in his task was close to 4. Sperling's subjects, however, were also required to remember the spatial location of the test consonants in the display. In this case, Sperling's subjects actually had to know two independent things about each item in order to recall it correctly. They had to remember the name and the spatial location and, therefore, their span of apprehension might be considered to be 8 rather than 4 items, in close agreement with Miller's estimate.

WORKING MEMORY We distinguish between the storage structure of immediate or short-term memory, and the recoding and rehearsal processes that operate on information held in short-term memory. The contribution of structure and process is sometimes difficult to isolate in a psychological task. The span of apprehension not only reflects the limited capacity of the short-term memory structure itself but also the limitations in the recoding and rehearsal processes. Since structure and process interact so closely in immediate memory, we often refer to it as working memory. Working memory is our stream of consciousness, which is central in the processing of information in the real world. William James said that for a state of mind to survive in memory, it must have endured for a certain amount of time; that to be able to retrieve information at a later time the information must first survive for some time in the stream of consciousness. Moreover, according to James, all improvement of memory consists of the improvement of one's habitual method of recording facts. It is through short-term memory that facts are recorded, and the efficiency of its operations determines how well they are stored and remembered.

The interaction of storage capacity and the processes of recoding and rehearsal in working memory are apparent in a task called the *QRST* task. The subject is told to set four counters in memory, corresponding to the letters *Q, R, S,* and *T,* at some numerical value such as zero. The experimenter then reads off a series of these letters in random order; for each letter read off, the subject must increment the appropriate counter by 1. Thus, if the list presented by the experimenter is *R, T, Q, R, S, S, T, S,* the correct answer at the end of the trial would be $Q = 1$, $R = 2$, $S = 3$, and $T = 2$.

QRST Task

The list is presented verbally and the subject cannot use paper and pencil to keep track of his counters. Thus, the subject is forced to keep a running mental account of the current status of each counter. When this task is analyzed in detail, it demonstrates many of the operations necessary in the working memory of normal cognitive functioning. First, the subject is required to perceive each item as it is presented. Second, after recognition he must search for the appropriate counter in his memory. One strategy is to keep the counters in alphabetical order; when the letter *S* is presented, the subject can move directly to the third counter. Then, once found, the counter value must be incremented so that the information in memory will be updated. Finally, the subject must rehearse —subvocally, for example—the values of all four counters or risk losing their information. Some sort of rehearsal appears to be absolutely necessary in this task for performance to be accurate. These four sequential operations necessary in the *QRST* task represent very well the usual operations involved in the learning or understanding of new information. Reading a book or listening to speech, we go through an analogous set of operations. The information must be perceived, recoded or integrated with what we already know, and rehearsed so that it can be utilized at some later time.

Figure 5 presents a flow diagram of the four operations involved in the *QRST* task. The most important thing to notice is that these operations must be performed in a time-sharing manner, since they cannot be performed simultaneously. Working memory

FIGURE 5. A flow diagram of the sequence of four processes or operations involved in the *QRST* task.

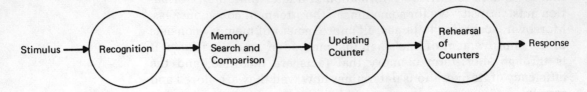

is a time-sharing system; to the extent the subject is engaged by one of these operations, he finds it difficult or perhaps impossible to carry out the other three. Even if the subject were able to do the operations simultaneously, the operations must be performed sequentially. Updating the appropriate counter is possible only after the item has been perceived and its appropriate counter found in memory.

If any one of the operations consumes most of the processing time available, the entire task can be disrupted. Very little meaning will be derived from a spoken message if one operation requires all the time available to the time-sharing system. This is analogous to the observation that children just learning to read derive very little meaning from the text. They are spending most of their time simply perceiving the words and phrases. Since for them this is a very difficult task, they do not have the time available to analyze the meaning of the message and integrate this meaning with what they already know. By the time they perceive the last word of a sentence, for instance, the first couple of words, having received no further processing, are forgotten. Certainly they would also have a processing deficit at other stages, but there are a number of reasons why perception is difficult for early readers. For example, they have not yet internalized the rules of the spelling patterns in the language and, therefore, cannot use this information to facilitate perception. Highly practiced readers, on the other hand, can carry out some of the operations simultaneously; words are perceived easily, allowing plenty of time for the other operations to take place concurrently.

Sequence of Psychological Operations

The functioning of each of these operations can be better understood when we find which independent variables influence each operation. Begin with the auditory presentation of a letter. The operation of recognition must transform some preperceptual representation of this stimulus into a name in short-term memory. One critical variable that should influence the time it takes for recognition is the signal-to-noise ratio of the letter. When we imagine the series of letters in the QRST task being spoken against a noisy background, it is obvious that this would increase the difficulty and, therefore, the time it takes for the recognition process. In the Sternberg task discussed in Chapter 4, we noted that a noise background increased the time for the recognition stage in the memory-search task.

The output of the recognition stage is the name of the letter that was presented. The second processing stage must find the counter that corresponds to this letter. Analogous to the Sternberg task, this requires a memory search and comparison of the names of the counters in memory. The time required for this stage can be increased by adding more counters in memory. For this reason a good strategy in this task, when the subject knows the total number of letters contained in the list, is to work with only three of the counters and infer the value of the fourth. The effect of number of counters in memory should be localized at the memory search stage; we would not expect it to affect the time it takes for perception of the letters. Analogously, when reading a book about a completely unfamiliar field, one may be able to perceive each word without effort. To recode and integrate the information, however, is very difficult in such a situation, consuming more of the working memory capacity and making less available for the other processes. Another important variable affecting the memory search operation would be the names of the counters themselves. In the QRST task, the fact that the four letters are in their correct alphabetical order increases the efficiency of memory scanning operations over what it would be if they were chosen at random from the alphabet.

The amount of processing required for the third operation, incrementing the value of the counters, depends upon the exact nature of this task. For instance, instead of setting each counter at zero and incrementing it by 1 for every appropriate letter, all the counters could be set at 9, and the subject could be instructed to subtract 3 for every letter. The first task corresponds to the well-learned experience of counting by 1's. The second involves a far less familiar task that most people could not perform without devoting some extra thought to each subtraction. Thus, the second task would consume extra time at this stage and less time would be available for the other operations.

Finally, increasing the amount of information in memory will affect the difficulty of the rehearsal operation. Rather than single digit counters, we could have the subjects set each counter at 78, a two-digit number. The subjects would now have to rehearse a two-digit number for each counter, which should take longer than rehearsal of a one-digit number.

Thus, the QRST task demonstrates the working memory at

work. Four psychological functions, each one critical to the process, must be carried out. The working memory allocates time to each; to the extent that one of the processes monopolizes the available time, the working memory process is disrupted. This experimental paradigm offers one possible method of exploring the nature of the operations involved in working memory.

WORKING AND LONG-TERM MEMORY

The most convincing evidence of working memory, usually called short-term memory, as a separate storage structure from the structure responsible for our long-term memories is phenomenological: we seem to be aware of an immediate present which is distinct from our memories of things that happened long ago. The process by which we recall what has happened within the last few seconds seems different from the process of recalling a more distant past. Recall from immediate memory seems to be based more on some sort of temporal dimension; one simply reaches back a few seconds; the item is there. We find it much more difficult to introspect about long-term memory. The processes by which it operates remain mysterious to us. There appear to be several kinds of long-term memory; some items require a series of logical steps to retrieve— for instance, what one was doing at a particular time. Other information, like memory for the meaning of words, seems to be accessed directly at the recognition stage.

Forgetting

In the laboratory, experimenters have attempted to establish evidence for two kinds of memory. For example, Murdock (1962) presented subjects with a list of 30 words, at 1 word per second, and asked for a free recall. In the free recall task, subjects attempt to recall as many words as they can in any order they choose. Figure 6 shows the percentage of correct recall as a function of serial position. First, note the orderly forgetting function for the last seven items in the list. Each item is recalled significantly better than the preceding item. Earlier items are recalled at a fairly low level of performance although significantly better than chance. Note also that the first two items are recalled better than the following items in the middle of the list.

Experimenters have concluded from these results that the last words in the list are retrieved from short-term memory; they have had insufficient time to fade or to receive much interference. They seem to be recalled first because they are the most accessible and recalling them first spares the necessity of rehearsal. The remaining words, it is argued, must now be recalled from long-term mem-

FIGURE 6. Percentage of correct recall in a free recall task as a function of the serial position of the test word (after Murdock, 1962).

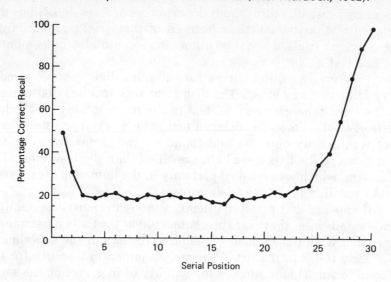

ory. The first words had a greater opportunity for rehearsal than the middle words, and so are recalled more accurately. When the first item comes in, the subject can selectively rehearse it. As the second item comes in, he has to share the available time between processing it and keeping the first word in memory. As more and more items come in, they receive less and less rehearsal. We would thus expect the first item, which had the system's complete rehearsal, to be better recalled than the third item, which had to share processing time with two others. When rehearsal must be shared across a number of items, very little information is transferred to long-term memory and performance asymptotes at a fairly low level in the middle of the list. Performance remains at this point until the end of the list, which has the immediate benefit of recall directly from short-term memory.

Another demonstration of the two kinds of memory is an experiment by Madigan and McCabe (1971). On each trial they presented subjects with five pairs of words at the rate of 2 seconds per pair. The probe test involved presenting the subject with the first member of one of the 5 pairs immediately after the list presentation and asking him to recall the second member. (Each pair is called a paired-associate because most researchers have seen the task as one that requires forming an association between the members of the pair, so that presentation of one member will bring the other to mind.) By giving the subjects a number of trials with different lists and randomly testing the subject with probes from the five different serial positions, a serial position curve could be generated. After 50 of these trials, subjects were given a final test on some of the items presented throughout the experimental session. Since this delayed test contained items from all of the serial positions from the previous trials, a serial position curve could also be computed for this test.

The serial position curves for the immediate tests showed a very large recency effect. The fifth item was recalled 100 percent of the time, whereas the first item in the list was only recalled 40 percent of the time. The delayed test gave a serial position curve that was exactly opposite that found on the immediate test. The first items in the lists were better recalled than the last items. The fifth item, which was recalled perfectly in the immediate test, could not be recalled at all in the delayed test.

It appears that these last items, although reported perfectly a few seconds after they were presented, did not get into a permanent store that would keep them available to the end of the experiment. The early items in the list, however, remained in memory for the second recall. This reinforces the validity of interpreting the serial position curve as the effect of two kinds of memory. If the last items in the list were retrieved from short-term memory, there would be no reason to rehearse them enough to transfer them to long-term memory. The first items, on the other hand, were presumably already in long-term memory at the first recall. The finding that they were better reported could only mean that they were more firmly fixed in long-term memory than the middle items. This effect should still be true at the second recall of the list.

This experiment appears to demonstrate what most memory models assume, that the stimulus comes into the system and enters some kind of preperceptual storage; then is recognized and placed in short-term memory; and then by means of rehearsal of this information in short-term memory, it is transferred into long-term memory. The model predicts that the more we rehearse the information, the more long-term memory builds up for it. The value of long-term memory is that its rate of forgetting is different from that of short-term memory. When recall is based on information in short-term memory only, forgetting is seen to occur very rapidly. Three or four interference items can drastically decrease memory for earlier items. Most investigators assume that in long-term memory, on the contrary, there is very little forgetting. Once information is placed in long-term memory, the items are forgotten at a very slow rate.

The problem with this memory model is the assumption that information must go through short-term memory before it makes contact with long-term memory. However, the process of reading out the information in preperceptual storage requires contact with long-term memory. It is possible, therefore, that as some maintain, what we call short-term memory isn't really another box in the system, but rather the process of directing consciousness to a particular part of long-term memory. An analogy might be drawn with a structure partly illuminated by a flashlight. Short-term memory is that part of the information that lies within the radius of the light; information in this model would go immediately from the recognition stage into long-term memory, and the learning and memory of the items would simply be a matter of how long the light remained on that area of long-term memory. This model can also describe the Madigan and McCabe findings that the last items in the list are not remembered at the end of the experiment. When the last item in the list comes in, the subject recognizes it and then reports it almost immediately, and the light moves elsewhere. With so little exposure, the last item is not learned and therefore is not remembered very well. In contrast, since the subject was trying to remember the earlier items in the list during the presentation of the later items, we can assume that the light was on these items for a much longer time. Therefore, the earlier items should have been learned better, allowing them to be recalled more accurately at the end of the experiment. A detailed analysis of memory and forgetting of recently presented verbal items is presented in Chapter 27, and long-term memory is studied in Chapter 28. It will be useful, not only to distinguish short-term from long-term memory, but also to distinguish different kinds of short-term memories (see Chapters 24, 25, and 26).

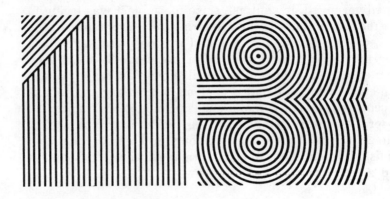

Attention and sensory channels

A shift of the selective process from one class of events to another takes a time which is not negligible compared with the minimal time spent on any one class.
—*Donald E. Broadbent (1958)*

The attitude of the experimental psychologist to attention provides an index of his theoretical biases. The introspectionists considered attention as a focal point for psychological study and studied such phenomena as sensory clearness and prior entry as a function of attention. That is, do we see something clearer or sooner when we are attending than when we are not attending? William James, for example, observed how the surgeon sees the blood flow before he observes the knife pierce the skin. James, more than anyone, made attention respectable, especially to the layman.

The Gestalt psychologists had no need for attention, since they believed that the properties of the stimulus array were sufficient to predict the perceptual response to it. The behaviorists dismissed the concept of attention as something unobservable and therefore not worthy of experimental study. Attention, a process, had no place in the description of stimulus-response relationships in these two later schools of psychology. So, in 1958, when attention was receiving little attention from American psychologists, Broadbent's book provided a renaissance for employing the concept of attention to describe how humans perceive and remember sensory inputs.

Broadbent's model, illustrated in Figure 1, focused on the flow of information between stimulus and response. Information enters this system through the senses and passes into a short-term store, a temporary buffer or storage structure whose purpose is to hold information until it can be processed further. The buffer, in effect, extends the duration of a stimulus; for example, the light from a camera flash maintains its effects beyond the time the light stimulus actually exists. Some structure of this sort is responsible for the fact that a lighted cigarette or a finger moved rapidly back and forth is perceived as being in several places at once (see Chapter 17).

BROADBENT'S MODEL

FIGURE 1. Flow of information between stimulus and response as illustrated by Broadbent (1958).

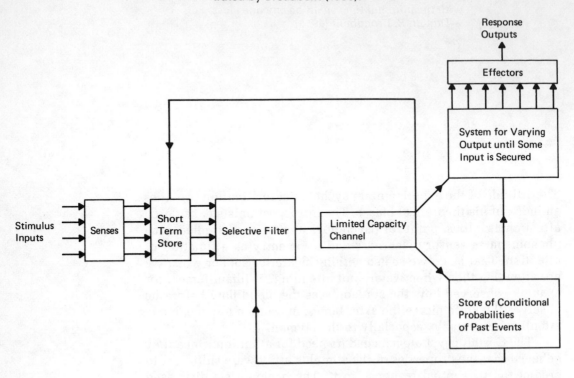

Broadbent assumed that stimuli could be partitioned into separate classes or channels of events as, for example, auditory and visual stimuli. Auditory stimuli coming from the left or the right could also be considered as different channels. As can be seen in Figure 1, Broadbent further assumed that the passage of information through the short-term store preserved these channels of information. A filter could then operate by selecting information on the basis of these separate channels or classes of information. All of the outputs from the buffer must pass through the selective filter device before reaching the limited capacity channel. The limited capacity processor is the workhorse of the system and operates on or processes the information made available by the selective filter. The limited capacity processor can be thought of as an analog of a computer's central processor. It also corresponds to James's span of consciousness—what is experienced as happening now. This process operates on the information in the short-term store and transforms it into more abstract or meaningful information. The processing of the limited capacity channel was equated with the process of attention; that is, to the extent a channel of information is being processed here, it is being attended to.

According to Broadbent, the processing that occurs up to the filter can take place simultaneously or in parallel across the different channels of information. In contrast, the processing of the limited capacity channel must operate serially across the different stimulus channels. That is to say, the processing by the senses into short-term store occurs simultaneously across the different stimulus channels, whereas the limited capacity processor can only operate on one channel at a time. The short-term store can hold the information from both auditory and visual inputs, or from two different speakers at a cocktail party; in short, from all the sensory stimuli that may surround one at a given time. This implies that the system is not limited in the amount of information that can be processed by the senses and stored in short-term store. The transformation and storage of the sound pressure vibrations of a symphony occur in the same way whether or not one is attending to the music. It is the limited capacity channel that is limited in the amount of information it can process. A filter between it and the buffer allows it to attend to only one source of information at a time. Thus, for example, at a cocktail party, the buffer may be storing the stimulus characteristics of two conversations, but the listener can pay attention to only one of them. Only one of them can pass through the filter to the limited capacity channel, where it can be recognized, possibly rehearsed, and then perhaps transferred to the motor effectors, where an appropriate response can be initiated.

Broadbent assumed that information could last in the buffer on the order of seconds without being processed by the limited capacity channel, after which it would decay away. Thus, the very fact that the limited capacity channel is processing one channel of information tends to ensure that the information from other channels will be lost. However, the central processor could switch attention and resolve the last couple of seconds of information on the unattended channel.

The filter has flexibility; obviously we can switch our attention from one stimulus source to another. The features that identify a channel of information also define channels of information in short-term store. The representation of these features in short-term store can be used by the central processor in switching attention. Broadbent proposed that the physical features of the stimuli are the critical features defining a channel of information. Thus the filter will be open to a certain spatial location in the environment, filtering out

Short-term Store

all other locations. It can also select a particular voice out of several, and the task of selecting will be easier if the selected voice is female and the other male. It can pass speech and filter out a pure tone that accompanies it; or it may pass the tone over the speech. In all cases, it has some physical feature to guide the central processor.

Limited Capacity Processor

Broadbent's processing system is limited at the stage of the limited capacity channel. The filter protects the processing at this stage by allowing it to concentrate its limited capacity on one channel. The buffer is utilized to hold information from other channels, so that when the serial processor is done attending one channel, it can return to process another. Attending to one thing does not necessarily mean, therefore, as James said, that everything else is lost. If the processor can get back to the buffer soon enough, before the second channel decays, it can process it. Thus the buffer provides some flexibility to the system; it allows it, in a sense, to deal with two simultaneous stimuli if the first can be processed before the second has decayed from the buffer. However, Broadbent further assumed that switching of attention between channels takes some substantial amount of time. In this case, processing the same information from two channels would always take longer than processing it from one channel.

SPLIT-SPAN EXPERIMENTS

Broadbent's theory was based on a series of experiments, now known as the split-span experiments. The studies took advantage of the subject's ability to distinguish easily the location of an auditory stimulus presented over a headphone on the left ear from another stimulus presented over a headphone on the right. The two ears can, therefore, function as two different channels of information in Broadbent's model. (This is not true of the eyes since, if both eyes are open, we cannot discriminate which eye is being stimulated.)

Broadbent (1954) presented auditory messages over the headphones, feeding a different message into each ear. In one ear he would present three digits, say, 7, 4, and 3. Simultaneously, he presented three other digits in the other ear, say, 8, 2, and 6. The rate of presentation to a given ear was two digits per second, so that the total presentation time was 1½ seconds. The task of the subject was to recall the digits in one of two different ways. In one condition, he was to recall the digits by ear of presentation; first, all three items presented to one ear, then the other three presented to the other ear. In our example, a correct response in this condition would be the serial recall 7, 4, 3, 8, 2, 6. In the second condition, subjects were asked to recall the items according to their chronological order of presentation. The digits had arrived in pairs, one at each ear simultaneously, and the subject could report the digits within each pair in either order. But he must report both before moving on to the next pair; thus, 7, 8, 4, 2, 3, 6 would be a correct recall by temporal order.

It was well known that subjects could serially recall a list of 6 digits, presented at a rate of 2 per second with a total presentation time of 3 seconds, with about 95 percent accuracy. The subjects could correctly recall 19 out of 20 lists. Broadbent's (1954) modification of this paradigm, by splitting the source of the digits, lowered performance significantly in both recall conditions. In the first condition, subjects were told to recall the digits by ear of presentation: first the digits fed into one ear, then the digits fed into the other; they were correct 65 percent of the time. In contrast, when subjects were required to recall the items by order of presentation—the first item in each ear followed by the second item in each ear, followed by the third—they were able to correctly recall the entire list only 20 percent of the time.

Broadbent interpreted this difference as reflecting the necessity of switching attention more frequently in the second recall condition than in the first. In the first condition, the subject could monitor one location and identify the items as they were presented. After identifying these three items, he must switch his attention to the information from the second ear before it decayed from the buffer or short-term store. The total time between the end of the list and its complete identification would include the time required to switch attention from the first to the second ear and the time to recognize the digits presented to that ear. Given that the items in short-term store could decay, this could reduce performance from that obtained when the list was presented over one source. In the second condition, the subject would have to switch attention at least three times. He could attend to one ear and recognize the first digit; then switch to the second ear to process the first digit on that channel. Next, the limited capacity processor could recognize the second digit on the second ear without switching, but would have to switch once again to read out the second digit of the first ear. The processor could remain on the first ear for the last digit and then switch to the second ear for the final digit. In all, the limited capacity processor would have to switch its attention three times in this condition, whereas when recall was by ear of presentation, it had to do so only once. This would increase the time required for identification of the items and would lower the chances of reaching the end of the list before the information in the short-term buffer faded away.

Broadbent (1954) repeated the experiment at a presentation rate of one pair every 2 seconds, a much slower rate that would allow the subject to switch his attention from channel to channel as the items were being presented. As predicted by the theory, the difference in performance as a function of recall order disappeared at this rate. The items were read out of the buffer as the items were being presented; therefore, the subject would have the names of all the digits at the time of recall and could report the items back in any order.

Gray and Wedderburn Study

Among the first to respond to Broadbent's publication of his model were two Oxford undergraduates, Gray and Wedderburn (1960). They took issue with the assumption of Broadbent that the two ears must function as channels that require switching time between them. It might be easier, they reasoned, to process information alternately across the ears if it was advantageous to do so. To bias the task in this direction, the experimenters made the lists more meaningful when they alternated across the ears than when they did not. They modified the split-span experiment by choosing the 6 stimulus items from two semantic categories: for example, 3 digits and 3 words. Each successive pair contained 1 word and 1 digit and the words and digits were alternated across ears. The words also had certain sequential constraints; for instance, one of their three-word sequences was *dear, aunt, Jane,* earning their experiment the name of *The Dear Aunt Jane Task.* In all other respects, they replicated Broadbent's experiment; the items were presented in pairs, one in each ear, at a rate of two pairs per second. A subject would hear '3, aunt, 8' in the right ear and 'dear, 2, Jane' in the left ear. His task was to recall all six items in any manner he wished. Gray and Wedderburn found that subjects were just as likely to recall the items correctly when they reported the items by alternating between the ears as when they reported the items by spatial location.

Gray and Wedderburn's results contradicted Broadbent's conclusions from his studies. Broadbent argued that channels of information are defined with respect to physical stimulus characteristics. The channels exist in the short-term store before the information is processed by the limited capacity processor. Since it is the central processor that is responsible for deriving meaning from the stimulus, meaning should not influence the switching time in the split-span studies. The semantic variables of semantic category and sequential constraints between words should not have influenced the results if Broadbent's original formulation were correct.

Broadbent and Gregory (1964) replicated the Gray and Wedderburn finding under more controlled recall conditions. As in Broadbent's earlier studies, the subjects were given the required order of report before the list presentation. Broadbent and Gregory also used the two categories, letters and digits, to eliminate any advantage of the sequential constraints in the three-word phrases of Gray and Wedderburn. On a given trial, a subject might hear '3, F, 8' presented on one ear simultaneously with 'A, 2, J' on the other. On some trials he was asked to recall them by spatial location, that is, by ear of presentation, so that in this instance he would respond correctly by saying '3, F, 8, A, 2, J.' On other trials he was asked to report back the items by meaning category. Thus, in the example he would respond correctly by saying 'F, A, J, 3, 8, 2.' According to Broadbent's original model, this second task should be considerably more difficult than the first, since in the first condition the central processor had to switch attention from one channel to another only once, while in the second it had to do so several times. Broadbent and Gregory found that dividing the lists into categories essentially eliminated the advantage of item recall by physical location over recall by meaning category.

How did Broadbent and Gregory interpret this result to make it compatible with Broadbent's general formulation? They admitted that perhaps the concept of channels was too narrowly defined in the original model. Broadbent may have begun with the strictly empirical notion that most of the meaningful order in our experience is out there in the stimulus. However, it appeared that a semantic category could influence performance in the same way as physical channels. In a second experiment, Broadbent and Gregory presented subjects with a single list of 6 items to the same ear. They showed that alternating digits and letters on the *same* ear decreased serial recall relative to presenting 3 items of one category followed by 3 items of another. Subjects could recall the list *AJL649* correctly 96 percent of the time, whereas the list *A6J4L9* only could be recalled correctly 4 out of 5 times. Broadbent and Gregory argued that a similar process to switching between ears was responsible for the effect. Selection of a class of an item must also take time to switch. Therefore, Broadbent and Gregory argued, switching between items on the same ear because of category class eliminated the advantage of recall by physical location in the split-span task with letters and digits. This means that recall by physical location should be disrupted when the items alternate between categories on a given ear. Contrary to this prediction, however, subjects recalled the entire list correctly about 65 percent of the time under both recall conditions, matching performance in the earlier recall by physical location in Broadbent's original (1954) study. Therefore, recall by physical location was not disrupted in Broadbent and Gregory's split-span study; rather, recall by meaning category was better than recall by temporal order in Broadbent's first study.

The channel concept and the filter notion were looking more complicated than Broadbent had assumed. The filter could no longer be thought of as always functioning before meaning was derived—as selecting and rejecting purely on the basis of physical cues. On the contrary, sometimes, at least, the filter held off its selection until items had been identified and categorized, and then selected some and rejected others on the basis of their meanings. This implied, for example, what may be intuitively known, that if one is listening to a single message out of several, it will be easier to attend to it if the others differ not only in physical characteristics, but also in content. Competing messages that are similar in content will interfere more with the attended message than will those that are very different in content. This suggested to some that the filter should be placed farther along the information-processing pathway.

Moray Study   Moray (1960) raised another problem with an experiment that cast doubt on Broadbent's assumption that the two ears always operate as separate channels of information. Moray modified the split-span design by presenting the pairs of digits successively, rather than simultaneously. Holding the total presentation time constant, he presented the digits at 4 per second and alternated them from ear to ear. Broadbent's assumption that the two ears function as two different channels predicts that report by temporal order in this task would be more difficult than recall by ear of presentation. In fact, to recall the items in temporal order, the subject must switch his attention for each digit no less than five times.

In Broadbent's original experiment, the switching time seemed to have been so large that multiplying it by 3 had reduced performance from 65 percent to 20 percent accuracy. In Moray's experiment, this large switching time should be multiplied by a factor of 5 and performance should be considerably poorer than the 20 percent correct obtained by Broadbent. In fact, however, performance in Moray's task was considerably better than the 20 percent found with temporal recall of simultaneous pairs of items. Even so, sequential recall across ears in Moray's experiment was still about

10 percent lower than a condition in which the 6 digits were presented to both ears at once. Therefore, although temporal recall of alternating digits is much better than predicted by Broadbent, the 10 percent decrement in an alternating presentation relative to a single channel presentation shows that separating the input across the two ears does disrupt processing. This result will be discussed in more detail below.

Broadbent and Gregory (1961) replied that the two ears may operate as a single channel in some situations and as two separate channels in others. When the auditory information is presented sequentially, the input could be processed as if it were coming from the same source, so that each item would pass through the filter in the actual order of arrival. Moray's results, therefore, were not incompatible with Broadbent's model of a serial processor dealing with a single channel or source of information at a time. The physical characteristics of the input determine how many channels there are; in the auditory case, the sequential versus the simultaneous nature of the item presentations seems to be the critical factor.

Broadbent and Gregory (1961) also used Moray's alternating task to demonstrate that the physical channel concept was a necessary one. Six digits were again presented sequentially, alternating between two channels of presentation. This time, however, Broadbent and Gregory chose both ears as one channel and the eyes as the other. In this case they found that subjects' recall of the 6 digits was much better if they could recall the 3 digits of one sensory modality before recalling the other 3. Recall by strict order of presentation, which in Broadbent's model meant five time-consuming switches in attention from one modality to the other, was poor.

Broadbent interpreted the results of the split-span experiments as supportive of his model. More specifically, he felt the results gave evidence for the concept of physical channels and a filter which operated along these channels. The critical concept used to explain the results was the notion of switching time—the time needed for the filter to switch from one channel to another. However, although Broadbent used the stage notion in his theoretical work, he did not apply it formally in his experimental studies. An analysis of the split-span experiments in the processing stage framework shows that alternative conclusions from the experiments are possible.

Let us analyze the split-span task in terms of our general information-processing model. We assume that recognition and memory are vital information-processing stages in the task. Each item must be recognized, that is, identified, and stored in memory from which it must be retrieved at the time of response. Performance in this task is, therefore, dependent upon both of these processing stages. The experimenter does not have a direct measure of performance at either of these stages; he only has some overall measure of performance. Unless the investigator can account for each stage of processing in the task, he cannot state with certainty the implications of the results.

The critical independent variable in the split-span experiments has been the order in which the subject is required to report the items. Broadbent assumed that this manipulation should affect only the recognition stage while not directly influencing the memory stage. In this assumption, Broadbent probably was influenced to a greater extent by his model than his intuition or his phenomenological experience in the task. Consider the split-span task from a generally naive point of view. The subject is presented with 6 digits, 3 to each ear, within 1½ sec. He is required to report the digits back in one of two ways: temporal order or ear of arrival. The performance differences may not reflect differences in recognition but rather differences in memory and retrieval. One question Broadbent did not ask was: How long does it take to perceive a digit? He assumed instead that the time could extend well beyond the presentation time; in fact, over 1½ sec. after a digit had been presented. Recall that subjects who reported by ear of arrival were assumed to recognize all of the digits in one ear before switching to the other.

As an alternative explanation, it could have been the case that all of the digits were recognized as they were presented in both recall conditions. The differences in performance reflected differences not in recognition, but in memory. Subjects in the split-span tasks must not only recognize and remember the names of the items but also their ear of arrival or temporal order, depending upon the recall condition. This interpretation of the split-span task locates performance differences at the memory stage, which makes the experiments irrelevant to Broadbent's model. We might argue that subjects would find it easier to remember the ear of arrival of the digits rather than their temporal order. Each digit must be stored in memory with some information relevant to recall. In the recall by temporal order condition, the subject must remember whether each digit came first, second, or third. In recall by order of arrival, he only has to remember if each digit came from the left or right ear. Since alternative interpretations are possible, the manipulation of order of report in the split-span experiments does not speak to Broadbent's model or any other model of the recognition process.

Savin Study   A study by Savin (1967) supports the idea that the memory and retrieval process could contribute to the performance differences in the split-span experiments. Savin presented pairs of digits simultaneously over only one location (a single speaker). According to Broadbent, subjects would be attending to a single physical channel, and it would not be necessary to switch attention from one to the other digit in a simultaneous pair; therefore, there should be no advantage to recalling the digits sequentially as in the split-span experiments. Yet given the choice, this is exactly what subjects did in Savin's experiment. Free to recall in whatever order they preferred, they usually recalled one digit of the first pair, followed by a digit of the second pair, and then recalled the other two digits in sequential order. The digits in each pair were not separated by location, so subjects chose at random between them as they proceeded from one pair to the next. Nevertheless, they much preferred to respond with one digit out of each pair followed by the other two, rather than to report both items in a pair before proceeding to the next pair.

Savin's results make viable another interpretation of the split-span experiments. It is possible that subjects in these experiments recognize the items on both ears simultaneously but maintain the items in memory according to their order on each physical location. That is to say, there is no filter that blocks out the items on one ear while the items on the other ear are being recognized. At the end of the list, the subject has stored in memory both lists and must recall them for the experimenter. He finds it easier to report the items by temporal order because this is the way the items are organized in memory. To recall the items by temporal order, he has to reorganize the list, which could cause some forgetting.

Treisman Study

To resolve the different interpretations in the split-span experiments, the investigator must locate the stage of processing responsible for the effects of his independent variable. Employing the methods developed in this book, this sometimes requires that the experimenter covary two independent variables, at least, instead of manipulating just one. An experiment by Treisman (1971) illustrates exactly the logic of this procedure in her followup of Moray's (1960) finding that temporal recall of items presented alternately across the two ears was poorer than recall of the digits presented successively to both ears at once.

Treisman (1971), aware of the fact that both recognition and memory are critical processes in the recall task, sought independent variables that might be expected to affect each of these processes, respectively. Treisman's central question was: Is recognition of a serial list of digits disrupted when they are alternated across the two ears relative to presenting them to one auditory location? Treisman reasoned that the method of presentation should affect the process of recognition, not memory or retrieval. Since the subject was required to recall the items in the order they were presented under both presentation conditions, there should be no differences in retrieval strategy, as there might be using the different types of report. In Treisman's experiment, the subject must simply remember and recall the items in their correct temporal order regardless of how they were presented.

To measure the contribution of the memory and retrieval process in this task, Treisman varied the number of items in the list by presenting a sequence of 6 or 8 items. We would expect that an eight-item list would be more difficult to remember than a six-item list. The critical question, however, was whether this variable interacted significantly with the independent variable of presentation condition. If there is a significantly large interaction between the two variables, they could be influencing the same psychological process. On the other hand, if their effects are relatively independent of one another, we have some evidence that they are affecting different processes in the task.

As a third independent variable, Treisman varied the presentation rate of the digits. Treisman reasoned that this variable should certainly affect the recognition stage, in that it directly controls how much time the subject has to perceive each item before the next one comes in. If both the type of presentation and rate of presentation affect recognition, we would expect a large interaction in their effects. On the other hand, if either of them affect the memory process rather than recognition, this variable should interact strongly with the variable of list length. Moray had used 250 msec. for each digit, the smallest possible time in normal speech. Treisman used a computer to reduce the duration of the digits to 150 msec. without the frequency distortion that accompanies the speeded-up playback of a tape recorder. Digits compressed in this way are still easily identifiable. Treisman presented the digits at either 4 or 6.7 digits per second.

To summarize, Treisman (1971) replicated Moray's comparison of binaural versus alternating presentations to study the time it takes to switch from one channel to another. (Unfortunately, Treisman compared the alternating dichotic presentation to a binaural one rather than to a monaural one. If the alternating vs. single-channel presentation is the critical comparison, it should not be confounded with whether the digits come in two ears or one. There is evidence that an auditory signal can be better resolved with two ears than with one.) Treisman improved on Moray's design by covarying list length and the rate of presentation with the type of presentation of the digits. Table 1 presents the observed results of Treisman's experiment.

TABLE 1

Percentage of Digits Recalled Correctly in Their Correct Serial Position in Treisman's (1971) Experiment

		Averaged over List Length	
		Type of Presentation	
		alternating	*binaural*
Rate of	6.7/sec.	51	73
Presentation	4 /sec.	75	85

		Averaged over Type of Presentation	
		List Length	
		six items	*eight items*
Rate of	6.7/sec.	73	51
Presentation	4 /sec.	90	70

		Averaged over Rate of Presentation	
		List Length	
		six items	*eight items*
Type of	*alternating*	73	52
Presentation	*binaural*	89	69

Treisman's dependent measure was the percentage of digits recalled correctly in their correct serial position. Overall, Treisman found that recall performance was 16 percent poorer in the alternating condition than in the single-channel binaural condition. These findings would be on more solid ground had Treisman used a non-alternating monaural condition instead of the binaural condition, but it seems unlikely that the difference she found would be eliminated entirely. Something in the task of perceiving and recalling digits that were alternated between the ears was more difficult than the same operation for digits presented binaurally. Treisman wanted to attribute this difference to the recognition stage of processing. More specifically, using Broadbent's model, subjects would not have to switch attention in the binaural condition as they did in the alternating case.

As we argued above, if the type of presentation is affecting recognition, this variable should interact strongly with the independent variable rate of presentation. Supporting this hypothesis, the top panel of Table 1 shows that the alternating condition was about 10 percent poorer than the binaural at the rate of 4 digits per second, whereas at 6.7 items per second, the alternating case was 22 percent poorer. Switching time, which would be constant whatever the rate of presentation, accounts nicely for this result.

Finally, Table 1 shows that the eight-digit list yielded poorer performance than the six-digit list, but this effect did not interact strongly with the other two variables. Overall, performance was about 20 percent better with the six- than the eight-item list but the size of the effect did not critically depend on the type of presentation condition or the rate of presentation. The result provides some evidence that the two variables that interacted—alternating vs. binaural condition and rate of presentation—affected one stage of processing and the number of items in the list affected a second stage of processing. Logically, these variables appear to be influencing the perception and memory stages, respectively.

Processing Stage Responsible for Attention Effects

To summarize, Broadbent had presented simultaneous pairs of digits and compared recall by strict order of presentation to recall by location. Finding that recall by location gave the best performance, he concluded that time was required to switch attention from one channel to another. Broadbent assumed, however, that the independent variable (recall order) in split-span experiments affects only the process of recognition. Yet a task that requires subjects to recall stimuli obviously involves a memory process. Broadbent had assumed without reason that the effects of the independent variable—order of report—influenced only one of these processes. The experimenter controls only the stimulus and the instructions he gives the subject about his response. He does not have a direct measure of each of the two stages of processing and must rely on inferences from the stimulus-response relationship. Until the investigator isolates the stage of processing that is responsible for the performance differences in the split-span experiments, these differences are open to alternative interpretations. Broadbent's model, like any model of the split-span experiments, must describe the two processes as they operate in this task in such a way that the effect of independent variables on each of them can be measured separately.

Experiments in the split-span task, prior to Treisman's, did not systematically covary second independent variables to determine the stage or stages of processing that were affected by the manipulation. Until these experiments are replicated with the proper manipulations, the results of the split-span studies cannot be located at either perception or memory. It is possible that under the two different recall instructions there may be no difference in the perceptual process at all, and subjects may process information by location as easily as they process it by order of presentation. Differences in the difficulty of memory retrieval could exist under the two conditions and could produce the differences that Broadbent found (Yntema & Trask, 1963).

Treisman (1971) wanted to show that the variables of alternating the items in the list from ear to ear and speeding up the rate of presentation would affect the recognition stage, while increasing the number of items in the list should affect the memory component. According to the additive-factor method presented in Chapter 3, if the effects of two variables interact, their effects could be influencing one stage in common. If the effects of two variables simply add, the two variables could be influencing separate stages. Treisman found that the first two variables did interact and their effects added with list length. Logically, then, it could be argued that the first two variables are affecting the perception stage and the third is affecting memory. In terms of Broadbent's model, Treisman's results show that the ears seem to act, at least partially, as separate channels of information, needing the attention of a central processor that can attend to only one ear at a time. There is really no other easy way that this result can be understood. The process responsible for auditory recognition and storage is sensitive to the spatial arrival of the inputs. Inputs coming in over one spatial location are more easily perceived and stored than inputs alternating between two spatial locations.

Axelrod and Guzy Experiments

Treisman's results, interpreted in the framework of Broadbent's model, imply that the subject has less time to recognize each digit when the digits are alternated between the ears than when they are presented binaurally. Given less time to recognize each digit, the subject should identify fewer digits in the alternating than the binaural presentation.

Recent results by Axelrod and his colleagues support Treisman's results and help locate the effect at the recognition stage of information processing. In their experiments, subjects are asked to follow a sequence of repetitive stimuli presented to the same or different locations. If the subjects must switch attention between locations to recognize each stimulus, they should be more accurate in recognizing the stimuli coming to one location than to two locations. More specifically, we might argue that the subjects would be more likely to miss stimuli when they come to a different than to the same location. Therefore, perceived rate of presentation should be slower and the perceived number of items presented should be fewer when the items are presented to different locations compared to the items presented to the same location.

Axelrod and Guzy (1968) used a method of constant stimuli (see Chapter 5) to determine the perceived rate of auditory click presentations as a function of monotic and dichotic presentations. An auditory click can be produced by presenting a pure tone for a very short duration, say under 10 msec., giving the tone a more clicklike than tonelike quality. In the monotic condition, the clicks were presented to the same ear. In the dichotic condition, the clicks were alternated from ear to ear. A standard train of clicks was presented first for 6 sec., followed by a silent interval of 2 sec., followed by a comparison train of clicks also lasting 6 sec. The subject had to judge whether the second comparison train of clicks was faster or slower than the standard train. The authors compared the monotic versus dichotic presentations by making one of the stimuli monotic and the other dichotic. If the standard was monotic, the comparison would be dichotic and vice versa. If dichotic clicks are perceived at a slower rate than monotic clicks, the point of subjective equality should occur when the dichotic clicks are presented at a faster rate than the monotic clicks. The point of subjective equality would be the point at which the subject responds faster and slower with equal probability.

Monotic and dichotic clicks

Comparing the dichotic versus the monotic click presentations at just one click rate for the standard train would not be a sufficient test of the attention-switching hypothesis. Some other process besides the recognition process may be responsible for perceiving the dichotic clicks differently than the monotic clicks. For example, the subject may simply have a decision bias which could produce differences in the results. To guard against this, the experimenters should test performance at a number of click rates so that they can show their results are sensitive to changes in a second independent variable, which should influence the perception rather than the decision stage. Ideally, we would want to find no differences in the perception of dichotic and monotic clicks at very slow rates when there is sufficient time for the switching of attention, and significant differences when the rate of click presentations is speeded up.

Analogous to Treisman's finding, then, we would expect the perceived slowing of dichotic clicks to be more pronounced at faster rates. This is exactly what Axelrod and Guzy (1968) and Axelrod, Guzy, and Diamond (1968) found. The monotic point of subjective equality is plotted as a function of the dichotic rate in Figure 2. This measure corresponds to the monotic rate that is needed to be perceived equal to the dichotic rate. If perception is veridical, the monotic rate would be equal to the dichotic rate and the results would lie along the line corresponding to the 45° diagonal. In contrast, if the dichotic clicks are perceived as occurring slower than the monotic clicks, the points would be below the diagonal. Also, if the perceived slowing of the dichotic clicks is directly related to the rate of presentation, the absolute distance between perceived equality and veridical perception should increase with increases in the click rate. This is the result shown in Figure 2. At a dichotic rate

FIGURE 2. Monotic point of subjective equality as a function of the dichotic rate of presentation. The 45° diagonal represents the point of objective equality (POE). (After Axelrod & Guzy, 1968, Experiment II.)

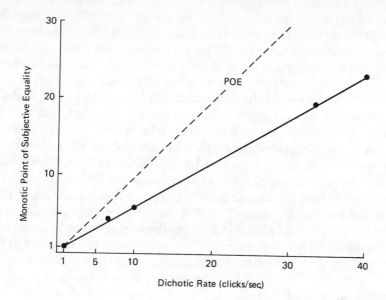

of 1/sec., its rate is not underestimated since the monotic rate perceived equal to the dichotic rate was also around 1/sec. However, at faster dichotic rates subjects perceived monotic trains, which were actually significantly slower than the dichotic trains, as equal to them. Furthermore, the amount of underestimation of the dichotic click rate increased with increases in rate.

The results shown in Figure 2 described a straight line with a Y intercept of .58 and a slope of .56. Accordingly, the point of subjective equality of a monotic click rate (PSE_m) to a dichotic click rate is given by the equation

$$PSE_m = .58 + .56 \times DR \tag{1}$$

where DR is the rate of dichotic clicks. Therefore, for a dichotic rate of 1/sec., Equation 1 predicts that subjects would perceive a monotic click rate of 1.14 as equal to it. With a dichotic rate of 10/sec. on the other hand, subjects would perceive a monotic train of 6.18 clicks per second at the same rate. The rate of dichotic clicks presented at 40/sec. is perceived equal to a monotic rate of 23.78 clicks/sec. Equation 1 states in effect that beyond the point where the intercept contribution becomes negligible, the perceived monotic rate is some fixed proportion of the actual dichotic rate.

If subjects underestimate the rate of dichotic clicks, we would also expect them to underestimate the actual number of clicks presented. Guzy and Axelrod (1972) asked subjects to estimate the number of clicks presented on each trial. The experimenters presented anywhere from 2 to 20 clicks at rates of 2, 4, 6, and 8 clicks/sec. The clicks were presented either monotically or dichotically. The estimated number of clicks was much lower in the dichotic than the monotic presentation. This effect increased with increases in the click rate and the total number of clicks presented. A good dependent measure is the estimated number of clicks of a dichotic train presented at a given rate divided by the estimated number given to the corresponding monotic train. If there is no difference between the estimates given the dichotic and monotic trains, this measure would be 1. If the number of dichotic clicks is underestimated, relative to the number of monotic clicks, the value would be less than 1. This measure is plotted in Figure 3 as a function of click rate and the number of clicks in the train. The results show that the number of dichotic clicks is underestimated relative to a monotic presentation when 4 or more clicks are presented at a rate of 4/sec. or faster. The underestimation of the dichotic train increases as the rate or the number of clicks is increased. These results support the original notion of Broadbent, which states that the separate ears operate as separate channels that can require a switching of attention of the limited capacity processor between them.

FIGURE 3. The estimated number of clicks given to a dichotic train divided by the estimated number given to the corresponding monotic train as a function of the number of clicks in the train. The parameter along each curve gives the rate of presentation of the click train (after Guzy & Axelrod, 1972).

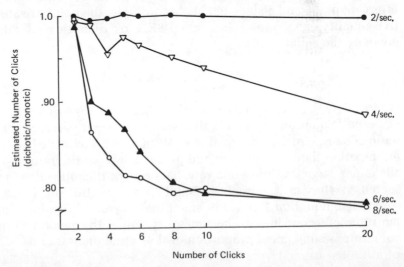

Axelrod and Nakao (1974) reasoned that if the effect is a central attentional one rather than some unique property of the auditory system per se, the effect should be found in other modalities. The subjects placed their hands about 7 inches apart on a table. Each hand could be vibrated independently through a hole in the table top. Subjects compared the rates of presentation of taps to the left hand alone to the rates of presentation of taps alternating between the two hands. The results exactly replicated the auditory experiments. The rate of alternating taps was underestimated relative to the rate of unimanual taps and the underestimation increased with increases in the rate of presentation of the taps. This result substantiates a central attentional interpretation of the auditory results rather than a modality-specific interpretation.

Vibratory taps

Pitch Channels

It appears that the pitch continuum can also be partitioned along channels. Composers and musicians know that the listener can follow successive notes within only a small range of frequencies. If the frequency differences between successive notes are greater than an octave (a ratio of 2 to 1), it is very difficult to follow the notes to organize the sequence into a melodic one. (See Chapter 20 for a discussion of the dimensions of sound.) Does this limitation in auditory processing result from the additional time needed for a central processor to switch between the appropriate pitch channels?

In order to see if listeners need time to switch between pitch channels we asked observers to count the number of tones in a sequence which alternated between the notes A_4 (440 Hz) and B_5 (988 Hz). Performance on this task was compared to the control condition in which all of the tones were the same in pitch (A_4 or B_5). On each trial, subjects were given a sequence of 5, 6, 7, or 8 notes; they responded with one of these four alternatives, and they were given feedback. Subjects counted the tones more accurately when they were all of the same frequency than when the tones alternated between the different notes. At a rate of 6½ tones/sec., subjects counted 94 percent of the control sequences correctly but only 81 percent of the sequences with alternating notes. The poorer performance with alternating notes could be due to the additional time needed to switch between the different pitches of the alternating notes.

Treisman's experiment with verbal items and the click, tap, and tone counting experiments can be taken as support for Broadbent's original information-processing model of attention. It appears reasonable to describe the two ears as channels and to speak of a limited capacity processor that can process or attend to only one channel at a time. A significant amount of time is required for the processor to switch between channels. This switching time appears to be the best explanation of the results of the experiments.

SHADOWING The experimental task known as shadowing, devised by Cherry (1953), also appeared to offer a flexible and reliable approach to the study of attention. Subjects were presented with a continuous auditory message, usually at a fairly rapid rate such as 150 words per minute. Their task was to repeat back every word of the message verbatim. This was found to be least difficult when the message was simple English prose that contained all the semantic and syntactic constraints of the language. Subjects in this case, instead of repeating each word as it came in, seemed to shadow by phrases, repeating two or three words at a time, so that a lag appeared between the message and the subject's response. When the words of the message were in random and unconstrained order, the shadowing task became much more difficult and subjects in this case repeated the message word by word, rather than phrase by phrase. In a sense they could not predict what was coming next and operated on each word separately. The central assumption underlying the shadowing task is that the difficulty of the act of shadowing absorbed the subject's attention.

Information Coming Through Unattended Channel The immediate problem that interested Cherry and others using his paradigm was the nature of information from an unattended channel that can get through to consciousness when subjects are devoting their attention elsewhere. Like Broadbent, Cherry used the two ears as separate channels and presented a different message to each ear through headphones. The subject shadowed one of the messages while the experimenter introduced various changes in the message on the unattended channel. After a brief period of shadowing the experimenter would break in and ask the subject if he had recognized anything peculiar on the unattended channel.

Cherry (1953) and Cherry and Taylor (1954) found that subjects noticed a change in voices on the unattended channel, especially changes in the sex of the speaker. They noticed a nonverbal event—for instance, a tone. More significant, however, was what they failed to notice. They missed changes in the nature of the material on the unshadowed ear; the investigator could switch the message from a passage in a science fiction novel to poetry, then to a physics text. He could reverse the speech for a while. He could even change the language of the message from English to French and back again without the subjects being able to report the change. These results were seen to support Broadbent's theory; they indicated that subjects, when attending to one channel, notice only gross changes in the physical characteristics of input on another channel. They notice a change from a male to a female speaker, and from speech to pure tones. But they miss changes that would require some perception of the meaning of the stimulus. The initial results of these rather informal experiments tended to locate the filter after the gross physical characteristics of the stimulus were detected, and before recognition of it.

Like Broadbent's split-span task, however, the shadowing task confounded the memory and recognition stages, as was pointed out by Norman (1969). He argued that, after all, subjects were required to *remember* what had occurred on the unshadowed message some unspecified time after it was completed. Moray (1959) previously had found that subjects could not remember English words that were repeated 35 times on the unshadowed channel. Norman (1969) pointed out that subjects in this experiment continued to shadow for roughly 30 seconds after the last test word was presented in the list. Rather than concluding from Moray's results that the words were not recognized on the unattended ear, one could argue that the words were perceived accurately but were forgotten by the time of the test.

In fact, there were some observations indicating that meaning did get through on the unshadowed channel, especially when very little memory was required. Some of Moray's (1959) subjects did remember hearing their names on the unattended channel, which we might expect to be easier to remember than random lists of words. Treisman (1960) showed that a meaningful series of words such as 'dear Aunt Jane,' when split between the two ears, could induce the subject to shadow the meaningful sequence rather than the sequence of words presented on the attended ear. Some subjects did not even notice that they had switched ears to follow the meaningful message.

Given the confounding of recognition and memory stages in the earlier shadowing experiments such as Moray's, an experiment was designed by Norman (1969) that would allow him to evaluate the recognition and memory stages separately. Practiced subjects shadowed a continuous sequence of monosyllabic words spoken in a female voice at a rate of 2/sec. In the memory conditions, a sequence of 6 two-digit numbers was presented in a male voice on the unshadowed channel at a rate of 1 item per sec. The test list was followed by a tone either immediately or after a 20-sec. delay. A probe number followed the tone and subjects indicated whether

Norman study

this number had appeared in the preceding list. On ⅔ of the trials, the probe number was equal to one of the numbers on the preceding list; on the other ⅓ it was not. This paradigm allows the investigator to obtain measures of the recognition and memory stages as discussed in Chapter 16. Using d' as a measure of memory performance, we can determine the memory for each item in the six-item list. The results in Figure 4 show a significant amount of memory for the last couple of items in the list if the subjects are tested immediately. This means that these items must have been recognized. However, if the probe test is delayed through 20 seconds of shadowing, no memory remains for any of the items. Clearly, delaying the test of memory is an invalid measure of whether the items on the unattended channel were recognized. To provide a true index of recognition the investigator must account for the forgetting that takes place between presentation and test.

Norman's result indicates that subjects are able to recognize the meaning of words on the unshadowed channel although we cannot be certain that they did so without the help of attention. Norman monitored the shadowing performance of his subjects carefully and did not report an increase in shadowing errors when the memory list was being presented. Even so there is simply no evidence that shadowing the message on one ear prevents attending to

FIGURE 4. Memory performance as indexed by d' values as a function of serial position when the probe item is presented immediately or after a delay of 20 seconds of shadowing (taken from Norman, 1969).

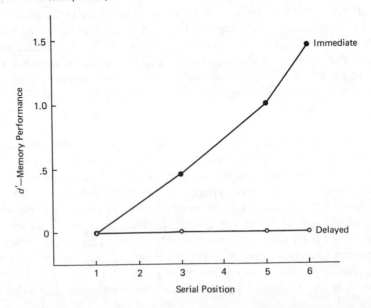

parts of the message on the unattended ear. The shadowing experiments, therefore, indicate that meaning can get through on the unshadowed channel, but we cannot say this occurred without some help from an attentive mechanism.

Broadbent's model of information processing generated a good deal of research, leading to refinement of the model and more research. Here we have an example of how the insights of a scientific investigator can influence the course of experimental research and theory. Although we criticized the basic experimental approach, it can be readily modified as demonstrated by the work of Treisman (1971) and Norman (1969). These modifications allow the investigator to disentangle the stages of information processing in the task and, more importantly, to determine which stages are influenced by an attention mechanism. The next chapter presents alternative theories of attention which were proposed to describe findings in disagreement with Broadbent's model, closing with an illustration of how the concept of attention can be incorporated into the general information-processing model developed in this book.

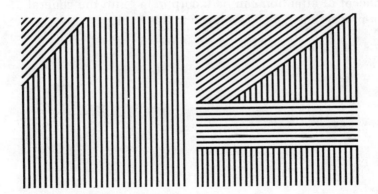

Models of attention

Every one knows what attention is. It is the taking possession by the mind, in clear and vivid form, of one out of what seem several simultaneously possible objects or trains of thought.
—William James (1890)

Experimentation and theory go hand in hand in scientific research. Broadbent's theory followed from the split-span studies and generated further research in this area. As might be expected, the results required further refinement in the theory. Rather than working within Broadbent's general theoretical formulation, other investigators developed contrasting theories. In this chapter, we discuss these alternative theories and show the interaction of research and theory in scientific study.

DEUTSCH/ NORMAN MODEL

Broadbent (1958) proposed that the attention of a limited capacity processor was necessary for recognition, whereas some research appeared to show that recognition could occur without complete attention. Treisman (1960) showed that subjects would shadow 'Dear Aunt Jane' even though the words were alternated across ears. Norman (1969) showed that some words were recognized on the unshadowed channel. These results spurred others to devise a model that could account for recognition without attention. Deutsch and Deutsch (1963) proposed that *all* information is recognized before it receives the attention of the limited capacity processor. Figure 1 presents a formal model of the Deutsch and Deutsch assumption as elaborated by Norman (1968).

In this model, recognition does not require the processing of a limited capacity processor. Rather, the meaning of all inputs can be derived simultaneously or in parallel. It is only then that the processing system becomes limited in capacity and the selective attention operation becomes necessary. Instead of using a physical channel as a basis for selection, however, the pertinence of the information is analyzed. The recognized items that have the highest level of relevance or pertinence are selected for further processing.

FIGURE 1. A model of information processing that assumes all inputs are recognized before selection occurs. All sensory inputs receive perceptual processing and are recognized; that is, they excite their representations (indicated by solid circles) in memory. Other factors influence which stored representations have high pertinence. The recognized items selected for attentive processing are those having the greatest pertinence to the task at hand (after Norman, 1968).

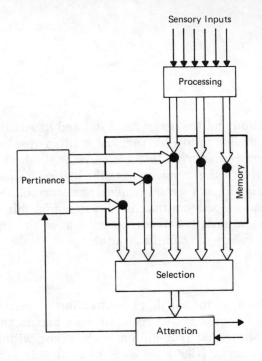

It is only at this stage that information processing becomes limited in capacity. The criterion for selection is pertinence, some ongoing aim of the processing system that enables it to select or reject information according to its relevance.

The central assumption of the Deutsch/Norman theory is that all items are recognized, even those presented to the unshadowed ear in a shadowing experiment. This means that the subject should know the words being presented on the unshadowed ear. If he is asked immediately, he should be able to repeat the word just spoken on that channel. But because he has been instructed to shadow the other message, which absorbs his attention, he cannot process the unattended message any further than recognition. The latter gets into short-term memory only for a brief period and is forgotten very quickly. These implications were supported by Norman's (1969) observations that subjects could remember the last couple of words on the unattended ear only if they were tested immediately, not after a short period of shadowing.

Location of Selective Filter

The critical difference between this theory and Broadbent's is the location of the selective attention mechanism. In Broadbent's model, all information available to the senses gets into the sensory buffer and remains there for two seconds or so. The limitation of the system is imposed between the sensory store and the recognition stage. Recognition is thus strictly limited by the selective filter since it needs the active attention of the central capacity processor. In the Deutsch/Norman model, on the other hand, information entering sensory store makes contact with meaning in long-term memory without the attention of a central capacity processor; all information available to the senses is thus identified and made meaningful before attention operates. Recognition does not require central processing capacity in this model, but remembering and/or responding to the information does require it. We are able to respond best when responding to only one channel of information, for example, a sentence; with more than one channel, performance deteriorates. We can, however, recognize all the stimuli entering the sensory store at the same time.

Figure 2 locates the filters of the two models in terms of our general information-processing model developed in Chapters 3, 12 and 13. Broadbent's theory says that the recognition process re-

FIGURE 2. The location of the filters of Broadbent and Deutsch/Norman models in terms of our general information-processing model.

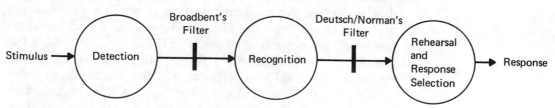

quires the attention of a central processor which is limited in capacity. Therefore, we cannot recognize two items as well as one. In contrast, the Deutsch/Norman theory says that only the rehearsal and response selection processes require the attention of a central processor which is limited in capacity; the process of recognition occurs without allocation of processing capacity. We, therefore, can recognize two items as well as one but can only rehearse and respond to a limited number.

TESTING THE BROADBENT AND DEUTSCH/ NORMAN MODELS Treisman and Geffen (1967) designed a test of the two models that made use of the Deutsch/Norman assumption that all incoming stimuli should be recognized by the system, whether or not they are allocated processing capacity. Their subjects shadowed a message in one ear while simultaneously another message occurred in the opposite ear. Besides repeating back one of the messages, they performed a second task at the same time. The subject was to tap whenever he heard one of a set of target words in the message. The target words would occur in either message, shadowed or unshadowed, and the subject was to make a tapping response in either case. The subjects thus had two tasks, to shadow the designated message, and to respond to targets occurring in either message.

The target words were of two kinds: specific words or categories. In one condition, the subjects simply were told to tap to a specific word, such as 'green.' In others they were told to respond to a class of words, such as any color, or any part of the face. On any shadowing trial there was only one target, or one class of targets.

Treisman and Geffen reasoned that, in Broadbent's model, recognition requires attention; therefore we can lock in the subject's attention by requiring him to shadow the message arriving at one ear, and he should not be able to notice target words or classes presented to the opposite, unattended ear. On the other hand, targets presented in the attended message should be easily recognized; they should get through the filter and should not require any additional processing to that necessary for the shadowing task itself. Broadbent's model predicts, therefore, that performance of the tapping response should be poor for targets on the unshadowed channel, and very good for targets in the shadowed message.

In the Deutsch/Norman model, there is no filter at the recognition level; recognition does not require attention, and therefore the words will be recognized as easily in the unshadowed as in the shadowed ear. On the other hand, it does take processing capacity to respond in this model, and in this case all the processing capacity might be used in the task of shadowing. Very little, if any, might be available for the tapping response for either ear. In this case, performance of the second task should be poor for both the shadowed and the unshadowed messages. A second possibility is that recognition of a target word would have high pertinence, which would be sufficient for the observer to switch his attention and tap to the target word in both channels. In this case, the tapping response obtains higher pertinence than shadowing, and tapping performance would be good at the expense of accurate shadowing. However, regardless of the pertinence of tapping, there is no apparent reason that tapping performance should differ in the attended and unattended ears since targets are recognized equally well in both ears.

The actual results of the Treisman and Geffen experiment fit the predictions of the Broadbent model. Subjects were able to respond to 87 percent of the target words in the shadowed message, but to only 8 percent of the targets in the unshadowed message. This was strong evidence for Broadbent and against Deutsch/Norman. Moreover, on most of the instances that went to make up the correct responses for the unshadowed message, performance of the shadowing task was disrupted; subjects made an error in the shadowing response, delayed it, said the wrong word, or skipped a portion of it entirely. This disruption seemed to indicate that when subjects did recognize and respond to targets on the unattended channel, the processing capacity available to the shadowed channel was reduced. In contrast, tapping to targets on the attended channel did not disrupt shadowing of that channel. Thus, it might be argued that the subjects had to switch attention to recognize the few targets that they did recognize on the unshadowed channel. Since subjects knew that targets would occur on the unshadowed channel, it seems reasonable that every now and then they would switch attention, checking for targets on that unattended channel.

Deutsch and Deutsch (1967) promptly responded that Treisman and Geffen's experiment was poorly designed. They had neglected the critical factor of pertinence in the Deutsch theory. The judgment of whether or not to respond to recognized information is influenced by anything that contributes to the subject's sense of what is relevant. By instructing subjects to shadow words in the message coming to one ear, Treisman and Geffen had emphasized the importance of words coming to that ear. They would be considered more relevant, in a general way, throughout the task. The data of this experiment were thus attributed to a tendency, induced by the experiment itself, to inhibit responses to words on the unattended channel, and not to a failure to recognize them. But why should subjects inhibit a simple tapping response to words recognized on the unattended channel when they could easily manage this response along with the shadowing response when the stimuli came in on the same channel?

Deutsch and Deutsch argued that it was the shadowing instructions that gave different pertinence values to targets on the different ears. A test of this criticism of the Treisman and Geffen study might be made by eliminating the shadowing instructions, thus having subjects attend to one message without repeating it. This would equate the pertinence of attended and unattended targets. If we could assume that their attention was indeed locked in on the designated message, even though they were not required to respond to it in a way that ensured this, then, according to Broadbent, performance of the tapping response ought to be the same as when the shadowing response is required. On the other hand, if we could assume that the instructions to tap the targets on both channels equated their pertinence, Deutsch and Deutsch would predict that subjects would respond to all targets in both the attended and the unattended messages. Moray and O'Brien (1967) actually did something similar. They had subjects attend to a random list of letters in one ear while simultaneously another list of letters was presented in the other. They were instructed to push a button to digits that could occur in either channel. In Moray and O'Brien's study more digits were recognized in the attended than unattended ear, even though no shadowing was required, thus continuing to support Broadbent.

If Treisman and Geffen's interpretation of the results is correct, supporting Broadbent's theory, then one would expect that non-verbal targets of distinctly different physical characteristics would produce a different effect. This experiment was done by Lawson (1966); the design was the same as Treisman and Geffen's except that instead of target words, subjects were told to tap to clicks or brief tones imbedded in both the shadowed and unshadowed messages. The task was identical to Treisman and Geffen's in all other respects. Nonverbal targets should be noticed, according to Broadbent, as they can be easily distinguished from the other verbal items in the messages without the attention of the limited capacity channel. They should not, however, according to Deutsch and Deutsch, be treated differently than verbal targets because Treisman and Geffen's earlier results were presumably due to differences in pertinence, which would be the same in this study. Lawson's results revealed that subjects were able to respond to the nonverbal items independently of the channel in which they were presented, adding weight to the Broadbent theory. It is difficult to see how the Deutsch/Norman theory can provide a consistent account of both the Treisman and Geffen results, and Moray's and Lawson's results.

TREISMAN MODEL

In spite of this additional evidence in its support, the Broadbent theory could still not account for the fact that some meaning does get through on unattended channels. It is evident that both theories interpret attention, or the limitation of the system, too narrowly. Treisman, whose experiments have been important in demonstrating the problem of both theories, has argued for a third one that incorporates elements of both (Treisman, 1960, 1964). Her alternative in a sense allows information to be selected at both the physical and meaningful levels, but there are important differences in the way she sees the operation of the selection process.

The primary difference in Treisman's model is that the filter is not all-or-none, as in the Broadbent and Deutsch/Norman models. A certain probability always exists that some information on the unattended channel can get through. Treisman used the concept of attenuation to describe the filter's operation on the unattended channels; information on these channels is attenuated, rather than filtered out. The word was an unfortunate choice, as it is usually understood as something done to the information content. It suggests that information is reduced by the filter; that a tone, for instance, is made less intense. This left Treisman open to the criticism that once a channel had been attenuated, a portion of its message could not get through in its original intact state, as it evidently could in shadowing and other experiments.

What Treisman actually meant, however, was not that the filter reduced the amount of information available in the unattended channel, but rather that it did not allow that information to be completely analyzed. A particular signal can have a number of features; if it occurs on the attended channel, most of them will be analyzed; if it occurs on the unattended channel, only a portion of them will be processed. Only a few features, however, are presumably necessary to identify highly meaningful or overlearned material, and therefore such material occurring on the unattended channel can be expected to be recognized. That is, a subject attending to one channel might be actually processing about 10 percent of the information coming in on the other channel. This might be enough to allow him to identify his own name, or a word that is highly predictable from preceding context, but it is usually insufficient for recognition of any of the other words in the unattended message. A better concept for this than attenuation would be that of a probabilistic filter. There is a much higher probability of words in the shadowed message being recognized than words in the unshadowed message, since a larger portion of the attended message is processed for recognition.

The second point about Treisman's model is that selective attention can operate on two levels. Selection can take place along certain channels of information as in Broadbent's original model. The filter is guided by distinctive physical characteristics; for example, the filter can select a particular voice out of several. Broadbent (1970, 1971) calls this stimulus set—subject is set to receive stimuli from a certain stimulus channel. Selective attention also can operate at the level of meaning, in which case the subject must recognize the stimulus before he selects or rejects it. For example, if subjects were instructed to remember only the animal names in a list of words, they would have to recognize each word before they could

Attenuation

Two Levels of Selection

decide whether they should study it further. Broadbent calls this response set. In this case, the subject is set to respond to stimuli that have a certain meaning. These two levels of selection correspond directly to Broadbent's and Deutsch/Norman's levels of selective attention. In Broadbent's (1971) most recent statement, Treisman's modification is accepted completely.

Thus, attention in Treisman's model is hierarchical. A stimulus can be first analyzed with respect to its gross physical features; if it occurs on a selected channel, a stimulus will have a higher probability of being recognized than if it occurs on an unselected channel. That is, if it occurs on a selected channel, a higher proportion of its features will pass through the filter than if it is on an unselected channel. The determining factor for the filter at this level is stimulus quality represented by physical location, voice characteristics, or any other gross stimulus characteristic. Information that is rejected at this level will not be perceived. Information that passes through the first level of the filter is recognized, but may still be rejected after its relevance is determined, as in the Deutsch/Norman model. Information that is rejected at this second level will not be rehearsed and remembered, nor acted upon.

NEISSER MODEL

Neisser (1967) offered an alternative explanation of the act of attention. Neisser sees most behavior as the result of two successive stages of processing. The first stage is preattentive, in which certain global aspects of the stimulus input can be determined. For example, an object may be isolated from its background, that is to say, detected without being recognized. To determine the exact shape of the object, however, the second stage of processing is required. Neisser calls this process analysis-by-synthesis and holds that this constructive process is what we normally refer to as the mechanism of attention itself.

Neisser assumes that the analysis-by-synthesis process can be completely focused on one channel regardless of the events occurring on the other channel. Consider an experiment carried out by Treisman (1964) in which the subject was required to shadow a message presented to the right ear. Treisman tested the subject at two interference conditions by presenting two additional messages that could be ignored. In the first, these two interfering messages were presented to two separate channels: to the left ear and to the middle of the head (by presenting this message to both ears simultaneously). In the second condition, both interfering messages were presented to the same channel together. The results showed that shadowing performance was much poorer when the interfering messages were presented to separate channels than when they occurred on the same channel. Processing on the unattended channels was found to require processing capacity (attention), so that two separate inputs would produce more interference than one. Neisser's model cannot handle this result since the analysis-by-synthesis process is assumed to operate only on the attended channel. Whatever analysis occurred on the unattended channels should have resulted from the preattentive process. In Treisman's experiment, it seems evident that some additional processing capacity was required to reject two irrelevant locations instead of just one. By equating attention with the single processing stage of analysis-by-synthesis, Neisser's model does not provide a process to deal with attentional effects at other stages of information processing.

We have presented four models of attention, each of which attempts to account for the selective nature of information processing. In Broadbent's original model, attention is controlled by a filter that regulates the amount of information flowing past one point in the information processing chain. At any point in time it permits only one channel of information to pass through to the processes that come after it; the system is always devoting 100 percent of its processing capacity to the selected channel, and none to those that are rejected. In the Deutsch/Norman model, all inputs are recognized completely, and selection takes place afterwards. Treisman combined these two levels of selection into one model and argued that information could be partially filtered (attenuated) at two levels of information processing. Neisser's model equates attention with the constructive process of analysis-by-synthesis.

There is little real dispute that the human information-processing system is limited in its capacity to handle multiple inputs. The issue among the information-processing models is where that limitation is imposed by the system, and upon what criterion. Indeed, it is the central issue among them because it is the central concept in their models. The Broadbent, the Deutsch/Norman, and the Treisman models were all conceived around the question: How are we able to select some inputs and reject others?

The concept of attention developed in this book takes a different tack. We first develop a model of the processing of information rather than of the selection of information to be processed. Our task then, with respect to attention, is to first clarify the stages necessary to the processing of information between stimulus and response. Then we can ask which stages of information processing have a limited capacity and, within each stage, which experimental and

ATTENTION AND PROCESSING STAGES

stimulus variables affect the processing capacity requirements of that stage. We can follow up by asking at each stage whether or not the system is limited here, whether it can perform this particular operation on more than one item at a time without loss of efficiency in the processing of any of them. If we have properly defined and distinguished each stage, it should be possible to devise experiments that test for the limitation at each stage, while controlling for the processing contributions of other stages.

In this model, the intervening processing between stimulus and response is made up of a series of processes, or stages, wherein the information undergoes ever more complicated analyses. Each stage receives its information from the last, acts upon it independently of the others, and sends it on to the next in a transformed state. Thus, information in this system is thought of as undergoing a series of transformations that, in a sense, ultimately transforms the stimulus input into the selected response.

The system is provided with a number of channels along which information can enter. The process of monitoring these channels is detection. Detection, the simplest of the stages we shall consider, asks merely whether something is out there or not. Its analysis consists of determining whether or not a change has taken place in the steady state level of a given channel. When a state of noise background changes to a state of signal plus noise and the system registers that change, the system is said to have detected it. Specific memory for a stimulus need not be involved at all in this process, which merely looks for any change in the environment. Thus we can detect a stimulus that is too faint to be recognized completely. We have often heard or seen something without determining *what* it was.

Two questions can be asked about the process of selective attention at the level of detection. First, is there a limited amount of processing capacity available for detection that can be allocated to a particular stimulus channel? For example, can we detect a visual and auditory stimulus simultaneously as well as either stimulus alone? Second, can the processing capacity demanded by other stages of information processing interfere with the detection process? For example, do we detect signals as well when we are also rehearsing a set of numbers for later recall?

In an analogous way, these same two questions can be asked about the recognition and rehearsal processes. The answers to these questions will determine to what extent attention operates at each stage of information processing.

To illustrate why it is so important to distinguish clearly between these processes, consider an experimental situation that we make more and more complex after the manner of Donders (see Chapter 3). For the stimuli in this series of tasks we choose the spoken letters *A* and *E* and we ask our subject to process these in increasingly complex ways.

In his first task, the subject is required simply to detect the stimulus by hitting a button whenever he hears anything over the head-phones. The experimenter presents one or the other stimulus at random from trial to trial and the intervals between the stimuli are randomly spaced so that the subject has no temporal cue. Every time the subject hears a signal he hits the button, and his reaction time (RT) is measured as the time between onset of the signal and onset of the response.

Subjects in this simple task can with practice get their RTs as low as 100 to 150 msec. Part of that time is taken up by the detection process, but some of the RT is required for other processes, such as response selection.

Recognition

To force the subject to make a more sophisticated judgment, we modify the above task by asking him to hit the button only if the stimulus is *E*. He is to ignore *A* when it is presented and to respond only to *E*. The stimuli are alternated at random so that, on the average, the subject will respond on only half the trials.

This is now a recognition task. In the detection task all the subject needed to decide between hitting or not hitting the button was the information either that something was out there or that nothing was out there. In this second task, however, he knows that some of the stimuli he is detecting require no response; that he will be wrong to respond not only when no stimulus is presented, but also when the stimulus is *A*. Therefore, after distinguishing between something-out-there and nothing-out-there, he must go on processing to distinguish *E* from *A*.

The RT in this task will go up to about 250 or 300 msec. As the reader will recall from the discussion of Donders' experiments in Chapter 3, the increase in RT for this task can be attributed only in part to the time required by recognition. The addition of the recognition task also changes the nature of the response-selection process, making it more difficult and therefore more time-consuming. Response selection is more difficult in the recognition task because, given a signal, the subject can only respond on 50 percent of the trials, whereas he always responds given a signal in the detection task.

Memory

The next level of complexity is reached when we add a memory task. For example, suppose we have the subject perform the same

MODELS OF ATTENTION   293

recognition tasks, hitting a button in response to *E* when *E* is alternated at random with *A*. Now, however, we stop every now and then in the course of the experiment and ask the subject to recall the last three stimuli that were presented. In order to respond correctly when interrupted, the subject must not only detect and recognize each stimulus as it comes in, but he must keep a running account of the three most recent stimuli. He must rehearse the list to remember it, and on every trial he has to update it with the letter presented on the current trial.

The new memory task puts a greater demand on the limited capacity system than did either the recognition or the detection tasks; therefore, RT to the letter *E* should increase. Note that in addition to the increase in overall complexity and sophistication, the role of memory has increased also. In the detection task the subject had to remember to hit the button every time an auditory stimulus was presented. In the recognition task he had to remember what *E* and *A* sound like, and to respond only to *E*. In the memory task he also has to remember the correct sequence of the three most recent stimuli, which means that he has to remember not only which stimuli he has heard, but in what order. Besides demonstrating that subjects make more errors or take longer to respond as task complexity is increased, the experimenter must demonstrate which stages of processing are responsible for the results. Accordingly, for each experiment in the literature, we must ask which stage of processing is responsible for any attentional effect.

ATTENTION RECONSIDERED   In our model, attention is a continuous modifying function that reassesses allocation of processing capacity at each link in the chain of information processing. Each level of processing produces a more sophisticated analysis of the information. At the level of detection, one knows that something is out there. At the level of recognition, one knows the identity of its smallest recognizable unit. At the level of rehearsal, one has linked those units into more meaningful and continuous concepts such as words and phrases.

In order to process an input like continuous speech, the system must be able to perform all these functions simultaneously. As you recognize the words in this line, you are also updating, rehearsing, and storing information from previous lines in short-term memory. We would expect the overall capacity of the system to be limited in this respect also. There is an upper limit to the speed at which we can comprehend speech, for instance. As the rate increases, understanding deteriorates.

The attention mechanism must therefore allow us to allocate

processing capacity among the different stages of the information-processing chain. That is, not only does it protect each stage by dividing its processing capacity among the various inputs, but it also protects the entire system by rationing the overall processing capacity allocated to each process at a given time. For example, conversing in a second language is difficult because so much capacity is required at the level of word recognition that very little is left for analysis of the meaning of the message. The allocation of attention across different processing stages is clearly illustrated in the QRST task discussed in Chapter 12.

The advantage of our conception of attention over previous formulations can be seen in the following interpretations to a number of experimental findings. Treisman (1964) showed that two messages interfered more with shadowing a primary message when the two messages were presented to spatially separate channels than when the two interfering messages were presented to the same channel. In one experiment, the subject was required to shadow a message presented to both ears, which localizes the message in the center of the head. In one condition, the two interfering messages were presented to a single ear; in the other, one message was presented to each of the two ears. Shadowing was much more difficult when the interfering messages were spatially separated, than when they were presented to the same ear. When the two messages are presented to the same ear, they sound garbled and very little can be recognized. When the messages are separated, they interfere less with each other, making it possible to recognize them. According to our model, the separated messages interfere more with shadowing because they require more processing capacity than the two messages presented to the same ear. According to the other attention models, however, there is no apparent reason for this result. In Broadbent's and Treisman's models, filtering is a process that protects the limited capacity system; it does not take its processing capacity away from the task at hand. Therefore, these models cannot explain why separating the two messages would interfere more with shadowing than presenting them to the same location. The Deutsch/Norman model cannot explain these results because, for them, recognition does not take processing capacity. Therefore, even if the subjects recognized more of the irrelevant messages when they were separated, shadowing should not have been affected, since the low-pertinence messages could be ignored.

In the Broadbent and Treisman models and the Deutsch/Norman model, the process of attention occurs after selection takes place. This is clearly illustrated in the diagrams of Broadbent's and

Competing Messages

Deutsch/Norman's model presented as Figure 1 of Chapters 13 and 14, respectively. What these models have failed to make clear is that filtering or selection are simply terms used to describe a psychological process—one that could require attention itself. Therefore, these concepts only disguise the issue the researcher faces when he studies attention. Selection and filtering seemed to have been employed as mechanisms that allow the subject to narrow down to a manageable size an already information-rich situation. In sharp contrast to this, we view attention as the distribution of processing capacity that allows the observer to impose information on a yet impoverished stimulus situation.

Consider the following experiment carried out by Lewis (1970). The subjects in his experiment were required to shadow a list of single-syllable words presented to one ear. Simultaneously with each word presentation, another word was presented on the other ear. The independent variable in the study was the semantic relationship between the two words presented simultaneously. The dependent variable was the RT to shadow each word, measured from the onset of the word to the onset of the subject's shadowing response. Subjects were specifically instructed to shadow word by word and to respond as rapidly as possible. Lewis found that the semantic, and, therefore, the conceptual relationship between the words had a significant effect on shadowing performance. For example, when the word presented to the opposite ear was a synonym of the word to be shadowed, RT was longer than when the opposite word was unrelated in semantic meaning.

These results cannot be explained by the Broadbent model because the word presented to the opposite ear should be rejected by the filter mechanism. Its meaning, therefore, can have no effect since it has not been recognized. At first glance, the results might seem to support the Deutsch/Norman model because the meaning of the unattended word did get in; the word was recognized. But, why, according to this model, did the meaning of the opposite word influence the shadowing response to the opposite ear? The answer to this question requires a stage analysis of the Lewis experiment.

Two important stages of information processing in the Lewis shadowing task can be located: recognition and response selection. Both of these stages contribute to the RT and either or both of them could be responsible for the results. It is possible that the time to recognize the word on the attended channel was dependent upon the meaning of the opposite word. We might think that the recognition of the word on the unshadowed ear sometimes occurred before recognition of the attended word. In these cases, it is possible that its meaning might somehow interfere with recognition of the word to be shadowed. If this is so, however, it implies that recognition is a process that requires a limited processing capacity which can be distracted or influenced in some way by the meaning of another word that has been recognized. The Deutsch/Norman formulation cannot make this assumption since recognition occurs, according to their model, without any processing capacity limitation. The second stage of processing that could be responsible for the Lewis result is the response-selection process. One might argue that it is more difficult to select a response to one word out of two when the words are similar in meaning. This seems entirely plausible if response selection can require, as it does in our model, processing capacity. However, according to the Deutsch/Norman theory, the selection of the appropriate word occurs before attention is operative and does not require attention (see Figure 1). Therefore, it is difficult to see how their model can account for the result.

The Lewis experiment is closely related to a surprising and fairly long-standing phenomenon, the Stroop color-word effect. In this task, subjects are asked to read off the color of the print in a vertical sequence of words. In one case, the subject is given a column of digit names; in the other, a sequence of color names. He finds that it is much more difficult and takes longer to read off the colors when the letters spell nonmatching color names than when they spell digits. The best explanation of this phenomenon is one originally given by Stroop (1935), and then by Klein (1964) in his well-known study. These results show that the meaning of the letter sequences "get in," even though the subject is trying to concentrate on the color of the letters themselves. The difficulty appears to be one of response selection. When the letters spell names of colors, the subject is aware of two color names and must select the appropriate one. In the digit condition, the subject is aware of one color name and one digit name and, since the digit is so dissimilar, he can more easily select the color response.

Words and Colors

The Lewis experiment and the Stroop color-word phenomena demonstrate that the process of selection itself appears to require processing capacity. Accordingly, we have tried to indicate that previous models have incorrectly formulated the attention problem. We do not need to come up with a mechanism that occurs somewhere in the processing chain, which protects a limited-capacity processor by filtering or selecting information. Rather, we must describe the temporal course of information processing and the rules that govern it. The rules of each of our processing stages will allow us to predict when attentional phenomena will be observed. A theory of attention should directly follow, not precede, a theory of information processing.

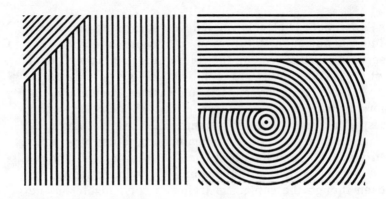

Attentional effects
within processing stages

The immediate effects of attention are to make us:
  a) perceive
  b) conceive
  c) distinguish
  d) remember
better than otherwise we could.
—*William James (1890)*

The concept of attention in our model depends on two criteria. First, the human processing capacity is limited; that is, there is a finite limit to the amount of cognitive or perceptual processing we can carry out at a given time. Second, given this limitation we can allocate this processing capacity to a particular stage of processing or to particular tasks within a stage of processing. When doing this, we say that we attend. The concept of attention would not be necessary if the system were not limited in capacity. Also, attention would not be possible if the system were not able to allocate a limited processing capacity to one task at the expense of another.

To validate this concept of attention one asks whether subjects can carry out two tasks as well as one. In the information-processing model we have presented, it is possible to make this question even more explicit. Having distinguished between the stages of processing, we first ask whether attention operates within each stage of processing. For example, can we recognize the information along one channel as well when we are simultaneously recognizing the input from another channel? The second question we ask is whether attention operates across or between processing stages. That is to say, can processing capacity available to one stage be reduced at the expense of processing at another stage? For example, is detection of a signal impaired by requiring the subject to remember a list of digits at the same time? In this chapter, we focus on the first question, deferring our discussion of the second question until the following chapter.

DETECTION

The process of detection is similar to the concept of sensation: the observer detects or senses something as being present. Much of the work studying detection has been concerned with the relationship between stimulus and sensation. However, one can also ask how the process of detection operates (see Chapters 5, 6, and 7). Can an observer detect a signal that might occur at two possible locations as well as in the case where it can occur at only one? Similarly, can an observer better prepare himself to detect a signal when he knows in advance exactly which signal will be presented than when he does not?

Auditory Detection Sorkin and Pohlmann (1973) studied the operation of attention in auditory detection. On each trial, an observation interval was defined and the subject reported whether or not a tonal signal was presented. The authors asked whether subjects could detect signals at either of two different frequencies as well as they could detect a signal at just one of them. In the selective attention case, subjects listened for a 630 Hz. tone and reported whether or not it occurred on a given trial. In the divided attention task, subjects were required to listen for either of two tones (630 Hz. or 1400 Hz.) and to report whether a signal was presented. It was found that subjects could detect the presence of a signal as well in the divided as in the selective attention task. Furthermore, Sorkin and Pohlmann showed that subjects could perform the divided attention task equally well if the two possible signals were presented to different ears. In this case, the subject had to listen for the 630 Hz. signal in the left ear and the 1400 Hz. in the right ear. The results show no evidence for an attentional process in the detection of auditory signals at different spatial locations or different frequencies.

It should be noted that both signals could not occur simultaneously in the Sorkin and Pohlmann task. Earlier studies (Sorkin, Pohlmann, & Gilliom, 1973) had shown that performance is disrupted in the divided attention condition when two signals could occur on a given trial. It appears that performance on one channel can be disrupted when a signal is presented on the other channel. In this case, a "signal" observation on one channel can lead to an interruption of detection processing on the other channel. Therefore, both studies taken together indicate that subjects can monitor at two frequencies and two locations for a signal as well as they could at just one, unless two signals are presented.

The Sorkin and Pohlmann study was a discrete trial signal-detection task with a well-defined observation interval. Moray (1970) has carried out auditory detection experiments in continuous detection tasks in which the subject must monitor a stream of signals occurring at a rate of 2 per second. This rapid rate of presentation could lead to performance differences in the selective and divided attention conditions that are not due to attentional effects at the detection stage, but could involve limitations at the later stages of information processing. For example, the response selection stage in Moray's task could take much longer in the divided attention task because the subject has to select twice as many responses in the divided than in the selective attention condition. The subject could easily fall behind when the signals are presented at a fast rate. Accordingly, Moray's results that subjects detect more signals in selective than divided attention cannot be interpreted unambiguously with respect to the stage of information processing responsible for the result.

Shiffrin, Craig, and Cohen (1973) studied attentional effects in the detection of vibrotactile stimuli. They asked whether observers could monitor three locations on the skin simultaneously for a tactile stimulus as well as they could monitor the three locations separately in sequential order. The three spatial locations were the palm of the right hand, the tip of the left index finger, and the surface of the forearm. Each vibrator protruded through a fixed surrounding frame attached to the locus of the skin. By activating one of the vibrators very slightly, a signal was presented, which was detected by the subject about 75 percent of the time. The task of the subject was to report which of the three locations contained the signal.

Tactile Detection

The question asked by the experimenters was whether the subjects could simultaneously monitor all three locations for a signal as effectively as they could monitor only one location at a time. Two experimental conditions were set up to answer this question. In the divided attention condition, there was a single observation interval during which the signal could occur at any of the three locations. On a given trial in the selective attention condition, the subjects were given three observation intervals, each associated with a particular location. Subjects knew that during the first observation interval, the signal could occur on the palm; during the second, on the finger; and during the third, on the forearm. The observation intervals were separated by 800 msec. On both selective and divided attention trials, only one signal was presented and the subjects were required to report its location. Subjects could monitor the locations one at a time in the selective attention condition, whereas they had to monitor the locations simultaneously in the divided attention condition. This experiment asks whether the detection of vibration is limited with respect to spatial location.

The experimental procedure used by these investigators was not arbitrary, but was necessary to control for differences in the operations of the decision system in the two tasks. Another procedure might have compared detection of a signal that could be presented to any of the three locations with detection of a signal to only one. On half of the trials the signal would be presented and the subject would simply state whether or not a signal occurred. In this task, the subject would have to make decisions about three locations in the divided attention case and about only one in the selective attention condition. The analysis presented later shows that this procedure confounds the operations of the decision system with that of detection. Therefore, the result would not be informative with respect to attention effects operating at the level of the detection process.

Shiffrin et al. (1973) found no differences in the selective and divided attention conditions. Performance averaged about 67 percent correct in both conditions. This means that subjects could not focus processing capacity on the relevant location to improve detection in the selective attention condition. Subjects essentially could monitor the three loci simultaneously as well as they could monitor one particular locus. This result shows that the concept of attention is not necessary to describe the detection of tactile stimuli across spatial location. It might be argued that a difference could still be found if the conditions were made more difficult, for example, by decreasing the intensity of the vibratory signal. This seems unlikely since the subjects were performing well below perfect performance where an actual difference could have been washed out by a ceiling effect. Even so, the procedure used in the author's laboratory, which is discussed later in this chapter, improves on the Shiffrin et al. procedure. It introduces a second independent variable that allows the experimenter to test his attention hypothesis at a number of different performance levels.

Visual Detection   Shiffrin, Gardner, and Allmeyer (1973) studied the detection of a single visual dot under selective and divided attention conditions. In divided attention, the subjects were required to monitor four locations simultaneously, whereas in selective attention they could monitor the locations successively. It would not be surprising to find a performance difference in the two conditions if the subjects were permitted to fixate on each location separately in the selective attention condition. In this case, each location would be viewed in foveal vision where acuity would be greater. Accordingly, the subject's performance might be better in the selective attention case just because the dots hit a more sensitive part of the retina, rather than because of selective attention. To control for acuity differences in the selective and divided attention conditions, Shiffrin et al. designed the following task. They defined a spatial array of two locations vertically by two locations horizontally. A fixation point was placed in the center of the display where subjects maintained their fixation. In the simultaneous case, a dot appeared in one of the locations during the observation interval and the subject reported which location contained the dot. In the successive case, there were two observation intervals: in the first, the dot could occur in either the upper left or lower right locations and in the second, the dot could occur in either the upper right or the lower left locations. The interval separating the two observation periods was 500 msec. The subject knew the relevant locations for each observation interval and at the end of the trial reported which location contained the dot.

The procedure is exactly analogous to the procedure used by Shiffrin, Craig, and Cohen in tactile detection. In both the selective and divided attention conditions, the subject must decide which one of four locations contained the dot presentation. The results showed no differences between the two conditions. In agreement with auditory and tactile detection, attentional effects do not appear to be operating at the processing stage of visual detection. The possibility remains, however, that attention effects might be found if the number of locations requiring monitoring is larger than the number used in this study.

The previous studies have shown that subjects can simultaneously monitor several channels of input in a given modality without a performance decrement. Shiffrin and Grantham (1974) studied whether subjects could monitor several modalities as well as one modality for detection of a signal. Again, they used the successive versus simultaneous paradigm. Subjects monitored visual, auditory, and tactile channels for a signal occurrence. On each trial, a signal was presented in one of the modalities and the subjects reported which modality contained the signal. There was one observation interval in the simultaneous task and three observation intervals separated by 500 msec. in the successive task, corresponding to the respective modalities. If detection were limited in processing capacity and observers could direct this limited capacity to a given modality, performance should have been better in the successive than the simultaneous conditions. This result did not occur, however, showing that the detection process appears to operate without attentional effects across the different modalities.

Detecting Signals in Different Modalities

Attention operating at the recognition stage of information processing has been called selective perception. Layman's usage of the concept of attention at perception is too general for experimental

RECOGNITION

purposes. For example, elementary school teachers might chide a pupil to "pay attention" when they mean that he should be looking at the blackboard rather than out the window. Contemporary psychologists have placed a more restrictive definition on attention. They are not impressed with the fact that an object is seen more clearly when attended to, if this means the subject changes his eye fixation from a peripheral to a foveal view. Our acuity in foveal vision is more sensitive than in peripheral vision and the concept of attention is not necessary to describe this phenomenon. The experimenter who wants to demonstrate attentional effects in perception must show that the amount of information available to the sensory system is constant in the two attention conditions.

Auditory Recognition

Massaro and Kahn (1973) studied whether attention is operative at the recognition stage of information processing. More specifically, they asked whether subjects could recognize the pitch quality of a tone without full attention to the tone. The tone recognition task was carried out in a backward recognition masking paradigm. In Chapters 21 and 22, we shall see that tone recognition is critically dependent upon the time between the test tone presentation and a second tone. Performance improves dramatically with increases in the silent interval between the first test tone and the second masking tone. Systematic variation of this second independent variable allowed Massaro and Kahn to test the attention hypothesis at a number of performance levels. On selective attention trials, the subjects simply had to identify the pitch quality of the first tone as sharp or dull. On any trial, the tone itself was equally likely to be of dull or sharp pitch quality. On the divided attention trials, the subjects were also required to identify as short or long the duration of a visual stimulus presented simultaneously with the test tone. The actual duration of the visual stimulus was also equally likely to be of short or long duration.

The selective and divided attention trials were presented in a completely random order. One second before each trial, the presentation of a visual cue indicated to the subject whether the upcoming trial was a selective or divided attention condition. The sharp or dull test tone was presented alone for 20 msec. in the selective attention condition and subjects identified it as sharp or dull. In the divided attention condition, the visual digit zero was presented simultaneously with the test tone presentation. The digit lasted 40 or 100 msec. The subjects in the divided attention condition were instructed to identify (1) the test tone as sharp or dull and (2) the duration of the visual symbol as short or long.

The results showed no effect of the attention manipulation.

Figure 1 shows that test tone identification did not differ under the selective and divided conditions averaging 73.5 and 73.7 percent, respectively. Performance did improve significantly with increases in the silent interval between the test and masking tones so that the attention hypothesis was tested at a number of performance levels. One reason that identification of digit duration did not interfere

FIGURE 1. Percentage of correct identifications of the test tone as a function of the intertone interval under both selective and divided attention conditions (after Massaro & Kahn, 1973, Experiment III).

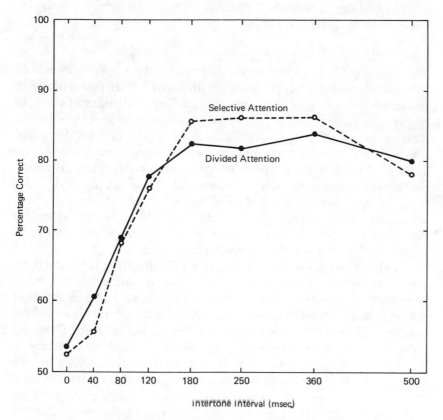

with tone recognition could be due to the ease of the duration identification task. Table 1 shows that identification performance averaged about 94 percent correct at all intertone intervals. To see if a more difficult task would interfere with tone recognition, the experiment was replicated while increasing the difficulty of the duration identification task. All experimental conditions were identical except that the duration of the visual symbol was either 100 or 160 msec. Identification of these durations should be more difficult than

TABLE 1
Percentage of Correct Identifications of the Duration of the
Digit "Zero" as a Function of the Duration of the Intertone Interval

Durations of Zero (msec.)	Intertone Interval (msec.)								Average
	0	40	80	120	180	250	360	500	
40–100	93	93	93	93	94	95	95	96	94
100–160	74	72	78	80	84	77	79	81	78

those in the first experiment since now the long stimulus is only about 1½ times as long as the short stimulus, whereas it was 2½ times as long in the first study.

Attention Effects Across Modalities

The first significant finding was that six of the twelve subjects in this experiment did not perform significantly better than chance in the test-tone identification task. This finding is significant since all of the nine subjects performed above chance in the first experiment. This result implies that identification of digit duration disrupted auditory recognition performance significantly. Analyzing the results of the other six subjects supports this conjecture. Although performance improved with increases in the silent interval under both the selective and divided conditions, Figure 2 shows that overall performance was significantly higher for the selective attention condition. Test tone identification was 5.4 percent better in the selective than the divided attention condition.

Table 1 indicates that the duration identification task was difficult—averaging 78 percent correct. Also, duration identification improved with increases in the intertone interval. This shows that when test-tone identification was more difficult due to a short intertone interval, duration identification also decreased. These results substantiate the operation of central processing capacity in auditory recognition. The amount of available processing capacity becomes limited as task difficulty increases. A visual identification task, if difficult enough, lowers performance on an auditory recognition task. This result is consonant with other investigations of single versus two-signal identifications (Lindsay, 1970). The findings suggest that the difficulty of the recognition task determines whether performance will be lowered in a divided attention situation.

Isolating Stages

It should be emphasized that this result can safely be located in the recognition stage rather than at another stage of information

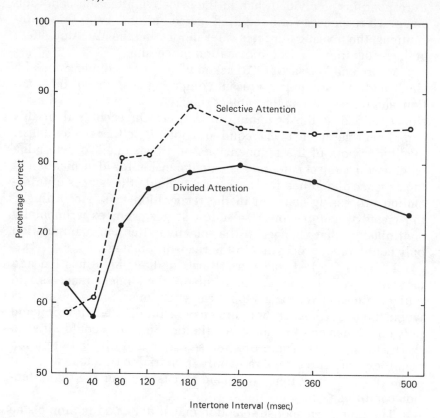

FIGURE 2. Percentage of correct identifications of the test tone as a function of the intertone interval under both selective and divided attention conditions (after Massaro & Kahn, 1973, Experiment IV).

processing. In the task, the selective versus divided attention conditions were manipulated on a within-subject basis and were presented randomly from trial to trial in an attempt to hold other processes necessary for tone identification constant in the two attention conditions. For example, memory for the test tones is critical for identification since subjects must learn and remember the tones to identify them accurately. When duration identification was difficult, it probably affected memory for the test tones as indicated by the overall deficit in performance in the second experiment. To the extent that the subject must process and identify the number duration, he has less time to identify and, therefore, remember the test tones. Of course, poorer memory for the tones will lead to poorer identification performance. By presenting the selective and divided attention conditions randomly from trial to trial, it was insured that memory for the test tones was held constant under the two attention conditions. Also, it seems unlikely that decision or response selection processes can account for the decrement in the divided attention condition. The subjects were given more time to respond in the divided than in the selective attention condition since two responses were required instead of one. With these precautions, the investigator feels safer in locating the attention effect at the recognition stage of information processing.

Moore and Massaro (1973) asked whether two dimensions of a single auditory stimulus represent competing channels of information, and if they do, can the subject selectively attend to one dimension specified at the beginning of a trial? On each trial of this experiment the subject was required to identify either the loudness, quality, or both of these dimensions of a test tone. To determine whether the subject can process one dimension for identification at the expense of another, it is necessary to hold other stages of information processing constant in the recognition task. Accordingly, the memory and response selection stages were experimentally controlled so that changes in the selective attention manipulation only could affect processing in the recognition stage.

Memory for test tones is critical for their identification and may vary with the amount of feedback the subject receives and with the time between trials to rehearse the tones. Since the subject would have to remember both dimensions for divided attention and only one dimension for selective attention, memory could differ in the two conditions. Therefore, the selective and divided attention conditions were presented randomly from trial to trial to insure that memory for the test tones was held constant under the two attention conditions.

The time for response selection may differ as a function of the attention manipulation. In the present experiment one response was required in the selective attention condition, while two were required in the divided attention condition. Accordingly, the subject was given more time to respond in the latter.

Given sufficient time, a limited capacity system could optimally process several dimensions of a signal simply by switching between them. Therefore, it is necessary to control the time available for the identification task. Although varying the duration of the test tone varies its clarity or the amount of information which it contains, it does not sufficiently control the perceptual processing time for that information (see Chapter 22). A preperceptual auditory image of the stimulus persists, extending the effective duration of perceptual processing. Presenting a masking tone after the test tone presentation can interfere with the processing of the preperceptual image. In the Massaro and Kahn experiment, we saw that if a short test tone is followed after some silent interval by a masking tone,

Studies previous to the Moore and Massaro (1973) study have not conclusively demonstrated that dividing attention between two dimensions of a tonal signal decreases identification performance. Lindsay, Taylor, and Forbes (1968) reported capacity limitations in a test measuring the discrimination of two auditory dimensions (frequency and intensity) under conditions where either one or two dimensions required attention. However, the findings are confounded by differences in the test stimuli used in the two attention conditions.

For example, in the selective attention condition when the subject identified which of two intervals contained the more intense tone, the irrelevant frequency dimension was the same in both intervals on a trial. In contrast, in the divided attention, both the frequency and intensity differed in the two intervals. In selective attention the subject identified the intensity of tones equal in frequency, whereas in divided attention he identified the intensity of tones unequal in frequency. It is well known that frequency has some effect on perceived loudness. Montague (1965) demonstrated that accurate identification of the intensity of a signal was reduced by varying the frequency of the tonal signal. It follows that, as in the Lindsay et al. (1968) study, an additional varying stimulus dimension in the divided attention condition may account for the lower performance relative to the selective attention condition. For informative results, experimenters must take care not to confound different stimulus conditions with their attention manipulation.

---

performance improves with increases in the duration of the silent interval. In the present experiment (Moore & Massaro, 1973), perceptual processing time was experimentally controlled using this recognition masking paradigm.

On each trial, the observer was presented with a test tone followed by a variable silent interval followed by a masking tone. The subject was required to identify either the loudness (soft or loud) or the quality (dull or sharp) or both dimensions of the test tone. The loudness of the tone was either soft or loud. The quality of the test tone was either dull or sharp. Each trial began with the presentation of a visual cue that preceded the test tone presentation by 2 sec, and signified whether the observer was required to identify only loudness, only quality, or both dimensions on the trial.

No Attention Effects Across Dimensions

There was very little advantage in performance for the selective versus the divided attention condition (1.75 percent averaged over subjects). Figures 3 and 4 present performance in the selective and divided attention conditions as a function of processing time (test

FIGURE 3. Percentage of correct identifications of the loudness of the test tone as a function of processing time under selective and divided attention. Results for best five subjects (after Moore & Massaro, 1973).

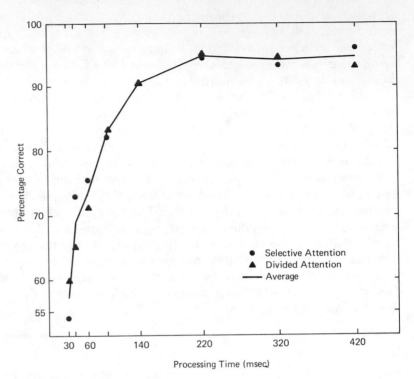

tone duration plus intertone interval). Performance improved significantly with increases in intertone interval, and the small difference between attention conditions did not change systematically with increasing processing time.

The large improvement in performance with increases in intertone interval demonstrates that processing time is critical for the auditory recognition process. The 1.75 percent difference in the two attention conditions is too small to be considered meaningful, and is negligible compared to the effect of processing time. The present study provided a strong test of selective attention, since it covaried a second independent variable, which controlled the duration of the perceptual process and thereby the level of performance. Even so, the attention variable did not affect performance. The results from the divided attention condition demonstrate that attention can be efficiently divided between dimensions of an auditory signal, and auditory recognition of one dimension cannot be enhanced by selectively attending to that dimension. A limited capac-

FIGURE 4. Percentage of correct identification of the pitch quality of the test tone as a function of processing time under selective and divided attention. Results for best five subjects (after Moore & Massaro, 1973).

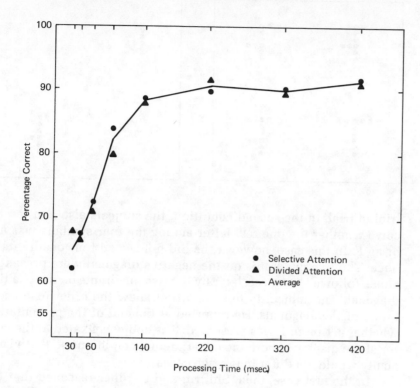

ity process appears to be unnecessary in describing recognition as a function of the number of dimensions in the present experiment. Future research requiring identification of more than two dimensions, however, may find evidence for such a limited capacity process.

Shiffrin and Gardner (1972) and Gardner (1973) asked whether attention effects operate at the visual recognition stage. We shall consider these studies in detail since they show how important it is to separate the recognition and decision stages of processing in perceptual tasks. Shiffrin and Gardner's visual display was a square divided into four quadrants. Each quadrant contained a letter; one of the four letters was a *T* or an *F*, and the other three were letter-like forms very similar to *T* and *F* (see Figure 5). The subject was told that each display contained a *T* or an *F* and instructed to say which letter was present on every trial. In one condition, the display was presented as described, the letter *T* or *F* varying from

Visual Recognition

FIGURE 5. Samples of typical displays used in the Shiffrin and Gardner (1972) study.

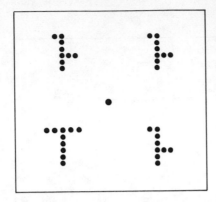 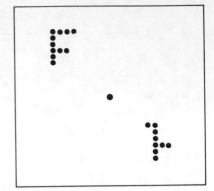

trial to trial. In the second condition, the subjects also had to perceive whether the one real letter among the four symbols was a *T* or an *F*. In this case, however, he did not see all four quadrants at once. The two quadrants on the negative diagonal were presented alone, followed 500 msec. later by the two quadrants on the positive diagonal. The subject in this condition knew the order of presentation of the diagonals. He reported at the end of the presentation whether a *T* or an *F* was presented. The subjects fixated at the center of the display in both the experimental conditions so that visual acuity would not differ in the two cases.

In the first case, then, Shiffrin and Gardner reasoned that the subject must divide his attention simultaneously among four letters to determine whether one of them is a *T* or an *F*. In the second case, only two of the quadrants require attention at one time. If recognition capacity is limited across spatial location, then the second condition, in which subject can devote all his attention to two quadrants at a given time, should enhance perception of the letters. It should be possible to process more of their features and to distinguish them more accurately. Performance, therefore, should be better in the second condition than in the first.

Gardner's decision model Why did not Shiffrin and Gardner simply compare the four-quadrant case to a two-quadrant case? In both cases, the subject would have to decide whether the display contained a *T* or an *F*. Therefore, the probability of guessing would be the same in the two tasks since there are two alternatives in both cases and chance performance is 50 percent. This, however, assumes an all-or-none guessing model. Other models of the task show that the decision system would be faced with a much easier task in the two- than the four-quadrant case. Gardner (1973) developed and tested a decision model of the task similar to the decision model we developed in Chapter 7.

The model of the task assumes that the subject evaluates each letter of the display independently at the recognition stage. The decision system makes its decision based on the values given by the recognition process. Analogous to the letter pandemonium model we shall discuss in Chapter 19, we can assume that each location of the display has a shouting demon who shouts T or F in direct proportion to the amount of T-ness or F-ness given by the symbol in that location. The decision system monitors the shouting from each location, chooses the loudest shouting demon, and responds with the letter he was shouting. Recall that the letter-like form was similar to T and F so we can assume that all symbols will produce some shouting.

The displays are presented for a very short duration, followed immediately by a masking stimulus so that the subjects make errors. We assume that the recognition process, analogous to the detection process, has a certain amount of background noise. This noise fluctuates from moment to moment so that a given symbol produces a different amount of information on different trials. Assuming that the information each symbol produces can be represented along a dimension of T-ness and F-ness, the letter T usually produces more T-ness than a letter-like form; sometimes, however, a letter-like form can actually produce more T-ness than the letter T. The noise in the system, assumed to correspond to a normal distribution, is responsible for this possibility. The amount of T-ness given by each symbol is shown in Figure 6.

The recognition and decision processes in the task can be described in terms of this model. The amount of T-ness or F-ness

FIGURE 6.   The amount of T-ness given by each of the test symbols follows a normal distribution (after Gardner, 1973).

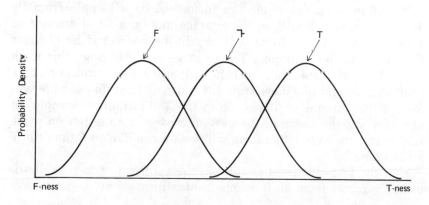

from a given location is given by a sample from the distribution corresponding to the symbol at that location. On the average, the sample will be at the mean of the distribution, but the noise in the system leads to errors. It is possible that a sample from the letter-like form will actually produce more T-ness or F-ness than the letters T and F themselves. Therefore, the letter-like form can produce more T-ness than the F-ness given by an F letter.

Analogous to our analysis of signal detection tasks, we assume that the decision system operates according to some decision rule. The decision system has available from recognition the amount of T-ness at each of the locations in the display. The simplest decision rule is that the decision system should place a criterion value at the mean of the distribution of the letter-like form. The amount of T-ness or F-ness from each location should be evaluated with respect to the criterion and the response should agree with the most extreme observation. In terms of the aforementioned pandemonium model, the decision system chooses the alternative shouted by the loudest shouting demon.

Given this model, what are the consequences when the number of locations and, therefore, the number of letter-like forms is increased? With two locations, the decision system evaluates the shouting of two demons, whereas it must evaluate the shouting of 4 demons when there are four locations. On F trials, most errors will occur because a particular letter-like form has more T-ness than usual and the F letter has less F-ness than usual. Similarly on T trials, most errors will occur when a letter-like form has more F-ness than the T-ness given by the T letters. If a T is presented in one quadrant and a letter-like form in the other, the decision system obtains a certain amount of information from each quadrant. The amount of information obtained on any trial from the T stimulus will be a single draw or sample from the T distribution. A draw or sample is exactly analogous to one roll of the dice in our dice game analogy of the signal-detection task in Chapter 7. Analogously, the information from the letter-like form will be a sample from its distribution, which will on the average have a neutral amount of T-ness/F-ness. The subject will usually be correct if he chooses the letter that has the most T-ness or F-ness. Although this is an optimal decision rule, however, he will still make errors; on some trials the amount of F-ness from the noise distribution sample will exceed the amount of T-ness from the T distribution sample. In other words, the noise in the system creates a situation on some trial where the letter-like form will look more like an F than the T looks like a T.

In the four-quadrant condition, the subject has to take distribution samples from all four quadrants. In this case, he must take two additional samples from the letter-like form distribution compared to the two-quadrant case. With three letter-like forms, the probability that the sample for one of them will be very high in F-ness increases considerably. Hence, if a T is presented, the subject is far more likely to perceive one of the letter-like forms in this condition as being more like an F than the T is like a T. Accordingly, the subject will make more errors in the four- than the two-quadrant condition.

This analysis shows that the decision system could be responsible for any performance differences when we increase the number of letter-like forms in the display. In our analysis, the recognition process was assumed to be constant in the two- and four-quadrant cases. That is to say, the amount of T-ness given by the test letter T did not change with changes in the number of noise letters. The operations of the recognition process were unaffected by the number of noise letters, but the subject made more errors in the four-quadrant case because the decision system was given a more difficult task. Faced with T-ness values from four locations instead of just two, it was more likely that one of the letter-like forms gave the most extreme value.

Shiffrin and Gardner (1972) were interested in attentional effects at recognition and did not want to contaminate their results with differences due to the decision stage. They controlled for the decision stage by requiring it to evaluate the output of four locations in both the selective and divided attention conditions. What differed was that the subject had to recognize only two of the locations at a time in the selective attention case, whereas he had to recognize all four locations simultaneously in divided attention. If attentional effects operate in recognition across spatial location, the amount of information given the decision system should differ in the two cases, thus producing a performance difference. The results showed, however, that performance averaged about 75 percent in both attention conditions. Subjects were able to recognize the T or F as well in the condition in which they had to process four locations simultaneously as in the condition in which they had two looks, with each look processing two locations.

The critical assumption we have been making is that the letter-like form is confused for a T or an F. This implies that the nature of the letter-like forms is critical for performance in this task. If the letter-like forms cannot be mistaken for a T or an F, increasing the number of alternatives in given display should not necessarily decrease performance. When the letter-like forms are extremely different than T or F, they will produce very little T-ness or F-ness.

No Attention Effects Across Spatial Location

Accordingly, the decision system could ignore these outputs in its determination of whether a *T* or *F* was presented. If attentional effects do not operate across spatial location in recognition, as shown in the Shiffrin and Gardner study, increasing the number of these very different alternatives in a simultaneous presentation with a *T* or an *F* should not degrade performance, because neither recognition nor decision will be affected.

The concept of attention refers to a central operation of allocating processing capacity and is not used to describe peripheral adjustments such as the increased acuity which results when an object is brought in foveal vision. Therefore, Gardner (1973) found it necessary to control for two operations in his task. Increasing the number of alternatives increases the spatial size of the array, which pushes the items towards the periphery where acuity is poorer. If the items are pushed together to give the same visual angle at all display sizes, the contours are pushed together, increasing the likelihood of lateral masking (see Chapter 17). Gardner's solution was the display presentation in Figure 7. Subjects fixated at a point placed at the center of an imaginary square and the items were presented at the corners of this square. Therefore, acuity is held constant in the different conditions since the distance

FIGURE 7. Sample displays used in Gardner's (1973) study which covaried the number of test letters in the display and the confusability of the nontarget letters.

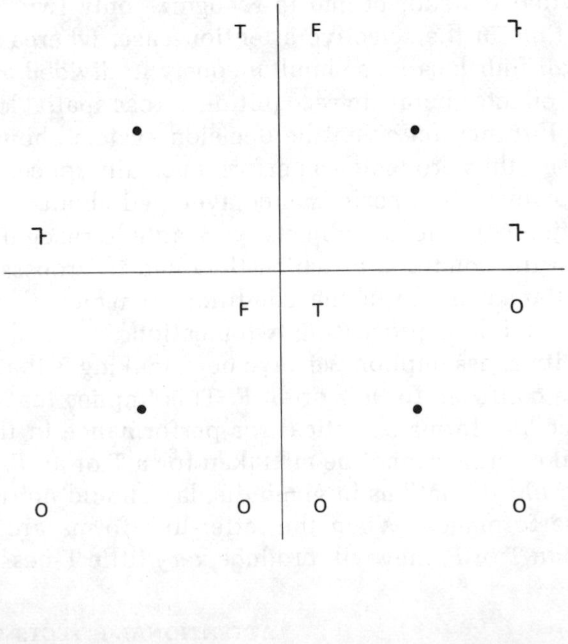

from the fixation point is the same for all display sizes between 1 and 4. Lateral masking is eliminated by making the square large enough so that there is no mutual interference between adjacent contours.

Gardner's (1973) experiment allowed him to evaluate the contribution of both the recognition and decision stages in his task. He systematically varied the number of alternatives in the display and the nature of the letter-like form. In the nonconfusable condition, the letter-like form was the letter O. In the confusable condition, the nontarget letters were letter-like forms used by Shiffrin and Gardner. On each trial, the subject saw a single display of 1 to 4 letters. There were three kinds of trials: T, F, or neither T nor F. On

FIGURE 8.   Probability of correct response as a function of the number of letters in the visual array for the "neither" trials in which neither a T nor an F was presented, and for the target trials in which either a T or an F was presented—with confusable or nonconfusable background letters.

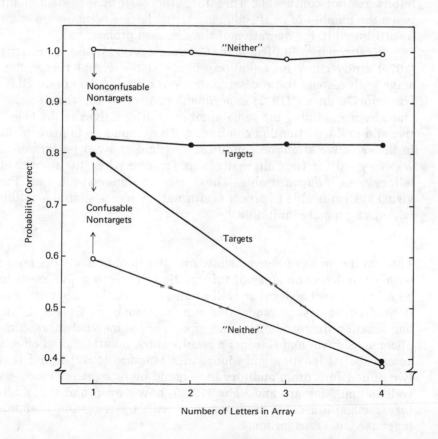

each trial, the subject responded *T, F,* or neither. Gardner (1973) reasoned that the decision system would not contribute to performance differences as a function of the number of alternatives in the nonconfusable condition since the letter *O* would produce very little T-ness or F-ness. The only cause of performance differences here could be the recognition stage. In contrast, both stages could produce differences in performance when the nontarget letters were the confusable hybrid *T–F.*

The results of Gardner's experiment, presented in Figure 8, show that increasing the number of letters in the display lowers performances if the nontarget letters are similar to *T* and *F*. This result can be attributed to either or both the recognition and decision stage. However, the results with the nonconfusable letters locate all of the effect at the decision stage. There was no performance decrement with increases in the number of letters when the letter forms were *O*'s. This result shows that the recognition process can recognize a *T* or an *F* out of four letters as well as out of one, and the decision system is not fooled when the nontarget letters are not confusable. Therefore, the performance decrement when the number of confusable nontarget letters is increased must be attributed to the operation of the decision process.

In summary, Shiffrin and Gardner's (1972) and Gardner's (1973) study show no attention effects at the visual recognition stage with respect to processing items at different locations. Shiffrin and Gardner's (1972) experiment controlled for the decision stage by maintaining the same number of alternatives in the selective and divided attention conditions. They found no improvement in the selective attention condition. Gardner showed performance was as good for four alternatives as for one when the nontarget letters were nonconfusable. These results demonstrate that the visual system is able to process information across spatial location without a capacity limitation.

The results we have viewed show no attentional effects operating within the detection stage of information processing. We seem to be able to detect a signal as well at any of a small number of locations, frequencies, or modalities simultaneously as we do at just one location. In recognition, the effects are somewhat more complicated. Shiffrin and Gardner's results show no attentional effects across spatial location and Moore and Massaro (1973) found that two dimensions of an auditory tone could be recognized almost as well as one. Massaro and Kahn (1973), however, found that auditory recognition could be interfered with by requiring a simultaneous visual recognition.

The apparently conflicting results of recognition make transparent the need for the two different criteria for attention in our model. Attentional effects are dependent upon a limited capacity and the ability to allocate that capacity to one task at the expense of another. Massaro and Kahn's subjects showed that recognition is limited in capacity and that the capacity can be allocated to a given modality. The results showing no attentional effects, on the other hand, illustrate that this limited capacity cannot always be allocated at will. More specifically, it seems difficult to allocate this capacity either to spatial location or to particular dimensions of a single stimulus. Finding the rule that predicts exactly when attentional effects will operate at recognition is the task faced by those who study attention.

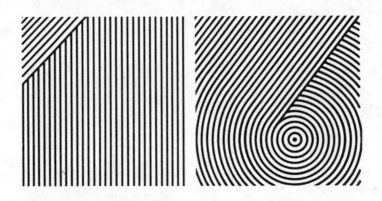

Attentional effects between processing stages

Selection is the very keel on which our mental ship is built. And in this case of memory its utility is obvious.
—William James (1890)

The last chapter examined attentional effects within the processing stages of detection and recognition. In this chapter, we study attentional effects between processing stages. Does processing at one stage influence the processing capacity available at another? If so, the addition of a task that requires processing in one particular stage should interfere with performance that is dependent upon the other information-processing stage.

Chapter 15 discussed studies of processing abilities within the process of detection. Another task is to determine if processing at another stage affects processing at the detection level. The logic is that if detection performance is limited in capacity it should be disrupted by additional processing requirements.

　　If detection requires processing capacity, performance of a detection task should be affected by the addition of a memory task, which also requires processing capacity. Broadbent and Gregory (1963) presented a list of six digits to one ear and a white noise burst to the other ear. The subject was required to monitor the noise burst for a pure tone that might be presented. In the selective attention condition, the subject could ignore the digits and concentrate on the tone presentation to the other ear. In the condition in which attention was divided, the subject was required to remember the digits, as well as to detect the tone. Subjects made more errors in detecting the signal when they were simultaneously required to remember the digits. This experiment demonstrates that attention was required for the detection process; if it were not, performance of the detection task would not be affected by adding a memory task. Broadbent and Gregory's study shows that the process of detection can be disrupted by a simultaneous memory task, although we do not know which stages of processing in the memory task disrupted detection.

DETECTION AND MEMORY

DETECTION AND IMAGINATION	The detection process also appears to be disrupted by imagination. This result was first demonstrated by one of Titchener's students in 1910. Titchener was concerned with describing the elements of consciousness; his student Perky was especially interested in the relationship between perception and imagery. By imagery Perky meant images brought to consciousness without reference to external stimuli, such as an imagined object or a remembered symphony. Perky felt that perception and imagination were closely related, involving the same processes and structures.

Perky Studies   To demonstrate this, she asked her subjects to fixate a white point on a translucent screen and then to form an image of a concrete object in their minds. Among the objects she suggested were apples, leaves, books, oranges, and so on. At the same time, Perky's assistant would project onto the screen, very near the fixation point, a colored patch in the shape of an object, at an intensity previously determined to be too dim to be seen. The intensity of the color on the screen was gradually increased to where it normally would be seen, while the subject completed forming the required image in his mind. He was then asked to describe it.

Perky found that when subjects were later questioned about what they had seen on the screen, few of them had been aware that anything was projected on the screen. Nevertheless, she found evidence that they had incorporated the color on the screen into their own images. On some trials, this finding was not conclusive. Perky unfortunately chose a red circle to project onto the screen when subjects were imagining an apple. With other objects, however, her results were not so easily discounted. When the color on the screen was blue, a book was imagined as blue more often than chance would dictate.

Two observations can be made about Perky's results. First, the ability to detect the color patch as being present apparently decreased during the imagination experiment. A level of intensity that was well above the previously determined "threshold" could not be detected by subjects engaged in forming an image. Thus it appears that imagination requires processing capacity that lowers our sensitivity to detect stimuli. Second, it seems that Perky's subjects confused two levels of information: the one from their mind's eye, and the one available to the sensory system.

These results generate two questions that must be answered in well-controlled experiments. The first question is, does imagery actually lower our sensitivity to a sensory signal? If both imagery and detection require central processing capacity, we should be less sensitive to the information coming in the sensory system while we are forming an image. The second question is related to Perky's assumption that the processes of perception are continuous with those of imagination. Does imagery require two kinds of processing capacity? The first would be a central processing capacity which could account for a positive answer to our first question. The second would be a modality-specific processing capacity peculiar to the nature of the image. Forming visual images may involve a different process than forming auditory images. Evidence for a modality-specific processing capacity ties the processes used in perception more directly with those used in imagination.

Segal and Fusella (1969) were specifically concerned with the first question: Does imagining lower our sensitivity to signals? In the selective attention condition, for example, the observer, looking at a fixation point in the visual field, was asked to detect whether a visual signal was presented. In the divided attention condition, the observer, looking at the fixation point in order to detect whether a signal was presented, was simultaneously required to form a visual image. The subjects might be asked to imagine a pair of shoes or a glass of orange juice. Colored geometrical forms were used as test signals. A standard signal-detection task and analysis were used to control for possible differences in the decision stage. A signal was presented on half the trials and the observers indicated on every trial whether or not a signal was presented. In the divided attention condition, the subject would first report whether or not a signal was presented, and then describe the image.

Segal and Fusella Studies

Replicating Perky's results, Segal and Fusella (1969) observed that the subjects' sensitivity to the visual signals was greater in the selective attention condition than in the divided attention condition. So we have, then, the process of imagination interfering with the process of detection. This result can be explained simply by a central processing capacity notion. That is, we have a certain amount of central processing capacity and we allocate it to different processing stages. Hence, if we allocate processing capacity for imagery, this will interfere with detection.

Segal and Fusella (1970) then asked whether there is a modality-specific processing capacity. Does the process of imagination require some of the same processes utilized by the process of perception? To test this, the investigators covaried the modality of the detection task with that of the imagination task in a factorial design. There were three imagination conditions: no imagination, visual imagination, or auditory imagination. These three imagination conditions were carried out under both visual and auditory detection tasks. If imagination also requires some modality-specific processing capacity, then observers should be better able to detect a visual signal under an auditory image condition than under a visual image condition. The poorest conditions for detection should be when one has to detect an auditory signal under an auditory imagination condition and a visual signal under a visual imagination condition.

Evidence was found by Segal and Fusella (1970) for both a central and a modality-specific processing capacity. Detection in the selective attention condition was better than detection when the subjects were required to form an image in the opposite modality. For example, detecting an auditory signal was disrupted when the subject had to form a visual image. This result was evidence for a central processing capacity. The modality-specific capacity is seen in the result that detecting a signal was significantly lower when the subject had to form an image in the same modality than in a different modality. These findings support Perky's early arguments for a processing relationship between perception and imagination.

Two different sets of experiments related to the detection process have been discussed. The first set of studies in Chapter 15 asked whether the detection process is limited with respect to the number of channels it can monitor simultaneously in order to detect a signal. The second set of studies discussed here asked whether a second task such as memory or imagination could interfere with the detection process itself. These two approaches to the study of attention effects at the level of detection lead to different conclusions. The first set of studies indicates that the detection process could operate without attentional effects. The second set of studies indicates that other processing requirements disrupted detection, leading to the acceptance of attentional effects at detection. Although these results appear to be contradictory at first glance, they are not necessarily so. The detection process may be constrained by a limited capacity as evidenced in the second set of studies. However, this processing capacity may be needed for the process of detection itself, not detection at a particular channel. The fact that we can process a number of letters simultaneously in visual word recognition does not mean that attention cannot operate at the level of this process. The first set of experiments tells us that the concept of attention is not necessary to describe detection performance as a function of the monitored number of channels. The locations can be monitored in parallel without any deficit in performance. The experiments do not say that the detection process itself is unaffected by the contribution of a limited capacity system.

In this section, we ask whether the amount of processing at other stages adversely affects visual and auditory recognition. Shulman and Greenberg (1971) asked whether memory for consonant letters interfered with visual recognition. Subjects were presented with 3, 5, 7, or 10 letters auditorily, followed by a short presentation of a visual digit. Subjects were asked to identify the digit and then to report the letters that had been presented. Digit recognition decreased significantly when the memory list increased to 7 or more items. A second experiment showed that the size of the memory list also affected the time it took for subjects to decide which of two lines were longer. These results support the idea that visual recognition and memory are both dependent upon a system that must share its limited capacity across the two processing stages.

In a class demonstration by the author, students were required to identify the syllables *da* or *ga*. The syllables were synthesized speech stimuli chosen to be fairly confusable so that errors would occur. Recognition was required under four different memory load conditions: 0, 1, 4, or 7 digits. Subjects were given a memory list of digits followed by a test syllable. They first stated which syllable had been presented, followed by recall of the digit list. The experimental question was: Does the process of recognition require processing capacity used by short-term memory? If it does, we would predict that increasing the memory load would interfere with recognition. The results indicated that memory load did interfere with the recognition process. Using d' as a measure of performance, recognition scores were 1.86, 1.67, 1.48, and 1.15 with 0, 1, 4, and 7 items in memory, respectively.

Chapter 12 showed that short-term memory was constrained by a limited capacity system. In fact, as we shall see later on, the best rule that describes processing in short-term memory will be based on the concept of a limited capacity. This theory, developed in Chapter 27, has two central assumptions (Massaro, 1970). Memory for an item is (1) directly related to the perceptual processing of that item, and (2) inversely related to the amount of perceptual processing of other items. Equating the concept of perceptual processing with processing capacity, we have a limited capacity rule for short-term memory. To the extent that some items require processing capacity, other items will be forgotten. The evidence that was presented in Chapter 12 and will be presented in Chapter 27 can be interpreted in favor of a limited capacity short-term memory. Here, we discuss one additional study that supports this idea

RECOGNITION AND MEMORY

DETECTION, RECOGNITION, AND MEMORY

and illustrates how specific quantitative models can be utilized to test experimental hypotheses. These same models help us locate experimental effects at particular processing stages.

Lindsay and Norman Study

Lindsay and Norman (1969) aimed to demonstrate how processing in short-term memory was limited. Their experiment involved two simultaneous tasks: a detection task and a short-term memory task. In the detection task, four noise bursts were presented in sequential order to the left ear. The noise bursts were 1 sec. in duration and were separated by 500 msec. of silence. A 100 msec. tone was presented in the middle of three of the noise bursts. On each trial, the three intervals that contained the tone were chosen randomly. The subject had to indicate which noise burst did not contain a tone.

Simultaneous with the train of noise bursts, the experimenters presented a list of six three-digit numbers at a rate of one number every second in the right ear. The list of numbers was followed by a probe number. On two-thirds of the trials, the probe item was an old item, identical to one of the previous six items. The old probe item was equally likely to be identical to any of the preceding six items. On the other one-third of the trials the probe item was a new three-digit number that had not been presented in the preceding list. The subject's task was to indicate by "yes" or "no" whether the probe item was an old item.

Stage model of memory task

Before discussing the operation of attention in this paradigm, we need to discuss a stage model of the short-term memory task used by Lindsay and Norman. This model is currently being used by a number of investigators studying short-term memory. The model describes the component stages or processes that are involved in the task and how these processes interact. The processes in the task are *acquisition, retention, retrieval,* and *decision.* The acquisition stage involves the perception and storage of each test item. After the items are perceived and stored, they must be maintained in memory. This stage is the retention process. At test, the subject is required to retrieve the necessary information from memory. The retrieval process is followed by a decision process which leads to the response.

Familiarity

It is necessary to postulate a dimension of judgment in the task. In the signal-detection task, we assumed that the observer made his decision along a dimension of intensity of sensation. If the sensation value exceeded his criterion value on any trial, he said that a signal was present. In the memory task the dimension of judgment is one that we shall call familiarity. The concept of a familiarity dimension is based on the very primitive notion that when a subject is asked whether a probe digit was a member of the preceding list, he bases his judgment on the relative oldness, or familiarity, of the digit. If he has just seen it on the preceding list, it should look very familiar to him. If it is a new digit, it should look strange, or different, from the preceding list of digits. If the familiarity of the probe item exceeds his criterion value, the subject says "old"; otherwise he says "new."

The model describes changes in the familiarity of potential probe digits in the task. When the subject is presented with a given memory item, that item gains α units of familiarity. The parameter α is an index of how much familiarity was gained from that presentation. The value of α is tied to the presentation conditions of the memory digits. The familiarity F of an item after presentation can be described by

$$F = \alpha \qquad (1)$$

Some independent variables that should affect α would be the presentation time, how long the subject has to perceive and encode the test item, the signal-to-noise ratio of the test item, and possibly the amount of attention that the observer can give to the test item. The α parameter provides an index of how familiar the test item is immediately after its presentation. It is reasonable to assume that an observer could only remember an item to the extent that the initial perception and storage of the item gave a high value of α.

Now we need to describe the retention of familiarity of one test item as new items are perceived and encoded. Experiments have shown that the familiarity of a test item will decrease with presentation of additional items (see Chapter 27). Every additional item the subject is presented with decreases the familiarity of an earlier item by a constant proportion. This result can be represented mathematically by

Mathematical representation

$$F = \alpha \phi^i \qquad (2)$$

where i is equal to the number of additional items presented after a test item. The value ϕ is a forgetting index that lies between 0 and 1. It is that proportion of familiarity of the test item that remains after each new item is presented. Equation 2 shows that the familiarity value F decreases geometrically with each additional presentation of a new memory item.

When the probe is presented, the subject perceives the item and determines its familiarity. This involves a retrieval process.

The decision process maintains a certain criterion familiarity value. If the familiarity value of the probe item exceeds the criterion, the subject says "yes"—he has seen the item in the preceding list. If the familiarity is less than the criterion value, the subject says "no"— the item is a new one.

Another way to describe the history of our test item is to take logarithms of Equation 2. In this case the log familiarity is equal to the log of α plus i times the log of ϕ.

$$\log F = \log \alpha + i \log \phi \qquad (3)$$

Since ϕ always has to lie between zero and 1, the log of ϕ will be either zero or a minus number. Bringing the minus sign out in front of the second term in Equation 3 gives

$$\log F = \log \alpha - i|\log \phi| \qquad (4)$$

where $|\log \phi|$ is the positive value of $\log \phi$.

Equation 4 shows that each additional item decreases log α, the initial familiarity, by a constant amount. If the F values are plotted on a semi-log plot, in which F is plotted on a logarithmic scale on the Y ordinate, and the number of intervening items i is plotted on a linear scale on the X abscissa, we would generate a straight line with a negative slope. A hypothetical function with $\alpha = 4$ and $\phi = .8$ is shown in Figure 1. The line intercepts the Y ordinate at α and the slope of the line becomes more negative (steeper) with decreases in ϕ.

It is now necessary to tie this familiarity measure to the dependent measure of performance in the task, using the signal-detection analysis presented in Chapter 7. Hence, we need a hit rate and a false alarm rate at each level of our independent variable —the serial position of the item equal to the probe item on old trials. Another equivalent way of expressing the levels of the independent variable is in terms of the number of intervening items between the original presentation of the item and its probe test. For example, in Lindsay and Norman's six-item list, an item presented in serial position 2 would have 4 intervening items between its presentation and the probe test. The hit rate is defined as the probability that the subject says "yes" given that the probe item was presented in the preceding list. This is written P(yes|old). A hit rate can be computed at each serial position. The false alarm rate is defined as the probability that the subject says "yes" given that the probe item was a new item, P(yes|new). This probability is not defined with respect to serial position, since a new item was not presented in the preceding list. Accordingly, we compute a

FIGURE 1. A hypothetical forgetting function which describes the changes in familiarity of an item as a function of the number of intervening items between its presentation and test.

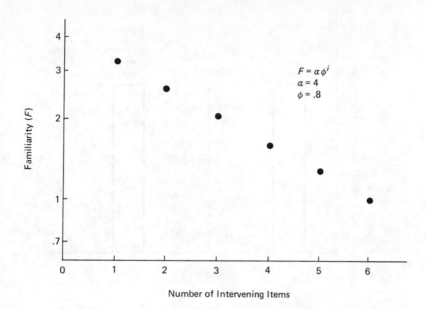

single false alarm rate, but a hit rate for each serial position. Performance is measured by the proportion of times the subject says "yes" on old trials, against the proportion of times the subject says "yes" on new trials. If the subject says "yes" equally on old trials representing a given serial position and on new trials, then he cannot distinguish these old items from new items. Hence, he has no memory for the old items at this serial position. Next we describe how these proportions relate to the familiarity values utilized in our model of the short-term memory task.

The test items on both old and new trials should have some familiarity. But on the average we would expect old test items that had been presented in the list to have more familiarity than new test items which had not been presented in the list. Figure 2 presents two histograms, showing that old items presented in the preceding list have a familiarity value greater than that for new items. Our measure of performance, how well the subject can discriminate old items from new items, is measured simply by the distance between these two familiarity values. If these two values are far apart, then old items can be discriminated very well from new items. Hence, performance in this task would be very good. In contrast, if there

Familiarity and performance

FIGURE 2. The familiarity values for old and new items are represented by two histograms. The distance between the histograms provides a measure of how well the old items are remembered.

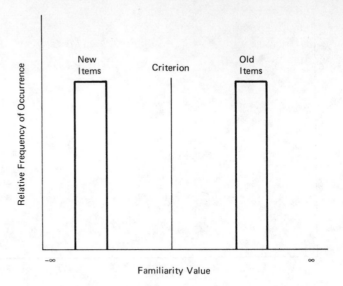

were very little or no distance between these two histograms, performance would be very poor in the memory task.

The subject makes his decision at test based on the probe item's value of familiarity. If this familiarity value is greater than his decision criterion C, the subject says "yes, it's old." If the familiarity value is less than C, he says "no, it's a new item." If the subject's criterion value is between the two histograms in Figure 2, his performance would be perfect. But subjects make errors. Thus, there must be some overlap in the two histograms shown in Figure 2. The familiarity of some new probe items exceeds the criterion value C and the subject incorrectly says "old." The familiarity values of some old probe items are less than the criterion value C and the subject incorrectly responds "new" to these items. Therefore, the familiarity values are probabilistic; a given probe item does not always produce the same value of familiarity. There is some random fluctuation in the value from trial to trial. We call this fluctuation "noise" because its statistical properties are assumed to be equal to those of auditory white noise.

The noise in the familiarity values can be described by a normal distribution on our familiarity scale. We now assume that a test item's familiarity value is a sum of two components: (1) the real value component shown in Figure 2, which differs for new and old trials, and (2) the value of the noise on that particular trial.

Figure 3 presents the probability distributions of the familiarity values for old and new test items when noise is added. As the figure shows, the distributions now overlap. On some trials, old items give familiarity values less than the criterion and some new items give familiarity values greater than the criterion value. Accordingly, with this model subjects should make errors in the short-term memory task.

FIGURE 3. Probability distributions for old and new items when noise is added to the distributions given in Figure 2.

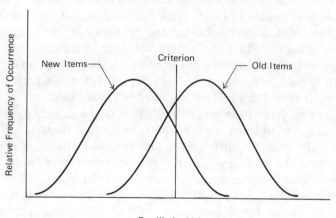

It is now possible to translate the subject's response probabilities into a familiarity value. The distance between the means of the old and new distributions is used as an index of how well the subject remembers. This method was described in detail in Chapter 7 for detection and recognition tasks. Here, the probability that the subject says "yes" to an old item is the hit rate, and the probability that the subject says "yes" to a new item is the false alarm rate. These two proportions uniquely determine the distance between the means of the two distributions as shown in Chapter 7. The distance is called d' and is taken as the index of memory performance in the task. The observed d' values can also be compared directly to the predicted values of familiarity F since they index the same dimension of familiarity.

According to the theory of the memory task presented, the subject would almost always recognize an old probe item correctly if it occurred very recently in the list. Figure 1 showed that F is large, with few intervening items between presentation and test. On the other hand, if the item occurred very early in the list and then was presented as a probe item, the subject would be less likely to call it old since it would seem less familiar. In terms of the representation in Figure 3, the distribution corresponding to old items will move towards the new distribution on its left. Therefore, the probability of "yes" given old, will decrease as we increase the number of items between presentation and test. There is only one value for the false alarm rate, since the location of the distribution of the new items and the criterion are fixed. Accordingly, d' will also decrease as we increase the number of intervening items.

Results and stage analysis   Lindsay and Norman's subjects performed both a memory task and a detection task. In the left ear, the subject had to detect which of four noise intervals did not contain a tone signal. In the right ear the subject determined whether the probe item was a member of the preceding list. In the divided attention condition, the subject performed both tasks, whereas in the selective attention condition, he simply had to perform the memory or detection task although the stimuli from both tasks were always presented.

The analysis of the results indicated that subjects could detect which interval did not contain the tonal signal just as well in the divided attention condition as in the selected attention condition. Performing the memory task did not interfere with detection. In contrast, memory performance was poorer in the divided than in the selective attention conditions. Requiring the subjects to monitor the noise bursts for detection interfered with their performance on the memory task.

The important thing is to locate the stage of processing that is interfered with by the detection task. In the model, this effect could be localized at either the acquisition and/or retention stage. The detection task could have interfered with the recognition of the memory items, in which case acquisition should differ in the selective and divided attention conditions. The predictions of the theory for the points where there are zero intervening items is our measure of α, the initial acquisition of the item. The detection task could have interfered with the retention of the memory items, in which case retention should differ under selective and divided attention. The slope of the forgetting function provides an index of ϕ, the measure of the retention stage. Therefore, it is necessary to plot the observed d' values and fit the forgetting functions of the selective and divided attention conditions with straight lines. A comparison of the intercepts and slopes will locate the attention effect at either or both acquisition or retention.

In Figure 4, the value d' is plotted on a log scale against the number of intervening items on a linear scale. Therefore, the theory predicts a straight line for both the selective and divided memory task conditions. In agreement with this, the two sets of points be-

FIGURE 4. Observed and predicted d' values as a function of the number of intervening items (after Lindsay & Norman, 1969).

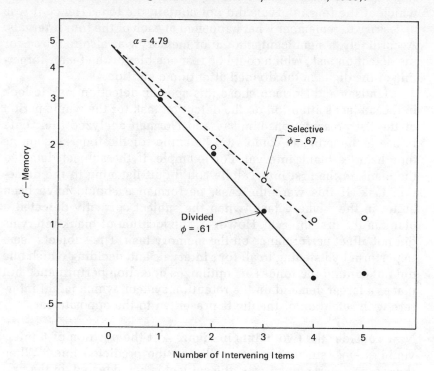

tween 0 and 4 intervening items are well described by two straight lines. The results shown in Figure 4 indicate that the intercept representing the value of α does not differ for the selective and divided attention conditions. This means that the detection task did not affect the initial acquisition stage of our memory model. However, the two lines describing performance diverge for the selective and divided conditions. In terms of the model, this means that the rate of forgetting, as measured by ϕ, differed in the two conditions. The value of ϕ is larger in the selective attention condition than in the divided attention condition, indicating that less forgetting occurred during the selective attention condition than during the divided attention condition. According to this analysis, the effect of attention is located at the retention stage of our model.

These results support the idea that there is a limited capacity at the level of retention in short-term memory. Retention requires processing capacity because the subject shows a faster rate of forgetting in the divided than in the selective attention condition.

Although the detection task interfered with the retention of the memory items, we cannot say that the detection process itself was responsible. The detection task of Lindsay and Norman (1969) required much more than merely detection. Subjects reported which of the four intervals did not contain the tone. Hence it was necessary to remember what happened at each of the four intervals. Accordingly, a significant amount of memory was also required for the detection task, which could be responsible for the faster forgetting of the digits in the divided attention condition.

Lindsay and Norman chose this specific detection task to lock in the subject's attention on the detection task for the whole period of the list presentation. Lindsay and Norman analyzed their data to see if the subjects could stop listening for the tone as soon as they heard a blank interval. For example, if the subject detected the blank in the first interval, he could quit listening to the detection task. If this were the case, performance should have been better in the memory task, when the subject correctly detected a blank in the first interval. However, the location of blank intervals did not affect performance on the memory task. The subjects seem to perform by listening to all four intervals and deciding which one did not contain the tone. This optimizes detection performance but places a larger demand on the retention system, which might interfere with retention of the digits presented to the opposite ear.

Primacy Now consider the two points in Figure 4 at the position of 5 intervening items, since they do not lie on the predicted lines. When there are 5 intervening items, the subject is being tested on the first item that was presented. Performance is higher at this position than it should be according to our memory model. This is known as a primacy effect, which has been located at the acquisition stage in the task (Wickelgren and Norman, 1966). Subjects seem to be able to learn more about the first item in the list than they can about following items (see Chapter 12). These points can be predicted by assuming that the first item is better acquired but then is forgotten at the same rate as the other items. This prediction locates the primacy effect at the initial acquisition stage and can be described by a simple change in α with no change in ϕ.

Recognition Lindsay and Norman's results contrast nicely with the results of the class demonstration carried out by the author. Our results showed that recognition requires processing capacity, whereas Lindsay and Norman's showed that it does not. The only difference between the two experiments is that the digits were very easy to recognize in Lindsay and Norman's study because they were not distorted in any way. The subject's hit rate was 100 percent when there were no interfering items. By contrast, in the *ba–ga* task, the two alternatives were very similar psychophysically, and they were very difficult to recognize. Performance only averaged about 75 percent correct. Accepting both results implies that recognition may not require processing capacity when the alternatives are easily distinguishable, but does when the task becomes difficult.

Our exploration into attention has been met with mixed success. We seemed to have learned more about how to study attention than about how attention operates. Our goal is to describe if and how attention operates at each stage of information processing. The answer to this question will follow from a description of each of the processing stages themselves. As alluded to earlier, the study of attention is secondary to the discovery of the operations of processing stages. The remainder of this book will clarify many of the questions raised here as we focus on the rules that describe specific processing stages between stimulus and response.

reading and Listening

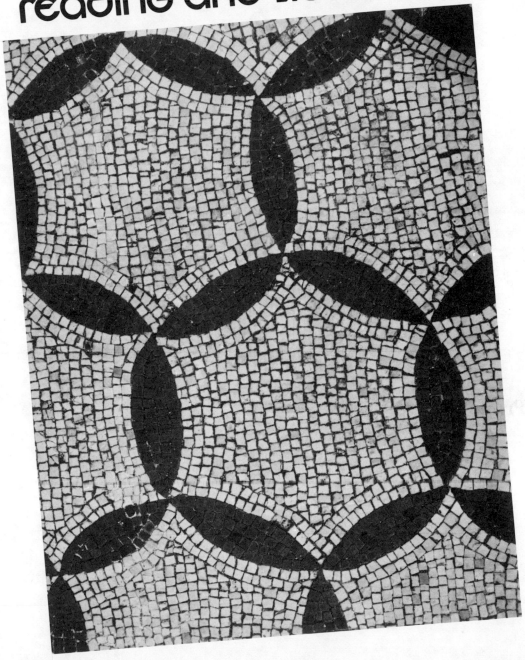

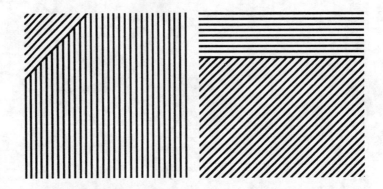

Preperceptual visual storage

As a rule sensations outlast for some little time the objective stimulus which occasioned them. If we open our eyes instantaneously upon a scene, and then shroud them in complete darkness, it will be as if we saw the scene in ghostly light through the dark screen. We can read off details in it which were unnoticed whilst the eyes were open.
—William James (1890)

The next three chapters provide a detailed analysis of the recognition stage of visual information processing. Experimenters in visual information processing hope eventually to describe the first stages of processing involved in the act of reading; a persistent goal in this field is to provide a model of how the reader goes from the figure-ground contrast of the letters on the page to meaning. The act of reading itself, however, cannot be studied directly until each of the discrete stages of mental events which it incorporates are well understood. Any attempt to study reading in an experimental design must account for a number of psychological processes that contribute to deriving meaning from text. For example, if we presented observers with a passage to read and measured comprehension as a function of the difficulty of the text, the poorer comprehension found with increased difficulty might be due to recognition, memorial, or decision processes. For this reason, experimenters have attempted to study directly the separate processes involved in the act of reading.

Consider the visual processing model diagrammed in Figure 1. This corresponds to a part of the general model developed in this book. The stimulus is a light-wave pattern which is transformed by the visual receptor system into a neurological code in preperceptual visual storage. The transformation by the receptor system is sufficient for detection to take place. Recognition, on the other hand, is the report that one out of a possible set of alternatives was

VISUAL PROCESSING MODEL

FIGURE 1. A flow diagram of the primary recognition stage of processing, which transforms a preperceptual visual image into a synthesized visual percept.

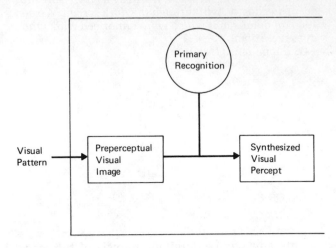

presented. To recognize what that something is, we must analyze the information held in preperceptual storage. This recognition processing takes time and its outcome is the transformation of the preperceptual visual image into a synthesized visual percept held in synthesized visual memory. The outcome of the recognition process is the phenomenological experience of seeing something of a particular size, shape, distance, and so forth. Chapter 11 discussed how the recognition process resolved the part of the figure-ground relationship available in each eye fixation. In this chapter, we study the recognition of letters in order to discover the properties of preperceptual visual storage and the operations of the recognition process.

Saccadic Eye Movements In the act of reading, these processes occur very rapidly, so that it would be difficult to study just the recognition stage in a continuous reading task. Fortunately, however, while we believe that our eyes move continuously across a page of text, the eyes actually make small discrete steps that are integrated into an illusion of continuous movement. Instead of moving continuously across the printed page, our eyes fixate at one point and then at another, at a rate of about four times per second. The eyes move so rapidly between one fixation and the next that they are often spoken of as being in flight between fixations. Studies of these saccadic eye movements in reading have revealed movement up to 400° per second; theoretically, this means that the eye could perform a complete rotation in 1 second. Normally in reading the distance covered in one saccadic eye movement is about 1½°, which takes between 10 and 20 msec. Thus, the image is sweeping across the retina at such a high speed that it would be very difficult for the system to resolve any figure-ground relationship while the eye is in flight. Experimenters have shown that, indeed, we cannot recognize patterns during saccadic eye movements.

Given that pattern recognition cannot occur during the time the eye is in flight, primary recognition must occur during the time the eye is fixated. Thus a single fixation sets the limit on the amount of time available to recognize the stimuli in the visual field during that fixation. The invention of the tachistoscope in the 1880's provided experimenters with a means of isolating the recognition stage of visual information processing. With the tachistoscope a stimulus can be presented for so short a period of time that we can be sure no eye movement has taken place, and that all the information derived about that stimulus has occurred within one fixation. In tachistoscopic studies, the experimenter is studying the readout of the information in preperceptual visual store—the processing of the information that uniquely characterizes a certain pattern. Nevertheless, other stages of processing are involved even in tachistoscopic studies; for example, the decision or response selection process will affect the actual response given by the observer.

Processing in a Single Eye Fixation

The goal here is to understand the recognition stage of visual information processing. The recognition process is critically dependent on the properties of preperceptual visual storage since it is the information held here that must be transformed. The properties of preperceptual storage, therefore, become important issues for research. In what form is the information held? How long does preperceptual visual storage hold the information? What is the capacity of preperceptual visual storage? These questions have led investigators to study the temporal course of the recognition process, since the operations of this process clarify the properties of preperceptual visual storage. One way is to study the recognition of a first stimulus when it is followed after some variable time by a second stimulus. If a second stimulus influences recognition of a previous stimulus, we can conclude that recognition of the first stimulus was not yet complete when the second stimulus was presented.

AVERBACH AND CORIELL STUDY

Averbach and Coriell (1961) carried out a series of experiments at Bell Laboratories that illuminate some of the properties of preperceptual visual storage and the temporal course of the recognition process. In all of the experiments the three observers were presented with an array of 16 letters arranged in two rows of 8, the letters having been drawn at random with replacement from the alphabet. The subjects were given a fixation point at the center of the test field which subtended a visual angle of 4° vertically by 5° horizontally. The duration of the test display was 50 msec. In all of the experiments, sometimes before or after the presentation, a visual marker appeared, indicating which letter was to be recalled. The marker was also presented for 50 msec.

Bar Marker

In the first experiment, the marker was a bar that appeared either above one of the letters in the top row, or below one of the letters in the bottom row, signaling that this letter was to be reported (see Figure 2). This marker could appear 100 msec. before the onset of the display, simultaneously with the onset of the display, or sometime after the offset of the display. This variation in

FIGURE 2. Typical array of letters and representations of the bar, circle, and grid indicators (after Averbach & Coriell, 1961).

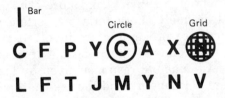

the onset time of the bar marker, then, was the independent variable in the experiment. The results were analyzed as percentage of correct identifications of the indicated letter as a function of the duration between the onset of the display and the onset of the bar marker.

What did Averbach and Coriell (1961) expect to find in this experiment beyond what was already known? In previous recognition studies, investigators required their subjects to report not only one but all of the items that were presented in the visual display. The results consistently indicated that subjects could recall 5 ± 2 of the items correctly. Averbach and Coriell reasoned, as did Sperling, that these results do not define how many letters the subject could see in the display, but how many he was able to remember and report correctly. The recall was constrained by a limitation in a later stage of information processing—short-term memory—and prevents direct study of the visual recognition process. Averbach and Coriell wanted to bypass this limitation by presenting a marker that indicated the only letter to be recalled. In this case, Averbach and Coriell hoped to show that subjects could report any of the letters in the display accurately by presenting the bar marker early enough in the sequence of events.

In terms of our visual-processing model, the information from the16-item display would be held in preperceptual visual storage. The bar marker, if it occurs early enough, directs the subject to the appropriate letter. The subject, on observing the location of the bar marker, processes the letter and reports it to the experimenter. However, the preperceptual storage of the16-item display would not remain indefinitely. If the bar marker is delayed until after the preperceptual image is gone, the subject will not be able to report the letter correctly unless he happened to encode and remember this particular letter when he was waiting for the marker. In agreement with our discussion of Sperling's experiment in Chapter 12, performance should not, therefore, decrease to zero, since the subject is recognizing and encoding some of the letters and their positions into short-term memory while he is waiting for the bar marker. The upper limit on the number of items that could thus be retained after the preperceptual visual information is no longer available is, therefore, the roughly 5-item limit of short-term memory. Thus we can expect that performance will decrease as the bar marker is delayed to a positive asymptote of about 30 percent, at which point the subject will have in short-term memory the name and location of roughly 5 of the 16 items.

Figure 3 shows the results for the three subjects in this experiment. As expected, performance was best when the bar marker preceded the display and decreased as the delay of the bar marker was increased, leveling off to a positive asymptote at a delay of 125 msec. for subject G.M. and 200 msec. for the other two subjects. The performance asymptote was between 25 and 35 percent, which supports the idea that performance at these delays was the result of the retrieval of recognized letters that were being held in short-term memory. The advantage in performance, at a delay of 125 msec., indicates that, even though the display had been off for 75 msec., the observers had access to the preperceptual visual information about a particular letter that had not been recognized and encoded in short-term memory. Furthermore, one might assume that the results define the duration of the preperceptual visual image to be about 125–200 msec. The duration cannot be estimated directly, however, since we cannot account for the time consumed by the identification and the location of the bar marker and the time required for recognition of the indicated letter. It is possible

FIGURE 3. Percentage of correct identifications of the letter indicated by the bar marker as a function of the time between the display and the bar marker. The three curves are results for three subjects (after Averbach & Coriell, 1961).

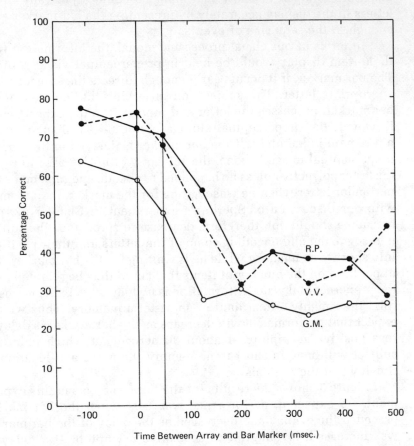

that the preperceptual image lasted for 250 msec. after termination of the display. But if location of the bar marker and recognition of the letter took 150 msec., recognition could not be completed before the preperceptual storage decayed when the bar marker was delayed more than 100 msec. after the offset of the display.

Acuity and Lateral Masking   Another result demonstrates two other processes that are important in visual recognition. Although the best performance was observed when the bar marker preceded the display, it was still significantly below complete accuracy. Therefore, not all of the letters in the display were perfectly legible. Figure 4 shows recognition performance as a function of letter position within the array.

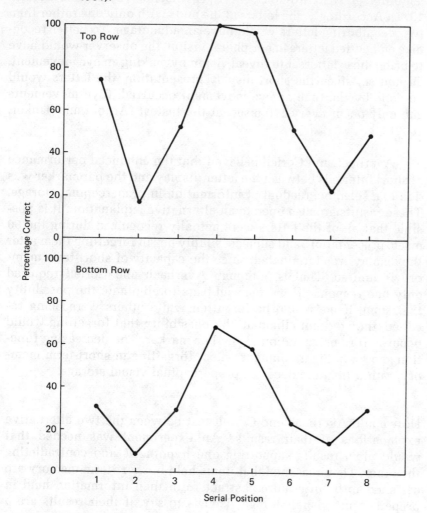

Recognition of letters in the upper row was consistently better than in the lower row, and the letters in the center and at the ends of the row were recognized better than the letters between these points. Averbach and Coriell point out that individual letters presented alone in any of the 16 positions were perfectly legible.

Two factors seem to be responsible for the serial position differences when the 16 letters are presented together. First, the advantage of the central letters can be attributed to the increased acuity found in foveal vision. Second, the poorest performance for the letters embedded between the center and ends could result from lateral masking where neighboring letters mutually decrease their legibility or signal-to-noise ratio (Townsend, Taylor, and Brown, 1971). Accordingly, the letters at the ends with only one rather than two neighboring letters would have an advantage. To better recognize embedded letters in peripheral vision, the observer would have to bring these letters into foveal vision by making an eye movement. Of course, given the short display presentation, the letters would be gone by the time an eye movement occurred. (Eye movements can only occur every 170 msec. at the fastest [Arnold and Tinker, 1939]).

Averbach and Coriell believed that the enhanced performance at short intervals between the letter display and the bar marker was due to a selective readout of information in preperceptual storage. These results are also open to an alternative explanation. It is possible that all of the letters were actually recognized during the 50 msec. presentation, and subjects simply began forgetting them after the display was terminated, since the capacity of short-term memory is limited. That is, although Averbach and Coriell required only one response from their subjects to eliminate the possibility that some items would be forgotten while others were being recalled, they did not eliminate the possibility that forgetting would occur before presentation of the bar marker. The decreasing function shown in Figure 3 might reflect forgetting in short-term memory, rather than the decay of preperceptual visual storage.

Grid Marker How could Averbach and Coriell test between the two alternative explanations of their results? An experiment was needed that would yield results supporting one hypothesis and contradicting the other. They reasoned that items held in short-term memory are assumed to be in a more abstract form than information held in preperceptual visual storage. That is to say, if their results are a function of the recognition process occurring after the display is terminated, they should be able to change the results by interfering with recognition at this point. On the other hand, if the items are in short-term memory after the display is terminated, performance should not be influenced by this manipulation. More specifically, if performance were dependent upon preperceptual visual storage after the display was terminated, the experimenters should be able to interfere with recognition by interfering with this storage. Averbach and Coriell reasoned that preperceptual visual storage should be sensitive to succeeding visual stimuli, whereas short-term memory should not. Preperceptual visual storage can be thought of as maintaining the original stimulus situation beyond its termination. Therefore, a second stimulus which would degrade the original stimulus might also degrade preperceptual visual storage if it occurred shortly after the first was terminated. To test these ideas, Averbach and Coriell changed the physical properties of the visual marker. Instead of a bar marker they chose a grid, which consisted of a circle containing lines drawn in the vertical and horizontal direction. The grid was presented in the same position as the letter to be recalled (see Figure 2).

The results were successful in distinguishing between the two hypotheses. The items do not appear to have been recognized by offset of the letter display since the grid interferes with performance when it immediately follows the display. Figure 5 shows that delaying the grid actually improved performance as opposed to the opposite result found with the bar marker. At a 250 msec. delay,

FIGURE 5. Percentage of correct identifications of the letter indicated by the grid marker as a function of the time between the display and the grid marker. The three curves are results for three subjects (after Averbach & Coriell, 1961).

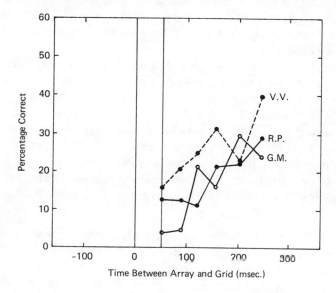

performance with the grid marker improved to the same positive asymptote given by the bar marker experiment. These results show that the grid must have degraded the information in the preperceptual visual image, preventing recognition of the appropriate letter. Delaying the grid gave the observers more time to recognize the letters, so that it was more likely that a letter could be reported correctly when the grid occurred, indicating the letter that had to be recalled.

One problem with the grid marker experiment is that Averbach and Coriell did not include sufficient levels of their independent variable to observe an asymptote in performance. We do not know if performance would continue to improve beyond the 250 msec. delay since the curves have not leveled off. If Averbach and Coriell had tested performance at longer delays, this experiment would have provided a good index of the useful duration of the preperceptual visual image.

PROPERTIES OF PREPERCEPTUAL STORAGE

The experiments of Averbach and Coriell established the existence of a preperceptual visual image that persists in the system for some time after the original stimulus is terminated. Further study of the visual image has centered around the following questions: What are its properties and characteristics? Specifically, how long does it last? Averbach and Coriell's experiments do not provide a direct answer to this question. Second, how do the properties of the preperceptual image depend upon the stimulus characteristics of the visual display? Finally, is the preperceptual visual information stored peripherally, for example, at the level of the retina, or is its storage more central?

Preperceptual storage can be demonstrated in a number of different ways. Move your finger rapidly back and forth across your field of vision; you should see it in more than one place at a given time. Or note the trail that a lighted cigarette leaves when it is waved in a darkened room. These demonstrations show that the sensation persists (is stored) after the stimulus is no longer present in the real world. The object is actually only in one place at a given time, but we are able to see it in two or more places. Therefore, we see it where it was some time ago and where it was some time later.

Slits and Pieces

Haber and Standing's (1969) experiment is a formal analog of these informal observations. Their visual display consisted of a black outline circle on a white background, over which they placed a piece of cardboard that completely covered the circle except for what was visible through a small vertical slit. The cardboard was oscillated back and forth, exposing the circle in small pieces. The slit exposed 1/20th of the circle. Obviously, if the cardboard were moved very slowly one would see the circle as a series of small line fragments. On the other hand, if there is some storage of visual information so that a preperceptual visual image persists after the stimulus has been terminated, then as the oscillation reaches a certain speed one would begin to perceive the circle phenomenologically as complete. Therefore, the minimum rate of oscillation necessary for the subject to cease perceiving the circle in bits and pieces and begin to see it as a whole would reveal the duration of preperceptual information. That is, if the subject sees the whole circle at an oscillation rate such that one complete loop takes 300 msec., then 300 msec. is a good estimate of the duration of the preperceptual storage in this situation.

The subjects were instructed to maintain their fixation at the center of the movement and told that they might be able to see a circle behind the slit. On each test, they were to report if they saw the circle, and if they did, whether it appeared complete or in bits and pieces. The subjects were informed that perceiving the circle as complete in this situation was illusory, but that there were no right or wrong judgments. The estimates of the oscillation rate necessary for perception of a complete circle were determined by a method of limits procedure.

With this procedure, Haber and Standing estimated the duration of preperceptual storage at about 330 msec. Thus every fragment of the circle had to be refreshed at least once every 330 msec., in order for the subject to perceive a complete circle continuously over time. A second independent variable, the luminance of the display, had an insignificant effect on this estimate when it was changed by a factor of 100. These results indicate that preperceptual storage lasts about 330 msec. in this situation. Furthermore, the fact that the luminance of the display was ineffective indicates that the visual stimulus starts a sequence of events that maintains the visual information for a time period that is not critically dependent upon the physical characteristics of the stimulus.

Haber and Standing assumed that the subject in this task could give a direct report of his perceptual experience without a confounding of other processes. We have seen that the decision system must be accounted for in all psychological tasks before any conclusion can be reached about the process of interest. Certainly, the attitude of the experimenter could influence how quickly the subjects "saw" continuous movement in this task. To correct the Haber and Standing procedure for this deficiency, we would have to employ catch trials to provide a check on the subject's honesty. The experimenter could include circles that were actually incomplete, to measure how often subjects would call these complete. The false alarm rate could then be used to correct the hit rate in order to provide a true measure of sensitivity (see Chapter 7).

One previous observation seems to support Haber and Standing's conclusion and provides information about preperceptual storage. Haber and Nathanson (1968) carried out a similar experiment in which subjects looked through a stationary slit, and an outline figure such as a camel was oscillated behind the slit, rather than the slit oscillating in front of the test figure. In this case, the test figure could not be perceived as complete. If the outline figure is oscillating behind the slit, different parts of the figure strike the retina on the same vertical axis and a complete projected image of the figure would not be available. This result indicates that the information in the preperceptual storage is a direct function of the temporal and spatial properties of the information in the retinal image. Finally, this result contrasts with the Haber and Standing (1969) result, providing some evidence that the phenomenological report is sensitive to differences in stimulus conditions and, therefore, cannot be completely due to decision biases.

In another demonstration of preperceptual visual storage, Haber and Standing (1969) gave repeated 10-msec. presentations of the complete circle with intervening blank fields that were half the luminance of the test field. Subjects perceived the circle as appearing present throughout the observation interval even though 200 msec. separated each 10 msec. flash. If the interval was longer than 200 msec., it appeared and disappeared alternately. Accordingly, this paradigm estimates preperceptual storage at roughly 200 msec. A second condition helps define the locus of preperceptual storage. In this condition, the test circle was presented to alternate eyes using Polaroid filters so that the circle appears at the same location in space. Subjects perceived the test circle as continuous with the same 200 msec. blank interval as in the first condition. Thus the circle could be perceived continuously even though each eye was stimulated only every 400 msec. This result distinguishes preperceptual visual storage from the positive afterimage discussed in Chapter 9. Preperceptual storage must be more central, given that it is not eye specific.

Perceived Duration Another technique that has been used to measure the duration of the visual image is to ask the subject how long the visual display appears to last (Sperling, 1967). One way to investigate this is to present the subject with a pattern followed by a click; the subject is to adjust the click so that it occurs simultaneously with what he believes to be the offset of the pattern. The subject also is asked to adjust the click to the onset of the display so that any temporal bias which would affect both perceived onset and offset should be eliminated. The difference between location of the click for onset and offset provides the estimate of perceived duration of the display. If the pattern appears to the subject to last longer than it actually does, then this additional duration represents the duration of the image after the stimulus is no longer present.

Both preperceptual visual storage and visual afterimages prolong the period of visual stimulation. In this chapter, we have seen how preperceptual storage maintains the information for recognition to take place. In Chapter 9 we saw how an afterimage from a previous eye fixation can mix with the current view of Riley's *White Discs I*. These storages appear to be qualitatively different given the following observations. A second visual stimulus can interfere with the pre-perceptual storage of the first, as demonstrated with the grid marker in the Aver-bach and Coriell paradigm. In contrast, Riley's painting shows that the visual information from a second eye fixation does not completely eliminate the after-image of the first. Furthermore, afterimages appear to be dependent upon a more peripheral storage, whereas preperceptual storage appears to be more central. Preperceptual visual storage has been shown to be a central phenome-non by Haber and Standing's finding that a second visual stimulus can refresh preperceptual storage of a first stimulus even if they are presented to different eyes. In exact contrast to this finding, afterimages can be eye-specific, as shown in the following demonstration based on a rediscovery by Wayne Shebilske.

In research for his master's thesis, Shebilske took pictures of a subject's eye in the dark, necessitating an electronic flash. What Shebilske observed was that he was still seeing the subject long after the picture was taken, even though there was no light in the room. (The electronic flash presents almost all of its light within 1 msec.) Now before questioning his own sanity, Shebilske brought in some colleagues whose judgment he could trust. Given a few moments of dark-adaptation, they too reported afterimages of the scene illuminated by the flash. These afterimages are extremely realistic and are seen in three-dimen-sional space. Given this basic finding, the variations on this theme are only limited by the creativity of the participants. In one, the observer keeps one eye closed during the flash and then tries to observe the afterimage with both eyes. He cannot: the image is only seen through the stimulated eye; the other eye feels as if someone has a fist in it. This demonstration shows that these visual afterimages are based on storage that is peripheral, in the sense that it is re-ceptor specific. It contrasts with Haber and Standing's demonstration that pre-perceptual visual storage is not receptor specific since it can be refreshed by alternating the stimulus between the eyes.

Haber and Standing (1970) used a 3 x 3 letter array as the test stimulus. In all conditions, the subject adjusted the time of the click until it appeared simultaneous with the onset of the test stimulus. Then, he adjusted the time of the click until it appeared simul-taneous with the offset of the test stimulus. When blank pre- and post-exposure fields possessed the same luminance as the test field, the subjects overestimated the duration of the test fields. Test fields presented for between 10 and 200 msec. were perceived to last between 175 and 225 msec. Longer test fields were not overestimated by more than roughly 25 to 50 msec. In a second set of conditions, the test field was followed after a variable interval by a second noise field made up of a montage of overlapping letters. If the noise field occurred within 200 msec. after the onset of the test field, the perceived duration of the test field was equal to the interval between the onsets of the two fields. If the noise field was delayed for more than 200 msec., the perceived durations were similar to those found in the first condition with no masking field. These results show that a short stimulus is perceived longer than it actually is and that a second stimulus can interfere with this visual persistence. Longer test stimuli are not overestimated significantly, indicating that a preperceptual visual image does not persist much after a relatively long visual stimulus.

These studies and others (e.g., Efron, 1970) provide independent evidence for preperceptual visual storage. A visual stimulus initiates a period of visual processing that appears to last between 200 and 300 msec. The information about the stimulus is held in preperceptual storage so that this processing can occur. The storage appears to have a central rather than a peripheral locus. A second stimulus, if presented within this critical time period, seems to interfere with the information in this storage, terminating the recognition process of the test stimulus. The next chapter will concern how the second stimulus interferes with the preperceptual image.

We give very little weight in this volume to the statistical test of significance in evaluating our results. Statistical tools were developed in order to estimate the extent to which any observed effects in an experiment are due to chance rather than to changes in the independent variable itself. If the investigator can eliminate chance as the contributing factor, he is safe in attributing the observed effect to changes in his independent variable. The psychologist usually performs his statistical tests as a matter of habit and because they are usually required by the psychological journals. However, it is a truism that one can lie with statistics. Whether or not the effects of an independent variable are statistically significant —not due to chance—transmits very little information. There are many uninteresting reasons for a significant effect of the independent variable, and the knowledgeable investigator carries out his experiment or finds a statistical test in ways that will give him the significance he so desires. For example, increasing the number of observations at each level of his independent variable increases the likelihood of getting statistical significance, and so on.

In order to safeguard against the statistical significance problem, we evaluate the *magnitude* of the effect of our independent variable, rather than whether it is statistically significant. Second, and more important, we are interested in the variable in terms of what it tells us about a psychological process, not simply in terms of whether the observed behavior differs under different levels of the independent variable. Consider the case in which we postulate a variable, say, processing time, as being critical for the psychological process of recognition. If we carry out an experiment that shows performance is at chance with very little processing time, and gradually improves to perfect accuracy with increases in processing time, there is no need to ask whether this variable is statistically significant. We have shown the variable to be psychologically significant by the way it illuminates the rules of a psychological operation or process. The discussion of experiment and theory in this book illustrates with many examples how research without statistical tests can increase our knowledge of psychological phenomena.

Perceptual processing time for seeing

Replicating experiments

The results obtained in Averbach and Coriell's experiments described in Chapter 17 are easily understood. The bar marker merely singles out the letter to be identified; it does not interfere with it. Performance decreases gradually with the fading of the preperceptual image, leveling off at 25 or 35 percent when the image is gone and the subject is limited to the information he has encoded into short-term memory. The grid, on the other hand, degrades the information in the letter it covers; in this experiment, therefore, performance is at its worst when the grid follows the letter immediately and improves as presentation of the grid is delayed. Again, performance should level off at 25 to 35 percent with larger delays reflecting the amount of information the subject has encoded into short-term memory.

AVERBACH AND CORIELL STUDY— Continued

Two other experiments carried out by Averbach and Coriell are more difficult to interpret. These experiments were identical to the others except for the marker, which was changed to a circle surrounding the letter to be recalled (see Figure 2 in Chapter 17). Instead of the monotonic decreasing function they had found with the bar marker or the increasing function with the grid marker, with the circle marker they found a U-shaped function (see Figure 1). Performance was very good when the circle appeared during or immediately after the display. When the onset of the circle was delayed beyond termination of the display by 50 msec., however, performance dropped very sharply to between 10 and 20 percent. Further increases in the delay of the circle marker led to an increase in performance which asymptoted roughly at the same level as in the bar marker experiment.

This result indicates that the circle marker functioned as the bar marker when it occurred during or immediately after the dis-

FIGURE 1. Percentage of correct identifications of the letter indicated by the circle marker as a function of the time between the display and the circle marker. The three curves are results for three subjects (after Averbach & Coriell, 1961).

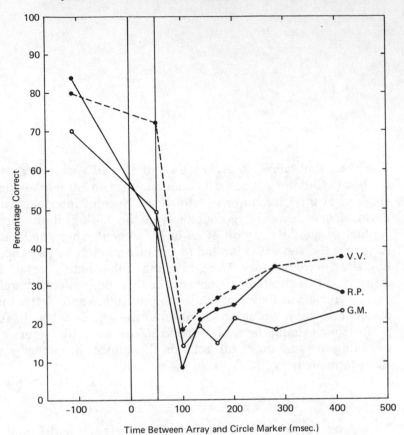

play and as the grid marker when it was delayed further. If the circle came on when the display was still on, it did not interfere with recognition. As can be seen in Figure 1, the letter can be recognized when the circle and the letter are simultaneously available. After the display is terminated, however, the circle interferes with the preperceptual image of the letter, preventing its recognition. If the first stimulus has not been recognized, a second stimulus can interfere with its recognition by interfering with the information being held in preperceptual visual storage.

In the last experiment of the series, both the bar marker and the circle were presented. One of them, the bar marker, was presented simultaneously with the display onset on all trials. The independent variable in the experiment was the time between the onset of the display and the onset of the circle surrounding the same letter that had been indicated by the bar marker. This experiment is the most direct study of preperceptual visual storage, since the experimenters have eliminated entirely the limitation of short-term memory in the task. The subject can concentrate on locating the bar marker and the appropriate letter at the onset of the display. In this case, maximum performance would not be constrained by a short-term limitation since the subjects could ignore all of the letters except the one indicated by the bar at the onset of the display. When the circle follows the display, it has no cue value; it can only interfere with the preperceptual image of the letter. Figure 2 shows that performance was very good if the circle came on during or immediately after the display and if the circle was delayed be-

FIGURE 2. Percentage of correct identifications of the letter indicated by the bar marker, which occurred simultaneously with the letter array onset, as a function of the time between the display and the circle marker. The three curves are results for three subjects (after Averbach & Coriell, 1961).

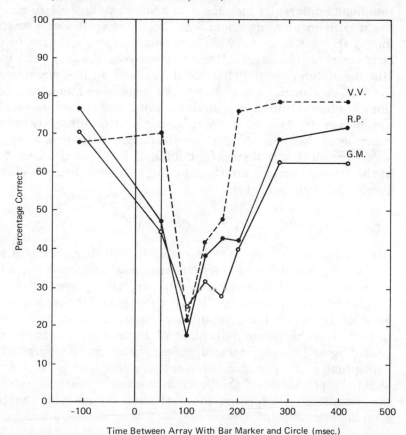

Time Between Array With Bar Marker and Circle (msec.)

yond 200 or 250 msec. However, the circle interfered with performance when it came on at the intermediate delays. The results show that it took the observers between 200 and 250 msec. to locate the bar and recognize the indicated letter. If the circle occurred before recognition was complete, it interfered with the representation of the letter in preperceptual storage. As in the earlier circle experiment, if the circle occurs before or immediately after the test display, it does not interfere significantly with the representation in preperceptual storage. If the circle and the letter presentations overlap in time, the circle does not interfere with the preperceptual storage of the test letter, as it does when it is delayed.

When the circle was presented only 100 msec. after onset of the display, i.e., 50 msec. after its termination, the very poor performance of 20 percent or less was again observed. In this case, the circle appeared at a time when the visual information was only present in preperceptual visual storage, and the recognition of the desired letter had probably begun but was not complete. Thus, the drastic drop in performance could only mean that the circle interfered with the information in the preperceptual image. The circle functioned differently than the grid marker. With the grid marker, the maximum masking effect was found when it was presented during the test letter presentation; this was not the case for the circle marker. The exact relationship between the first and second stimulus determines the effect of the second on the perception of the first. A general rule might be that increasing monotonic functions are found if the test stimulus is not legible when the test and the marker are presented simultaneously. The grid marker is an example of this case. If simultaneous presentation does not decrease legibility, a U-shaped function may be found if the contours of the second stimulus are close to and surround the first—for example, the circle indicator.

VISUAL MASKING Besides cueing the appropriate response, Averbach and Coriell's circle and grid indicators functioned as masking stimuli, since they interfered with the information in the test letter presentation. This chapter will be concerned with experiments and theories of visual masking in which the test and masking stimuli do not coexist in time. The changes in perception of a stimulus, as a function of preceding or following stimuli, reflect the temporal course of the perceptual process which, in turn, should provide information about the properties of the process. Backward masking refers to the paradigm of following the test stimulus presentation by a masking stimulus. In forward masking, the masking stimulus precedes the test stimulus presentation. The interval between the two stimuli is referred to as the interstimulus interval.

Averbach and Coriell proposed two processes to explain their results. Consider the last experiment, in which the circle had no cue value since the bar marker always was presented at the onset of the display. When the circle occurs within a certain very brief period after onset of the test letter, the two stimuli are integrated and treated as one by the system. Thus, the subject perceives a letter surrounded by a circle which does not significantly affect the legibility of the letter. A second process, interruption, occurs if the onset of the circle is delayed after this critical integration period. The circle cannot be integrated with the letter now, but instead interferes with its preperceptual visual storage. The effect of interruption is greatest when the onset of the circle occurs fairly soon after termination of the display. Later, as recognition of the letter progresses and is eventually encoded in short-term memory, interference with preperceptual visual storage has less and less effect on performance.

Integration

The integration process proposed by Averbach and Coriell was not new to experimenters of visual perception; it had been observed in a number of other types of experiments. The visual system appears to integrate the energy from a stimulus over time. In our discussion of the Hecht, Shlaer, and Pirenne experiment in Chapter 8, we saw that a light was equally detectable when the energy was spread out over 100 msec. as when all of the energy was presented in 1 msec. Accordingly, the detectability or legibility of a stimulus could be affected by another stimulus if they occur together within the period of integration. We refer to the legibility of a stimulus as its *figure-ground contrast* or the *signal-to-noise ratio* of the stimulus.

The integration process plays an important role in the temporal course of visual perception. The signal-to-noise ratio of a particular stimulus is influenced by the signal-to-noise ratios of other stimuli that occur within the integration period. The preperceptual representation in the visual system does not have available the signal-to-noise ratio of the stimulus as it exists in the outside world. Rather, that original ratio has been integrated with preceding and following stimuli. Consider, for example, a test stimulus of a given figure-ground contrast which we denote as X:Y. Assume that as X increases or Y decreases, the figure-ground contrast is enhanced and the test figure is clearer and more easily perceptible. Thus, an

X:Y ratio of 1:1 gives no contrast, whereas a 10:2 ratio gives good legibility. In the test display, assume that the test letter has a good contrast of 5:1. Prior to presentation of this display, however, a blank white field of 1:1 figure-ground ratio appears and reappears again following offset of the test figure. Integration theory maintains that in effect the figure-ground ratio of the test figure is not 5:1, but is an average over some time period of the contrasts of the images that occurred within that period. Thus, in this case the 5:1 ratio of the letter averaged with the 1:1 ratios of the background might be lowered to an effective figure-ground ratio of 3:1 and the letter would now be more difficult to perceive.

Figure-ground contrast   Figure 3 presents an example of the figure-ground ratio of a test stimulus presented for 30 msec. when the period of integration is equal to 60 msec. The black letters painted on a white background are preceded and followed by a white field equal to the background white. Since the test figure lasts 30 msec. and the period of integration is 60 msec., the two displays contribute equally to the signal-to-noise ratio of the test figure. The effective intensity of the background would be equal to the background white since it is the same in both displays. To determine the effective intensity of the letters, we should mix the black paint with the background white

FIGURE 3. The presented and perceived visual displays according to integration theory. The perceived outlines of the letters are partially washed out, due to the preceding and following white field.

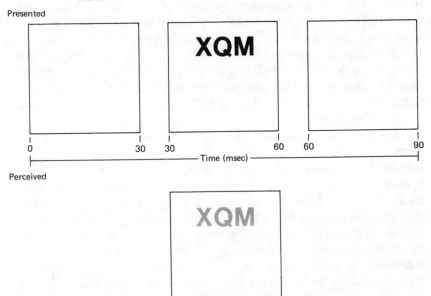

and paint the figure with this mixture. The effective figure-ground contrast is, therefore, gray letters on the background white.

The effective figure-ground contrast can also be computed mathematically. In this case, the actual figure-ground ratio is a weighted average of the figure-ground contrast of each of the three fields. The weight given to each of the fields is directly proportional to the time it is present during the period of integration. In this case, the effective figure-ground contrast E [X:Y] is equal to

$$E [X:Y] = [X:Y]_1 \left(\frac{t_1}{t_I}\right) + [X:Y]_2 \left(\frac{t_2}{t_I}\right) + [X:Y]_3 \left(\frac{t_3}{t_I}\right) \quad (1)$$

where $[X:Y]_1$, $[X:Y]_2$, and $[X:Y]_3$ are equal to the figure-ground contrast of the three displays and t_1, t_2, and t_3 are the times each display is on during the period of integration. The value t_I is the duration of the integration period. Substituting the appropriate values in Equation 1 gives

$$E [X:Y] = [1:1] \frac{15}{60} + [5:1] \frac{30}{60} + [1:1] \frac{15}{60}$$

$$= [1:1] \frac{1}{4} + [5:1] \frac{1}{2} + [1:1] \frac{1}{4}$$

$$= \left[\frac{1}{4} : \frac{1}{4}\right] + \left[\frac{5}{2} : \frac{1}{2}\right] + \left[\frac{1}{4} : \frac{1}{4}\right]$$

$$= [3:1]$$

Accordingly, the pre- and post-fields have effectively lowered the test field from a 5:1 to a 3:1 figure-ground contrast.

Averbach and Coriell's display lasted for 50 msec. If the integration time exceeds this 50 msec. presentation, one would have to take into account the figure-ground contrast in the preceding and following period of integration to determine the actual figure-ground contrast represented in the preperceptual visual image. Thus, to understand how a second stimulus interferes with a first, we have to compute the effective signal-to-noise (S/N) ratio of the two stimuli combined. Since recognition is dependent upon the signal-to-noise ratio of the letter display, reduction of that ratio by a second stimulus would reduce letter recognition.

Interruption

The second process proposed by Averbach and Coriell was new to psychologists at the time and many were unwilling to accept it. The interruption process predicted that a second stimulus could remove the perceptual visual image of a previous stimulus completely from preperceptual storage. Averbach and Coriell actually used the word "erasure" to describe this process. Therefore, a second stimulus could interfere with recognition of a previous stimulus since it could remove its information from preperceptual visual storage before recognition is complete.

U-SHAPED FUNCTIONS

Psychologists responded that the integration process was sufficient to understand the effect of one stimulus on the perception of another. However, this single-process explanation of the interference of a second stimulus with a first cannot account for the U-shaped function. For example, according to a theory based only on the process of integration, the largest effect of the second stimulus upon the first in the Averbach and Coriell studies should have occurred when the second stimulus was presented immediately afterwards. The circle decreases the effective S/N ratio of the test letter to the extent that the circle and the test letter occur together in the same period of integration. If the circle is delayed, its detrimental effect should have decreased steadily in a monotonic fashion.

Integration theorists have replied by questioning whether the U-shaped function actually exists. One experimental result is not sufficient to reject any theory, so replications of the masking experiment are required. In 1965, Weisstein and Haber replicated the Averbach and Coriell design in miniature. They presented the subject on each trial with one of two letters, D and O, lasting 20 msec. After a variable blank interval, they presented a 50 msec. circle around the previous location of the letter. Thus, instead of 16 letters, they presented only the one to be reported, followed by the circle. Their results confirmed the existence of the U-shaped function. Performance was minimal, not when the circle followed the letter immediately, but when it followed the offset of the letter after 25 msec. Thus the U-shaped function was replicated.

When Eriksen, Becker, and Hoffman (1970), prominent proponents of integration theory, replicated the Weisstein and Haber experiment, they faced the problem that exact replication was not possible. As is usual in tachistoscopic studies, there are large subject differences and the smallest differences in apparatus and stimulus variables can affect performance so that it is either at chance or perfect under the different levels of the independent variable of interest. Eriksen et al. found that their subjects required a much shorter duration of the test letter in order to make errors. Accordingly, these investigators adjusted the duration of the test letter for each subject individually so that performance in a pretest was roughly 85 percent correct at a zero interstimulus interval. Now each subject's performance could be mapped out across the levels of the independent variable of interest, the interstimulus interval.

Numerous problems face an investigator who wants to replicate another psychological study. First, the investigator must realize that he is carrying out his experiment at another point in time and with a different population of subjects than in the first study. Also, his apparatus and experimental setup will probably differ significantly. All of these differences make an exact replication of the results impossible. Most importantly, there are large intersubject differences in all psychological tasks, and one subject might perform perfectly under the same condition under which another subject cannot perform better than chance accuracy. Therefore, even in the same experiment, the investigator might not be able to maintain the same stimulus conditions for all subjects. The experimenter must sometimes arrange different experimental conditions for each subject to test his hypothesis of interest.

Suppose an experimenter wanted to test the hypothesis that if a letter is followed after some variable interval of time by a circle mask, performance will follow a U-shaped function with respect to the duration between the letter and the circle mask. If the subjects performed at chance or perfect in the task, this hypothesis could not be tested. The experimenter must adjust his experimental conditions so that performance is in a range that will be sensitive to changes in his independent variable. In the Weisstein and Haber study, subjects had two alternatives, so that performance must be between 50 and 100 percent. Therefore, the experimenter should attempt to insure that performance in the task averages about 75 percent correct. At this level, performance will be most sensitive to changes in the independent variable.

The results for each of four subjects appeared to Eriksen et al. to be rather noisy, but when they averaged them, as is commonly done, they found clear indications of a function different from that found by Weisstein and Haber. Performance as a function of interstimulus interval started out poorly, remained relatively flat, and then rose fairly sharply. This monotonic function was compatible with integration theory and contradicted the findings of a U-shaped function by other experimenters.

In their publication of these results, Eriksen et al. presented the individual points at each interstimulus interval around the line that they generated as an average. The reader could thus examine individual performances, and discover that these individual points described a U-shaped function for three of the four subjects. As can be seen in Figure 4, the U-shaped curves are not noisy, but are very orderly, since they are monotonically increasing in both directions from their minimum. This demonstration should be interpreted as a warning against averaging results from subjects that show extremely different individual functions. The Eriksen et al.

FIGURE 4. Percentage correct recognition as a function of the interstimulus interval between the *D* or *O* test letter and the masking circle (after Eriksen, Becker, & Hoffman, 1970).

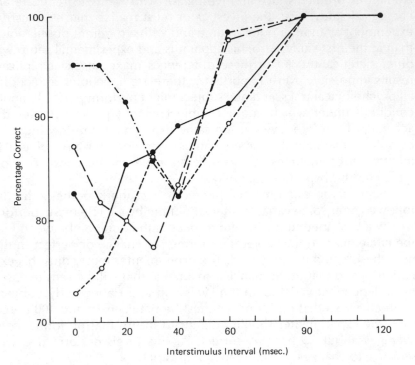

data do not necessarily support rejection of the U-shaped function as an accurate description of performance in Weisstein and Haber's task.

FORWARD vs. BACKWARD MASKING   There is another way to provide a critical test of the two theories, however. Integration theory maintains that preceding as well as following stimuli affect the signal-to-noise ratio of the test stimulus (see Equation 1). Forward masking (when the masking stimulus precedes the test) should thus be symmetrical with backward masking. The minimum performance should be obtained when the test and masking stimuli are presented simultaneously; performance when a masking stimulus precedes the test stimulus by 50 msec. should be equal to performance when it follows the test stimulus by 50 msec. The two-process theory of integration and interruption not only predicts that forward masking can occur within the period of integration, but that backward masking can occur beyond the period of integration until the process of recognition is complete.

Spencer and Shuntich (1970) carried out an experiment in

which the effects of forward and backward masking were directly compared. The display in this experiment consisted of 12 letters arranged around an imaginary circle, with a simultaneous bar marker indicating the letter to be reported. Either before presentation of this display, in the forward masking condition, or after it in the backward masking condition, they presented a pattern mask made up of a series of Xs linked together. This pattern masked the entire display. The independent variable is expressed by the stimulus onset asynchrony (SOA) which is the time between the onsets of the test and masking stimuli (test minus mask interval).

When the test and masking stimuli were presented at the same intensity, Spencer and Shuntich found that minimum performance was obtained not when the mask and the test stimulus occurred simultaneously, as predicted by integration theory, but rather when the mask followed the test by 50 msec. Figure 5 shows that performance improves in both directions from this minimum. However, performance in the forward masking condition reached the asymptote of the no-mask condition at an SOA of —100 msec., whereas an SOA of 300 msec. was required in the backward masking condition to reach this same level of performance. Thus, the

FIGURE 5. Percentage of correct identifications as a function of SOA between the 12-letter display and the pattern mask.

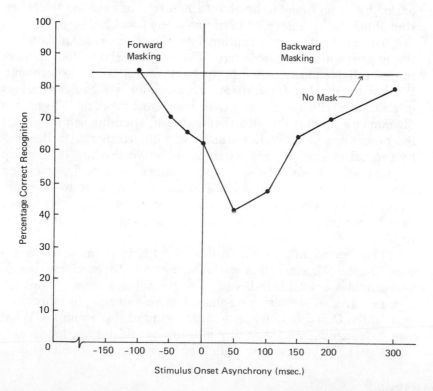

forward and backward masking functions were definitely not symmetrical; the minimum point occurred in the backward masking condition, and the temporal course of the backward masking function was much longer than that of forward masking. This critical test allows us to reject integration theory and any other that would explain the effect of a second stimulus upon the first simply by an integration of the stimulus information in the preperceptual image. The theory must also account for the temporal course of the recognition process and the interrupting effect of a second stimulus.

TWO-PROCESS MODEL   Although the integration process is not sufficient to account for forward and backward masking, the concept of integration of visual information over time is, in itself, a good one. It is demonstrable in a number of situations, for instance, in the trade-off that occurs between the presentation time of a stimulus and its intensity (see Chapter 8). A stimulus presented at an intensity of 10 per 1 msec. is detected as well as the same stimulus presented at an intensity of 1 per 10 msec. The intensity must be summated over time to explain the result. The time/intensity trade-off can suggest an estimate of the duration of the temporal integration period as the time beyond which the trade-off relationship breaks down. This period has been found to be about 100 msec., as seen in the discussion of the Hecht, Shlaer, and Pirenne study (see Chapter 8).

The concept of interruption has also been substantiated in the experiments discussed here. The U-shaped function appears to be a reliable phenomenon in the backward masking experiment. We have seen that forward masking produces significantly less interference with recognition than backward masking. These two phenomena support the idea that a second stimulus can terminate the processing of an earlier stimulus by interfering with the preperceptual storage of this stimulus. It is worthwhile to develop a quantitative model of the temporal course of visual perception based on these two processes. The model forces us to be more explicit in describing the phenomena and should, therefore, lead to a better understanding of the temporal course of visual perception.

The dependent variable in the model is in terms of d' values (see Chapter 7), since this measure controls for decision biases and provides a reliable index of what the subject knows about the stimulus. (As an exercise, you should be able to compute this measure in the D and O letter recognition studies, for example. What two independent response probabilities would be needed in this situation?) The central assumption of the model is that recognition is a temporally extended process, not an instantaneous occurrence. We also assume that the information in preperceptual storage is in the form of visual attributes or features. Recognition involves a readout of the visual features represented in preperceptual visual storage. Recognition also follows a very simple quantitative rule: in each unit of time, a fixed proportion of the remaining unanalyzed features are read out or synthesized. Assume that there are 10 features, and the recognition process reads out 20 percent of the unprocessed features every 30 msec. In the first 30 msec., then, two features are processed; in the second 30 msec., 20 percent of 8 or $1\%_0$ of a feature is processed, and so on, as shown in Figure 6.

Recognition performance is directly proportional to the number of features processed. Therefore, our measure of performance (d') is a negatively accelerating growth function of presentation time (t):

$$d' = \alpha \left(1 - \theta^t\right) = \alpha - \alpha\theta^t \tag{2}$$

in which θ indexes the rate of gain of information per unit of processing time, and α the maximum information that the subject can derive from the stimulus, given unlimited time to process it. In

FIGURE 6. The number of features processed as a function of recognition time according to the rule given in Equation 2.

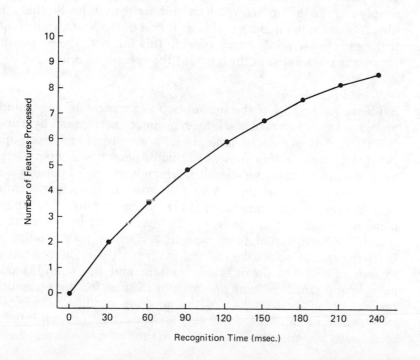

Equation 2, θ must lie between 0 and 1. If θ is close to 0, d' will approach α very rapidly, that is, the value $\alpha\theta^t$ will approach zero quickly. If θ is close to 1, on the other hand, d' will approach α very slowly, since θ will have to be raised to a larger power (t must be large) before θ^t approaches zero. According to the model, then, the recognition of a stimulus is a continuous process which involves an analysis of a number of features in the stimulus. The more features available and the more time the observer has to extract these features, the better performance should be.

In this context, then, α indexes the effective signal-to-noise ratio of the test item in the preperceptual visual image. If the test stimulus is preceded or followed during the critical integration period by a stimulus which decreases the signal-to-noise ratio, then α will decrease. The value of α is dependent upon the clarity of the test stimulus itself, and upon those stimuli that precede or follow it during the critical period of temporal integration.

For a given α, changes in d' are a negatively accelerating function of t, the time available to process the information. Recognition takes time and the rate of this process is indexed by the value of θ. As θ decreases, the recognition process is able to extract a larger proportion of unanalyzed features per unit of time. According to interruption theory, the masking stimulus interrupts recognition of the test stimulus by erasing all the visual information in the preperceptual image before the recognition process is complete. We simply require that interruption cannot occur until the second stimulus falls outside the period of integration of the first. Accordingly, if the second stimulus occurs outside this interval, the recognition process is terminated at the onset of the second stimulus.

Turvey Study   Evidence in support of the formal two-process model presented is provided by a backward masking experiment carried out by Turvey (1973). Turvey presented subjects with a test pattern made up of three consonant letters and asked them to identify as many letters as they could. A masking stimulus, which was a noise pattern made up of random bits of lines, was presented in the same location. Both the test and the masking patterns lasted for 10 msec. The dependent measure in the task was the number of letters correctly recalled, which varied from zero to 3. Turvey manipulated two independent variables: the ratio of the intensity of the test pattern to the intensity of the masking pattern and the stimulus onset asynchrony which reflects the amount of time for the recognition process before presentation of the masking stimulus. There were two levels of stimulus intensity: the ratio of test pattern intensity to masking pattern intensity was 2:1 in the first condition and 1:2 in the second. The stimulus onset asynchrony was varied between 0 and 184 msec. in the backward masking paradigm.

In terms of our model, α should be affected by the intensity of the test stimulus. As the intensity of the test pattern is increased, its signal-to-noise ratio is increased. If a book is viewed with very little light, it is difficult to discern the figure-ground contrast of the letters. As the light is increased, the letters become clearer, making them easier to read. The second variable, stimulus onset asynchrony (SOA), should not change the value of α or θ, since it only affects the amount of time the subject has to read out the information in the test pattern before presentation of the masking pattern.

The formalized model given by Equation 2 predicts the following results for this experiment. At zero SOA, the subject has an infinite time to process the test stimulus, because the masking stimulus does not fall outside of the integration time and recognition is not interrupted. Therefore, d' at this SOA is equal to α, since t is very large. Work out Equation 2 to show that $d' = \alpha$ when t becomes large (approaches ∞). In this case, α indexes the signal-to-noise ratio when the test and masking stimuli are presented simultaneously.

When the intensities of both patterns are integrated, the intensity of the test stimulus is reduced by that of the noise stimulus. The effect of the latter is greater when it is twice as intense as the test pattern than when it is one-half as intense. Thus we would expect d', which at zero SOA is equal to α, to be high in the 2:1 condition and low in the 1:2 condition. Turvey's results indicated that, indeed, when the ratio of test pattern intensity to masking pattern intensity was 2:1, subjects could report almost all 3 of the letters, whereas when it was 1:2, subjects could report none.

At an SOA of 184 msec., on the other hand, we would expect that performance would be good under both intensity conditions. If 184 msec. is sufficient for the recognition process, it would be complete by the time the masking stimulus occurs. To map out the functions in between, we would expect performance to show a monotonically increasing function in the condition in which the intensity of the masking stimulus is twice that of the test stimulus. As the SOA increases, the subject not only has more time to process the test stimulus but, in addition, the signal-to-noise ratio should improve, as the masking pattern becomes less and less likely to fall within the critical integration period. Performance in this condition can only improve with increases in SOA.

In the other condition, in which the test pattern is twice as intense as the masking pattern, performance follows a somewhat more complicated course. As we have said, when the two stimuli are presented simultaneously, performance is near perfect. Information in the two stimuli are integrated and the more intense test stimulus is read easily against the faint noise background. As the stimulus onset interval increases, however, the second stimulus begins to fall outside the integration period. Now it begins to interrupt the recognition process and performance should drop off sharply. In this case, performance is disrupted as the masking stimulus moves outside the integration period. However, with further SOA increases the subject has more and more time to process the features of the preperceptual image before the onset of the mask, and thus recognition should start improving at some point. Performance, therefore, drops off as the mask falls outside the integration period and then improves again as more time for the recognition process becomes available. The result should be a U-shaped curve.

When the results of the two conditions were plotted (Figure 7), they described the two functions predicted. Under the 2:1 condition, performance was near 3 letters recalled at zero SOA and dropped to a little over 1 letter recalled at 50 msec. SOA. At an SOA

FIGURE 7. Mean number of letters correctly identified as a function of SOA and the ratio of the test pattern intensity to the masking pattern intensity (T:M). (After Turvey, 1973.)

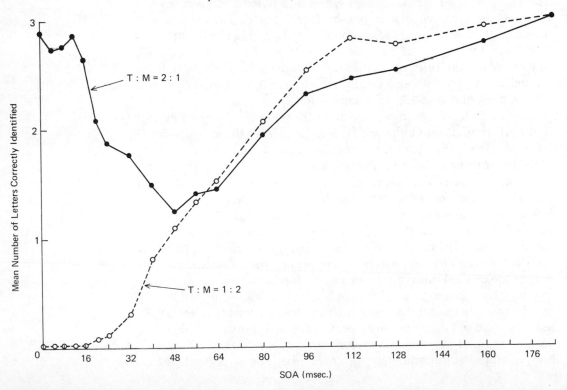

of 50 msec. we may suppose that the masking stimulus is occurring just outside the critical period of temporal integration, and functions therefore as a new stimulus interrupting the processing of the old. The subject has had only 50 msec. to process the test stimulus and therefore he possesses very little information about it. As the SOA increases, however, more and more information is available before the masking stimulus erases the preperceptual image, and performance gradually improves to 3 letters recalled at 184 msec. Under the 1:2 condition when the masking stimulus is twice the intensity of the test stimulus, no letters could be recalled at zero SOA, but as more and more time elapsed before the masking stimulus was presented, performance rose to all 3 letters recalled at 184 msec. SOA. Notice that the two curves come together at the 50-msec. SOA. In this case, both stimuli function to interrupt processing and the only critical variable is the amount of processing time before the masking stimulus presentation.

RECOGNITION TIME

We have seen many times that perception of a visual stimulus takes time. Exactly how much time this process requires has been studied by a number of experimenters, beginning with Baxt in 1871 (Sperling, 1963). Baxt presented himself, as subject, with a display containing a number of letters for a very short period of 5 msec., followed by a bright light flash. Baxt recorded the number of letters he could see in the display as a function of the time between presentation of the display and presentation of the light. He could apparently see one additional letter every 10 msec.; for every increase in time of 10 msec. he was able to read an additional letter.

Sperling Study

In the early 1960's Sperling investigated the problem with some procedural improvements (Sperling, 1963). First, he rejected the bright light flash as a means of terminating processing of the letters, since the bright light may not interfere with the image, but may actually produce a negative afterimage. Sperling found that, if the display letters were black on white, the bright light might produce an afterimage of white on black which the subject could continue to read out. The 10 msec. figure obtained by Baxt could thus have been an underestimation if the bright light did not terminate processing. Sperling used a noise mask of a series of random bits of letters to terminate processing. However, instead of presenting the display for a fixed duration and varying the blank interval before the noise mask, he kept the display on throughout the variable interval before onset of the noise mask. Despite these procedural changes, Sperling replicated Baxt's results exactly. For every increase in presentation time by 10 msec., the subject was able to read out 1 more letter up to about 4 or 5 letters when the limitation of short-term memory intervened.

The validity of this 10 msec. estimate rested on the assumption, admitted by Sperling, that his noise mask (which was ⅔ as intense as the test) was sufficient to erase the information from the letter matrix completely. However, if the noise mask was integrated with the test letter display, then the remaining trace might continue to be read for some unknown time after the mask occurred. There is no reason to assume that the mask erases all traces of the image of the test letters. Turvey's experiment above showed that test letters can be perfectly legible when a dimmer masking stimulus follows the test stimulus immediately. Furthermore, given the process of integration, one would expect that the longer the test stimulus is left on, the less the mask will interfere with the signal-to-noise ratio of the test letters. This follows from the fact that the test stimulus would contribute more and the masking stimulus less to the effective signal-to-noise ratio as we increase the duration of the test stimulus (see Equation 1). In Sperling's experiment, then, the on-time of the test stimulus was confounded with the interval between onset of the stimulus and onset of the mask. The improvement of letter recognition could be due to either or both the increase in processing time before the onset of the mask or the enhanced signal-to-noise ratio with longer presentation times. By varying his independent variable t (presentation time), Sperling confounded two psychological processes, affecting not only how long the subject had to process the information in the display, but also the clarity of the preperceptual image.

Eriksen and Eriksen Study

The Sperling estimate of 10 msec. per letter could be too small because of his invalid measure of processing time. Eriksen and Eriksen (1971) pursued the issue in an experiment in which they presented subjects with three successive visual symbols to be identified. Each one of the three was one of a pair, and which member of a given pair was presented on a given trial was varied randomly from trial to trial. Thus, there were a total of six stimuli in the experiment, three presented on each trial. The first pair consisted of *A* and *H*; either one of these could be presented as the first stimulus on the trial. The second stimulus was either a 5 or an 8, and the third was either an upward- or a downward-pointing arrow. Each of the three symbols was presented at the same spatial location in the visual display.

The three symbols on a trial were presented one by one on a tachistoscope, after which the subject was required to identify them. The dependent variable in the experiment was the number of trials on which the three symbols were reported correctly. The question of interest was the amount of time subjects needed to identify the symbols; to study this, two independent conditions were used.

First, time between presentation of the three stimuli was varied from trial to trial, affecting the amount of time the subject had available to read out each symbol. In this condition, presentation time was held constant at a very short duration—the minimal time to correctly identify the three symbols 90 percent of the time when they were presented at an interstimulus interval of 350 msec. This time was between 2 and 9 msec. for the different subjects. The remainder of the time between stimuli was made up of a blank dark fixation field. This was the silent condition in the experiment; the subject in this condition carries on the processing of the preperceptual visual image in the absence of information in the real world. This condition holds constant the signal-to-noise ratio, since the actual duration of the stimulus is not confounded with recognition time (the time between the onsets of each stimulus).

The second condition is analogous to Sperling's study since the stimulus was left on throughout the interstimulus interval. Thus, if the interval on a given trial was 50 msec., each symbol appeared for 50 msec. plus the 2–9 msec. presentation time. This is referred to as the continuous condition, since the stimuli remain on during the processing interval. Accordingly, the two conditions (silent and continuous) can be compared directly as a function of interstimulus interval (ISI). In one case, the stimulus stays on during the interval; in the other, the stimulus is turned off.

Plotting the results, one would expect that at the zero ISI, when the stimuli follow each other immediately, the effect would be a montage which the subject would have difficulty discriminating. Performance should, therefore, be very low. The actual results showed a performance of 33 percent, meaning that the subject was able to get 1 out of the 3 trials correct. Therefore, the subject did have some information available, given that guessing alone would account for a performance of only about 12 percent. (The probability of guessing all 3 of the symbols correctly is $(\frac{1}{2})^3$ or about 12 percent.) Why was performance better than chance at this condition? Nothing followed the last symbol so that the subject actually had infinite processing time to disambiguate the montage given by the three symbols. The experiment would have gained in validity by the addition of a noise mask at the conclusion of the third symbol presentation.

Figure 8 shows performance in the two conditions as a function of the interstimulus interval. Zero ISI is equivalent to a 2 to 9

msec. presentation time in both the continuous and silent processing conditions. Performance improves with increases in recognition
time but at diverging rates for the continuous and silent processing
conditions. The results indicated that in the silent condition, when

FIGURE 8. Percentage of trials on which all three stimuli were correctly
identified as a function of the interstimulus interval and the
silent and continuous processing conditions (after Eriksen &
Eriksen, 1971).

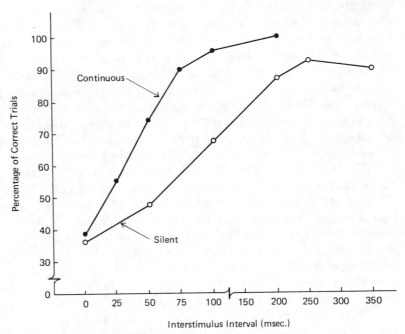

the time between stimuli was filled with a blank interval, performance reached 90 percent correct at 250 msec. ISI. That is, after a
very short presentation of each symbol, subjects needed a 250 msec.
blank period before presentation of the next symbol, in order to
report the symbol correctly. In the continuous condition, however,
when the time between stimuli was completely filled by presentation of the stimulus, only a 200 msec. presentation time was needed
to reach perfect identification of all three symbols.

The criticism of Sperling's study was thus confirmed; when
the stimulus is left on throughout the processing time, the effect of
the integration of energy over time results in a clearer image, a
greater signal-to-noise ratio. The subjects were able to identify the
symbols perfectly in the continuous condition, whereas they could
only reach 90 percent correct in the silent condition. In terms of the

formal quantitative model, the continuous/silent manipulation affects α, the amount of information available in the test stimulus. The greater the value of α, the less time is required to read out the information necessary for a given level of recognition performance.

We would expect that the estimate of processing time in any task would be dependent to some extent on the difficulty of the recognition task. Eriksen and Eriksen's experiment employed pairs of stimuli that were relatively difficult to discriminate: A and H, for instance, can be differentiated by the analysis of only one or two features, perhaps closure at the top. Nevertheless, even though discrimination was relatively difficult, it probably was not as difficult as Sperling's study where the letters had many more alternatives. Even so, the estimate arrived at is ¼ sec., much higher than the estimates of Baxt and Sperling.

The experiments of Averbach and Coriell, Spencer and Shuntich, Turvey, and Eriksen and Eriksen have shown that subjects need roughly 250 msec. to read out the information in a visual display. This estimate agrees remarkably well with our estimate of the duration of preperceptual visual storage in the last chapter. In terms of the preperceptual visual storage and the perceptual processing time relevant to reading, it is interesting to note that the estimate agrees with the ¼ sec. that the eye remains fixated at a given point during reading. We noted before that all the information derived from the text must be acquired during these fixation intervals, since the intervening movements from one point to another occur at too great a speed for recognition to take place during eye movements. The reason these fixation periods last for 250 msec. could mean that this is the length of time necessary to process the information available within 1 fixation.

An alternative reason for 4 eye movements per second in reading has been suggested, i.e., that the eye movement system is limited in such a way that it cannot move any faster. However, Arnold and Tinker (1939) found that subjects could move their eyes significantly faster than this rate when they were required to fixate successively on a horizontal array of dots. Therefore, the first explanation, that roughly 250 msec. is needed at each fixation to perceive the information available in the preperceptual image, is the only acceptable one. Once the information has been processed and synthesized, the eye can jerk to another point of fixation; another visual image can be formed in the system, and processing of it can begin.

Perceptual units in reading

*The brain—our prior knowledge of the world—
contributes more information to reading than the visual
symbols on the printed page.
—Frank Smith (1971)*

Chapters 17 and 18 outlined the temporal course of the recognition process. The preperceptual visual storage preserves the visual characteristics of the stimulus for roughly 200 to 300 msec. It is during this period that the recognition process must occur. In this chapter, we study the size of the units that are utilized by the recognition

FIGURE 1. A schematic drawing of the recognition process and the two properties of signs defining perceptual units in long-term memory.

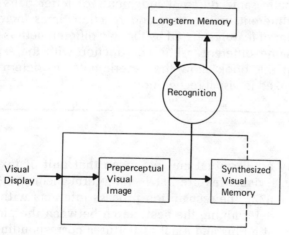

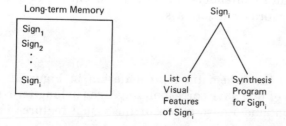

Visual Features

We have utilized the concept of visual features to define the information held in preperceptual storage. Although some of the visual features utilized in visual perception of shape, size, and distance were discussed in Chapter 9, we have not concerned ourselves with the features used in reading. Here we shall discuss a few studies aimed at isolating the visual features utilized in reading to demonstrate the types of experiments that can be used for this purpose.

The search task discussed in Chapter 4 can be employed to determine which visual features are critical in reading. For example, Neisser (1964) had subjects search for the letter Z in a list of either curved (e.g., O, D, U) or uncurved letters (e.g., M, T, X). The logic of the experiment is that it should take longer to reject background letters that have features in common with the test letter. When searching for a Z, it should take more time to reject an X than to reject an O, since X and Z share a slanted line while Z and O do not. In agreement with this logic, more search time per letter was required when the features of the background letters were similar to those of the test letter.

Gibson, Pick, Osser, and Hammond (1962) showed how confusion errors can be used to test which visual features are used in letter recognition. The idea is that letters should be confusable to the extent they have the same features in common. Subjects made same–different judgments of letter pairs presented simultaneously. On different trials, errors and reaction times increased with increases in the number of features shared by the two different letters. The visual search task and the same–different task in conjunction with the experimental methods discussed in this book allow the experimenter to determine which visual features are utilized in visual recognition.

process. By a perceptual unit we mean that unit of text which is defined by a visual-feature list in long-term memory. As seen in Figure 1 (p. 377), the recognition process interacts with long-term memory by determining the best match between the physical features in the stimulus and a list of features corresponding to a sign in long-term memory. These signs in memory define perceptual units; the major contenders for perceptual units are letters, spelling patterns, words, and phrases.

SIGNS According to the schematic representation in Figure 1, the perceptual units of text have corresponding signs in long-term memory. Each sign contains a description of the visual features in its per-

Jasper Johns' *Alphabets* come in different sizes, shapes, and colors.

ceptual unit. The recognition process determines which sign best describes the actual visual features in preperceptual storage. In other words, the recognition process makes the best bet given the visual information, and chooses a particular sign in memory. The recognition process then initiates the corresponding synthesis program for this particular sign and a synthesized percept enters synthesized visual memory.

EARLY READING RESEARCH

What are the perceptual units in reading? That is to say, do our signs in long-term memory correspond to letters, words or phrases? Much of the work on this question was done during the early period of experimental psychology, shortly after the invention of the tachistoscope and Emile Javal's discovery of saccadic eye movements in the 1870s. Until then it had been assumed that the eye moved continuously across the page, identifying each letter as it appeared. Now it was revealed that the eye moved in a series of discrete steps across the page. This finding generated the question of how much could be read in a single fixation between steps. In 1879, James M. Cattell, the first American to write a dissertation directed by Wilhelm Wundt, did a tachistoscopic study of letter, word, and phrase recognition showing that subjects could read out words, or even phrases and short sentences, from a display presented for so short a time that an eye movement was not possible.

In the 1890s, Erdmann and Dodge found that subjects could read words at distances too great to permit the identification of the component letters when they were presented alone. Acuity breaks down with increasing distance as the letters in preperceptual storage become smaller. This is another experimental technique which can be used to obtain errors; it does not limit the amount of processing time but decreases the S/N ratio. This method should produce the same qualitative results as a method which manipulates processing time to obtain errors. Erdmann and Dodge also found that subjects could read sentences at a distance too great to permit the recognition of the words presented alone.

All this suggested that the perceptual unit of recognition was not the letter, as might be supposed, but some larger unit. Further evidence was provided by the work of Pillsbury, a disciple of Wundt, who in 1897 devised an experiment to test Wundt's theory of apperception. Wundt, influenced by the philosophy of Kant, argued that what one perceives is dependent upon a pre-existent structure of knowledge. Pillsbury's demonstration of apperception in reading involved presenting subjects with visually distorted words. For instance, the word WORD might be presented with a slash drawn through the O. Other stimulus words might simply be missing a letter. These displays were presented very briefly to subjects, who were then asked to report what they had seen. Subjects were able to identify the distorted words correctly; and some of them failed to perceive anything unusual in the display. The apperceptive process enabled them to perceive the words as accurately as if they were complete and undistorted. These results convinced many people that word recognition was not dependent upon the recognition of individual letters.

A great deal of excitement in psychological and educational circles was generated by this work. Many educators, convinced that the basic unit of recognition was not the letter—as had always been assumed—but the word and even the phrase, began to advocate the whole-word method of teaching. Thus began the controversies that have raged ever since around the proper method for teaching children to read. If skilled readers perceive entire words and phrases, it was reasoned, the method of teaching children spelling patterns and phonetics could only interfere with their developing the optimal technique for deriving meaning from the text.

Psychologists meanwhile intensified their study of reading, convinced that it held the key to a great many crucial psychological issues. The American psychologist, Edmund Huey, wrote in 1908:

> ... to completely analyze what we do when we read would almost be the acme of a psychologist's achievements, for it would be to describe very many of the most intricate workings of the human mind, as well as to unravel the tangled story of the most remarkable specific performance that civilization has learned in all its history.

In spite of such grand expectations, most of the work done on reading in this period concerned the measurements of eye movements. A great deal of time was spent on devising apparatus of varying degrees of ingenuity to record the flight of the eye from one fixation to the next.

In 1900 Wilhelm Wundt objected. To understand reading, he pointed out, one would have to understand far more than the duration of eye fixations and the speed of eye movements. Crucial psychological processes, such as attention and expectancy, were being ignored by the reading psychologists in their study of how the reader derives meaning from printed text. For instance, the reader brings to the reading task a variety of sources of knowledge. As he reads, the skilled reader is able to predict the next word or words to some extent. This could result from either of two causes. (1) He has the information available in his peripheral vision; although he is focused on one point on the page, he can actually see words that occur further on in the text. (2) The knowledge of the observer enables him to guess at what is coming on the basis of what he has already read. It is possible, therefore, that reading efficiency is due not to an effect of the peripheral processing, but rather to the reader's ability to construct hypotheses about what lies ahead on the basis of what he already knows.

VISUAL INFORMATION AND REDUNDANCY

Wundt's criticism of the reading experimentalists of his time brought to light the crucial requirement of a valid study of reading: the separation of the effects of two different contributions to the process. The first contribution is that of the stimulus, the visual symbols on the page of text. The second is nonvisual information possessed by the sophisticated reader and stored in long-term memory.

There are three sources of nonvisual information that can aid the reader in decoding the written message. These sources are the orthographic, syntactic, and semantic structures that exist in English prose. The orthographic constraints define the valid spelling patterns in English. We know that words are separated by blank spaces and must have at least one vowel. Syntactic rules establish the permissible sequences of different parts of speech. For example, "The boy down fell the hill" is grammatically incorrect. Finally, semantic rules allow the reader to predict the word or words that make sense in a given sentence context. "The hill fell down the boy" is syntactically correct but semantically anomalous. All of these rules allow us to agree on the missing word in "Please clean the dirt from your s _ _ _ s before walking inside." This chapter will concern the ways visual and orthographic information interact in reading during a single eye fixation. Both of these components operate in the reading task, and the effect of each must be sorted out by the experimenter.

In terms of the information-processing approach, the visual stimulus is transformed by the visual system and a list of features is recorded in preperceptual visual storage. Recognition, or the read-out of this information, depends on the features of the information in preperceptual store and on the information possessed by the reader about the valid spelling patterns in English. Figure 2

FIGURE 2. The same visual configuration can be interpreted as two different letters, depending on the meaningful context.

demonstrates how two identical visual patterns can be interpreted as different letters because of meaningful context. Thus, although the visual information available about the last letter of the first word is the same as the first letter of the second word, the contribution of what one knows about the valid spelling patterns in English text demands that they be interpreted as different letters. (The knowledge of these rules is sometimes referred to as redundancy, since it reduces the number of valid alternatives a particular visual configuration can possess.) In reading, we would expect that this knowledge of rules of English spelling would enable us to extract meaning from a page of text without analyzing all the visual information present, or to identify words even when some of the visual information is missing.

It should be stressed that orthographic rules involve more than simply a knowledge of the spelling of each word in our vocabulary. For example, we know that *cht* does not spell a word, not because the meaning of *cht* is unknown, but because we know that *cht* is an invalid spelling sequence for a three-letter word. To illustrate, consider the spelling configuration *cit*. Even though one may not have this word in his vocabulary, it would be incorrect to conclude that this configuration could not spell a word.

Given that the reader may utilize orthographic, syntactic, or semantic rules, two interpretations emerge from the early experiments of Erdmann and Dodge, and Pillsbury. In the Erdmann and Dodge study, subjects were able to read words and sentences better than they could read isolated letters and words, respectively. One interpretation is that words are easier to read because our signs in long-term memory correspond to whole words, making them easier to perceive. For example, words may have unique visual characteristics which make them easier to perceive than individual letters. The alternative interpretation is that even though signs in long-term memory correspond to letters, subjects were able to guess correctly more often when the impoverished letters formed word sequences than when they did not. Consider the example in Figure 2. If the subject is presented the letter *c* at a very great distance, he may be unsure if it is a *c* or an *e* and would have to guess randomly between the two. On the other hand, if he is presented with *cool,* the *c* may be just as ambiguous visually, but if *ool* is interpreted as such, he can guess correctly with the word *cool*. In this case, the results would show better recognition for words than for isolated letters. We can also develop an analogous explanation for the results that sentences are better recognized than isolated words, using the syntactic and semantic rules.

Similarly, we do not know why the subjects in the Pillsbury experiment were able to identify words when a letter was missing or distorted. It is possible that they actually perceived the intact word, and that they did not need each letter to be present and intact in order to perceive the word. On the other hand, it is possible that they did not perceive it as complete and intact, but that their knowledge of the rules of English spelling enabled them to make a good guess at the word. We cannot conclude from these experiments, therefore, that the signs in long-term memory correspond to words; only that subjects need not perceive every letter before they can correctly identify the word.

Reicher Paradigm   Contemporary experimenters are aware that the knowledge of the rules of English orthography must be isolated in order to study the process of extracting information from the visual display. Reicher (1969) developed an experimental design that has been assumed by a number of investigators to control for orthographic redundancy. Reicher's purpose was essentially the same as Cattell's—to demonstrate whether subjects could recognize words in the same amount of time that they could recognize letters. Whereas Cattell had permitted his subjects to use their knowledge of English text, Reicher, at least implicitly, attempted to control for this knowledge by forcing a choice on every trial between one of two alternatives, either one of which would satisfy the requirements of English text (see Figure 3). For example, on one trial the subject might be presented with the word WORD for a very brief time, followed immediately by a visual noise mask made up of overlapping X's and O's. The masking stimulus also contained a cue to report one of the four letters. When his task was to name the fourth letter in the word, two alternatives would be presented at the time of the cue, D and K. The subject would have to choose one of these alternatives. In this task, then, the subject must make his choice only on the basis of the information he has obtained from the visual display. Knowledge of the rules of English spelling will not help him; both alternatives D and K form words given the information WOR—. Of course, a different word was presented on each trial and the subject did not know which letter position would be tested until the cue appeared.

Performance in this condition was compared with performance when the subject was presented with a single letter at any of the four serial positions defined by the word. For example, the subject could be presented with D alone and asked whether it was D or K. If the word rather than the letter is the perceptual unit, then a letter presented in a word should be better recognized than a letter presented alone. According to our model, the signs in long-term memory would correspond to words, making their identification easier. Of course, by definition we must also have signs in long-term

FIGURE 3. The visual displays used in the Reicher study (1969).

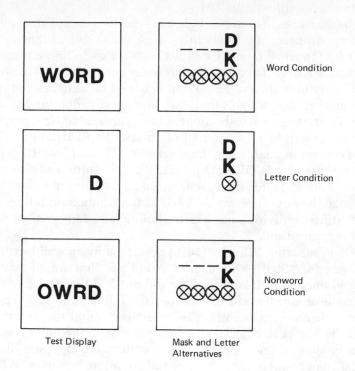

Test Display   Mask and Letter
                        Alternatives

memory which correspond to letters, since they can be recognized when they are presented alone. The idea would be that words function as perceptual units because their signs are more readily used and available in reading. Also, the description of words would involve more than a simple description of the letters that make them up. For example, the general word shape of WORD and WORK could be a visual feature, which could make these words much easier to recognize than D or K alone. There is more information in the perceptual unit, and it should be recognized more rapidly and accurately.

The third condition allowed Reicher to compare word versus nonword recognition. On some trials, the subject was presented with a nonsense word that did not conform to the spelling rules of English, for example, OWRD or OWRK. Again, if the word is the perceptual unit, it should be more easily identified than a nonword, even though the contribution of the rules of English spelling is controlled by using Reicher's forced choice test. Despite the care with which Reicher seemed to have controlled for this knowledge, his subjects identified the letter about 12 percent more often when it was imbedded in the word than when it was presented alone or imbedded in a nonword. The letter alone and the letter in the nonword were identified equally well.

Reicher's results have been interpreted as a demonstration that the common perceptual unit in reading is the word; that is, it is easier for the word to make contact with a sign in long-term memory than a letter. If experienced readers recognize text word-by-word, letter identification of D and K would be unusual and might take longer. The word was therefore more easily identified than the letter. The nonsense words could not be represented by signs, making it necessary to recognize all of their individual letters. Given that signs are available for the words WORK and WORD but not the nonsense words OWRD and ORWK, recognition of the words should proceed faster than recognition of the nonsense words. To recognize the nonsense words, each of the component letters must be identified individually, which should take longer than single word identification.

One year later, Wheeler (1970) described five possible artifacts in Reicher's (1969) experimental paradigm that might have influenced the result. Like others, he did not feel that Reicher's findings made sense; therefore, he expected to find, when he repeated the experiment controlling for these artifacts, that the letter alone would be recognized at least as well as the letter imbedded in a word. In spite of the pains he took to control for any possible artifactual component in the experimental situation, however, Wheeler found the same result that Reicher had found.

Nevertheless, Reicher's and Wheeler's results are inadequate as a demonstration that the perceptual unit is a word, because an alternative conclusion from the experiment is possible. In visual perception, as in any psychological behavior, there is a sequence of mental processes that exists between stimulus and response, and the experimenter's model of how these processes operate determines his interpretation of his results. The conclusion one reaches from Reicher's and Wheeler's results is, therefore, dependent upon the processing model assumed. When the Reicher paradigm model is made explicit, it becomes clear that an alternative model is possible. The alternative model leads to a different interpretation of the experimental findings.

TWO MODELS OF REICHER PARADIGM

We know that the visual pattern presented to the observer is transformed by the visual system into a preperceptual visual image. Recognition is the process by which the observer synthesizes a percept from this preperceptual visual image. By this process the information in preperceptual storage is analyzed and transformed into a percept, which is held in synthesized visual memory. In order to provide the experimenter with some measurable indication of the information that he has about the stimulus, the observer must make a response. This response is all that is available to the experimenter. The percept cannot be measured directly; for example, Pillsbury was not able to determine whether his subjects actually saw the configurations as words or made a good guess. The process of response selection intervenes between the percept which the experimenter wishes to study and the response which is available to him. The effect of orthography, which Reicher and Wheeler took pains to eliminate from the response, could operate at either the recognition stage or at the response-selection stage.

To control for the contribution of the rules of English orthography, Reicher and Wheeler limited the subject to two response alternatives, both of which spelled words. Why does equating the number of valid response alternatives under the different conditions control for the knowledge of English orthography? The answer to this question makes explicit the model the investigators employed. First of all, the model assumes two stages of processing between stimulus and response: recognition and response selection. The central feature of the model, however, is that it can be interpreted as the all-or-none guessing model traditionally employed in psychophysical tasks (see Chapter 6). The subject either correctly recognizes what was presented, or he does not; if he does not, he guesses at the response-selection stage. The two stages of processing assumed in this model—recognition and response selection—correspond directly to the detection and decision stages in Chapter 6.

Redundancy at Response-Selection Stage

This model assumes that the rules of English orthography can operate at the response-selection stage. If the subject does not know what was presented at the recognition stage, the spelling rules of English can be used at the response-selection stage to enhance the accuracy of his guesses. When a letter is presented in a word, rather than alone, the subject by means of the rules can reduce the population of valid alternatives and, hence, will be more likely to be correct. For example, if the subject has recognized WOR__ and is asked to report the fourth letter, he can reduce his guessing set from 26 letters to 5 because only 5 letters spell words given WOR__. Accordingly, the subject's guessing rate would go from 1/26 to 1/5 and performance based on guessing alone would be enhanced in the word, relative to the nonword or letter conditions. In order to control for different guessing probabilities, then, the subject is forced to guess from two alternatives in all conditions. This should set the probability of a correct guess at 1/2 in all conditions. Given this model and the precautions taken, any advantage observed in letter recognition performance in the word condition must be due to an increase in the amount of information transmitted by the recognition process.

A formulation of this model in our general information-processing model is shown in Figure 4. In the model, a light-wave pattern is

FIGURE 4. Model of visual recognition in which the knowledge of valid spelling patterns can be utilized only at the response-selection stage.

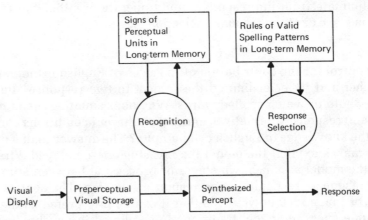

held in preperceptual storage and the recognition process operates on the information to find a match with a sign or signs in long-term memory. Reicher and Wheeler used a mask to terminate recognition before it was complete, so that errors would occur. The output of the recognition process produces some synthesized percept in synthesized visual memory. The synthesized percept is made available to the response-selection stage, which has access to the rules of English orthography. To control for redundancy on word trials, the subject is limited to two response alternatives that both spell words. Accordingly, since the knowledge of these rules should be superfluous, orthography should be eliminated as a contributing factor in the comparison between word and nonword recognition. Given this model and the Reicher paradigm any advantage in word recognition must be due to the recognition process, which is dependent on the signs of perceptual units in long-term memory.

Redundancy at Recognition Stage Figure 5 presents an alternative model which assumes that the effect of redundancy operates at the recognition stage, not at the response-selection stage of information processing. Accordingly,

FIGURE 5. Model of visual recognition in which the knowledge of valid spelling patterns can be utilized at the recognition stage.

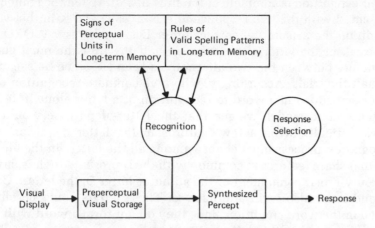

the subject can employ the rules of English orthography during the readout or synthesis of the preperceptual visual image. This model can describe Reicher's results even if it is assumed that the letter is the basic perceptual unit of analysis. Redundancy serves to enhance letter recognition when the letter is embedded in a valid spelling pattern, since it reduces the number of possibilities that can occur. This model assumes that the signs of perceptual units are letters and that, therefore, the visual features are defined with respect to letters. The recognition process is an analysis and synthesis of the individual features held in preperceptual visual storage. In a typical trial, because of the brief duration of the preperceptual visual image, the recognition process has only partial information about the letters in the display. However, the recognition process can utilize the rules of English orthography and synthesize a correct percept based on partial visual information.

Consider a particular trial in which the word WORD is presented. Assume that the subject has some visual information about each letter. The visual features that were processed reduce the alternatives to V or W, C or O, R or P, and D or B in the four positions, respectively. However, if the subject believed that the letter configuration must spell a word, he could synthesize the word WORD since it is the only valid spelling pattern given this visual information in each of the serial positions. In the letter-alone case or in the nonsense word, the recognition process could not use the spelling rules of English to reduce the number of alternatives for the tested letter. If the visual information limits the alternatives to D or B in the letter-alone case, the subject's synthesis or best guess will be correct only half the time. On half the trials, he sees a D; on the other half, he sees a B.

Recognition is complete at the time of test. When the subject is presented with the two response alternatives D and K in the word condition, he selects the correct letter D since he saw WORD. In contrast, in the letter-alone case, on half the trials he must guess randomly between the two alternatives D and K since he sees a B on half the trials. Accordingly, when we compare recognition of a letter embedded in a word to recognition of a letter alone in terms of the second model, we see that the letter-alone case would be more difficult. Given a few features in the letter condition, the recognition process must choose among all the letters in the alphabet that share features in common with the D presented. Thus, given the curvilinear component of the stimulus letter D, the letters C, O, Q, and P are also valid alternatives. These letters could be eliminated in the word condition since they do not form a word with the features from the other letters in the word.

Partial information   If the subject could retain the partial information he possesses about the letter until the experimenter gave him the alternatives, he would be able to benefit from them. For example, if he could remember that the letter was curvilinear, given the alternatives D or K, he could correctly choose D. However, Thompson and Massaro (1973) showed that subjects do not appear to be able to function in this way. They replicated the Reicher task while simultaneously manipulating the similarity of the response alternatives. Table 1 presents some of the stimulus items and the similar and dissimilar response alternatives in the task. Consider the word REAL when the subject is cued to report the first letter of the word. In one case, the subject is given the alternatives R and P, in the other, the alternatives R and M. Under the comparable letter condition the letter R would be presented with the similar response alternatives R and P or the dissimilar alternatives R and M. The experiment, therefore, involves a factorial design with two independent variables: letter vs. word and dissimilar vs. similar response alternatives.

The subjects were tested for five days. On the first day a stimulus duration for each subject was determined that gave an overall level of performance of near 75 percent accuracy. On the next four days, the subject was tested repeatedly under the different experimental conditions. The results replicated the previous findings, since a 9 percent word advantage effect was found. However, performance did not change as a function of the similarity of the response alternatives in either the word or letter conditions.

The failure to find a similarity effect indicated that the subjects were not able to utilize the partial visual information they had dur-

TABLE 1
An Example of Stimulus Items and the Similar and Dissimilar Response
Alternatives in the Letter and Word Recognition Tasks

Letter position tested	Base word	Alternatives	
		Similar	Dissimilar
1	REAL	P	M
	BEND	R	L
	PLOW	B	G
	NAIL	M	P
	CASH	G	R
	EAST	F	C
2	SNUG	M	L
	WAIT	H	R
	AGES	C	P
	SHIN	A	P
	SHIP	K	N
	SKIM	H	W
3	PACE	G	N
	LANE	M	C
	ROBE	P	S
	CURE	B	T
	MOPE	R	L
	TOLL	I	O
4	SLAP	B	M
	STAB	R	Y
	HALE	F	L
	HEAR	P	L
	RICH	K	E
	GRIM	N	P

ing the recognition stage in selecting between the response alternatives. Thus it appears that recognition or synthesis of the percept eliminates any earlier information in the preperceptual visual image on which that synthesis was based. If the recognition process mistakenly synthesizes the letter P, for instance, that percept replaces the preperceptual visual information from the D stimulus. This is essentially the transfer of information from preperceptual storage to synthesized visual memory. When the observer is then given a forced choice between D and K, he is unable to refer back to the information in preperceptual storage, since it is no longer there. He knows only that his identification was wrong and, therefore, guesses from the two test alternatives.

To sum up so far, there are two different models with differing interpretations of the results of the Reicher paradigm. One maintains that the perceptual unit is something larger than a letter, i.e., that the visual features that are analyzed in the recognition process correspond not to letters but to larger units such as a spelling pattern or word. This model assumes that the process of recognition is such that the amount of information it produces is independent of the effect of redundancy, and that redundancy's effect of reducing the possible number of alternatives operates only at the response-selection stage. The second model maintains that the features analyzed in the recognition process are defined with respect to individual letters. Redundancy, however, enhances recognition itself in this model, so that recognition of a letter embedded in a word may be better than that of the same letter presented alone, even though the experimenter has controlled for its effect at the response-selection stage.

Experimental Tests

What is needed now is an experiment that can distinguish between our two alternative interpretations of the advantage of recognizing letters when they are imbedded in words. The second model based on letters as perceptual units has assumed that the recognition process is able to utilize the rules of English orthography. When the alternatives are given after the stimulus presentation, the recognition of words has an advantage because presenting the alternatives after recognition cannot affect the operations of this stage. We might expect, therefore, that presenting the alternatives before the stimulus presentation might eliminate differences between the word and letter conditions, since the utilization of English orthography would be ineffective. Using our previous example of the word WORD, the subject is now given the alternatives D and K for the fourth letter position before the stimulus presentation. If the subject could utilize this information at recognition, there should be no advantage in the recognition of the word WORD versus the letter D. If the subject has recognized WOR— he still knows that the fourth letter must be D or K. More importantly, on letter-alone trials, he does not have to choose from all 26 letters but can synthesize D or K depending on the visual information available. This interpretation leads us to expect that the advantage of words would, therefore, be eliminated when we present the alternatives before the stimulus presentation.

In fact, Reicher had also employed a precue condition in which the two alternatives were given verbally before each trial. However, this study is not sufficient to test the effect of presenting the alternatives beforehand, because Reicher did not tell his subjects the position of the test letter referred to by the two alternatives. Accordingly, the subjects might know that the alternatives were D and K, but would not know that this applied to a given letter position until the alternatives were presented after the trial. This must have been very confusing for the subjects and, in fact, performance on the precue condition was roughly 10 percent poorer than the condition in which the alternatives were presented only after the stimulus trial. The precue disrupted performance equally on word, letters, and nonword trials.

Even if Reicher's subjects had been given the location of the to-be-reported letter in the precue condition before the trial, they may not have been able to utilize this information at the recognition stage. On the other hand, the rules of English orthography are highly overlearned, so that they may be employed easily at recognition. That is to say, although we tell the subject a given letter will be a D or a K, he cannot incorporate this information in recognition whereas he does utilize the spelling rules in the language. Therefore, the advantage of recognizing words may still be due to the utilization of the rules of English orthography on word trials even though the alternatives are presented before the stimulus trial.

We have argued that subjects could not utilize the information given by the two alternatives when they are presented immediately before the trial as in Reicher's task. In a second experiment, Thompson and Massaro (1973) taught their subjects the possible alternatives before the experiment session. In this case, they hoped to control for the utilization of redundancy at recognition while providing a test between word and letter recognition. The subjects were taught four alternatives before the experimental session. Given sufficient practice with this set of alternatives, the investigators expected the subject to incorporate the knowledge of the alternatives into the recognition process, eliminating the effects of redundancy. In the letter condition, the test letter could be any of the four alternatives P, R, C, or G. In the word condition, the test word could be the words APE, ARE, ACE, or AGE. Accordingly, in both conditions the subject knew that the presented letter or word must be one of four alternatives.

The four alternatives in Thompson and Massaro's experiment were also chosen so that two alternatives were highly similar to each other and highly dissimilar from the other two alternatives. The letters P and R are identical except for the downward slash of the R, and their physical features differ significantly from the features of C and G. Analogously, C and G have the same features except for those additional ones that change a C into a G. If recognition of the letters is dependent upon an analysis of the visual features of the letters held in preperceptual storage, then the letters R and P should be confused for each other more often than for C or G. Similarly, when the letters C or G are misidentified, the subjects

*Equating
redundancy
rules*

should be more likely to respond with the other similar alternative than with the letters R or P. More importantly, if the letter is the perceptual unit, the visual confusions on the word trials should be the same as on the letter-alone trials. On both kinds of trials, the signs of letters would be referenced in long-term memory so that the visual confusions should be identical on letter-alone and word trials. If the word is the perceptual unit, however, it seems likely that the type of confusions might differ on letter-alone and word trials. In this case, we would expect the words to have different feature lists stored with the signs of words in long-term memory.

In contrast to previous findings, the results indicated that letters presented alone were better recognized than letters imbedded in words by 11 percent. The second finding was that when subjects reported the wrong letter, they were far more likely to have mistaken the stimulus for the similar letter among the other three, than for one of the two very different letters. If subjects chose their responses randomly on error trials, each of the three error alternatives should be equally likely and should occur about 33 percent of the time. However, the similar alternative was given on error trials 63 percent of the time. Secondly, the subjects were as likely to confuse similar letters when they were presented in words as when the letters were presented alone. This supports the idea that subjects used visual features that were defined with respect to individual letters and not with respect to the word.

Thompson and Massaro's experiments, therefore, seem to show that a letter is not better recognized in a word than presented alone when the operation of redundancy is eliminated at the recognition stage. Smith and Haviland (1972) made a word–nonword comparison while attempting to control for redundancy at the recognition stage. Subjects were presented with three-letter trigrams, the first letter of which was always either R or B, and the third letter of which was always G or M. For the middle letter of the trigram they had two conditions: in one the middle letter was either A or U, and in the other condition it was either S or D. That is, in the first condition the letters chosen on any trial would always form a word; eight combinations were possible, all of which constituted meaningful words in English in this condition. In the second condition, in which the middle letter was one of two alternative consonants, all of the eight possible combinations were meaningless strings of consonants. Smith and Haviland taught their subjects how the stimulus sequences were made. Subjects were also tested to make sure that they knew the possible alternatives at each position in the word and nonword condition.

Essentially then, Smith and Haviland's subjects learned a new set of rules for the spelling patterns in their experiment. Now if these rules were utilized equally on word and nonword trials, any differences in recognition must be attributed to the existence of perceptual units for words but not for nonwords. In both conditions, the subject learned the possible alternatives for all three letters and had the same number of alternatives available at the time of recognition. If the learning was successful, knowledge of spelling rules would not give recognition in the word case an advantage over recognition in the nonword case. Thus, the second model, which assumes that perceptual units are letters and redundancy operates at the recognition stage, would predict no differences in performance in the two conditions. On the other hand, the first theory, that the permanent feature lists of signs in long-term memory are defined with respect to spelling patterns or words rather than letters, would predict that the letters would be better recognized when embedded in a word than when embedded in a nonsense string. The fact that the same number of alternatives exist in either case would eliminate the effect of redundancy but would not affect the advantage of having signs for the words in long-term memory.

Smith and Haviland tested subjects under the word and nonword conditions in different blocks of trials. They also used the Reicher cueing procedure so that only one letter was tested per trial. In the analysis of their results, they compared performance on the first and third letters in the word and nonword conditions. The results of the middle letter were not analyzed since they differed in the word and nonword condition and any differences observed might be due to the actual letters used rather than the word–nonword difference itself. The actual results of this experiment showed a difference of about 4 to 7 percent in favor of recognition of letters in words. It is difficult to evaluate a result of this size, but the experimenters were satisfied that it represented support for the theory that the perceptual units are larger than a single letter. However, it is possible that another process besides the recognition process is responsible for the advantage of recognizing letters in words over nonwords. Although the subjects knew the response alternatives before each session, they were not cued with respect to the position of the letter to be reported until after the test presentation. The cue was presented on a choice card outside of the tachistoscope. It is possible that there was differential forgetting between the stimulus presentation and processing of the choice card on word and nonword trials. Even though the subject recognizes the letters, he must remember them correctly in order to be correct on a given trial. If the subject recognizes all three letters correctly on word trials, he can rehearse the word during the interval between recognition and the processing of the cue card. In contrast, the subject must rehearse three consonant letters in the nonword condition. Therefore, a slight forgetting difference might account for the differences between word and nonword trials.

Resolving conflicts Given the apparent conflict between the Smith and Haviland findings and Thompson and Massaro's results, the author replicated both the letter versus word and the word versus nonword comparison (Massaro, 1973). These studies only tested performance at one accuracy level and did not obtain many observations under each experimental condition. One reason for this is that a manually operated tachistoscope is a slow and tedious method for presenting test stimuli. Because of variability in the data, therefore, some of these studies may not have obtained a valid measure of performance in the different conditions. Hence, Massaro (1973) took a large number of observations from each subject.

Another precaution which was taken by the author in his (1973) study, was to manipulate a second independent variable which was known to affect performance in a certain way. This variable was the amount of time the subject had for recognition. By allowing recognition time to take on one of eight possible values, performance could be observed at a number of accuracy levels. This essentially allows the investigator to test his hypothesis repeatedly in the same experiment. Furthermore, if there is a significant difference between recognition of a word and a nonword, this difference should be dependent upon the amount of recognition time. With a very short time for recognition, performance should be near chance and there should be very little difference between the stimulus conditions. As recognition time is increased, the differences between the two conditions should increase until no errors are made and performance should once again be similar under the two conditions.

Massaro (1973) first replicated the stimulus conditions of the Thompson and Massaro (1973) study. The test letters were P, R, C, and G and the test words were APE, ARE, ACE, and AGE. The test stimulus duration was 1 msec. The test stimulus was presented alone or followed by a masking stimulus after a variable blank interval of 10, 20, 40, 70, 110, 160, or 240 msec. A small computer controlled the experimental events and the test stimuli were presented over visual displays made of light-emitting diodes. Four subjects were tested for five days each. On the first day, subjects were given one session of 300 trials under the letter condition and a session of the same length under the word condition. The letter and word conditions were then alternated on the next four days. Two subjects were given the letter conditions on the second day, the other two were given the word condition. Two sessions of 300 trials each were given each day. The 4 test alternatives and the 8 processing conditions occurred randomly with equal probability in each session.

In the second experiment, a word–nonword comparison was made. The above experiment was replicated except that the alternatives VPH, VRH, VGH, and VCH, were the stimuli used in the nonword condition. The letters V and H were chosen because their inside features are similar to the letters A and E used in the word condition. Four new subjects were tested for five days during which the word–nonword comparison was carried out exactly analogous to the letter–word comparison in the first experiment.

The results showed that the recognition time variable had its expected effect in both experiments. Performance improved about 40 percent with increases in the blank interval showing that recognition time was critical for correct performance. The results of the first experiment showed that letters presented alone were better recognized than letters in words replicating the findings of Thompson and Massaro. The results of the second experiment showed no differences in the word and nonword conditions, failing to replicate the findings of Smith and Haviland. A letter seems to be better recognized alone than when embedded in a word because of lateral masking (see Chapter 17). The outside letters decrease the clarity in the middle letter, giving an advantage for letters presented alone. In the word–nonword comparison, lateral masking should be identical in the two conditions so that no difference should be expected if the operations of redundancy are controlled at the recognition stage.

One explanation of the differences in the Smith and Haviland (1972) and the Massaro (1973) study is that Massaro's subjects were much more practiced in the redundancy rules than were those of Smith and Haviland. Therefore, it is possible that the slight advantage of word trials in the Smith and Haviland study may have been eliminated if the subjects were tested for a larger number of trials under each condition.

In the author's opinion, the results to date define the letter as the perceptual unit in reading. Recognition involves a readout of the visual features that make up individual letters. The knowledge of English orthography or redundancy operates at the recognition stage, which facilitates recognition by reducing the number of valid alternatives when only partial information is available. This model correctly predicts when a letter embedded in a valid spelling pattern will and will not be better recognized than when presented alone or in a nonsense word.

Assuming that letters are the perceptual units in reading, it is interesting that subjects can identify 4 letters in a nonsense word as well as a single letter (Reicher, 1969). Since redundancy cannot account for this result, it appears that a string of letters can be processed in parallel without capacity limitations (see Chapter 15). The feature analyzers defined with respect to individual letters can operate efficiently on a string of letters while simultaneously keeping track of serial positions. Accordingly, although the perceptual unit in reading is a single letter, the recognition process operates simultaneously across the string of letters available in preperceptual visual storage.

SELECTIVE PERCEPTION REVISITED

The analysis of the above experiments shows that the experimenter must make explicit his model of performance in the task. These experiments and analysis are also relevant to another set of experiments which have systematically varied the number of alternatives in a recognition task. The experiments were developed because of an interest in selective perception, the extent to which perception is enhanced when the observer is prepared for just that event. For example, when you are looking for a particular friend in a crowd, will that person be easier to see compared to the situation when you are looking for no one in particular? One experimental task that has been used to answer this question was first used by Lawrence and Coles (1954) and is illustrated by a recent experiment carried out by Gummerman (1971).

Gummerman (1971) attempted to show that preparation facilitates visual perception by the following experiment: Gummerman's subjects were asked to identify letters of the alphabet presented one at a time on a visual display. On some trials he told them that the letter coming up was one of two specific alternatives. Performance on these trials was compared to performance on others in which the 2 alternatives were not presented until the visual display had ended.

In one condition, the letters were chosen from a master set of four letters. Thus, the subject knew on every trial that the coming letter would be, for example, either A, L, N, or T. In the BEFORE condition the subject saw two of these letters, one of which would be presented on this trial. In the AFTER condition the subject did not see the two alternatives until after the test letter was presented. The test letter was presented for 120 msec., followed by a masking stimulus and two stimulus alternatives. The subject reported which of these two letters was presented on that trial. In a second condition, the master set of letters was 16 instead of 4.

Gummerman hoped to prove that subjects could enhance their perception of stimuli if they were prepared for them in advance; this means that subjects would do better in the BEFORE condition than in the AFTER condition. In the latter case their attention would be spread among either 4 or 16 anticipated stimuli; in the BEFORE condition, on the other hand, their attention could be concentrated on the perception of only two stimuli. On the trials using 4 stimuli, the subject's performance did not differ under the BEFORE and AFTER conditions and averaged 85 percent. With 16 stimuli they averaged 88 percent correct in the BEFORE condition, but only 73 percent correct in the AFTER condition. As we might have expected, then, performance in the BEFORE condition was the same whether the master set of 4 or 16 alternatives was used. With a 4-alternative stimulus set, no difference was found in the BEFORE or AFTER conditions. With 16 alternatives, however, performance dropped significantly in the AFTER condition.

One might conclude from the results that narrowing down the alternatives allowed the observers to perceive the letter alternative more clearly. This means that the subject had more visual information about the test alternative in the BEFORE case than in the AFTER. Unfortunately, Gummerman's experiment illustrates a major problem in accounting for the decision stage in this sort of task. Analogous to the recognition task discussed above, the experimenter must make explicit how the decision process operates in his task. The AFTER condition was Gummerman's attempt to control for the decision stage. Perceiving the problem to be that it is much easier to guess the correct answer in a two-alternative task than in a 16-alternative task, the AFTER condition equalized the chances of guessing correctly. If the subject did not know the answer and had to guess, he had two alternatives and a 50/50 chance in either case. Therefore, the BEFORE and AFTER conditions were assumed to be equivalent because it would not be easier to guess correctly in one than in the other condition. Gummerman (1971), like other investigators before him, assumed that he had thereby adequately controlled for the decision system, and that any differences in performance between the two conditions could be safely attributed to the recognition process.

It seems unlikely, however, that this model is the correct one for the decision system in this experiment. Gummerman, in fact, has made exactly this point in a recent paper (1973). The model implies that there are two kinds of trials, those on which the subject knows what was presented, and those on which he knows nothing. He has either all of the information about the letter or none of the information. When he has it all, he responds correctly; when he has none he guesses randomly. The probability of a correct response on guessing trials then would be $1/n$ where n is the number of alternatives in the task. Thus, when the subject is choosing between the two alternatives, M and R, there are three possible situations. Subject knows the stimulus is an M; subject knows that it is an R; or subject knows nothing and guesses at random. In the last case, limiting the possible alternatives should increase his chances, but it will make no difference whether these alternatives are given before or after presentation.

This model is the all-or-none guessing model and there appears to be no strong evidence to it. In fact, observers in a task such as this report that there is no such thing as a trial in which they are perfectly certain that a given stimulus was presented. Moreover, there are very few trials in which they know nothing at all. On the contrary, usually they have some information about the stimulus, and they make a decision based on that partial information.

Decisions and Demons In our model, we assume that recognition involves a readout of the visual features of the letter held in preperceptual visual store. These features are checked against the signs of letters in long-term memory. The observer has a set of rules according to which he can match visual information from a stimulus to the name of a letter of the alphabet. One way to think about letter recognition is analogous to Selfridge's (1959, 1966) Pandemonium model, in which the 26 signs of letters are each hooked up with an egotistical demon. Each demon looks for visual features of the letter it represents. The demon shouts in direct proportion to the number of visual features that match its letter. For example, the experimenter presents an A; a number of the demons begin to yell, some more loudly than others. The A- and the H- demons are both shouting above the rest, and the A-demon is probably shouting the loudest. The shouting of the demons is monitored by a decision demon. The easiest way for the decision demon to choose among the shouting demons is to choose the letter corresponding to the loudest shouting demon: the A-demon wins, the others retire from the competition, and the observer perceives the letter A.

This model conforms to our persistent belief that perceptual tasks involve two processes: recognition and decision. Figure 6 illustrates the psychological processes in the letter recognition task in terms of the model. Recognition is assumed to output a value X for each of the 26 letters. The value X for each letter is a direct function of the shouting of the appropriate demon. The decision system monitors the shouting of the demons and chooses that letter which is represented by the largest value of X. It is now possible to reformulate the question of whether preparation enhances perception in terms of this model. The effects of presenting the alternatives before the test stimulus presentation can occur at either or both the recognition and decision stages.

FIGURE 6. Two stages of processing involved in the letter recognition task. The recognition process is assumed to transmit a value X for each of the 26 letters, and the decision process chooses that letter represented by the loudest shouting demon.

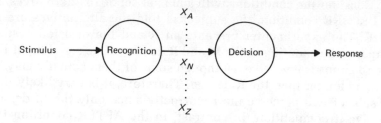

Recognition

If presenting the alternatives before the test affects recognition, the values of X transmitted by the recognition process will be more accurate than the values in the AFTER condition. Presenting the alternatives before the trial should prime the appropriate demons and all of the recognition capacity is devoted to these demons. If the subject is given the alternatives M and R, these demons are much more accurate in their shouting because of the recognition capacity devoted to them. Whereas the M demon might shout only at 70 dB for an M presentation without the alternatives in advance, he shouts at 90 dB if the alternatives are limited to M and R before the trial. Similarly, whereas the R demon normally might shout at 35 dB to an M presentation, the advance cueing of the two alternatives reduces the shouting of the R demon to an M presentation. Presenting the alternatives BEFORE the test stimulus, could, therefore, change the values of X given by the recognition process.

Decision

In addition to affecting the recognition stage, presenting the alternatives before the test stimulus could influence the decision stage of processing. The decision demon could selectively attend to the shouting of the appropriate demons cued by the two alternatives given before the trial. Given the alternatives M and R in advance, the decision demon only has to compare the shouting of these two demons. The shouting of the letter demon N to an M presentation can be ignored because it is not a valid alternative. Therefore, even though the values of X do not differ under the BEFORE and AFTER conditions, the decision system could behave more optimally when it only has to compare the shouting of a limited number of demons indicated by the alternatives in the BEFORE condition.

The effects found in Gummerman's study could be due to either or both recognition and decision processes. Although subjects were always given two alternatives after the trial to eliminate any differences between the BEFORE and AFTER conditions in the decision stage, a decision operation with a limited memory could account for Gummerman's findings completely.

Consider the conditions with a master set of 16 alternatives. In the BEFORE condition, the subject is told the alternatives are M and R. The experimenter presents an R and the decision system compares the shouting of the M and R demons. The shouting of the other demons is ignored even though some of them actually may be shouting louder than the R demon. Therefore, it is very likely that the subject will perceive the R correctly since only the M demon can give it competition. In contrast, in the AFTER condition the decision system must compare the shouting of 16 demons representing the 16 letters. Since the subject does not have complete visual information, on some trials the wrong demon will shout the loudest. The experimenter presents an R, and while demons representing all 16 letters shout at various intensities, the decision system listens and chooses P, the loudest shouting demon. The subject perceives P as the shouting subsides. The display is terminated and the experimenter announces that the stimulus was either an M or an R. Now the subject knows that P was the wrong demon, that he should have chosen either M or R. But the M and R demons are no longer shouting and he cannot remember the intensity of shouting, so the subject no longer has the necessary information to decide between them. Therefore, he is forced to guess between the two alternatives. This example shows that the subject may make more errors in the AFTER condition even though the recognition process did not differ in the two tasks.

Gummerman's subjects performed equally well in the BEFORE and AFTER conditions when the master set contained 4 letters. This means that the subjects could remember the shouting of the 4 relevant demons until the two alternatives were presented after the stimulus presentation. However, with a master set of 16 alternatives, the observer was unable to remember the intensity of the shouting of all the demons until the two alternatives were presented. This result is consistent with a limited capacity memory and with our interpretation of the recognition of letters presented alone, in words, or in nonwords. Accordingly, Gummerman's results are also consistent with the idea that the decision stage is responsible for the differences between the BEFORE and AFTER conditions.

Both the letter, word, and nonword recognition studies and the BEFORE-AFTER experiment demonstrate that recognition performance is dependent upon the number of valid response alternatives in the task. Logically, reducing the number of valid alternatives can facilitate performance at two processing stages and the experimenter must devise his experiment to determine which process is responsible for his results. To do this, he must define explicitly the psychological processes in a model of a particular experimental task and interpret the effects of his independent variables in terms of this model. Only then can he begin to evaluate the contributions of each of the different stages of information processing.

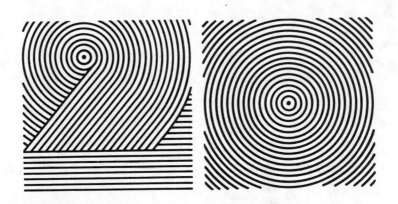

Dimensions of hearing

*. . . But for thee who looks to understand me, it is first
the sound that comes into thine ear in order to insinuate
the word into thy mind.*
—St. Augustine

Speech perception and music appreciation are the most impressive
demonstrations of auditory information processing. Consider the
spoken sentence: "He was seen running from the scene of the ob-
scene crime." By what rules do we process these sounds, so that
we are able to discriminate not only the different sounds in the
sentence, but also the three different meanings of one sound? In
time experimenters hope to accumulate enough understanding of
each of the simpler component processes of auditory perception to
begin to describe the complex operations by which we perceive
such a sentence.

The stimulus that the auditory system processes is an atmospheric **SOUND**
sound wave. The atmosphere is composed of small particles that
are highly sensitive to the motion of the other particles around
them. When one particle is displaced from its stable resting position, and thus moves closer to a neighboring particle, the two particles are said to be in a state of compression. In this state they repel
each other. The second particle moves away, and its direction is the
same as that of the original motion of the first particle. The first
particle, however, is in the meantime compelled by this state of
compression to reverse its direction and move back towards its
original position.

   At some point the two particles are farther away from each
other than normal; a state of rarefaction now exists between them,
and they are drawn back together. Thus, the motion of any particle
influences its neighbor, and the motion induced in its neighbor influences the first particle in turn, so that the two oscillate in close
relation to each other. Meanwhile, the motion of the second particle
has set a third one to oscillating, which in turn affects a fourth, and
so on until the motion of the air particles adjacent to the ear pushes
the eardrum back and forth.

Consider the schematic diagram presented in Figure 1. As the prong of a vibrating tuning fork moves out from its resting position, it pushes a neighboring air particle ahead of it, and the return movement of the prong toward the center of the fork sets up a state of rarefaction that draws that particle back with it. The oscillation of the prong induces a corresponding oscillation in this neighboring air particle. Next to the neighboring particle, particle A, is particle B. As the outward moving prong drives A toward B, a point is reached at which A and B repel each other. A moves back, pushed by its reaction against B and drawn by the returning prong, while B moves outward, repelled by A. Eventually A and B are in a state of rarefaction and are attracted toward one another again; meanwhile the outward push of B has set in motion particle C. Gradually the original motion of the tuning fork prong is transmitted to one particle after another, until the particles adjacent to the ear receive it, and the eardrum is pushed back and forth in the same way.

The representation of such a periodic motion over time is a sine wave. Think of an oscillating particle as a pencil point resting

FIGURE 1. The propagation of a sine wave along the particles of the atmosphere (after Denes & Pinson, 1963).

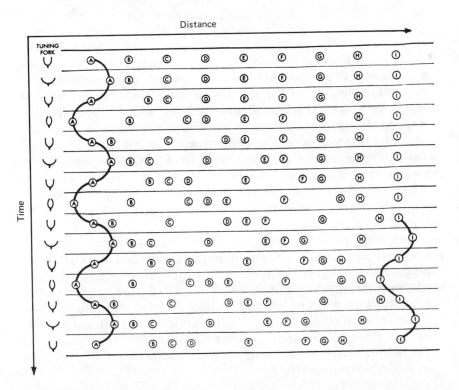

on a sheet of paper. The paper is being drawn along at a constant rate in a direction perpendicular to the direction of particle movement. The particle will describe a continuous line in the form of a wave back and forth across the stable position of the particle. This is the sound wave pattern, a representation over time of the motion that is reproduced in particle after particle until it reaches the ear. Note that it is the movement pattern that flows from the sound source to the receptor, not the particles themselves. On the contrary, the particles simply oscillate around their original distance from the source (see Figure 1).

The tuning fork prong is actually surrounded by adjacent air particles, so that each of these particles carries the message to its neighbors, and the sound radiates in concentric circles from the source. The speed at which the message is transmitted from particle to particle is the velocity of sound. The velocity is dependent on the atmospheric pressure; in our atmosphere at sea level, sound travels 1130 ft. per second, or 770 miles an hour.

SINE WAVES

One way to think of a wave is to imagine a man running around a circle painted on the floor of a dark room. A light attached to the top of the man's head throws a small circle of light onto the wall behind him as he runs. Suppose that we place a roll of photographic paper horizontally on the floor next to the wall and have a student pull it upward at a constant rate. The paper is sensitive to light and dark so that it records the tracing of the light reflected by the man. As the man runs around the circle, the light reflected on the paper moves back and forth, and since the paper is moving upward the light describes a wave upon it. The design recorded on the paper will be a sine wave pattern as shown in Figure 2. The amplitude of the sine wave, or the height of the wave's crest measured from the center, is equal to the radius of the circle. As we increase the radius of the circle we increase the amplitude of the sine wave. Analogously, the amplitude of an oscillating air particle varies according to the amount of energy expended in the oscillation. A sound source of great energy displaces air particles far from their resting position, and the amplitude of the sound wave is correspondingly large. A very faint sound stimulus displaces the air particles by only a small distance, and the amplitude of the sound wave is therefore very small.

Amplitude

The amplitude of a sound wave is given by its sound pressure, which is the amount of force acting over a unit area and is mea-

FIGURE 2. Sine wave pattern. The amplitude of the wave is given by A. The frequency is measured by the number of complete cycles per unit of time. The phase is the position in the wave cycle with respect to the beginning of the cycle.

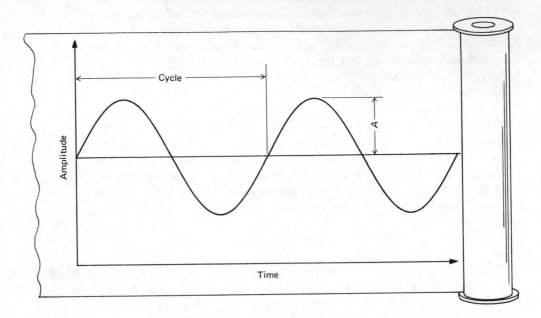

sured in dynes per square centimeter (dynes/cm²). One dyne is the amount of force required to give a mass of 1 gram an acceleration of one cm/sec². (The computed sound pressure is actually the amount of pressure change in the oscillations of the air particles.) We can hear sounds within the range of roughly .0002 to 2000 dynes/cm². Since this scale contains a range on the order of a million units, a smaller, more useful scale has been devised. The measure used is a decibel (dB), which specifies the sound pressure of a sound stimulus relative to some reference sound pressure level. The amplitude in decibels of a sound stimulus is given by the equation

$$A = 20 \log_{10} \frac{P_1}{P_0}$$

where P_1 is the sound pressure of the sound stimulus and P_0 is the sound pressure of a reference sound pressure level, usually taken as .0002 dynes/cm². Using this measure, the range of audible sound can be expressed within the range of 140 dB. Every time the sound pressure is increased by a factor of 10, we add 20 dB. Changes in amplitude primarily affect the perceived loudness of the sound pattern. Speech is normally in the range of 60 to 80 dB.

The second property by which the sound wave can be described is its frequency. If the man in the dark room runs very slowly—perhaps pondering how he got into this situation—he may complete a circuit only once a minute. If he then begins to run twice as fast, he will complete two full circuits in a minute and describe two wave cycles on the moving paper in the same space as had earlier been required for only one. The frequency of the sound wave then is equal to the number of complete cycles traced out by the running man per unit of time. It corresponds to a measure of the rate of oscillation of the air particles per unit of time.

Frequency

The frequency of sine waves is measured in cycles per second, technically referred to as Hertz (Hz.) after the 19th-century German physicist. Sound patterns can usually be heard if they have sine waves in the range of 20 to 20,000 Hz. The psychological experience of pitch quality is primarily determined by the frequency of the wave. The musical note middle C is roughly 261 Hz., and A above middle C is 440 Hz. The musical scale is an octave scale; a note that is an octave higher than another note is twice its frequency. When a note is played on most musical instruments, sound pressure variations are also present at the frequencies that are some multiple of the frequency of the note. These frequencies are called harmonics of the fundamental note.

The final dimension of the scene of the man running around the circle is his position at any point in time. The position can be described independently of the amplitude and the frequency by specifying the number of degrees traversed from the beginning of a wave. Accordingly, position or phase is a measure of position in a wave and can vary between 0 and 360 degrees. A phase of 90 degrees corresponds to a point on the positive crest of a wave.

Phase

The pure tones generated by a tuning fork are described by true sine waves, making their description very easy. However, most sound patterns are represented by much more complex waves. The French mathematician Fourier showed that any complex wave could be analyzed into component sine waves. By the method of Fourier analysis, then, one can both break down and rebuild complex waves into the sine waves whose amplitude and frequency can be specified precisely. Figure 3 shows a complex wave broken down into its component sine waves.

COMPLEX SOUND PATTERNS

Another method of representing a complex sound pattern is in terms of its power spectrum. The power spectrum plots the ampli-

Power Spectra

FIGURE 3. A complex wave (top panel) broken down into its component sine waves (bottom panel).

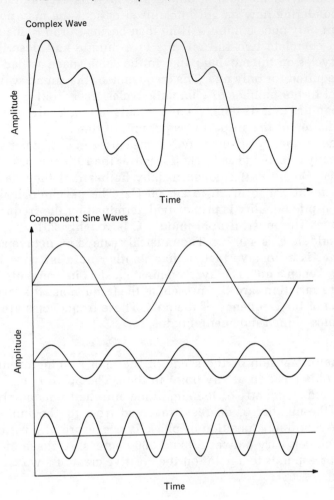

Complex Wave

Amplitude

Time

Component Sine Waves

Amplitude

Time

tude of the component waves on the Y ordinate as a function of their frequency on the X abscissa. Figure 4 shows the power spectrum of a musical note of 261 Hz. played by a violin. The power spectrum is not only a simpler method of representing complex sound patterns; it is also in a sense more accurate. The next three chapters on auditory information processing will show that we do not perceive sounds continuously, that is, we do not attach meaning to each small change in the continuous wave pattern. Rather, we perceive a set of discrete meaningful units such as musical notes or speech syllables. This means that the power spectrum of short sound patterns sometimes represents sound as we perceive it more

FIGURE 4. Power spectrum of the note middle C, 261 Hz., played on a violin.

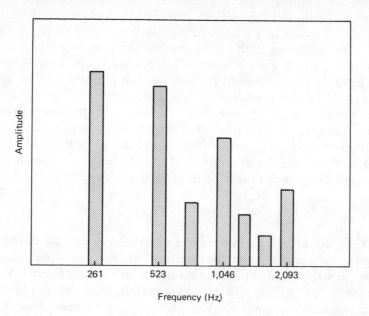

FIGURE 5. The power spectra of white noise (top panel) and the sound /sh/ as in *sugar* (bottom panel).

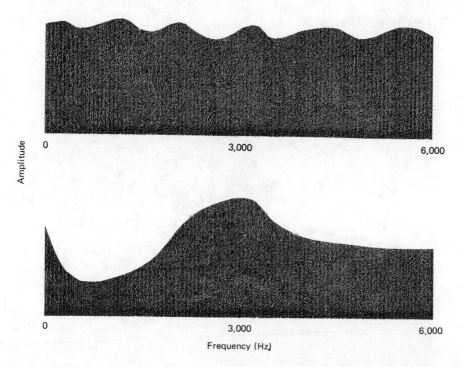

accurately than does the continuous wave representation. Somehow the auditory system preserves the sound pattern over some finite chunk of time and we perceive that segment of the sound pattern as a unitary whole, or a gestalt.

White noise, with which we are familiar as radio static, is a complex sound that has some interesting properties. When analyzed into its component sine waves, white noise will be found to have its energy distributed evenly throughout all the frequencies within its frequency spectrum. The wave shape and power spectrum of a white noise pattern is shown in the top panel of Figure 5. Other sounds such as the /sh/ sound in the bottom panel of the same figure usually have much of their energy concentrated within certain frequency ranges of the frequency spectrum.

THE EAR When the atmospheric pressure variations reach the potential listener, they pass through the auditory canal and set the eardrum into motion (see Figure 6). The auditory canal not only funnels the pressure vibrations but also amplifies certain sound waves because of its resonance properties. The phenomenon of resonance refers to one body being set into motion by the vibrations of another. One

FIGURE 6. The ear.

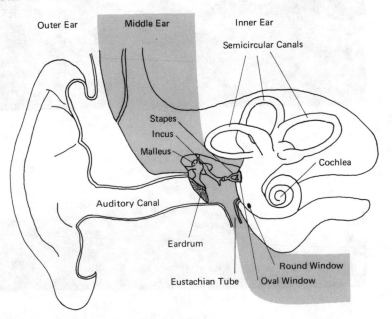

body resonates to the vibrations of another when they have the same natural frequency of vibration. For example, a tuning fork will resonate to the vibrations of another fork equal to it in frequency. The ear canal amplifies sound near its natural resonance, which lies between 3000 and 4000 Hz. In fact, we seem to be most sensitive to sounds within this frequency range.

The vibrations of the eardrum set into motion the three components of the middle ear that provide the mechanical linkage to the inner ear. The malleus is rigidly attached to the eardrum so that motions of the eardrum are carried to the incus and to the stapes which covers the entrance to the inner ear. The middle ear also amplifies the signal from the eardrum to the inner ear in two ways. First, the components of the middle ear function as a lever mechanism, which produces a greater force at the stapes than that applied at the malleus. Second, the total force of the stapes is applied over a much smaller area than the area at the eardrum. The amplification of the signal in the middle ear increases our sensitivity to pressure variations by roughly a factor of 1000.

The stapes carries the message to a bone opening of the inner ear called the oval window. Vibrations from the stapes set into motion the membrane of the oval window—the entrance into the cochlea—a cavity which resembles a snail's shell. The cochlea contains the basilar membrane with its attached hair cells. The vibrations of the oval window set the fluid in the cochlea into motion, producing wave motion in the basilar membrane. The vibration pattern along the membrane causes neural activity in the fibers connected to the hair cells on the membrane. The transformation of the mechanical vibrations into nerve impulses takes place here. These impulses then stimulate fibers of the auditory nerve which carries the message to the brain.

SPEECH SOUNDS

The sounds of speech are a direct consequence of the manner in which the sound is produced by the human vocal apparatus. The speech organs, illustrated in Figure 7, are the lungs, the trachea, the vocal cords, the larynx, the pharynx, the mouth, and nasal cavity. The sound pattern depends on three factors: 1) a source of energy, 2) a vibrating body, and 3) a resonator. The steady stream of air coming from the lungs and trachea when we exhale, provides the source of energy for speech sounds. This original stream of air is given its specific character during its passage past the vocal cords and through the resonating cavities of the vocal tract—the pharyngeal, oral, and nasal cavities.

FIGURE 7. The human vocal organs.

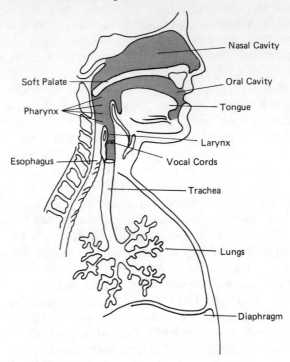

Voiced   The vocal cords are two elastic folds of tissue controlled by movable cartilages in the back wall of the larynx. The opening between the two cords can be controlled by changing the position of the cartilages. In the voicing position, the vocal cords vibrate with the air stream as it flows past. The frequency of vibration is controlled by the size of the vocal folds and their degree of tension. The frequency of the vocal fold vibration determines what we perceive as the individual pitch quality of a speaker's voice. Generally, males have lower voices than females since the mass of the male vocal folds is usually larger than its female counterpart. Similarly, we have all noticed an increase in the pitch of a person's voice when he becomes excited. Excitement increases the tension of the vocal folds, which in turn increases their rate of vibration in the same way the tension of a guitar string determines its pitch quality.

Figure 8a shows the pressure variations in the breath stream caused by vibration of the vocal cords. The frequency of vibration varies between 60 and 350 Hz. in normal speech. The wave shape in Figure 8a is called periodic because the pattern of pressure variations repeats itself over time. The pattern repeats itself at the rate of the vocal cord vibration. As mentioned earlier, a complex sound pattern such as the one in Figure 8a can be represented in terms of its power spectrum, which presents the frequencies and amplitudes of the component sine waves. (The power spectrum of the wave in Figure 8a is given in Figure 8b.) The largest frequency component corresponds to the rate of vibration of the vocal cords and is called the fundamental frequency. Frequencies of the other components are integer multiples of the fundamental frequency, called har-

FIGURE 8. The pressure variations in the breath stream during a voiced sound and its power spectrum.

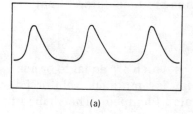

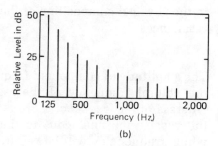

(a)

(b)

monics of the fundamental. The second harmonic is twice the fundamental frequency, the third is three times the fundamental, and so on. The amplitude of the harmonics decrease as the harmonics get large at the rate of 12 dB/octave. In this instance, the amplitude of the second harmonic is 12 dB less than the fundamental, the amplitude of the fourth harmonic is 24 dB less than the fundamental, the amplitude of the eighth harmonic is 36 dB less than the fundamental, and so on.

Voiceless

In a second position of the vocal cords, they do not vibrate with the air stream flowing past. In this case, speech sounds are produced by producing turbulence in the air stream during its passage through the vocal tract. For example, the sound /sh/ is produced by forcing the outgoing air stream at a high enough velocity through a constriction formed by the tongue and the roof of the mouth. The wave shape produced by the sound source when the vocal cords do not vibrate is aperiodic since no regular pattern exists in the sound wave. Because the wave shape is not periodic but is highly irregular, the waves contain all frequencies rather than just the harmonics of a given fundamental. Since all components have roughly equal intensity, this defines the sound as white noise comparable to radio static.

The wave shape of both voiced and voiceless sounds is modified by its passage through the throat, oral, and nasal cavities, which together make up the upper vocal tract. The vocal tract extends from the vocal cords to the lips, a distance of about 17 cm. As we see in Figure 7 (p. 414), the width of the tract is variable and can be changed by placement of the lips, jaw, tongue, and soft palate. The soft palate controls the passage of air through the nasal cavity, which is about 12 cm. long. The vocal tract functions as a series of resonance chambers which respond differentially to sounds of different frequencies. Each resonator has a preferred or natural resonance frequency. Two different violins playing the same note will have different pitch qualities because the inevitable differences in the physical composition of the violins produce different natural resonances.

Formants The amplitude of component frequencies which are equal to or near the natural frequency of the resonator is amplified (reinforced) whereas other frequencies are attenuated (damped). The shape of the vocal tract, analogous to the shape of the violin, determines which frequencies will be reinforced or damped. Hence, the final sound wave is uniquely determined by the shape of the vocal tract. These natural resonances of the vocal tract are called formants. Since the resonances change with changes in the shape of the vocal tract, each configuration of the vocal tract has its characteristic formants.

The sound source and its modification by the vocal tract can be approximated by a two-stage process. The sound which can be periodic or aperiodic passes through the vocal tract and is modified depending on its shape. These two components can be varied independently to produce different sounds. For a fixed sound source, we can change the speech sound by changing the configuration of the vocal tract. Conversely, for a fixed shape of the vocal tract, we can modify the speech sound by changing the sound source, for example, from periodic to aperiodic. The sounds /s/ as in see and /z/ as in zoo are articulated with very similar configurations of the vocal tract. However, the sound source in /s/ is aperiodic, whereas the sound source for /z/ is produced by vibrating the vocal cords. Figure 9 shows that the power spectra of the sounds are different. The fact that /s/ has some energy across the entire frequency spectrum gives its noise-like quality. The speech sound /z/, on the other hand, is much more tone-like, since most of the energy is concentrated at the formant frequencies.

For voiced sounds produced with a periodic sound source, the overall shape of the power spectrum is a function of the configuration of the vocal tract and is relatively independent of changes in

FIGURE 9. Power spectra of /z/ as in *zoo* (top panel) and /s/ as in *see* (bottom panel).

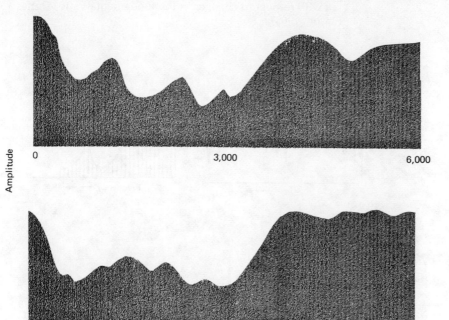

the frequency of vocal fold vibration. Figure 10 presents the wave patterns and power spectra of the vowel /ah/ pronounced with two different rates of vocal cord vibration (90 and 150 Hz). The vertical lines in the power spectra give the amplitude at the fundamental and harmonic frequencies. Connecting these lines, we get the same overall shape for both sounds. In this case, the formant frequencies indicated by the spectral peaks are the same under both frequencies of vibration. These peaks, of course, correspond to the natural resonances of the configuration of the vocal tract in producing the sound /ah/.

Vowel Sounds

The sounds of speech can be divided between the two classes of vowels and consonants. Vowels are spoken with a relatively fixed configuration of the vocal tract and the vocal folds are vibrated with the outgoing breath stream. The exact vowel sound is produced by the position of the tongue in the mouth. Tongue position is usually described according to the location of the tongue and the height of the highest part of the tongue. Tongue location is usually classified as in the front, central, or back part of the mouth. The

FIGURE 10. The sound /ah/ produced with two frequencies of the fundamental, showing that the power spectrum is relatively invariant with respect to changes in the fundamental (after Denes & Pinson, 1963).

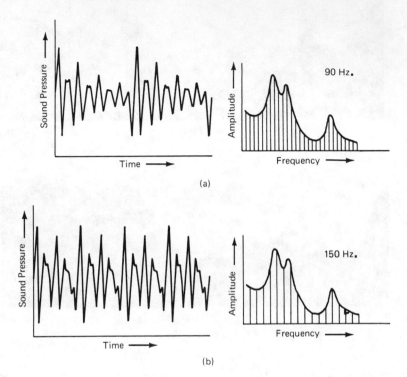

(a)

(b)

highest point of the tongue can be in the high, middle, or low part of the mouth within each of these three regions. Figure 11 presents the configuration of the vocal tract during the articulation of some vowel sounds.

Since the shape of the vocal tract and the resulting vowel sound does not change over time, it is convenient to represent the vowel sounds in terms of their respective power spectra. Figure 11 also presents the power spectra of the vowel sounds. The peaks of energy in the power spectra correspond to the formants of the vowel. That is to say, the frequencies of the natural resonances of the vocal tract are determined by the shape of the vocal tract. For vowels, the primary determinants of the first and second formants are the location and height of the tongue.

Consonant Sounds

Consonant sounds are more complex than vowels for a number of reasons. One reason is that, unlike vowels, a number of consonants

FIGURE 11. The positions of the vocal organs (based on X-ray photographs) and the spectra of the vowel sounds in the middle of the words *heed, hid, head, had, hod, hawed, hood, who'd* (after Ladefoged, 1962).

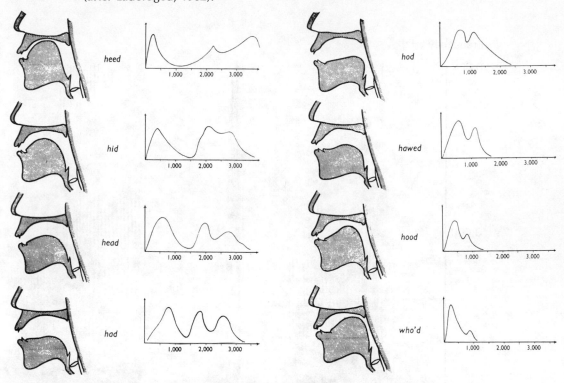

cannot be spoken in isolation. For example, try to articulate the consonant /d/ as in *dog* without an accompanying vowel. In the articulation of /d/, we actually say a consonant-vowel syllable. The consonant must, therefore, be isolated out of the consonant-vowel syllable. The articulation of consonants can be described according to three attributes: the point of articulation, the manner of articulation, and whether or not the vocal cords are vibrated. The point of maximum closure in the vocal tract during articulation of a consonant is referred to as the point of articulation. The manner of articulation describes how the speech sound is produced. Independent of the point of maximum closure and the manner of articulation, the vocal cords may or may not be vibrated during production of the speech sound.

The consonant sounds in English can be divided roughly into stops, fricatives, nasals, and glides. Stops, sometimes called plosive sounds, are produced by closing the vocal tract completely (usually

FIGURE 12. Sound spectrogram of the phrase, "That you may see." The phrase lasts roughly 2.2 sec.—the standard duration of a spectrogram.

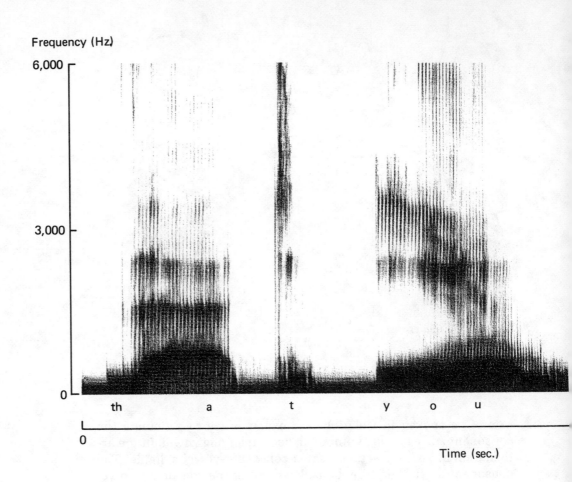

with the lips or tongue), building air pressure up behind the closure, and then suddenly opening the closure. The stop consonants in English are /b, p, d, t, g/ and /k/. In fricative sounds, such as /s/ or /f/, the vocal tract is only partially closed at some point and the air forced through the constriction produces a unique fricative sound, depending on the point of constriction and whether the vocal folds are also vibrating. Nasal sounds such as /m/ and /n/ are produced when the breath stream is allowed to pass through the nasal cavity (by lowering the soft palate) as well as through the

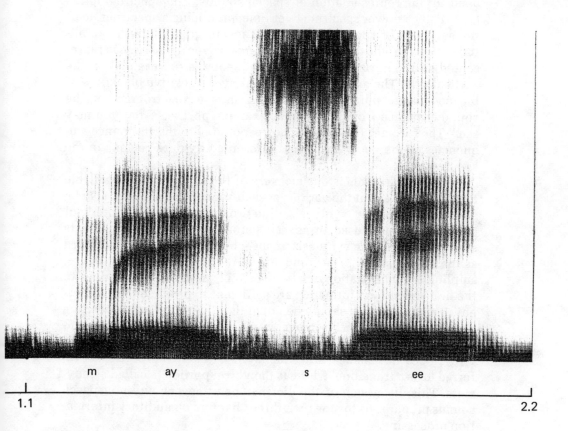

m   ay   s   ee

1.1   2.2

oral cavity. Finally, the glides are characterized by changing the
point of articulation during their production. The sound source for
the glides is accompanied by vocal cord vibration and the vocal
tract is relatively open, giving the glides such as /l/ and /r/ vowel-
like properties.

In representing consonant sounds or a series of speech sounds,
the power spectrum is no longer sufficient since it loses temporal
information. The power spectrum of a sound is the average intensity present at each frequency over some period of time. Since

vowel sounds do not change significantly over time, the power spectrum gives a realistic representation. For sounds that change over time, or for a sequence of sounds, it would be convenient to represent the sound in a successive sequence of power spectra. This is accomplished by a sound spectrograph, specifically developed for the representation of speech sounds. The spectrograph is essentially a power spectrum over time, producing a spectrogram of the sequence of speech sounds. The spectrogram plots the amplitude of each of the component frequencies over time. Time is represented on the horizontal axis and frequency is represented on the vertical axis. The amplitude is indexed by the relative blackness of the coordinate points. Figure 12 presents a spectrogram of the sound sequence from the popular example phrase, "That you may see." The formant frequencies, corresponding to the resonance frequencies of the vocal tract, are represented by dark regions in the spectrogram.

The spectrogram is one measure of the acoustic cues available to the listener about the various speech sounds. Speech can also be produced artificially (synthesized) to provide a more direct study of the acoustic cues used in speech perception. Figure 13 presents spectrograms of the synthesized speech syllables which are heard as the syllables /di/, /da/, and /do/. As can be seen in the figure, amplitude concentrations at two distinct areas, corresponding to the first and second formants, are sufficient to produce these different speech sounds. It should be noted that the sound corresponding to the consonant portion moves rapidly across different frequencies, whereas the later portion of the sound corresponding to the vowel does not change in frequency. The changing portion is referred to as a transition, whereas the vowel portion is called steady-state. This discussion of the dimensions of speech and nonspeech sounds prepares us for the next three chapters on auditory information processing.

FIGURE 13. Spectrographic patterns that produce the syllables /di/, /da/, and /do/.

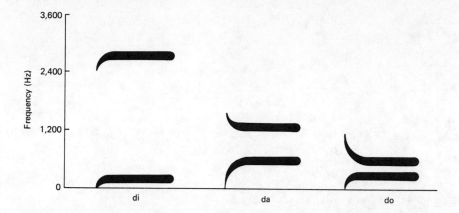

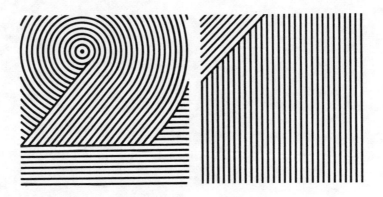

Preperceptual auditory storage

Incoming information may be held in a temporary store at a stage previous to the limited capacity channel: it will then pass through the channel when the class of events to which it belongs is next selected.
—*Donald E. Broadbent (1958)*

The assumption of preperceptual storage played a central role in our discussion of visual information processing. Some storage is deemed necessary for perception to take place because the perceptual process cannot be immediate. It follows that the information in the storage must be maintained in a fixed form for operations of the perceptual process. In vision, the information is held in a steady-state form during the eye fixation between saccadic eye movements. The perceptual process must occur during each fixation since the next fixation introduces a different pattern into preperceptual storage, interfering with the preperceptual information from the previous fixation.

The concept of preperceptual storage in audition is even more critical than in vision. An auditory stimulus has a temporal dimension, whereas a visual stimulus does not. Accordingly, auditory perception cannot be immediate because there is not enough information in each small segment of the acoustic input for a consistent mapping of stimulus information to percept. The complete sound pattern must be held in some preperceptual form for the perceptual or recognition process. Similar to vision, after the sound pattern is available in preperceptual storage, it must be recognized before the next sound pattern presented interferes with the preperceptual information from the previous sound pattern.

What are the properties of preperceptual auditory storage and how long does it last? Broadbent (1958) postulated the existence of such a storage system; it was assumed to hold preperceptual information on the order of two seconds (see Chapter 13). Evidence for this assumption was based on the now classic dichotic listening experiments. In these studies, listeners were presented a list of six items, three to each ear. The items occurred simultaneously on the

EARLY ASSUMPTIONS

two ears and the rate of presentation was 2 items/sec. on a given ear. The results indicated that observers found it easier to report the six items by ear of presentation rather than by temporal order. Broadbent (1958) interpreted these results to mean that the preperceptual storage maintained the information from the two ears in a preperceptual form along different channels. Recognition of the items required a serial central processor which could recognize the information on only one channel at a time. Therefore, the optimal strategy would be to perceive the items on one channel (ear) before proceeding to the other channel, rather than continually switching between the channels to recognize the items by order of presentation. Employing this strategy, the preperceptual storage would have to hold the information from one ear until all of the items along the other ear were recognized. Since the entire list was presented in 1½ sec., the items on the second channel would not receive the attention of the central processor until at least 1½ sec. after their presentation. Using this logic, preperceptual storage must last at least 1½ sec. plus recognition time. In Chapter 13 we discussed Broadbent's theory along with these experiments in detail.

Two important assumptions about the auditory recognition stage are made by Broadbent's model. (1) Preperceptual storage lasts on the order of 2 seconds before it decays. (2) The ears functioned as separate channels in the storage and the limited capacity processor could only read out one of these at a time. After reading out one channel, it could switch to another. We now consider a number of experimental paradigms employed to test Broadbent's model and to define the temporal characteristics of preperceptual auditory storage.

PARTIAL REPORT PARADIGM

Broadbent's model leads directly to an experimental test in the partial report paradigm, which requires the subject to report only a subset of the stimuli presented. If the information is maintained in preperceptual auditory storage along certain channels, then recognition of a given channel can be enhanced if the subject is cued before the information has decayed in the preperceptual store. Logically, the only partial report cues that should be beneficial are those cues that refer directly to the channels in storage. For example, if the subject is asked to report the items presented to one ear, this should enhance performance relative to asking him to report the items from both ears. On the other hand, if the subject is asked to report back only the digits in a group of digits and letters, the report cue should not be beneficial. In this case, the central processor would have to recognize the items from both ears before knowing which ones to report. Since the amount of work by the central processor would not be diminished, a partial report should not be more efficient than a whole report.

Sperling's Study

Sperling (1960) and Averbach & Coriell (1961) were the first to use the partial report to study sensory storage in vision (see Chapters 12 and 17). In one condition Sperling presented subjects with a visual display of 3 rows of 3 letters in each row. A partial recall cue indicating which of the 3 rows should be recalled was presented either before or sometime after the 50 msec. display presentation. Sperling found that recall of the cued row was almost perfect if the cue occurred simultaneously with the display presentation and decreased with increases in the delay of the cue. Sperling reasoned that if a subject, when cued by row, could report all 3 items in the row correctly, then he must have had access to all 9 items in the display since the cue was randomly chosen. Therefore, the number of items available for report is obtained by multiplying the number of items recalled by the number of possible cues in the experiment. Using this dependent measure, Sperling found that the decline in recall in the partial report accompanied by increases in the delay of the location cue asymptoted at the number of letters that subjects can give in whole reports when they attempt to report all of the items in the display. The advantage of the partial report at short delays was taken as evidence that the subject retains a visual representation of the display after the display presentation is terminated.

The critical question is whether the visual information in this representation is actually preperceptual. In another of Sperling's experiments, the partial report cue referred to item category rather than physical location. In this study, 2 letters and 2 numbers were presented in each of 2 rows. Immediately after the display presentation, one of the two report cues was randomly presented, designating whether the number or the letters in the display were to be recalled. In contrast to the experiments using partial recall by location, the partial report score multiplied by two (the number of possible cues) did not exceed the whole report score. This result indicated that subjects could not selectively read out the items in the visual representation according to item category. Logically, if the visual representation were preperceptual, category information would not be available and each item would have to be recognized before it could be accepted or rejected for recall. In this case, the subject would be limited by the span of immediate memory as in the whole report condition. This result, in conjunction with the positive results with recall by location, supports the hypothesis that the visual representation remaining after the short display presentation is a preperceptual one.

We have reviewed Sperling's study in detail because the partial report paradigm in audition utilizes the same logic. The paradigm was first used in audition by Moray, Bates, and Barnett (1965) and more recently by Darwin, Turvey, and Crowder (1972) and Treisman and Rostron (1972). There have been a number of general methodological problems with using this paradigm in audition and discussion will show that "positive" results do not necessarily demonstrate the existence of a preperceptual auditory storage.

An Auditory Analog

Darwin et al. (1972) attempted to replicate the Sperling partial report procedure in audition. The investigators presented simultaneously 3 lists of 3 consecutive items (letters and digits) to each of 3 spatial locations (left ear, middle of the head, and right ear). The rate of presentation was 3 items per sec. at a given location. On each list, either 4 or 5 items were digits and the other 5 or 4 items were letters. The subject was then cued with a visual marker to report the items with respect to either spatial location or item category (digits or letters). When the subject was cued by spatial location, a bar was presented visually either to the left, in front of, or to the right of the subject, indicating that he should recall only the items presented to the left, middle, or right. When the subject was cued by category class, the marker was presented to one of two locations, instructing the subject to recall only the digits or the letters that were presented. The independent variable of interest was the delay of the cue marker from the end of the test presentation. Performance under partial recall was also compared to a whole report condition in which the subjects were required to report all of the items presented on a given trial.

In their first experiment Darwin et al. cued partial recall by spatial location 0, 1, 2, or 4 sec. after presentation of the auditory lists. To determine the number of items available for recall, they multiplied by 3 the items correctly recalled from a cued location. Using this dependent measure, partial recall performance decreased with increases in the delay of the report cue, and was superior to the whole report condition if the partial report was cued within 2 sec. after presentation of the test list.

These results indicate that subjects had more information available immediately after presentation of the test lists than they could recall in a whole report or with a delayed cue. The critical question, as Darwin et al. point out, is whether this information is preperceptual. If the information is preperceptual, a partial recall cue based on meaning or category information should not be as effective as the spatial location cue. Broadbent's model predicts that preperceptual information should not be accessed as easily along meaning dimensions as along stimulus dimensions. The stimulus dimensions such as spatial location correspond to channels in preperceptual storage, whereas the meaning dimensions do not. Therefore, a second experiment was carried out in which the report cue indicated whether the category letters or digits should be reported. Subjects were required to recall the items indicated by the category cue and also had to report the spatial location of the items. Darwin et al. derived the number of items available from the partial report case by doubling the number of items correctly recalled from a cued category, since there were only two categories. In this case, partial report at all delays was significantly poorer than the whole report condition. Darwin et al. concluded from these results that category name is a poorer method of cueing the partial report than is spatial location.

This conclusion, however, is not justified because the design and the data analysis of the second experiment were inappropriate. For some reason, Darwin et al. also required the subjects to report the spatial location of each item they recalled in the second experiment. Therefore, the subjects had to know exactly as much in this experiment as in the first to perform the partial report task accurately. In the first experiment, the subject had to know both the location and the name, in order to recall an item correctly. In the second, the subject also had to know both the name and the location of the item for correct recall. The only difference between the two experiments was how the subject was cued for recall. He was directed to access the items either by spatial location or by category name. Therefore, a direct comparison between the two experiments provides a test of whether the information accessed for partial report is preperceptual. If it is preperceptual, it should be more easily accessed by location than by category. If it is perceived or categorized, then location may not necessarily be a better retrieval cue than recall by category name.

The performance differences between the two experiments can be compared by simply computing the mean number of items correctly recalled in both experiments. Such a re-analysis indicates that partial recall is actually poorer when subjects are cued by location than when cued by category name. This result provides some evidence against the assumption that the cue directs recall from a preperceptual auditory storage. The third experiment of

Darwin et al. substantiates the present interpretation of the results. In this task, subjects were cued by category name as in the second experiment, but were not required to also report the location of the items. By computing the uncorrected partial recall score, we see that performance is significantly better in the third than in the first experiment. Subjects averaged between 1.4 and 1.9 items correct in the first experiment, in which the report cue referred to the location of the items. When the report cue referred to category name, in the third experiment, subjects averaged over 3 items correct. The number of items available for report can be obtained by multiplying the number of items recalled by the number of report cues. Given that there were 3 possible locations and 2 possible categories, the number of items available for report was under 6 items in the first experiment and over 6 items in the third. Our present re-analysis of the results of Darwin et al. indicates that retrieving the items by location is not easier than retrieval by category name.

One critical objection to the Darwin et al. procedure is that the authors did not equate the number of possible report cues in the two report tasks. There were only two possible categories in the recall by category name, whereas there were three possible locations in recall by spatial location. Accordingly, it might be easier for the subject to decode the partial report cue under the category name than under the spatial location condition. This confounding could bias the results in favor of the recall by category name condition. On the other hand, a second problem with the experimental design would work in favor of the report by spatial location condition. Forgetting from immediate memory may have operated differently in the two partial report conditions. In recall by category, subjects had to recall either 4 or 5 items—the number of letters or digits presented—whereas they had to recall only 3 items in recall by spatial location.

Location or Category

Since the present analysis is post hoc and there is no way to account for the methodological problems in the Darwin et al. study, another experiment is needed to provide a direct comparison between recall by spatial location and recall by category name. This author carried out an experiment that provides a test of whether preperceptual auditory information is present immediately after presentation of auditory lists of items. If it is, and we accept that preperceptual information is more easily accessed along stimulus rather than meaning dimensions, partial recall should be better when recall is cued along location than category dimensions.

The first study (Massaro, 1972a) was designed to provide a direct test of the existence of a preperceptual storage that lasts

1 or 2 sec. and is more easily accessed along stimulus dimensions than along name dimensions. Two lists of 4 items each were recorded by different speakers at a rate of 4 items/sec. These lists were presented simultaneously to the two ears. Only these two locations were used, and a different speaker was used on each ear to keep the lists as distinctive as possible. Each list on each ear contained 2 digits and 2 consonants. The report cues were 2 tones (a high tone and a low tone). On any trial, a high tone or a low tone was equally likely to be presented. When subjects were asked to recall by location, the pitch of the tone indicated whether they should report the items presented to the left or right ears. When subjects were asked to recall by category, the pitch of the tone indicated whether they should report the digits or consonants. Given these two report conditions (location and category) the results are directly comparable. In both report conditions there were 2 possible report cues and the subjects were required to report 4 items. The exact same lists and report cues were used in both report conditions. The cue was presented immediately after the last item in the list. Therefore, if the items contain preperceptual auditory information that is more easily accessed along stimulus than name dimensions, recall should be superior in the location than in the category condition.

The results of the experiment showed that recall by category was significantly better than recall by location. The percentage of items recalled correctly by category was 75 percent, compared to 62 percent correct recall by location. This result was consistent across all eight subjects independent of the order of presentation of the two conditions. Thus, the present analysis of the Darwin et al. (1972) experiment is supported by showing that recall by location is not a more effective retrieval cue than recall by category name.

Forgetting

Massaro (1972a) did not determine whether the corrected partial report obtained by multiplying the number of items recalled times the number of report categories would have been superior to a whole report, and did not map out a decline of the partial report with delay of the report cue. Neither of these comparisons can eliminate the contribution of immediate memory effects. The corrected partial report might be somewhat superior to the whole report simply because subjects would have to recall twice as many items in the whole report as in the partial report condition. Similarly, a decline in the corrected partial report with increases in cue delay might be contaminated by forgetting in immediate memory. Some forgetting might occur while the subjects were rehearsing items before presentation of the report cue. Accordingly, neither of these "positive" results would necessarily reflect the decay of preper-

Experimental Method

It is worthwhile to discuss some of the methodological detail of Massaro's (1972a) partial report experiment to illustrate its complexity and the procedural precautions that must be taken. The recording of the tapes was controlled by a small computer. The computer controlled visual readouts placed in front of the two female speakers. The test lists were read by the speakers according to the pacing of symbols presented over the visual display. Each speaker was seated in a separate sound-attenuated chamber. On each trial, each speaker read a list of 4 items at a rate of 4 items/sec. into one channel of the tape recorder. The items in the list were read in a way that maintained the distinctiveness of the individual items. Simultaneously with the reading of the lists, the computer controlled the presentation and timing of the warning tone and recall cue tones. The tones were recorded on both channels of the tape recorder.

After recording, the tapes were monitored to determine how accurately the two test lists were synchronized. Lists that did not begin and end together were rerecorded. Each list contained 4 digits and 4 consonants with the restriction that 2 digits and 2 consonants occur on each channel. The digits and consonants were randomly selected without replacement from the respective master sets of 1, 2, 3, 4, 5, 6, 8, 9 and F, J, K, N, Q, T, V, Y.

Eight observers participated in the experiment for five days. Four observers were tested simultaneously in separate sound-attenuated rooms. Each day of the experiment consisted of two sessions for a total of 162 trials. On the first practice day, subjects were given one session of recall cued by location and one session cued by category. On the following four experimental days, the two cueing conditions were alternated from day to day. Four of the subjects received the location condition first; the other four subjects received the category condition first. The first 15 and last 5 trials of each session were eliminated in the data analysis.

The tapes were presented over matched headphones at a normal listening intensity. Each trial began with a 250 msec. warning tone presented binaurally 500 msec. before the list presentation. The frequency of the warning tone was 1200 Hz. The test lists were presented simultaneously to the left and right ears

ceptual acoustic information but rather would reflect interference effects in short-term memory.

Guessing   Our own study was slightly biased in favor of category recall since it is impossible to control exactly for set size when comparing spatial location and category name recall cues. When subjects were asked to recall by location, they knew beforehand that they had to recall 2 letters and 2 digits. In this case, they were recalling 4 items out of a possible set of 16 alternatives (8 letters and 8 digits). In at a rate of 4 items/sec. There were 4 test items on each ear; therefore, the 8 items were presented within 1 sec. Immediately after presentation of the last 2 test items, a cueing tone was presented. The cue tone was presented binaurally at the same loudness as the test items and lasted 50 msec. The binaural presentation localizes the tone in the middle of the head. On any trial the cue tone could be either high (3000 Hz.) or low (300 Hz.) with equal probability. After presentation of the cue tone the subjects had 13 sec. to write their answers on an answer sheet. The master sets of items were available to the subjects who were asked to try to respond with 4 items in both the category and location cue conditions.

The results were determined by computing the mean number of items correctly recalled on each of the four experimental days. This score could be between 0 and 4. The percentage correct on each day was then determined by dividing the mean number of items correct by 4, the total possible that could be recalled. The results for each subject and average results are presented in Table 1.

TABLE 1.

Percentage correct recall of 8 subjects under the category and location recall conditions across the four experimental days. (The first four observers recalled by location on Days 2 and 4; the second four observers recalled by category on Days 2 and 4.)

	Location	Category	Location	Category
S_1	70	75	65	78
S_2	69	75	74	80
S_3	49	59	57	84
S_4	48	63	47	73
S_5	69	81	68	77
S_6	67	76	77	81
S_7	56	79	54	71
S_8	61	71	63	80
Mean	61	72	63	78

recall cued by category, subjects knew they had to recall either 4 digits or 4 letters. In this case, they were recalling 4 items out of a possible set of 8 alternatives. Accordingly, the guessing rate would be higher in recall by category than recall by location. Assume that the subject knew nothing on both kinds of trials and randomly selected his responses from the valid set of alternatives given by the cue on that trial. When he was cued by category, he would choose randomly 4 out of the 8 possible valid alternatives and would be 50 percent correct on the average. When the subject was cued by location, he would randomly choose 2 items from both the digit and letter sets. In this case, it can be shown that when he knew nothing, he would average 25 percent correct.

Therefore, we see that performance is favored in the category condition because of differential guessing rates. However, as the subjects remember some of the items, the differences in guessing rates is reduced. For example, if subjects remember 3 out of 4 of the items, they would only have to guess on the final item. In recall by category, the subject could randomly select 1 from the remaining 5 alternatives. In recall by location, the subject would have to select his final alternative from a set of 13. Hence, the correct guessing rates for the last item would equal 20 percent and approximately 8 percent in the category and location conditions, respectively. Therefore, although the subject actually knew 3 out of 4 items in both conditions, his observed probability correct would be somewhat larger than 75 percent. Furthermore, percentage correct on category trials would be larger than on location trials simply because of differences in guessing rates. On 1 out of 5 trials, we said that he would recall the fourth item correctly in recall by category. Therefore, his overall probability correct (P_c) would be the weighted average of the guessing-correctly and guessing-incorrectly trials.

$$P_c = \frac{4}{5}\ (75\%) + \frac{1}{5}\ (100\%)$$
$$= 60 + 20$$
$$= 80\%$$

In recall by location, using the same logic, we have

$$P_c = \frac{12}{13}\ (75\%) + \frac{1}{13}\ (100\%)$$
$$= 69.3 + 7.7$$
$$= 77\%$$

Therefore, although the subject actually knew as much in both recall conditions, performance shows a 3 percent advantage in the recall-by-category condition because of different guessing rates in the two conditions. Given that there is only a 3 percent difference that can be accounted for by guessing at a level of performance near the observed performance level in Massaro's study, it is unlikely that the advantage of the category condition can be completely accounted for by guessing differences. Therefore, we can, at least, conclude that recall by location is *not* easier than recall by category in the partial recall experiment in audition.

There is no way to eliminate the guessing differences entirely, since the location set must be twice the category set if the same lists are used on both kinds of trials. One way to reduce guessing differences is to increase the master set sizes so that the guessing rate approaches zero in both conditions. We have replicated the above experiment using letters and one-syllable words as test items with master set sizes of 25 items each. In this case, the guessing rates cannot differ by more than 2 percent and performance can be compared directly without depending on a method to correct for guessing differences. The results of two additional experiments using these master sets indicated that location and category recall did not differ significantly. In summary, the results support the idea that recall is *not* easier along a location dimension than along a category dimension in the auditory partial report experiments. Accordingly, the experiments contradict Broadbent's assumption of a preperceptual auditory storage that preserves for 1 or 2 sec. the information along a number of channels determined by stimulus characteristics such as spatial location.

A second paradigm to consider in the study of preperceptual auditory storage is the backward recognition masking task. This paradigm is the exact auditory analog of the backward masking experiment in vision that was discussed in detail in Chapters 17 and 18. It was argued that a visual preperceptual representation of the visual display was maintained during an eye fixation. A second fixation after an eye movement replaces the information available in the first, thus terminating perceptual processing of the first input. This sequence of events was assumed to be modeled in a recognition masking task, in which a second visual stimulus follows a first after some blank processing period. Although the situation is not as obvious, there is also an analogous case in auditory perceptual processing. If a sound pattern is presented and held in a preperceptual auditory storage, a second sound pattern should interfere with the information in the first and, therefore, terminate the perceptual processing of the first sound pattern. This paradigm was devised by the author to study the duration of preperceptual auditory images and to determine the temporal course of the auditory perceptual process (Massaro, 1970c).

The duration of the preperceptual auditory storage was first investigated experimentally using the following logic: If the stimulus information resides in the system for a finite period of time, and if processing of that information is dependent upon its presence in the system, then it should be possible to halt processing by interfering with the preperceptual information. A second auditory stim-

BACKWARD RECOGNITION MASKING

ulus entering preperceptual auditory storage while the image of the first stimulus is still present might interfere with the earlier image. In the perception of speech or music, the preperceptual auditory image holds the first part of an auditory stimulus until the pattern is complete and recognition occurs. A second pattern does not usually occur until the first pattern has been recognized. However, if the second pattern is presented soon enough, it should interfere with recognition of the first pattern. By varying the delay of the second pattern, we can determine the duration of the preperceptual auditory image and the temporal course of the recognition process. The experimental task is referred to as a recognition masking paradigm. A test sound presentation is followed by a masking sound after a variable silent interstimulus interval.

Control for Loudness In the recognition masking task, the test and masking sounds must be presented at the same loudness, so that the time between the onsets of the test and masking sounds provides a true measure of the perceptual processing time available for the test sound. If the masking stimulus were presented at a different intensity than the test stimulus, the time between the onsets of the two sounds would no longer be an accurate measure of the available processing time for the first sound. Consider the following stage model of auditory processing presented in Figure 1. The auditory stimulus must be

FIGURE 1. A stage model of the processes of detection and recognition in auditory information processing.

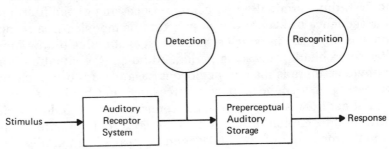

transformed by the auditory system and detected before the preperceptual representation is placed in preperceptual auditory storage. The loudness of the stimulus affects the amount of time it takes for this detection process.

McGill (1961) studied the time required for the detection process as a function of stimulus intensity. On any trial, the subject heard a pure tone of 1000 Hz. and hit a button as soon as he heard the tone. The independent variable was the intensity of the tone, which was varied randomly from trial to trial. McGill (1961) found that decreasing the intensity of the tone from 100 to 30 dB increased the RT from 120 to 216 msec. In our discussions of the duration of mental events in Chapter 3, we reasoned that stimulus loudness affects detection time, not response-selection time in the RT task. McGill's results, therefore, must indicate that detection time is highly dependent upon stimulus loudness. In terms of our model, stimulus loudness affects the time between the presentation of the stimulus and the onset of its representation in preperceptual auditory storage. Accordingly, when the two sounds in the masking paradigm differ in loudness, the time between the onsets of the two stimuli is not a valid measure of the duration of the representation of the first stimulus in preperceptual auditory storage. By keeping the loudness of the two stimuli equal, we insure that the detection time is the same for both sounds and the differences in onset time provide a measure of recognition time. In the backward recognition task with equally loud sounds, the test stimulus is always detected (heard), but its recognition may be disrupted by the second sound if it occurs before the first is completely recognized.

In the recognition paradigm, the subject first learns to identify or recognize two or more test signals. For example, the test signals could be two short tones differing in frequency. The subject's task is to identify the higher tone as high and the lower tone as low. In the backward masking paradigm, one of the test tones is presented, followed by a silent interval, followed by a masking tone.

Identifying Pitch Quality

In the study that illustrates the method and results of the recognition masking experiment, one of two pure tones (a 20 msec. sine wave of 770 or 870 Hz.) was presented and the observer's task was to identify the tones as low and high, respectively. The masking tone was equal to 820 Hz. and lasted 500 msec. All tones were presented at a normal listening intensity, 81 dB. The silent intertone interval lasted 0, 20, 40, 80, 160, 250, 350, or 500 msec.

Each subject was tested in a sound-insulated chamber and the experimental events were controlled by a small computer. The pure tones were produced by an oscillator controlled by the computer and were presented over high quality headphones. The observer recorded his decision by pushing one of two pushbuttons labeled "high" and "low," respectively. Following the response period, feedback was given by illuminating a small light above the correct response button. Each trial began with a test tone followed by the masking tone after a variable silent interval. The subject had 2 sec. to identify the test tone as "high" or "low" and was then informed of the correct answer for that trial. The intertrial interval was 2½ seconds. The subject was given two sessions of 400 trials each per day.

Percentage correct and *d'* values

Averaging performance on both kinds of trials allows the investigator to have a measure of performance that is relatively unaffected by decision biases. For example, if the subject knew nothing and guessed randomly from trial to trial, he would average 50 percent correct, which is chance performance in the task. If he knew nothing but had a strong bias to say "high," his performance would be very good on high trials but very bad on low trials. Averaging these two trials would still give 50 percent. This percentage correct measure is based on the same logic as the *d'* measure since it weights performance from both high and low trials. Considering performance on one kind of trial independently of performance on the other is incorrect in both cases. The results given here in terms of percentage correct lead to the same conclusions as when *d'* values are calculated from the hit and false alarm probabilities.

The observers first learned to identify the test tones accurately by performing in the experiment without the masking tone. After the subjects learned the tones, they were given some practice in the experiment itself before the results were recorded. In this experiment, as in all recognition masking experiments, all of the experimental conditions are randomly presented to control for differential contributions of other processes such as memory or motivation. Therefore, in Massaro's study, any of the 16 (2 test tones x 8 intertone intervals) conditions could be presented with equal probability on every trial. For the results, the observers were tested every day for 4 days so that there are about 200 observations at each of the 16 experimental conditions. The dependent measure, percentage correct, is determined by averaging the proportion correct on the high and low tone trials at each level of the intertone interval.

Figure 2 shows that for each of the three subjects in the task, recognition performance improved with increases in the silent intertone interval up to 250 msec. Further increases in the silent interval beyond 250 msec. did not significantly facilitate recognition performance. These results provide information about the duration of the preperceptual auditory image of the test tone, the vulnerability of the auditory image to new inputs, and the temporal course of recognition. Given that the test tone lasted only 20 msec., some preperceptual storage must have remained for the perceptual processing necessary to improve recognition performance with increases in the silent intertone interval. This same result indicates that the masking tone terminated perceptual processing of the image. Since recognition performance levels off at about 250 msec., the image probably decayed within this period. These results also indicate that the subjects required roughly 250 msec. of silence—

FIGURE 2. Percentage of correct identification of the test tone as a function of the intertone interval. The three curves are the results for three subjects (after Massaro, 1970c).

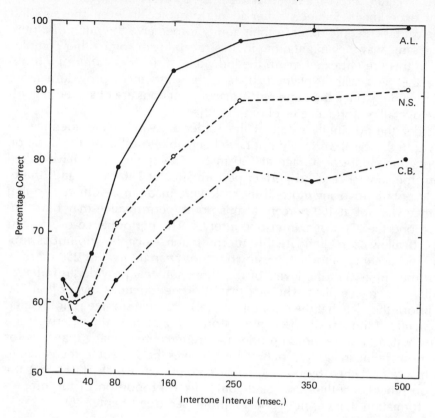

besides the 20 msec. of the test tone presentation—for the recognition process.

These results provide evidence for a preperceptual auditory image that lasts for roughly 250 msec. and is extremely vulnerable to a second tone. This study and a number of studies discussed in Chapter 22 estimate the duration of preperceptual auditory storage at 250 msec. Since performance does not improve beyond 250 msec., the image probably decayed within this period so that no further information could be extracted. Although these experiments estimate the maximum duration of preperceptual auditory storage at 250 msec., it is still logically possible that preperceptual auditory storage lasts longer than this duration but that the recognition process cannot utilize the information beyond 250 msec. after it is presented. However, this alternative does not add anything in terms of our analysis, since we can still conclude that the *effective* duration of preperceptual auditory storage lasts on the order of 250 msec.

Individual differences

The results in Figure 2 reveal a fact that has plagued every investigator in a psychological experiment. Subjects differ in performance in even the simplest psychological task. People differ in their ability to perceive the pitch of a pure tone in the same way they might differ in musical ability or some other complex function. In this present experiment, the individual differences are not a problem since they are easily explained. In fact, the differences provide a more substantive finding, since the same performance functions are observed regardless of the overall performance level of the subject.

Consider the possibility of all of the subjects giving results identical to subject A.L. In this case, we would not have been able to estimate the duration of preperceptual auditory storage at 250 msec. The storage may have lasted longer but the subject reached perfect performance at 250 msec. and, therefore, could not improve any more. If the task were made more difficult so that performance was not at 100 percent at this point, performance may have improved beyond the 250 msec. intertone interval. The performance of subjects N.S. and C.B. allow us to eliminate this interpretation, since they do not asymptote at perfect accuracy although improving stops at an interval of 250 msec.

The different asymptotic levels of the three subjects provide an index of their ability to perceive pitch. The fact that all three functions level off at 250 msec. supports the idea that the duration of preperceptual storage is not related to the difficulty of the task. Preperceptual storage is a structural property of the processing system: a tone should produce a preperceptual image that lasts for a fixed period of time, regardless of how long it takes the subject to recognize it. The results are explained by our model of recognition, which states that the recognition process continuously reads out a fixed proportion of the preperceptual information that has not yet been processed (see Chapter 18).

PERCEIVED DURATION   The third task asks the observer to estimate the duration of auditory sounds. This paradigm is similar to one employed by Haber and Standing (1969) for visual stimuli, which was discussed in Chapter 17. Efron (1970a, b) provided an analysis of the perceived duration of tones and noise. In his experiment, the observer judged the temporal overlap between two stimuli presented sequentially. The subject states whether or not the onset of the second index stimulus (e.g., a light) occurred before the offset of the first auditory stimulus (a tone). The interval between the offset of the auditory stimulus and the onset of the index stimulus is adjusted until the observer perceives the offset of the tone and the onset of the light as occurring simultaneously. The independent variable of interest is the duration of the first auditory stimulus. The results indicate that the minimal perception of an auditory stimulus lasts about 130 msec. Decreasing the duration of the first auditory stimulus below 130 msec. increased its perceived duration by a similar amount. For example, if a first noise burst lasted 30 msec., the observer did not perceive a temporal interval between its offset and the onset of the index stimulus until there was an interstimulus interval longer than 100 msec. If the duration of a sound is overestimated because of preperceptual auditory storage, it should be possible to eliminate this overestimation by interfering with the storage. Gol'dburt (1961) asked subjects to estimate the duration of a tone that was followed after some variable interval by a second tone. This experiment is analogous to the backward masking task. The results indicated that the subjects overestimated the duration of short tones, but that if a second tone occurred within the period of overestimation, it shortened the perceived duration of the first tone. Gol'dburt's results show that a second tone interferes with the preperceptual storage of the first, supporting the conclusions reached in the backward masking experiment.

The results of perceived duration support the assumption of a short preperceptual auditory storage. If a short tone produces an auditory image for perceptual processing, the observer should be able to estimate its duration. Analogous to the visual image (see Chapter 17), the duration of an auditory image is inversely related to the duration of the stimulus producing the image. If perceptual processing usually takes about 250 msec., there would be no need for an image to remain if the presentation time of the stimulus exceeds this value. Processing the information in the stimulus seems to be sufficient to eliminate any afterimage of the stimulus presentation.

We have considered three paradigms that have been employed to study a preperceptual auditory storage. The partial report task failed to demonstrate such a storage lasting on the order of 1 or 2 seconds. The recognition task using backward masking demonstrated that preperceptual auditory storage lasts about 250 msec. Finally, the perceived duration tasks estimate the duration at somewhat less than 250 msec. In Chapter 17, some methodological problems with the perceived duration task were discussed, such as the fact that it does not allow us to account for the subject's decision criterion. Therefore, this paradigm cannot be used for providing an exact quantitative measure of preperceptual storage. At this time, the recognition masking task seems to provide the best tool for studying preperceptual auditory storage. In the next chapter, our study of recognition masking asks what psychological processes are necessary to describe performance in the task.

Perceptual processing time for hearing

But if we assume that every stimulus starts a process in the brain which lasts perhaps 200 milliseconds, we can make backward inhibition acceptable if we further suppose that this process can be inhibited at any moment during the 200-millisecond interval by the onset of the second stimulus.
—*Georg von Békésy (1971)*

In the previous chapter, we saw how the temporal course of auditory recognition could be studied in a recognition masking paradigm. The results showed that a short tone presentation produced a preperceptual image that outlasted the tone presentation. This image was necessary for recognition since the recognition process itself exceeded the tone presentation. A second tone interfered with recognition of the first when it occurred before recognition was complete or the image had decayed. This result generates a number of questions which must be answered in order to clarify the properties of preperceptual auditory storage and the nature of the recognition process.

How, we first ask, does the masking tone interfere with the recognition of the test tone? First, the masking tone might interfere with recognition without actually interfering with the preperceptual storage of the test tone. It is possible that the preperceptual storage can hold two successive tones without any mutual interference with the second tone simply distracting the recognition process from processing the first tone. So it is necessary to ask whether the masking tone interferes with the preperceptual image itself or simply terminates the recognition process without interfering with preperceptual storage.

AUDITORY MASKING

The distinction can be clarified by considering the recognition masking task in terms of Broadbent's (1958) model discussed in Chapter 13. In terms of this model (see Figure 1, Chapter 13), the recognition of the tone is dependent upon a central processor which is limited in capacity and can read out only one channel at a time. In this model, it is logically possible that the masking tone in the recognition masking task distracted the attention of the central processor away from the test tone, interfering with recognition of the test tone. Recognition performance improves with increases of the silent interval before the onset of the masking tone, because it measures the time of undisturbed attention for identifying the tone. Accordingly, recognition masking might occur even if the masking tone does not interfere with the preperceptual storage of the test tone.

What sort of experiment is needed to decide this question? In the recognition masking experiment, the masking tone could have interfered with preperceptual auditory storage or simply distracted the central processor. We must develop an experiment in which the masking tone does *not* interfere with preperceptual auditory storage, but does distract the central processor, at least to the same extent as in the typical recognition masking task. If no masking or a significantly reduced amount of masking occurs in this condition compared to the prototypical masking study, we can conclude that the masking tone *must* interfere with preperceptual storage.

Tone vs. Light Masking Stimuli

Massaro and Kahn (1973), using the above logic, reasoned that a nonauditory stimulus should not interfere with the preperceptual auditory storage of an earlier tone since preperceptual storage is modality specific. If subjects were required to process a nonauditory stimulus at varying times after the test tone presentation, would this produce a masking function? To answer this question, recognition masking was compared when the test tone was followed by auditory and visual masking stimuli, respectively. It was also necessary to ensure that the auditory and visual masking stimuli were processed equally to insure the attention of the central processor. Therefore, light and tone masks were employed and subjects were required to identify the duration (long and short) of the masking stimulus on each trial.

Each trial began with a 20 msec. presentation of one of two possible test tones. The seven observers were required to identify a saw-toothed tone of 800 Hz. as "sharp" and a sine wave tone of 800 Hz. as "dull." (The wave shape of a saw-toothed tone resembles the teeth of a saw, and the tone sounds sharp because of energy at higher harmonics of the fundamental frequency. The sine wave sounds dull by comparison.) A masking stimulus followed the test tone after a variable blank interval which lasted 0, 40, 80, 120, 180, 250, 360, or 500 msec. The masking stimulus was a square wave tone of 800 Hz. or a small light on the panel in front of the observer.

(The wave shape of a square wave tone traces out a sequence of rectangular shapes. The square wave tone has a buzzlike quality.) The duration of the masking stimulus was 100 or 160 msec. The subject was also required to identify the duration (short or long) of the masking stimulus. On any trial, therefore, a test tone was followed, after a variable blank interval, by a masking stimulus. The subject was instructed to look at the light and listen on every trial, since he would have to identify both the quality of the test tone and the duration of the masking stimulus. As in the prototypical backward masking study, all 64 experimental conditions (2 test tones x 2 masking stimuli x 2 masking stimulus durations x 8 interstimulus intervals) were presented randomly with equal probability. Furthermore, the subjects were well-practiced in the task and were tested for 4 days.

The results indicated that subjects processed the masking stimulus, since identification performance of its duration averaged about 80 percent correct. This means that the masking stimulus did

FIGURE 1. Percentage of correct identifications of the test tone as a function of the masking stimulus and the intertone interval (after Massaro & Kahn, 1973).

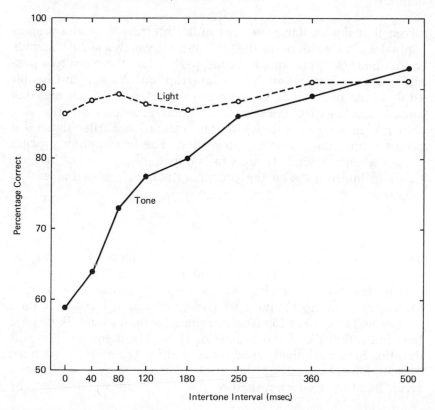

require the attention of Broadbent's central processor and the results can be used to test the central processing account of backward recognition masking. If processing of any stimulus at all—regardless of modality—is sufficient for masking, there should be no difference in the tone and light masking function. By contrast, if the second stimulus must interfere with the preperceptual auditory storage of the first, only the auditory stimulus should produce a masking function.

Figure 1 presents the percentage correct identification of the test tone as a function of the masking stimulus and interstimulus interval. Identification performance with a tone masking stimulus increased 34 percent with increases in the blank interstimulus interval. By contrast, with a masking light identification performance was at a high level and did not increase significantly with increases in the blank interstimulus interval. These results indicate that the disruption of a central processor cannot account for the backward masking function when a tone is used as a masking stimulus. This finding is consistent with the hypothesis that a second auditory stimulus interferes with recognition of an earlier one because it interferes with the information held in a preperceptual auditory image.

Given that the masking stimulus must interfere with the preperceptual auditory storage of the test tone, why is this so? Analogous to the theories of masking in visual perception, there are two possible reasons, integration and/or interruption. We saw in Chapter 18 that both of these processes were important in visual masking and we would expect the same in audition. A second stimulus was shown to influence the signal-to-noise ratio of an earlier signal if it occurs within the period of integration. The interruption process occurs when a second stimulus falls outside the period of integration and interferes with the preperceptual storage of the earlier stimulus.

INTEGRATION PROCESS

The auditory system, like the visual system, integrates acoustic energy over time within the period of integration. The integration process functions to combine acoustic energy across time in order to give an auditory stimulus its perceived sound quality. A pure tone of less than 10 or 15 msec. duration does not sound like a pure tone but rather like a short noise or click. Tones longer than this duration have a relatively good tonal quality. Accordingly, we need to integrate at least 10 or 15 msec. of acoustic energy occurring at a given auditory frequency before the tone sounds tone-like. The important thing to note is that extending the duration of the pure tone changes its perception categorically from a noise-like sound to a tone-like sound. It does not produce the perception of a noise sound followed by a pure tone sound. Rather, it allows us to perceive a single sound of a certain sound quality.

A finding by Creel, Boomsliter, and Powers (1970) has shown that the integration process may last much longer than normal in people who have a deficient blood supply to the brain. For these persons, tones must last much longer than 15 msec. to be perceived as tone-like. For example, pure tones lasting 200 msec. or less may be perceived as noise sounds. The amazing finding is that tones lasting longer than 200 msec. are perceived as pure tones *without* being preceded by a noise-like sound. This result is a powerful demonstration of how the acoustic information is integrated across time in audition.

Tone Duration

How can we determine the temporal period of integration in tone perception? Having said that increasing the duration of a tone increases its tone-like quality, it follows that accurate pitch perception should improve with increases in tone duration. If we ask a subject to distinguish between two tones of different frequencies, the duration of the tones should be critical. At very short durations, both tones would sound noise-like, making them difficult to discriminate. With increasing duration, the tones would sound more tone-like, and more importantly, the pitch of the tones would sound different. Increasing the duration of the tones should improve pitch perception only within the period of integration, since we assume that only the acoustic information within the integration period can affect the signal-to-noise ratio of the stimulus. Using this logic, the accuracy of tone perception as a function of tone duration should allow us to measure the integration period.

Task considerations

Previous investigators have determined the accuracy of pitch perception as a function of tone duration by computing barely noticeable differences in frequency at different durations. The task used was a successive comparison task in which one tone is immediately followed by another tone and the subject reports whether the tones differ in pitch. The frequency difference between the two tones is varied, using one of the classical psychophysical methods discussed in Chapter 5. The experimenter then determines the frequency difference between the tones that is correctly recognized as different 75 percent of the time. The independent variable of interest is the duration of the tones. But the successive comparison task is not appropriate to measure perception, since the tone duration cannot be systematically varied without confounding some other process. Consider the task in which the first and second tones are presented at the same duration, one immediately after the other. When the experimenter systematically varies tone duration, he also varies the amount of processing time available for the first tone. A second tone interferes with the perception of an earlier tone if it occurs before the first tone is completely processed. Therefore, the results are uninformative since they are a function of tone duration and/or processing time.

One modification of the task would be to hold processing time of the first tone constant by keeping it at a fixed duration. For example, the first tone could be presented for 250 msec., followed immediately by a second tone of varied duration. Now the experimenter faces the problem that a short second tone may sound different from the first tone because the two tones differ in duration. Accordingly, the successive comparison task is also inappropriate when the duration of the first tone is fixed. The just noticeable difference may be larger for tones of shorter duration, not because the pitch of the second tone was perceived less accurately, but because it is more difficult to compare the pitch of two tones that differ in duration.

The appropriate task for determining the accuracy of pitch perception is the absolute judgment task used in the backward masking studies. Two tones that differ in frequency are used as test stimuli in the task. The subject is instructed to call the higher tone "high" and the lower tone "low." Since there are two possible stimulus trials and two possible responses, we can use the methods developed in Chapter 7 to derive a dependent measure that is independent of decision biases. Either "percentage correct responses" or d' values will provide a good index of the subject's ability to perceive pitch.

The independent variable in the experiment is the duration of the test tones. This variable must be systematically varied within an experimental session rather than between experimental sessions. Memory plays an important role in the absolute identification task. The subject can identify the tones accurately only to the extent he remembers what they sound like. This is why it is necessary to practice the subject and to give him feedback in the task before the experiment itself can be carried out. It is possible that tone duration could influence the memory for the test tones. Longer tones might allow the subject to remember the tones more accurately, which would lead to more accurate pitch recognition. Accordingly, if an experimenter varies tone duration between experimental sessions, he does not know to what extent the differences in tone recognition are dependent upon differences in memory in the different conditions. When the duration of the tones is varied within a session, any tone duration is equally likely to be presented on any trial. Accordingly, memory for the pitch of the test tones would be relatively constant throughout the experiment and would not be confounded with tone duration.

One anecdotal observation illustrates the danger of varying the duration of the test stimulus between sessions. An experimenter found that performance continued to improve with increases in the duration of the test stimulus out to 1 sec. This was particularly disturbing since the subject always made his response within ½ sec. The improvement in performance observed with increases in duration from ½ to 1 sec., therefore, could not be a direct function of the effect of duration on recognition, since recognition must have been completed before the second ½ sec. of the tone. It seems more likely that the longer durations allowed the subject to study the test stimulus longer on each trial after he made his response. The resulting improvement in his memory for the test stimulus would facilitate his recognition performance on the next trial.

Pitch perception

The author utilized the absolute judgment task to determine the temporal period of integration in pitch perception. Two test tones of 1000 and 1010 Hz. were employed as test stimuli. The tones were presented at one of 8 stimulus durations: 5, 10, 20, 40, 60, 80, 100, and 120 msec. All 16 experimental conditions (2 test tones x 8 tone durations) were equally likely to occur in an experimental session. The subjects identified the higher tone as "high" and the lower tone as "low" and feedback was given on each trial. The first day of 600 trials was considered as practice and the results of the last 2 days were used in computing the percentage correct at each of the 8 stimulus durations.

Figure 2 presents the average results of four observers tested in the experiment. The results show that recognition performance improved with increases in tone duration up to between 60 and 80 msec. Our estimate of the integration period, therefore, is of this order of magnitude. Acoustic energy within this period is integrated, increasing the signal-to-noise ratio of the test tone. Duration increases beyond this interval have no effect since the stimulus falls outside the period of temporal integration.

Blips and blaps

The results of the experiments discussed so far have shown how the process of integration affects the sound quality of a stimulus when it is increased in duration. We now consider how integration operates when two stimuli occur within the period of temporal integration. The first experiment by Hirsh (1959) also deserves con-

FIGURE 2. Percentage of correct recognitions of the test tone as a function of its duration. (Unpublished data of the author.)

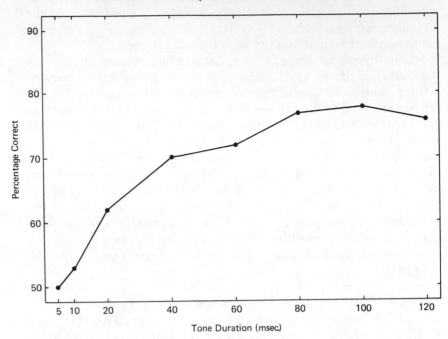

sideration because it provides an apparent contradiction of the results found in the backward recognition masking task. Hirsh's subjects heard two successive and overlapping tones that differed in frequency. One tone was high (for example, 1200 Hz.) and the other was low (1000 Hz.). On any trial, the first tone could be either high or low and the subject's task was to indicate which one came on first. Hirsh systematically varied the onset differences of the two tones, but kept their offsets simultaneous. (If the two tones were kept on for the same duration, subjects would know which came on first by simply knowing which was turned off last.) Thus, on a given trial, a 1000 Hz. tone might come on and a few msec. later a 1200 Hz. tone would be added; both tones would remain on for some time (roughly 500 msec.) and then terminate simultaneously.

Hirsh varied the difference in onset time using a method of constant stimuli to find the point at which subjects could reliably discriminate which tone came on first. The results showed that performance improved very rapidly from 50 percent chance accuracy to perfect performance with increases in the onset differences. At zero onset difference, the onsets could not be discriminated since they were, in fact, the same. At a difference in onset of 17 msec., subjects were able to say which of the tones came on first 75 percent of the time. At a 50 msec. onset difference, performance was perfect.

Hirsh's subjects would appear to be much sharper than those employed in the backward masking paradigm, for they were able to tell perfectly whether the first tone was high or low when it was presented alone for only 50 msec. before the onset of the second tone. If the second tone interfered with the preperceptual storage of the first, subjects must have recognized the pitch of the first tone before the second tone was presented. Hence, the pitch of the first could be recognized in 50 msec. This estimate of recognition time is too short and contradicts our earlier conclusions. But the contradiction is only apparent, because in the Hirsh paradigm, the second tone overlapped with the first. The first tone remained on for some time, and did not terminate until the second one did also. By contrast, in the backward recognition masking task, the first tone is turned off before the second tone is presented.

This stimulus difference between the two tasks is critical and accounts for the performance differences. In Hirsh's paradigm the subject actually perceives one complex sound, not two successive pure tones. Therefore, he does not make his decision about the first tone before the second is presented. Actually, the subject does not perceive the pitch of the first tone directly, but he can deduce it correctly on the basis of the complex sound and the feedback given by the experimenter throughout the task. A different sound is given by the tones when the high tone precedes the low tone than when the order is reversed. The sounds of the tones might be described as 'blap' or 'blip.' Given the feedback in the task, subjects could learn that the 'blap' sound means that low preceded high, whereas 'blip' means the reverse.

Since Hirsh's study, further experiments have been undertaken with this paradigm. Patterson and Green (1970) tried leaving the tones on for only about 10 msec. The minimum interval that subjects needed for accurate reports of temporal order was only 2 to 4 msec. in this task. With so small a difference it is possible to distinguish 'blip' from 'blap.' Nevertheless, subjects still should require ¼ sec. to read out either complex sound. These experiments measure not the perception time of the first tone, but the perceived differences between complex acoustic stimuli. The tones appear to be integrated when they overlap in time, giving the perception of a complex sound. Subjects learn that the perception of 'blip' means that the experimenter presented a low-high sequence and 'blap' means the opposite. Although the subject is doing the task correctly, he is not identifying the pitch of the first sound in the way that Hirsh believed. Here is where a phenomenological report from the subjects could have been helpful in Hirsh's interpretations of these results.

An integration process can explain why performance would improve with increases in the onset differences in the two tones in Hirsh's task. The two pure tones contribute independently to the perceived quality of the complex sound. With no onset separation, both tones contribute equally to the sound quality. As one tone precedes the other, the sound quality becomes more bliplike or blaplike, depending on which sound came first. This follows from the fact that the larger the temporal separation between the onsets of the two sounds, the longer one tone is on relative to the other. To the extent that one tone is on longer than the other, the perceived quality will be determined by that tone and not the other, making the sound more blip- or blaplike.

The integration process accounts for the differences in the onset difference needed for accurate recognition as a function of the overall duration of the tones. In Hirsh's task, the tones lasted roughly 500 msec., whereas they only lasted 10 msec. in the Patterson and Green (1970) study. The overall duration affects recognition since the subjects needed a 17 msec. onset difference in the first case and only a 2 to 4 msec. difference in the second. Assume that the period of integration lasts roughly 50 msec. from the onset of the first tone. In Hirsh's study, then, one tone would be on for 50 msec. and the other on for 33 msec. during the period of integration at an onset difference of 17 msec. In contrast, the longest tone was on for only 10 msec. in the Patterson and Green study, so that the second tone is on for a much shorter period, for example, 7 msec. for an onset difference of 3 msec. What seems to be critical in determining the blip- or blaplike sound quality is the *relative* rather than the absolute durations of the tones during the period of integration. Accordingly, Patterson and Green's results show that roughly a 30 percent difference in duration is sufficient for 75 percent recognition. Using this result, we can predict the period of integration based on Hirsh's finding of 17 msec. The value 17 msec. is 30 percent of 57 msec., which provides an estimate of the period of integration in audition. The results discussed earlier and other results presented below also support an estimate of this order of magnitude for the period of temporal integration.

INTERRUPTION PROCESS The findings discussed in this chapter have illustrated the properties of the integration process. However, it is apparent that the process of integration alone cannot account for the backward recognition masking results. We have estimated the temporal period of integration at between 50 and 80 msec., whereas recognition masking occurs out to 250 msec. The interruption process accounts for the rest of the masking function that occurs outside the period of integration. A second stimulus presented outside the period of integration interferes with the preperceptual storage of a first stimulus, preventing any further processing of the first. The role of both integration and interruption processes in perception can be illustrated in a comparison of backward and forward recognition masking (whether the test tone precedes or follows the masking tone). Analogous to our discussion in Chapter 18, there should be no difference between backward and forward masking if the masking results are simply dependent upon integration. In contrast, if the interruption process is essential to the masking results, there should be significantly more backward masking than forward masking.

A recent experiment by the author (Massaro, 1973a) illustrates the proper procedure for comparing forward and backward masking. The duration of the test tones and the masking tone was 20 msec., and the tones were presented at the same loudness. On the first day of the experiment, the subjects learned to identify the test tones in an absolute judgment task without the masking tone present. The forward and backward masking conditions were presented on the next three days. The intertone interval lasted 0, 20, 40, 80, 140, 220, 340, or 480 msec. All experimental conditions (2 test tones x 2 masking conditions x 8 intertone intervals) were presented randomly with equal probability within a test session. Each trial began with the presentation of a visual cue indicating to the subject whether the test tone would be the first or second tone on that trial. The subjects were instructed to identify this test tone and to ignore the other tone. The cue occurred 1½ sec. before the tone presentation to give the subject plenty of time to prepare himself for the appropriate tone. All other procedural details followed the typical masking experiment.

Forward vs. Backward Masking

The average results of five subjects are presented in Figure 3. The masking functions are not symmetrical and there is significantly more backward masking than forward masking. At the zero intertone interval, there is no difference between the forward and backward masking conditions. In contrast, at a 20 msec. intertone interval, performance is roughly 12 percent better in the forward than in the backward masking condition. Furthermore, perform-

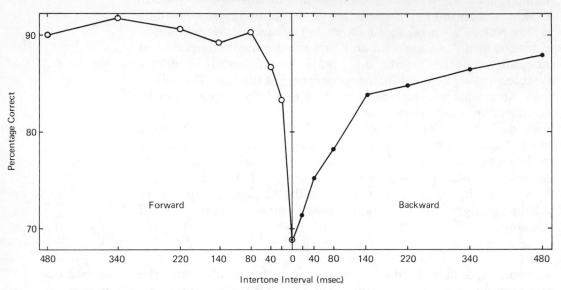

FIGURE 3. Percentage correct identifications of the test tone as a function of the intertone interval in the forward and backward masking conditions (after Massaro, 1973a).

ance has essentially reached asymptote in the forward masking condition at the 80 msec. interval, whereas performance continues to improve out to 340 msec. in the backward masking condition.

TWO PROCESSES IN ACTION Analogous to our description of visual masking, the results of auditory recognition masking must be described by both integration and interruption processes. Integration is responsible for the forward and backward masking found at the zero intertone interval. The integration of the acoustic information of the test and the masking tones reduces the signal-to-noise ratio of the test tone, disrupting recognition performance. The interruption process is necessary to describe the finding of no forward masking but significant backward masking at intertone intervals outside the period of temporal integration. No forward masking is found because the second test tone is stored in preperceptual storage without interference from the first masking tone. In contrast, significant backward masking is found because the preperceptual storage of the first test tone is interfered with by the second masking tone.

Another way to show integration and interruption processes in operation is to demonstrate how both the actual stimulus duration and the processing time before the masking stimulus presentation are important for auditory recognition. This procedure is somewhat analogous to the Eriksen & Eriksen (1971) study presented in Chapter 18. The backward recognition masking task was carried out under two different conditions (Massaro, 1972c). In the first, a short tone was presented, followed by a variable silent interval, followed by a masking tone. In the second condition, the test tone was left on for some variable period and the masking tone followed immediately. The variable of interest in both conditions is recognition time. In the first, recognition time equals the 20 msec. tone presentation plus the duration of the silent interval. In the second, recognition time is equal to the duration of the first tone. Therefore, we have performance being tested under two different conditions and as a function of a second independent variable—recognition time.

The operation of the integration and interruption processes in this task can be clarified using the quantitative model developed for visual recognition in Chapter 18. Measuring recognition performance in terms of d' values, we said that it was a negatively accelerating growth function of recognition time t

$$d' = \alpha(1 - \theta^t) \tag{1}$$

In this equation, the parameter value α provides an index of the clarity or signal-to-noise ratio of the test stimulus. The parameter value θ indices the rate of processing the information in the test stimulus presentation. This equation should describe the results of both recognition conditions in Massaro's (1972c) task.

In the silent processing condition, the test tone was presented for 20 msec. followed by silent intervals of 30, 50, 80, 130, 190, 250, 340, or 430 msec. In the continuous processing condition, the test tone was left on for these processing intervals. If we assume that the temporal period of integration is roughly 50 msec., then even the shortest tone presentation in the continuous processing condition produces the largest possible signal-to-noise ratio of the test tone. Therefore, the performance in this condition can be described by Equation 1 with a fixed value of α and θ. In the silent condition, we would expect the α value to be small, since the test tone is left on for only 20 msec. It is also possible that the value of θ, the rate of processing, could differ in the two experimental conditions.

In order to test this model, the results must be presented in terms of d' values. The observed d' values were computed from the hit and false alarm rates. The predicted d' values from Equation 1 were obtained by estimating the parameter values, using the pro-

FIGURE 4. Discriminability of the test tones in terms of d' values as a function of processing time under the silent and continuous processing conditions (after Massaro, 1972c).

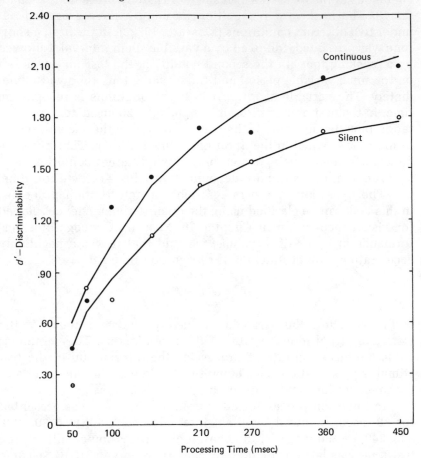

cedure discussed in Chapter 10, which minimizes the squared deviations between the predicted and observed d' values. Figure 4 presents the observed and predicted d' values as a function of recognition time under silent and continuous processing conditions. The α values were 1.90 and 2.30 for the silent and continuous conditions, respectively. These values show that the signal-to-noise ratio of the test tone was larger in the continuous than in the silent processing condition, supporting the integration hypothesis. The results show also that recognition time was critical in both conditions out to a period of at least 250 msec., supporting the interruption process. If a second stimulus occurs before the first is recognized, it interferes with the preperceptual storage of the first stimulus, disrupting its recognition.

Our preceding discussion concentrated on results from the backward recognition masking experiment to develop a model of the process of auditory recognition. A strong and healthy theory must be capable of demonstration by more than one paradigm. It cannot be limited to one isolated experiment, but must be able to describe the phenomena of a number of experimental and real-life situations. We have shown that the perception from a preperceptual storage of auditory information takes roughly 250 msec. in auditory backward masking experiments. A different paradigm was used by Warren, Obusek, Farmer, and Warren (1969) in search of perceptual processing time in audition.

PERCEPTUAL PROCESSING TIME

Warren et al. presented their observers with four auditory stimuli, one after the other: a low tone, a buzz, a high tone, and a hiss. The high and low tones were 2,000 and 300 Hz. respectively, very distinguishable, and of course the buzz and the hiss were easily distinguished from each other and from the tones. These sounds were presented in any of the possible orders on a given trial and repeated in a loop in that same order. The subject heard them as, for instance: buzz, high tone, hiss, low tone, buzz, high tone, hiss, low tone, buzz, etc. The subject's task was to identify the sequence in which they were presented. He could begin anywhere in the sequence in reporting them, but he had to get them in correct order from that point, for instance, "low tone, buzz, high tone, hiss."

Nonsense Sounds

The independent variable in this experiment was the duration of each stimulus. If identification of a stimulus requires a certain amount of time, then we would expect that each stimulus in this task would have to last the full time required in order to be correctly identified. If it takes 100 msec. to perceive the hiss, and each stimulus is presented for 50 msec., then the low tone would replace the hiss before the latter could be recognized. Thus, the duration of each stimulus in the sequence which results in the correct recognition of the temporal order of the sounds would correspond to the minimum time required to perceive each stimulus.

Warren et al. found that subjects on the first trial needed about 700 msec. per stimulus to perform the task correctly. After a short practice period, this time dropped down to 300 msec. The first longer estimate cannot be a true estimate of the time it takes to perceive these sounds, but must reflect the role of forgetting in short-term memory or some other factor. For example, although the sounds are easily distinguishable, the totally unpracticed subject might have difficulty remembering the order of the sounds already perceived while recognizing the others. This hypothesis is supported by the finding that unpracticed subjects do much better in the task if they can respond by arranging 4 cards with the stimulus names in serial order during the repeating sequence than if they are required to simply remember them and respond verbally. Practice eliminates the short-term memory problem, which leaves 300 msec. as an acceptable estimate of the recognition time for each stimulus.

Speech Sounds

Thomas, Hill, Carroll, & Garcia (1970) used vowel stimuli in the Warren paradigm. Four vowels were repeated in a loop, and subjects were asked to identify the temporal order of the vowels. In this experiment, the estimate of recognition time was much shorter than the estimate found with nonsense sounds. When the four vowels were presented at a rate of 125 msec. per stimulus, the temporal order could be correctly reported. Digits have also been used in this task (Warren and Warren, 1970) and, like the vowels, can be identified more rapidly than the nonsense sounds.

The differences between the recognition times for nonsense and speech sounds reveal that recognition time can vary with the difficulty of the task. The test stimuli employed in the backward masking tasks were chosen to be very similar, so that recognition time would be maximal and limited only by the duration of preperceptual auditory storage. If the test stimuli had been more distinctive, our estimates of recognition time would have been much shorter. For example, if the two test tones differed more in frequency, perfect recognition could occur in much less than 250 msec. Using this logic, we would expect to increase our estimates of recognition of speech sounds by choosing speech stimuli that were more similar and, therefore, more difficult to distinguish from one another.

In the 1860s, Donders hoped to measure the time it takes for certain psychological processes by using the RT task (see Chapter 3). The backward recognition masking task achieves what Donders hoped to do because it provides a method of measuring the recognition time. The temporal order task developed by Warren and his colleagues can also be used to estimate recognition time. (One way to combine the two tasks would be to use very short stimuli in the temporal order task and vary the silent interval between the successive stimuli.) Accordingly, the experimenter hoping to trace out the temporal course of psychological processes is not limited to the RT task. These relatively new paradigms discussed above provide additional tools for defining the operations of psychological processes.

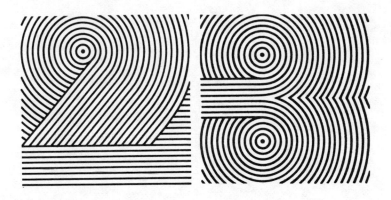

Perceptual units in speech

*The irreducible acoustic stimulus is the sound pattern
corresponding to the consonant-vowel syllable.*
—*Alvin Liberman, Pierre Delattre, and Franklin Cooper
   (1952)*

Chapters 21 and 22 presented evidence in favor of a particular view
of auditory perception. The auditory stimulus is transformed by
the auditory receptor system and sets up a neurological code in
preperceptual auditory storage. This storage holds the information
in a preperceptual form for roughly 250 msec. during which time the
recognition process must take place. The recognition process transforms the preperceptual image into a synthesized percept held in
synthesized auditory memory (see Figure 1). In this chapter, we analyze the sound units that are functional in the recognition stage of
speech processing.

SIGNS

These sound patterns are referred to as perceptual units. Analogous
to those in reading, every perceptual unit in speech has a representation in long-term memory, which is called a sign. The sign contains a list of acoustic features that define the acoustic features of
the sound pattern as they would be represented in preperceptual
auditory storage. As each sound pattern is presented, its corresponding acoustic features are held in preperceptual auditory storage. The recognition process operates to find the sign in long-term
memory which best describes the acoustic features in preperceptual
auditory storage. The outcome of the recognition process is the
transformation of the preperceptual auditory image of the sound
stimulus into a synthesized percept held in synthesized auditory
memory. Figure 1 presents a schematic diagram of the recognition
process.

According to our model, preperceptual auditory storage can
hold only one sound pattern at a time for a short temporal period.
The recognition masking studies have shown that a second sound
pattern can interfere with the recognition of an earlier pattern if the
second is presented before the first is recognized. These results

FIGURE 1. A schematic drawing of the recognition process and the two properties of signs defining perceptual units in long-term memory.

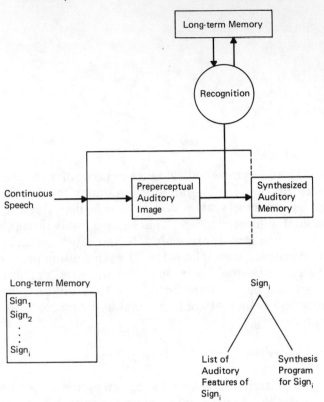

show that each perceptual unit in speech must occur within the temporal span of preperceptual auditory storage and must be recognized before the following one occurs for accurate speech processing to take place. Therefore, the sequence of perceptual units in speech must be recognized one after the other in a successive and linear fashion. Finally, each perceptual unit must have a relatively invariant acoustic signal so that it could be recognized reliably. If the sound pattern corresponding to a perceptual unit changes significantly within different speech contexts, recognition could not be reliable, since one set of acoustic features would not be sufficient to characterize that perceptual unit. Perceptual units in speech as small as the phoneme or as large as the phrase have been proposed.

Determining the acoustic features utilized in speech perception is more difficult than determining the visual features in reading, since the speech signal is much more complicated than printed text. Here we discuss one approach to the study of the acoustic features used in vowel perception. In Chapter 20, vowel sounds were described by a power spectrum, which gives the amount of sound energy at each frequency of the sound. The different vowels are characterized by having their peaks of energy, called formants, at different frequencies. Therefore, the acoustic features utilized in vowel perception could be the frequency location of their formants. The question is the extent to which each of the vowel formants contributes to vowel recognition, that is to say, which vowel formants are critical acoustic features in vowel recognition.

Klein, Plomp, and Pols (1970) had 50 people pronounce 12 different vowels in a b–vowel–t context. The test vowels were obtained by removing 100 msec. segments of the steady-state vowel sound. In order to describe the physical properties of these vowels, the investigators measured the sound intensity across the audible frequency spectrum and determined the location of formant frequencies for each of the vowels. The next step was to obtain perceptual judgments of the vowels. Observers identified each of the 100 msec. vowel segments as one of the 12 alternatives, getting 74 percent correct. The critical dependent variable in this test, however, is the confusion errors between vowel stimuli. To the extent that a listener confuses one vowel for another, it can be said that these vowels are perceptually similar. According to our analysis, this implies that similar vowels share or have in common a number of acoustic features.

Now the task was to determine if the location of the formant frequencies of the vowel stimuli could describe the perceptual confusions between the vowels. The results indicated that locations of the first two formants were critical for vowel perception. That is to say, two vowels were confused with each other to the extent the first two formant frequencies of the vowels were similar. In Chapter 20, we noted that these formants are mainly determined by the location and height of the tongue in vowel articulation. This study provides one example of how confusion errors in a recognition task can be utilized to determine what stimulus features are used in perception.

PHONEMES

The first candidate we consider for the perceptual unit is the phoneme. Phonemes represent the smallest functional difference between the meaning of two speech sounds. Given the word ten we can change its meaning merely by changing the consonant /t/ to /d/. The two sounds form two different words when they are combined with /–en/; they are therefore different phonemes. On the other hand, sounds are said to be within the same phoneme class if substitution of one for the other does not change the meaning of the sound pattern. One example is the word *did*. The two *d*'s in the word are not the same acoustically and, if their sound patterns were extracted and interchanged with each other, the word would not sound the same. Yet they are not functionally different since interchanging them should still give the word *did*. In this case, they are called different allophones of the same phoneme. Thus, if the substitution of one minimal sound for another changes the meaning of the larger unit, then the two sounds are phonemes. If such substitution does not change the meaning of the larger unit, then the sounds are allophones of the same phoneme class.

Consider the acoustic properties of vowel phonemes. Unlike some consonant phonemes, whose acoustic properties change over time, the wave shape of the vowel is considered to be steady-state or tone-like. The wave shape of the vowel repeats itself anywhere from 75 to 200 times per second depending on the fundamental frequency of the speaker (see Chapter 20). Figure 2 presents the wave shapes of some common vowels; as can be seen in the figure,

FIGURE 2. Wave shapes of the vowels /I/ as in *hit* (top panel) and /i/ as in *heat* (bottom panel), as pronounced by the author.

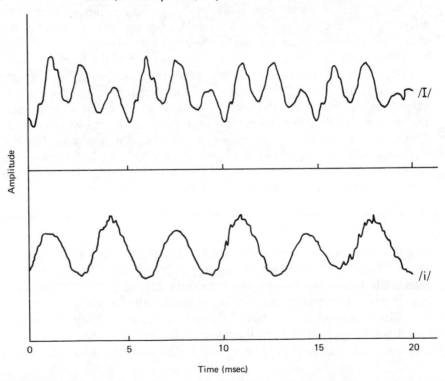

different vowels have uniquely different wave shapes. In normal speech, vowels last between 100 and 300 msec. and during this time, the vowels maintain a fairly regular and unique pattern as seen in Figure 2.

Although vowels usually last between 100 and 300 msec. in normal speech, vowels presented for much shorter durations can still be recognized (Gray, 1942; Suen & Beddoes, 1972). It should not be surprising that short vowels can be recognized easily since the extended duration of the vowel does not add new information. We saw how the wave shape of the vowel repeats itself at the fundamental frequency of the speaker. Another method of analyzing the acoustic characteristics of vowel sounds is to take a power spectrum which plots the amount of energy at each component frequency (see Chapter 20). When we take the power spectra of different vowel sounds, the vowels can be distinguished on the basis of the peaks of energy called formant frequencies. The important point for our present discussion is that these peaks do not change significantly with increases in the duration of the vowel beyond 4 or 5 fundamental repetitions, that is, about 20 to 40 msec. Therefore, if recognition of the vowels was based on the location of the formant frequencies, it should be unaffected by increases in vowel duration beyond this lower limit.

In contrast to the above demonstration, continuous speech would become unintelligible if its vowels were shortened by a similar amount. One hypothesis that accounts for these two apparent discrepancies is that subjects in the vowel identification experiments were able to continue processing the vowel during the retroactive silent interval, whereas in real speech a second sound occurs before the vowel is recognized. This hypothesis implies that observers should be able to identify shortened vowel sounds only if they are given enough time afterward to process the vowel. If we were to follow the abbreviated vowel pattern with a second sound stimulus, we should interfere with the recognition of the vowel. This hypothesis follows directly from our model of auditory processing developed in the last two chapters. The necessary experiment to test it, therefore, is the backward recognition masking paradigm.

A series of vowel recognition studies have been carried out by Massaro (1974). In order to have precise control over the duration of the vowels, their loudness, and the masking intervals, it was necessary to utilize a small digital computer both to record the vowel stimuli

VOWEL RECOGNITION

Recognition Masking

and to play them back during the experiment. It is possible to record sounds in the computer by using an analog-to-digital converter. The sounds are spoken into a microphone, which transduces the sound pressure changes into electrical changes that can be stored in the computer in digital form. The duration and loudness of the vowels can then be set at whatever values the experimenter desires. For example, it is necessary to adjust the loudness of the vowels so that they are equal in loudness as required by the backward recognition masking task. During the experiment, the sound can be presented by playing back the digital representation of a sound pattern through a digital-to-analog converter into a set of headphones.

The test alternatives used in the first experiment were the vowels /i/ pronounced as in the word *heat,* /I/ as in *hit,* /a/ as in *hat,* and /U/ as in *put.* The duration of the test vowels was 20 msec. The masking vowel was also chosen from the 4 vowels, /i/, /I/, /a/, and /U/, and lasted 20 msec. There were eight different silent intervowel intervals. Presentation of the 4 test alternatives, the 4 masking alternatives, and the 8 intervowel intervals was completely random and each of the 128 conditions was programmed to occur with equal probability. On each trial, the subject heard a test vowel followed after some interval by a masking vowel. He indicated which of the 4 vowel alternatives occurred and was given feedback on each trial. Twelve people were tested for 5 days and the results of the last 3 days were used in the data analysis.

Measure of Performance

When 4 vowel alternatives are used in the recognition task, it is possible that some of the vowels would be more intelligible than others. For example, if three of the vowels were very similar acoustically and the fourth vowel differed significantly from the other three, recognition of the fourth vowel should be much better than the other three. Therefore, it is informative to derive how well the subject recognizes each of the 4 vowel alternatives rather than computing an average percentage correct. What dependent measure can we use for this analysis? The percentage of correct recognitions of each vowel is not a good measure because it could be influenced by decision biases. In Chapter 7, we saw how performance on one of two test alternatives could not be considered independently of performance on the other alternative. The same logic applies here. A person may correctly recognize a given alternative more often than the other alternatives, not because the vowel is more intelligible, but rather because he has a decision bias to respond with that particular vowel. Accordingly, to eliminate the influence of a decision bias, it is necessary to correct or adjust his performance on one trial type by his performance on the others.

Consider the case in which the subject correctly identifies the test alternative /i/ 90 percent of the time. In this case, the probability of responding i given the stimulus alternative /i/, written as $P(i|i)$, would be .9. If the subject performed at this high level on i trials simply because he had a response bias to say i, then the probability of responding i to non /i/ trials, written as $P(i|\bar{i})$, should also be very large. On the other hand, if /i/ was actually recognized at a high level, $P(i|\bar{i})$ should be very low. This is exactly the same logic we used in our development of the data analysis in Chapter 7. Using this logic, the d' measure provides the best index of the intelligibility or recognizability of a vowel alternative in the 4-alternative task. We can derive a d' value for each of the 4 test alternatives. The probability of identifying a vowel correctly is designated a hit, and responding with that vowel alternative to any other test alternative is designated a false alarm. For example, for the d' value for the vowel i, $P(i|i)$ would be a hit, whereas $P(i|\bar{i})$ would be a false alarm. The hit and false alarm rates can then be used to derive a d' value as shown in Chapter 7. Using this method, we can derive a d' value for each of the 4 test alternatives in the task.

Figure 3 presents the d' values for each of the test vowels as a function of the intervowel interval. The results show that the overall level of performance differs significantly for each of the 4 vowels. The rank ordering from least to most intelligible was /a/, /I/, /U/, and /i/. The results for each of the vowels shows that performance improved significantly with increases in the intervowel interval up to about 220 msec.

Masking Functions

The continuous lines in the figure are the predicted results given by our recognition equation:

$$d' = \alpha(1 - \theta^t) \qquad (1)$$

where t is the amount of recognition time between the onset of the test and masking vowels. In order to estimate the parameter values α and θ, it was reasoned that a different value of α should be estimated for each of the 4 vowel alternatives. The parameter value α indexes the intelligibility or signal-to-noise ratio of the test vowel. Accordingly, the more intelligible vowels should have higher values of α. As an added constraint on the model, it was assumed that θ, the rate of processing, should not differ for the 4 different vowels. Regardless of the intelligibility of the vowel, the rate of processing per unit of time should be fixed. Accordingly, predicted d' scores were determined by estimating a different parameter value of α for each of the 4 test vowels and a single value of θ. We are, there-

FIGURE 3. Discriminability values (d') for the four test vowels as a function of the silent intervowel interval. (The lines are drawn through the predicted points given by Equation 1.)

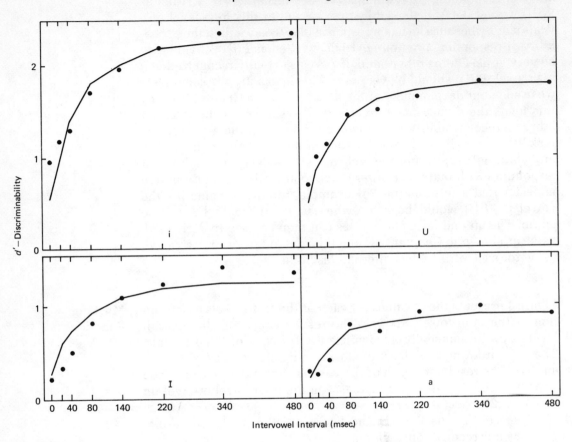

fore, predicting the 32 points in Figure 3 only on the basis of estimating 5 different parameters. The parameter estimates of the α values were 2.29, 1.77, 1.31, and .88 for the test vowels /i/, /U/, /I/, and /a/, respectively. The parameter value for θ was $.3 \times 10^{-6}$ when t is expressed in seconds.

One additional finding of the experiment was that the similarity relationship between the test vowel and masking vowel did not influence the backward masking functions. Each vowel was effective in masking every other vowel, even itself, in the task. This means that observers could not discriminate any better on the trials on which the test and masking vowels were the same vowel, than on the trials on which the masking vowel differed from the test vowel. These results support our idea of an interruption process that is responsible for the masking vowel interfering with the representation of the test vowel in preperceptual auditory storage.

The vowels masking experiment has shown that short vowel sounds can function as perceptual units in the recognition masking paradigm. In continuous speech, however, the vowels are much longer in duration and recognition must occur during the extended vowel duration rather than during a retroactive silent interval. In terms of our model, vowels could function as perceptual units in continuous speech if processing of the sounds could occur during the extended vowel duration. To show that processing can occur during this time, it is necessary to employ longer vowels in the backward masking paradigm.

Employing the 4 vowels used in the above study, Massaro (1974) compared recognition of a short vowel to the same vowel left on during the processing interval before the onset of the masking vowel. In the silent processing condition, the test vowel was presented for 26 msec., followed by the masking vowel after a variable silent interval. In the continuous processing condition, the test vowel was left on for the processing interval before presentation of the masking vowel. According to our model, increasing the duration of the test vowel should increase its intelligibility until the temporal period of integration is exceeded. However, recognition of a continuous vowel presentation will still require the same amount of recognition time as required by a short vowel followed by a silent interval. In terms of Equation 1, the value of α should be larger in the continuous than in the silent processing condition but θ, the rate of processing, should be very similar in the two conditions. The predicted results were determined by estimating an α value for test vowels that lasted 26 msec. and another α value for test vowels that lasted 52 msec. or more. In other words, it was assumed that increases in vowel duration beyond 52 msec. did not increase the signal-to-noise ratio of the vowel. Even so, we would expect continued improvement in performance with further increases in vowel duration, since this increases the amount of recognition time before the onset of the masking vowel. The results showed that it took roughly 200 msec. to recognize the vowel in both the silent and continuous processing conditions, supporting our recognition model.

These experimental results demonstrate that the vowel phonemes could function as perceptual units in speech. Next let us consider consonant phoneme sounds. Consonant sounds are more complicated than vowels and some of them do not seem to qualify as perceptual units. We have noted that a perceptual unit must have a relatively invariant sound pattern in different contexts. However, some consonant phonemes appear to have completely different

Processing During Vowel Presentation

CONSONANT RECOGNITION

sound patterns in different speech contexts. In the earlier example of the stop consonant phoneme /d/, the same phoneme has different acoustic representations in the two allophones in the word *did*.

To clarify this point, it would be profitable to analyze synthesized speech stimuli (see Chapter 20). Liberman, Cooper, Shankweiler, and Studdert-Kennedy (1967) have shown that sounds with the acoustic patterns shown in Figure 4 are sufficient for the recognition of the syllables /di/ as in *deed* and /du/ as in *do*. Since the steady-state portion corresponds to the vowel sounds, the first part, called the transition, must be responsible for the perception of the consonant /d/. As can be seen in the figure, the acoustic pattern

FIGURE 4. Spectrograms of the synthesized speech syllables /di/ and /du/ (after Liberman et al., 1967).

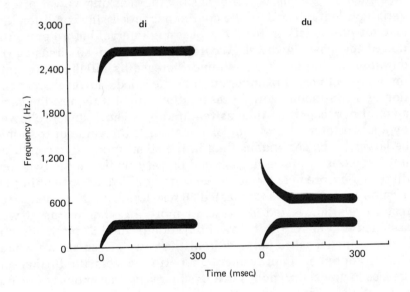

corresponding to the /d/ sound differs significantly in the two syllables. Although the first formant is identical in the two syllables, the transition of the second formant rises from approximately 2200 Hz. to 2600 Hz. in /di/, whereas it falls from 1200 to 700 Hz. in /du/. Hence, one set of acoustic features would not be sufficient to recognize the consonant /d/ in the different vowel contexts. Therefore, we must either modify our definition of a perceptual unit or eliminate the stop consonant phoneme as a candidate.

CV Syllables There is another reason why the consonant phoneme /d/ cannot qualify as a perceptual unit. In our model perceptual units are recognized in a successive and linear fashion. But Liberman et al. have also shown that the consonant /d/ cannot be recognized before the vowel. They used the following procedure to demonstrate this: the duration of the vowel in the consonant-vowel syllable (CV) is gradually decreased and the subject is asked when he hears the stop consonant sound alone. The CV syllable is perceived as the complete syllable until the vowel is eliminated almost entirely. At that point, however, instead of the perception changing to the consonant /d/, a nonspeech whistle is heard. Liberman et al. show that the sound pattern corresponding to the stop consonant /d/ cannot be recovered by itself. Therefore, it seems unlikely that the /d/ sound would be perceived before the vowel sound; it appears, rather, that the CV syllable is perceived as an indivisible whole or gestalt.

These arguments lead to the idea that the CV syllables /di/ and /du/ function as perceptual units rather than containing two perceptual units each. One way to test this hypothesis is to employ the CV syllables in a recognition masking task. Liberman et al. found that subjects could identify shortened versions of the CV syllables when most of the vowel portion is eliminated. Analogous to our interpretation of vowel perception, recognition of these shortened CV syllables also should take time. Therefore, a second syllable, if it follows the first soon enough, should interfere with perception of the first. Consider the three CV syllables /ba/, /da/, and /ga/, which differ from each other only with respect to the consonant phoneme. Backward recognition masking, if found with these sounds, would demonstrate that the consonant sound is not recognized before the vowel occurs and also that the CV syllable requires time to be perceived.

Recognition Masking

Both Massaro (1974) and Pisoni (1972) have employed the three CV syllables /ba/, /da/, and /ga/ as test items in the backward recognition masking task. These items were synthetic speech stimuli that lasted 40 msec.; the first 20 msec. of the item consisted of the CV transition and the last 20 msec. corresponded to the steady-state vowel. The masking stimulus was also chosen randomly from this set of three stimuli. In one condition of Pisoni's study, the test and masking stimuli were presented to opposite ears, that is, dichotically. All other procedural details followed the prototypical experiment.

Figure 5 shows the percentage of correct recognitions for 9 observers as a function of the silent interval between the test and masking CVs. The results show that recognition of the consonant is not complete at the end of the CV transition, nor even at the end

FIGURE 5. Percentage correct recognitions of the test CV syllables as a function of the duration of the silent interstimulus (intersyllable) interval (after Pisoni, 1972).

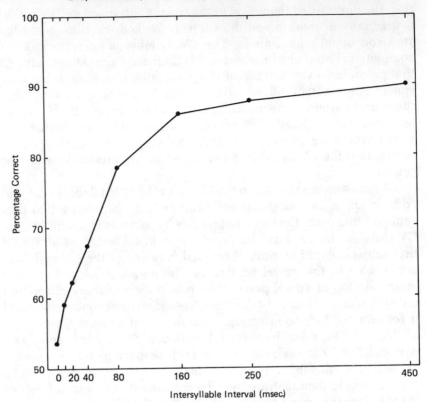

of the short vowel presentation. Rather, correct identification of the CV syllable requires perceptual processing after the stimulus presentation. These results support our hypothesis that the CV syllable must have functioned as a perceptual unit, because the syllable must have been stored in preperceptual auditory storage and recognition involved a transformation of this preperceptual storage into a synthesized percept of a CV unit. The acoustic features necessary for recognition must, therefore, define the complete CV unit. Our signs in long-term memory would correspond to the complete CV syllable.

Pisoni's results are also informative with respect to one of the properties of preperceptual storage. Even though his test and masking stimuli were presented to opposite ears, recognition masking occurred in the same way as it did for a binaural condition in which the two stimuli were presented to both ears. Preperceptual storage must be located somewhere after the information from the two ears is combined in the auditory system. Therefore, a second sound is just as effective in interfering with the storage of an earlier sound, even though the sounds are presented to different ears. Recall that Broadbent (1958) assumed that the ears functioned as physical channels in preperceptual storage so that the inputs along these two channels could be maintained relatively independently of each other. The results discussed in Figure 5 argue against this type of formulation.

Processing During CV Syllables

Analogous to the discussion of vowels, it must be shown that CV syllables can function as perceptual units in continuous speech. In this case, too, processing of the CV syllable would occur during the extended vowel duration in continuous speech. Accordingly, we should be able to show that CV syllables of the duration found in continuous speech also require time for recognition. If the longer CV syllables are recognized in the same way as the shortened ones in the masking studies, we should be able to interfere with recognition by presenting a second stimulus before recognition is complete. This experiment remains to be carried out.

We have demonstrated how a vowel phoneme or a CV syllable could function as a perceptual unit in speech. Next we must ask whether perceptual units could be larger than vowels, CV, or VC syllables. Miller (1962) argued that the phrase of two or three words might function as a perceptual unit. According to our criteria for a perceptual unit, it must correspond to a sign in long-term memory which has a list of features describing the acoustic features in the preperceptual auditory image of that perceptual unit. Accordingly, preperceptual auditory storage must last on the order of one or two seconds to hold perceptual units of the size of a phrase. But the recognition masking studies usually estimate the effective duration of preperceptual storage to be about 250 msec. Therefore, perceptual units must occur within this period, eliminating the phrase as the perceptual unit.

The recognition masking paradigm developed to study the recognition of auditory sounds has provided a useful tool for determining the perceptual units in speech. If preperceptual auditory storage is limited to 250 msec., the perceptual units must occur within this short period. This time period agrees nicely with the durations of syllables in normal speech. Massaro (1972b; in press) presents other evidence indicating that vowels, consonant-vowel, and vowel-consonant syllables are the perceptual units in continuous speech.

Memory and Learning

Los Angeles County Museum of Art, Eye-dazzler, 1885–1895, Anthony Berlant, Santa Monica (detail).

Synthesized auditory memory (nonspeech sounds)

*But there are people whose voices change constantly.
I frequently have trouble recognizing someone's voice
over the phone, and it isn't merely because of a bad
connection. It's because the person happens to be
someone whose voice changes twenty to thirty times in
the course of a day. Other people don't notice this but
I do.*
—*An unidentified mnemonist quoted in
Alexander R. Luria (1968)*

Our discussion of auditory recognition pointed out how this stage
of information processing involves a read-out of the information in
the preperceptual auditory storage. In our model, the read-out
produces a synthesized percept in synthesized auditory memory.
This chapter focuses on the properties of synthesized auditory
memory. How can we characterize the information in this memory?
What is the capacity of synthesized auditory memory? How long
does the information last in this memory? Does following information interfere with synthesized memory and/or is it simply subject
to a passive decay over time?

How do we test the forgetting of our subject's synthesized percept of the test tone in the recognition masking task? If we present
the test tone without a mask, the subject processes the tone and has
available two dimensions of information: what the tone sounds like
and its name (high or low). Intuitively, we might expect that the
subject would forget what the tone sounded like much faster than
he would forget the name that he gave it. We forget the sound of a
friend's voice before we forget his name. When he telephones, the
sound of his voice is not sufficient for recognition and he must
identify himself before we know who he is. The sound of a friend's
voice is very difficult to codify or reduce to a simple abstract dimension. Imagine trying to page someone at an airport by announc-
ing a description of his voice rather than his name.

These examples clarify the distinction we make between synthesized auditory and generated abstract memory in our model.
Figure 1 presents a flow diagram of the two recognition stages of
auditory information processing. We call primary recognition the

FIGURE 1. Flow diagram of the two recognition stages of auditory information processing.

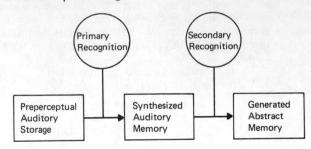

transformation of the preperceptual auditory image into a synthesized percept in synthesized auditory memory. Secondary recognition occurs when a name is given to the synthesized percept and placed in generated abstract memory. This model clarifies the interaction between synthesized auditory and generated abstract memory. We may recognize a voice of a certain quality but may not know its name. In this case primary recognition occurred but the secondary recognition process failed. Primary recognition occurred because we have a synthesized percept which we can utilize in later processing. For example, after hearing the voice and failing to recognize its name, we could be told that it was John's voice. Now we may recognize the voice as John's if it is presented at some later time.

DELAYED COMPARISON TASK

Returning to our test tone example, it would be informative to test the subject's memory for its sound quality at varying times after the test tone presentation. One paradigm that has been used successfully is the delayed comparison task. In this task, a test stimulus called the standard is presented for some finite period of time, followed by an interval of a certain duration, followed by a second stimulus—the comparison—that may or may not differ from the standard stimulus. The subject's task is to indicate whether the second stimulus is the same as or different from the first. He makes a delayed comparison between the two stimuli. Since the standard stimulus is no longer in the real world when he makes the comparison judgment, it is his memory for it that he compares to the comparison stimulus. Thus, the delay between the two stimuli makes this a memory task, in which the changes in memory can be isolated by measuring performance at different times after the standard tone presentation.

As in all other tasks, this one involves a series of processing stages, each of which must be analyzed and understood before any inference can be drawn from the results. First, the subject must perceive and in some way store the standard stimulus. Second, he must preserve this representation for the period of time necessary; he must remember it. Third, he must process the comparison stimulus and retrieve the information about the standard in order to make his comparison judgment. Finally, he must make a decision; that is, he must select a response based on the outcome of his comparison judgment.

The questions we ask in this task, then, begin with the perception stage; how do we perceive and prepare an auditory item for memory? The second question we ask, the one of most interest in this chapter, is What happens to the representation of a stimulus held in synthesized auditory memory? More precisely, what are the rules of the forgetting process in synthesized auditory memory? Third, how does the subject perform the comparison judgment in the delayed comparison task? Finally, we need to know the decision rule that the subject uses at the response-selection stage.

Let us consider a concrete example of a delayed comparison task, in which the subject is asked to compare two tones that may differ in frequency. The experimenter presents him with a tone for 250 msec; during this time he processes it and stores it in synthesized auditory memory. After the presentation, a forgetting interval of some definite duration occurs. At the end of the interval, the subject is presented with a second tone. The subject's task is to tell whether the second tone is the same or different in pitch quality as the first one. On half of the trials, the experimenter presents a comparison tone that is either higher or lower in frequency than the standard tone. On the other half of the trials, he presents a comparison tone that is equal in frequency to the standard tone.

MEMORY FOR PITCH

One critical variable is how different the comparison tones are on different trials. If they are significantly different, the subject should make no errors. If, on the other hand, they are relatively similar to the standard tone, the subject will make errors. Assume that the standard tone is 1000 Hz. What difference in frequency can the observer discriminate? The just noticeable difference that a listener can discriminate about 75 percent of the time under optimal conditions is 3 or 4 Hz. This is in a comparison task with no delay between the standard and comparison tones. However, it is necessary to make the comparison tone differ by about 10 or 20 Hz. from the

Task Considerations

standard on different trials since we want maximum performance to be near 90 or 95 percent, allowing us to measure forgetting over a wider range of accuracy. Ideally, performance should go from this high level to near chance as the subject forgets the sound quality of the standard tone.

Although the subject can discriminate tones that differ by 10 Hz., he cannot successfully label them in the task. For example, suppose the subject were a musician and besides synthesizing the sound quality of the tone he also encoded it in generated abstract memory as being in the range of the musical note B_5, which is about 988 Hz. on the piano. This label will not help him, however, in the same-different task unless the different comparison stimuli are labeled differently than the same comparison stimulus. When the 990 or 1010 Hz. comparison is presented, he will synthesize this tone and most likely encode it as also being in the range of B_5, since the nearest alternative notes $A\#_5$ and C_6 are equal to 932 and 1046 Hz., respectively. Accordingly, his verbal label held in generated abstract memory will not allow him to perform the task accurately. He must rely on the information in synthesized auditory memory. His question must be: Does the sound quality of the comparison tone differ significantly from my memory for the sound quality of the standard tone? Accordingly, the experimenter has a task that provides a measure of the synthesized auditory memory for the standard tone without being influenced by any information in generated abstract memory.

The experimenter is interested in memory and forgetting of the standard tone as a function of its presentation time and the forgetting interval. To study this, he must present a different standard on every trial. If he does not, the subject will learn the stimulus with repeated presentations and will not evidence any forgetting of it during the forgetting interval. That is, a subject will not compare the comparison tone to his memory of the standard tone on that trial; rather, he will compare the tone to a memory of the standard based on all of the trials he has heard so far. Therefore, performance will not be systematically related to the forgetting interval on that trial. The experimenter could select randomly a standard between 900 and 1100 Hz. on every trial. Accordingly, the observer cannot learn the sound quality of one particular standard with repeated presentations, but must attend to and process a new standard for memory on every trial.

How are the data analyzed? There are four possible events on every trial: two trial types × two responses. The subject can respond "same" given a same trial, "same" given a different trial, "different" given a same trial, or "different" given a different trial. This gives a two-stimulus, two-response forced choice task that can be analyzed using the method of signal detection theory discussed in Chapter 7. This analysis allows the experimenter to disentangle what the subject actually remembers about the standard tone from any possible decision bias. He can designate the probability of a "same" response given a same trial, $P(s|S)$, as the hit rate and the probability of a "same" response given a different trial, $P(s|D)$, as the false alarm rate. According to this analysis, a high hit rate could reflect either a very good memory for the standard stimulus, or a decision criterion biased in favor of saying "same." In the latter case, to interpret the high hit rate as revealing very good performance would be misleading because the subject has simply set his criterion so that he is very likely to say "same" whatever he perceives. Accordingly, that fact will be reflected in a high false alarm rate. On the other hand, if his good performance on same trials accurately reflects a good memory, not only would the hit rate be high but the false alarm rate would be low. Since we want to discover his ability to discriminate the two kinds of trials, the true index of performance in this task is derived from both the hit rate and the false alarm rate, giving the measure d' as the index of performance.

Familiarity

The task has been constructed so that the subject cannot use verbal labels; his memory for the standard stimulus must be auditory, rather than abstract, if he is to respond correctly. This is the sort of auditory memory by which we remember the voice quality of friends with a degree of detail and discrimination that we find impossible to communicate by words. A voice we can recognize in this way is familiar to us. Familiarity is a concept that describes the dimension the subject uses to evaluate the comparison stimulus. A difference in familiarity will represent the difference between a stimulus that is recognized as "same" and one that is recognized as "different." The subject begins the trial with a certain amount of familiarity with the pitch of the standard; presentation of the standard increases its familiarity. When the comparison tone is presented he processes the comparison tone and evaluates its familiarity. He perceives a comparison equal to the standard as very familiar, and he responds accordingly. An unequal comparison he perceives as less familiar than it would be if it were equal; therefore, it is different.

Similarity

Another concept we employed is perceived similarity. We say that two things are perceived as similar if they are perceived as being alike or can be confused for one another. The perceived similarity of the pitch of tones is a direct function of the physical similarity of their frequency. This relationship only breaks down at octaves in which a tone of 1000 Hz. may seem more similar to a tone of 2000 Hz. than to a tone of 1700 Hz. (Shepard, 1964). Since our tones are well within a range that is not influenced by the octave effect, we can say that perceived similarity is a direct function of physical similarity in the pitch judgment task. Accordingly, since very similar tones are perceived as such, to increase the familiarity of one tone by presenting it as the standard is also to increase the familiarity of other tones very close to it in frequency. Therefore, when we present a comparison tone that is identical to the standard except for a small difference in frequency, the comparison tone will sound almost as familiar as if it were the same. If the standard tone has X units of familiarity, then we can say that the unequal comparison tone has βX units where β is some value between 0 and 1. In this case, β provides an index of the similarity between equal and unequal comparison tones. If β were less than 1, subjects should be able to perform at 100 percent accuracy in the task, merely by determining whether the amount of familiarity of a given comparison stimulus was best represented by X or by βX. In this case, the subject can choose a criterion value of familiarity represented by C units where $\beta X < C < X$. If the familiarity of the comparison tone is less than C, he responds "different." If the comparison tone has a familiarity larger than C, he responds "same." Table 1 lists the stimulus events and the psychological processes involved in the comparison judgment task.

TABLE 1.
The Stimulus Events and the Psychological Processes Involved
in the Delayed Comparison Task

Stimulus Events	Psychological Processes
1. Present standard	1. Perceive and encode standard in synthesized auditory memory
2. Wait during some forgetting interval	2. Maintain information in synthesized auditory memory
3. Present comparison	3. Perceive and encode comparison
4. Wait for response	4. Does its familiarity exceed criterion value? If yes, respond "same"; if no, respond "different."

Distribution of Familiarity   This simple model, however, in which the equal comparison always has X units of familiarity and the unequal one βX units, is not sufficient to describe the results found in this experiment. Subjects make errors; sometimes an unequal comparison tone sounds familiar enough to the subject so that he mistakenly calls it equal, in which case the familiarity of the unequal tone must have exceeded his criterion value C. Likewise, on some proportion of trials the familiarity of a comparison stimulus that is equal to the standard falls below his criterion, and he is misled into calling it different. Thus, although on some trials the value along the familiarity dimension will be located at X or βX, on many trials the value will occur at some other place along the familiarity dimension. Analogous to our development of signal detection theory, we assume that a certain amount of noise is added to the familiarity value on each trial. The noise added on any trial will be a sample from a normal distribution with a mean of zero. Accordingly, the familiarity value for a given comparison stimulus over a sufficient sample of trials will also follow a normal distribution. On the average, when the comparison is equal, the value along the familiarity index will be X; when the comparison is unequal, the average familiarity value will be βX.

Figure 2 shows a graphical representation of these two distributions placed along the familiarity dimension. The mean of the equal comparison distribution is indicated by X; βX is the mean of the unequal distribution. The subject's decision rule is that every comparison tone whose familiarity is larger than (to the right of) the criterion value is called "same"; everything to the left is called "different." Thus, the proportion of the equal distribution to the right of the criterion represents the probability that the subject says "same" given same, $P(s|S)$. The proportion of the unequal distribution that is also to the right of the criterion represents the probability that the subject says "same" given different, $P(s|D)$.

FIGURE 2. Familiarity distributions for comparison (C) tones that are equal and unequal to the standard (S) tone.

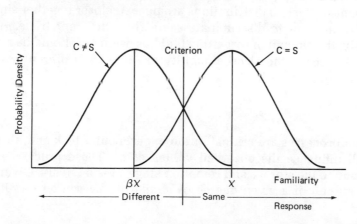

If the standard and comparison stimuli are chosen so that their familiarity distributions are close together, the hit rate is decreased and the false alarm rate increased. If a series of trials with another set of stimuli result in distributions that are farther apart with little overlap, then the false alarm rate will drop to near zero and the hit rate will be close to 100 percent. That is, in the first case, the two stimuli chosen would have been more difficult for subjects to discriminate; whereas they could discriminate the second pair with almost perfect accuracy. As the means of the two distributions are moved closer, the greater the overlap between them, and the more similar the hit and false alarm rates become.

Decision Process On the other hand, changes in the criterion value do not change the distance between the means. Hence, this distance, represented by d' provides an index of performance that is not confounded with decision biases. We allow the subject to place his criterion arbitrarily since its placement represents another process—the decision process—which should not change in an orderly fashion with changes in synthesized auditory memory. The d' value corrects for any decision bias; if C is set at a high familiarity value, the false alarm rate will decrease but only at the expense of a diminished hit rate. Setting the criterion at a low familiarity value increases the hit rate, but also increases the false alarm rate. Hence the distance between the two means, d', is a direct measure of the differences in familiarity of the equal and unequal comparison stimuli used in the experiment.

This analysis establishes d' as our dependent measure in the experimental situation. Accordingly, we expect decreased d' values when we increase the similarity of the different comparison tones to the standard tone. Moreover, as the subject forgets the standard, his familiarity judgment becomes more unreliable; in effect, the means of the two distributions are pushed closer together since it is more difficult to discriminate same from different trials. Accordingly, the amount of forgetting that has occurred should be reflected in changes in the discriminability of same and different trials and hence in changes in d'.

STORAGE PROCESS Two processes are critical in the experimental task and, therefore, will influence the observed values of d'. These processes correspond to the storage and retention stages, respectively. Given a pair of stimuli of a given degree of similarity, presented one immediately after the other so that forgetting is not a factor, the basic independent variable affecting the storage process is the duration of the standard stimulus. The longer the standard tone is presented, the more time the subject has to process the tone and the more information he will be able to derive from it. If presentation time, t_s, is equal to zero, the subject knows nothing about the standard and is unable to discriminate it from any other tone. As t_s is increased, the subject learns more and more about the stimulus, until he has reached the limit of the information this particular subject is able to derive from this particular stimulus. Roughly, then, d' is an increasing function of t_s, since the synthesized percept is a direct function of the information read out of the preperceptual image. In the previous chapters, the growth of the percept was described by an increasing negatively accelerating geometric curve:

$$d' = \alpha(1 - \theta^{t_s})\qquad(1)$$

in which α represents the limit of the amount of information available to this subject from this stimulus and θ is a parameter describing the rate at which d' reaches α with increases in t_s. The value of α will vary from one subject to another. Some people have a higher sensitivity to tone pitch than others, and the value of α that describes their performance will be correspondingly higher. The value of θ lies between 0 and 1, and determines how fast the curve reaches asymptote. Some subjects might acquire the maximum amount of information faster than other subjects. If d' reaches asymptote very rapidly, then the value of θ is relatively small; if the curve grows slowly, θ is correspondingly large.

This part of the model is very familiar. It describes the readout of preperceptual store into synthesized auditory memory. From it we know the amount of information the subject has stored away in synthesized auditory memory, after a given presentation time. In the previous chapter we were mainly concerned with the readout of a very short tone during a silent interval before presentation of the masking tone. Performance asymptoted at roughly 250 msec. because the preperceptual image had effectively decayed. In the delayed comparison task, the standard tone is left on, and it is possible that the readout can occur beyond 250 msec. If presentation time is very short, d' is small; the distributions of the familiarity of the equal and unequal comparison stimuli are close together. As presentation time increases, d' increases and the distributions draw apart. At some point, further increases in presentation time cease to affect d', which remains at the value of α.

RETENTION PROCESS Let us assume that the presentation time was sufficiently long so that $d' = \alpha$ after its presentation. Now we wish to know what will happen when a forgetting interval is introduced between the standard and the comparison stimulus in the delayed comparison task. Intuitively, we might think that the forgetting interval, t_i, will decrease d'. Over time, whatever amount of information was stored in memory during presentation of the standard would decrease during the forgetting interval. This is the prediction of a simple decay theory of forgetting.

Decay Theory The simplest quantitative decay theory postulates geometric forgetting. The central assumption of this theory is that the subject loses or forgets a certain fixed proportion of his memory during each unit of time. In this case, the equation that describes the relationship between d' and t_i is:

$$d' = \alpha \phi^{t_i} \qquad (2)$$

where ϕ is a value between 0 and 1 that indexes the rate of forgetting. The value of ϕ is estimated to permit the curve to change with the experimental situation. For example, there may be individual differences in the rate of forgetting over time, making it necessary for the experimenter to estimate different values of ϕ for different subjects. If ϕ is 1, the subject does not forget at all since

$$d' = \alpha 1^{t_i} = \alpha \qquad (3)$$

whatever the value of t_i. A very low value of ϕ on the other hand, indicating a high rate of forgetting, would quickly drive α down toward zero.

When values are given for this equation and the forgetting curve is plotted, we get a negatively decelerating function. Assume 3 units of α and ϕ equal to .5. At $t_i = 0$ (that is, immediately after presentation of the standard), d', or discriminability between the equal and unequal comparisons, is equal to $3 \times .5$ to the zero power, or $d' = 3$. With an interval of 1 sec., d' is equal to $3 \times .5^1$, or 1.5. At 2 sec., d' is equal to $3 \times .5^2$ or .75. With a ϕ of .5, then, each second of t_i decreases d' by one-half the remainder, as shown in the top panel of Figure 3.

This geometrical curve can also be represented graphically on semilogarithmic graph paper in which the Y ordinate is scaled logarithmically and the X abscissa is linearly. When we take the logarithm of a geometric equation,

FIGURE 3. Geometric forgetting function plotted on linear scale (top panel) and semilogarithmic scale (bottom panel).

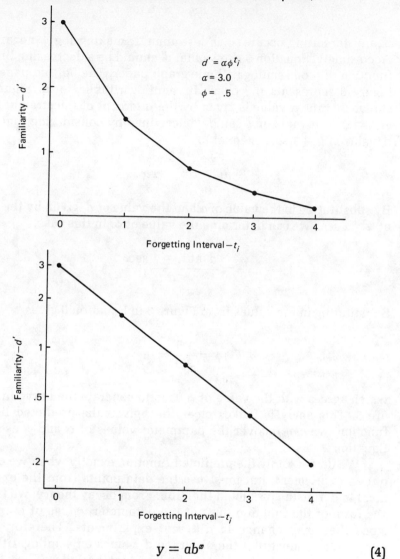

$$y = ab^x \qquad (4)$$

we have a linear function of the form

$$\log y = \log a + x \log b \qquad (5)$$

where the log y is some linear function of x. Therefore, if y is plotted logarithmically and x linearly, Equation 5 describes a straight line.

Taking the logarithm of Equation 2 in the same way gives

$$\log d' = \log \alpha + t_i \log \phi. \tag{6}$$

If any forgetting occurs, ϕ is less than 1, making $\log \phi$ negative. Accordingly, Equation 6 shows that d' should be a decreasing linear function of t_i on semilogarithmic graph paper. The bottom panel of Figure 3 represents the curve in semilogarithmic form. Figure 3 shows that the α value is given by the intercept of the straight line at $t_i = 0$. The value of ϕ can be determined by considering that the d' value at $t_i = 1$ sec. is equal to

$$d' = \alpha\phi^1 = \alpha\phi. \tag{7}$$

By substituting in the value of α and the value of d' given by the line at $t_i = 1$ sec., we can determine the value of ϕ. In this case,

$$\phi = \frac{d' \text{ at } t_i = 1 \text{ sec.}}{\alpha}. \tag{8}$$

Substituting in the values from Figure 3 in Equation 8 gives

$$\phi = \frac{1.5}{3.0} = .5 \tag{9}$$

which agrees with the value of ϕ used to generate the curve in Figure 3. This analysis makes clear that, given the predicted linear function, we can recover the parameter values of α and ϕ used in Equation 2.

We do not know the predicted function exactly when we carry out an experiment, but must use the data points from the experiment to derive the predicted function. From decay theory, we know the form of the function but not the parameter values of α and ϕ, since they may change in different experiments. Therefore, the experimenter must plot the observed d' values on semilogarithmic graph paper and find the straight line that best describes these points. The best line will be the one that minimizes the vertical deviations between the line and the observed points. Usually, simply fitting the line to the points by eye provides a good fit and a mathematical solution is not necessary. The estimated values of α and ϕ can then be determined from the predicted points on the straight line. The value of α will be equal to the predicted d' value at the intercept ($t_i = 0$). The value of ϕ can be determined by dividing the predicted d' value of $t_i = 1$ sec. by the predicted α value

(Equation 8). This example demonstrates how the investigator utilizes the observed data to estimate the parameter values of a quantitative theory in a particular experimental situation.

Interference Theory

Decay theory predicts changes in performance as a function of t_i. This theory assumes a passive decay over time. By contrast, interference theory does not accept the assumption that the critical independent variable affecting memory for the standard is the time since the standard was presented. Rather, new information must have been processed during that interval, interfering with memory for the standard. Thus, the independent variable of importance for the interference theorist is the nature of the stimulus in the forgetting interval.

The central assumption of interference theory is that the rate of forgetting should be directly related to the similarity of the intervening stimulus to the test stimulus. For example, another tone should interfere considerably, whereas a visual stimulus might produce very little forgetting of a tonal stimulus. Decay theory predicts that the nature of the intervening stimuli should not affect the forgetting functions since time alone is the critical variable. Decay and interference theories, therefore, make different predictions about forgetting in the delayed comparison task.

TESTING ALTERNATIVE THEORIES

One way to test decay and interference theories is to manipulate the stimulus events that occur during the t_i interval. In one experiment (Massaro, 1970d, Experiment II), the standard tone was presented for 1 sec. followed by a 1, 2, or 4 sec. interval, followed by a 1 sec. comparison tone. The forgetting interval was either silent, filled with white noise, or filled with another tone that was 90 Hz. higher in frequency than the standard tone. If forgetting were simply a matter of time as postulated by decay theory, the forgetting functions should be the same under the three different conditions during the forgetting interval. In contrast, if forgetting were due to interference, there should be more forgetting when the forgetting interval is filled with another stimulus, and the rate of forgetting should be a direct function of the similarity of the stimulus in the forgetting interval to the standard stimulus.

The quantitative decay theory predicts geometric functions with equal values of ϕ under the three forgetting conditions. In contrast, interference theory predicts that the value of ϕ will be near 1 during the blank interval and less than 1 when a stimulus is presented in the interval. Figure 4 presents the results of the experiment plotted on semilogarithmic graph paper.

Nature of Intervening Stimuli   In this experiment, the forgetting functions should intercept the Y ordinate at the same point, since t_s was constant under the three conditions. That is to say, storage and retention are different processes and varying the nature of the stimulus in the forgetting interval might affect the retention process but should not affect storage. In agreement with this, Figure 4 shows that the points can be described reasonably well by straight lines that intercept the

FIGURE 4.   Forgetting curves plotted as a function of the type of material in the forgetting interval. The predicted lines are from Equation 2 with one value of α and different values of ϕ for each type of interference material (after Massaro, 1970d).

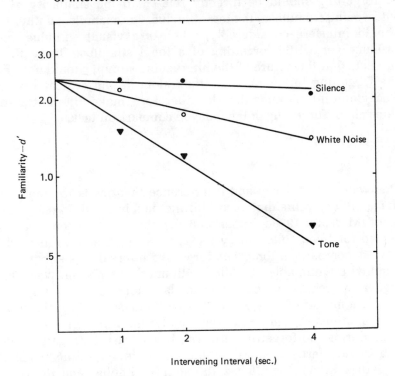

Y ordinate at the same point. Figure 4 also shows that the type of forgetting interval had a substantial effect on the slopes of the best fitting straight lines. The estimated values of ϕ were .98, .87, and .69 for the blank, noise, and tone intervals, respectively. Clearly, a simple decay process is not sufficient to describe forgetting in synthesized auditory memory, since the decay rate as indexed by ϕ should have been the same under all stimulus conditions.

Some forgetting did occur during the blank interval. Interference theory might account for that slight forgetting by assuming that, since the room was not completely quiet, some background noise was available. Most "sound-proof" rooms do still have a low level of background noise from the ventilating system in the building. Also, the subjects may have introduced noise themselves by trying to silently hum or rehearse the sound of the standard tone. Therefore, the small amount of forgetting during the blank interval is not necessarily incompatible with the interference theory.

Can the decay theory also be salvaged given the negative results? One possible problem is the absence of apparent control over the subject's rehearsal in the experiment. Rehearsal is a process that allows the subject to reinstate the stimulus during the forgetting interval, slowing down its passive decay. The decay theorist might argue that the blank interval enabled the observer to rehearse the stimulus, whereas it was more difficult to rehearse during the noise and tone forgetting intervals. However, Massaro (1970d) has also shown that one form of rehearsal (silent humming) does not improve performance but actually disrupts it in this task. In that study, subjects instructed to silently hum the tone during the forgetting interval performed significantly poorer than subjects not given rehearsal instructions. Furthermore, the rehearsal instructions disrupted performance, regardless of the stimulus in the forgetting interval. Of course, some other form of rehearsal may be more effective but even so, it is not clear why it should be easier to rehearse during the white noise than during the tone interval. The weakness of this decay-rehearsal theory, is that it cannot specify when rehearsal would be more difficult. Differences in rehearsal do not appear to account for Massaro's results and cannot easily salvage the decay theory.

Number of Intervening Items

The experiment described above demonstrates that information in synthesized auditory memory is forgotten as a function of the similarity of a new stimulus and its duration. In this experiment, however, only one stimulus was presented in the forgetting interval and its duration was systematically varied. It is also necessary to ask if forgetting is dependent on the number of stimuli that occur in a fixed interval. In a followup study, Massaro (1970a) covaried the duration of the forgetting interval with the number of tones presented during this interval in a factorial design. The duration of the forgetting interval was 1.2, 2.4, or 3.6 sec., with 1, 2, 3, or 4 different tones presented in the forgetting interval. For example, if

3 tones were presented in a forgetting interval of 2.4 sec., each tone would last .8 sec. The 12 different conditions were presented randomly from trial to trial. Subjects were instructed to decide whether the last tone was same or different in pitch as the first tone. In agreement with the previous studies, forgetting increased with increases in the duration of the forgetting interval. The new important finding was that forgetting increased with increases in the number of tones in a fixed interval. This result cannot be handled easily by decay theory. Rehearsal should not differ in the different conditions since there is always a tone present during the forgetting interval. Accordingly, decay theory has no mechanism to explain why increasing the number of tones in a fixed interval increased forgetting. The result is compatible with an interference theory that assumes each new tone produces some new interference with memory for a previous tone.

Familiarity of Intervening Items

In our analysis of the memory-for-pitch task, we assume that the subject operates along a dimension of familiarity in making his comparison judgment. An experiment by Deutsch (1970a) provides some direct evidence for this, by showing that intervening tones presented during the forgetting interval also build up some familiarity which later influences the same-different judgment of the comparison tone. She presented a 200 msec. standard tone, followed by four 200-msec. intervening tones separated by 300 msec., followed by a two-second silent period before presentation of the comparison tone that lasted 200 msec. In the control condition, none of the four intervening tones were equal to the standard or the comparison. The hit rate was 80 percent and the false alarm rate was 6 percent. In the repeated condition, the standard tone was repeated as either the second or third tone in the sequence of the middle four tones. This increased the hit rate to 97 percent and decreased the false alarm rate to 2 percent. These results are straightforward according to our familiarity model. If d' values are calculated for the nonrepeated and the repeated standard tone conditions, performance improves from 2.39 to 3.93 with the standard tone repetition. Repeating the standard increased its familiarity, which improved the same-different judgment on both same and different trials.

On some of the different trials in the same experiment, Deutsch also presented the unequal comparison tone in the second or third intervening position. This manipulation increased the false alarm rate to 35 and 24 percent, respectively. In contrast to repeating the standard tone, then, repeating an unequal comparison lowered performance by increasing the false alarm rate. This follows from our interpretation, since the unequal comparison tone would have an increased familiarity due to its recent presentation as an intervening tone. Therefore, the observer says he has heard it before more often, thus increasing his false alarm rate. Deutsch's results indicate that subjects cannot reliably remember the temporal order in which the tones occurred. Although a certain tone can reliably sound familiar or unfamiliar, we are not exactly sure of when we heard it before. These observations support our construct of familiarity as the dimension of judgment in the pitch memory task.

We assume that preperceptual auditory storage and synthesized auditory memory operate at two successive stages of auditory processing. Preperceptual auditory storage is revealed in the backward masking task, whereas synthesized auditory memory is studied in the delayed comparison task. In both tasks, a first test tone is followed by an interference tone. In the masking task, the second tone interferes with the preperceptual storage of the first, terminating the recognition process. The subject then makes his decision on the basis of what had been processed before the second tone presentation. In addition to terminating the recognition process, the second tone in the memory-for-pitch task also affects performance by interfering with the synthesized storage of the first tone over time. Therefore, increasing the duration of the interference tone decreases performance in the memory-for-pitch task. In contrast, the subject does not have to remember the test tone, given that he can make his judgment immediately in the masking experiment; therefore, the duration of the masking tone should have no effect on the masking function.

PREPERCEP- TUAL AND SYNTHESIZED AUDITORY STORAGE

Massaro (1971, 1972c) systematically varied the duration of the masking tone in the recognition task. In one experiment, the test tones were a sine wave and a sawtooth wave of 800 Hz. These two tones differ with respect to the higher harmonics of 800 Hz. and the sawtooth wave sounds high or sharp relative to the low or flat sound of the sine wave. The duration of the test tones was 20 msec. The masking tone was a square wave of 800 Hz. that lasted 20, 60, 120, or 240 msec., possessing a buzzlike quality. The test and masking tones were presented at a normal listening intensity. The masking tone followed the test tone after a variable silent intertone interval, which lasted 20, 40, 70, 120, 180, 250, 330, or 420 msec. In a given session, all 64 experimental conditions (2 test tones × 4 masking tones × 8 silent intertone intervals) were presented ran-

Duration of Masking Tone

domly with equal probability. All other procedural details followed the prototypical masking experiments (see Chapter 21).

Figure 5 presents percentage correct identifications of the test tone for four observers in the experiment as a function of the silent intertone interval and the duration of the masking tone. The continuous lines are drawn through means averaged over the durations of the masking tone. For all four of the observers, performance improved with increases in the duration of the silent intertone interval. The improvement in performance reached asymptote at an interstimulus interval of either 180 or 250 msec. For each of the four observers, the masking tone duration had no significant effect on performance. The failure to find a significant effect of the masking tone duration contrasts with the effects of the second tone in the delayed comparison task. These results support the distinction between preperceptual and synthesized auditory storage.

Memory-for-pitch Task

One nice example of the different roles of preperceptual and synthesized auditory memory is seen in the memory-for-pitch task. Consider the case in which observers are presented with a standard tone, followed immediately by an intervening tone, followed by a comparison tone. The observer reports whether the comparison tone is the same as or different in pitch than the standard tone. Preperceptual and synthesized auditory memory are responsible for different stages of processing in the experimental task. The information available in the preperceptual auditory image and the time this information is available for perceptual processing determines the perception and storage of the standard test tone. The perceptual processing of the information in the preperceptual auditory image produces a synthesized percept that enters synthesized auditory memory. Synthesized auditory memory is responsible for remembering what the standard test tone sounded like during the intervening tone presentation. The subject bases his decision on a comparison between the perception of the comparison tone and the representation of the standard tone in synthesized auditory memory.

If preperceptual auditory storage and synthesized auditory memory are different structures in the pitch memory task, these should be affected differently by changes in independent variables in the experiment. If preperceptual storage is only responsible for original perception and synthesis of the test tone, it should only be affected by the signal-to-noise ratio of the test tone presentation and the time the information is available for perceptual processing. It should not be affected by variables that affect the memory for the test tone. Conversely, the temporal course of synthesized memory

FIGURE 5. Percentage of correct identifications of the test tone as a function of the intertone interval and duration of the masking tone (after Massaro, 1972c).

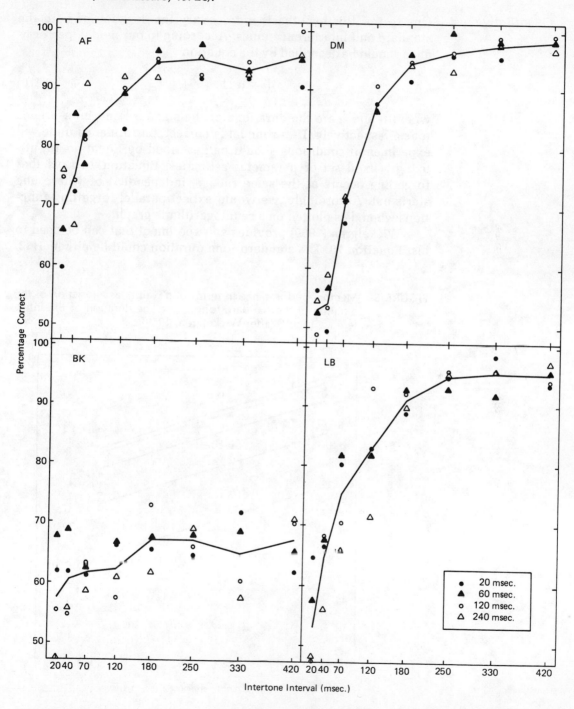

should be affected by mnemonic variables and not by the variables that affect the perception and storage of the standard tone.

Quantitative test   One test of this hypothesis is to covary the duration of both the standard and interference tones. According to our model, performance should be described by the equation

$$d' = \alpha \, (1 - \theta^{t_s}) \phi^{t_i} \qquad (10)$$

where t_s and t_i are the durations of the standard and interference tones, respectively. If our model is correct, performance under all experimental conditions should be described by Equation 10, utilizing a fixed set of parameter estimates. Equation 10 says that forgetting occurs at the same rate, ϕ, independent of where one starts out. Accordingly, we would expect parallel forgetting functions when d' is plotted on a semilogarithmic graph.

Wickelgren (1969) provides an experiment that can be used to test Equation 10. The standard tone duration could be either .1, .2,

FIGURE 6.   Memory performance in terms of d' values as a function of the duration of the standard tone t_s and the duration of the interference tone t_i (after Wickelgren, 1969).

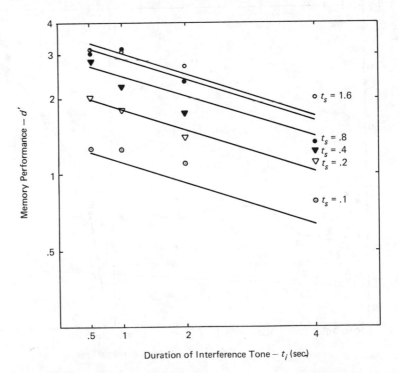

.4, .8, or 1.6 sec. The interference tone lasted .5, 1, 2, or 4 sec. These 20 experimental conditions were presented repeatedly to three subjects. The average performance is shown in Figure 6 along with the predictions given by Equation 10. The estimated parameter values were $\alpha = 3.62$, $\theta = 0.12$, and $\phi = .83$ when t is measured in seconds.

The results, although somewhat noisy, show that increasing the duration of the standard test tone enhances the original perception and storage of that test tone but does not affect the rate of forgetting of the test tone during the interference tone presentation. Similarly, increasing the duration of the interference tone increases the forgetting of the test tone but does not affect the original perception or storage of the test tone presentation. These results support the present model by showing that two successive stages of auditory information processing are operative in the pitch memory task.

Now it becomes necessary for us to demonstrate also that synthesized auditory and generated abstract memory are different storage structures. Recent results have shown that synthesized auditory memory operates independently of generated abstract memory in the pitch memory task. Deutsch (1970b) presented either a blank period, a series of intervening tones, or a series of digits during the forgetting interval in the pitch memory task. The standard tone was presented for 200 msec. followed by a 5-sec. interval, followed by a 200-msec. comparison tone. Six intervening tones or 6 digits were played during the forgetting interval. They were equated for loudness and spaced equally in the 5-sec. interval. Deutsch first selected subjects who performed perfectly in the silent interval condition. Then they were presented with four different conditions: (1) intervening tones that could be ignored, (2) intervening numbers that could be ignored, (3) intervening numbers to be recalled in serial order after the same-different pitch judgment, and (4) no pitch judgment but recall of the 6 digits. Performance dropped to 68 percent in the first condition but only to 98 percent in the second. This shows that synthesized auditory memory for the test tones is highly specific and is only interfered with by similar auditory items.

The third and fourth conditions demonstrate the independence of information in synthesized auditory and generated abstract memory. Requiring the subjects to remember the intervening digits did not appear to disrupt pitch memory performance. Having the subjects recall the digits in Condition 3 only dropped performance in the pitch judgment task to 94 percent. Similarly, the pitch memory task did not disrupt recall of the digits. In Condition 3, subjects recalled 75 percent of the digit lists correctly after they performed the pitch judgment, whereas in Condition 4, when the subjects could devote all their attention to the digits, recall did not improve (73 percent). Accordingly, subjects could perform as well on both tasks simultaneously as they could when concentrating on only one task. One explanation of this is that the sound quality of the standard tone was held in synthesized auditory memory; it did not interfere with, nor was it interfered with, by the names of the digits in generated abstract memory.

The procedure of the Deutsch experiment has an aspect that keeps one from concluding that the intervening digits produced no additional interference on pitch memory. Since she selected subjects who scored perfectly with a blank interval, it is difficult to determine the exact amount of interference produced by the different conditions. While a significant amount of forgetting could have been produced by the intervening digits, a ceiling effect could have prevented the observation of a noticeable amount of forgetting. That is to say, a significant amount of forgetting could have occurred, but the subject still remembered enough about the tone to perform accurately. Hence, it is necessary to compare performance in Deutsch's task under the easiest conditions at below perfect accuracy. Then, any forgetting will be directly observable in the results.

Memory for the perceived sound of an auditory stimulus is an important storage structure in the sequence of processing auditory inputs. The delayed comparison task proved to be informative in studying the storage, retention, and decision processes operative in synthesized auditory memory. The concepts of similarity and familiarity were employed to describe performance in the memory-for-pitch task. The formalization of these concepts along with a model of the decision process allowed us to test between decay and interference theories of forgetting. Forgetting of sound is influenced by the type, number, and familiarity of sounds processed during the retention interval.

Given evidence for a synthesized auditory memory, it was necessary to distinguish it from other storage structures. Whereas preperceptual auditory storage maintains the acoustic features for a short time so that a sound can be perceived, synthesized auditory memory allows us to retain the perceived sound of the stimulus. In learning a new sound, we must process the features of the sound to experience it and then remember that particular sound experience. Synthesized auditory memory maintains the sound experience, whereas any meaningful label given it would be held in abstract form in generated abstract memory. In speech, we usually go from sound to meaning without much attention to our sound experience. The next chapter attends to the sound experience in obtaining meaning from sound, and clarifies the properties of synthesized auditory memory by analyzing its role in the processing of speech.

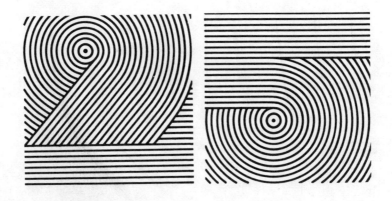

Synthesized auditory memory (speech sounds)

In the colorful terminology of one such subject, the most recent items in a verbal series reside temporarily in a kind of "echo box" from which they can be effortlessly parroted back.
—Nancy C. Waugh and Donald A. Norman (1965)

The previous chapter dealt with a number of studies that have demonstrated synthesized auditory memory for pure tones. Conceivably, the information processing of these sounds could differ considerably from processing more complicated speech sounds. In this chapter, we shall show that synthesized auditory memory is also a critical memory structure in speech processing. A series of studies are discussed that provide evidence for synthesized auditory memory for speech sounds and demonstrate how this memory code differs for different kinds of sounds.

The contribution of synthesized auditory memory (SAM) is apparent in a number of different experimental studies of short-term memory. When subjects are presented with a short auditory list of words to be remembered, auditory information in SAM might supplement the name information in generated abstract memory (GAM). It is conceivable that subjects could remember the sound of a word in SAM without the necessity of holding the name of the word in GAM. Accordingly, the subject could use the sound of the word to generate the name during recall.

One way to measure the contribution of SAM in recall is to compare recall of lists of items presented either auditorily or visually. In one task, 7 or 8 words are presented sequentially at a rate of 2 words/sec. The subject's task is to recall the list in serial order after it is presented. A subject recalling in serial order must begin recall at the start of the list and proceed in order through the list. If he cannot recall a word at a particular serial position, he can skip that position (for example, by placing a dash in written recall) and continue recalling the remaining items. Of course, once the subject responds at a particular serial position he cannot backtrack to

SERIAL PRESENTATION AND RECALL

change his answer at earlier positions. This task is referred to as a serial presentation and serial recall task.

A number of studies using this paradigm have been carried out, demonstrating some contribution of SAM to recall in this task. As an example study, Murray (1966) presented lists of 8 consonant letters visually, one at a time on a memory drum at a rate of 1 item/sec. The subject either repeated the items subvocally or vocally during the test list presentation. When a person repeats the consonants out loud, he hears himself saying them, which is not the case in the silent repetition condition. The subject's out-loud repetition of a letter produces an acoustic stimulus which leads to a preperceptual auditory storage of the test letter. A read-out of this storage produces a synthesized percept in synthesized auditory memory. In the subvocal rehearsal case, no acoustic stimulus is produced and these events cannot take place. Therefore, repeating the items out loud should produce information in synthesized auditory memory, whereas the subvocal repetition should not. We assume that the contribution of synthesized visual memory is constant and relatively negligible in both conditions (see Chapter 26).

Serial Position Curves Figure 1 presents the percentage of items correctly recalled under the overt (out loud) and covert (silent) repetition conditions as a function of their serial position in the list. The results show a fairly typical serial position curve in this task. Recall tends to decrease in a fairly monotonic fashion as a function of serial position. This result is primarily a function of the serial recall task: the earliest items are recalled first so that there is less intervening recall between their presentation and test. As the subject begins recalling the items, he forgets the names of later ones. This phenomenon is called output interference. The first item or two in a serial list also appear to have some advantage because they are better stored than the later items in the list (see Chapter 12).

Performance is significantly better in the overt than the covert repetition condition. This advantage has been attributed to the added information in SAM because the items are repeated aloud. More importantly, as an index of the capacity of SAM, previous investigators have used the differences between the two curves as a function of serial position. As can be seen in Figure 1, the difference between the two curves increases with increases in serial position. From these curves, investigators have concluded that there is more information in SAM about the later than about the earlier items in the list. This conclusion seems entirely reasonable in view of our studies of pitch memory in the last chapter. There is more infor-

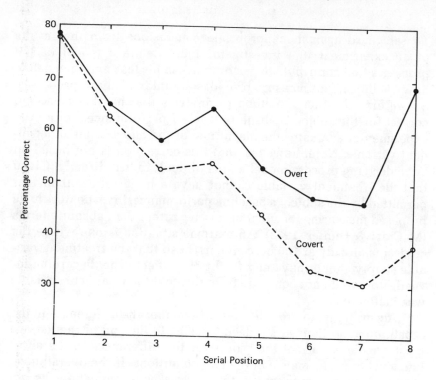

FIGURE 1. Percentage of letters recalled at each serial position as a function of the repetition condition (after Murray, 1966).

mation in SAM about later items because these items have fewer interfering items between their presentation and recall.

While this conclusion appears reasonable and may even be correct, it is not justified given the results in Figure 1. This is because the percentage of correct items recalled may not be the appropriate dependent variable for comparing the two curves from the covert and overt repetition conditions. The basic issue is that the size of the effect of an independent variable is limited by the subject's absolute level of performance. Assume that two subjects are given the same experimental treatment but their baseline levels of performance differ. The first subject performs at 50 percent without the treatment and improves to 75 percent when tested under the treatment variable. The other subject improves from a baseline level of 70 percent to 85 percent when given the treatment variable. The treatment improved performance of the first subject by 10 percent more than for the second subject (25 to 15 percent). However, it does not follow that the treatment variable had a larger effect for the first subject, since the subjects' levels of performance differed to begin with.

Absolute and Relative Scales

To safeguard against inappropriate conclusions from the results of an experiment, the investigator must define a model of the processes that contribute to performance in his task and then define how his dependent measure provides an index of these processes. So we first consider a method of analysis that has been used to correct for the subject's absolute level of performance, before the experimenter evaluates the magnitude of the effect of his independent variable. Note, however, that this correction is not based on an underlying process model and is difficult to test directly. Given that the treatment variable cannot have a larger effect than that permitted by the subject's baseline performance, investigators have proposed measuring its effect in relative rather than absolute terms (McCrary & Hunter, 1953). An extreme situation is one where the subject is already at 100 percent correct so that the treatment variable simply cannot have any facilitating effect. The discerning investigator would not conclude from this that the treatment variable was ineffective.

Accordingly, to provide a test of whether the differences in the repetition conditions are, indeed, specific to the end of the list, we must somehow correct the scores for the differences in the absolute level of performance in the two conditions. If the overall level of performance between the two curves could somehow be accounted for, we could compare the curves directly. One way to do this is to determine the percentage of total errors $P(E)$ at each serial position (McCrary & Hunter, 1953). In this case,

$$P(E) = \frac{E}{TE} \tag{1}$$

where E is equal to the number of errors at a particular serial position and TE is equal to the total number of errors made on the list. This procedure equates the overall level of performance in two different conditions and allows the experimenter to compare the serial position curves directly. In both conditions, adding the percentage of errors across all serial positions will equal 100 percent.

Figure 2 plots the data in Figure 1 in terms of percentage of total errors at each serial position. We can see the effect of the correction of McCrary & Hunter by comparing Figures 1 and 2. A very small difference in absolute performance when performance is very good is given as much weight on the relative error scale as a larger difference in performance when absolute performance is

FIGURE 2. The results in Figure 1 plotted in terms of the percentage of total errors made at each serial position.

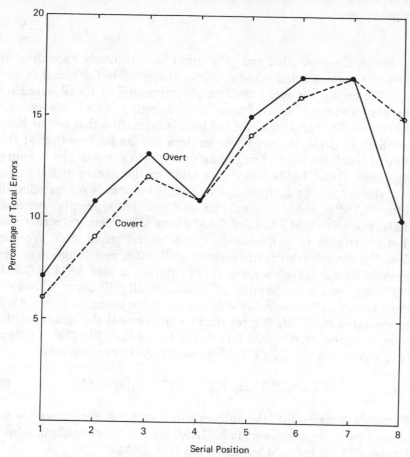

much poorer. Therefore, the serial position curves do not differ significantly at the first 7 serial positions when performance is measured relatively in terms of percentage of total errors. The last serial position shows a definite advantage for the overt repetition condition. By comparing the points of the last two serial positions in Figure 1, we see that although the performance level does not change significantly in the covert repetition condition, it shows a marked improvement from the penultimate to the last serial position in the overt repetition condition. Therefore, we can conclude, using this model, that the vocal repetition showed the largest advantage in performance only at the last serial position. This analysis also shows that the differences between the two conditions at the other serial positions can be accounted for by differences in the absolute level of performance. The later positions in the list have more errors to start with and, therefore, more room for improvement.

SAM and GAM Components

Although the preceding analysis might be intuitively appealing, it does not make explicit the processes responsible for recall in the task. To do so, we now present a formal model of recall based on the assumptions of our information-processing model. We assume that either SAM and/or GAM can hold information that can be later recalled. In SAM, the sound of an item can be held so that at the time of recall the subject can transform it into a name. The memory structure, GAM, holds a representation of the names of the items for later recall. We further assume that if an item is represented in either SAM or GAM, the subject will recall it correctly. Accordingly, assuming that SAM and GAM are two independent structures that contribute to performance in the serial recall task, we can describe the probability of correct recall, $P(C)$, as a function of the probabilities that the sound quality or the name is in SAM or GAM, respectively. The probability of correct recall will occur whenever the name of an item is in GAM. However, even though an item is not represented in GAM, correct recall will occur if the sound of the item is represented in SAM. Defining the probability that the item is in GAM and SAM as $P(GAM)$ and $P(SAM)$, respectively,

$$P(C) = P(GAM) + [1 - P(GAM)]P(SAM). \qquad (2)$$

Equation 2 states that the subject can recall the item correctly on those trials when its name is in GAM, and on those trials in which its name is not in GAM but its sound is in SAM.

As Equation 2 shows, having the sound of the item in SAM increases $P(C)$ only to the extent that the name is not in GAM. To the extent that $P(GAM)$ is large, $1 - P(GAM)$ is small and the right side of Equation 2 contributes very little to $P(C)$. Accordingly, having the sound of an item in SAM can facilitate performance only to the extent its name is not in GAM. For a fixed $P(SAM)$, the improvement in recall $P(C)$ is an inverse function of $P(GAM)$. Consider an experimental condition in which $P(SAM) = .5$, compared to a condition, $P(SAM) = 0$, in which there is no information in SAM. Figure 3 plots $P(C)$ for these two conditions as a function of $P(GAM)$. The figure shows that the absolute gain in performance given the added information in SAM decreases to the extent the corresponding name is in GAM. That is to say, the increase in $P(C)$ due to a fixed amount of information in SAM decreases as $P(GAM)$ increases.

The above analysis shows that determining the contribution of SAM in a serial recall task is a complicated matter. The investi-

FIGURE 3. Predicted results of two experimental conditions that produce values of .5 and 0 for P(SAM). The figure shows that the absolute gain in performance because of a SAM advantage is critically dependent on the overall level of performance when there is no information in SAM.

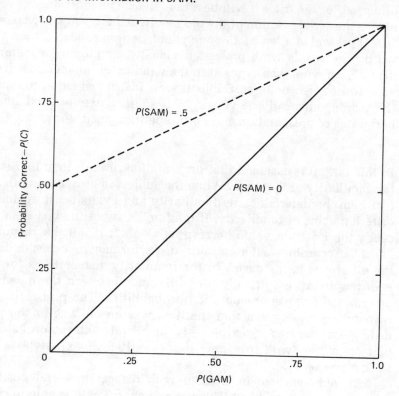

gator, therefore, cannot use the absolute differences as a measure of the relative contribution of SAM, since these differences will change with differences in the overall level of performance, even though the contribution of SAM is fixed. Accordingly, since we do not have a model of how P(GAM) changes with the serial position in the serial recall task, we cannot estimate the contribution of SAM at each serial position. We cannot rely on the serial recall task as a measure of SAM since it confounds recall from two memory structures, SAM and GAM, which cannot be disentangled in the dependent measure.

To determine the contribution of SAM we need an experimental task that can be described by an explicit process model. Employing a probe recognition testing procedure (see Chapter 16), we have

PROBE RECOGNITION STUDY

developed a process model for a memory task. The subject is presented with a sequence of items followed by a test item and reports whether the test item was in the preceding list. On half the trials the test item will be equal to one of the items in the list; on the other half of the trials it will be a new item. The independent variable is the serial position of the old test item. McNabb and Massaro (1973) presented a list of 15 one-syllable words followed by a test word. The words were presented visually, employing a memory drum. Each word was exposed in the window of the memory drum at a rate of 1/sec. or 2/sec. Subjects were instructed either to repeat the words subvocally or vocally. All subjects were tested under both rates of presentation and both repetition conditions.

Familiarity   In this task, it is assumed that presentation of each item increases the familiarity of that item. When the subject is presented with the test item, he determines its familiarity and evaluates it against a criterion value of familiarity. If the familiarity of the test item exceeds the criterion value he responds "old"; if not, he responds "new." Accordingly, the measure of performance corresponds to the difference in the means of the familiarity distributions for old and new items. Empirically, the difference between the means is determined from the recognition probabilities. The probability of responding "yes" given that the item was an old one in the preceding list—written P(yes|old)—is the hit rate and the probability of responding "yes" to a new item—written P(yes|new)—is the false alarm rate.

An old item can be defined with respect to serial position whereas a new item cannot. The experimenter will be able to compute a different hit rate at each serial position and the false alarm rate will be constant. We would, at first glance, expect the hit rate to be somewhat higher for items presented very early in the list. This primacy effect reflects the fact that the first items are perceived and learned better than later items. However, even though the first items have this advantage, they should be forgotten the most since they have the most intervening items between presentation and test. The critical independent variable is the number of intervening items between original presentation and test. Our quantification of this theory predicts that forgetting is a decreasing geometric function of the number of intervening items n. If presentation of an item increases its familiarity to α and presentation of each new item decreases the familiarity of earlier items to a proportion ϕ of α, forgetting can be described by the equation

$$d' = \alpha\phi^n \qquad (3)$$

where $0 \leqq \phi \leqq 1$. The parameter of α indexes the amount of familiarity obtained during presentation and the parameter ϕ indexes the rate of forgetting caused by new items. Taking logarithms of Equation 3 gives

$$\log d' = \log \alpha + n \log \phi \qquad (4)$$

Since ϕ must be less than 1 if forgetting occurs, $\log \phi$ will be negative. Accordingly, Equation 4 shows that each new item decreases the log of d' by a fixed amount. Plotted, this gives a straight line on a log-linear graph of d' as a function of n.

Overt vs. Covert Repetition

This model defines the basis for the theoretical analysis of the McNabb and Massaro (1973) study. The probe recognition task was carried out under two experimental conditions. In the covert repetition condition, the subjects repeated the words to themselves whereas in the overt repetition condition they repeated the words aloud. The overt repetition condition should have an advantage of synthesized auditory memory, whereas the covert repetition should not. When the subjects repeat the words aloud, they can remember

FIGURE 4.   Memory performance measured by d' values as a function of the number of intervening items for the overt and covert repetition conditions. The lines are predicted functions given by Equation 4 (after McNabb & Massaro, 1973).

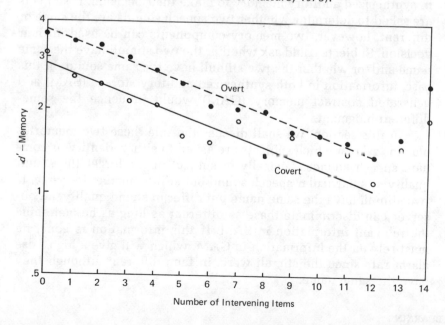

not only the name of the word but, also, what the word sounded like when they repeated it. We are still interested in whether synthesized auditory memory will be constant across all serial positions or will be more prevalent at the later serial positions with few intervening items. The answer will be determined from the parameter estimates of α and ϕ in the two experimental conditions. If saying the word aloud gives the subject more information by adding the sound in SAM, α should be larger under the overt than under the covert conditions. If the information in SAM is interfered with by new items, more forgetting should occur in the overt than in the covert conditions.

The results obtained gave a higher parameter estimate for α in the overt than in the covert repetition condition, whereas the parameter value of ϕ did not differ in the two cases. The results in Figure 4 show that forgetting is described reasonably well by Equation 4 and that the best fitting lines are parallel, reflecting a constant rate of forgetting. The higher intercept in the overt condition shows the extra familiarity obtained by the overt repetition which places the sound of the item in SAM. These results indicate that the contribution of SAM does not necessarily have to be serial position specific, but could enhance recall of all of the items in the list.

SPEECH PROCESSING In the memory-for-pitch task (see Chapter 24), the experimental situation was arranged so that subjects had to rely on the information in synthesized auditory memory to make their decision. If subjects are asked to determine whether two speech sounds are the same or different, however, two memory components can be used in their decision. Subjects could ask whether the two stimuli have the same name and/or whether the two stimuli have the same sound. In this case, information in both synthesized auditory storage (SAM) and generated abstract memory (GAM) would influence the same-different judgment.

In this section, we shall discuss the role these two memories play in tasks in which subjects are asked to either identify or compare speech sounds. Logically, a subject might forget the sound quality of a particular speech sound but still remember its name. If two stimuli have the same name but differ in sound quality, an observer can discriminate these as different as long as he maintains the relevant information in SAM. If this information is gone, he must rely on the information in GAM, which will give a high false alarm rate since the stimuli were, in fact, different although they have the same name.

SAM and GAM structures are relevant to the phenomenon of categorical perception in speech processing. Perception is said to be categorical if the subject can only make judgments about the name of a stimulus, not its particular sound quality. For example, the same speaker may repeat the same syllable a number of times. The acoustic patterns representing this syllable would differ from each other since he cannot repeat the same sound exactly. A listener who perceives the sounds categorically would not be able to discriminate any difference in the particular sound quality of each repetition of the syllable. The same listener, on the other hand, would be able to recognize a difference between any of these sounds and another syllable spoken by the same speaker. In categorical perception, the listener can recognize differences when the syllables have different names but not when they have the same name. Upon examination of the stimuli, we may find that the acoustic differences were as large when the same syllable was repeated as were the acoustic differences between two different syllables. In this case, we say that discrimination is limited by identification; the observer only discriminates that two sounds differ if he identifies them as having different names.

Subjects certainly were not limited in this way in the memory-for-pitch task. They were able to discriminate two tones as different even though they could not differentially label them. This is true for all sound dimensions: subjects can discriminate many more differences than they can identify successfully. This phenomenon, in fact, was one of the observations that convinced George Miller (1956) of the magical number 7 ± 2. Miller observed that although we could make many discriminations along a unidimensional stimulus continuum, we can identify accurately about 7 ± 2 of these stimuli. In this case, discrimination is not limited by identification, since subjects can discriminate differences along a stimulus continuum which they cannot identify absolutely.

How do we assess the relative roles of synthesized auditory and generated abstract memory in the discrimination of speech sounds? Going back to our hypothetical experiment in the penultimate paragraph, we could provide a set of stimuli by having a speaker repeat the syllables /ba/ and /da/ 3 times each (the vowel is pronounced /a/ as in hat). These sounds are recorded and used in our experiment. We must determine whether the subject's discrimination of every pair of sounds is limited by his identifying them as "different." Accordingly, we must determine how well he identifies the sounds and, also, how well he discriminates them.

CATEGORICAL PERCEPTION

SAM and GAM Contributions

In the first part of the experiment, we present one of the 6 stimuli on each trial and ask the observer to identify it as /ba/ or /da/. We obtain a number of repeated observations by selecting the stimuli randomly from trial to trial for a sequence of many trials. The dependent measure is the percentage of times each stimulus is identified as one of the two alternatives. After this identification task, we present pairs of the stimuli in a discrimination task. On each trial, we present one stimulus followed by a second one and ask the observer to report whether the stimuli were the same or different in sound quality. We warn the subjects to respond on the basis of how the sounds sound, not on the basis of their names. If they notice any difference whatsoever between the two sounds, they should respond "different" even if the sounds have the same name. Also, we tell the subjects that, on 50 percent of the trials, the two sounds will be different.

Process Model   Let us now define a process model of the two tasks in terms of our information-processing model. In the identification task, the speech stimulus initiates a preperceptual auditory storage of its sound. The primary recognition process involves a read-out of the acoustic features held there and produces a synthesized percept in synthesized auditory memory. The secondary recognition process, then, involves an analysis of the synthesized percept for its meaning, which would enter generated abstract memory. In this case, the sound quality information would be available in the synthesized percept, whereas the name information would be contained in generated abstract memory. The subject, then, would make his identification response on the basis of the name held in abstract memory.

In the same-different task, these same processes occur for each stimulus but now the subject must compare what he knows about the two sounds themselves. In this case, his memory for the sound quality of the first sound is critical, since this is what he must compare to the sound quality of the second in order to perform the task accurately. If the subject forgets the sound quality of the first sound and only remembers its name, and responds on this basis, he would show categorical perception. That is to say, he would respond "same" if he had given both sounds the same name; otherwise, he would respond "different." In contrast, if the subject remembered the sound quality of the first sound exactly, he could discriminate it as being different from the sound quality of the second sound even though they both had the same name.

In the ba–da example, we simply recorded the sounds from natural speech and did not have specific control over the physical differences in the stimuli. Usually, in this kind of experiment, synthesized speech sounds are used to control exactly the stimulus properties. Also, the stimuli differ from each other along an acoustic dimension or continuum that changes the sound gradually from one syllable into another, for example, from /ba/ to /da/. This experiment can also be carried out with nonspeech sounds, which provide a better example of how the experiment is carried out and how we can test for categorical perception.

Consider the following experiment with 7 auditory stimuli that differ along some continuum. We choose 7 pure tones from 880 to 1000 Hz. in 20-Hz. steps and randomly present one of these stimuli on each trial. The observer identifies it as either high or low. We record the percentage of times the subject responds high or low to each of the seven stimuli. The discrimination test then presents adjacent pairs of the stimuli in the same-different comparison task in which a standard stimulus is followed by a comparison stimulus. The instructions to the subject are to respond "different" if he notices any difference whatsoever in the sounds of the two stimuli. That is to say, if the two stimuli have the same name but have different sounds, the correct response is "different." Of course, we shall include "same" trials on 50 percent of the trials to keep the subjects honest.

> By comparing performance in the two tasks, we can determine to what extent the subject utilizes synthesized auditory memory in the task. If no synthesized auditory memory is employed, the subject's performance in the same-different task can be predicted exactly by his performance in the identification task. If discrimination performance is completely predicted by identification performance, then a subject should discriminate two different sounds as different only to the extent he identified them differently in the identification test. To derive the quantitative predictions, we first denote the successive stimuli used in the task as S_1, S_2, $\cdots \cdot S_7$, respectively. The probability that the subject calls one of the stimuli "high" in the identification task is denoted $P(h|S_i)$ where $i = 1$, 2, $\cdots \cdot$ 7. Similarly, $P(l|S_i)$ is equal to the probability the subject called S_i "low."

Prototypical Experiment

Now we want to predict "same" and "different" responses in the discrimination task as a function of these probabilities. Consider the case of two adjacent stimuli, S_1 and S_2, used in the same-different task. There are three kinds of trial types: S_1 could be paired with itself; S_2 could be paired with itself; and S_1 could be paired with S_2. The probability that the subject responds "same" or "different"

Quantitative Formalization

on each of these trial types can be predicted from the observed probabilities, $P(h|S_1)$ and $P(h|S_2)$, in the identification task. The probability that the subject responds "same"—$P(\text{same})$—is the probability the subject identified the standard and comparison with the same name. This could occur in two ways; he could call both the standard and comparison high or both of them low, so that

$$P(\text{same}) = P(h|\text{standard})\, P(h|\text{comparison})$$
$$+ P(l|\text{standard})\, P(l|\text{comparison}) \qquad (5)$$

The above equation states that the subject responds same if he gives both stimuli the same name. This occurs in two independent ways: he calls them both high or both low. The probability that he says "different" is the probability that he gives them different names.

$$P(\text{different}) = P(h|\text{standard})\, P(l|\text{comparison})$$
$$+ P(l|\text{standard})\, P(h|\text{comparison}) \qquad (6)$$

According to the two above equations, $P(\text{same}) + P(\text{different}) = 1$, as it should, since the subject makes one of these responses on every trial and there are only these 4 possible events that can occur on any trial.

Consider the case in which S_1 is followed by itself in the same-different task. The probability that the subject responds "same" given that the standard is equal to the comparison, $P(\text{same}|S = C)$, can be derived from Equation 5 by substituting the appropriate values:

$$P(\text{same}|S_1 = S_1) = P(h|S_1)\, P(h|S_1)$$
$$+ P(l|S_1)\, P(l|S_1) \qquad (7)$$

Analogously,

$$P(\text{same}|S_2 = S_2) = P(h|S_2)\, P(h|S_2)$$
$$+ P(l|S_2)\, P(l|S_2) \qquad (8)$$

The probability that the subject calls S_1 and S_2 "different" when one follows the other in the same-different task is equal to

$$P(\text{different}|S_1 \neq S_2) = P(h|S_1)\, P(l|S_2)$$
$$+ P(l|S_1)\, P(h|S_2) \qquad (9)$$

These equations, therefore, predict performance in the same-different task as a function of performance in the identification task, assuming that categorical perception occurs. It should be worthwhile to work out a concrete example utilizing the above predictions. Assume that the subject called S_1 and S_2 "high" 10 percent and 30 percent, respectively, in the identification test. If discrimination performance were predicted by identification performance, Equations 7, 8, and 9 would give

$$P(\text{same}\,|\,S_1 = S_1) = .1^2 + .9^2 = .01 + .81 = 82\% \qquad (10)$$

$$P(\text{same}\,|\,S_2 = S_2) = .3^2 + .7^2 = .09 + .49 = 58\% \qquad (11)$$

$$\begin{aligned} P(\text{different}\,|\,S_1 \neq S_2) &= (.1)(.7) + (.9)(.3) \\ &= .07 + .27 = 34\% \end{aligned} \qquad (12)$$

In the discrimination task, "same" trials would be presented 50 percent of the time. If we carry out a discrimination experiment with S_1 and S_2, the predicted percentage correct, $P(C)$, in the task would be the weighted average of the percentage correct for each of the three trial types.

$$\begin{aligned} P(C) &= .25(.82) + .25(.58) + .5(.34) \\ &= .205 + .145 + .17 \\ &= 52\% \end{aligned} \qquad (13)$$

If the subject consistently called both S_1 and S_2 high, predicted performance should be at chance (50 percent correct). Equations 7, 8, and 9 predict that performance should be at 100 percent, 100 percent, and 0 percent correct for the three conditions, respectively. Averaging these conditions (as we did in Equation 13) gives 50 percent, which is at chance in this task. If the subject consistently identified S_1 and S_2 differently, the equations predict that $P(C) = 100\%$.

The above predictions give performance levels when discrimination performance is limited by identification performance. In contrast, if subjects were not limited to the use of the names of the stimuli, but could reliably employ the information in synthesized auditory memory, we would expect $P(\text{different}\,|\,S_1 \neq S_2)$ to be well above that predicted by these equations. That is to say, even though subjects gave stimuli S_1 and S_2 the same name, they might discriminate the sounds as different and respond "different."

A number of early studies have shown that some speech sounds appear to be perceived categorically. Eimas (1963) used a speech synthesizer to make 13 sounds that ranged from /ba/ to /da/ to

Experimental Studies

FIGURE 5. Spectrograms of the stimuli /ba/, /da/, and /ga/, with /a/ pronounced as in *hat*. (Note that the stimuli differ only with respect to the transition of the second formant (F₂), since the first (F₁) and third (F₃) formants are the same.) (After Eimas, 1962.) Eimas (1963) made 10 other stimuli by varying the beginning point of the second formant in equal steps within the /ba/, /da/, /ga/ range. This gave a total of 13 stimuli used in the experiment.

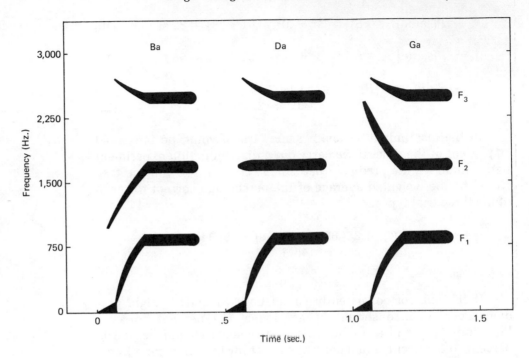

/ga/ with the vowel /a/ pronounced as in *hat*. Figure 5 shows 3 of the sounds which are always heard as /ba/, /da/, and /ga/, respectively. The figure shows that the starting point of the second formant (F₂) transition is the only acoustic difference between the 3 sounds. Therefore, it was possible to make a sound between /ba/ and /da/ by simply starting the F₂ transition at a point somewhere between the starting points of F₂ for these stimuli. Eimas, in fact, divided the range between the F₂ starting points of /ba/ and /ga/ into 11 equal steps, giving him 13 stimuli that differed only with respect to the starting frequency of the second formant. Observers first identified the stimuli as /b/, /d/, or /g/; they were then asked to discriminate them.

In Eimas' study, the subjects always heard the syllables in triads. Subjects were instructed to listen to a complete trial before making their three identification responses. For discrimination,

Eimas employed an ABX task rather than a same-different comparison task. In the ABX task, subjects are presented with a sequence of three sounds, A, B, and X, and are asked to state whether the last sound, X, is equal to sound A or to sound B. Unfortunately, the ABX paradigm may encourage the verbal encoding of the stimuli A and B since it would be very difficult to remember their auditory sound quality. Studies in the previous chapter demonstrated how a second sound interferes with the synthesized auditory memory of a previous sound. This interference is directly related to the similarity between the two sounds. In the ABX task, the B stimulus should interfere with the auditory memory of the A stimulus, leaving only its name in GAM.

Consonant and Vowel Differences

Eimas' results indicated that subjects' performance in the ABX discrimination task was limited by identification. This result was not entirely due to the ABX procedure, however, because in the same kind of experiment Fry, Abramson, Eimas, & Liberman (1962) and Pisoni (1971) showed that synthetic vowels were not perceived categorically. The spectrograms of the vowels heard as /i/ as in *heat,* /I/ as in *hit,* and /e/ as in *met* are shown in Figure 6. Pisoni (1971) showed that subjects could discriminate differences in vowel stimuli much better than was predicted by identification performance. Accordingly, these subjects showed that vowels can be held in synthesized auditory memory and that this information can improve performance in the ABX task. Pisoni's results indicate that even though the ABX procedure may encourage verbal encoding, some synthesized memory may be used in this task. The findings seem to imply that vowels can be maintained better in synthesized auditory memory than can stop consonants.

Pisoni (1973), in a same-different comparison task, has essentially replicated the differences between consonants and vowels found by Eimas and by Fry et al. For both vowels and consonants, discrimination performance with sounds that had been given different names was better than performance with sounds that had been identified as the same. However, the differences were larger for the stop consonants than for the vowels. Pisoni also employed durations of 200 and 50 msec. for the vowel stimuli. The short vowels behaved more like consonants in that discrimination functions were more accurately predicted by the identification performance. This result is reasonable, assuming that a short vowel places less information in synthesized auditory memory than a long vowel.

Why do vowels have a better representation in synthesized auditory memory than stop consonants in CV syllables? As shown

FIGURE 6. Spectrograms of the vowels /i/ as in *heat,* /I/ as in *hit,* and /e/ as in *met.* Pisoni (1971) made the 10 other stimuli by varying the location of the three formants in equal steps within the /i/, /I/, /e/ range. This gave a total of 13 stimuli used in the experiment.

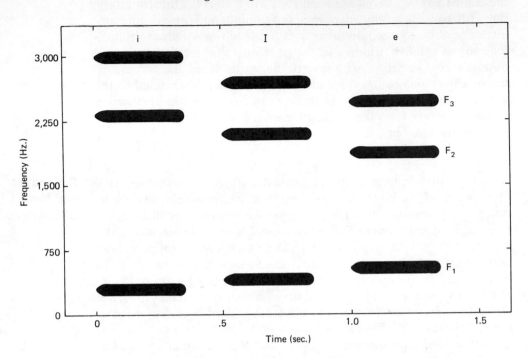

in Figure 5, stop consonants are characterized by rapid transitions of the formants toward the steady-state vowel formants. The auditory pattern of the transition would seem to be more difficult to maintain in synthesized auditory memory than the steady-state pattern of the vowel. Note also that, whereas in Figure 5 the first and third formants do not differ for the different stop consonants, in Figure 6 all three formants differ for steady-state vowels. Steady-state vowels are more pitchlike and it is easier to maintain that sound quality than the rapid transition sound of the stop consonant.

SAM for Consonants Can within-category discriminations be made with stop consonants at all? Although synthesized auditory memory is limited for stop consonants, can it be employed at some level to facilitate discrimination over that predicted by identification? Two recent demonstrations have shown that subjects can discriminate the auditory differences between stop consonants that are given the same name in identification.

Categorical perception means that if subjects give different stimuli the same label, they cannot discriminate differences among these stimuli. To test this, Barclay (1970) first had subjects identify stimuli along the /ba/, /da/, and /ga/ continuum, with the vowel /a/ pronounced as in *hat*. As in previous experiments, subjects were given the alternatives /ba/, /da/, and /ga/. The subjects consistently labeled 3 sets of the stimuli as /ba/, /da/, and /ga/, respectively. The next day, the subjects were brought back, were given a description of the stimuli, and were told that the /da/ stimuli lay between /ba/ and /ga/. The subjects were then given another identification test with the same stimuli, but were limited to the alternatives /ba/ and /ga/. If perception of /da/ were indeed categorical, the subjects should not have been able to respond differentially to the stimuli called /da/ on the previous day. We would, therefore, expect a random assignment of the responses /ba/ and /ga/ to the /da/ stimuli. However, the results indicated that the subjects did differentiate between the different /da/ stimuli. The /da/ stimuli near the /ga/ boundary were more frequently called /ga/, and the identification response, /ba/, increased reliably as the /da/ stimuli approached the /ba/ end of the stimulus continuum.

Pisoni and Lazarus (1974) showed that special training and a sensitive discrimination test can eliminate the categorical perception of stop consonants found in ABX tasks after the regular identification task. The special training involved presenting the stimuli in sequential order across the continuum and instructing subjects to listen carefully to the differences between the successive stimuli. The discrimination test involved presentation of two pairs of stimuli; one pair was always the same and one pair was always different. Subjects reported which of the two pairs was the same. These subjects, then, were trained to utilize information in synthesized auditory memory and were given a discrimination test that made it easy to do so. The subjects given the special training showed improved discrimination performance and no categorical perception. Discriminating between sounds that are usually given different names was not significantly better than discriminating between sounds that are usually given the same name.

MEMORY FOR VOICE QUALITY

The foregoing studies demonstrate synthesized auditory memory for the sound quality of speech sounds. Evidence also exists that demonstrates we can preserve a memory for the characteristics of the speaker's voice. Cole, Coltheart, and Allard (1974) presented subjects with a sequence of two letters and had them report as quickly as possible whether or not the second letter had the same name as the first. The independent variable of interest was whether the two letters were presented by same or different speakers. Since subjects would almost always be correct in this task, the reaction time (RT) of the "same" or "different" response to the second letter was the dependent variable. Certainly this task could be performed utilizing the information in abstract memory, which would simply involve a comparison of the names of the letters. In this case, it should not matter whether the letters are spoken in same or different voices. But if the sound quality of the first letter can be preserved in synthesized auditory memory, it might enhance the original recognition of the second letter and/or facilitate the comparison process.

The results indicated that subjects could respond faster on both "same" and "different" name trials when the letters were in the same voice than when spoken by different voices. Also this advantage was independent of the duration of silence separating the two letters (½ to 8 sec.). Unfortunately, these results do not locate the effect at the recognition or comparison stage of processing. It should be worthwhile to analyze a simple stage model of this task

FIGURE 7. A flow diagram of the stimulus events and the processing stages in the same-different RT task.

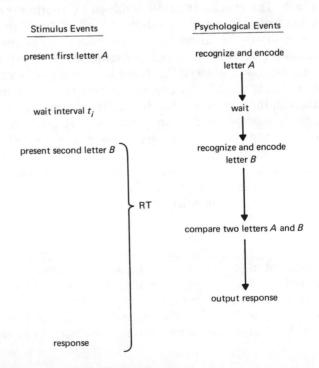

and to ask what results would isolate the facilitating effect of speaking the two letters in the same voice. Figure 7 presents a flow diagram of the stimulus events and the processing stages in the task.

The time needed to perform the three processes of recognition, comparison, and response selection contributes to the RT to the second letter. Which stage of processing is responsible for the facilitating effect of speaking the second letter in the same voice? We can be fairly sure of eliminating the response selection stage as a causal factor (see Chapters 3 and 4). The answer is known before response selection is begun and the voice of the speaker should have no effect on this process. However, the facilitation could occur at either or both the recognition and comparison stages. If facilitation occurred at recognition, this would mean that subjects can synthesize what a speaker says, remember the characteristics of the speaker's voice in synthesized form, and use this information to enhance decoding of a second signal. This interpretation agrees with the observations of Ladefoged and Broadbent (1957) that a listener's perception of a particular speech sound is influenced by the voice characteristics of the earlier speech input.

Recognition or Comparison Stage

Facilitation could also occur at comparison if the subject utilized the sound characteristics when he compared the two letters after recognition of the second letter was completed. In this case, having the letters in the same voice would facilitate their comparison. To isolate this effect would certainly be important because it would also provide substantial information about the comparison stage of processing (discussed in Chapters 3 and 4). In point of fact, the methodology studied there is the key to isolating which process is critical in the task. The additive-factor method can be used to test whether voice quality affects the recognition or comparison stage. The experimental paradigm used is the memory search task in which subjects are presented with a test list of items followed by a probe item. The subjects respond "yes" or "no" as quickly as possible, indicating whether the probe item was in tho previous list.

The significant result in this memory search paradigm is the linear increase in RT with increases in the number of items in the test list (see Chapter 4). The slope of the function provides an index of the time for the memory search and comparison of each letter. The time needed to recognize the probe item is independent of search and comparison time and contributes to the intercept value. To set up a definitive experiment would involve replicating the memory-search task with letters, while simultaneously varying the identity of the voice presenting the probe letter.

FIGURE 8. Three possible results when the number of test letters is co-varied with the identity of the voice of the probe letter. Panels A, B, and C indicate that sound quality affects recognition, comparison or both of these psychological processes, respectively.

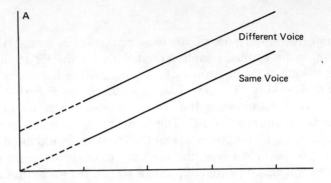

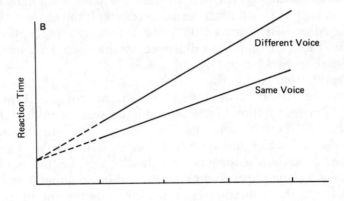

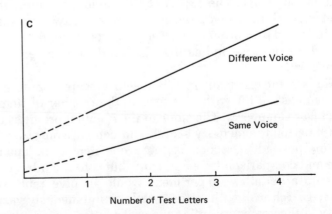

Accordingly, we covary two independent variables: the number of letters in the test list and whether the probe is in the same or different voice as the test list. Sternberg's classical finding is that RT increases linearly with increases in the number of items in the test list. How will the effect of same or different voice combine with this effect? The RT in the task can be described as a sum of three components: the time for recognition (t_R), search and comparison (t_C), and response selection (t_{RS}):

$$RT = t_R + Kt_C + t_{RS} \qquad (14)$$

where K is the number of items in the test list. The components t_R and t_{RS} contribute to the intercept, and the size of t_C determines the slope. Given this model, there are three possible results, each of which would be informative (see Figure 8). If having the letters in the same voice only facilitates recognition of the probe letter, the two curves will differ in intercept, but not in slope (Panel A). If the sound quality is only critical at the comparison stage, the slope of the function will be steeper for a probe letter in a different voice than in the same voice with no intercept effect (Panel B). Both slope and intercept will change if voice quality affects both the recognition and comparison stages of information processing (Panel C). This study remains to be carried out.

SYNTHESIZED AUDITORY AND GENERATED ABSTRACT MEMORY

We have shown that information held in synthesized auditory memory can facilitate information processing in a number of experimental tasks. Bryden (1971) has presented some evidence for our central assumption of the relative independence of synthesized auditory memory (SAM) and generated abstract memory (GAM). Subjects were instructed to attend to one ear during a dichotic presentation of numbers. Subjects listened to 4 digits coming in on one ear while simultaneously 4 digits were being presented to the other ear. The pairs of numbers were presented at a rate of 2 pairs/sec. One group of observers was required to recall the items on the attended channel first and the items on the unattended channel second. Another group of observers recalled the items in reverse order.

Overall, performance was much better for recall of the attended than the unattended digits. Figure 9 shows that the serial position curves also differed for the two kinds of items. The unattended items showed a significant amount of forgetting as new items were presented during the list presentation, whereas the attended digits did not. The basic differences between the level of

FIGURE 9. Percentage of items recalled at each serial position for the attended and unattended lists as a function of whether the list was recalled first or second. Data from those trials on which subjects reported that they followed the attention instructions (after Bryden, 1971).

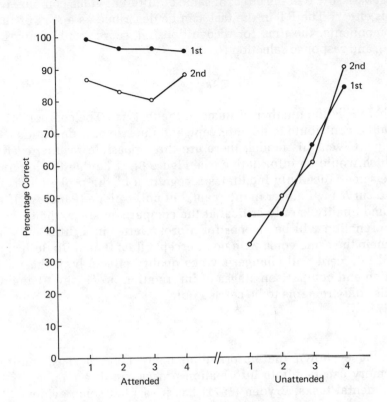

performance and the serial position curves show that the unattended digits were stored differently than the attended digits. It seems likely that the names of the attended digits were transferred from synthesized auditory memory into generated abstract memory, whereas the names of the unattended digits were not. Therefore, subjects could recall the names of the attended digits directly from GAM, whereas they had to transfer the sound of the unattended items in SAM to names in GAM before they could be recalled.

Independent Memory Structures Given that the attended and unattended items were assumed to be in GAM and SAM, respectively, at the time of recall, the forgetting functions might be used to determine the respective capacities of SAM and GAM. The rapid forgetting of the unattended items supposedly held in SAM shows that its capacity is under 4 items. In contrast, no forgetting was found for the attended items, supporting the idea that GAM can hold at least 4 items. Bryden's results, therefore, reveal very nicely the differences between SAM and GAM.

It should also take more processing capacity to recall the items from SAM than from GAM. One way to measure the amount of processing capacity that is used for recall is to compare performance as a function of whether the items are recalled first or second. To the extent that recall of some items interferes with recall of the others, we can assume that recall requires processing capacity. Accordingly, we would expect the act of reporting the unattended items from SAM to interfere more with the attended items held in GAM than recall of the attended items in GAM should interfere with the unattended items held in synthesized auditory memory. Indeed, Figure 9 shows that when the unattended items were reported first, recall of the attended items was interfered with, whereas no interference was observed with recall of the unattended items when they were recalled after the attended items. These results support the idea that SAM and GAM are two relatively independent memory structures that hold information at two different levels. In agreement with the earlier results discussed in this chapter, information in SAM can supplement the limited capacity of GAM. Such storage is extremely helpful in the processing of auditory speech sounds, since the sounds arrive sequentially; they must be held in some storage until a sufficient number of sounds come in so that meaning can be derived and placed in GAM.

Synthesized visual memory

For me 2, 4, 6, 5 are not just numbers. They have forms.
1 is a pointed number . . . 2 is flatter, rectangular . . .
3 is a pointed segment that rotates . . .
—An unidentified mnemonist quoted in
  Alexander R. Luria (1968)

Preperceptual and synthesized auditory storage have their analogous counterparts in visual information processing. Preperceptual visual images have been demonstrated in recognition masking tasks by a number of investigators (see Chapters 17 and 18). Synthesized visual memory (SVM) is memory for the visual properties or dimensions of the visual stimulus read out of preperceptual storage. This is the memory that is responsible for recognizing a familiar face or visual scene that one may not have seen for years. Although many obvious examples of synthesized visual memory exist, relatively few demonstrations have taken place in the experimental laboratory.

Color memory is critically dependent upon SVM. We have some memory for the color spectrum and have (arbitrarily) defined category names for groups of colors. We have also denoted the categories to agree with those of our neighbors so that it is possible to communicate verbally about color. Even someone who is colorblind has learned that a particular shade of gray is called green when it is the color of a lawn.

COLOR MEMORY

Early studies of SVM for color usually employed the psychophysical method of adjustment (Burnham & Clark, 1955). In this task, the subject is given a color to memorize and then sometime later must find that color among a number of stimulus alternatives. The subject must look at a number of colors before he finds the color he thinks is correct. Accordingly, although the experimenter can systematically vary the time and events before the subject is tested, he has no control over the duration of the actual forgetting interval or the number of colors perceived and processed before the subject makes his choice. Since both time and items have been found to be important in synthesized auditory memory for pitch (see Chapter 24), we might expect that they will also contribute to forgetting of color information. Furthermore, the measures of memory performance can be influenced by decision factors (for example, response biases) of the subject, which cannot be partitioned out in the method of adjustment task. Therefore, the early results are not adequate to measure memory for color given that the studies did not control these important variables.

Delayed Comparison Task

It is necessary to study color memory in a task that allows the experimenter to isolate perception, memory, and decision factors so that the forgetting of color can be accurately described. The author (unpublished) studied recognition memory for hue in a delayed comparison task. The procedure and data analysis were exactly analogous to the experiments of memory for pitch discussed in Chapter 24. The procedure, theoretical model, and data analysis discussed there can be used to work out an analogous methodology for the hue memory task.

In one experiment, a standard color was presented for .5 sec. followed by a gray color for 0, .5, or 2 sec., followed by a comparison color presented for .5 sec. The standard and comparison colors were blue-greens that differed very little in wavelength. The stimuli were Munsell color patches that are precisely specified with respect to the three visual stimulus dimensions. The value or chroma of a stimulus corresponds to its brightness, that is how much light it reflects. The saturation or purity of a stimulus provides an index of how much of the color is made up of a given wavelength and how much is contributed by white light. Light at a single wavelength is fully saturated, whereas white light has zero saturation. Finally, hue corresponds to what is usually called color and is determined by the wavelengths of the light.

As in the memory-for-pitch studies, the standard and comparison colors were very similar and could not be differentially labeled. The subject had to remember what the color looked like, not its name, on every trial. Furthermore, the standard color was randomly selected from a population of colors on every trial to prevent the subject from learning what a given standard looked like over a series of trials. These precautions insure that the experimenter is studying the storage and retention of the color that is presented on each trial.

If the subject forgot a fixed proportion of what he remembered about the standard color in each unit of time, we should be able to describe the results by our geometric forgetting equation (see Chapter 24). Plotting the d' values as a function of time on semilogarithmic graph paper, the geometric equation describes a straight line. Figure 1 presents the results of the performance of three practiced observers in this task on such a log-linear graph. Geometrical forgetting was indicated for two of the subjects since their results are described fairly well by straight lines.

FIGURE 1. Memory performance for three subjects as measured by *d'* values as a function of the duration of the forgetting interval (after Massaro, unpublished).

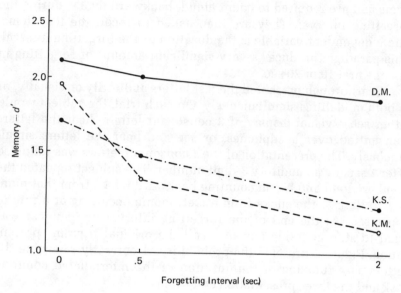

The third subject's results cannot be described accurately by a straight line. The subject appears to have forgotten much more than she should have between 0 and .5 sec., than between .5 and 2 sec., if forgetting was geometric. Hopefully, the present procedure and experiment will stimulate researchers to study memory for color, given how little we can currently say about this common function.

We have assumed that SVM is a memory structure that holds information about how things look as opposed to what they sound like or their names. Analogous to SAM, SVM has a limited capacity and information in SVM can be interfered with by requiring the observer to process new information. If interference describes the forgetting in SVM, then similarity should play a role in the amount

LETTER MEMORY

of forgetting that occurs. We would expect that visual stimuli should interfere more than auditory stimuli with items held in SVM.

Peterson and Peterson Task

Two experiments have shown that letters held in SVM can decrease the interference usually found from subsequent auditory information processing. Scarborough (1972b) presented observers with a list of letters to remember in a Peterson and Peterson (1959) memory task. In this task, subjects are presented with a list of test items and are required to count aloud, backward by 3's, during the forgetting interval. They are then asked to recall the test items. The independent variable is the duration of the forgetting interval. This paradigm produces a very significant amount of forgetting in just the first 10 or 20 sec.

Scarborough presented the test letters auditorily or visually, or in both modalities simultaneously. On each trial, the subject would either see a visual display of 3 consonant letters, hear the letters transmitted over headphones, or see and hear the letters simultaneously. The presentation of the 3 consonant letters was followed after 1 sec. by an auditory 3-digit number. The subject repeated the number aloud and began counting backward by 3's from that number, in time to the clicks from a metronome occurring at a rate of 1 per sec. At the end of the forgetting interval, the subject was cued to stop counting and to recall the original trigram presentation. Figure 2 presents the probability of correctly reporting the letters as a function of the duration of the interpolated counting task and the three presentation conditions.

Auditory vs. Visual Presentation

There are two psychological processes operating in the Peterson and Peterson task. The consonant letters must have been perceived and stored upon presentation and then remembered during the counting-backward task. Since Scarborough systematically varied the duration of the counting interval, it is possible to locate the differences between auditory and visual presentation at either or both the storage and retention stages. The figure shows that the curves intercept the Y ordinate at roughly the same point and then diverge significantly. The intercept value at zero sec. provides a measure of the original perception and storage of the stimuli, since it measures how much information the subject has immediately after the presentation of the stimuli, when no forgetting has taken place. The rate of forgetting can be determined from the slopes of the forgetting functions. According to this analysis, Figure 2 shows that the items presented auditorily are forgotten much faster than

FIGURE 2. Probability of a correct report of the stimulus trigram as a function of three presentation conditions and the duration of the interpolated counting task (after Scarborough, 1972b).

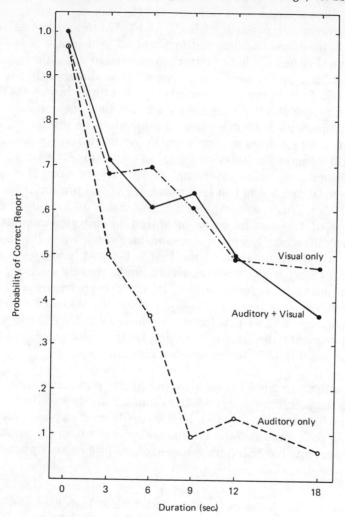

tho items presented visually. Furthermore, adding an auditory presentation to a visual one does not facilitate performance in this task. These results indicate that the items presented visually were stored differently than those presented auditorily. A good hypothesis is that the visual items were held in SVM, which would be less susceptible to interference from counting aloud than the auditory items, which would have to be held in either or both synthesized auditory (SAM) or generated abstract memory (GAM).

Shadowing   Another recent series of experiments also has isolated a visual storage mechanism with the properties of SVM (Kroll, Parks, Parkinson, Bieber, & Johnson, 1970; Parkinson, Parks, & Kroll, 1971; Salzberg, Parks, Kroll, & Parkinson, 1971). This memory appears to be relatively independent of SAM and GAM and is not as susceptible to interference from auditory verbal processing. The subjects in the task heard a list of letters presented in a female voice at a rate of 2/sec. The subjects were required to shadow, that is, to repeat back each letter as it occurred. Sometime during the list presentation, a test letter was inserted in the list. Besides shadowing, the subjects were also required to remember the test letter. The test letter was presented in a male voice for auditory presentations and on a photographic slide for visual presentations.

Auditory shadowing interfered more with memory for auditory presentations of the test letter than for visual presentations of the test letter. This result implies that the visual and auditory presentations of the test letter were stored in different memories, which are differentially sensitive to auditory shadowing. It appears that the visual presentation of the test letter was held in a visual form for memory which was relatively unaffected by auditory letters that had to be repeated aloud. It would be interesting to see whether subjects, trained to visually imagine the shape of auditory test letters, would show less forgetting during auditory shadowing. The experiments discussed later imply that this manipulation would be successful in the auditory shadowing task.

Phonemic similarity   The investigators cited above also varied the phonemic similarity between the test letter and the letters that are shadowed during the forgetting interval. Usually two letters are defined as phonemically similar if their pronunciations share a vowel sound in common. Table 1 presents the 26 letters grouped according to their phonemic

TABLE 1
Letters of The Alphabet Grouped According to Their Phonemic
Similarity. (Two Consonants are Phonemically Similar
if They Share a Vowel Phoneme in Common)

A	B	F	Q	I	O	R	W
H	C	L	U	Y			
J	D	M					
K	E	N					
	G	S					
	P						
	T						
	V						
	Z						

similarity. The results indicated that shadowing phonemically similar letters produced more interference than shadowing dissimilar letters, but only if the test letter was presented auditorily. This finding supports the hypothesis that the items presented visually were held in SVM, since we would not expect this memory to be susceptible to acoustic similarity. It remains to be seen whether the visual similarity of the letters would be a critical variable affecting storage of letter information in SVM.

Posner and his colleagues (Posner, Boies, Eichelman, & Taylor, 1969; Posner & Keele, 1967) have studied the contributions of visual codes held in SVM, using a same-different reaction time (RT) task. In this task, subjects are presented with a sequence of two letters and asked to report whether the second letter has the same name as the first. The independent variables are the temporal interval separating the two letters, and whether the second letter is physically identical to the first letter or simply has the same name. Of course, the letters have different names on half of the trials in order to keep the subject honest. The dependent variable is the time it takes the subject to make the same-different judgment.

RETENTION OF VISUAL CODES

In one experiment (Posner & Keele, 1967), a capital letter was followed by (1) a letter which had the same name but was either capital or small, or (2) a letter with a different name. The experimenters (1967) reasoned that a comparison between the RTs on the two kinds of "same" trials would provide an index of the memory code utilized by the subject. If the memory codes were identical on both kinds of "same" trials, there should be no difference in the RTs. If the memory codes were different, then the time to make the "same" judgment could differ in the two cases. Therefore, Posner and Keele looked at the RT differences between the two kinds of "same" trials. When the second letter followed the first immediately, "same" RTs were 80 msec. faster if both letters were capitals, than if a capital letter was followed by a small one. This advantage decreased with increases in the interstimulus interval. With a 1.5 sec. interval, the "same" RTs did not differ on the two kinds of trials. In another study, Posner et al. (1969) showed that the advantage of having both letters physically identical was not peculiar to matching capital letters, since small-letter physical matches facilitated "same" RTs in the same way.

These results show that presenting two letters that are both capitals or both small can facilitate the time it takes observers to

Letter Matching

determine whether the letters have the same name. This means that the observers could have utilized the visual code of the letter held in SVM in order to facilitate their comparison task. Since this advantage disappears very quickly with increases in the interletter interval, subjects probably make their comparison on a strictly name basis at longer interletter intervals. If the second letter has the same upper or lower case as the first, does it also facilitate comparison on "different" trials? Recall that in the Cole et al. study discussed in Chapter 25, having a second letter in the same voice facilitated both "same" and "different" name matches. This result does not obtain in visual letter matches; in fact, Posner et al. (1969) found that different RTs were consistently about 20 msec. longer on trials when the first and second letters were both either capitals or small than when they were not. This result indicates that the SVM for letter case is much more letter-specific than the SAM for a speaker's voice.

Interference with SVM   In a second experiment, Posner et al. presented two kinds of interference during the interletter interval. The first letter was presented for 1 sec. followed by a .5 sec. interval before presentation of the second letter. The forgetting interval was either empty, or with a visual noise field of black and white squares, or with an addition task in which the subject had to add a pair of digits. The RT advantage of responding "same" when the letters were physically identical as opposed to only nominally identical was 52 msec. when the letters were separated by the empty or noise intervals, but dropped to 14 msec. when the subjects had to perform the addition task. This result might indicate that the subject's processing capacity is necessary to maintain the visual information about the shape of the letter in SVM. If the subject is required to add two numbers, this interferes with holding the information in SVM. However, the digits to be added were also presented visually and it is possible that the recognition of the digits rather than their addition produces the interference. If processing of similar visual information interferes with SVM, it is not surprising that the noise field produced no interference, since it is qualitatively different than visual information about letter names.

How necessary is it for the subject to see the first letter to facilitate physical matches? According to our model, visual information can be placed in SVM without a visual stimulus, but through the recoding process. We can all visualize the differences between upper and lowercase letters with our eyes closed. Posner et al. (1969) and Beller (1971) have shown that the subject does not have to see the first letter to operate on the basis of a visual instead of a name code in making his same-different judgment. On some trials, the experimenters told their subjects that the second letter would definitely occur in uppercase, although it could be same or different as the first. On other trials, subjects knew it could occur in either upper or lower case. The investigators found that "same" RTs were faster in the first-mentioned kind of trials even though the first letter was presented auditorily. The result might mean that subjects generated a visual code of the uppercase form of the letter that was presented auditorily, facilitating their comparison judgment of whether the second letter was "same" or "different."

Subjects in the letter comparison task can direct their attention to either the visual form of the first letter or to its name, whichever seems to be the best strategy in the particular task. If they know that the second letter is likely to occur one way—either upper or lower case—they might concentrate on the shape of the first letter. Therefore, it will be easiest to respond "same" to the second letter when it is physically identical to the first letter. Recall that the advantage of "same" RTs on trials with same-case letters decreased with increases in the interletter interval. This result could have occurred because it is not optimal to operate solely on the basis of the visual form of the letter, since half of the same trials will be different in letter case although they have the same name.

FACES AND NAMES

Posner and his colleagues have shown how subjects could utilize information in SVM or generated abstract memory (GAM) for making a same-different comparison judgment. Subjects can maintain the visual quality of the form of an item as well as its name in SVM and GAM, respectively. If the subject focuses on the visual form of the item, this will decrease the time it takes to make "same" judgments when the form of the comparison stimulus agrees with the form of the item held in SVM. If the stimulus differs from the form held in SVM, the subject must base judgment on whether the two things have the same name.

An experiment by Tversky (1969) supports and clarifies our interpretation of how SVM and GAM operate in a same-different judgment task. In her experiment, subjects first became acquainted with different persons by learning to give different names to the schematic faces shown in Figure 3. After the names were learned, both the schematic faces and the names were used in a same-different RT task. Subjects were presented with a test stimulus for 1 sec., followed by a 1-sec. blank interval, followed by a second stimulus. The subjects were instructed to report whether the second stimulus was the same or different from the first with respect to the identity of the person, regardless of his physical representation. This experi-

FIGURE 3. The representations used as stimuli in the Tversky (1969) study.

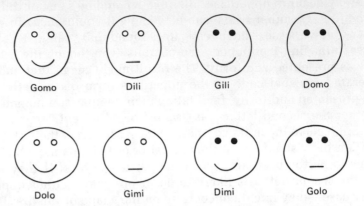

ment, then, is exactly analogous to the letter matching experiments. The experiment was partitioned into blocks of trials. In a given block of trials, the first stimulus was always presented in one representation, picture or name. The second stimulus could occur in either representation, but one representation was 4 times as likely to be presented as the other. Therefore, there are 4 possible blocks of trials. The first stimulus could always be a picture or could always be a name, and the second stimulus could more likely be a picture or a name. Practiced subjects were used and the 4 types of trial blocks were presented in a counterbalanced manner to eliminate any differences due to temporal order. A large number of trials was presented within each block of trials so that it was easy for the subject to learn whether the second stimulus was more likely to be a name or a picture. On half of the trials, the two stimuli had the same name; on the other half, they were different in name.

The same and different RTs were primarily a function of the likelihood that a particular representation would be presented as a second stimulus, regardless of the representation of the first stimulus. Both same and different RTs were faster when the second stimulus had the representation that was the most likely in that particular block of trials. For example, when a name always occurred as the first stimulus and a picture was most likely to occur as the second stimulus, RTs were faster for pictures than names on both same and different trials. Accordingly, although subjects were presented with the name of a person, they generated his pictorial representation, since the second stimulus was more likely to be a picture. In this case, when a picture was presented as the second stimulus, they would compare the picture with the representation in SVM; such comparison was very easily made. In contrast, if a name was presented second, they would be faced with comparing the name to a picture held in SVM. This would require some sort of transformation of the picture into a name or the name into a picture so that comparison could take place. The subjects took an average of 156 msec. longer when the second stimulus was presented in the unexpected than the expected representation, regardless of the representation of the first stimulus. This length of time provides an estimate of how long it took for the appropriate transformation that made a comparison possible.

Potter and Levy (1969) studied recognition memory for color pictures of typical scenes of people, animals, food, etc. Each subject viewed a sequence of 16 pictures at rates of presentation that varied from 8 pictures/sec. to 2 sec./picture. The subject was then given 32 pictures, 16 identical to those in the list and 16 new pictures. He went through this group of pictures indicating whether or not each picture was in the preceding list. The results showed a very low false alarm rate (saying a picture was in the preceding list when it was not) at all presentation rates. In contrast, the hit rate improved substantially from 15 percent at 8 items/sec. to 93 percent at 2 sec./item. The first 333 msec. of the picture appeared to be the most critical for retention; the hit rate was almost 60 percent at this rate of presentation. The last item in the list was better recognized at all presentation rates, showing that the subjects were able to continue processing this item after the slide was turned off, in agreement with the visual processing studies discussed in Chapters 17 and 18.

PICTURE MEMORY

Potter and Levy's results show that subjects have a good memory for pictorial information even when this information is presented at relatively fast rates of presentation. With slower rates of about 5 sec./item, Nickerson (1965) and Shepard (1967) showed extremely good recognition memory for lists of hundreds of pictures. In Nickerson's task, the hit rate was .87 and the false alarm rate was .02. Shepard showed increased sensitivity by using a two-alternative forced-choice task. In this case, the subject was presented with an old and a new picture and was asked to indicate which one was in the preceding list. Subjects in this task were 97 percent correct. Haber (1970) carried Shepard's study to an extreme by asking his subjects to look at 2560 photographic slides over the course of several days. Haber's patient and courageous subjects averaged about 90 percent correct in a forced-choice recognition task. These experiments demonstrate that visual memory for complex scenes is extremely good when we are tested with a recognition procedure. This visual memory also seems to improve memory performance substantially when subjects form images of words rather than trying to remember the words in purely linguistic form (Paivio, 1971).

INDEPENDENCE OF SVM AND GAM

In our model, we have assumed that the information in SVM is relatively independent of the information in GAM. Supporting this, Scarborough (1972a) has shown that subjects can retain a list of visually presented digits without a visual preperceptual image and without implicitly speaking them (placing them in GAM). Subjects were given a list of about 7 auditory digits presented at a rate of 2 items/sec. followed by a visual display of 6 letters or digits presented for 250 msec. The 250 msec. presentation and a letter-noise masking stimulus presented immediately after the display presentation insured that the items did not remain in preperceptual visual storage after presentation. Subjects were required to remember both the auditory and visual lists of items. Immediately after the visual display presentation, subjects were signalled by the experimenter to recall either the visual or auditory list. The cue signal was randomly varied from trial to trial so that subjects could not predict which signal would occur. Percentage of correct recall in this condition was compared to a condition in which subjects were told in advance to remember only the auditory or only the visual items.

The results showed no decrement in performance when the subjects were required to remember both lists instead of just one. Percentage of correct recall of the visual items was not lowered when the subjects were also required to remember the auditory items. Analogously, recall of the auditory items was not affected by whether or not the subjects were also required to remember the visual items. Since the auditory list was relatively long and probably exceeded the capacity of synthesized auditory memory, we can assume that it was held in GAM. Since GAM has a limited capacity, the auditory list should have decreased recall of the visual items if the visual items were also held in abstract memory. Since correct recall of visual items was not lowered, we have some evidence that the visual list was held in SVM independent of storage in GAM.

Scarborough also varied the delay of the report cue after the visual display offset. If the report cue was delayed, recall of the items in the visual display decreased significantly only when the subjects were also required to remember the auditory items. This result shows that, although information in SVM can supplement the information in GAM, SVM cannot hold a visual representation of a list of items indefinitely. With a delayed recall, the subject had to divide his attention between the items in GAM and SVM, since either the auditory or visual list could be cued for recall. When subjects were not required to remember the auditory items, recall of the items in the visual display did not decrease with increases in the delay of the report cue. In this case, they were able to direct their attention completely to the items from the visual display held in SVM.

The studies discussed here provide some support for the existence of a storage structure that holds visual information in perceived or synthesized form for a short time. Scarborough's (1972a) study provides one method of overcoming the span of apprehension in an experimental task. His results show that a visual list of items can be held for a very short period of time in SVM, which increases the span of apprehension. However, the information in SVM can only be held in this form for a very short period of time. When the report cue was delayed, the subjects probably found it necessary to begin transferring the items held in SVM to GAM. Since GAM has a limited capacity, they would forget some of the items already held there. The storage structure SVM plays an important role in reading, since it allows the subject to hold the visual information from the last two or three eye fixations before meaning is derived and transferred in GAM. Recall from Chapter 11, also, the importance of SVM in the perception of objects rotated in depth. There we found that the subject was able to integrate the information from the last couple of eye fixations to perceive a figure in depth.

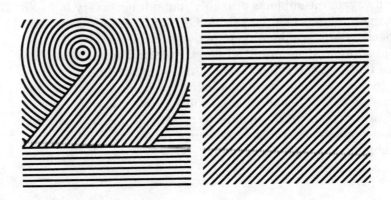

Generated abstract memory

> Ghost: *Adieu, adieu! Hamlet, remember me.*
> Hamlet: *Remember thee!*
> *Ay, thou poor ghost, while memory holds a seat*
> *In this distracted globe. Remember thee!*
> *Yea, from the table of my memory*
> *I'll wipe away all trivial fond records*
> *All saws of books, all forms, all pressures past,*
> *That youth and observation copied there;*
> *And thy commandment all alone shall live*
> *Within the book and volume of my brain*
> *Unmix'd with baser matter: yes, by heaven!*

In our model, synthesized visual and auditory memory can be transformed by the secondary recognition process into names held in generated abstract memory. This memory is called *abstract* because it is not modality-specific; it is called *generated* because the secondary recognition process involves an active generation of the synthesized information into abstract form. In this chapter, we attempt to analyze the way the forgetting of name information happens in generated abstract memory. Analogous to other memories, there are two primary causal contenders: decay and interference. Decay theory was first presented systematically in Broadbent's (1958) model of information processing (see Chapter 13). Interference theory has its origin in the concept of association outlined by the British Empiricists. Both of these theories will be presented, followed by experimental tests between the theories.

DECAY THEORY

In Broadbent's model, incoming stimuli are held in a preperceptual form along various channels. The recognition process reads out the information along one channel at a time, so that identification can take place. However, rather than passing on this transformed information to another storage structure, it is recirculated back through the original storage. This assumption eliminates the value of the information-processing approach. Information in preperceptual form certainly differs from the name information after recognition has taken place, and the storage characteristics and forgetting of both kinds of information should be both qualitatively and quantitatively different. Given this qualification, it is still possible to evaluate how forgetting of name information is assumed to occur in terms of Broadbent's model.

In Broadbent's formulation of decay theory, name information decays passively over time unless it is operated on; that is, unless it is rehearsed by the central processor. To cause forgetting, it is sufficient to distract the central processor away from this information so that its decay takes place. The activities of the central processor in the processing of new information do not in any way interfere with the previous information; only the neglect of the old causes forgetting. No forgetting will occur if the central processor is allowed to devote attention to the relevant information during the forgetting interval. Because the central processor is limited in capacity, some forgetting usually occurs, as the processor is incapable of processing new information and maintaining its attention on the old.

INTERFERENCE THEORY

In contrast to decay theory, interference theory assumes that no forgetting will occur unless intervening activity has a direct effect on the information in memory. The interference theory of forgetting assumes that two events occurring together in time become associated or linked together. Memory in this context functions to maintain the association between the two events. Using a stimulus-response model, interference theorists interpreted the two events as consisting of a stimulus and a response. The subject learns to associate stimulus (S_1) with response (R_1). This means that he has learned to associate certain features of that stimulus to that response. Now when he learns to respond to a second stimulus, S_2, with the response R_2, it is probably safe to assume that the second stimulus has some features in common with the first. This similarity between the two stimuli means that there are features in one stimulus that are associated with the response of the other. S_2 is like S_1 in some respect, and when S_2 is presented, the features that it has in common with S_1 will evoke not only R_2, but also R_1. Thus the similarity in the two stimuli produces competition between the two responses. In this way the learning of a new set of associations interferes with memory for an older set.

The critical difference between decay and interference theory, therefore, is in the way people forget. Decay theory says that one forgets when one is unable to rehearse, or chooses not to do so. The memory trace fades automatically over time unless it is renewed. Interference theory assumes that forgetting occurs when a stimulus-response association is weakened by learning of another association. If no new material was learned, the subject would remember a given association permanently. This does not happen because we continuously learn new information that interferes with the old.

In 1965, Broadbent and Gregory showed how forgetting seemed to be more dependent on the attention of the central processor than on the learning of new associations. On each trial, subjects listened to 10 letters presented at a rate of 1 letter every 5 sec. Within each set of 10 letters, 1 letter occurred twice, whereas none of the other letters were given more than once. At the end of the presentation, the subject reported which letter had occurred twice. This task required the subject to recognize and remember each letter and to determine if it was presented previously. This task is analogous to the QRST task discussed in Chapter 12, since it requires the same working memory processes.

Broadbent and Gregory Study

Simultaneously with this task, subjects were also required to perform a choice RT task. Subjects held the index finger of each hand on one of two buttons during the experiment. The buttons consisted of a ring, through the center of which a vibrating rod projected. The rod vibrated from time to time between the letter presentations. Under one condition, whenever one of the rods was felt to be vibrating, the subject was to press down on that same button. Under a second condition, when one rod vibrated, the subject was required to press the button under the finger of the opposite hand. The authors reasoned that the first task should be easier than the second because the response is more compatible with the stimulus. Thus, under the compatible response condition, when the left button vibrated the subject pressed it with the finger of the left hand. Under the incompatible response condition, when the left button vibrated the subject pressed the right button. If the second condition is more difficult than the first, this means that in a limited capacity system it requires more processing capacity than does the compatible response condition.

According to Broadbent's decay theory if the task of responding to the vibrating buttons reduces the processing capacity available for the letter memory task, then the second condition should reduce it more than the first. Subjects had longer RTs on the button-punching task in the incompatible response condition, showing that this condition was indeed more difficult. Performance in the memory task should, therefore, be worse when the button-pushing task is being done under the incompatible response condition. This is in fact what Broadbent and Gregory found: memory performance was 85 percent and 59 percent correct under the compatible and incompatible response conditions, respectively. According to Broadbent's model the subject had more time to perceive, rehearse, and update the letters in memory in the response-compatible condition. It is plausible that performance in the button-pushing task prevented rehearsal of the test items in the memory task. But it is very difficult to see how the vibration in the second task could have enough features in common with the letter stimuli to cause response competition and hence forgetting.

Mackworth Experiment

Mackworth (1964) devised an experiment in which subjects were visually presented with a row of 6 letters that they read aloud from left to right. After reading the letters, they were also required to read either a row of 5 digits or 5 color patches. In both cases, the subject had to recall the letters in sequential order immediately after reading the digits or colors. It is more difficult, as measured by RT, to identify a color patch than to name a digit. According to Broadbent, given that recognition requires processing capacity, reading the colors should take more processing capacity than reading the digits. If processing capacity is limited, requiring more of it for identification of the color patches should reduce the capacity available for rehearsal of the letters. Mackworth found that memory for the letters was, indeed, better in the case in which they were followed by the naming of digits than by the naming of color patches. Identifying new items, therefore, interfered with memory for old items as a direct function of the difficulty of recognition. Again, it is easy to understand these results in the framework of the Broadbent model. Interference theory, however, which would account for forgetting as the result of similar stimuli triggering the same response, does not fit this situation.

Interference theory might explain the Broadbent and Gregory result by assuming that performance in the button-pushing task requires some subvocal rehearsal on the part of the subject. The subject may have to instruct himself continuously, "Remember, push the right button when the left hand is vibrated." If this were the case, it seems likely that the incompatible response condition required more rehearsal than the compatible response condition. Forgetting of the letters, then, was not caused by the intervening task itself, but by the rehearsal required for the task. In this case, subvocal rehearsal, because of its similarity to letter processing, would cause interference with letter memory. Whereas in the Mackworth experiment, the similarity of the digit and color names to the letters might be proposed as the basis for interference.

Given the necessity of these post hoc explanations, the interference theorist may want to discard the assumption that similarity is absolutely necessary for forgetting. He may simply assume that intervening activity can interfere with memory even though there is no apparent similarity between the intervening processing and the memory items. Even though this assumption makes interference theory much more similar to the decay theory, the two theories still differ and can be distinguished, at least logically. Although the interference theorist cannot offer so explicit an explanation of the nature of the interference, he does not have to concede the interference assumption itself. Interference theory attributes forgetting directly to interfering activity, whereas decay theory attributes forgetting to a lack of rehearsal.

TESTS OF DECAY AND INTERFERENCE THEORIES

This makes interference theory more difficult to distinguish from decay theory but, in principle, it can be done. One difference is that, according to decay theory, forgetting must occur if rehearsal is prevented whereas, according to interference theory, it should not occur if no intervening information was processed. Providing a clear test between the two theories thus depends upon demonstrating (1) that subjects either do or do not forget over time when no new material is presented, but (2) that rehearsal of the memory items does not take place. The experimenter must prevent rehearsal, so that forgetting can occur if it is a matter of passive decay, but he must not present new material, since forgetting in this situation can be explained by decay or interference. The only way to be sure one has done this is to engage the subject's attention with another task. The catch here is that the interference theorist can always say that the new task, whatever it might be, could interfere with memory for the test items. If the subject forgot the test items, the experimenter would not know whether it was because he had prevented rehearsal or because he had required new intervening activity that interfered with memory.

Reitman Study

Reitman (1971) provided a nice experimental attempt at distinguishing between decay and interference theories. Subjects were required to remember three concrete words presented visually for 2 sec. and then were asked to recall the items at some later time. In previous applications of this task (called the Peterson and Peterson [1959] task after the investigators who first used it), the subjects counted aloud, backward by 3's, during a variable forgetting interval before recall. Results usually show about a 30 or 40 percent decrease in performance in the first 15 sec. of the forgetting interval. Both the decay and interference theories can explain this result: decay theory explains it by the amount of time that has passed while the subject was prevented by the backward counting task from rehearsing, and interference theory explains it by the interference of the counting task itself.

The counting backward task prevented rehearsal, but in doing so the subjects had to process new information. Reitman saw that the problem would be solved if the experimenter could find some means of locking the subject's attention onto a channel clear of input. That is, if the subject could be made to attend to nothing in the period between perception of the test items and recall of them, any forgetting that appeared in the results could only be attributed to decay. Reitman hit upon the task of having the subject monitor an auditory channel for a barely detectable signal. It was true that at times there would be information coming in over that channel; there would have to be an occasional input to hold the subject's attention. If the signals were properly randomized, however, there would be some trials on which nothing would occur, yet the subject would have no way of predicting this and would have devoted as much attention to monitoring the auditory channel as on any other trial. These trials, Reitman reasoned, would fulfill the condition of preventing any rehearsal of the test items while at the same time avoiding presentation of any new material.

Employing this logic, the Peterson and Peterson task was modified so that subjects were required to attend to the input coming in over headphones and to hit a button whenever they detected a 100 msec. tonal signal. The intensity of signal was adjusted so that it was just barely audible in the continuous background of white noise. With no memory task, subjects were able to detect the tone about 50 percent of the time. Here, 50 percent is much above chance since the false alarm rate was negligible. Presentation of the tone over the auditory channel was randomized in such a way that at any point in time a signal had a constant probability of occurring independent of when it last occurred. Under these conditions, it was impossible for the subject to predict when a signal would come on. The monitoring interval was 15 sec., and any number from zero to 14 tones could occur during that interval. The probability of a tone occurrence during any interval of time was set so that a trial without a tonal signal would occur 14 percent of the time. On these trials no tone would occur, but the subject should have devoted as much attention to monitoring the auditory channel on these trials as on the others. On each trial, at the end of the monitoring interval the subject recalled the three test words presented before the interval began.

Reitman was mainly interested in the small set of trials on which no tone was presented during the monitoring interval. She reasoned that here she had succeeded in engaging the subject's attention, so that rehearsal was impossible without presenting him with new material or allowing him to think of other things on his own. This situation, then, closely approximated the ideal test of decay and interference theory. Any forgetting that was observed when nothing was presented in the forgetting interval would have to be attributed to passive decay of the memory trace. Nothing had happened during the interval between perception and recall except the passage of time.

Reitman tested 18 subjects, and 13 of them showed absolutely no forgetting. At 15 sec. after perception of the display, these subjects could recall the items with 100 percent accuracy. The remaining five subjects performed between 67 and 89 percent accuracy, giving an average performance of 92 percent for the 18 subjects, much higher than performance found in the counting backwards task. A second important finding was that recall did not even decrease with increases in the number of tonal detections. Therefore, monitoring the auditory channel and tonal detection itself did not appear to interfere with memory for the test words.

It is possible that the subjects did not devote full attention to the auditory monitoring task but spent some time rehearsing the test items. To check on this, Reitman looked at performance in a control condition of the monitoring task when the subjects were not required to remember the test words. No rehearsal should have occurred here; therefore, if some rehearsal was taking place during the memory task and if rehearsal interfered with the auditory signal detection, then signal detection performance should be poorer in the recall than in the control condition. Reitman found that subjects detected the signal about 50 percent of the time in both conditions. Detection performance did not deteriorate when subjects had to recall test words at the end of the interval; therefore, Reitman reasoned, they were not rehearsing the items during this time. As a second check on rehearsal, she asked the subjects after the experiment if they were aware of being able to rehearse during the monitoring interval, and they replied that they were not.

At first glance, Reitman's study appears to provide evidence against a pure decay theory of forgetting. Subjects apparently did not rehearse and yet forgetting did not seem to occur. However, interference theory must account for the fact that detection performance does not interfere with memory for the test words. The theory could fall back on the concept of similarity but we saw that this variable is not always critical. If anything, Reitman's experiment seems to present a problem for both decay and interference theories.

A number of problems in Reitman's experiment will be quickly noticed by both decay and interference theorists. Most critical is the incomplete experimental design, since she did not measure performance at different forgetting intervals, but only at 15 sec. after the word presentations. To show that no forgetting occurred, it is necessary to show that the subject recalled as much 15 sec. after the monitoring interval as he did immediately after presentation of the test list. Reitman believed she had done this by showing that 15 sec. after the test word presentations, performance was 100 percent correct. The problem here is that this "ceiling" effect could have hidden any forgetting that did take place. Subjects may have learned the words so well that, even though some forgetting occurred, performance was still perfectly accurate 15 sec. after presentation. The test would have been more powerful if the experimenter could have presented a larger number of words for memory so that performance would not have been perfect even if tested immediately. Then, if memory were tested after different monitoring intervals, the rate of forgetting could have been determined by looking at the slope of the forgetting function. Shiffrin's (1973) study corrects for these methodological difficulties.

Shiffrin Study Shiffrin (Experiment III) made four modifications of the basic Reitman procedure. First, he presented 5 consonants for the test items for 3 sec. Second, he systematically varied the duration of the signal detection task at 1, 8, and 40 sec. Third, after the signal detection task, the subjects were also required to perform an addition task for 5 or 30 sec. Subjects saw a 3-digit number followed by a single digit every 2 sec. The subject's task was to perform a running addition of the numbers. Fourth, subjects were given monetary incentives to perform the detection and addition tasks as accurately as possible.

Given that the addition task is similar to counting backwards, we would expect it to interfere with memory, whereas the signal detection task should not interfere if Reitman's findings were valid. This expectation was obtained, as can be seen in the forgetting functions shown in Figure 1. The duration of the signal detection task had no significant effect on performance, whereas increasing the duration of an addition task lowered performance significantly. In agreement with Reitman's study, signal detection performance was also not affected by the addition of the memory task. These results support our interpretation of Reitman's findings: time without rehearsal is not sufficient for forgetting.

The ultimate acceptance of either decay or interference theory will depend on which theory best describes forgetting. In decay theory, time is the critical independent variable, whereas interfering activity is critical for interference theory. One popular test between

FIGURE 1. Probability of recalling the test items as a function of the duration of the signal detection task and the duration of the addition task (after Shiffrin, 1973).

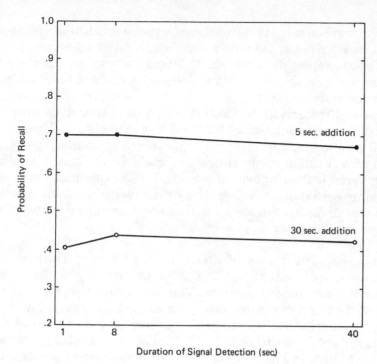

these two theories has been to vary the rate of presentation of a list of verbal items and to ask subjects to recall them immediately. Experimenters reasoned that faster rates should lead to less forgetting according to decay theory since there would be less time between presentation and test. However, these experimenters failed to realize that there were two important psychological processes in the task: perception and memory. The rate of presentation might affect both of these processes in different ways so that the results would not be informative with respect to the nature of the forgetting process.

A second problem with these studies is that subjects were permitted a free recall; hence their rehearsal and recall strategies were not under experimental control. This paradigm does not allow one to describe the forgetting that occurs, since the actual forgetting interval and the interference activity varies, depending upon the strategy of the subject. It is necessary to devise an experimental paradigm that can measure perception and memory directly as a function of either time or the number of interfering items. The suitable paradigm is a probe recognition or recall task in which the subject only responds with 1 item per trial.

Probe Recall   Waugh and Norman (1965) employed a probe recall study in which subjects were presented with a list of items followed by a test item and had to report the item that followed the test item in the preceding list. Waugh and Norman explicitly instructed their subjects to concentrate on the current item being presented and not to rehearse earlier items in the list. This instruction was given to eliminate differences in rehearsal for the different items as a function of serial position. Accordingly, any differences in memory performance as a function of serial position could be attributed to some other variable than amount of rehearsal. The experimenters could, therefore, determine whether time or number of items is a better predictor of changes in memory, thus providing a test between interference and decay theories.

Waugh and   Waugh and Norman's test of interference and decay theories was to
Norman Study   vary the rate of presentation of the list and to compare the forgetting functions under two rates. The forgetting function was determined by systematically testing the subject for different items in the preceding list. A list of 15 digits was presented at a rate of 1 or 4 digits per sec. There were 1, 2, 3, 4, 5, 6, 8, 10, or 12 digits between the tested item and its presentation in the list. Figure 2 presents the percentage of correct recall as a function of the number of interpolated digits between a digit's original presentation and its test under two rates of presentation. The results show how quickly forgetting occurs at both rates of presentation. However, the two curves drawn through the points illustrate a systematic difference between the forgetting functions under the two rates of presentation.

The function describing forgetting at a rate of presentation of 4 items/sec. starts out lower and ends up higher than the function describing forgetting when the items are presented at 1/sec. The intersection at the Y ordinate provides some measure of the original perception and storage of the digits, whereas the slope of the curves should provide an index of the rate of forgetting. According to this analysis, the items presented at 1/sec. were better stored but forgotten faster than the items presented at 4/sec. Thus, the results illustrate the importance of our stage analysis of the memory task. Every memory task contains both storage and retention stages which must be isolated in both the experimental design and theoretical description. The Waugh and Norman task allows us to see

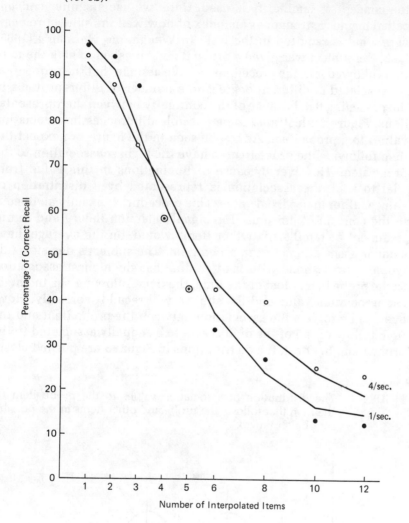

FIGURE 2. The percentage of correct recall as a function of the number of interpolated items between presentation of the digit and its test under two rates of presentation (after Waugh & Norman, 1965). The lines are predicted functions given by Massaro (1970b).

the effects of each of these stages independently, whereas the earlier free recall experiments did not. Accordingly, it is clear that the results must be described by a theory that can account for the differences in the original storage and the differences in forgetting rates under the two rates of presentation. A simple decay or interference theory based on time or items will not suffice.

PERCEPTUAL PROCESSING THEORY

One theory that describes these results has been presented by the author (1970b). The theory is similar to the analysis presented in the previous chapters on auditory and visual memory. In describing storage and forgetting in synthesized auditory and visual memory, the concept of familiarity is used. Here, we use a similar concept called memory strength as an index of how well the subject remembers what is required in the task. In Waugh and Norman's (1965) task, the subject was given a probe item and asked to give the item that followed it in the preceding list. We assume that the probe item is associated in different degrees to a number of different items in the preceding list, because of the contiguity between their presentations. Figure 3 illustrates some possible differences in association values to a probe item. As can be seen in the figure, we expect the item following the probe item to have the highest association to the probe item. However, because of fluctuations in this value from trial to trial, the association is represented by a distribution of values rather than a fixed value. This procedure is exactly analogous to the concept of noise used in signal detection theory and in our treatment of familiarity. Other items would, on the average, have smaller associations to the probe item. The subject's decision rule would be to respond with the item that has the highest association to the probe item. Most of the time, the item following has the highest association value and the subject will recall it correctly. However, as he forgets the association between the probe item and the item following, all of the digits seem to be equally associated to the probe item. In effect, the distributions in Figure 3 are pushed closer

FIGURE 3. The distribution of association values to the probe item for the item that follows the probe and other items in the possible set of alternatives.

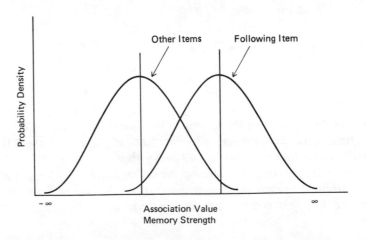

together so that the subject becomes more likely to respond with a wrong item.

The two main assumptions of the above-mentioned theory describe changes in memory strength of an item as a function of perceptual processing. Perceptual processing simply refers to the analysis of information in a sensory input used to recognize and remember the stimulus. We have seen that recognition requires an analysis of the input held in storage so that a match can be found in long-term memory. After identification of the item, further perceptual processing is necessary to remember or store the item. For example, to perform correctly in the Waugh and Norman study, the subject must remember the sequential order of the items so that he will be able to recall the item that followed the probe item in the preceding list. The first assumption of the theory is that memory for an item is directly related to the amount of perceptual processing of that item. Since an item is processed during its presentation, memory strength will increase with increases in the presentation time of the item. The second assumption is that memory for an item is inversely related to the amount of perceptual processing of other items. Accordingly, the amount of interference that a retroactive item produces will increase as the duration of the retroactive item increases.

These two assumptions qualitatively predict Waugh and Norman's results. The first assumption predicts that the items presented at 1/sec. will have more memory strength after their presentation than will items presented at 4/sec. The longer the presentation time of an item, the more time the subject rehearses it, providing a stronger memory trace at presentation. The second assumption predicts that the degree of interference with earlier items produced by a new item is directly related to the amount of processing the new item receives. Since items presented at 1/sec. receive more processing, they will interfere more with earlier items than items presented at 4/sec. We now develop a quantitative formulation of the theory to see if these assumptions can also give a quantitative description of the results.

The first assumption in quantitative form is that the perceptual processing of an item increases its memory strength according to a negatively accelerating growth function of time:

Quantitative Description

$$s(t_s) = \alpha(1 - \theta^{t_s}) \tag{1}$$

where $s(t_s)$ is the memory strength of the item after a presentation time of t_s sec. Presentation time includes both the duration of the item and the silent interval afterwards. Equation 1 indicates that the memory strength of a single item approaches a finite asymptote α at a rate θ.

Equation 1 is the same growth function used earlier in describing the recognition of visual and auditory items in Chapters 18 and 22. Memory for an item parallels its recognition. To the extent that an item is perceived clearly, it will be stored clearly in memory. Therefore, if a subject recognizes an item better, we expect him to recognize or recall it better in a later memory test. The parameter values of α and θ can also be interpreted as they were in the analysis of recognition. The parameter value α provides an index of the amount of available information in the stimulus. The rate at which this information is processed for memory is reflected in the value of θ.

The second assumption is that the perceptual processing of a new item decreases the memory strength of earlier items. The amount of interference of a new item, however, is positively related to the amount of perceptual processing that a new item receives. From Equation 1, it can be seen that the total amount of processing of an item increases with increases in its presentation time. However, perceptual processing eventually reaches an asymptote α, so that no further information can be derived from the item. In this case, the item produces no further interference on the memory of earlier items. More specifically, Equation 1 shows that the absolute amount of processing decreases during the presentation time of the item. This means that each additional unit of presentation time adds a smaller absolute amount to the item's memory strength. Since there is a direct trade-off between processing a new item and forgetting an old, each additional unit of presentation time of a new item subtracts a smaller amount from an old item's memory strength.

To put this assumption into quantitative form, consider first the case where a test item is presented for memory followed by a single retroactive interference item. The proportion $\phi(t_I)$ of memory strength of the test item remaining after presentation of the retroactive item for t_I sec. is given by the equation:

$$\phi(t_I) = 1 - \lambda(1 - \gamma^{t_I}) \tag{2}$$

where $0 \leq \lambda \leq 1$ and $0 \leq \gamma \leq 1$. Equation 2 shows that the proportion of memory strength $\phi(t_I)$ remaining after presentation of a new item is inversely related to the duration of the new item. However, a new item's interference does not increase continually with increases in its presentation time. Equation 2 shows that the proportion $\phi(t_I)$ of memory strength remaining must be at least $1 - \lambda$, regardless of the duration of the interference item. This follows from the fact that γ^{t_I} goes to zero with large increases in t_I.

Equation 1 gives the memory strength $s(t_s)$ resulting from a presentation time of t_s sec. The value $\phi(t_I)$, given by Equation 2 is the proportion of memory strength retained after presentation of a retroactive item lasting t_I sec. Therefore, the memory strength $s(t_s, t_I)$ of an item presented for t_s sec. followed by a retroactive item presented for t_I sec. is equal to:

$$s(t_s, t_I) = s(t_s)\phi(t_I) \qquad (3)$$

where $s(t_s)$ and $\phi(t_I)$ are given by Equations 1 and 2, respectively.

Next, consider the present case in which a complete list of items is presented. We assume that the items are homogeneous so that each item in the list of items has a fixed amount of information. Furthermore, subjects are instructed to process the items in the same way; therefore, α should be the same for all items. If the items are processed at a constant rate within a list, each new item is learned to the same degree and produces the same amount of interference with earlier items. It follows that the memory strength $s(t_s, t_I, n)$ of an item of presentation time t_s after n retroactive items, each lasting t_I sec., is given by the equation:

$$s(t_s, t_I, n) = s(t_s)\phi(t_I)^n \qquad (4)$$

The values of $s(t_s)$ and $\phi(t_I)$ are given by Equations 1 and 2, respectively. Equation 4 indicates that each retroactive item decreases memory of an earlier item to some constant proportion, $\phi(t_I)$, of its previous memory strength.

Equation 4 is in the same form as the quantitative theory presented in Chapter 16. We saw there that taking logarithms simplified our analysis. Taking the logarithm of Equation 4 gives:

$$\begin{aligned} \log s(t_s, t_I, n) &= \log s(t_s) + n \log \phi(t_I) \\ &= \log s(t_s) + n \log [1 - \lambda(1 - \gamma^{t_I})] \end{aligned} \qquad (5)$$

Consider a list of items given at a fixed rate of presentation. In Equation 5, $\log s(t_s)$ is the memory strength immediately after an item's presentation. Given that $[1 - \lambda(1 - \gamma^{t_I})]$ will be less than 1 if either λ or γ are less than 1, $\log [1 - \lambda(1 - \gamma^{t_I})]$ will be negative. Accordingly, Equation 5 can be written

$$\log s(t_s, t_I, n) = \log s(t_s) - n|\log[1 - \lambda(1 - \gamma^{t_I})]| \qquad (6)$$

where the verticals represent the positive value of $\log [1 - \lambda(1 - \gamma^{t_I})]$. Equation 6 shows that $\log s(t_s, t_I, n)$ will be equal to $\log s(t_s)$ immediately after its presentation, that is, when $n = 0$. When $n = 1$ with 1 intervening item, $\log s(t_s)$ is reduced by the positive value of $\log [1 - \lambda(1 - \gamma^{t_I})]$. With each intervening item, $\log s(t_s)$ is decreased by this same fixed amount. Thus, $\log s(t_s, t_I, n)$ should be a linearly decreasing function of n with a Y intercept of $\log s(t_s)$ at $n = 0$.

Experimental Tests The independent variable—rate of presentation—will affect the Y intercept and the slope of the linear function in the following way. Since $\log s(t_s)$ increases with increases in the presentation time of an item, the intercept of the function should increase with decreases in the presentation rate. Since the amount forgotten due to another item's presentation is directly related to t_I, the slope of the forgetting function should be steeper as the presentation time (t_I) increases. That is, subjects should forget at faster rates as we decrease the rate of presentation.

Theory quantitative predictions of the theory were tested against Waugh and Norman's results. The observed data are in terms of percentage of correct recall as a function of serial position and rate of presentation. The theory describes changes in memory strength values—the distance between the means of the two memory strength distributions in Figure 3. The subjects had 10 possible response alternatives in the task and were forced to recall a digit on each trial. Therefore, the proportions correct can be translated into strength values using a method analogous to the calculation of d'. The strength values were taken from a set of tables given by Elliot (1964), who has computed strength values as a function of percentage correct and the number of alternatives in the response set. The predictions of the theory (Equation 4) were determined by finding the parameter values for α, θ, λ, and γ that minimized the squared deviations between the predicted and observed d' values. The computer search routine described in Chapter 10 was also used here. This routine searches a parameter space defined by the experimenter for the optimal parameter values.

Predicted d' values can then be translated back into percentages for comparison with the observed percentages of recall (see Figure 2). The predicted and observed d' values of the Waugh and Norman study are shown in Figure 4. The memory strength values are plotted against the number of interpolated items as a function of the rate of presentation. As predicted by Equation 5, the figure indicates that log memory strength is a simple linear function of the number of interpolated items (n). Furthermore, the forgetting function is steeper for the slower than for the faster rate of presentation.

FIGURE 4. The predicted and observed memory strength values for the Waugh and Norman (1965) study as a function of the number of interpolated items and the rate of presentation.

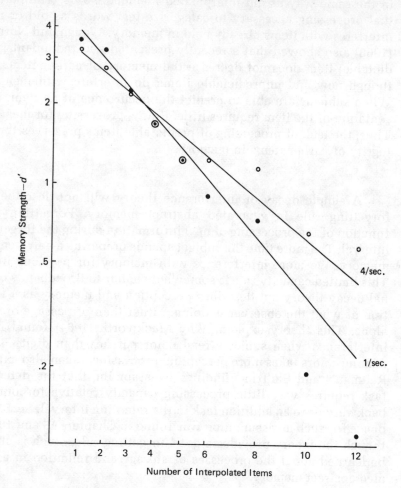

This result indicates that, as predicted, the rate of forgetting as a function of the number of items increases as the rate of presentation is decreased.

The analysis of the Waugh and Norman (1965) study supports the idea that perceptual processing of new items interferes with retention of old items in memory. Norman and Waugh (1968) presented a list of 16 memory words followed by a test list of 10 words. The subject's task was to indicate whether each test word had occurred in the preceding list. With this procedure the experimenters were able to evaluate the interference effect of both interpolated memory items and test words. The results showed that each additional test word decreased retention of the memory words in the same way as did interpolated memory words. The perceptual processing necessary to categorize test words as old or new interferes with items already held in memory. Waugh and Norman (1968) also showed that a recently presented and redundant (predictable) item does not decrease the memory of earlier items, although new and unpredictable items do interfere with memory. When subjects are able to predict the occurrence of an item, presentation of the item requires little, if any, processing for memory. Thus, the lack of processing of predictable items preserves the integrity of earlier items in memory.

A simple decay or interference theory will not describe the forgetting rule in generated abstract memory. Forgetting is a function of the processing of new information during the forgetting interval. The more time the subject spends preparing a new item for memory, the more interference with memory for previous items. This limited capacity rule is somewhat similar to Broadbent's original decay theory but describes perception and memory as a function of what the observer is doing, rather than of passage of time alone. This theory explains why Mackworth (1964) found more interference when subjects read color patches than digits, since naming colors takes more perceptual processing. It can also explain Reitman's and Shiffrin's findings by assuming that the detection task requires very little processing capacity relative to counting backward or to an addition task in the retention interval. Some evidence for such an assumption was found in Chapters 15 and 16. Although the theory provides a good forgetting rule, much is still to be learned about the processes of storage and retention in generated abstract memory.

In our study of memory, we have relied on experimental procedures that control exactly the events between presentation of a memory item and its later test. There are critical design problems with other procedures, such as a free recall test in which the subject recalls all of the words in whichever way he chooses. Faced with the free recall protocol of a subject, the experimenter cannot isolate the psychological processes responsible for performance. Memory for an item is a joint function of perceptual, mnemonic, and decision processes and each of these must be evaluated exctly to make sense of the results.

As an example, consider the problem confronting the experimenter when he varies the rate of presentation in a free recall task. Subjects might be presented with a list of 24 words at a rate of 1 or 2 sec. per item. We know that the additional study time should enhance the storage of each of the items in memory. This same additional time, however, will probably produce additional interference with the retention of other items in the list. The helpless experimenter has no way of determining the operations of each of these processes; hence, he cannot develop an understanding of how each of these processes operates.

Long-term memory

*If an object did not appear similar to itself, if
recurrences of an event did not seem the same, if
members of a class bore no resemblances to one another,
if relations could never be seen as alike, in short, if
every event was new and unfamiliar, the commonplace
stability of the perceptual universe could never be
constructed out of the raw material of our experience
and the world would necessarily remain a blooming,
buzzing confusion.*
—George A. Miller (1956)

Our study of the early stages of information processing is heavily
dependent upon certain implicit assumptions about long-term memory. The psychological processing of a stimulus event is continually
interpreted in terms of the knowledge the observer brings to the
given task. For example, we saw how subjects could utilize the
spelling rules of English orthography to facilitate the perception of
letter strings. Language users also utilize phonological, syntactic,
and semantic rules in the processing of language. All of this information must be stored in long-term memory, making its capacity
much larger than the other storage structures studied earlier.

How do we go about studying long-term memory? One method is to **FORGETTING**
present subjects with material to be learned, and then wait a sufficiently long period of time before testing to ensure that whatever
information is recalled must be recalled from long-term memory.
Analogous to our short term memories, this approach should allow
us to determine how forgetting occurs in long-term memory, the
nature of memory search strategies in long-term memory, and possibly the form of the structure of long-term memory. Wickelgren
(1972) has traced out long-term memory forgetting over a time span
up to 2 years. These studies utilize the same methodological and
procedural techniques that we analyzed in studies of short-term
memory. The interested reader is referred to the original paper for
the methodological details and results. This chapter concentrates

on experimental paradigms that have not yet been discussed for our studies of long-term memory.

TIP OF THE TONGUE One unique approach to the study of long-term memory is to ask subjects what they already know, rather than to have them learn something new. Brown and McNeill (1966) capitalized on a phenomenon that we all have experienced: a "tip of the tongue" (TOT) state. In this state, an individual is unable to remember a word that he is sure he knows. The experience that he knows this particular word is usually accurate, because he may eventually recall the word days later, be able to recognize it correctly, or be able to give partial information about the word. Brown and McNeill successfully induced the TOT state in some subjects some of the time by presenting them with a definition of an uncommon English word and asking for the word. Subjects, given the definition of a word, sometimes entered the TOT state. In this state, subjects were in mild torment trying to recall the correct word. Brown and McNeil encouraged their subjects to give all of the words that came to their mind; the subjects were also asked the first letter and the number of syllables of the word they were trying to remember.

Given the definition of *sextant,* "a navigational instrument used in measuring angular distance, especially the altitude of the sun, moon, and stars at sea," the TOT state was induced in 9 out of 56 subjects. Some of the words subjects gave were *astrolabe, compass, dividers, protractor, secant, sextet,* and *sexton.* The first four words are similar in meaning to the target word, whereas the last three are similar in sound and spelling. Some of the words similar in meaning could be traced directly to certain parts of the definition. For example, *protractor* is used in measuring angular distance but, of course, not of the stars at sea. The semantic confusions show that words with similar meanings can be thought of as being stored and/or retrieved together or substituted for each other.

The similar sounding items show that the perceptual description of words must be stored along with their meaning. We can assume that some subjects were able to retrieve the correct concept given the meaning, but had only partial information about the perceptual properties of the word corresponding to that concept. Analyses of the physical similarity between the correct word and the words recalled that were similar in sound indicated that the number of syllables of the word, the primary stress of the word, and its first and possibly its last letter were the most prevalent features. This result shows that subjects can have partial information about the sound of a word corresponding to a concept, with certain attributes more prevalent than others. The final interesting result of the Brown and McNeill (1966) study is that subjects knew how much they knew. That is, subjects knew that similar sounding words were not correct but that they were, in fact, similar sounding.

Brown and McNeill's results can be used to develop a model of the way the meanings of words are stored in long-term memory. This model is compatible with the model we developed earlier for visual and auditory recognition. We assume that long-term memory contains the equivalent of a dictionary or a lexicon with two distinct dimensions. These dimensions are perceptual and conceptual representations. The perceptual representation describes the sound of the word and the sight of the word. Brown and McNeill's results reveal that the number of syllables, the primary accent, and first and last letters are important attributes of this perceptual representation. The conceptual representation contains, in some abstract form, the meaning of the word. Each perceptual code is associated with one or more conceptual codes and each conceptual code is associated with one or more perceptual codes. A perceptual code can be associated with more than one conceptual code because the English language contains homophones (seen, scene); the same conceptual code can be associated with different perceptual codes because of synonyms. Figure 1 illustrates our model of the secondary recognition process.

In the processing of language, we have postulated that subjects attempt to find perceptual codes in long-term memory that match the information held in synthesized auditory or visual memory. This is the process of secondary recognition, the outcome of which is the location of a perceptual and, therefore, a conceptual code in long-term memory. Location of the perceptual code is usually sufficient to take us directly to meaning, since the perceptual and conceptual codes are stored together. Brown and McNeill reversed the process by presenting subjects with information that should be contained in the conceptual code and then asking them for the associated perceptual code.

How can this model explain Brown and McNeill's results? We must explain both the semantically related and perceptually related confusions. For the perceptually related confusions, we can assume that the subject was able to locate the correct conceptual and, thus, the perceptual code in long-term memory, but that the attributes of the perceptual code were not completely available. Therefore, the subjects simply generated whatever words they could bring to mind, based on this partial information. Subjects were not sure of

PERCEPTUAL AND CONCEPTUAL CODES

FIGURE 1. A model of the secondary recognition process. The process attempts to achieve a match between synthesized visual and/or auditory information with a representation in long-term memory.

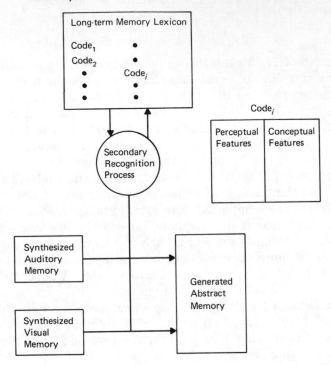

their responses because they knew all of the attributes were not available. Conceptual confusions show that the correct conceptual code was not always located given the definition. If the correct conceptual code corresponding to a definition was only partially defined, a subject might find a better match of the definition with another "incorrect" conceptual code. In this case, the meaning of the word would be semantically similar to the correct word even though it was incorrect.

Henley (1969) provided another important technique that can be used to study the structure of long-term memory. She was interested in the relationship between animal names. A dog has certain properties or features that distinguish it from a horse and so on. Henley asked, What dimensions are important in the meaning of animal names? For example, how does a mouse differ from an elephant? Most people would agree that size is the most distinguishing factor between these two animals. In contrast, a deer and a gorilla seem to be about the same size, but differ in ferocity. To get subjects to compare animals in this way, Henley asked them to rate the amount of dissimilarity between two animals on a scale from 0 (no difference) to 10. She used 30 animals and presented subjects with all possible pairs, one pair at a time.

DISSIMILARITY RATINGS

The dependent measure in this experiment is a matrix of dissimilarity ratings. The dissimilarity of each animal to every other animal would be represented by a number between 0 and 10. The investigator faced with a dissimilarity rating for all possible pairs of 30 animals is unable to determine how many dimensions were important in the subject's ratings. There is a mathematical procedure called multidimensional scaling which aims to represent the animals in an n-dimensional Euclidean space so that the distance between two animals would be directly related to the rated amount of dissimilarity. In addition, the analysis provides the representation with the smallest number of dimensions possible. In our earlier examples, we said that subjects might judge the dissimilarity of the animals on the basis of only size and ferocity. In this case, the multidimensional scaling routine would indicate that the animals can best be represented in a two-dimensional space. The multidimensional routine cannot label the dimensions but simply places animals in the space. The experimenter must use his ingenuity in finding dimensional names or concepts that describe the placement of the animals. The experimenter would be justified in labeling the two dimensions *size* and *ferocity* if the animals were arranged from small to large and gentle to fierce, respectively, on the two dimensions. The relationship between the animals could then be seen directly on a simple two-dimensional plot. Animals judged to be very dissimilar would be very distant spatially, whereas animals judged to be similar would be represented very close together.

Animal Space

Henley found that three dimensions were necessary to describe the dissimilarity ratings of the animals. Three dimensions or attributes seemed to be important to the subjects in rating dissimilarity. Figure 2 plots the spatial relationship between her selected set of animals in a way that best describes the dissimilarity ratings. The three dimensions seem to correspond to the attributes of size, ferocity, and humanness although it may not be possible to describe each dimension in terms of a single word. The dimensions may be more complex and difficult to specify exactly. This spatial structure was also found when other methods, such as a method of association

FIGURE 2. Spatial relationship between the animals along the dimensions that best describe the dissimilarity ratings (after Henley, 1969).

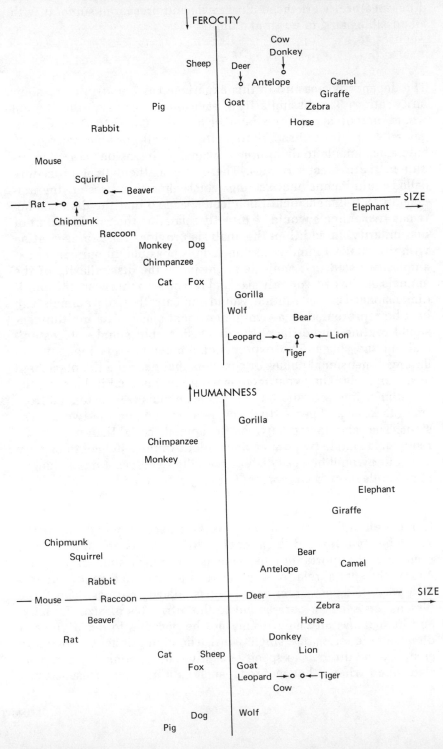

were used. In this case subjects were required to respond with the animal word that came to mind upon presentation of a test word. The test words were the 30 animals' names. In this instance, animals were considered to be similar to the extent they were given as responses to each other. The multidimensional scaling routine revealed the same structure for these responses as for the dissimilarity ratings.

In terms of our model, subjects performed the dissimilarity rating task by comparing the conceptual codes corresponding to the animal names. Subjects could evaluate the overlap in the definitions and respond accordingly. In the association task, their response rule might be to respond with the word whose conceptual code overlaps the most with the test word. Since, in both cases, three dimensions seemed to be important, the organization of the conceptual codes might be said to be structured along only these three dimensions. Henley's results reveal that it is reasonable to represent the conceptual codes of animals in a multidimensional space with roughly three dimensions. Given this structure, investigators have devised experimental studies to determine how we operate on the stored information in order to carry out certain cognitive tasks.

ANALOGIES

In the first task we shall study (Rumelhart & Abrahamson, 1973), subjects were required to complete analogies of the form A:B as C:——. For example, a subject might be given the problem:

> fox:horse as chipmunk:——.
> Answer with one of these alternatives:
>   a. antelope
>   b. donkey
>   c. elephant
>   d. wolf

Rumelhart and Abrahamson formulated a model that predicts the solution to the analogy is an animal that has the same relationship to chipmunk as horse has to fox. Therefore, the subjects' solutions to these animal analogies would be described in the framework of the semantic space given by Henley's analysis. Consider the relationship between fox and horse in the above analogy. According to Henley's multidimensional analysis, a fox can be considered to be about 60 units smaller, 65 units fiercer, and about 10 units less humanlike than a horse. A chipmunk can also be represented along these three dimensions, and the ideal solution would be an animal that is 60 units larger, 65 units less fierce, and 10 units more humanlike than a chipmunk. Of the four alternatives the best solution to this problem is antelope. Wolf is a particularly bad choice since it is much less humanlike than a chipmunk. Elephant is too large. Donkey is the next poorest choice because it is significantly less humanlike than the chipmunk. The best solution is antelope, although it need not be considered an ideal one. The ideal solution would be a nonexistent animal with the properties described above. The results of the experiment generally supported Rumelhart and Abrahamson's model of analogical reasoning.

MEMORY SEARCH AND COMPARISON

Homa (1973) has shown how memory search and retrieval can be influenced by semantic properties. Semantic similarity was manipulated by defining items as semantically similar if they belong to the same superset category and semantically dissimilar if they belong to different superset categories. The categories used were taken from the Battig and Montague (1969) norms, constructed by presenting subjects with names of semantic categories and asking them to generate all of the instances that came to mind. Some examples of semantic categories used were four-footed animals, fruits, trees, items of furniture, and family relations. Homa took the popular instances that were given to the category names and used them as target and test items in the Sternberg memory search task (see Chapter 4).

Homa varied the size and the number of categories in the target list by covarying the two independent variables: the number of categories in the target list and the number of words per category. This factorial design is shown in Figure 3. The list could contain either 2, 3, or 5 categories of either 2, 3, or 5 words per category.

FIGURE 3. The factorial design used by Homa (1973) in generating target lists in the Sternberg task. The entries give the number of items in each target list.

Number of Categories

Number of Words per Category		2	3	5
	2	4	6	10
	3	6	9	15
	5	10	15	25

Consider two different target lists of size 15. In one condition, the target members would be drawn from 3 categories of 5 members each. In the other, the target members would be drawn from 5 categories of 3 members each. Any differences in RT between these two conditions would reveal some influence of category membership in the search task.

Homa (1973) also specifically varied the semantic relationship of the test item to the target list. One of three types of test items could be presented. The positive item would be a test item that was contained in the target list. The negative item could either belong or not belong to one of the categories defined by the target list. For example, the target list might contain the items *dog, cat, pig, chair, stool,* and *couch* defining the categories animal and furniture, respectively. The negative item *lion* would belong to the same semantic category as some of the target items but would not be a specific member of the target set. Therefore, the correct response would be "no." The negative item *doctor* would be semantically unrelated to the target set, since its members define the categories animals and furniture, respectively. Accordingly, Homa's subjects were tested on positive (P), negative but same (NS) category, and negative but different (ND) category items. Homa's experiment allowed him to test a number of specific models of the search process.

In Chapter 4, we said that the serial exhaustive search model described the results of experiments using digits as target and test items. This simple model predicts that the critical variable in Homa's experiment is the absolute number of items in the target set. The number of categories and the number of words per category should not be critical over and above their effect on the absolute size of the target list. Furthermore, the type of negative item should have no effect on the functions relating RT to the number of items in the target set.

Alternative models can be developed which assume that category membership can affect the memory search and comparison process. Figure 4 shows the target list as an organized hierarchical structure that the subjects could store. Homa's subjects were given the positive target set a day before the experiment so that they had sufficient time to organize it optimally. Subjects could define the categories in the target set and store all of the instances under the appropriate category name. This organization could facilitate the memory search and comparison process with the use of the following search algorithm: Upon presentation of a test item, determine its superset category. Then search the category names in the target set. If the category of the test item does not match any of the categories of the target items, respond "no." If the category of the test item does agree with one of the target categories, search

FIGURE 4. A hierarchical organization for storing the target items in Homa's (1973) experiment.

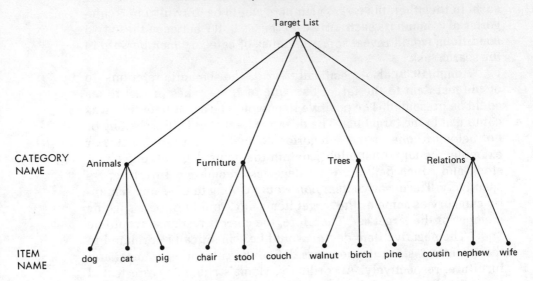

the instances of that target category. If the test item matches one of the target items under the positive category, respond "yes." Otherwise, respond "no." This search strategy is presented graphically in Figure 5. The reader might try to write a computer algorithm (analogous to those written in Chapter 4) for storing and searching the target list.

FIGURE 5. A search algorithm of the memory search task based on the hierarchical organization given in Figure 4.

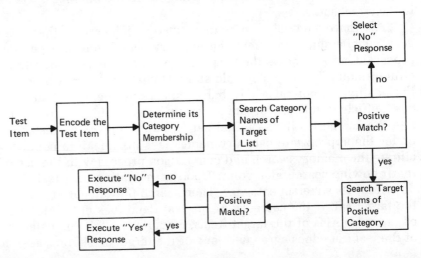

The organization of the target items allows subjects to respond faster to ND items as opposed to NS items. Subjects presented with a test item could first compare the category membership of that item with the categories represented in the target list. If the test item did not belong to the same category as any of the target items, the subject could select a "no" response. But if the test item was a member of the same category as some of the target items, a "no" response would be premature at the end of the search through category names. The subject would have to examine the members of the category of the test item represented in the target list. This strategy predicts that responses to ND items should be faster than responses to NS items. Figure 6 plots the RT as a function of the number of categories for ND and NS items when category size was equal to 5. The figure shows that category membership influenced the search

FIGURE 6. Mean RT as a function of the number of categories for negative test items of (1) the same superset category as some of the target items (NS), and (2) a different superset category (ND). Size of each category was 5 items (after Homa, 1973).

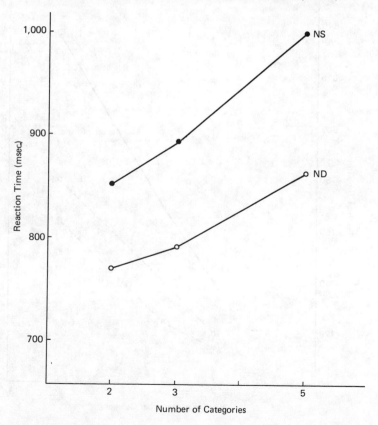

strategy in the predicted direction. Subjects were able to reject ND items faster than NS items presumably because they were able to reject ND items on a search through the category names, whereas they could not reject NS items until they also searched the members of the category given by the negative item.

Figure 7 presents another plot of the Homa data when there were two categories in the target list. The figure plots RT as a function of the number of items in each category for each of the three test items. If subjects search category names, as was described in the organized search strategy, then the number of target items in each category should have no effect on the RT for ND items. Subjects can terminate their search (as shown in the search algorithm) after they exhaust the search of the category names, since the cate-

FIGURE 7. Mean RTs as a function of the number of items per category for negative but same (NS), positive (P), and negative but different (ND) test items. The target list was made up of two categories (after Homa, 1973).

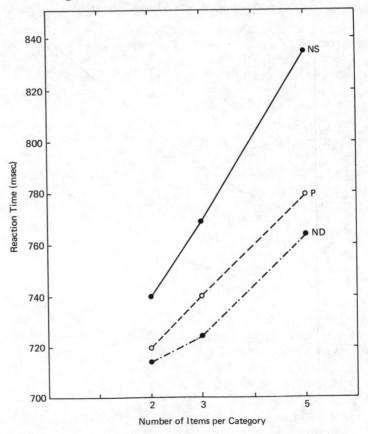

gory of an ND item will not match any of the category names of the items in the target set. Given that the RT for ND test items increases with the number of items per category, it appears that subjects do not always perform an organized search through the category names, especially with small target lists (Atkinson, Herrmann, & Wescourt, 1974). Although Homa's data show a significant role for semantic similarity in memory search and comparison, his quantitative data are not easily described by the organized search strategy.

WORD RECOGNITION

Much of the information we have stored in long-term memory can be discovered in very simple demonstrations. For example, consider what we know about the lexical rules of English, that is, the relationship between letter strings and meaning. Consider the following letter strings: dampness, dempster, demgster. Do these letter strings spell words? A typical answer might be "yes," "maybe," and "no," in that order for the three respective words. We are sure that *dampness* is a word since we use it and know its meaning. Most of us might not know the meaning of *dempster* but we realize that it could be a word. In contrast, *demgster* is difficult to pronounce and, therefore, it is difficult to believe that it would be a word. This example demonstrates that we know which words we can define and also, at some level, which letter sequences are valid in English. We have a rule in English which says that a nasal phenome **m, n,** or **ŋ** as in *me, no,* or *sing,* followed by a stop consonant *p, b, t, d, k,* or *g* must share the same point of articulation where the mouth is closed, or occluded. Therefore, *demp* can be a word, since both *m* and *p* are articulated by occluding the mouth at the lips. On the other hand, *demg* is an invalid syllable since the consonant *g* is articulated by occluding the mouth towards the back. Therefore, *demg* cannot be easily pronounced.

Lexical Decisions

This demonstration shows that two decisions can be made about a string of letters; (1), whether the letter sequence obeys the rules of English orthography, and (2), the meaning of a valid sequence of letters. Subjects might know that a sequence of letters could spell a word but not know the meaning of the word.

Meyer and Schvaneveldt (1971) showed how the semantic meaning of words could affect the time required to determine whether or not a string of letters spelled a word. They presented 2 strings of letters; 1 string of letters was centered above the other. Each string of letters spelled or did not spell an English word, so that the subject might see 2 words, 2 nonwords, or a word and a nonword. The subject's task was to respond "yes," as quickly as possible if both strings spelled words, and "no," otherwise. The major independent variable of interest was the relationship of the two words on "yes" trials. Half of the word pairs were commonly associated words such as *bread-butter* and *doctor-nurse*. The other half of the word pairs were associatively unrelated, such as *bread-doctor* and *butter-nurse*. The second independent variable was the position of the nonword (top or bottom) when it occurred with a word string. Table 1 gives possible trial types in the experiment and the probability of occurrence of each type. Of course, each trial type was presented randomly from trial to trial so that subjects could not predict their responses in advance.

The first interesting result was the large effect of the position of the nonword when it occurred with a word string. The RT of the "no" response was 183 msec. faster when the nonword occurred in the top than in the bottom string (see Table 1). This result indicated that subjects performed a serial self-terminating search of the 2 letter strings, beginning with the top letter string. Since subjects could respond "no" as soon as they found 1 nonword, performance was faster when the nonword occurred in the top position, which

TABLE 1.

The Possible Trial Types, their Probability of Occurrence, and the Observed Results in the "Yes-No" Meyer and Schvaneveldt (1971) Task.

Type of stimulus pair		Correct response	Proportion of trials	Mean RT (msec.)	Mean % errors
Top string	Bottom string				
word	associated word	yes	.25	855	6.3
word	unassociated word	yes	.25	940	8.7
word	nonword	no	.167	1,087	27.6
nonword	word	no	.167	904	7.8
nonword	nonword	no	.167	884	2.6

was searched first. When the top string was a word, it was necessary to determine the status of the bottom string before a decision could be made. Figure 8 presents a diagram of the operations in this task. The self-terminating search is also supported by the finding that 2 nonwords were not responded to significantly faster than were a nonword and a word, when the nonword occurred in the top row. The lexical status of the bottom row should not matter when the top string is a nonword.

FIGURE 8. Flow diagram of the sequence of operations involved in the "yes-no" lexical decision task (after Schvaneveldt & Meyer, 1973).

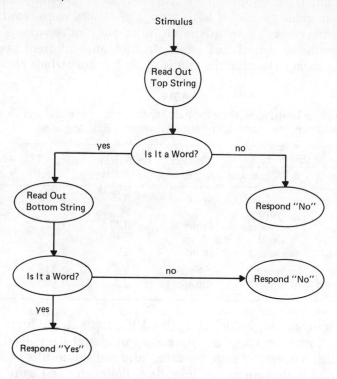

The significant variable on "yes" trials is the associative relationship between the two words. Given that the top string is a word, the bottom string must be processed before a response is executed. The question is whether the meaning of the top word influences processing of the bottom word. Meyer and Schvaneveldt (1971) found that RTs were 85 msec. faster when the words were associatively related than when they were unrelated. This result indicates that the semantic meaning of the first word string can facilitate recognition of the second string. That is to say, the subject can determine more quickly that the sequence of letters *doctor* is a word if he has just read *nurse*, than if he has just read *butter*.

Meyer and Schvaneveldt (1971) carried out another type of experiment to show that this phenomenon was not unique to a particular experimental task. The psychological processes discussed in this book have made themselves visible in a number of experimental tasks and can be considered reliable phenomena. To be

Associations

psychologically meaningful, a phenomenon must be robust, so that we can conclude it plays a role in normal everyday processing. In the second experiment subjects saw the same letter strings, but now they responded "same" if both strings of letters were words or if both strings were nonwords, and "different," otherwise. Table 2 presents the design of this study. In the same-different task, the subjects must determine the status of both letter strings regardless

TABLE 2.

The Possible Trial Types, their Probability of Occurrence and the Observed Results in the "Same-Different" Meyer and Schvaneveldt (1971) Task.

Type of stimulus pair		Correct response	Proportion of trials	Mean RT (msec.)	Mean % errors
Top string	Bottom string				
word	associated word	same	.125	1,055	2.1
word	unassociated word	same	.125	1,172	8.7
nonword	nonword	same	.25	1,357	8.9
word	nonword	different	.25	1,318	11.6
nonword	word	different	.25	1,386	12.0

of the outcome of the decision about the top string. Figure 9 presents a flow diagram of the necessary operations involved in the same-different task. As an exercise, interpret the results in Table 2 in relation to the processing operations delineated in Figure 9.

In terms of our model, recognizing that a letter string spells a word requires a sequence of psychological processes. First, the primary recognition process transforms the preperceptual visual image into a synthesized percept in synthesized visual memory. The secondary recognition process must now analyze the synthesized percept for meaning. If it spells a word, the conceptual code must be found that gives the word meaning. The association effect seems to facilitate the secondary recognition process, that is to say, the location of the conceptual code in long-term memory.

Semantic Features Schvaneveldt and Meyer (1973) propose two explanations of how the association can facilitate the secondary recognition process. The first model assumes that the conceptual codes of words are made up of a number of semantic features. According to this conceptual priming model, retrieval of a word in memory facilitates retrieval of associated words because the conceptual codes of the words share a number of semantic features or have them in common. That the concept of a word can be represented by an inter-

FIGURE 9. Flow diagram of the sequence of operations involved in the "same-different" lexical decision task (after Schvaneveldt & Meyer, 1973).

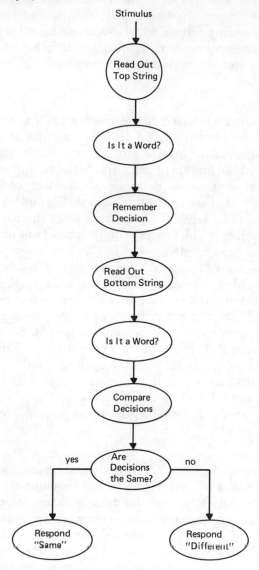

section list of semantic features is illustrated by the following example. When asked to think of something bubbly, no definite answer comes to mind. When asked, independently, to think of something pink, again no unique answer comes to mind. However, when asked to think of something bubbly and pink, many people respond with champagne. The concepts of doctor and nurse share certain semantic features such as medical profession, white uniforms, hospital, pain, etc. If the secondary recognition of the letter sequence *doctor* activates all of the semantic features which define doctor, this activation would facilitate retrieval of the conceptual codes of semantically related words such as *nurse*. Doctor and butter do not share many semantic features and, therefore, recognition of one of these words does not facilitate retrieval of the conceptual code of the other.

Discrete Nodes

A second hypothesis is based on the assumption that the conceptual code of each word is stored at a discrete location or node. In this case, the conceptual code of a word has a single representation rather than a whole bundle of semantic features. In this model, the association between words determines the distance between the representations of their conceptual codes. Secondary recognition occurs in this model when the process locates the correct conceptual code in memory. The process can only read out one location at a time and the time needed to shift from one conceptual code to another increases with the distance between conceptual codes. This model predicts the effects of association in the Meyer and Schvaneveldt study by assuming that the conceptual codes of associated words are stored closer together in long-term memory than are the conceptual codes of unassociated words. Since secondary recognition must shift from the conceptual code of the first letter string to the second, recognition time of the second word is a direct function of distance of their conceptual codes. Hence, location shifting time and RT will be shorter for associated words than for unassociated words. Figure 10 presents a graphic representation of these two models.

Features or Nodes

Both the semantic-features and the discrete-node models predict the positive results of association in the previous studies. To discriminate between these two models, Schvaneveldt and Meyer (1973) carried out an ingenious experiment. They presented 3 horizontal strings of letters in a vertical array and manipulated the locations of the 2 associated words. The letter strings could either spell 3 words or any combination of words and nonwords. Subjects were requested to respond "yes" if all of the letter strings spelled words, and "no," otherwise.

The central assumption of this experiment is that subjects will process the letter strings in a top-down order. This assumption can be tested by observing the RTs for "no" responses as a function of the position (top, middle, or bottom) of the first nonword. If subjects self-terminate the search as soon as they find a nonword, the

FIGURE 10. A graphic rendition of the semantic-features and discrete-node models representing conceptual codes.

Semantic – features model

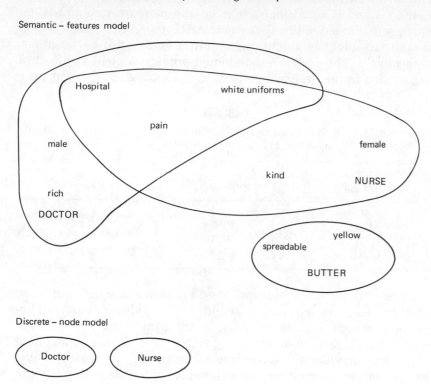

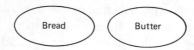

Discrete – node model

responses should be systematically ordered as a function of the position of the nonword. Letting W and N represent words and nonwords, respectively, the three possible sequences (NWW), (WNW), and (WWN) gave large and orderly differences in RT, 846, 1020, and 1187, respectively. This result supports the assumption that the subject read the strings in a top-to-bottom order and that reading time for each additional string averaged about 170 msec. Therefore, we can assume the subjects read the strings in a top-to-bottom order in our test of the two models of the association effect.

The RTs to the four kinds of "yes" trials can be used to differentiate the two models. These trial types are presented in Table 3. Letting A and U stand for associated and unassociated words, respectively, consider the two trials AAU and AUA. Examples of these trials might be doctor-nurse-butter and doctor-butter-nurse, respectively. The discrete-node model predicts a positive effect of association in the first case but not in the second. In the first case,

TABLE 3.

Average RTs of a "Yes" Response as a Function of the Different Kinds of "Yes" Trials in the Schvaneveldt and Meyer (1973) Study.

Trial type	RT (msec.)	Mean % errors
AAU	1093	3.4
AUA	1090	4.4
UAA	1073	3.1
UUU	1175	3.8

the associated words will be processed in immediate succession, so that the time to recognize the second word should be shortened because of the close distance between the conceptual codes of the words. In contrast, given the string AUA, there should be no effect of association since the secondary recognition process must travel to the conceptual code of an unrelated word before it gets back to the conceptual code of an associated word. Therefore, the short distance between the conceptual codes of the two A words should play no role in an AUA sequence and should not shorten reaction time. In contrast to the predictions of the discrete-node model, the semantic-features model predicts that the secondary recognition of the second A word in the sequence AUA could still be facilitated if the semantic features of the first A word remain present during the readout of the third letter string. We would expect the features to be still available since secondary recognition of the middle word requires only another 170 msec. The results supported the semantic-features model. The "yes" RTs were about 90 msec. faster when 2 of the 3 words were associated than when all 3 words were unrelated. However, the position of the two A words had no significant effect, contradicting the prediction of the discrete-node model.

Temporal Course of Association   Meyer, Schvaneveldt, and Ruddy (1972) have substantiated the above results by tracing out the temporal course of the association effect. They also modified the experimental paradigm to assure that the subjects processed the letter strings in sequential order. In this paradigm, subjects were presented a sequence of letter strings, one at a time, and responded "yes" or "no" to each string individually, with respect to whether or not the letter string spelled a word. Subjects responded to each word individually and a following word was presented 250 msec. after the subject's response. Again, we can test the semantic-features model and the discrete-node model by comparing "yes" RTs to unassociated words, separated associates, and adjacent associates by comparing performance on the trials UUU, AUA, and UAA. In this paradigm, the dependent variable is the RT to the third word, depending on its relationship to the previous two words. Examples of UUU, AUA, and UAA trials might be nurse-star-butter, bread-star-butter, and star-bread-butter. The results show that the association effect is attenuated with an intervening word but not eliminated completely, supporting the results of the Schvaneveldt and Meyer (1973) study.

In another experiment, the investigators varied the time between 2 words in the sequential task. In this task, the subject saw a sequence of 2 letter strings on each trial and responded "yes" or "no" to each letter string, depending upon whether or not it spelled a word. The independent variable was the delay interval between the first response and second letter string. The dependent variable is the RT to the second word. The measure of the association effect is the difference in RTs to the same word when it follows an associated and nonassociated word. This difference at each of the delay intervals measures the temporal course of the association effect. The results showed that the association effect decreased with increases in the delay between the two words, but a significant effect remained even after 4 sec. The reason for the positive result at a long delay is probably that the subject was not required to process any new information during the delay interval and could continue thinking about the first word. This study should be repeated when the subject is required to perform an interfering task during the delay interval.

Long-term memory remains one of the least explored areas using the techniques of information-processing methodology. We have seen a number of techniques that appear to be successful in discovering the structural properties and processing rules of long-term memory. In contrast to the paucity of experimental work, there has been a large increase in theoretical work, influenced by recent studies in linguistics. Perhaps the methods developed here will begin to bring together the theoretical and empirical approaches to the investigation of long-term memory.

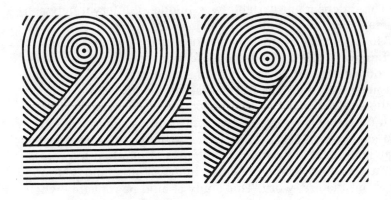

Learning

*. . . and it is no wonder that she [the soul] should be able
to call to remembrance all that she ever knew about
virtue, and about everything; for as all nature is akin,
and the soul has learned all things, there is no difficulty
in her eliciting, or, as men say, learning, out of a single
recollection all the rest.*
—Plato's Meno.

Implicit throughout the book is the assumption that man is continually learning, and this learning process plays a factor in normal
perceptual and cognitive functioning, as well as in experimental
tasks. In our experiments subjects usually show a remarkable improvement in performance during the first few or even the first few
hundred trials. In a pitch discrimination experiment subjects' identifications improve remarkably during the first 20- or 30-minute
session, leveling off thereafter. In our studies we have eliminated
the contribution of learning as a possible confounding by (1) practicing the subjects before the experiment proper so that performance is asymptotic during the trials of interest, or (2) randomizing
all conditions within experimental sessions and among subjects so
that, on the average, all experimental conditions are tested equally
at all levels of learning. As a result, our studies are informative with
respect to the study of perceptual and cognitive functioning for a
relatively fixed learning level.

Learning itself is, of course, an interest to the experimental psychologist. However, learning, as traditionally studied, appears to
be a result of the interaction of a number of psychological processes
rather than a distinct process itself, analogous to recognition or
decision. In fact, learning typically results when we recombine
many of the processes discussed throughout this book. Hence, we
actually know more about learning and how to study learning than
might be inferred from our disuse of the term. The verbal short-
term memory studies provide a good case in point. If a subject correctly recognizes that an item was presented earlier in a previous
list of items, we can say he has *learned* that it was presented earlier.

INTERACTION OF PROCESSES

Accordingly, a description of the learning process will be exactly the same as our descriptions of perception and storage, retention and retrieval, and decision that were necessary to describe performance in the short-term memory task.

LEARNING CONCEPTS

The concept of learning has been discussed here without defining it explicitly; we have relied on the fact that our interpretations of this word are sufficiently similar to make this dialogue worthwhile. In fact, the use of a word or concept in this way presents a significant challenge to the learning psychologist or the philosopher of knowledge. For example, how do we come to know "learning"—an abstract concept—having had contact with nothing more than a series of relatively unrelated concrete instances of the learning process? This problem was posed by Plato in the *Meno* and has yet to be explained adequately. His explanation was that the soul or mind has already been acquainted with abstract concepts from a previous reality, so that all present signs of learning are actually signs of anamnesis (recollections). Plato solved the problem of learning by redefining it so that no explanation was necessary. Since we know everything there is to know, there is no need to describe how we come to know.

Aristotle rejected his mentor's solution and proposed, instead, that learning and knowledge are derived from experience with concrete particulars. Aristotle reformulated the problem so that the question to be answered was: How does experience with a sequence of learning acts lead us to the generic concept of learning? His solution was one of abstraction; we isolate out common elements of learning scenarios to derive what is critical to the learning process. Aristotle's common elements will not enable us to abstract enough information to define learning, mainly because perception is not a passive process but an active, constructive one. For example, we have discussed how the rules of English orthography are utilized to help make unambiguous a sequence of written letters. By constructing the relevant dimensions, we seem to be able to derive concepts from particulars. In philosophical terms, we arrive at universals on the basis of experience with particulars. This chapter will concern the rules by which one comes to learn a concept or schema as a function of his experience with concrete particulars.

PROTOTYPE LEARNING

Plato was concerned with the acquisition of the concept of virtue. Since virtue is difficult to bring into the laboratory, however, recent experimenters have studied the learning of visual and auditory concepts that can be specified precisely. The task is to have subjects classify instances of prototypical patterns while varying the similarity between the prototype and the instance to be classified. Consider two prototype patterns, A and B; these patterns can be distorted to various degrees and presented to subjects for classification. The experimenter seeks to determine which stimulus attributes are critical for classification and, more importantly, how the subject comes to know these stimulus attributes.

How does learning fit into our general information processing model? Learning occurs when the subject imposes a transformation in the processing sequence that leads to more accurate performance on subsequent trials. Consider *insofarasicansee,* the sequence of letters presented one at a time to a subject who is to learn them in sequential order. This task could be relatively difficult, since the number of letters exceeds the span of immediate memory. If the observer learns, however, that the letter sequences spell a common and simple phrase, his learning rate should increase dramatically. In this case, calling on his lexical memory structures the task so that learning is facilitated. Whether or not the subject applies this rule, the sequence of processes is easily understood in terms of our information-processing model. In one case, the transfer from synthesized visual memory to generated abstract memory is in terms of letters; in the other, the transfer is in terms of words. However, the question here is how the subject comes to know that the letters spell words; and when he does, how does he recognize the correct words?

One way to ensure that the reader will interpret the sequence of letters as words is to put blank spaces in the appropriate places. Here we have changed a structural aspect of the stimulus to obtain this effect. By varying the number of blank spaces in the sequence of letters, we should be able to systematically influence the probability that the subject will read the letters as words. Even with no blank spaces, however, he will have some probability of interpreting the letters as words. This probability could also be influenced by context variables; for example, the subject could be given the appropriate set by first presenting other letter sequences that spell words. However, the best index of performance the experimenter can get is a probability; he cannot predict exactly whether a particular person will see words or unrelated letters on a particular trial. This is no different from our probabilistic interpretations of detection, recognition, and retention discussed in detail throughout this book.

Insofarasicansee

Dot Patterns The discussion above implies that learning is critically dependent upon perception, which is critically dependent upon the structural aspects of the stimulus situation. One demonstration of this has been a series of experiments carried out by Posner and his colleagues in which they distorted dot patterns that were then categorized by college students. In the Posner, Goldsmith, and Welton (1967) study, subjects were required to classify visual dot patterns as an instance of either a triangle, the letter *M*, the letter *F*, or a random pattern. The instances presented to the subjects were distorted from their prototypical pattern (shown in Figure 1), so that classification was not easy. Four levels of distortion were employed in generating instances from the prototypical patterns. The instances corresponding to these four levels of distortion of the triangle are shown in Figure 2.

Each prototypical dot pattern was represented on graph paper divided into squares. The dot would essentially fill one complete square. Each dot of the prototype would be moved according to a probabilistic schedule that differed for the different levels of distortion. The space was partitioned into five areas by defining a series of rings around the prototypical cell. The cell containing the prototypical dot was called zero, the eight surrounding cells called 1, and the next sixteen cells surrounding these eight were called 2, and so on until five such areas were defined. For each level of distortion, the dot could move into any of these five areas with a certain proba-

FIGURE 1. The four prototypical patterns used in the Posner, Goldsmith, & Welton (1967) study.

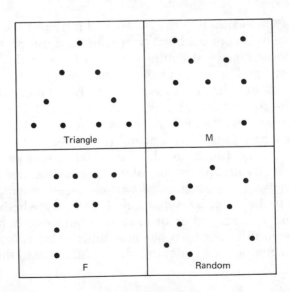

FIGURE 2. Four examples of distortion of the prototypical triangle. The numbers define the average number of squares each dot was moved for that level of distortion (after Posner, Goldsmith, & Welton, 1967).

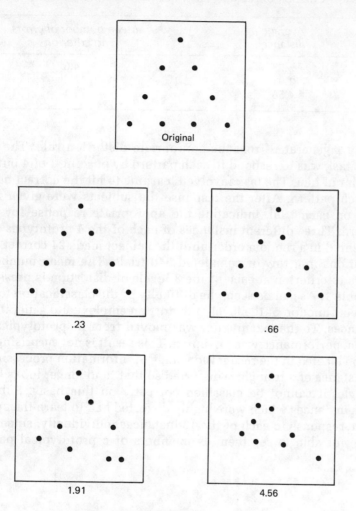

Original

.23

.66

1.91

4.56

bility. Once it entered an area, it was equally likely to enter any of the cells defined by this area. By varying the probabilities that a given dot can enter any of the five areas, the experimenter has direct control over the average distance each dot in the pattern will move. In one experiment (Experiment III, replication) Posner et al. (1967) chose 3 levels of distortion. Table 1 gives the average number of squares moved for each of the 3 levels of distortion.

In the experiment subjects were assigned to 1 of the 3 levels of distortion and presented instances of the 4 prototypes shown in

TABLE 1

Three Levels of Distortion Defined by the Average Distance (number of squares) Each Dot was Moved and the Mean Number of Classification Errors to a Criterion of Learning (after Posner, Goldsmith, & Welton, 1967).

Average distance	Mean number of errors to criterion
.23	4.6
1.91	12.2
4.56	71.1

Figure 1 generated from the appropriate distortion rule. The subject's task was to respond to each pattern by pushing 1 of 4 buttons in front of him. The task involved learning to hit the correct button to each pattern. After the response the subjects were given feedback on each trial, indicating the appropriate response for each pattern. Three different instances of each of the 4 prototypes were presented in a random order until the subject made 24 correct classifications in a row or completed 240 trials. The mean number of errors to criterion at each of the 3 levels of distortion is presented in Table 1. As can be seen, the difficulty of the classification task is a direct function of the level of distortion employed to generate the instances. To the extent a dot was moved from its prototypical location, performance was disrupted. This result is not surprising and can be located in the recognition stage of information processing. If an instance of a triangle is distorted so that it no longer looks like a triangle, it cannot be classified correctly on this basis. Subjects given instances which were highly distorted had to learn the appropriate response to each of the 12 instances individually, since they were not able to see them as members of a prototypical pattern class.

TEMPORAL COURSE OF LEARNING

Although these experiments tell us that structural aspects of the stimulus are critical in prototype learning, we still do not know how the observers come to know the concept. Throughout the history of psychology there have been two major theories of the learning process. One theory assumes that learning occurs in a gradual incremental fashion; the subject slowly builds up the relevant information required for the task. The incremental learning theory can be viewed as a multistate process in which the subject goes through many successive learning states. In each learning state the probability of a correct response is slightly higher than it was in the preceding learning state. The other theory is that the subject learns, or comes to know, in an all-or-none fashion. He tests out certain rules describing the situation and operates according to these rules or hypotheses until he settles on one that leads to accurate performance. The all-or-none learning theory is a two-state process. In the first state the subject knows very little and the probability of a correct response is near chance. In the second state the subject has solved the problem and the probability of a correct response is as high as is possible in the learning task. (The asymptotic probability may not be 1, since problems might not be capable of a perfect solution.)

How do we test between these two theories of learning? The task seems easy enough. We devise an experimental task and plot out a learning curve—performance across successive learning trials. The incremental learning theory predicts that percentage of correct responses should increase gradually across learning trials, whereas the all-or-none theory predicts that learning should occur in a single step at some point in the training session. However, when we look at the responses of a subject across trials, it is difficult to tell which theory gives a better description of performance. On each trial, performance is either correct or incorrect, and a trend in the data is

Learning Curves

FIGURE 3. A group learning curve demonstrating gradual learning, but based on the all-or-none results in Table 2.

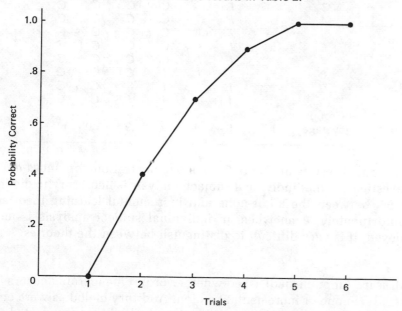

not directly apparent. For this reason investigators have pooled the results over a number of subjects and have plotted group learning curves as shown in Figure 3. Here the curves plot the probability of a correct response on each trial derived from dividing the number of correct responses on each trial by the total number of subjects. These results invariably show incremental learning, rather than all-or-none learning curves.

Unfortunately, the group learning curves say nothing about the learning of individual subjects. As pointed out by a number of investigators (e.g., Estes, 1956), the individual subjects may actually have learned the problem in an all-or-none fashion, but by pooling the results this effect is washed out, giving a gradual learning curve. That is to say, pooling the results could give the incremental data shown in Figure 3, even if subjects learn in all-or-none fashion on different trials. Table 2 is an example of the individual results of ten subjects who learned the problem in an all-or-none fashion but gave

TABLE 2

When Pooled, Individual Protocols which Show All-or-None Learning Give the Gradual Incremental Curve Shown in Figure 3. The Letters *I* and *C* Refer to Incorrect and Correct Responses, Respectively.

Subject	Trial number					
	1	2	3	4	5	6
1	*I*	C	C	C	C	C
2	*I*	C	C	C	C	C
3	*I*	C	C	C	C	C
4	*I*	C	C	C	C	C
5	*I*	*I*	C	C	C	C
6	*I*	*I*	C	C	C	C
7	*I*	*I*	C	C	C	C
8	*I*	*I*	*I*	C	C	C
9	*I*	*I*	*I*	C	C	C
10	*I*	*I*	*I*	*I*	C	C
Group average *P*(C)	0	.4	.7	.9	1.0	1.0

the pooled results of Figure 3. This demonstration convinces most investigators that individual subject analysis is necessary to distinguish between the all-or-none and incremental learning theories. Unfortunately, even when an individual subject analysis is employed, it is very difficult to distinguish between the theories.

Auditory Melodies Massaro (unpublished) asked whether prototype learning occurs in an all-or-none or incremental fashion. Auditory melodies were employed as stimuli. Each melodic pattern had 6 notes that lasted 50 msec. each, with 250 msec. of silence separating each note. Figure 4 presents the prototypes for the two patterns A and B. On each trial the stimulus pattern was determined by randomly choosing the pattern A or B. Then each successive note of the pattern was determined by choosing the prototypical note with a probability of 10/16; a tone one note higher or lower than the prototypical tone

FIGURE 4. The prototypical auditory patterns used by Massaro (unpublished).

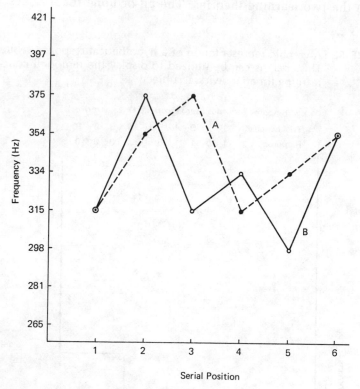

with probability of 2/16 each; and a tone two notes higher or lower than the prototypical tone with probability of 1/16 each. As can be seen in the figure, the first and last notes are the same for the prototypes of both patterns. Accordingly, these notes cannot provide reliable information for identification, and recognition must be based on the middle four tones.

Listeners were instructed to classify the auditory pattern on each trial as A or B by pushing the appropriate button on a panel in front of them. Subjects were informed that the melody would be a variation of either A or B, and they were to classify it as an instance of A or B. They were told that they could learn the patterns, since feedback would be given after they made their response on each trial. Each trial began with the presentation of an auditory pattern followed by a 3 sec. response interval. The subject responded by pushing one of two buttons labeled A and B, respectively. Feedback was given at the end of the response interval by presenting the letters A or B for .5 sec. on a visual display. The intertrial interval was 1.5 sec.

Testing Theories It is necessary to analyze individual subject data in order to test between the two learning theories. The all-or-none theory says that

FIGURE 5. A graphic representation of a hypothetical response sequence. This analysis can be utilized to display the temporal course of learning for an individual subject.

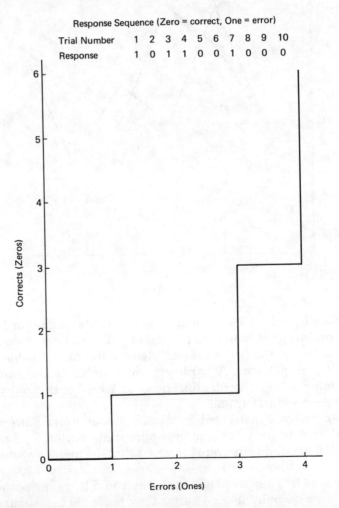

Response Sequence (Zero = correct, One = error)

Trial Number	1	2	3	4	5	6	7	8	9	10
Response	1	0	1	1	0	0	1	0	0	0

performance will begin at chance accuracy (.5 in this case) and then jump to some asymptotic level (not necessarily 1.0). By contrast, the incremental learning theory says that performance will gradually improve over the course of learning. The experimenter can process the data to give a sequence of Zeros and Ones, respectively. In this case, Zeros refer to correct responses and Ones refer to errors. The subject's response protocol will, therefore, represent a sequence of Zeros and Ones. The incremental learning theory says that the probability of a Zero occurring should increase gradually over trials, whereas the all-or-none theory says that the probability of a Zero occurring should remain fixed for some number of trials and then jump to some higher value when learning occurs.

Viewing the sequence of Zeros and Ones, the experimenter will find it difficult to tell which theory describes the response protocol best. One graphic method involves plotting the sequence of Zeros and Ones on linear graph paper as shown in Figure 5. The X and Y axes are marked off in unit steps. The experimenter starts in the lower left-hand corner and goes up one unit for each correct response and to the right one unit for each incorrect response. If the subject is performing at chance accuracy (.5), then the steps traced out should follow a straight line with a slope of 1. As accuracy improves beyond .5, the slope of the line through the steps should become steeper and steeper. If the improvement in performance occurs in an all-or-none manner, the change in slope should be a sudden one.

The graphic analysis of the learning of an actual subject presented in Figure 6 shows that the change in slope might be interpreted as sudden rather than gradual. For this typical subject there appears to be a change in slope at Trial 36. The interpretation of the graphic representation is based on a mathematical analysis of the data developed by Theios (1968). The analysis indicated that the best description of the learning of this subject can be given by the two-state process predicted by the all-or-none learning theory. In the first state the subject's correct response probability is fixed at some value, g, across trials. Then, on some trial, the subject learns or transits into a second state where his correct response probability is fixed at some value k, where $k > g$. The correct response probability then remains constant for the rest of the experimental session. For this subject the probability of a correct response was .61 during the first 36 trials and .89 thereafter.

Can we conclude with some confidence that this subject learned to identify the patterns in an all-or-none as opposed to an incremental manner? One way to check on our conclusion is to generate some hypothetical data according to incremental learning theory and to compare this data to the observed data, employing

FIGURE 6. Response protocols for a typical subject tested in Massaro's prototype learning study and a simulated subject behaving according to an incremental model.

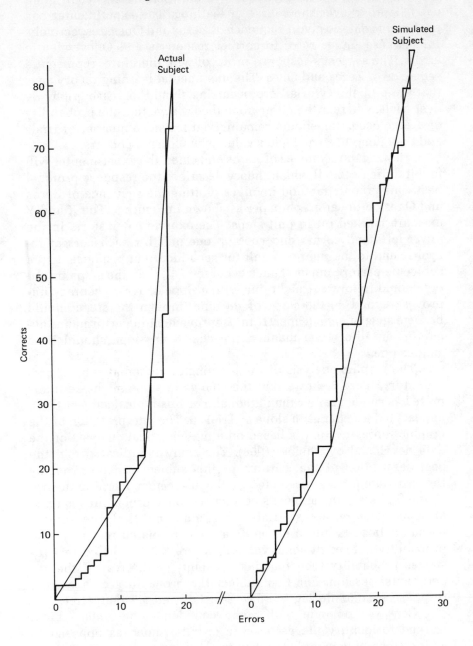

both our graphic and mathematical analyses. We would expect and hope that the response sequences generated by the incremental model could not be described by the all-or-none model. Thus, there would be no sharp change in slopes in the graphic analysis and the response sequences could not be described with two probabilities (g and k) of being correct before and after a given trial.

A large number of incremental learning models could be generated since incremental learning might occur in a number of ways. For example, the subject could learn a small fixed amount on each trial. In this case, the probability of being correct should also increase by a fixed amount on each trial. Accordingly, performance could be described by the equation

$$p_n = p_{n-1} + \alpha \qquad (1)$$

where p_n is the probability of being correct on Trial n and α would represent the increment in correct performance. In our prototype experiment p_1 would be .5, since the subject will be correct half the time even if he knows nothing and p_n must asymptote below 1, since the subject cannot master the task completely. If we assume that maximum performance is about 85 percent and $\alpha = .01$, the task would be learned in 35 trials. This would correspond roughly to the time it took the actual subject in Figure 6 to learn. We can generate hypothetical or simulated response protocols according to this model by randomly drawing a Zero (success) or One (error) with p_n representing the probability of a success. In this case, $p_1 = .5$, $p_2 = .51, \cdots p_{36} = .85, p_{n > 36} = .85$.

Using a random number table, we can look at a new two-digit number for every trial. If the number is less than $p_n \times 100$, we give the subject a success (Zero) on that trial. If it is larger, he gets an error (One). Also graphed in Figure 6 is a hypothetical response protocol according to this learning model. As can be seen in the simulated subject's slope, this data can also be interpreted as all-or-none learning, even though it was actually generated by an incremental learning theory. The mathematical analysis interpreted the learning sequences as arising from a two-state process with the probabilities of g and k equal to .61 and .77, respectively, with learning occurring after Trial 37.

Our short exploration into all-or-none vs. incremental learning indicates how difficult it is to distinguish between these two theories in actual experimental situations. Research in learning in the 1960s was focused on this controversy, and it has remained unresolved. According to the thesis developed in this book, our knowledge about learning will increase as we find out more about the component processes that make it up. After we define the operations of these processes, it will then remain to be seen if a description of learning is possible.

WHAT IS LEARNED? What do subjects learn, remember, and utilize in normal cognitive functioning? The prototype learning experiments have shown that subjects learn to utilize certain dimensions or attributes of the stimulus for their categorization response. Bransford and Franks (1971, 1972) have carried out a series of interesting experiments to study what is learned and remembered when subjects are presented with a series of sentences. More specifically, they asked whether we retain specific sentences or whether we integrate these into a more holistic concept, forgetting details of sentence type.

Ants and Jelly Bransford and Franks had to develop an experimental paradigm to test their ideas. They presented subjects with a list of sentences. These sentences were not unrelated, but consisted of subsets of sentences each of which made up part of an arbitrarily chosen complete idea. The investigators asked whether the subjects would remember the sentences separately or whether they would integrate related sentences into a more holistic representation of the complete idea.

Consider this sentence: *The ants in the kitchen ate the sweet jelly which was on the table.* This sentence could be broken into basic propositions, each representing one fact, two facts, and so on as shown in Table 3. In a series of experiments, subjects were given

TABLE 3

A Sample Sentence and Examples of its Component Sentences Used in the Bransford and Franks (1971) Study.

Sample Sentence		The ants in the kitchen ate the sweet jelly which was on the table.
	Component Sentences	
Type One:	1 fact:	The jelly was sweet. The ants were in the kitchen.
Type Two:	2 facts:	The ants in the kitchen ate the jelly. The sweet jelly was on the table.
Type Three:	3 facts:	The ants ate the sweet jelly which was on the table. The ants in the kitchen ate the sweet jelly.

sentences from 4 different complete ideas. During the acquisition phase of the experiment, subjects were given sentence types One, Two, or Three from each of the 4 ideas. The sentences were randomly intermixed before presentation so that the relatedness of the sentences would not be completely obvious. Bransford and Franks also chose to use an incidental learning task. That is to say, subjects were *not* told that their memory for the sentences would be tested later or that the experimenters were interested in how they remembered the sentence. Subjects were merely asked a simple question about each sentence immediately after it was presented. For example, given the sentence *The jelly was sweet*, the experimenters might ask how the jelly tasted. In all, 24 sentences were presented.

Following the acquisition phase of the experiment, subjects were given a recognition test. They were presented sentences one at a time and told to indicate whether the sentence was old or new, that is, whether it had been presented earlier. They also rated the confidence in their decision on a five-point scale. Besides old sentences, two kinds of new sentences were presented during the test. Some of the new sentences were not presented during acquisition, but their meaning was part of one of the complete ideas generated by the old sentences. The meaning of other new sentences could *not* be derived from one of the complete ideas. The results indicated that the subjects seem to remember the overall meanings of the complete ideas rather than the specific sentences that were presented. Subjects easily mistook new sentences, with the same meaning as one of the complete ideas, as having been presented before. By contrast, new sentences that had a different meaning were correctly recognized as new most of the time. These results are especially convincing given the fact that many of the new sentences with different meanings were subtle distortions of the complete ideas. For example, subjects incorrectly answered "old" for the new sentence *The scared cat running from the barking dog jumped on the table* when it agreed with the complete idea, and correctly answered "new" for the sentence *The scared cat was running from the barking dog which jumped on the table* when it disagreed with the complete idea. These results show that subjects easily forget sentence length and complexity but remember an integrated meaning derived from a number of sentences.

Turtles and Logs

The Bransford and Franks experiments show that the individual sentences are not treated separately if they are semantically related. The information from different sentences is integrated to form an interrelated structure which is remembered and used in later processing. Bransford and Franks also show that subjects use what they know, to add to whatever linguistic information is given. They distinguish between the following two sentences:

    (1) Three turtles rested beside a floating log and a fish swam beneath them.

    (2) Three turtles rested on a floating log and a fish swam beneath them.

Even though the two sentences are very similar linguistically, they express different things about the state of the world of turtles, a fish, and a log. Sentence (2) specifies that the fish must have swum beneath the log since it swam beneath the turtles which were on the log. Sentence (1) does not imply or deny this possibility. Using what they know about spatial relations, then, subjects could infer that the fish swam under the log given Sentence 2, but not given Sentence 1.

Subjects were given sentences of either type in acquisition and tested for recognition memory using old and new sentences. New sentences corresponding to (1) and (2) above would be: *Three turtles rested beside a floating log and a fish swam beneath it* and *Three turtles rested on a floating log and a fish swam beneath it,* respectively. The results indicate that new sentences corresponding to (2) were recognized as old as often as actual old sentences. By contrast, new sentences corresponding to (1) were recognized as old significantly less often than the actual old sentences. These results show that subjects used what they knew to encode the sentences and were later interpreting a new sentence as old since it agreed with what they actually inferred and remembered. For example, if the subjects used visual imagery to remember the sentences, different visual images would be constructed for sentences (1) and (2), respectively. The visual image constructed given sentence (2) would have the fish swimming under the log; this would not necessarily be the case for sentence (1). Given the new test sentence, subjects reviewing their visual images would err in one case but not the other. The Bransford and Franks paradigm should prove to be highly useful for studying learning and remembering in a situation that closely approximates the way information is usually processed.

While the information-processing approach has not contributed many techniques to the study of the temporal course of learning itself, many of the studies throughout this book actually illuminate the learning function or its parts. Learning has maintained its behavioristic influence longer than other areas of experimental psychology and has lagged in its application of the information-processing approach. Indices taken from recent research in learning suggest a reversal of this trend.

Summary and speculation

By itself, a study of motion can tell us almost nothing about that which, in any given instance, is being moved. Similarly a study of behavior can, by itself, tell us almost nothing about the individual mind-body that, in any particular instance, is exhibiting the behavior.
—Aldous Huxley (Brave New World Revisited)

We have traveled a long, laborious road utilizing the information-processing approach to experimental psychology. What have we learned and what remains to be learned? Here we summarize our experimental approach and our information-processing model; and then we speculate about what remains ahead.

We have continually stressed that the experimenter must account for each of the processing stages in his psychological task. The information-processing analysis demands that the experimenter make explicit the implicit assumptions inherent in any experimental situation. Failure to do so severely limits what can be learned from the results. Such a fine-grain analysis is more than an exercise in esoteric argument. Rather, the information-processing methodology can be thought of as a microscope: it allows us to see what is not directly observable.

In this book, man is conceptualized as an information-processing system. The psychological phenomena we study begin with some stimulus and end with some observable response. One goal is to understand the stimulus-response relationship. A stimulus has potential information and in order to understand the response to the stimulus it is necessary to account for the operations initiated by the stimulus. The central assumption of our information-processing model is that a number of processing stages occur between stimulus and response. These processing stages are assumed to be successive and each stage operates on the information available to it. The operations of a particular stage take time and transform the information, making it available to the next stage of processing. Two theoretical constructs are important in this approach. First, the structural construct describes or defines the nature of the information at a particular stage of processing. Second, the functional construct describes the operations of a stage of information processing.

This book utilizes a specific processing model as a theoretical and experimental guide for experimental psychology. The model is structured around experiments employing a particular experimental methodology. It is also used as a heuristic to incorporate data in some coherent manner from a number of different studies. In this way the model also functions as an organizational structure for the state of the art in experimental psychology. The main advantage of the theoretical framework is that it forces consistency in methodology, interpretations, and conclusions.

Figure 1 presents a flow diagram of the temporal course of visual and auditory information processing. The sound and light wave patterns are transformed by the auditory and visual receptor systems, respectively. We call this process feature detection, and this operation transduces the physical signal into a neurological code in preperceptual storage in the form of features. The features are described as acoustic or visual, since we assume that there is a direct relationship between the nature of the auditory or visual signal and the information in preperceptual storage. This one-to-one relationship between the signal and the information in preperceptual storage distinguishes the feature detection process from the succeeding stages of information processing. There is no one-to-one relationship between the input and output of the processing stages that follow, since these later stages actively utilize information stored in long-term memory in the sequence of transformations. For this reason the passive transduction of feature detection contrasts with the active construction of the later processing stages.

The outcome of the feature detection process is the information of whether or not a particular feature is present. We assume that the feature detection process sets up a list of features in preperceptual storage. These features are held there for a very short time—on the order of 250 msec. The primary recognition process involves a readout of the features in preperceptual storage and a transformation of these features into a synthesized percept in synthesized memory. Three sources of information are available to the primary recognition process: (1) the features in preperceptual storage, (2) knowledge in long-term memory, and (3) other contextual or situational knowledge. Perception requires an analysis and synthesis of the information made available by the detection of features in the sound or light pattern.

FIGURE 1. A flow diagram of the temporal course of auditory and visual information processing.

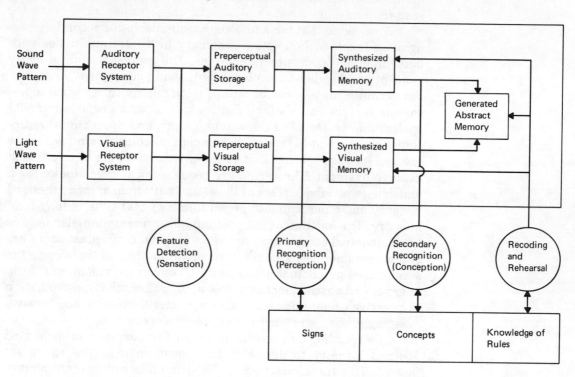

The minimal sound or light patterns that can be recognized are referred to as perceptual units of information. Perceptual units correspond to those patterns that are uniquely represented by signs in long-term memory. Each sign contains a list of features that describe the perceptual unit. The primary recognition process finds the sign with the best description in long-term memory that matches the features held in preperceptual storage and the current contextual information. The location of this sign initiates a synthesis program for seeing or hearing this particular sign, that is, for transforming the information into synthesized memory.

The secondary recognition process transforms the synthesized memory into meaningful units in generated abstract memory. This process also involves recognition in the sense that the observer chooses which of several alternatives is presented; it is called secondary recognition (conception) to distinguish it from the primary recognition process. Although conception is an uncommon term for this stage of processing, it seems to be an appropriate description, since it involves an analysis of synthesized memory for meaning. This conceptual stage of processing involves finding a match between the synthesized percept and information held in long-term memory.

We assume that the knowledge responsible for secondary recognition is stored in long-term memory in the form of codes with perceptual and conceptual attributes. The representation of every concept has a code with both perceptual and conceptual attributes. For example, the perceptual code of *wind* might contain some representation of the sound of the word *wind,* the look of the letters that spell *wind,* the sound of the wind blowing, and the pictorial representation of a windy scene. The conceptual code of wind would be the variety of properties that constitute the meaning of wind, such as air movement. The secondary recognition process looks for a match between the percept of the sound pattern held in synthesized memory and a perceptual representation of that code in long-term memory. The location of the perceptual representation also locates the conceptual code, since the perceptual and conceptual codes are stored together. The secondary recognition process transforms the synthesized perceptual pattern into a conceptual meaningful form in generated abstract memory, so called because the transformation is an active generation rather than a passive derivation and because meaning is abstract rather than modality-specific.

The recoding process operates on the concepts in generated abstract memory to derive further meaning from the entire sequence. This transformation of the string of meanings into a more specific and abstract form does not change the specific nature of the information. Hence, this information is recirculated back through generated abstract memory. The recoding process has access to whatever knowledge of rules the system has available in long-term memory—for example, the semantic and syntactic rules of a language. The recoding process can also operate in reverse. Given an abstract idea, it can transform this concept into a sequence of words in generated abstract memory or a perceptual representation in synthesized auditory or visual memory. Finally, the processing at this stage may be a simple regeneration or repetition of the information in generated abstract memory, in which case the operation is called rehearsal.

This general model serves as a heuristic to study each information-processing stage and how the stages work together. The utilization of this model has met with preliminary success in the study of speech perception and reading (Massaro; in press). We believe that the information-processing approach can bring the psychologist from experimental research to a greater understanding of difficult, meaningful, and important psychological phenomena.

Hopefully, the reader has been able to impose a structure on this journey, making our trip a worthwhile experience. One can consider a good book to be analogous to a good symphony. It must have a prelude which first attracts the observer's attention. Then its movements—light and heavy—occur at the appropriate times to keep the participant engaged. Finally, the work should have a grand finale. Having here completed the prelude and many light and heavy movements, what about the finale? To reach the finale, the information-processing approach to experimental psychology must still complete its long-term test of increasing our knowledge of ourselves.

Suggested readings

Many of the questions raised in the two monumental volumes of William James (1890) remain central to experimental psychology. Almost a century after they were written the volumes make particularly good reading. The mind-body problem has recently become the object of renewed interest by psychologists. Sperry (1969), known for his fascinating work among patients with surgical separation of the two hemispheres, has argued against the epiphenomenalism currently fashionable in the neurosciences. His solution to the mind-body problem is very similar to the monistic theory developed here. A recent analysis of consciousness is provided by Mandler (in press), and reviews of the work in biofeedback training can be found in Miller, Barber, DiCara, Kamiya, Shapiro, and Stoyva (1973).

Chapter 1

Hadamard's (1954) eclectic treatment of the nature of discovery was influential in developing the stage analysis of discovery. Albert Einstein's reflections on the thought processes involved in the creation of the theory of relativity were the source for a chapter in Wertheimer's classic study (1945, reissued in 1959). McCormick (1959) provides an introduction to digital computers, and Wooldridge (1963) gives an exciting treatment of the machinery of consciousness and its similarities to the operations of inanimate information-processing systems.

Some relevant sources for the history of experimental psychology can be found in Boring (1950), Bruno (1972), and Rancurello (1968). Radford (1974) contains a recent reflection on introspection and Norman (1970, 1973) analyzes questions such as the one we discuss, "in the house you lived in two houses ago . . . ."

Chaptor 2

The time it takes to decide "What day is today?" is the subject of a study by Koriat and Fischoff (1974). McCain and Segal (1973) introduce the student to the psychology of the scientist and his game of science, while Kuhn (1970), in an important work, covers the nature of scientific discovery.

Chapter 3   Donders' original paper has been translated and republished (1969) in the same volume as Sternberg's (1969b) presentation of the additive-factor method. A good introduction for the beginning student is Sternberg (1969a), and a review of the applications of the additive-factor method to a number of psychological problems is provided in Sternberg (1971). Woodworth (1938) devotes a chapter to the early work on reaction times. Murray (1970) and Grice (1968) have studied how stimulus intensity influences reaction time.

Chapter 4   The memory search task has developed into one of the most popular paradigms of current psychological research (e.g., Atkinson & Juola, 1974), and the serial-exhaustive search model has not gone unchallenged (J. A. Anderson, 1973; Murdock, 1971; Theios, 1973). A comprehensive review of many of the recent studies utilizing reaction times is contained in Nickerson (1972). Kristofferson (1972a,b,c) and her colleagues (Kristofferson, Groen, & Kristofferson, 1973) have explored the effects of practice and error rates in both the Sternberg and Neisser search tasks and show that differences in these variables are responsible for many of the differences originally found in the two tasks. A visual search task that eliminates the necessity of eye movements has been developed by Sperling, Budiansky, Spivak, and Johnson (1971).

Chapters 5, 6,   Krantz (1969) has developed a threshold theory with three sensory
and 7   states and Stevens (1972) argued for a neural quantum model of sensory discrimination. The question of whether or not confidence judgments could be used as a test between two-state and multistate theories can be followed in a series of papers by Watson, Rilling, & Bourbon (1964), Larkin (1965), Watson & Bourbon (1965), Broadbent (1966), Wickelgren (1968), and Massaro (1969). Massaro provides an experiment that uses the dice game to analyze the operations of the decision system.

Chapter 8   The treatment of the Hecht et al. (1942) experiment is similar to that provided by Cornsweet (1970), who presents an excellent treatment of brightness and color vision. The Hecht et al. study is reprinted in Cain and Marks (1971) along with other historical papers on sensation.

Chapter 9   Most of the relevant readings or, more appropriately, viewings can be found in the picture credits. Also, your local art museum is a great resource center. For op (optical) art Barrett's (1970) book provides a nice introduction. Kanizsa (1974) provides an intriguing treatment of illusory contours, and Coren (1972) makes the case that these contours are seen because of depth cues such as interposition in the visual array. Metelli (1974) presents a lovely treatment of the perception of transparency. Yarbus (1967) and Alpern (1971) are recommended for further reading on eye movements.

A particularly fine treatment of visual illusions by Luckiesh in 1922 has been reprinted (Luckiesh, 1965). Gardner (1970) devotes one of his sections on mathematical games in *Scientific American* to optical illusions, and a variety of illusions are explained by Day (1972), who utilizes so-called perceptual constancies such as size constancy. Robinson (1972) gives the most complete and exhaustive coverage of research and theory in illusion. The influence of psychological research on M. C. Escher's creative work is discussed in Teuber (1974). A fun exhibition called *Illusion in Science, Nature, and Art,* which opened in London in 1973 and is scheduled for an international tour, was the basis for a book of related essays edited by Gregory and Gombrich (1973).

Chapter 10

The phenomena of size and shape constancy are reviewed by Epstein, Park, and Casey (1961) and Epstein and Park (1963), respectively. Helmholtz's treatise of the last century has been reissued, as has Hering's work, allowing the reader to follow their disagreements (Helmholtz, 1962; Hering, 1964; Warren & Warren, 1968). Presentations of high excellence are provided by Hochberg (1971) on the invariance hypothesis of size and shape perception, and by Cornsweet's (1970) treatment of brightness and hue constancy. A good historical and theoretical account of the horopter is given by Shipley and Rawlings (1970), and, for further reading on binocular vision, Ogle's (1964) book is recommended, as are Sperling's (1970) and Julesz's (1971) advanced treatments. Gibson (1950, 1966) focuses on the structural information defining our visual world.

Chapter 11

Sperling's (1960) partial report task has been replicated and extended by a number of investigators (Turvey & Kravetz, 1970; von Wright, 1968, 1970, 1972). In contrast, Dick (1969, 1971) has demonstrated how short-term memory processes may play the significant role in the partial report task. Our analysis of the Averbach and Coriell (1961) experiments in Chapters 17 and 18, however, substantiates our interpretation of Sperling's results and is not open to Dick's criticisms. Nonetheless, his point of view is well taken and is particularly applicable to utilization of the partial report task in audition (see Chapter 21). One of the most influential memory models is that of Atkinson and Shiffrin (1968). A number of recent experiments have focused on immediate and delayed tests of memory as a way of investigating the fate of memorized items (e.g.,

Chapter 12

Bartz, Lewis, & Swinton, 1972; Craik, 1970; Darley & Murdock, 1971; Light, 1974). The readings given for Chapters 24–28, which provide a more extensive treatment of memory, are also relevant.

Chapters 13, 14, 15, and 16　　In the recent literature, attention has received a great deal of exactly that. The latest are the books by Kahneman (1973) and Keele (1973), and Broadbent (1971) has an excellent review and treatment of the attention literature. Hochberg (1970), Norman (1968), Swets and Kristofferson (1970), and Treisman (1969) are recommended for further reading.

Chapters 17, 18, and 19　　Experimental psychologists have lately shown renewed interest in the reading process. Woodworth (1938) still remains one of the best treatments of psychological processes fundamental to reading. Smith (1971) is a good introduction to reading, while Huey's book (1908; reissued in 1968) provides a refreshing, insightful treatment focusing on many of the problems still current today. Turvey's (1973) article is a trenchant empirical and theoretical analysis of visual masking. Some recent studies in letter and word recognition are found in Estes (in press). Massaro and Schmuller (in press), present a review of the visual features utilized in letter and word recognition. In the same volume, Massaro (c) presents a summary and evaluation of current theories of reading and Shebilske analyzes the implications of reading eye movements from an information-processing point of view.

Chapters 20, 21, 22, and 23　　Denes and Pinson's (1963) introduction to sound and speech can be profitably followed by Wilder's (in press) review of the characteristics of speech production and the physical properties of speech sounds. The processing model developed here has been extended to account for many aspects of speech processing. Massaro (in press, a) provides an analysis of the acoustic features that are functional in speech perception and (b) analyzes the temporal course of processing speech. Paap, in the same volume, sets forth a detailed analysis of the current theories of speech perception and an evaluation of these theories against empirical data. In another approach Cole and Scott (1974) tackle the same questions. Thurlow (1971) and Lindsay and Norman (1972) cover some aspects of auditory perception—such as spatial localization—that are not discussed in this book.

Chapters 24, 25, and 26　　The delayed comparison task has been used by Siegel (1974) to study persons with absolute pitch. Synthesized auditory memory has been the focus of a number of recent experiments (Crowder & Morton, 1969; Darwin & Baddeley, 1974) and investigators have also shown renewed interest in categorical perception (Pisoni, 1973). Paap (in press) reviews these studies with special emphasis on the role of synthesized auditory memory in processing speech and Freund (in press) covers recent research on prosodic information—intonation and stress—that is presumably held in synthesized auditory memory for processing. Highly relevant to the concept of synthesized visual memory is the recent empirical and theoretical work on visual imagery by Bower (1970) and Paivio (1971).

The structures and the processes operating in short- and long-term memory are central to much of current research. The greatest impact has come from the influence of artificial intelligence and linguistics (Shank, 1972; Fodor, Bever, & Garrett, 1974; Anderson & Bower, 1973). Smith, Shoben, and Rips (1974) have utilized semantic features to describe reaction times to analytic statements. The development in linguistics in terms of an information-processing approach is reviewed in Solberg (in press). Bower, Garner, Mandler, and Tulving have contributed to our knowledge of organization factors in memory and learning (e.g., Bower, 1972; Garner, 1974; Mandler, 1972; Tulving & Thomson, 1973). A comprehensive coverage of theory and data in human memory is presented in Murdock (1974), and Kausler (1974) has a refreshing treatment of verbal learning and memory. Hellige (in press) analyzes the role played by generated abstract and long-term memory in sentence processing. Recent work in learning (Estes, 1973; Grant, 1972, 1973) has taken on an information-processing outlook.

Chapters 27, 28, and 29

Journals provide the most current coverage of experimental psychology. Articles relevant to the philosophy of science and such topics as the mind-body problem can sometimes be found in *American Psychologist, Psychological Review, Psychological Bulletin,* and *Cognition.*

Recommended journals

Behavioral Research Methods and Instrumentation presents papers dealing with methodology and instrumentation. The scientist in the twentieth century is critically dependent on the most technologically advanced equipment. This journal gives the reader a good idea of the state of the art in the relevant technology. Research in psychophysics and perception can be found in *Journal of the Acoustical Society of America, Vision Research, Perception and Psychophysics, Journal of Experimental Psychology: Human Perception and Performance, Perception,* and *American Journal of Psychology.*

Articles on attention, auditory and visual information processing, memory, learning, and decision making are published in the same journals recommended for psychophysics and perception and also can be found in *Journal of Experimental Psychology: Human Learning and Memory, Journal of Verbal Learning and Verbal Behavior, Cognitive Psychology, Memory and Cognition, Journal of Mathematical Psychology, Acta Psychologica, British Journal of Psychology,* and *Quarterly Journal of Psychology.* Theoretical articles are more likely to be found in *Psychological Review,* whereas review articles are presented in *Psychological Bulletin, Annual Review of Psychology,* and *Journal of Experimental Psychology: General.* Articles of general interest to psychologists sometimes are published in *Science, Scientific American, The American Scientist,* and *Nature.*

References

Alpern, M. Effector mechanisms in vision. In J. W. Kling and L. A. Riggs (Eds.), *Experimental Psychology*. New York: Holt, Rinehart, and Winston, 1971.

Anderson, J. A. A theory for the recognition of items from short memorized lists. *Psychological Review,* 1973, *80,* 417–438.

Anderson, J. R., & Bower, G. H. *Human associative memory.* Washington, D.C.: V. H. Winston, 1973.

Anderson, N. H. Averaging model applied to the size-weight illusion. *Perception and Psychophysics,* 1970, *8,* 1–4.

Arnheim, R. Art in bits and chunks. *Contemporary Psychology,* 1971, *16,* 459–461.

Arnold, D. C., & Tinker, M. A. The fixational pause of the eyes. *Journal of Experimental Psychology,* 1939, *25,* 271–280.

Atkinson, R. C., Herrmann, D. J., & Wescourt, K. T. Search processes in recognition memory. In R. L. Solso (Ed.), *Theories in cognitive psychology: the Loyola symposium.* Potomac, Md.: Lawrence Erlbaum Associates, 1974.

Atkinson, R. C., & Juola, J. F. Search and decision processes in recognition memory. In D. H. Krantz, R. C. Atkinson, R. D. Luce, & P. Suppes (Eds.), *Contemporary developments in mathematical psychology.* San Francisco: Freeman, 1974.

Atkinson, R. C., & Shiffrin, R. M. Human memory: a proposed system and its control processes. In K. W. Spence and J. T. Spence (Eds.), *Advances in the psychology of learning and motivation research and theory.* Vol. II. New York: Academic Press, 1968.

Averbach, E., & Coriell, A. S. Short-term memory in vision. *Bell System Technical Journal,* 1961, *40,* 309–328.

Axelrod, S., & Guzy, L. T. Underestimation of dichotic click rates: results using methods of absolute estimation and constant stimuli. *Psychonomic Science,* 1968, *12,* 133–134.

Axelrod, S., Guzy, L. T., & Diamond, I. T. Perceived rate of monotic and dichotically alternating clicks. *Journal of the Acoustical Society of America,* 1968, *43,* 51–55.

Axelrod, S., & Nakao, M. Apparent slowing of bimanually alternating pulse trains. *Journal of Experimental Psychology,* 1974, *102,* 164–166.

Ballard, J. G. The subliminal man. In H. A. Katz, P. Warrick, & M. H. Greenberg (Eds.), *Introductory psychology through science fiction.* Chicago: Rand McNally, 1974.

Barclay, J. R. Noncategorical perception of a voiced stop consonant: a replication. *Proceedings of the 78th Annual Convention of the American Psychological Association,* 1970, 9–10.

Barlow, H. B. Temporal and spatial summation in human vision at different background intensities. *Journal of Physiology,* 1958, *141,* 337–350.

Barrett, C. *Op art.* New York: Viking Press, 1970.

Bartz, W. H., Lewis, M. Q., & Swinton, G. Serial position effects for repeated free recall: negative recency or positive primacy? *Journal of Experimental Psychology,* 1972, *96,* 10–16.

Battig, W. F., & Montague, W. E. Category norms for verbal items in 56 categories: a replication and extension of the Connecticut Category Norms. *Journal of Experimental Psychology Monograph,* 1969, *80,* 1–46.

Beck, J., & Gibson, J. J. The relation of apparent shape to apparent slant in the perception of objects. *Journal of Experimental Psychology,* 1955, *50,* 125–133.

Békésy, G. von. Auditory inhibition in concert halls. *Science,* 1971, *171,* 529–536.

Beller, H. K. Priming: effects of advance information on matching. *Journal of Experimental Psychology,* 1971, *87,* 176–182.

Boring, E. G. The moon illusion. *American Journal of Physics,* 1943, *11,* 55–60.

Boring, E. G. *A history of experimental psychology.* (2nd Ed.). New York: Appleton-Century-Crofts, 1950.

Bower, G. H. Analysis of a mnemonic device. *American Scientist,* 1970, *58,* 496–510.

Bower, G. H. A selective review of organizational factors in memory. In E. Tulving and W. Donaldson (Eds.), *Organization of memory.* New York: Academic Press, 1972.

Bransford, J. D., & Franks, J. J. The abstraction of linguistic ideas. *Cognitive Psychology,* 1971, *2,* 331–350.

Bransford, J. D., & Franks, J. J. The abstraction of linguistic ideas: a review. *Cognition,* 1972, *1,* 211–250.

Broadbent, D. E. The role of auditory localization and attention in memory span. *Journal of Experimental Psychology,* 1954, *47,* 191–196.

Broadbent, D. E. *Perception and communication.* New York: Pergamon Press, 1958.

Broadbent, D. E. Two-state threshold model and rating scale experiments. *Journal of the Acoustical Society of America,* 1966, *40,* 244–245.

Broadbent, D. E. Stimulus set and response set: two kinds of selective attention. In D. I. Mostofsky (Ed.), *Attention: contemporary theory and analysis.* New York: Appleton-Century-Crofts, 1970.

Broadbent, D. E. *Decision and stress.* London: Academic Press, 1971.

Broadbent, D. E., & Gregory, M. On the recall of stimuli presented alternately to two sense organs. *Quarterly Journal of Experimental Psychology,* 1961, *13,* 103–110.

Broadbent, D. E., & Gregory, M. Division of attention and the decision theory of signal detection. *Proceedings of the Royal Society,* 1963, *158,* 222–231.

Broadbent, D. E., & Gregory, M. Stimulus set and response set: the alternation of attention. *Quarterly Journal of Experimental Psychology,* 1964, *16,* 309–317.

Broadbent, D. E., & Gregory, M. On the interaction of S-R compatibility with other variables affecting reaction time. *British Journal of Psychology,* 1965, *56,* 61–67.

Brown, R., & McNeill, D. The "tip of the tongue" phenomenon. *Journal of Verbal Learning and Verbal Behavior,* 1966, *5,* 325–337.

Bruno, F. J. *The story of psychology.* New York: Holt, Rinehart, & Winston, 1972.

Bryden, M. P. Attentional strategies and short-term memory in dichotic listening. *Cognitive Psychology,* 1971, *2,* 99–116.

Burnham, R. W., & Clark, J. R. A test of hue memory. *Journal of Applied Psychology,* 1955, *39,* 164–172.

Cain, W. S., & Marks, L. E. *Stimulus and sensation: readings in sensory psychology.* Boston: Little, Brown, 1971.

Cattell, J. M. The time it takes to see and name objects. *Mind,* 1886, *11,* 63–65.

Cherry, E. C. Some experiments on the recognition of speech, with one and with two ears. *Journal of the Acoustical Society of America,* 1953, *25,* 975–979.

Cherry, E. C., & Taylor, W. K. Some further experiments on the recognition of speech with one and two ears. *Journal of the Acoustical Society of America,* 1954, *26,* 554–559.

Cole, R. A., Coltheart, M., & Allard, F. Memory of a speaker's voice: reaction time to same- or different-voiced letters. *Quarterly Journal of Experimental Psychology,* 1974, *26,* 1–7.

Cole, R. A., & Scott, B. Toward a theory of speech perception. *Psychological Review,* 1974, *81,* 348–374.

Conant, J. B. *On understanding science.* New Haven: Yale University Press, 1947.

Coren, S. Subjective contours and apparent depth. *Psychological Review,* 1972, *79,* 359–367.

Cornsweet, T. N. *Visual Perception.* New York: Academic Press, 1970.

Craik, F. I. M. The fate of primary memory items in free recall. *Journal of Verbal Learning and Verbal Behavior,* 1970, *9,* 143–148.

Creel, W., Boomsliter, P. C., & Powers, S. R. Sensations of tones as perceptual forms. *Psychological Review,* 1970, *77,* 534–545.

Crowder, R. G., & Morton, J. Precategorical acoustic storage. *Perception and Psychophysics,* 1969, *5,* 365–373.

Darley, C. F., & Murdock, B. B. Effects of prior free recall testing on final recall and recognition. *Journal of Experimental Psychology,* 1971, *91,* 66–73.

Darwin, C. J., & Baddeley, A. D. Acoustic memory and the perception of speech. *Cognitive Psychology,* 1974, *6,* 41–60.

Darwin, C. J., Turvey, M. T., & Crowder, R. G. An auditory analogue of the Sperling partial report procedure: evidence for brief auditory storage. *Cognitive Psychology,* 1972, *3,* 255–267.

Day, R. H. Visual spatial illusions: a general explanation. *Science,* 1972, 175, 1335–1340.

Denes, P. B., & Pinson, E. N. *The speech chain.* Bell Telephones Laboratories, 1963.

Deutsch, D. Dislocation of tones in a musical sequence: a memory illusion. *Nature,* 1970, *226,* 286. (a)

Deutsch, D. Tones and numbers: specificity of interference in immediate memory. *Science,* 1970, *168,* 1604–1605. (b)

Deutsch, J. A., & Deutsch, D. Attention: some theoretical considerations. *Psychological Review,* 1963, *70,* 80–90.

Deutsch, J. A., & Deutsch, D. Comments on "Selective attention: perception or response?" and reply. *Quarterly Journal of Experimental Psychology,* 1967, *19,* 362–363.

Dick, A. O. Relations between the sensory register and short-term storage in tachistoscopic recognition. *Journal of Experimental Psychology,* 1969, *82,* 279–284.

Dick, A. O. On the problem of selection in short-term visual (iconic) memory. *Canadian Journal of Psychology,* 1971, *25,* 250–263.

Donders, F. C. On the speed of mental processes. 1868–1869. In W. G. Koster (Ed.), *Attention and performance II: Acta Psychologica,* 1969, *30,* 412–431.

Efron, R. The relationship between the duration of a stimulus and the duration of a perception. *Neuropsychologia,* 1970, *8,* 37–55. (a)

Efron, R. The minimum duration of a perception. *Neuropsychologia,* 1970, *8,* 57–63. (b)

Eimas, P. D. A study of the relation between absolute identification and discrimination along selected sensory continua. Ph.D. dissertation, University of Connecticut, 1962.

Eimas, P. D. The relation between identification and discrimination along speech and non-speech continua. *Language and Speech,* 1963, *6,* 206–217.

Elliot, P. B. Tables of d'. In J. A. Swets (Ed.), *Signal detection and recognition by human observers.* New York: Wiley, 1964.

Epstein, W., & Park, J. N. Shape constancy: functional relationships and theoretical formulations. *Psychological Bulletin,* 1963, *60,* 265–288.

Epstein, W., Park, J. N., & Casey, A. The current status of the size-distance hypothesis. *Psychological Bulletin,* 1961, *58,* 491–514.

Eriksen, C. W., Becker, B. B., & Hoffman, J. E. Safari to masking land: a hunt for the elusive U. *Perception and Psychophysics,* 1970, *8,* 245–250.

Eriksen, C. W., & Eriksen, B. A. Visual perceptual processing rates and backward and forward masking. *Journal of Experimental Psychology,* 1971, *89,* 306–313.

Estes, W. K. The problem of inference from curves based on group data. *Psychological Bulletin,* 1956, *53,* 134–140.

Estes, W. K. Memory and conditioning. In F. J. McGuigan (Ed.), *Contemporary views in learning and conditioning.* Washington: V. H. Winston, 1973.

Estes, W. K. Memory, perception, and decision in letter identification. In R. L. Solso (Ed.), *Information Processing and Cognition: the Loyola symposium.* Potomac, Md.: Lawrence Erlbaum Associates, in press.

Evans, C. R., & Marsden, R. P. A study of the effect of perfect retinal stabilization on some well-known visual illusions using the after-image as a method of compensating for eye movements. *British Journal of Physiological Optics,* 1966, *23,* 242–248.

Fechner, G. T. *Elements of psychophysics.* Vol 1, 1860. Translated by H. E. Adler. D. H. Howes and E. G. Boring (Eds.). New York: Holt, Rinehart, & Winston, 1966.

Fodor, J. A., Bever, T. G., & Garrett, M. F. *The psychology of language: an introduction to psycholinguistics and generative grammar.* New York: McGraw-Hill, 1974.

Freund, A. Word and phrase recognition in speech processing. In D. W. Massaro (Ed.), *Understanding language: an information processing analysis of speech perception, reading, and psycholinguistics.* New York: Academic Press, in press.

Fry, D. B., Abramson, A. S., Eimas, P. D., & Liberman, A. M. The identification and discrimination of synthetic vowels. *Language and Speech*, 1962, *5*, 171–189.

Galanter, E., & Galanter, P. Range estimates of distant visual stimuli. *Perception and Psychophysics*, 1973, *14*, 301–306.

Gardner, G. T. Evidence for independent parallel channels in tachistoscopic perception. *Cognitive Psychology*, 1973, *4*, 130–155.

Gardner, M. Mathematical games: Of optical illusions from figures that are undecidable to hot dogs that float. *Scientific American*, 1970, *222*, No. 5, 124–127.

Garner, W. R. *The processing of information and structure*. Potomac, Md.: Lawrence Erlbaum Associates, 1974.

Gibson, E. J., Pick, A., Osser, H., & Hammond, M. The role of grapheme-phoneme correspondence in the perception of words. *American Journal of Psychology*, 1962, *75*, 554–570.

Gibson, J. J. *The perception of the visual world*. Boston: Houghton Mifflin, 1950.

Gibson, J. J. *The senses considered as perceptual systems*. Boston: Houghton Mifflin, 1966.

Gol'dburt, S. N. Investigation of the stability of auditory processes in micro-intervals of time (new findings on back masking). *Biophysics*, 1961, *6*, 809–817.

Graboi, D. Searching for targets: the effects of specific practice. *Perception and Psychophysics*, 1971, *10*, 300–304.

Graham, C. H., & Margaria, R. Area and the intensity-time relation in the peripheral retina. *American Journal of Physiology*, 1935, *113*, 299–305.

Grant, D. A. A preliminary model for processing information conveyed by verbal conditioned stimuli in classical conditioning. In A. H. Black and W. F. Prokasy (Eds.), *Classical conditioning II: current theory and research*. New York: Appleton-Century-Crofts, 1972.

Grant, D. A. Cognitive factors in eyelid conditioning. *Psychophysiology*, 1973, *10*, 75–81.

Gray, G. W. Phonemic microtomy: the minimum duration of perceptible speech sounds. *Speech Monographs*, 1942, *9*, 75–90.

Gray, J., & Wedderburn, A. Grouping strategies with simultaneous stimuli. *Quarterly Journal of Experimental Psychology*, 1960, *12*, 180–184.

Green, D. M., & Swets, J. A. *Signal detection theory and psychophysics*. New York: Wiley, 1966.

Gregory, R. L. Distortion of visual space as inappropriate constancy scaling. *Nature*, 1963, *199*, 678–680.

Gregory, R. L. *Eye and brain: The psychology of seeing.* New York: McGraw-Hill, 1966.

Gregory, R. L. Visual illusions. *Scientific American,* 1968, *219,* No. 5, 66–76.

Gregory, R. L., & Gombrich, E. H. (Eds.), *Illusions in nature and art.* London: Duckworth, 1973.

Grice, G. R. Stimulus intensity and response evocation. *Psychological Review,* 1968, *75,* 359–373.

Gummerman, K. Selective perception and the number of alternatives. *American Journal of Psychology,* 1971, *84,* 173–179.

Gummerman, K. A model of selective perception: The effect of presenting alternatives before or after the stimulus. *Bulletin of the Psychonomic Society,* 1973, *2,* 365–367.

Guzy, L. T., & Axelrod, S. Interaural attention shifting as response. *Journal of Experimental Psychology,* 1972, *95,* 290–294.

Haber, R. N. How we remember what we see. *Scientific American,* 1970, *222,* No. 2, 104–112.

Haber, R. N., & Nathanson, L. S. Post-retinal storage? Some further observations on Parks' Camel as seen through the eye of a needle. *Perception and Psychophysics,* 1968, *3,* 349–355.

Haber, R. N., & Standing, L. G. Direct measures of short-term visual storage. *Quarterly Journal of Experimental Psychology,* 1969, *21,* 43–54.

Haber, R. N., & Standing, L. G. Direct estimates of apparent duration of a flash. *Canadian Journal of Psychology,* 1970, *24,* 216–229.

Hadamard, J. *The psychology of invention in the mathematical field.* New York: Dover, 1954.

Hamilton, W. *Lectures on metaphysics and logic.* 1861–1866. 4 vols. Reprinted by Adler's Foreign Books.

Hecht, S. Vision: II. The nature of the photoreceptor process. In C. Murchison (Ed.), *A handbook of general experimental psychology.* Worcester, Mass.: Clark University Press, 1934.

Hecht, S., Shlaer, S., & Pirenne, M. H. Energy, quanta, and vision. *Journal of General Physiology,* 1942, *25,* 819–840.

Hellige, J. B. An analysis of some psychological studies of grammar; the role of generated abstract memory. In D. W. Massaro (Ed.), *Understanding language: an information processing analysis of speech perception, reading, and psycholinguistics.* New York: Academic Press, in press.

Helmholtz, H. von. *Treatise on physiological optics.* 1856–1866. Translated from the 3rd Ed. by J. P. C. Southall (Ed.). New York: Dover, 1962.

Helmholtz, H. von. A series of lectures delivered in Frankfurt and

Heidelberg, 1867. Reprinted in R. M. Warren & R. P. Warren (Eds.), *Helmholtz on perception: its physiology and development.* New York: Wiley, 1968.

Henley, N. M. A psychological study of the semantics of animal terms. *Journal of Verbal Learning and Verbal Behavior,* 1969, *8,* 176–184.

Hering, E. *Outlines of a theory of the light sense.* 1878. Republished by Harvard University Press, 1964.

Hirsh, I. J. Auditory perception of temporal order. *Journal of the Acoustical Society of America,* 1959, *31,* 759–767.

Hochberg, J. Attention, organization and consciousness. In D. I. Mostofsky (Ed.), *Attention: contemporary theory and analysis.* New York: Appleton-Century-Crofts, 1970.

Hochberg, J. Perception I: color and shape. Perception II: space and movement. In J. W. Kling and L. A. Riggs (Eds.), *Experimental Psychology.* New York: Holt, Rinehart, and Winston, 1971.

Holway, A. H., & Boring, E. G. Determinants of apparent visual size with distance variant. *American Journal of Psychology,* 1941, *54,* 21–37.

Homa, D. Organization and long-term memory search. *Memory and Cognition,* 1973, *1,* 369–379.

Huey, E. B. *The psychology and pedagogy of reading.* New York: Macmillan, 1908. Republished by M.I.T. Press, 1968.

Huxley, A. *Brave new world revisited.* New York: Harper & Row, 1958.

James, W. *The principles of psychology.* New York: Holt, 1890. Republished as Dover paperback, 1950.

Julesz, B. *Foundations of cyclopean perception.* Chicago: University of Chicago Press, 1971.

Kahneman, D. *Attention and effort.* Englewood Cliffs, N.J.: Prentice-Hall, 1973.

Kanizsa, G. Perception, past experience, and the impossible experiment. *Acta Psychologica,* 1969, *31,* 66–96.

Kanizsa, G. Contours without gradients, or cognitive contours. *Italian Journal of Psychology,* 1974, *1,* 93–113.

Kaufman, L., & Rock, I. The moon illusion, I. *Science,* 1962, *136,* 953–961.

Kausler, D. H. *Psychology of verbal learning and memory.* New York: Academic Press, 1974.

Keele, S. W. *Attention and human performance.* Pacific Palisades, Calif.: Goodyear, 1973.

Keesey, U. T. Effects of involuntary eye movements on visual acuity. *Journal of the Optical Society of America,* 1960, *50,* 769–774.

Klein, G. S. Semantic power measured through the interference of words with color-naming. *American Journal of Psychology*, 1964, *77*, 576–588.

Klein, W., Plomp, R., & Pols, L. C. W. Vowel spectra, vowel spaces, and vowel identification. *Journal of the Acoustical Society of America*, 1970, *48*, 999–1009.

Koffka, K. *Principles of gestalt psychology*. New York: Harcourt, 1935.

Kohler, W. *Gestalt psychology*. New York: Liveright, 1929.

Koriat, A., & Fischoff, B. What day is today? An inquiry into the process of time orientation. *Memory and Cognition*, 1974, *2*, 201–205.

Krantz, D. H. Threshold theories of signal detection. *Psychological Review*, 1969, *76*, 308–324.

Kristofferson, M. W. Effects of practice on character-classification performance. *Canadian Journal of Psychology*, 1972, *26*, 54–60. (a)

Kristofferson, M. W. Types and frequency of errors in visual search. *Perception and Psychophysics*, 1972, *11*, 325–328. (b)

Kristofferson, M. W. When item recognition and visual search functions are similar. *Perception and Psychophysics*, 1972, *12*, 379–384. (c)

Kristofferson, M. W., Groen, M., & Kristofferson, A. B. When visual search functions look like item recognition functions. *Perception and Psychophysics*, 1973, *14*, 186–192.

Kroll, N. E. A., Parks, T. E., Parkinson, S. R., Bieber, S. L., & Johnson, A. L. Short-term memory while shadowing: recall of visually and of aurally presented letters. *Journal of Experimental Psychology*, 1970, *85*, 220–224.

Kuhn, T. S. *The structure of scientific revolutions*. Chicago: University of Chicago Press, 1970.

Ladefoged, P. *Elements of acoustic phonetics*. Chicago: University of Chicago Press, 1962.

Ladefoged, P., & Broadbent, D. E. Information conveyed by vowels. *Journal of the Acoustical Society of America*, 1957, *79*, 98–104.

Larkin, W. D. Rating scales in detection experiments. *Journal of the Acoustical Society of America*, 1965, *37*, 748–749.

Lawrence, D. H., & Coles, G. R. Accuracy of recognition with alternatives before and after the stimulus. *Journal of Experimental Psychology*, 1954, *47*, 208–214.

Lawson, E. A. Decisions concerning the rejected channel. *Quarterly Journal of Experimental Psychology*, 1966, *18*, 260–265.

Lefton, L. A. Metacontrast: a review. *Perception and Psychophysics*, 1973, *13*, 161–171.

Lewis, J. L. Semantic processing of unattended messages using dichotic listening. *Journal of Experimental Psychology*, 1970, *85*, 225–228.

Liberman, A. M., Cooper, F. S., Shankweiler, D. P., & Studdert-Kennedy, M. Perception of the speech code. *Psychological Review*, 1967, *74*, 431–461.

Liberman, A. M., Delattre, P., & Cooper, F. S. The role of selected stimulus variables in the perception of the unvoiced stop consonants. *American Journal of Psychology*, 1952, *65*, 497–516.

Light, L. L. Incentives, information, rehearsal, and the negative recency effect. *Memory and Cognition*, 1974, *2*, 295–300.

Lindsay, P. H. Multichannel processing in perception. In D. I. Mostofsky (Ed.), *Attention: contemporary theory and analysis.* New York: Appleton-Century-Crofts, 1970.

Lindsay, P. H., & Norman, D. A. Short-term retention during a simultaneous detection task. *Perception and Psychophysics*, 1969, *5*, 201–205.

Lindsay, P. H., & Norman, D. A. *Human information processing: an introduction to psychology.* New York: Academic Press, 1972.

Lindsay, P. H., Taylor, M. M., & Forbes, S. M. Attention and multi-dimensional discrimination. *Perception and Psychophysics*, 1968, *4*, 113–117.

Linker, E., Moore, M. E., & Galanter, E. Taste thresholds, detection models, and disparate results. *Journal of Experimental Psychology*, 1964, *67*, 59–66.

Luce, R. D. A threshold theory for simple detection experiments. *Psychological Review*, 1963, *70*, 61–79.

Luckiesh, M. *Visual illusions: their causes, characteristics, and application.* New York: Dover, 1965.

Luria, A. R. *The mind of a mnemonist.* New York: Basic Books, 1968.

McCain, G., & Segal, E. M. *The game of science.* Monterey, Calif.: Brooks/Cole, 1973.

McCormick, E. M. *Digital computer primer.* New York: McGraw-Hill, 1959.

McCrary, J. W., & Hunter, W. S. Serial position curves in verbal learning. *Science*, 1953, *117*, 131–134.

McGill, W. J. Loudness and reaction time. *Acta Psychologica*, 1961, *19*, 193–199.

MacKay, D. M. Moving images produced by regular stationary patterns. *Nature*, 1957, *180*, 849–850.

Mackworth, J. F. Interference and decay in very short-term memory. *Journal of Verbal Learning and Verbal Behavior*, 1964, *3*, 300–308.

McNabb, S., & Massaro, D. W. Recognition memory for synthesized auditory information. Unpublished paper, 1973.

Madigan, S. A., & McCabe, L. Perfect recall and total forgetting: a problem for models of short-term memory. *Journal of Verbal Learning and Verbal Behavior,* 1971, *10,* 101–106.

Mandler, G. *Organization and recognition.* In E. Tulving and W. Donaldson (Eds.), Organization of memory. New York: Academic Press, 1972.

Mandler, G. Memory storage and retrieval: some limits on the reach of attention and consciousness. In R. L. Solso (Ed.), *Information processing and cognition: the Loyola symposium.* Potomac, Md.: Lawrence Erlbaum Associates, in press.

Massaro, D. W. The role of the decision system in sensory and memory experiments using confidence judgments. *Perception and Psychophysics,* 1969, *5,* 270–272.

Massaro, D. W. Forgetting: interference or decay? *Journal of Experimental Psychology,* 1970, *83,* 238–243. (a)

Massaro, D. W. Perceptual processes and forgetting in memory tasks. *Psychological Review,* 1970, *77,* 557–567. (b)

Massaro, D. W. Preperceptual auditory images. *Journal of Experimental Psychology,* 1970, *85,* 411–417. (c)

Massaro, D. W. Retroactive interference in short-term recognition memory for pitch. *Journal of Experimental Psychology,* 1970, *83,* 32–39. (d)

Massaro, D. W. Effect of masking tone duration on preperceptual auditory images. *Journal of Experimental Psychology,* 1971, *87,* 146–148.

Massaro, D. W. Preperceptual and synthesized auditory storage. Studies in human information processing, University of Wisconsin, 72–1, 1972. (a)

Massaro, D. W. Preperceptual images, processing time, and perceptual units in auditory perception. *Psychological Review,* 1972, *79,* 124–145. (b)

Massaro, D. W. Stimulus information vs. processing time in auditory pattern recognition. *Perception and Psychophysics,* 1972, *12,* 50–56. (c)

Massaro, D. W. A comparison of forward versus backward recognition masking. *Journal of Experimental Psychology,* 1973, *100,* 434–436. (a)

Massaro, D. W. Perception of letters, words, and nonwords. *Journal of Experimental Psychology,* 1973, *100,* 349–353. (b)

Massaro, D. W. The perception of rotated shapes: a process analysis of shape constancy. *Perception and Psychophysics,* 1973, *13,* 413–422. (c)

Massaro, D. W. Perceptual units in speech recognition. *Journal of Experimental Psychology,* 1974, *102,* 199–208.

Massaro, D. W. Acoustic features in speech perception. In D. W. Massaro (Ed.), *Understanding language: an information processing analysis of speech perception, reading, and psycholinguistics.* New York: Academic Press, in press. (a)

Massaro, D. W. Preperceptual images, processing time, and perceptual units in speech perception. In D. W. Massaro (Ed.), *Understanding language: an information processing analysis of speech perception, reading, and psycholinguistics.* New York: Academic Press, in press. (b)

Massaro, D. W. Primary and secondary recognition in reading. In D. W. Massaro (Ed.), *Understanding language: an information processing analysis of speech perception, reading, and psycholinguistics.* New York: Academic Press, in press.(c)

Massaro, D. W., & Anderson, N. H. Judgmental model of the Ebbinghaus illusion. *Journal of Experimental Psychology,* 1971, *89,* 147–151.

Massaro, D. W., & Kahn, B. J. Effects of central processing on auditory recognition. *Journal of Experimental Psychology,* 1973, *97,* 51–58.

Massaro, D. W., & Schmuller, J. Visual features, preperceptual storage, and processing time in reading. In D. W. Massaro (Ed.), *Understanding language: an information processing analysis of speech perception, reading, and psycholinguistics.* New York: Academic Press, in press.

Metelli, F. The perception of transparency. *Scientific American,* 1974, *230,* No. 4, 90–98.

Meyer, D. E., & Schvaneveldt, R. W. Facilitation in recognizing pairs of words: evidence of a dependence between retrieval operations. *Journal of Experimental Psychology,* 1971, *90,* 227–234.

Meyer, D. E., Schvaneveldt, R. W., & Ruddy, M. G. Activation of lexical memory. Paper presented at the meeting of the Psychonomic Society, St. Louis, November, 1972.

Miller, G. A. The perception of speech. In M. Halle, H. G. Lunt, H. McLean, C. N. van Schooneveld (Eds.), *For Roman Jakobson.* The Hague: Mouton, 1956.

Miller, G. A. The magical number seven, plus or minus two: Some limits on our capacity for processing information. *Psychological Review,* 1956, *63,* 81–97.

Miller, G. A. Decision units in the perception of speech. *Institute of Radio Engineers (IRE) Transactions on Information Theory.* New York: 1962, Information Theory–8, 81–83.

Miller, N. E., Barber, T. X., DiCara, L. V., Kamiya, J., Shapiro, D., & Stoyva, J. (Eds.), *Biofeedback and self-control.* Chicago: Aldine, 1973.

Millodct, M. Influence of accommodation on the viewing of an illusion. *Quarterly Journal of Experimental Psychology,* 1968, *20,* 329–335.

Montague, W. E. Effect of irrelevant information on a complex auditory-domination task. *Journal of Experimental Psychology,* 1965, *69,* 230–236.

Moore, J. J., & Massaro, D. W. Attention and processing capacity in auditory recognition. *Journal of Experimental Psychology,* 1973, *99,* 49–54.

Moray, N. Attention in dichotic listening: affective cues and the influence of instructions. *Quarterly Journal of Experimental Psychology,* 1959, *11,* 56–60.

Moray, N. Broadbent's filter theory: postulate H and the problem of switching time. *Quarterly Journal of Experimental Psychology,* 1960, *12,* 214–220.

Moray, N. Introductory experiments in auditory time-sharing: detection of frequency and intensity increments. *Journal of the Acoustical Society of America,* 1970, *47,* 1071–1073.

Moray, N., Bates, A., & Barnett, I. Experiments on the four-eared man. *Journal of the Acoustical Society of America,* 1965, *38,* 196–201.

Moray, N., & O'Brien, T. Signal detection theory applied to selective listening. *Journal of the Acoustical Society of America,* 1967, *42,* 765–772.

Murdock, B. B. The serial effect of free recall. *Journal of Experimental Psychology,* 1962, *64,* 482–488.

Murdock, B. B. A parallel processing model for scanning. *Perception and Psychophysics,* 1971, *10,* 289–291.

Murdock, B. B. *Human memory: theory and data.* Potomac, Md.: Lawrence Erlbaum Associates, 1974.

Murray, D. J. Vocalization-at-presentation and immediate recall, with varying recall methods. *Quarterly Journal of Experimental Psychology,* 1966, *18,* 9–18.

Murray, H. G. Stimulus intensity and reaction time: evaluation of a decision theory model. *Journal of Experimental Psychology,* 1970, *84,* 383–391.

Nachmias, J., & Steinman, R. M. Study of absolute visual detection by the rating-scale method. *Journal of the Optical Society of America,* 1963, *53,* 1206–1213.

Neisser, U. Decision time without reaction time: experiments in visual scanning. *American Journal of Psychology,* 1963, *76,* 376–385.

Neisser, U. Visual search. *Scientific American.* 1964, *210,* No. 6, 94–102.

Neisser, U. *Cognitive psychology.* New York: Appleton-Century-Crofts, 1967.

Neisser, U., Novick, R., & Lazar, R. Searching for ten targets simultaneously. *Perceptual and Motor Skills,* 1963, *17,* 955–961.

Nickerson, R. S. Short-term memory for complex meaningful visual configurations: a demonstration of capacity. *Canadian Journal of Psychology,* 1965, *19,* 155–160.

Nickerson, R. S. Binary-classification reaction time. A review of some studies of human information processing capabilities. *Psychonomic Monograph,* 1972, No. M65.

Norman, D. A. Toward a theory of memory and attention. *Psychological Review,* 1968, *75,* 522–536.

Norman, D. A. Memory while shadowing. *Quarterly Journal of Experimental Psychology,* 1969, *21,* 85–93.

Norman, D. A. Remembrance of things past. CHIP–11. Center for human information processing, University of California, San Diego, 1970.

Norman, D. A. Memory, knowledge and the answering of questions. In R. L. Solso (Ed.), *Contemporary issues in cognitive psychology: the Loyola symposium,* Washington, D.C.: V. H. Winston, 1973.

Norman, D. A., & Waugh, N. C. Stimulus and response interference in recognition experiments. *Journal of Experimental Psychology,* 1968, *78,* 551–559.

Ogle, K. N. *Binocular vision.* New York: Hafner, 1964.

Paap, K. Theories of speech perception. In D. W. Massaro (Ed.), *Understanding language: an information processing analysis of speech perception, reading, and psycholinguistics.* New York: Academic Press, in press.

Paivio, A. *Imagery and verbal processes.* New York: Holt, Rinehart, and Winston, 1971.

Parkinson, S. R., Parks, T., & Kroll, N. E. A. Visual and auditory short-term memory: The effects of phonemically similar auditory shadow material during the retention interval. *Journal of Experimental Psychology,* 1971, *87,* 274–280.

Patterson, J. H., & Green, D. M. Discrimination of transient signals having identical energy spectra. *Journal of the Acoustical Society of America,* 1970, *48,* 894–905.

Perky, C. W. An experimental study of imagination. *American Journal of Psychology,* 1910, *21,* 422–452.

Peterson, L. R., & Peterson, M. J. Short-term retention of individual verbal items. *Journal of Experimental Psychology,* 1959, *58,* 193–198.

Pillsbury, W. B. A study in apperception. *American Journal of Psychology,* 1897, *8,* 315–393.

Pirenne, M. H. *Vision and the eye.* London: Associated Book Publishers, 1967.

Pisoni, D. B. On the nature of categorical perception of speech sounds. (Supplement to status report on speech research) Haskins Laboratories, 1971.

Pisoni, D. B. Perceptual processing time for consonants and vowels. Haskins Laboratories Status Report on Speech Research, SR 31/32, 1972, 83–92. Also appears in *Journal of the Acoustical Society of America,* 1973, *53,* 369.

Pisoni, D. B. Auditory and phonetic memory codes in the discrimination of consonants and vowels. *Perception and Psychophysics,* 1973, *13,* 253–260.

Pisoni, D. B., & Lazarus, J. H. Categorical and noncategorical modes of speech perception along the voicing continuum. *Journal of the Acoustical Society of America,* 1974, *55,* 328–333.

Plato. *Meno.* In A. Sesonske and N. Fleming (Eds.), *Plato's Meno: text and criticism.* Belmont, Calif.: Wadsworth, 1965.

Plato: *Theaetitus.* Translated by B. Jowett. Indianapolis: Bobbs-Merrill, 1959.

Posner, M. I., Boies, S. I., Eichelman, W. H., & Taylor, R. I. Retention of visual and name codes of single letters. *Journal of Experimental Psychology Monograph,* 1969, *79* (No. 1, Pt. 2).

Posner, M. I., Goldsmith, R., & Welton, K. E. Perceived distance and the classification of distorted patterns. *Journal of Experimental Psychology,* 1967, *73,* 28–38.

Posner, M. I., & Keele, S. W. Decay of visual information from a single letter. *Science,* 1967, *158,* 137–139.

Potter, M. C., & Levy, E. I. Recognition memory for a rapid sequence of pictures. *Journal of Experimental Psychology,* 1969, *81,* 10–15.

Potter, R. K., Kopp, G. A., & Kopp, H. G. *Visible speech.* New York: Dover, 1966.

Radford, J. Reflections on introspection. *American Psychologist,* 1974, *29,* 245–250.

Rancurello, A. C. *A study of Franz Brentano.* New York: Academic Press, 1968.

Reicher, G. M. Perceptual recognition as a function of meaningfulness of stimulus material. *Journal of Experimental Psychology,* 1969, *81,* 275–281.

Reitman, J. S. Mechanisms of forgetting in short-term memory. *Cognitive Psychology,* 1971, *2,* 185–195.

Restle, F. Moon illusion explained on the basis of relative size. *Science,* 1970, *167,* 1092–1096.

Robinson, J. O. *The psychology of visual illusion.* London: Hutchinson & Co., 1972.

Rock, I., & Kaufman, L. The moon illusion, II. *Science,* 1962, *136,* 1023–1031.

Rumelhart, D. E., & Abrahamson, A. A. A model for analogical reasoning. *Cognitive Psychology,* 1973, *5,* 1–28.

Salzberg, P. M., Parks, T. E., Kroll, N. E. A., & Parkinson, S. R. Retroactive effects of phonemic similarity on short-term recall of visual and auditory stimuli. *Journal of Experimental Psychology*, 1971, *91*, 43–46.

Savin, H. On the successive perception of simultaneous stimuli. *Perception and Psychophysics*, 1967, *2*, 479–482.

Scarborough, D. L. Memory for brief visual displays of symbols. *Cognitive Psychology*, 1972, *3*, 408–429. (a)

Scarborough, D. L. Stimulus modality effects on forgetting in short-term memory. *Journal of Experimental Psychology*, 1972, *95*, 285–289. (b)

Schvaneveldt, R. W., & Meyer, D. E. Retrieval and comparison processes in semantic memory. In S. Kornblum (Ed.), *Attention and Performance, IV*, New York: Academic Press, 1973, 395–409.

Selfridge, O. G. Pandemonium: A paradigm for learning. In *Symposium on the mechanization of thought processes*. London: HM Stationary Office, 1959.

Selfridge, O. G. Pandemonium: A paradigm for learning. In L. Uhr (Ed.), *Pattern recognition*. New York: Wiley, 1966.

Segal, S. J., & Fusella, V. Effects of imagery and modes of stimulus onset on signal-to-noise ratio. *British Journal of Psychology*, 1969, *60*, 459–464.

Segal, S. J., & Fusella, V. Influence of imagined pictures and sounds on detection of visual and auditory signals. *Journal of Experimental Psychology*, 1970, *83*, 458–464.

Shank, R. C. Conceptual dependency: a theory of natural language understanding. *Cognitive Psychology*, 1972, *3*, 552–631.

Shebilske, W. Reading eye movements from an information processing point of view. In D. W. Massaro (Ed.), *Understanding language: an information processing analysis of speech perception, reading, and psycholinguistics*. New York: Academic Press, in press.

Shepard, R. N. Circularity in judgments of relative pitch. *Journal of the Acoustical Society of America*, 1964, *36*, 2346–2353.

Shepard, R. N. Recognition memory for words, sentences, and pictures. *Journal of Verbal Learning and Verbal Behavior*, 1967, *6*, 156–163.

Shepard, R. N., & Metzler, J. Mental rotation of three-dimensional objects. *Science*, 1971, *171*, 701–703.

Shiffrin, R. M. Information persistence in short-term memory. *Journal of Experimental Psychology*, 1973, *100*, 39–49.

Shiffrin, R. M., Craig, J. C., & Cohen, U. On the degree of attention and capacity-limitations in tactile processing. *Perception and Psychophysics*, 1973, *13*, 328–336.

Shiffrin, R. M., & Gardner, G. T. Visual processing capacity and attentional control. *Journal of Experimental Psychology,* 1972, *93,* 72–82.

Shiffrin, R. M., Gardner, G. T., & Allmeyer, D. H. On the degree of attention and capacity limitations in visual processing. *Perception and Psychophysics,* 1973, *14,* 231–236.

Shiffrin, R. M., & Grantham, D. W. Can attention be allocated to sensory modalities? *Perception and Psychophysics,* 1974, *15,* 460–474.

Shipley, T., & Rawlings, S. C. The nonius horopter, I. History and theory. *Vision Research,* 1970, *10,* 1225–1262.

Shulman, H. G., & Greenberg, S. N. Perceptual deficit due to division of attention between memory and perception. *Journal of Experimental Psychology,* 1971, *88,* 171–176.

Siegel, J. A. Sensory and verbal coding strategies in subjects with absolute pitch. *Journal of Experimental Psychology,* 1974, *103,* 37–44.

Skinner, B. F. Are theories of learning necessary? *Psychological Review,* 1950, *57,* 193–216.

Smith, E. E., & Haviland, S. E. Why words are perceived more accurately than nonwords: inference versus unitization. *Journal of Experimental Psychology,* 1972, *92,* 59–64.

Smith, E. E., Shoben, E. J., & Rips, L. J. Structure and process in semantic memory: A feature model for semantic decisions. *Psychological Review,* 1974, *81,* 214–241.

Smith, F. *Understanding reading.* New York: Holt, Rinehart, and Winston, 1971.

Solberg, K. B. Linguistic theory and information processing. In D. W. Massaro (Ed.), *Understanding language: an information processing analysis of speech perception, reading, and psycholinguistics.* New York: Academic Press, in press.

Sorkin, R. D., & Pohlmann, L. D. Some models of observer behavior in two-channel auditory signal detection. *Perception and Psychophysics,* 1973, *14,* 101–109.

Sorkin, R. D., Pohlmann, L. D., & Gilliom, J. D. Simultaneous two-channel signal detection. III. 630- and 1400 Hz signals. *Journal of the Acoustical Society of America,* 1973, *53,* 1045–1050.

Spencer, T. J., & Shuntich, R. Evidence for an interruption theory of backward masking. *Journal of Experimental Psychology,* 1970, *85,* 198–203.

Sperling, G. The information available in brief visual presentations. *Psychological Monographs,* 1960, 74 (11, Whole No. 498).

Sperling, G. A model for visual memory tasks. *Human Factors,* 1963, *5,* 19–31.

Sperling, G. Successive approximations to a model for short-term memory. In A. F. Sanders (Ed.), *Attention and performance. Acta Psychologica,* 1967, *27,* 285–292.

Sperling, G. Binocular vision: a physical and a neural theory. *American Journal of Psychology,* 1970, *83,* 461–534.

Sperling, G., Budiansky, J., Spivak, J. G., & Johnson, M. C. Extremely rapid visual search: the maximum rate of scanning letters for the presence of a numeral. *Science,* 1971, *174,* 307–311.

Sperry, R. W. A modified concept of consciousness. *Psychological Review,* 1969, *76,* 532–536.

Sternberg, S. High-speed scanning in human memory. *Science,* 1966, *153,* 652–654.

Sternberg, S. Two operations in character recognition: Some evidence from reaction-time measurements. *Perception and Psychophysics,* 1967, *2,* 45–53.

Sternberg, S. Memory-scanning: mental processes revealed by reaction-time experiments. *American Scientist,* 1969, *57,* 421–457. (a)

Sternberg, S. The discovery of processing stages: Extensions of Donders' method. *Acta Psychologica,* 1969, *30,* 276–315. (b)

Sternberg, S. Decomposing mental processes with reaction-time data. Copy of invited address, Midwestern Psychological Association, Detroit, May, 1971.

Stevens, S. S. A neural quantum in sensory discrimination. *Science,* 1972, *177,* 749–762.

Stroop, J. R. Studies of interference in serial verbal reactions. *Journal of Experimental Psychology,* 1935, *18,* 643–662.

Suen, C. Y., & Beddoes, M. P. Discrimination of vowel sounds of very short duration. *Perception and Psychophysics,* 1972, *11,* 417–419.

Swets, J. A. Is there a sensory threshold? *Science,* 1961, *134,* 168–177.

Swets, J. A., & Kristofferson, A. B. Attention. *Annual Review of Psychology,* 1970, *21,* 339–366.

Swets, J. A., Tanner, W. P., & Birdsall, T. G. Decision processes in perception. *Psychological Review,* 1961, *68,* 301–340.

Teuber, M. L. Sources of ambiguity in the prints of Maurits C. Escher. *Scientific American,* 1974, *231,* No. 1, 90–104.

Theios, J. Finite integer models for learning in individual subjects. *Psychological Review,* 1968, *75,* 292–307.

Theios, J. Reaction-time measurements in the study of memory processes: theory and data. In G. H. Bower (Ed.), *The psychology of learning and motivation,* Vol. 7. New York: Academic Press, 1973.

Thomas, I. B., Hill, P. B., Carroll, F. S., & Garcia, B. Temporal order in the perception of vowels. *Journal of the Acoustical Society of America,* 1970, *48,* 1010–1013.

Thompson, M. C., & Massaro, D. W. Visual information and redundancy in reading. *Journal of Experimental Psychology,* 1973, *98,* 49–54.

Thurlow, W. R. Audition. In J. W. Kling and L. A. Riggs (Eds.), *Experimental Psychology* (3rd Ed.). New York: Holt, Rinehart & Winston, 1971.

Titchener, E. B. *Outline of psychology.* New York: Macmillan, 1899.

Townsend, J. T., Taylor, S. G., & Brown, D. R. Lateral masking for letters with unlimited viewing time. *Perception and Psychophysics,* 1971, *10,* 375–378.

Treisman, A. M. Contextual cues in selective listening. *Quarterly Journal of Experimental Psychology,* 1960, *12,* 242–248.

Treisman, A. M. The effect of irrelevant material on the efficiency of selective listening. *American Journal of Psychology,* 1964, *77,* 533–546.

Treisman, A. M. Strategies and models of selective attention. *Psychological Review,* 1969, *3,* 282–299.

Treisman, A. M. Shifting attention between the ears. *Quarterly Journal of Experimental Psychology,* 1971, *23,* 157–167.

Treisman, A. M., & Geffen, G. Selective attention: perception or response? *Quarterly Journal of Experimental Psychology,* 1967, *19,* 1–17.

Treisman, M., & Rostron, A. B. Brief auditory storage: a modification of Sperling's paradigm applied to audition. *Acta Psychologica,* 1972, *36,* 161–170.

Tulving, E., & Thomson, D. M. Encoding specificity and retrieval processes in episodic memory. *Psychological Review,* 1973, *80,* 352–373.

Turvey, M. T. On peripheral and central processes in vision: inferences from an information processing analysis of masking with patterned stimuli. *Psychological Review,* 1973, *80,* 1–52.

Turvey, M. T., & Kravetz, S. Retrieval from iconic memory with shape as the selection criterion. *Perception and Psychophysics,* 1970, *8,* 171–172.

Tversky, B. Pictorial and verbal encoding in a short-term memory task. *Perception and Psychophysics,* 1969, *6,* 225–233.

von Wright., J. M. Selection in visual immediate memory. *Quarterly Journal of Experimental Psychology,* 1968, *20,* 62–68.

von Wright, J. M. On selection in visual immediate memory. In A. F. Sanders (Ed.), *Attention and performance,* III. *Acta Psychologica,* 1970, *33,* 280–292.

von Wright, J. M. On the problem of selection in iconic memory. *Scandinavian Journal of Psychology,* 1972, *13,* 159–171.

Waite, H., & Massaro, D. W. A test of Gregory's constancy-scaling explanation of the Müller-Lyer illusion. *Nature,* 1970, *227,* 733–734.

Wald, G. Human vision and the spectrum. *Science,* 1945, *101,* 653–658.

Warren, R. M., Obusek, C. J., Farmer, R. M., & Warren, R. P. Auditory sequence: confusion of patterns other than speech or music. *Science,* 1969, *164,* 586–587.

Warren, R. M., & Warren, R. P. *Helmholtz on perception: its physiology and development.* New York: Wiley, 1968.

Warren, R. M., & Warren, R. P. Auditory illusions and confusions. *Scientific American,* 1970, *223,* No. 6, 30–36.

Watson, C. S., & Bourbon, W. T. Rating scales and two-state threshold models. *Journal of the Acoustical Society of America,* 1965, *38,* 667–668.

Watson, C. S., Rilling, M. E., & Bourbon, W. T. Receiver-operating characteristics determined by a mechanical analog to the rating scale. *Journal of the Acoustical Society of America,* 1964, *36,* 283–288.

Watson, J. B. Psychology as the behaviorist views it. *Psychological Review,* 1913, *20,* 158–177.

Waugh, N. C., & Norman, D. A. Primary memory. *Psychological Review,* 1965, *72,* 89–104.

Waugh, N. C., & Norman, D. A. The measure of interference in primary memory. *Journal of Verbal Learning and Verbal Behavior,* 1968, *7,* 617–626.

Weisstein, N., & Haber, R. N. A U-shaped backward masking function in vision. *Psychonomic Science,* 1965, *2,* 75–76.

Wertheimer, M. *Productive thinking.* New York: Harper, 1945.

Wheeler, D. D. Processes in word recognition. *Cognitive Psychology,* 1970, *1,* 59–85.

Wickelgren, W. A. Testing two-state theories with operating characteristics and a posteriori probabilities. *Psychological Bulletin,* 1968, *69,* 126–131.

Wickelgren, W. A. Associative strength theory of recognition memory for pitch. *Journal of Mathematical Psychology,* 1969, *6,* 13–61.

Wickelgren, W. A. Trace resistance and decay of long-term memory. *Journal of Mathematical Psychology,* 1972, *9,* 418–455.

Wickelgren, W. A., & Norman, D. A. Strength models and serial position in short-term recognition memory. *Journal of Mathematical Psychology,* 1966, *3,* 316–347.

Wilder, L. Articulatory and acoustic characteristics of speech sounds. In D. W. Massaro (Ed.), *Understanding language: an information processing analysis of speech perception, read-*

ing, and psycholinguistics. New York: Academic Press, in press.

Winnick, W. A., & Rosen, B. E. Shape-slant relations under reduction conditions. *Perception and Psychophysics,* 1966, *1,* 157–160.

Woodworth, R. S. *Experimental psychology.* New York: Holt, 1938.

Wooldridge, D. E. *The machinery of the brain.* New York: McGraw-Hill, 1963.

Yarbus, A. L. *Eye movements and vision.* New York: Plenum, 1967.

Yntema, D. B., & Trask, F. P. Recall as a search process. *Journal of Verbal Learning and Verbal Behavior,* 1963, *2,* 65–74.

Credits

Acknowledgment is made to the following for their kind permission to reprint copyrighted material:

Fig. 4.5 from John N. Antrobus, *Cognition and affect.* Copyright © 1970 by Little, Brown and Co. (Inc.), p. 23. Reprinted with permission of publisher.

Fig. 4.8 from Ulric Neisser, "Visual search." Copyright © 1964 by *Scientific American,* Inc. All rights reserved.

Fig. 8.9 from George Wald (1945). Copyright 1945 by the American Association for the Advancement of Science.

Fig. 10.4 from Massaro & Anderson, "Judgmental model of the Ebbinghaus illusion." *Journal of Experimental Psychology,* 1971, *89,* 147–151; Fig. 18.8 from Eriksen & Eriksen, "Visual perceptual processing rates and backward and forward masking." *Journal of Experimental Psychology,* 1971, *89,* 306–313; Tables 28.1 and 28.2 from Meyer & Schvaneveldt, "Facilitation in recognizing pairs of words: evidence of dependence between retrieval operations." *Journal of Experimental Psychology,* 1971, *90,* 227–234. Copyright 1971 by the American Psychological Association. Reprinted with permission.

Figs. 11.8 and 11.9 from Shepard & Metzler (1971). Copyright 1971 by the American Association for the Advancement of Science.

Figs. 12.1, 12.2, and 12.3 from George Sperling, "Information available in brief visual presentations." *Psychological Monographs,* 1960, *74,* No. 11 (Whole No. 498). Copyright 1960 by the American Psychological Association. Reprinted with permission.

Fig. 12.6 from Bennett Murdock, "The serial effect of free recall." *Journal of Experimental Psychology,* 1962, *64,* 482–488. Copyright 1962 by the American Psychological Association. Reprinted with permission.

Fig. 13.1 reprinted with permission from Donald E. Broadbent, *Perception and Communication,* 1958, Pergamon Press, Ltd

Fig. 13.3 from Guzy & Axelrod, "Interaural attention shifting as response." *Journal of Experimental Psychology,* 1972, *95,* 290–294; Fig. 15.5 from Shiffrin & Gardner, "Visual processing capacity and attention control." *Journal of Experimental Psychology,* 1972, *93,* 72–82; Fig. 26.2 from Don Scarborough, "Stimulus modality effects of forgetting in short-term memory." *Journal of Experimental Psychology,* 1972, *95,* 285–289. Copyright 1972 by the American Psychological Association. Reprinted with permission.

Fig. 14.1 from Donald Norman, "Toward a theory of memory and attention." *Psychological Review,* 1968, *75,* 522–536. Copyright 1962 by the American Psychological Association. Reprinted with permission.

Name Index

Abrahamson, A. A., 567–68
Abramson, A. S., 517–18
Aguilonius, Franciscus, 233
Albers, Josef, 174, 175
Allard, F., 519–20
Allmeyer, D. H., 302–03
Alpern, M., 607
Anderson, J. A., 606
Anderson, J. R., 606
Anderson, N. H., 201–05, 206, 609
Aristotle, 23, 584
Arnheim, Rudolf, 23
Arnold, D. C., 375
Atkinson, R. C., 573, 606, 607
Averbach, E., 342–47, 355–58, 427, 607
Axelrod, S., 273–77

Baddeley, A. D., 608
Barber, T. X., 605
Barclay, J. R., 519
Barnett, I., 428
Barrett, C., 606
Bartz, W. H., 608
Bates, A., 428
Battig, W. F., 568
Baxt, N., 371
Beck, J., 216
Becker, B. B., 362–64
Beddoes, M. P., 465
Beethoven, Ludwig von, 9
Békésy, Georg von, 443
Beller, H. K., 534–35
Berkeley, George, 12
Bernini, Giovanni, 26–27
Bever, T. G., 609
Bieber, S. L., 532–33
Birdsall, T. G., 140

Boies, S. I., 533–35
Boomsliter, P. C., 447
Boring, E. G., 191, 209–11, 605
Borromini, Francisco, 185
Bourbon, W. T., 606
Bower, G. H., 609
Bransford, J. D., 596–98
Brentano, Franz, 26–27
Broadbent, Donald E., 30, 259–64, 265–66, 267, 268, 272, 285, 286, 289–90, 321, 425–26, 443, 446, 473, 541, 543–44, 521, 606, 608
Brown, D. R., 346
Brown, R., 562–64
Bruno, F. J., 605
Bryden, M. P., 523–25
Budiansky, J., 606
Burnham, R. L., 527

Cain, W. S., 606
Carroll, F. S., 458
Casey, A., 607
Cattell, James M., 380
Cherry, E. C., 278–79
Clark, J. R., 527
Cohen, U., 301–02
Cole, R. A., 519–20, 608
Coles, G. R., 398
Coltheart, M., 519–20
Conant, J. B., 231
Cooper, Franklin, 461, 470
Coriell, A. S., 342–47, 355–58, 427, 607
Coren, S., 606
Cornsweet, T. N., 150, 151, 606, 607
Craig, J. C., 301–02
Craik, F. I. M., 608
Creel, W., 447

James, William, 9, 11, 16, 24, 170–71, 251, 283, 299, 321, 339, 605
Javal, Emile, 380
Johns, Jasper, 379
Johnson, A. L., 532–33
Johnson, M. C., 606
Johnson, Samuel, 12
Julesz, B., 607
Juola, J. F., 606

Kahn, B. J., 304–08, 444–46
Kahneman, D., 608
Kamiya, J., 605
Kanizsa, G., 186–87, 606
Kant, Immanuel, 25, 380
Kaufman, L., 192, 195, 207
Kausler, D. H., 609
Keele, S. W., 533–35, 608
Keesey, U. T., 165
Klein, G. S., 297
Klein, W., 463
Koffka, K., 29, 216
Kohler, W., 29, 35
Koriat, A., 605
Krantz, D. H., 606
Kravetz, S., 607
Kristofferson, A. B., 606, 608
Kristofferson, M. W., 608
Kroll, N. E. A., 532–33
Kuhn, T. S., 605
Külpe, O., 49

Ladefoged, P., 419, 521
Larkin, W. D., 606
Lawrence, D. H., 398
Lawson, E. A., 288
Lazar, R., 78
Lazarus, J. H., 519
Levy, E. J., 537
Lewis, J. L., 296
Lewis, M. Q., 608
Liberman, Alexander, 168–69
Liberman, Alvin, 461, 470, 517–18
Lichtenstein, Roy, 172, 209
Light, L. L., 608
Lindsay, P. H., 309, 326, 332–34, 608
Linker, E., 140
Locke, John, 24
Luce, R. Duncan, 103, 112
Luckiesh, M., 607

Ludwig, Wolfgang, 163–64
Luria, Alexander R., 477, 527

McCabe, L., 255–56
McCain, G., 605
Mackworth, J. F., 544
McCormick, E. M., 605
McCrary, J. W., 504
McGill, W. J., 436–37
MacKay, D. M., 164
McNabb, S., 508–10
McNeill, D., 562–64
Madigan, S. A., 255–56
Mandler, G., 609
Marks, L. E., 606
Marsden, R. P., 164
Massaro, D. W., 198–99, 206, 216–20, 223–30, 304–11, 318, 325, 390, 393, 396, 430, 432, 437–39, 444–46, 455, 469, 489, 493–94, 508–10, 552, 590, 606, 608
Metelli, F., 607
Metzler, J., 221–23
Meyer, D. E., 573–76, 577–81
Miller, George, 249–50, 473, 501, 511, 561
Miller, N. E., 605
Millodot, M., 164
Monet, Claude, 172
Montague, W. E., 309, 568
Moore, J. J., 308–11
Moore, M. E., 140
Moray, N., 266–67, 270, 279, 288, 300, 428
Morton, J., 608
Müller, Johannes, 42
Murdock, B. B., 254–55, 606, 608
Murray, D. J., 502–03
Murray, H. G., 606

Nachmias, J., 140
Nakao, M., 277
Nathanson, L. S., 349–50
Neisser, U., 78, 81–83, 290–91, 606
Nickerson, R. S., 537, 606
Norman, Donald A., 279–81, 283–88, 326, 332–34, 501, 550, 553, 556–58, 605, 608
Novick, R., 78

Obusek, C. J., 457
Ogle, K. N., 607

Teuber, M. L., 607
Theios, J., 61, 593, 606
Thiebaud, Wayne, 173, 174
Thomas, I. B., 458
Thompson, M. C., 390, 393, 397
Thomson, D. M., 609
Thorndike, E. L., 28
Thurlow, W. R., 608
Tinker, M. A., 375
Titchener, Edward B., 1, 322
Townsend, J., 346
Trask, F. P., 272
Treisman, A. M., 269–72, 279, 286–87, 288–91, 295, 608
Treisman, M., 428
Tulving, E., 609
Turvey, M. T., 368–71, 428–30, 607, 608
Tversky, B., 535–37

Vasarely, Victor, 168, 170, 175, 176, 178, 179
von Wright, J. M., 607

Waite, H., 198–99
Wald, G., 155
Warren, R. M., 457, 607
Warren, R. P., 457, 607
Watson, C. S., 606
Watson, John B., 28
Waugh, Nancy C., 501, 550, 553, 556–68
Wedderburn, A., 264–65
Welton, K. E., 586–88
Wertheimer, Max, 29, 605
Wescourt, K. T., 573
Wheeler, D. D., 386
Wickelgren, W. A., 496–97, 561, 606
Wilder, L., 608
Winnick, W. A., 216
Woodworth, Robert S., 463, 200, 606, 608
Wooldridge, D. E., 605
Wundt, Wilhelm, 25, 26, 380, 381

Yarbus, A. L., 607
Ynetema, D. B., 272

Subject Index

d'—(Cont.)
    as measure of memory, 280, 331–34, 486–89, 507–10, 552–57
    as measure of memory for pitch, 490, 496–97
    as measure of visual perception, 366–69
    and percentage correct, 438
Dark-adaptation, 146–48, 166–67
dB. See Decibel
Decay theory, 486–89, 541–42, 543–45
    vs. interference theory, 545–50
    quantitative representation of, 486–89
Decibel, 94
Decision bias, 97, 448
    measure of, 134–35
Decision criterion:
    in multistate theory, 120
Decision process:
    in delayed comparison task, 484
    in letter recognition, 400–03
    in memory task, 330
    in psychophysical task, 104
Delayed comparison task, 478–79
    memory for color in, 528–29
    memory for pitch in, 479–99
    task considerations in, 479–81
Demons, 400–03
Dependent variables, 31
Detection, 16, 39–41, 293
    attentional effects in, 299–302
    and imagination, 322–24
    of light, 142–59
    and memory, 321
    stage of, 104
    tactile, 301–02
Detection time, 39
Deutsch-Norman model, 283–85, 286–87
Dice game, 121–30
    as analogy to signal detection task, 121–22
Dichotic listening. See Split-span tasks
Dichotic presentation:
    defined, 471
Dissimilarity ratings, 564–67
Divergence. See Vergence eye movements
Dominant hand, 53

Dot patterns, 586–88
Dumbbell illusion, 196
Dynes, 93, 408

Ear, 412–13
Eardrum, 413
Ebbinghaus illusion, 200, 206–07
Echo box, 501
Empiricism:
    British empiricists, 24
    as theory of knowledge, 24–25
English language, 382
    consonant sounds in, 418–21
    rules of, 573
Epiphenomenalism, 12, 14
    see also Mind-body problem
Eriksen and Eriksen study, 372–75
Errors in RT tasks, 81, 219
Estimating parameters. See Parameter estimates
Euclidean space:
    animal, 565
Exhaustive search, 67–70
Experimental control, 33
Experimental design, 34–36, 78
Experimental method, 31–37
    and between-subjects designs, 218
    and confounding processes, 36
    and counterbalancing, 52
    and data analysis, 135–36
    and dependent variables, 31
    for evaluating memory processes, 559
    and factorial designs, 52
    of partial report, 432
    for replicating experiments, 363
    and stimulus confoundings, 309
    and within-subject designs, 218
Eye:
    accommodating of the, 164–66
    high frequency tremor of the, 163–64
    structure of, 144
Eye movements:
    accommodation, 164–66
    nystagmus, 163–64
    saccadic, 166–69, 235, 340–41, 379
    vergence, 235

Poisson process, 157
Power function, 193–95
Power spectrum:
  of sound, 409–12
Practice, 35, 52, 127, 218, 445, 583
  see also Learning
Preperceptual auditory image. See Preperceptual auditory storage
Preperceptual auditory storage, 424–41, 493–97
  and GAM, 497–99
  properties of, 348–50
  and SAM, 493–97
Preperceptual visual image. See Preperceptual visual storage
Preperceptual visual storage, 338, 339–41,
  and afterimages, 351
  properties of, 348–52
Primacy, 334
Primary recognition, 477–78
Prior entry, 259
Probabilistic threshold. See Threshold
Probability distribution, 95
  and dice game, 121–31
  see also Normal distributions
Probe recall, 550
Probe recognition, 326, 507–10
Processing capacity. See Attention
Projected shape, 227
Prototype learning, 584–85, 586–88, 590–92
PSE. See Point of subjective equality
Psychophysical method:
  of adjustment, 90
  attitude of observer in, 97–98
  choice of stimulus levels, 91–93
  of constant stimuli, 91
  keeping observer honest in, 98–99
  of limits, 89–90
  motivation of observer in, 99–100
  in signal detection task, 98
Psychophysical task:
  stage model of, 103–04
  see also Psychophysical method

QRST task, 251–52, 253
Quantum theory, 143, 151–53

Randomization, 33, 218, 583
Reaction time:
  and attention, 543–44
  choice vs. simple tasks, 44–47, 58
  in letter matching, 533–35
  of lexical decisions, 573
  and memory, 543–44
  and mental rotation, 233
  for naming, 58–61
  in Neisser task, 78–83
  and number of alternatives 57–61
  in same-different task, 535–37
  and semantic similarity, 568–73
  of shadowing, 296–97
  of shape perception, 216–38
  in Sternberg task, 73–78
  and stimulus intensity, 436–37
  tests of invariance hypothesis, 216–38
  of word recognition, 573–81
  see also Additive-factor method, Subtractive method, 39, 42–51
Reading, 339, 376–403
  visual features, 378
  see also Letter recognition, Word recognition
Recall, 501–07
Recoding, 249–50
Recognition masking. See Auditory backward masking, Auditory forward masking, Visual backward masking, Visual forward masking
Recognition, 40–42, 293, 339–40
  attentional effects in, 303–19, 325, 334–35
  and memory, 242, 325, 334–35
  temporal course of, 341, 366–71
  time, in visual perception, 371–75
  of words, 373–81
  See also Auditory perception, Visual perception
Recognition time, 41
Redundancy:
  in reading, 382–84
  in word recognition, 387–92, 393–98
Rehearsal, 248–49, 255
  subvocal, 73–74
Reicher paradigm, 384–86
  and letter similarity, 390–91
  models of, 386–90

Threshold theory:
    Fechner's, 93–95
    general two-state, 112–16
    high threshold, 106–12
"Tip of the tongue" state, 562–63
Total impression theory, 200–06, 207
Trachea, 413
Transition matrices, 107
    and two-stage theories, 106–11, 112–16, 118–29
Treisman model, 288–90
Treisman study, 269–72
Turtles and logs, 597
Turvey study, 368–71
Two-process model, 366
Two-state theory, 112–17
    and multistate theory, 139–41

Unattended channels, 278–79
U-shaped functions, 355–57, 362–64, 368–71

Variables, 31–35
    control of, 32–35
    dependent, 31
    independent, 31
Vergence angle, 234
Vergence eye movements, 235
Vibratory taps, 277
Violin note, 410–11
    power spectrum of, 411
Virtue, 584–85
Vision:
    acuity, 344–46
    lateral masking, 344–46
    see also Visual perception
Visual acuity, 344–46
    and color mixing, 168–69
    individual differences, 34
    and nystagmus, 165
Visual angle, 152–53
Visual codes, 533–35
Visual detection. See Light detection
Visual features, 367, 378
Visual imagery, 598
Visual masking, 358–59
    backward masking, 358–59
        vs. forward masking, 364–66
        and masking stimulus, 371–72

Visual masking—(Cont.)
    backward masking—(Cont.)
        and test stimulus duration, 371–75
        two-process model of, 366
    forward masking, 358–59
        vs. backward masking, 364–66
        two-process model of, 366
    see also Lateral masking
Visual perception:
    and art, 162
    binocular, 208–38
    and eye movements, 162–69
    of illusory contours, 178–79
    of impossible scenarios, 180–81
    and knowledge, 161–62
    and lateral masking, 344–46
    and memory, 170–72
    monocular, 160–81
    and perspective cues, 173–78
    reversibility of, 179–80
    and sensation, 24, 209
    and stimulus duration, 348–52
    see also Illusions, Recognition, Reading
Visual scanning. See Neisser task
Vocal cords, 413, 414–15
Vowel recognition, 465–68, 469
Vowel sounds, 417–18, 464–65
    wave shapes of /I/ and /i/, 464

Waugh and Norman study, 550–57
Waves
    Sine waves, 407–09
    sound waves, 407–09
White noise, 412–15
    and normal distribution, 95
    power spectrum of, 411
Within-subject designs, 218
Word recognition, 379, 382, 384–86, 392–98, 573–81
Working memory, 250
    and long-term memory, 254
    see also Immediate memory, Short-term memory

z scores:
    and d' values, 136–38
    and normal distribution, 132–35
    table of, 133
Zeros and Ones, 593